A Prophet from Amongst You

A PROPHET FROM AMONGST YOU

The Life of Yigael Yadin:
Soldier, Scholar, and Mythmaker
of Modern Israel

NEIL ASHER SILBERMAN

Addison-Wesley Publishing Company
Reading, Massachusetts   Menlo Park, California   New York
Don Mills, Ontario   Wokingham, England   Amsterdam   Bonn
Sydney   Singapore   Tokyo   Madrid   San Juan
Paris   Seoul   Milan   Mexico City   Taipei

The title *A Prophet from Amongst You* is adapted from Yadin's reconstruction of the missing text of the Temple Scroll, column LXI, line 02.

נביא אקים להם מקרב אחיהם...אליו תשמעון

"I will raise up for you a prophet . . . from among you, from your brethren—him you shall heed . . ."

Library of Congress Cataloging-in-Publication Data

Silberman, Neil Asher, 1950–
    A prophet from amongst you : the life of Yigael Yadin : soldier, scholar, and mythmaker of modern Israel / Neil Asher Silberman.
      p.   cm.
    Includes bibliographical references and index.
    ISBN 0-201-57063-7
    1. Yadin, Yigael, 1917–1984.   2. Statesmen—Israel—Biography.
3. Generals—Israel—Biography.   4. Israel—Armed Forces—Biography.
5. Archaeologists—Israel—Biography.   6. Israel—Antiquities.
I. Title.
DS126.6.Y3S55   1994
956.94′04′092—dc20
[B]   93-5406
                                              CIP

Jacket design by Barbara Atkinson

Text design by Richard Oriolo

Map by Amy Elizabeth Grey

Set in 10-point Galliard by Weimer Graphics

1 2 3 4 5 6 7 8 9 10-MA-9796959493

First printing, November 1993

Handwritten library call number in margin: DS 126.6 .Y3 S55 1993

TO MY PARENTS

CONTENTS

ACKNOWLEDGMENTS

T he life of Yigael Yadin was so deeply involved in three distinct spheres of specialized knowledge—military affairs, biblical archaeology, and politics—that any biographer must become familiar with the various archives and libraries in Israel whose collections contain primary sources on his contributions to these fields. The most important of these sources are in Hebrew, and where I have quoted from documents, correspondence, or interviews conducted in Hebrew, the translations are my own. Since this biography is intended primarily for a general rather than a scholarly readership, I have avoided the citation of many secondary bibliographic references that are either highly technical or of limited availability. The specialized literature on subjects such as the Haganah, the 1948 war, and the early years of the State of Israel is so vast that I have attempted to list only the most basic works. In cases where an English translation exists for a memoir or other work, I have sometimes cited it—even though it may contain less detail than the Hebrew original. And rather than phonetically transliterate titles of books and articles that have appeared only in Hebrew, I have translated them into English to offer general readers a sense of the scope of Israeli research. I trust that specialists in the history of Israel will recognize the works I have cited. Earlier versions of my accounts of the battles of Latrun and the 1949 armistice negotiations were published in *Eretz* magazine. A full list of the archives I consulted and interviews I conducted is included in the bibliographic notes at the end of the book.

The transliteration of Hebrew and Arabic names into English remains a difficult problem. Although I have tried to be consistent in transliteration, I have chosen variant spellings when they are more commonly used in English and are thus more familiar to a general readership. Likewise I have used the more familiar chronological designations A.D. and B.C.—rather than the more neutral terms C.E. ("Common Era") and B.C.E. ("Before the Common Era"), which have become accepted in scholarly writing.

I owe thanks to many individuals and institutions for their help during the course of this three-year project. I would like to express my gratitude to the John Simon Guggenheim Memorial Foundation, which supported my research and travel with a 1991 fellowship. The staff of the Sterling Memorial Library of Yale University were, as usual, of great assistance. The library's collections once again served me as an invaluable and nearby resource. In Jerusalem, Joseph Aviram of the Israel Exploration Society offered continual advice and guidance and shared with me many insights from his close thirty-year friendship and professional collaboration with Yadin. I also want to express my gratitude to Amos Elon, who was the first to encourage me to undertake this biography. I continue to cherish his friendship and benefit from his political, historical, and philosophical insights.

Professors Moshe and Trude Dothan made my work immeasurably easier (once again) by sharing with me their wisdom and continuing friendship. Over the years, they have deeply influenced my understanding of Israeli archaeology and of Israel itself. Their tolerance of my endless questions, requests, and uncertainties is boundless. And their living room in Jerusalem—with its antique copper table, book-lined walls, and never-failing good company—has always been a scene of stimulating conversation and comfortable refuge for me.

My thanks also go to Naomi Kaplansky of Israel Television, who from the beginning of this project has been a welcome source of encouragement and help. Gideon Eshet and Yael Chen were, as usual, good sounding boards for my work-in-progress and keen observers of the current Israeli scene. Jonathan and Pamela Lubell and Avi and Ora Gan-Bar offered hospitality and encouragement in numerous trips to Israel. Ambassador Richard Nolte was an excellent source of advice and experience on the modern history of the Middle East, as was the late Professor Albert Glock of Bir Zeit University. My research also benefited from extended conversations with Professor Eric Meyers of Duke University, Professor Sy Gitin of the Albright Institute in Jerusalem, Professor Amnon Ben-Tor of the Hebrew University, and Professor Israel Finkelstein of Tel Aviv University. Over the years, I have greatly benefited from discussions with Professor Aharon Kempinski of Tel Aviv University on the interaction of archaeology and ideology.

At the Annenberg Research Institute in Philadelphia, Dr. David Goldenberg and Jonathan Brumberg-Kraus were of enormous help in researching the early phases of Eleazar Sukenik's career. At Yale University, Dr. David Stagg offered patient, constant advice on matters relating to computer systems and electronic information retrieval. I would also like to thank Zvi Schneider for help in utilizing the resources of the library and photo archives of the Hebrew University Institute of Archaeology. Alan Bitker shared his professional expertise in my analysis of Yadin's background. Rabbi Howard Sommer was helpful in reading an earlier version of the manuscript and offering perceptive literary and historical comments. I would also like to express my gratitude to Littal Yadin and Orly Yadin for permission to use the photograph of their father that appears on the cover.

My continuing thanks go to my agent Carol Mann, who with her usual skill and sound judgment facilitated the publication of this book. At Addison-Wesley, I have had the benefit of not one but *three* editors, each of whom contributed to this book in their own way: Jane Isay (who persuaded me to write it); Nancy Miller (who helped me through the unexpectedly long period of formulation); and Amy Gash (who helped me bring it to what I hope is a successful conclusion). My thanks also go to Production Supervisor Pat Jalbert, who brought the text, illustrations, and design elements together—efficiently and reassuringly.

These acknowledgments would not be complete without mentioning the invaluable contribution of Janet Amitai. As an experienced and skillful editor, researcher, and writer, she provided outstanding research assistance over the past two and a half years. Janet's enthusiasm; her ingenuity in tracking down promising archival leads, doing background research, arranging interviews, and locating photo sources; and her perceptiveness in pointing out mistakes and misinterpretations in my preliminary drafts made this book far better than it would have been otherwise. The value of her contribution to this project is, needless to say, far greater than these brief thanks can possibly express.

To my parents, I hope that this book's dedication will at least partially repay years of devotion and encouragement. And to my sister, Ellen Silberman Lemoine, I offer my appreciation for continuing moral support and welcome assistance in the formulation of travel plans.

Finally, I want to express my love for my wife Ellen and daughter Maya and thank them—yet again—for putting up with canceled weekend trips, missed vacations, and a generally preoccupied husband and father who sometimes seemed to prefer working or traveling to normal family life. I hope that the final product will justify their patience. Only they know how difficult and all-consuming the writing of this complex life story has been.

Branford, Connecticut
April 5, 1993

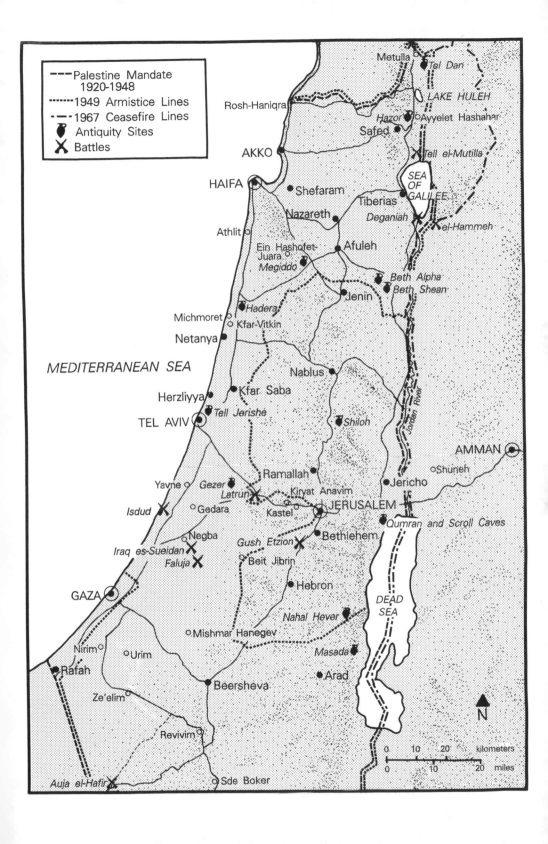

	Palestine Mandate 1920-1948
	1949 Armistice Lines
	1967 Ceasefire Lines
	Antiquity Sites
	Battles

Metulla
Tel Dan
LAKE HULEH
Rosh-Haniqra
Hazor
Ayyelet Hashahar
Safed
Tell el-Mutilla
AKKO
HAIFA
SEA OF GALILEE
Shefaram
Tiberias
Nazareth
Deganiah
Athlit
el-Hammeh
Ein Hashofet-Juara
Afuleh
Megiddo
Beth Alpha
Beth Shean
Jenin
Hadera
Michmoret
Kfar-Vitkin
Netanya
MEDITERRANEAN SEA
Nablus
Herzliyya
Kfar Saba
Shiloh
TEL AVIV
Tell Jerishe
AMMAN
Ramallah
Shuneh
Yavne
Gezer
Jericho
Latrun
Kiryat Anavim
Isdud
Gedara
Kastel
JERUSALEM
Qumran and Scroll Caves
Negba
Bethlehem
Gush Etzion
Iraq es-Sueidan
Faluja
Beit Jibrin
Jordan River
Hebron
GAZA
DEAD SEA
Nahal Hever
Mishmar Hanegev
Nirim
Masada
Urim
Arad
Rafah
Beersheva
Ze'elim
Revivim
N
0 10 20 kilometers
0   10   20 miles
Auja el-Hafir
Sde Boker

A Prophet from Amongst You

Prologue:
The View from
Masada

Beneath the fallen columns and shattered frescoes of King Herod's once-luxurious northern palace at Masada lay the grim evidence of destruction and death. Bronze arrows, tattered clothing, straw mats, leather sandals, and hundreds of silvered armor scales of an officer's battle corselet were suddenly exposed in the rubble as a group of volunteer diggers cleared away a thick blanket of ash and charred beams. The day was November 14, 1963, and Yigael Yadin's ambitious excavations were under way all across the summit of the remote mountain fortress built two thousand years before by the Judean king. Yadin, summoned urgently from another excavation area, made his way cautiously down a makeshift wooden stairway to the lowest level of the palace, built on a small, square terrace overlooking the arid gullies and salt flats of the western shore of the Dead Sea. It was a moment of high drama and unforgettable emotion. Yadin watched in silence as the volunteer diggers cleared the debris from a small bathing pool, whose smoothly plastered surface was darkly stained with what seemed to be blood. Nearby were the jumbled bones of two young men and a young woman, whose long hair, still neatly braided, had been miraculously preserved in the dry atmosphere of the region around the Dead Sea for almost two thousand years.

By 1963, Masada had become a modern myth in Israel, the symbol for a nation that felt itself surrounded and under siege. For decades, Jewish youth groups had made the difficult pilgrimage up the steep slopes of the flat-topped mountain in the Judean Wilderness to declare their connection with an ancient tale of heroism. It was there at Masada—according to the ancient Jewish historian Josephus Flavius—that during the great Jewish revolt against Rome in A.D. 66–74 a desperate band of Jewish rebels had stubbornly held out against a massive Roman siege and had taken their own lives rather than fall into Roman captivity. The story of Masada had taken on great significance in the modern Zionist movement; many had adopted as their watchword the slogan "Masada Shall Not Fall Again!" Yet while a succession of explorers and archaeologists had studied and mapped the ruins on the summit of Masada—and the Roman siegeworks around it—none before Yadin had been able to mobilize the resources and muster the manpower to excavate its palaces, administrative buildings, and storerooms. More to the point, there was no other archaeologist in Israel with the talent and charisma to spark the imagination of the nation—and to bring the story of the Jewish zealots' last stand to life.

Now with Yadin's discovery of the splendor of Herod's desert palace, the violence of the Roman conquest, and the grim evidence of the last Jewish defenders, Masada would become one of Israel's greatest tourist attractions and one of the world's most famous archaeological sites. Its significance was not to be strictly archaeological. By apparently verifying an ancient story of unrelenting military resistance, Yigael Yadin had contributed a powerful element to modern Israel's national consciousness. At a time when Israel was preoccupied with hit-and-run attacks on its borders, a political scandal of major proportions, and the traumatic passing of a generation of founding fathers, Masada served as one of the most powerful and evocative symbols for the country's sense of isolation and its precarious physical existence. Such was the modern symbolic power of Yadin's message that few dared challenge his conclusions or contest his evidence.

Masada was only one of Yadin's triumphs. In the mid-1950s at the Galilean site of Hazor, he led a large expedition that uncovered the remains of a vast Bronze Age city—called "the head of all those king-doms" in the Book of Joshua—and found what he believed was evidence of a victory of the children of Israel over the Canaanites there. In the burnt layer amid ruins of sacked temples and smashed idols, he brought to life the conquest of the vast Canaanite city by the ancient tribes of Israel, a message with enormous contemporary resonance to a nation so recently established in the midst of a modern war for its Promised Land. Later, at the site of Megiddo in the western Jezreel Valley, Yadin capti-vated the nation with his discovery of the spacious palaces and public works of King Solomon. And in 1960 in the caves of the Judean wilder-ness, he led a daring—and spectacularly successful—search for remains and hidden possessions of the followers of the legendary Jewish hero Bar-Kokhba. Throughout his career ran yet another continuing obsession: his name would always be linked closely to the intrigue and mystery of the Dead Sea Scrolls.

As a prophet of national rebirth and archaeological discovery, Yadin was rivaled by few other archaeologists of the twentieth century. His was not merely a message of ancient treasure recovered (though his excava-tions uncovered many priceless artifacts) or of ancient mysteries solved by modern science (though he proposed many intriguing solutions to puzzling historical questions). Rising to the lectern with the confidence of a master, he would look out over audiences of eager listeners, charm them with his wit and erudition, and inspire them to see in the modern State of Israel a poetic culmination of all Jewish history. When the house lights lowered in lecture halls and auditoriums from Hong Kong to Cin-cinnati, Yadin became the hero of his own perfectly crafted adventure as his brilliant color slides were projected upon the screen. Flashing power-ful images of ancient battlements and fortifications, enigmatic cult ob-jects, Hebrew scrolls, and jumbled human skeletons, he was a persuasive orator and international celebrity. And as one of Israel's most famous military leaders and public figures, he understood that in many ways the past is merely a projection of the present, and he used his archaeological insights to describe and defend his view of the modern State of Israel. Although he was interested in and knowledgeable about archaeological developments in other parts of the world, Yadin had no interest in exca-vating the ruins of the other peoples' ancestors. For him, archaeology would always be a profoundly patriotic activity.

Yadin was no conventional scholar. Though archaeology was always his first love, it was in another sense a second profession for him. While he was still in his thirties, he had attained a place in the highest circles of power in Israel, helping formulate policy, craft strategy, and plan mili-tary operations whose effects reverberated throughout the region—and the world—for decades thereafter. As one of the young leaders of the Haganah during the last years of the British Mandate, as chief of operations in Israel's War of Independence, as head of the Israeli military delegations to the Rhodes and Lausanne peace conferences, and as first peacetime chief of staff of the Israel Defense Forces, Yadin enjoyed enormous prestige and national honor. Yet in 1952 he abandoned that promising public career, freely giving up the power for which so many young men lust, to devote himself to the quiet joys of studying and teaching about the past.

The slender, prematurely bald, but supremely self-assured Yadin was a brilliant point of light among the cautious, old-style antiquarians who populated the world of biblical archaeology. While other faculty members in the archaeology department of Hebrew University drilled students on coins and letter forms, on dates, details, and specifics, Yadin created an atmosphere of excitement as he described ancient battles, kings, weapons, and wars. His flowing, lucid lectures, delivered with the arrogant flair for which he was famous, offered students a welcome respite from the modern realities of 1950s Israel, with its economic austerity plans and a state of siege that were unrelenting in their ferocity. Into his vivid descriptions of ancient Near Eastern civilization, with its kings, battles, and charioteers, he wove tales of hard-headed combat, wise policies, efficient administration, cynical alliances, and great territorial conquests. In the dreamlike world of biblical antiquity, he and his students could use archaeology to mold reality. In the triumphs and defeats of ancient Egyptians, Assyrians, Babylonians, and Israelites, they constructed a world with meaning for the present as well.

Behind the scenes as always, Yadin's wife Carmella, daughter of one of Israel's most aristocratic families, devoted her life to making every detail of Yadin's public persona seem effortlessly elegant. Again and again in the 1950s and early 1960s, the tight circle of political insiders and party professionals around Prime Minister David Ben-Gurion attempted to persuade Yadin to reenter the public arena and resurrect the fortunes of Ben-Gurion's party, Mapai. Yet Carmella constantly reassured Yadin that his place was not in the smoky meeting rooms of the Knesset but at the lectern in academia, aloof from the wildly changing fortunes of those who entered Israeli politics. Later, after Carmella's death, in the midst of political upheaval, Yadin again succumbed to the lure of the public life, only to suffer his deepest humiliation and personal setback. When he left the dreamland of the past, where he could mold the world as he wished it, the realities of social change and the political combativeness of modern Israel came to have a sobering effect on his extraordinary career.

Throughout his life, Yadin remained a symbol to the people of Israel. His parents were among the wave of Zionist settlers of the Second Aliyah, the second great wave of modern Jewish immigration to Palestine at the turn of the century. And as the son of one of Israel's first archaeologists—and of one of its pioneering kindergarten teachers—Yadin was raised to believe that both the past and the future could be molded at will. His life embodied the enormous transformation that took place in the historical and political consciousness of the Jewish people, from the sacred texts and sacred history of a persecuted religious community to the sovereign consciousness of a modern nation-state. In a sense, that had been the dream of the turn-of-the-century Zionist movement; the transformation of the Jewish people from helplessness and persecution to independence and modernity. What the movement's leaders had not anticipated was a national awakening among the Palestinian Arabs—and the psychic costs to themselves and their children of becoming accustomed to using violence and threat of violence as a means of defending their own sovereignty.

The harried Jews of the Russian Pale of Settlement in the late nineteenth century bore utopian dreams of *ge'ula,* the ancient Jewish concept of redemption, the dawning of a millennial time. Although the ingathering of the Jews in their holy land was now described and implemented in the secular terms of nationalism, modernism, and historical destiny, the metaphysical, visionary dimension remained. The faith of Yadin's parents and their generation in redemption would be sorely tested over the coming decades as they confronted physical hardship, political opposition, and mounting violence. Yet it would never be entirely abandoned. On March 21, 1917, when a Hebrew kindergarten teacher named Chassiya Feinsod-Sukenik gave birth to a frail baby boy two months premature in a small house on the Street of the Prophets in Jerusalem, she and her husband Lipa gave him a name that underlined their faith that *ge'ula,* redemption, would come to the next generation if not to their own. The baby's given name, Yigael, was an uncommon passive future form of that same Hebrew word, meaning "*he* will be redeemed." The child's destiny was to be deeply intertwined with that of his people. Only time would tell if the name represented a prophetic premonition—or was simply an idle yearning, destined to end in disillusionment.

Chapter One

LOST IN
THE RUINS

E ven as an infant, Yigael Sukenik attracted attention. Passersby
on Jaffa Road and shoppers among the piled cabbages and carrots of the vegetable market at Mahane Yehuda would often re-
mark to his mother Chassiya—as if she needed convincing—that her son
was an exceptionally beautiful child. A stiffly formal baby photograph
taken by a photographer in Jerusalem around 1920 shows Yigael's delicate expression. Against the photographer's painted studio backdrop,
the three-year-old's arms are positioned carefully; one hand rests grace-
fully on a prop ottoman, while his pudgy legs are crossed elegantly at the
knees. That sepia image bespeaks a pampered childhood in which turn-
of-the-century Eastern European respectability had not yet completely
faded into an aggressive, combative Middle Eastern reality. Indeed, as a
result of his mother's constant supervision, guidance, and encourage-

ment, Yigael would always carry with him a sense of gentility and propriety that derived from her own childhood home in Bialystok.

To the Sukeniks in the 1920s, that middle-class Jewish society in far-off Lithuania, ravaged by the battles of the Great War and under attack by Soviet commissars, was little more than a fairytale setting for fond family memories and anecdotes. Chassiya often spoke of her parents' home, with its modern middle-class elegance and its traditional, prayerful reverence for distant, almost heavenly Eretz Israel, the "Land of Israel." Yigael's maternal grandfather, Matthias Feinsod, had owned an elegant furnishing store on Gildova Street in Bialystok's commercial center, offering expensive, imported furniture and elegant chandeliers for sale to the city's wealthiest residents. But Chassiya—Chashka, her family called her—had had no desire to remain in Bialystok and become a respectable businessman's wife. Like many other idealistic young Jews throughout Eastern Europe, she was captivated by the rising Zionist movement. Even though her father's personal connections with provincial authorities enabled him to shield his family, elegant home, and social standing from the mounting violence and arbitrary exactions against Jews under the reactionary tsars Alexander and Nicholas, Chassiya intended even as a teenager to become a teacher of Jewish pioneers' children among the palm trees of Eretz Israel.

Yigael's father, Lipa Sukenik, also hailed from Bialystok, but he rarely spoke of his background or his boyhood friends. His family was neither as prosperous nor as effectively shielded from the harsh realities of Jewish life in the Pale of Settlement as the Feinsods were. The name *Sukenik* (meaning "dry goods seller" or "cloth peddler" in Polish) branded the family with the image of a wandering hawker, and over the decades, they had maintained a precarious existence, progressively restricted in residence, livelihood, and physical security. All that Yigael knew of his father's early life he learned years later, not from fond recollections but from bitter memories of a painful personal history. Yadin's paternal grandfather, Moshe Sukenik, was a workman with nothing more to sell than his own labor, living in a completely different world from the prosperous merchants and leaders of Bialystok's Jewish community. To escape the drudgery and poverty of his earthly existence, he immersed himself in the interior world of ritual, tradition, and spirituality. His son Lipa, the eldest of eight children, was sent off at an early age to a traditional *cheder* to learn prayers and passages of Talmudic law. Although most of his brothers and sisters were forced to end their formal education at ten or eleven to become craftsmen's apprentices or factory workers, Lipa, having an apparent talent for learning, was enrolled as a rabbinical student in the huge Slobodka yeshiva located in the river town of Kovno, some two hundred miles north of Bialystok.

Lipa Sukenik was not destined, however, to become a rabbi. During his four years of study at Slobodka, he was deeply influenced by the older students' hushed but heated debates. Over the previous decade the Jewish socialist movement, the Bund, had gained strength in manufacturing centers like Bialystok, promising far-reaching changes in the lives of the thousands of Jewish men and women who worked in factories and textile mills. The Bund activists preached tirelessly to workmen's circles and mutual aid societies that a revolution against capitalism offered a sure path to *ge'ula*—redemption—that obedience to haggard, gray rabbis and timid civic leaders could not possibly provide. The world outside the yeshiva walls became harder to ignore as outbreaks of anti-Jewish violence spread through nearby cities and towns. In June 1906 came news of a campaign of violence in Bialystok itself. A shot had reportedly been fired at a church procession, and a rumor that a Jew had fired it set off two days of attacks against the Jewish quarters. Members of the municipal police took an active part in the looting, rape, and anti-Jewish violence, participating in the destruction of dozens of homes and businesses, the murder of dozens of innocent men, women, and children, and the serious injury of hundreds more.

To seventeen-year-old Lipa Sukenik, the Bialystok pogrom of 1906 occasioned a decisive break with his own past. Religious study could no longer provide escape from the horrors of the outside world. Sometime in the fall of that year he left Slobodka "to the great consternation" of his parents, to return to Bialystok. By year's end, having replaced his Torah and Talmud studies with Marxist study circles and union agitation, Lipa Sukenik had joined Poalei Zion, "the Workers of Zion," and met Chassiya Feinsod. Neither set of parents could have been happy about the match or its political setting, for in the intensifying official repression, membership in any socialist organization, including Poalei Zion, was a serious political offense. While Chassiya remained in the background, confining her activities to the Poalei Zion's programs in Hebrew education, her new friend Lipa became, by his own less-than-modest admission, one of the party's "able young lecturers" and was soon dispatched to other cities to give speeches and organize new Poalei Zion cells. After five years of off-and-on courtship, tireless commitment to spreading the message of seditious activity, Chassiya and Lipa decided to leave Lithuania forever, get married, and make a future together in Palestine.

Redemption, however, was not to be achieved merely by making the sea passage from Trieste to Jaffa. To be sure, both Chassiya and Lipa soon found employment as teachers in the Hebrew school system in Jerusalem (she had spent two years in Berlin gaining professional training as a kindergarten teacher, and he received certification after a brief period of study at the Hebrew Teachers' College). But World War I—with its famine, pestilence, and persecution of Jewish activists—sorely tested their faith in the Zionist ideal. Soon after the start of the war in 1914, the couple had exchanged their Russian passports for Ottoman nationality certificates, but that merely made them vulnerable to the arbitrary confiscations and conscriptions ordered by the increasingly desperate Turks. Even after Yigael's birth—and after the British conquest of Palestine in 1917 and the publication of the Balfour Declaration, with its official sponsorship of the establishment of a "Jewish national home," dreams of redemption still seemed distant. During the early years of the British mandate, Chassiya, Lipa, and their two sons (a second son, Yosef, or Yossi, was born in 1920) lived a modest albeit peripatetic existence, moving frequently through the older neighborhoods of western Jewish Jerusalem. In 1921 they were forced to leave a solid stone house on the Street of the Prophets for a more modest apartment in the Geula neighborhood (that onomastic hope for redemption again) and after a year or two, on to Schneller, a more distant suburb that had been constructed around the looming buildings of a nineteenth-century German-Protestant orphanage. In 1928, Chassiya gave birth to a third son, Mattatyahu, named after her merchant father who could never quite understand his daughter's stubborn obsession with Palestine.

Home life for the Sukeniks was not particularly happy. While Chassiya remained a dedicated kindergarten teacher, Lipa was never satisfied as a high school instructor in mathematics and geography. From his first days in Jerusalem he displayed an intense interest in antiquarian subjects; he would go off on his own to explore the surrounding countryside of Judea, hiking through villages and hidden valleys, seeking biblical identifications for ruins and ancient tumbles of stones. Sukenik's interest in the past was inspired by the radical Hebrew novels he had read years before, smuggled into the yeshiva like biblical pornography. Written in modern Hebrew and freely combining melodramatic romance and high adventure with familiar biblical stories, they offered him a dreamland of wish-fulfillment. Like the religious texts that he and his fellow students pored over, they represented a body of sacred knowledge whose basic truth was never to be questioned, yet they were at the same time capable of endless reinterpretation. In his daydreams about the heroes of the biblical period—and in his study of the scattered archaeological remains they had left behind—Lipa Sukenik found an alternative reality in which there were no disappointments, no boredom or tedium, no unrealizable ideals. In his vision of antiquity, confident Jewish warriors bravely defended their land and their freedom. Hebrew judges battled Canaanites and Philistines; Maccabean freedom fighters defeated huge Greek armies; and even the desperate, doomed struggle of the defenders of the ancient desert fortress of Masada and the followers of the great rebel leader Bar-Kokhba served as timeless models of strength, determination, and fearlessness.

Sukenik was determined to become an archaeologist, though that was a ludicrously unrealistic ambition for a Palestinian Jew in the early 1920s. At that time, *real* archaeology was undertaken only by Great Institutions, Great Fortunes, and Great Powers. The prototypical Near Eastern archaeologist of that era was a refined European or American gentleman-scholar who had the leisure or financial support to travel widely and hire native guides and workmen to facilitate his archaeological research. As was the case in Egypt, Greece, and Mesopotamia, the serious exploration of Palestine was conducted by the staff and students of European and American archaeological schools. Clustered around Ethiopia Street, near other diplomatic, educational, and cultural institutions of New Jerusalem, were the local headquarters of the American School of Oriental Research, the British-sponsored Palestine Exploration Fund, and the Deutscher Palästina Verein. Even now with the war over and a new British-administered Department of Antiquities established, the past still seemed to belong to others besides Palestinian Jews. A huge, well-funded expedition from the University of Pennsylvania was preparing to excavate the towering mound of Beth Shean in the northern Jordan Valley. The British School of Archaeology had laid claim to the ruins of the ancient coastal city of Ashkelon. And the orientalists of the University of Chicago had set their sights on a resumption of the dig at Megiddo—with the generous support of John D. Rockefeller. A golden age of archaeology was apparently dawning, but it was golden only for outsiders. Even the most promising Palestinian students had little to look forward to other than patronizing lectures by European and American scholars and occasional employment as junior assistants on digs. As a result, Lipa Sukenik had to content himself with organizing field trips for the small Jewish Palestine Exploration Society and with researching and writing a Hebrew guidebook to the antiquities of Jerusalem.

Lipa's constant exploration in many ways symbolized a personal dissatisfaction. After only a few years in Palestine, he had grown disenchanted with the socialist theories of the Poalei Zion party and began to feel stifled in his personal life. As the years went on, his relations with Chassiya cooled; at times they reached the breaking point when rumors—justified or contrived—reached Chassiya of her husband's infidelities. To the boys, their father often seemed detached and isolated, maintaining his own affairs in careful order in the privacy of his study. He was attached to certain personal possessions—his leatherbound diary, desk calendar, stationery, and Waterman pen in particular—as if his external propriety had to be shored up continually with material objects. Throughout his career he sought the public recognition that he could never find among his scholarly colleagues. "They'll never forget that I was an algebra teacher," Lipa Sukenik complained for years, in disgust.

Such sentiments were lost on young Yigael. As the tensions within his family mounted, he retreated into a private world. As his mother devoted herself single-mindedly to her kindergarten in Nahlat Sheva and his father to his antiquarian studies, Yigael—even as a small child—formed the preference for solitary reflection that would characterize him for the rest of his life. "It's strange what you recall from age two or three," he noted years later in a long autobiographical interview. "I remember the big garden with trees behind the house." That hidden garden in the backyard of the house at number 23 Street of the Prophets provided four-year-old Yigael an island of serenity and play in an increasingly violent world. In the fall of 1921, however, the small boy saw a frightening scene unfold on the other side of his garden wall: A sullen procession of Arab Palestinians with shepherds' clubs bared and angrily shouting nationalist slogans marched down past the closed garden. It would remain among the most vivid of his earliest childhood memories.

Years later, as a public figure and national celebrity, Yigael Yadin visited the place, with journalists, on a pilgrimage to the scenes of his earliest childhood. He wandered into the enclosed garden behind the house, which now seemed so much smaller than he had remembered. As he walked through the cramped apartment, he pointed out the rooms where he had been delivered by Dr. Kagan the midwife, where he had played with his brothers, where the family had sat together for dinner, and where the Russian nanny and housekeeper Maria had kneaded dough for Russian pastries for the family. Maria had obviously been an important figure in the family—she was recalled fondly by both Yigael and Yossi in later years. A middle-aged woman, she was one of the thousands of poor non-Jewish Russians who had come to Palestine in the mass pilgrimages encouraged by the tsarist government at the turn of the century. But now she was stranded, with neither hope nor desire to return to the new Soviet state. Maria would take the Sukenik boys on adventures through the crowded covered bazaars of the Old City. As light streamed into the darkness through skylights, she haggled with bedouin women over the price of vegetables, gossiped with other Russians about the latest news from the old country. And they faithfully visited the dark, musty-smelling rotunda of the Church of the Holy Sepulcher, traditional site of the crucifixion, where she and the two little Jewish boys partook of holy water and pungent clouds of incense and mumbled Russian prayers to her Saviour above.

The color and variety of these trips to the Old City were eventually overshadowed by the disturbances and violence that marked the early years of the British Mandate. In an atmosphere of tension and mutual suspicion, each of Jerusalem's ethnic communities turned inward. What had seemed alien before was now often regarded as threatening, and despite the ideals of international and intercultural solidarity so proudly expressed by both Chassiya and Lipa, the openness of their household eventually underwent painful contraction. As Yossi recalled, Chassiya returned from work one day to find Maria drawing water from the cistern in the courtyard and crossing herself to bless its purity. The sight of her own two little boys standing behind her and reverently mimicking the sign of the cross seemed symbolically to undermine her hopes for a Jewish renaissance in Palestine. The boys were shooed away, and Chassiya spoke with Maria frankly. Her place as nanny and surrogate mother was soon taken by a succession of Jewish girls.

Long after Yigael Yadin had become a famous and respected national figure, his mother, long retired, often told a story that unintentionally revealed his inner vulnerability as a boy. The young Yigael had prided himself on being able to evoke his mother's praise or laughter, but there was something silently fragile about him. So it was that one day—the precise date is lost but is no less vivid for its mythic timelessness—Chassiya, again coming home from work and occupied with a dozen other things, asked Yigael to bring her an orange. The precocious child didn't hesitate in bringing her a tomato—and thus, the story went, she discovered that her son was color-blind, like so many other members of her husband's family. But the color-blindness was not the important point of the story; far more significant was Yigael's reaction. On being chided mildly that this was a tomato, not an orange—that he had thus not carried out the instructions precisely and elegantly—Yigael's self-confidence suddenly crumbled, and he burst into tears.

The atmosphere in which Yigael grew up was overshadowed by uncertainty and foreboding, for by 1920, optimistic hopes for the imminent establishment of a Zionist commonwealth under British auspices were fading. Agitation among the Palestinian Arab population against the Balfour Declaration was rising, and the British administration, fearing backlash throughout the region, perceptibly cooled its ardor for the itation of a Jewish National Home. A younger generation of Palestinian Arab intellectuals looked northward to Damascus and worked for the incorporation of Palestine into a vast Arab kingdom under the Emir Faisal of the Hashemite line. Both Arabs and Jews were bracing themselves for violence. In January 1920 an attack by Arab irregulars on the Jewish settlement of Tel Hai in the Upper Galilee resulted in the death of the Russian Jewish war hero and military leader Yosef Trumpeldor. The entire Jewish community in Palestine was terrified and outraged; Tel Hai and Trumpeldor became powerful symbols. In fact, the Sukeniks' second son Yosef, who was born later that year, was named after him.

The day of blissful field trips was now over; the dreams of a peacefully built Zionist homeland in Palestine could no longer be so easily entertained. No longer could anything—even archaeology—be unconnected with politics. In the summer of 1921 Lipa Sukenik left home for what would be the first of many explorations. He had been asked by the Commission for Educational Work among Jewish Laborers in Palestine, an organization of the Zionist labor union Histadrut, to deliver a series of lectures on archaeology to the settlers and road builders along the southwestern shore of the Sea of Galilee. Preaching in makeshift dining halls and in open-air encampments, Sukenik tried to impress upon the young people the sanctity of archaeological remains and their shared national responsibility to investigate them. The modern Jewish pioneers of Galilee, he noted with considerable (yet characteristic) rhetorical flourish in his journal, were "the descendants of the owners of these destroyed, ancient buildings, who have returned from great distances to the land of their forefathers to rebuild it and raise up its ruins." The trip north also offered Sukenik a chance to make some archaeological discoveries of his own. Arriving at the communal settlement of Kinneret, he at once observed that the new road being constructed by the young workers cut through the edge of an ancient city mound known as Khirbet Kerak. Extensive remnants of collapsed walls, floors, and aqueducts lay exposed. Sukenik collected some pottery fragments, several Greek and Arabic inscriptions, and a marble head of the Greek goddess Tyche that he brought back home to his wife and sons proudly, intending to publish on them himself.

four-year-old Yigael might have thought of the white
an's head on which his father lavished so much atten-
took his father more and more often away from the
e time through the fall of 1921, Sukenik combed the
eign archaeological schools for ancient references to
Kerak and for artifacts that stylistically paralleled the
red there. Particularly helpful was a thirty-year-old

American scholar named William Foxwell Albright, who had recently been appointed director of the American School of Oriental Research. Despite their vastly different backgrounds (Albright had been born in Chile, son of pious American Methodist missionaries), Albright and Sukenik hit it off immediately. On Albright's recommendation—and apparently with his bibliographical assistance—a densely documented article on the history of Khirbet Kerak was published the following year in the *Journal of the Palestine Oriental Society,* under the simple byline "L. Sukenik, Jerusalem." Sukenik knew that he would have to gain some scholarly credentials to fulfill his long-range career plan. Even as he continued to teach in the public schools through the academic year 1921–22, he worked hard to polish his reading, writing, and speaking skills in German. With the help of the Jewish Palestine Exploration Society he obtained a modest scholarship for archaeological study abroad. At the end of the school year he ended his career as a Zionist teacher. And in the autumn of 1922 he left his wife and two young sons in Jerusalem, setting off for a year of study at the University of Berlin.

Sukenik's absence was by this time a routine aspect of the family's life. During the boys' early childhood their father was away for weeks, sometimes months at a time. While their mother was always there to nurture and reassure them, their father was aloof and often angry and in most cases simply not there. Yigael's early memories of time spent with his father were vivid perhaps because of their very rarity. He fondly recalled the Sabbath walks from the center of the city to the new Jewish suburb of Talpiot to visit the historian Joseph Klausner and the poet S. Y. Agnon. Yet in at least one case there was a far less pleasant childhood memory of time spent with his father that Yigael would carry with him for the rest of his life. The time was the summer of 1922; Sukenik was preparing to depart for Berlin in just a few weeks to begin his first proper archaeological training. His American friend, William Albright, was undertaking excavations on the biblical site of Tell el-Ful, "the Mound of the Bean," only a short distance north of Jerusalem, a site that he identified with the ancient palace of King Saul. Sukenik could hardly refuse Albright's invitation to visit him there, and for some reason he brought along his five-year-old son. Many years later, Yadin remembered the leisurely walk north from Jerusalem, with his father holding his hand, then carrying him on his shoulders, a detail of shared experience and physical contact that seems from the very vividness of its recollection to have been relatively rare. This moment of shared experience was, however, suddenly shattered. Arriving at Albright's excavation, with the dust rising and the local workers hacking the soil from the foundations of the ancient fortress, Sukenik's relationship to his son suddenly, unknowingly changed. Eager to greet and speak with Albright and above all to make a respectable, collegial impression, he absentmindedly put Yigael down in one of the trenches and quickly walked off with his American friend.

The five-year-old, suddenly alone in strange surroundings, with the Beit Hanina villagers hacking at the soil with their picks and hoes and speaking among themselves, was struck with the panicked fear that his father had forgotten him and left him behind. "I still remember how traumatic it felt," Yadin confided to a journalist in his last public interview, in the spring of 1981. "I ran among the ruins, crying and looking for my father. I was sure that I'd be left there forever." The hysterical child was not easily calmed; as Chassiya remembered many years later, late that same afternoon her husband returned home from the visit with the boy still crying, still red, and reflexively drawing in breaths between sobs. The excursion to Tell el-Ful became a family legend, but it was only in the recalling, years later, at the end of his career, that Yigael Yadin could fully appreciate the power of that vision of sudden abandonment by his father among the ancient, tumbled stones of the Land of Israel.

———

With a mother like Chassiya Feinsod-Sukenik, it is little wonder that Yigael later made many idealistic calls for educational reform and cultural renaissance. His friends and colleagues recalled the fond admiration in which he held her, as one of the nation's true educational pioneers. Indeed, during the first decade of British rule in Palestine, Chassiya emerged as the most powerful and persistent exponent of kindergarten education. As early as 1918, she drafted a detailed memorandum for the leaders of the world Zionist movement urging that modern kindergartens be established in every Jewish neighborhood. Deeply influenced by the latest theoretical developments—particularly the Montessori method, which was introduced into Palestine right after the war—Chassiya successfully mobilized official support. With the establishment of kindergartens in Jewish neighborhoods throughout Jerusalem and Chassiya's appointment as their supervisor, however, she found herself embroiled in the politics of competing conservative, socialist, secular, and religious ideologies. Rather than embroil her own sons in the turbulent public schools of the city, she used all the family resources to pay tuition for a private academy founded by an American expatriate.

Thus it was that Deborah Kallen, a stern, gaunt teacher from Baltimore, became a major influence in the Sukenik boys' lives. Like so many Americans who saw the passions and the medieval prejudices of the Middle East as problems to be overcome through the light of American progressive education, Kallen wanted to bring a unique educational program to Palestine. "It is dangerous," she once remarked to Zionist leader Arthur Ruppin, "to tell children that they do not know enough." With her own open curriculum and staff of dedicated teachers, Kallen applied to primary education what she believed was a scientific plan. To many, hers was a strange school where the children learned "nothing and everything," for with an outspoken prejudice against memorization of facts and numbers, the Kallen School concentrated above all on developing its students' self-confidence. Instead of formal classes and lessons, there were projects. Carpentry was used to teach mathematics, physical dexterity, and aesthetics; gardening, for both science and nutrition. Indeed, the students were encouraged to establish and maintain a bank, store, restaurant, and storeroom in a miniature idealized community watched over by Deborah Kallen and her staff.

From an early age, Yigael and Yossi were bundled off to attend this school where self-reliance was the watchword and where the environment was strictly controlled. To set her students apart from other children, Kallen insisted that they wear "playsuits"—uniform, short-legged jumpsuits that blurred the usual dress distinctions between boys and girls. Gender roles were mixed evenly in cooking, in tending flower and vegetable gardens, in carpentry, sculpture, and furniture-making, and in creating scenery and costumes for school plays. While other students in the city studied Talmud, the Koran, or alphabets and multiplication tables, the Kallen pupils dashed off impressionistic drawings and creatively expressed their feelings about family associations and significant events. Always keeping her distance from her pupils, Kallen inspired fearful respect among them; although her philosophy was progressive, her discipline was stern and uncompromising, for teachers and pupils alike. She tolerated no romances among her staff, nor any of the teachers receiving parents' gifts or excessive praise. Her educational goal was to encourage self-reliance in each child.

Actually, self-reliance became an important asset in light of the hostility that other schoolchildren in Jerusalem often expressed toward the pupils of the Kallen School. Coming to school in their playsuits, the Kallen pupils were often teased by other children as spoiled little aristocrats. There was more than a little truth to the characterization, for although scholarships were given to a few poorer children, the bulk of the students were children of the community's elite—professionals, academics, and Zionist functionaries. Their parents were receptive to unorthodox, modern ideas of progressive education, a closed community of intellectual free-thinkers in a city where fanatical religious orthodoxy was—and still is—an acceptable norm. Had the Kallen School been situated in a quiet Baltimore suburb, it might have merely raised eyebrows. Located as it was in a big house in the mixed Jewish-Arab neighborhood of Musrara, the strange school's customs raised the anger of zealots on both sides of the fence. Kallen girls riding their bicycles to school through the orthodox Meah Shearim neighborhood more than once became targets for rocks and tomatoes; insults and jeers were an everyday occurrence. As a result, the children of the Kallen School learned to shield themselves with the smug self-assurance that they were going to a special institution—one far better than the public elementary schools. Despite the ideology of egalitarianism and national revival that so thoroughly permeated the Jewish community in Palestine, the two hundred Kallen pupils were taught to consider themselves a besieged intellectual elite.

In grade school Yigael Sukenik did not make much of an impression on his schoolmates; most remembered him as a quiet, average student who kept largely to himself. Like all the other children, he joined the game On the Border at every recess, in which two teams vied to conquer each other's territory. Prisoners would be captured, and daring raids would be staged to free them. If Waterloo was won on the playing fields of Eton, however, it is not at all clear that the Israeli War of Independence was won on the playground of the Deborah Kallen School. Classmates' memories of Yigael Sukenik in this period are fragmentary—his longtime friendship with a girl named Hemda Feigenbaum, his unusually thick hands for his slender body, and most of all his emerging interest in history. As fellow students recalled years later, Kallen delighted in the historical pageants like *The Exodus from Egypt*. The participants had to do research to design the costume of the high priest, the symbols for the Twelve Tribes, and the arms and armor of the Israelite warriors. In typical Kallen fashion the students were less concerned with dates, facts, and figures than with communicating emotion vividly.

Outside school hours, Yigael's natural shyness inhibited his attempts to mix in the wider society. For the most part he remained an observer, going every Saturday to watch soccer games in a big field near the police headquarters, where teams made up of British police—stolid roughnecks from Scotland and the Midlands—vied with teams of Polish boys and workers from the "Maccabee" Athletic Club of Jerusalem. Years later, Yigael recalled his hero—a Jewish defenseman named Fiedler—but he could never quite share his enthusiasm or recreate the man's plays and heroism along with the other boys of his neighborhood. There was always a gulf between Yigael and the children of poor, observant Jews who went to the Tachemoni School in the neighborhood. As the eldest son of the kindergarten teacher and the archaeologist, Yigael's sense of detachment was often confused, as shyness often is, with an attitude of superiority. "He always kept his distance," recalled boyhood acquaintance Chaim Rivlin, who never saw Yigael join in the games of the neighborhood boys; "he was always with his books and select circle of friends."

Chassiya and the boys remained in Jerusalem during Lipa's year of study at the University of Berlin, sending off money to support him, faithful that somehow his dream would come true. In the meantime, Lipa was taking on a new identity and adopting concepts that would later exert enormous influence on Yigael. These basic archaeological concepts, which Sukenik would utilize in his study of the antiquities of the Land of Israel, were those most common and most powerful in Weimar Germany—a society of outsiders, in which cultural pretensions and aggressive patriotism masqueraded as respectability. Within the cafés and student meeting places of the busy, cosmopolitan city lurked a dashed and twisted version of the nation's prewar megalomania. Generalizations about races and peoples came easily; social scientists and historians alike turned to the geographer Friedrich Ratzel's theories of the inevitable competition of all races for *Lebensraum,* "living space." In collective shock at the destruction of German national pride at the hands of the Allies, many turned to a grim ideology of struggle: the idea that the destiny of every people was either to conquer or be enslaved. These themes recurred in crowded university lecture halls and in scholarly debates and essays, even in surveys of ancient history and literature.

For years afterward, Yigael would listen with avid attention as his father recalled his student days in classical archaeology classes with Professors Noack, Farbner, Rodenwalt, and Goldschmidt; in Semitic languages with Professors Ebling, Mittwoch, and Brockelmann—he could not help but encounter the belief that race and racial conflict were the moving forces in all human history. Segregating the human past according to ethnic cultures, each with its own language, art forms, and unchanging racial characteristics, it was all too easy to declare that what was familiar was superior and what was different was somehow deficient or bad. At the University of Berlin, there was little argument about where the apex of human achievement was to be found. Attending the lectures of the famous classical historian Ulrich Wilcken (later to receive both power and recognition from the Nazis), Sukenik heard for himself the pompous platitudes about the sublime genius of Aryan civilization that would, in time, help bring about a period of darkness and horror in modern Germany. For Sukenik, of course, the message of Aryan superiority was unacceptable; yet the technique of seeing a people's essence in their ancient material remains would have enormous utility.

The history of the Jews had always been expressed abstractly. But in the material remains of the Land of Israel—like the bricks, pottery, and inscriptions Lipa Sukenik had found by the roadside at Kinneret—were the raw materials of an archaeological history of the Jewish people. In the tangible relics of antiquity, Yigael's father came to see a timeless national longing, self-reassuringly phrased in modern Zionist terms. "I'll never forget those days I spent in the papyrological department of the Berlin Museum," Sukenik later recalled of his study of the ancient Jewish papyri from Elephantine Island in Egypt. "Twenty-five centuries ago, one of my people sat in far-off Egypt, his pen poised over the very same documents I now held in my hands. And just like me today, his eyes were turned to the land of our forefathers, the nation's heart." The archaeology of golden ages and chosen peoples stressed unchanging national characteristics embodied in artworks and material artifacts. So after gaining a year's training in the jargon and concepts of *Kulturgeschichte,* in its implicit contrast between culturally creative peoples and culturally passive peoples, there was no question on which side of that great divide Sukenik would place the Jews. Sukenik now saw it as his mission to find the Jews' national history and natural genius expressed in the archaeology of their Promised Land.

Ancient synagogues rather than papyri quickly became his main subject of interest. The remains of Late Roman and Byzantine-era synagogues in the Galilee symbolized for him a last golden autumn of Jewish autonomy in Palestine, centuries after the Temple of Jerusalem had been destroyed. There one could still see the timeless Jewish symbols engraved on their tumbled stones: the menorah, the lulav, the ethrog, the shofar. Many of the ruins still bore the names of the donors who had contributed funds for the sanctuary's upkeep and blessings for the peace of all the people of Israel. Most important of all in Sukenik's mind, the ancient synagogues represented a brilliant adaptation of an essentially foreign architectural form. Through the genius of ancient Jewish architects, the Roman basilica of the forum and marketplace, with its large central hall divided lengthwise by rows of columns, was transformed into a building for prayerful worship, not commerce. This Jewish architectural innovation would be adopted by Christians for their churches as well.

Sukenik's hypothesis about the origin of the synagogue—from foreign form to national expression—can be seen as his own metaphorical resolution of an important issue of Zionist ideology. It explained how the Jewish community of Palestine could borrow from the Western world yet still maintain its cultural integrity. The study of the ancient synagogue was for him both a process of discovery and a means of self-reflection, and so it would also be for his son. While he was in Berlin, Sukenik submitted an article on this subject to the Hebrew literary magazine *Rimon*. That article, published in the spring of 1923, brought Sukenik before a far wider public. Deciding to use a Hebrew name for his byline, he would be known as Eleazar L. Sukenik from then on.

For Chassiya—not to speak of Yigael and Yossi—Sukenik's homecoming was hardly cause for celebration. Back in Jerusalem for the academic year 1923–24, he spent little of his leisure time at home. Still encouraged by his American friend Albright, Sukenik attended classes at the American School, helped organize field trips, and mingled amiably with the tightly knit group of conservative American Protestant scholars who had come to study there. In the fall of 1923, Sukenik helped one of Albright's students, William Carroll of Yale, explore and record the archaeological remains at Bittir, a few miles south of Jerusalem, identified as ancient Beitar, the site of the ancient Jewish hero Bar-Kokhba's last stand against the Romans in A.D. 135. In February 1924, Albright invited Sukenik to join an ambitious expedition to the Dead Sea region, a project conceived and financed by the Reverend Melvin Grove Kyle of the Xenia Theological Seminary of St. Louis, Missouri, whose guiding passion in life (in those days leading up to the Scopes "monkey" trial) was to use archaeology to prove the Bible true. Setting off from Jerusalem in mid-February, the ecumenical team included Albright, Kyle, two of his students from Xenia, William Carroll, geologist Alfred Day from the American University in Beirut, flint expert Père Alexis Mallon, director of the Pontifical Biblical Institute, Inspector Nai'im Makhouli of the Department of Antiquities as expedition liaison, and Eleazar Sukenik, in the unlikely positions as expedition surveyor and field botanist. The project was fruitful. In a month of exhausting search for the cities of Sodom and Gomorrah, this eclectic group of scholars crossed the Jordan, traveled from Amman down to Kerak and the Ghor es-Safi, discovered the important Early Bronze remains at Bab edh-Dhra, and concluded that the wicked cities of the plain, so vividly described in the Book of Genesis, lay submerged somewhere at the southern end of the Dead Sea.

Sukenik emerged from that expedition with new credentials. "The collaboration of Mr. Sukenik, in particular," wrote Director Albright in the school's 1923–24 annual report, "was stimulating and helpful to all." But Sukenik had little interest in merely providing material for American Bible Belt ministers' sermons; he was anxious to move on in his own archaeological career. For him, the Bible was not a religious tract but a national epic, and Palestine was not the Holy Land but Eretz Israel. Continuing his exploration of the ancient synagogue ruins of

Galilee, Sukenik also collaborated with Dr. Leo Arieh Mayer, a recent German Jewish immigrant who had been hired as an inspector for the Department of Antiquities in some important excavations around Jerusalem. In uncovering a massive fortification wall to the north of the Old City and in opening several distinctive Jewish tombs from the Roman period, Sukenik entered the bitter debates about the topography and customs of Jerusalem at the time of Jesus that had traditionally been the province of Christian scholars. What was more, he gave his interpretations of this last period of Jewish political independence a distinctly patriotic spin.

Sheer ambition and a tireless bullishness were the keys to Sukenik's success. By the summer of 1924, the character of the Jewish community of Palestine was dramatically changing. Tens of thousands of middle-class Jewish immigrants from the large cities of Eastern Europe, uprooted by stringent economic edicts and fears of anti-Semitism in Poland and blocked by new immigration restriction laws in the United States, swelled the populations of Haifa, Jerusalem, and Tel Aviv. In contrast to the ultraorthodox sector of the community (who relied solely on sacred texts for their understanding of Jewish history) and in contrast to the idealistic young farmers and road builders (who were primarily concerned with the country's future), these middle-class immigrants had been raised in an urban milieu in which appreciation of history, attendance at antiquarian lectures, and visits to museums were all standard components of polite respectability.

Sukenik found a ready audience in these new arrivals. In articles that often appeared in the popular press, he presented reports of recent discoveries and urged the immediate establishment of an archaeological museum in Tel Aviv. He tirelessly tried to rouse public interest. "How amazing it is," he wrote in 1925 in the Tel Aviv daily *Ha-Doar,* "that the nation that gave this land its glory, that poured out its spirit and soul on the mountains and valleys," is so far behind in its exploration of the land. "The time has come for us, the Jewish people," he continued, "to fulfill our obligation to the Jewish past and to the exploration of the Land of Israel, cradle of our faith."

Fulfilling this dream required of Sukenik yet another absence from his wife and family. In the early 1920s some of the most distinguished Jewish scholars in the world convened to select a faculty for the soon-to-be-opened Hebrew University in Jerusalem, and to make the university an international intellectual showplace. Sukenik's public reputation as an up-and-coming scholar had impressed American-born university chancellor (and later president) Judah Magnes, who now did what he could through his American contacts to see that the ambitious young archaeologist was not left out in the cold. In the summer of 1925, on the recommendation of Magnes, Sukenik was given a modest stipend and appointed a research fellow at Dropsie College in Philadelphia, an institution of higher learning for modern Hebrew and Jewish scholarship. Leaving his young family behind, Sukenik spent the 1925–26 academic year at Dropsie, giving lectures based on his fieldwork on Roman-Byzantine synagogues, and writing them up as a modest dissertation entitled *The Ancient Palestinian Synagogue*. For this he was awarded a quick—not to say unprecedented—doctor of philosophy degree. The following year, he was formally appointed to the ill-defined post of "archaeologist" on the faculty of humanities of the Hebrew University. He had no immediate teaching responsibilities and he devoted all his considerable energy to pleading for a suitable budget, collecting equipment for a small laboratory, and continuing his explorations of the synagogues of Galilee. He hired a young immigrant from Czechoslovakia, an engineering graduate named Nahman Reiss, as draftsman and his general assistant. In the course of time, Reiss would adopt the Hebrew name Avigad and serve as Sukenik's faithful if rarely appreciated assistant for the next twenty-six years.

One project closely followed another in the excavation of synagogues and tombs. In the summer of 1927, Dr. Sukenik hired Jewish workers for his first season of excavation at the Bronze and Iron Age mound of Tell Jerishe, on the outskirts of the swollen yet depressed metropolis of Tel Aviv. Every summer Yigael and his brothers had accompanied their mother to Tel Aviv to spend their vacation by the sea. But this summer and in the months that followed, Yigael began to spend more time watching his father's excavations and sensing their importance. For by this time, the elder Sukenik saw his future in far more sweeping terms than pedantic scholarship. "The important work that lies before me," Yigael's father jotted in his journal in July 1928, "is the creation of Jewish Archaeology."

Chapter Two

FATHER AND SON

T he way to Beth Alpha was not easy early in 1929, yet Yigael
savored the chance to go on an adventure with his father—and
to share in the excitement of what would be his greatest discovery. Much more than his brothers, Yigael had begun at an early age to
show serious interest in his father's explorations. Dr. Sukenik's assistant,
Nahman Avigad, recalled fondly more than sixty years later that when
ten-year-old Yigael was brought along to excavations by his father, he
"would look at what we were doing with great curiosity—at the site, at
everything around it, how we did the work." Now Yigael was about to
share in his father's greatest archaeological triumph, at a site far to the
north. From Jerusalem, father and son drove in a hired auto along the
narrow asphalt road that wound northward through the hill country,

past dozens of Arab villages and through the major cities of Ramallah, Nablus, and Jenin.

Because of the distance and slow pace of travel, Yigael and his father were forced to spend the night in a small hotel in Afuleh, a town that had been planned several years before as a great metropolitan hub for Jewish agricultural settlements in the Jezreel Valley. The developers' plans proved to be far too ambitious; with immigrants slow in coming and jobs nonexistent, only a few houses now dotted the extensive, neatly surveyed grid of avenues and streets. For the time being, Afuleh remained only a way station for those trying to reach more remote sites of the Jezreel Valley. So it was for Dr. Sukenik and his son; on the following morning a horsecart arrived from the nearby communal settlement of Beth Alpha to take them to the site of Sukenik's latest archaeological dig.

The project had begun unexpectedly, less than a month before. On the evening of December 30, 1928, Dr. Sukenik had returned home from a day at the university to find a young man waiting on his doorstep, a young man who would unwittingly transform Sukenik's professional career. Seven years before, while preaching to the road builders along the shores of the Sea of Galilee, Sukenik had impressed upon the young settlers the importance of archaeological remains and the necessity of reporting their discoveries to the proper authorities. Little wonder then that when a group of the young people, now settled on their own kibbutz—Beth Alpha, in the eastern Jezreel Valley—came upon a spectacular find, they contacted the only Zionist archaeologist they knew. Dr. Sukenik invited the young kibbutznik in from the doorstep, and the young man explained that just a few days before, while digging an irrigation channel, some of the Beth Alpha settlers had uncovered a brilliantly colored mosaic floor. In the narrow strip of the mosaic that had been exposed, they could make out the signs of the zodiac and some Hebrew inscriptions. Although they understood that this was an important discovery, they needed to complete the irrigation channel and could not halt work indefinitely. What should they do?

Based on the young man's sketchy description, Sukenik realized that the Beth Alpha settlers had come upon the floor of an ancient synagogue. The next day he contacted both the official representatives of the World Zionist Organization and Chancellor Magnes at the university. Both institutions immediately filed formal applications with the Department of Antiquities, and on January 2, 1929, Sukenik received excavation permit number 73. Within a few days, he and Avigad traveled north to begin the excavations, despite the unusually heavy winter rains. Arriving at the site of the discovery, they found a gaping hole in the wet earth, the colorful signs of the zodiac still visible. Sukenik quickly recruited volunteer workers from among the kibbutz members, and as the days passed and the entire mosaic was gradually revealed, the excitement among them grew. Sukenik later recalled with obvious satisfaction this striking demonstration of the political and spiritual power of archaeology for the Zionist enterprise. "Suddenly these people saw things that were never so tangible before," he remembered. "There was suddenly a feeling that this very parcel of land—for which they had suffered so much—wasn't just any piece of land but the place where their fathers and grandfathers had lived and died fifteen hundred or two thousand years before. All their work now had a different significance. Their history had been uncovered, and they could see it with their own eyes."

Unlike known examples of ancient Jewish mosaics, the intricate, colorful patterns of this pavement were complete. At the northern end of the main sanctuary was a vivid depiction of the sacrifice of Isaac, as described in the Book of Genesis. Rendered with the liveliness of folk art, it presented a haloed, bearded Abraham and the other figures in the story in an animated style that contrasted pleasingly with the somberness and avoidance of human figures characteristic of Jewish art of the Diaspora. In the center of the floor was a colorful circle of the zodiac, surrounded by personifications of the four seasons. In its center was the Greek god Helios, driving the chariot of the sun. To make the juxtaposition of motifs even more intriguing, the southern end of the hall—the side facing Jerusalem—featured a depiction of an Ark of the Law flanked by two menorahs and other ritual implements and guarded by fancifully rendered lions. Since this unique mosaic had to be carefully recorded, Avigad was assigned to make life-size tracings of the patterns. Sukenik hurried back to Jerusalem to summon a photographer—and to spread the word about the great discovery.

By the time Sukenik returned to the site with Yigael, the Beth Alpha mosaic had become a local sensation. In addition to the mosaic's main motifs, the portion near the synagogue entrance bore an Aramaic inscription that listed the names of the ancient benefactors of the congregation, in an uncanny parallel to the plaques that named the patrons of the modern Zionist enterprise. Visitors from the neighboring settlements were already flocking to see it. As word of the discovery spread throughout the country, it soon took on something of a spiritual significance for the Jewish community. Journalists and Histadrut officials made the long journey from Tel Aviv. Chancellor Judah Magnes of the Hebrew University also came to see the ancient synagogue, arriving from Afuleh on horseback. Because of the constant flow of visitors and the danger posed to the mosaic by exposure to the elements, the director of the government Department of Antiquities, Ernest T. Richmond, authorized the sizable appropriation of £650 for the construction of a protective building over the site.

Here was a sacred landmark in the making. The synagogue at Beth Alpha could be all things to all people: for the settlers of the Jezreel Valley, it was validation of their physical presence; for the nonreligious Jews of the country, it revealed a lively Judaism that freely borrowed motifs from other cultures; for the religious, it demonstrated the continuity of their religious rituals over millennia; and for the politically minded, it evoked a period in which the Jewish community of Palestine had maintained at least nominal autonomy.

For Eleazar Sukenik, the discovery of the Beth Alpha mosaic was a crucial turning point. The find's vast publicity made him a national celebrity. He gave lectures, presided over openings of exhibitions of excavation photographs and drawings, and received acclaim from the scholarly world. His long period of professional struggle appeared to be over. His ambitions for the establishment of "Jewish archaeology" as a tool of national rebirth had seemingly been validated. The skepticism of his friends and acquaintances toward his obsession with archaeology was now transformed to grudging admiration. On March 15 he lectured to the humanities faculty of the Hebrew University and received an enthusiastic welcome from colleagues who had never quite taken him seriously before. Even more gratifying was his reception abroad. Just six years before, he had been a silent auditor at the University of Berlin. In the spring of 1929, however, in the wake of the find at Beth Alpha, he became one of its distinguished guests. At the end of April he traveled to Germany to lecture on Beth Alpha at the festive Centennial Congress of the Archaeological Institute of Berlin. All over the world Sukenik's discovery was trumpeted: "Old Mosaics Trace the Origin of the Jews," ran a *New York Times* headline on April 29, 1929; "Dr. Sukenik Excavates a Synagogue in Palestine Which Makes New History in Judaism." In ten years Dr. Eleazar L. Sukenik had achieved nearly all his personal ambitions. He was the first Jewish Palestinian scholar to demonstrate archaeology's awesome potential. It was a lesson that would deeply impress itself upon the consciousness of his eldest son.

———

Through 1928 and 1929, as Yigael entered adolescence, he became more conscious of political concerns. Tensions were growing throughout the country. In the fall of 1928 a small riot occurred at an ancient site in Jerusalem that would transform the modern history of Palestine. It began with an incident that might have amounted to nothing if not for the interethnic tensions waiting to explode. On the Eve of Yom Kippur, September 23, 1928, a Jewish sexton placed a large ark, straw mats, lamps, and a screen to separate male and female worshippers in the narrow alley along the Western Wall. That wall, a surviving vestige of the ancient Jewish temple, also served as an outer retaining wall for the Muslim shrines of the Haram esh-Sharif, the "Noble Sanctuary," built on the Temple Mount. Conflicts for possession of shared sacred spots throughout the Holy City had always been an index of religious discord in Jerusalem, and at this time the index was high. The following morning, British officers, summoned by Muslim authorities, demanded that the Jewish worshippers remove the screen and other furnishings. When they refused to perform such labor on this holy Day of Atonement, the policemen attempted to remove the screen themselves and a violent melee ensued.

This small riot at the Western Wall quickly became an international cause célèbre. Haj Amin el-Husseini, the mufti of Jerusalem, convened a General Muslim Conference, stressing the wall's sanctity to Islam and suggesting that the Zionists' ultimate goal was the acquisition of the entire Haram esh-Sharif. On the other side of the conflict, the Zionist Organization mustered documentary evidence to prove Jewish ownership of the sacred alley, and Dr. Joseph Klausner, one of the Hebrew University's foremost historians and political essayists, urged his fellow Jews to form Western Wall Committees to insist on their national and religious rights to this shrine.

In this era of growing agitation, other ancient symbols were also being raised on the banners of militant political movements. Palestinian Arab nationalists turned increasingly to the slogans and emblems of Islam, while a growing conservative Zionist faction (led by Vladimir Jabotinsky and soon to be called the Revisionist party) effectively mobilized heroic symbols of Jewish antiquity in uncompromising and increasingly strident demands for immediate Jewish sovereignty. Their youth movement was known as Betar—an acronym for *Brit Yosef Trumpeldor,* "the Covenant of Yosef Trumpeldor," in honor of the fallen Jewish military hero. The movement's name could also be understood as a reference to ancient Beitar, the site of Bar-Kokhba's last stand.

The struggle for possession of the Western Wall continued to be a powerful rallying point for both Jewish and Arab nationalists through the spring and summer of 1929, and the youth in all of Jerusalem's neighborhoods were drawn into it. From the beginning of August 1929, young men on both sides showed their muscle. The soccer-playing heroes of the Maccabee Athletic Club (many of them were members of the underground Haganah Defense Force of the Labor movement) marshaled crowds at the Western Wall on the Eve of the Ninth of Av. The Revisionist youth had a more overt political agenda: to make this Ninth of Av commemoration—celebrated on the evening of August 15—the high point of the yearlong agitation to secure Jewish rights to the Western Wall. Incident followed incident, and the British were unable to contain the ethnic conflict. On the following day, Friday, August 16, a crowd of Muslims came out of the mosque and attacked Jews praying at the Western Wall, beating up several and burning some Torah scrolls. Anger built on both sides through the days that followed, but the event that led to the explosion occurred far from the sacred places of Arabs and Jews. In the course of a Saturday soccer game, some Jewish youths happened to kick their ball into an Arab's garden. Words led to blows, blows led to a stabbing, and the funeral that followed was transformed into a riot by the hotheads on both sides.

Even for the closed community of the Deborah Kallen School, the following Friday, August 23, 1929, was a day seared into memory forever. After speeches and the prayers at the el-Aqsa Mosque in which the existence of the Arab people in Palestine was said to be threatened with mortal danger, a crowd of young men from Jerusalem and the surrounding villages streamed out of the Haram esh-Sharif compound into the city streets. At the Jaffa Gate, a few of them fell upon those Jewish passersby so fatally unlucky as to have gotten in their way. The attempts of the police to stop the rampaging throng was futile, and after a few pitiful shots were fired into the air, the youths were allowed to go on their way. One group proceeded into the valley to attack the Jewish neighborhood of Yemin Moshe. Another group left the Damascus Gate and raged toward Meah Shearim, butchering some poor Jewish families who lived in the Georgian quarter on the way.

The bloodcurdling cries of murder and violence remained in the consciousness of an entire generation, as was the Jewish community's response. Forces of the underground Haganah militia mobilized hurriedly, leaving homes and workplaces in response to frantically conveyed reports of the disturbances, to stand on roofs, open windows, and alleys armed with hand grenades and guns. In some places the defense was effective. In some others, there was no time for a defense to be properly organized. In the relatively isolated southern suburb of Talpiot, innocent people were killed, their libraries were set afire, and kitchen machines and other gadgets that they had brought from Warsaw, Berlin, or St. Louis were carried off as prizes by rampaging villagers. With difficulty, the British gained control of the situation in Jerusalem, only to receive word that another crowd had fallen upon the Jewish community of Hebron, causing the utter destruction of an ancient community and dozens of deaths. The violence spread to Tel Aviv, where outlying settlements were attacked and abandoned. The adjoining kibbutzim of Beth Alpha and Hefzibah were among the many that were forced to fight off violent assaults. Slowly the violence died down and life returned to normal, but the consciousness of everyone had changed.

The shock waves echoed for months throughout both Jewish and Arab communities, marking a new era of increasing hostility and giving the lie to the progressive ideas of logic, ethnic coexistence, and compromise. Haj Amin el-Husseini, the mufti of Jerusalem, offered neither remorse nor even an explanation for the violence and killing, sensing that this graphic demonstration of Arab determination to fight Zionism was making some headway with the British government. By ordering a general strike of Arabs throughout the country on Yom Kippur that fall, he pressured the government—in an effort to avoid a pretext for another riot—to prevent the traditional blowing of the shofar at the Western Wall. On the Jewish side of the city there was a corresponding stiffening of position as hard-liners of the Revisionist party declared war on those whom they considered Jewish appeasers, collaborators, and moderates. Chancellor Judah Magnes's opening speech at the Hebrew University was interrupted by catcalls; he and other members of the Jewish peace group Brit Shalom were harassed and accosted on the street. The grim situation in the outside world penetrated even the walls of the sheltered, progressive Deborah Kallen School. An essay written by twelve-year-old Yigael Sukenik described the fear, loathing, and humiliation of the time, now turned against all Arabs. It was inspired by a disturbing image of the Mahane Yehuda market, once the scene of shopping expeditions of a mother and her eldest son among the piled cabbages and carrots of the Bedouin and fellahin.

"When I remember the scenes at the Jerusalem vegetable market at the time of the disturbances," the young Sukenik wrote, "the image that comes to my mind is of a deserted market, empty of all vegetables. I have to ask myself: What would have happened if the disturbances had lasted for half a year, instead of just a month? Will we always be so dependent on those same Arabs, who at each and every disturbance withhold vegetables from us, and who will start to make fun of us for not being able to survive on our own vegetables, and for our dependence on them? Couldn't we fill the market with vegetables ourselves? Who can say if more disturbances won't break out in the future, and maybe we'll be without vegetables again and the same Arabs will ridicule us for being so dependent on them. . . . In every settlement and in every neighborhood we have to grow vegetables and send them to the markets of the cities, and then the Jews in the cities will not have to buy their vegetables from

Arabs. And then the Arabs will no longer ridicule us, since we will not be dependent on them. And then it will seem to them that we are able to exist on our own. May this time come soon. Although the disturbances showed us the need for vegetables, we should learn from them other things as well."

The Laemel School, perched on a ridge to the west of Old Jerusalem, with its Hebrew-lettered clock above the main entrance, had undergone a far-reaching transformation in the three decades since its establishment by the Berlin-based Hilfsverein der Deutschen Juden. Both Lipa and Chassiya Sukenik had worked there as teachers before World War I, and both had participated in the struggle to make Hebrew—not German— the main language of instruction, in what was known as the War of the Languages. Now, in the 1930s, there was no longer any question of what language would be used for instruction, or whether it would become the focus of a Hebrew cultural renaissance. The Laemel School was now firmly a part of the Hebrew public school system; located in the heart of an expanding city, it was surrounded by institutions of a distinctly modern character—the Edison Cinema, a subsidized cafeteria for Histadrut workers, and the Eastern European–style Laemel Café, with its streetside gramophone endlessly blaring a crooning rendition of the Yiddish standard "Mein Shtetl at Belz."

Despite all the changes, the Laemel School retained a central role in the life of the Sukenik family. Even though the boys were students at Deborah Kallen's, they spent several afternoons every week in the school's courtyard, which had become the meeting place of a troop called the "Mattatyahu tribe" of the Organization of Hebrew Scouts. Scouting, in fact, was one of the most formative experiences of Yigael's childhood; the uniform of khaki shirt, shorts, and knee socks, with neckerchief tied neatly at the collar, attracted Yigael from an early age. Joining the tribe as a cub at age ten, he continued rising through the ranks of the organization, earning medals and patches and commendations, and eventually becoming a youthful scout leader himself.

Like everything else in the Holy City, the character of its scouting movement was marked by the growing tensions between Arabs and Jews. Soon after the establishment of the Mandate, the first high commissioner, Sir Herbert Samuel, had been eager to instill the principles of good citizenship among Palestinian young people and had proposed a scouting union of Muslims, Christians, and Jews. At the time, the leaders of the Jewish scouts were eager to cultivate their own brand of good citizenship and national feeling, and they rejected the suggestion, preferring to remain autonomous, display Jewish symbols, and instill Jewish values. In contrast to other youth movements sponsored by various political parties in the Jewish community, the scouts distinguished themselves as relatively nonideological. During the 1920s a new organization, the Legion of Scouts, was founded by Hebrew University classics professor Moshe Schwabe, who had once been a leader of Zionist youth movements in Eastern Europe. But Schwabe's insistence on encouraging heartfelt philosophical discussions—his "salon of ideas"—among the cubs and their leaders proved too esoteric for most. In the late 1920s, when the atmosphere in the city was more politically volatile, Schwabe became increasingly active in the Brit Shalom Arab-Jewish conciliation movement, and broke off his connections with the scouting movement, which to his taste had become far too preoccupied with tying knots, taking hikes, and wearing uniforms.

But that was just what the scouts wanted to be doing. A high school teacher named Zion Ha-Shimshoni had given the movement new life in 1930, in the aftermath of the riots. Ha-Shimshoni cared more about hikes and outings and sports than about philosophical or political speculation; an extraordinarily charismatic leader with a sense of the power of romantic symbols, he founded the Mattatyahu tribe in honor of the father of the ancient Maccabees. Placing stress on physical development and adventure, he organized hikes, campfires, and overnight trips in which only the most practical subjects were discussed: geography, nature lore, and fitness. In the twice-weekly afternoon meetings and weekend excursions, Yigael Sukenik grew to love the intricacies of uniforms, of hierarchy, of rules and regulations. For the summer encampments, scout groups from the entire area would convene at the rural communal settlement of Kiryat Anavim in the pine forests of the Jerusalem hills. There Yigael Sukenik first experienced freedom from the closely watched home of his hovering, if always well-intentioned mother, in a world of songs, tent craft, rope craft, and other military arts. In the swirling smoke of the campfires and in the group hikes, he experienced a life very different from the regime of the Deborah Kallen School.

In the scouts, Yigael also met very different sorts of people. He met a small circle of boys his own age—Alex Ziloni, Israel Ben-Yehuda (known to his friends as Abdu), Yitzhak Saidoff, and Zvi Spector—who were always ready to go off on a hike among unexplored hills, to wander through rural villages or Bedouin camps, to fight to repay a real or imagined insult—ready for adventures of every kind. Like Yigael, these boys were products of respectable middle-class families, but their impetuous and adventurous nature contrasted with Yigael's more cautious personality, as would become more and more evident as the years went on. At first their interactions were uneasy, but it was among this circle of un-likely types that Yigael gradually emerged from his childish shell. Even-tually, he was accepted in their tight circle, though never as a complete equal. Abdu recalled many years later their clear differences in personal-ity. "He was such a pedant, such a spoiled boy," he remembered. "When we would all go off for an outing with nothing more than our lunches, jackknives, and hiking staffs, Yigael would bring along his toothbrush and toothpaste."

Under the guidance of Zion Ha-Shimshoni, the scouts grew up to-gether, filling their weekends and holidays with hikes and outings in the vicinity of Jerusalem, coming to know at close hand the terrain, the vil-lages, and the historical monuments. Little by little their familiarity with the region expanded. From their headquarters at the Laemel School they might set off southward for an afternoon's hike toward Bethlehem or the hillside town of Beit Jala—or northward past the Jewish settlements of Neveh Yaacov and Atarot to the market towns of Ramallah and el-Birah. Eventually they learned to cook their own meals and set up encamp-ments in the open air. Wandering through Arab villages and biblical sites, they would hike through the hill country as far north as Wadi Farah, or they would wind their way through the Kidron Valley, past Bedouin tents and increasingly arid terrain, down to Jericho and the Dead Sea. By the shores of those dead waters where the weather is warm even in mid-winter, they would explore the ancient city conquered by Joshua and leveled by the Israelites' trumpets. Sheltered by makeshift tents of blan-kets, they would remain for three or four days. And it was also there in the Dead Sea region that the scouts visited a site that would later have enormous importance both for Yigael Sukenik and for the State of Israel.

That site was Masada, the newly adopted symbol of Zionist aspira-tions. As related nearly two thousand years before by the first-century Jewish historian Josephus Flavius, a band of Jewish zealots made a des-perate defense of the mountain—and ultimately a grim decision to com-mit suicide rather than fall into Roman hands. In a world turned cruel and threatening for a people fighting for its very survival, the Masada story struck a deep and sympathetic chord with the Fourth Aliyah, the new wave of pioneering Jewish immigrants coming to Palestine. For those who fled the Soviet Union after dreams of a worker's paradise turned into a bloody nightmare with the civil war and the resurgence of anti-Semitic pogroms, the ancient Jewish zealots emerged as symbolic ancestors, bearing the possibility, the hope, that this time the struggle for freedom might be crowned with victory. Since the early 1920s, the writings of historian and political activist Joseph Klausner had given the history of the Second Temple and the revolt against Rome modern nationalist significance. The archaeological discoveries of Eleazer Sukenik and others had given this history tangible illustration through hundreds of Jewish ossuaries and coins and Jerusalem's ancient outer fortification wall. But it took a poet to evoke the most vivid and horrifying tale in all of Josephus Flavius' histories. In 1927 the Russian immigrant poet Yitzhak Lamdan, the voice of the new generation, metaphorically depicted the Jewish National Home as the towering plateau of Masada rising in the wilderness as a last barren refuge. The story of the mass suicide contrasted sharply with Lamdan's poetic image, in which the pioneers of the Fourth Aliyah dance on the summit with the cry, "Masada Shall Not Fall Again!"

Years later, former members of the Mattatyahu tribe recall their overnight field trips to Masada as pilgrimages as much as scouting journeys, in which they combined physical, geographical, historical, and even spiritual studies. The hiking club of the Jerusalem Teachers' College had first undertaken the difficult trek to the mountain in the Judean wilderness decades before (and it is certainly possible that Eleazar Sukenik, an avid hiker and leader of the Maccabee Society, went along on those early expeditions). But by the late 1920s, the trip took participants not only across the physical landscape of modern Judea but, as Yossi recalled, over a human and cultural landscape as well. Marching out from the heart of the modern city, passing through poorer Jewish neighborhoods where black-coated yeshiva boys hurried off to prayers or lessons, the scouts would board an Arab bus at the Jaffa Gate, where fellahin and bedouin women hawked fresh vegetables. The bus trip wound southward through the hills to Hebron, where bedouin guides met them and took them to a nearby village to spend the night. Roused before dawn, the scouts were led through the ravines of the wilderness to the coast of the Dead Sea. After another night spent in the open, they made their way southward along the shore and climbed to the summit of Masada, a site that some thirty years later Yigael would make famous all over the world.

Poetry of ancient heroism against the Romans, however, was not enough to resurrect a Jewish commonwealth, for the large native Arab population was utterly unmoved by the poetry of Issac Lamdan. Their growing resistance was a political fact that nervous policy planners in London began to take more seriously into account. Despite the assurances of supporters of the Balfour Declaration that the influx of Jewish immigrants and the modernization of the country could not but help raise the standard of living of the Arab population, the economic decline of the rural areas continued, traditional patterns of family and community were shattered as young men flocked in search of jobs to the cities, and resentment simmered, even after the bloody anti-Jewish riots of August 1929 had been put down. An official commission sent by the British government to investigate the causes of the riots underlined the danger (for British interests in the region) of underestimating Arab resistance to the idea of a Jewish National Home. This British attempt to balance the favors it bestowed on Arabs and Jews merely intensified the suspicious and political maneuvering of both. In the autumn of 1930, Colonial Secretary Lord Passfield issued a White Paper announcing that thenceforth Jewish immigration would be more closely controlled, land sales from Arabs to Jews closely monitored, and every effort be made to alleviate the economic distress of the traditional rural economy of Palestine. For the Zionists around the world this White Paper was seen as a betrayal. Despite the lip service given by Prime Minister Ramsay MacDonald to the ideals and aspirations of the Jewish people, the handwriting was on the wall.

Even the least political of the scouts grew concerned with their future and came to believe that familiarity with the countryside might someday play an important role in the Jewish struggle to possess it as a national home. Though other Jewish youth movements trumpeted more explicit political programs—Revisionists, socialists, utopianists, and others—the basic ideology of preparedness, good citizenship, and national historical traditions like the story of Masada had their effect. In those years Yigael Sukenik was slowly moving toward the leadership of the Mattatyahu tribe in Jerusalem, and his personality was evolving as well. Abandoning his earlier silent aloofness, he began to step forward—at least in scouting circles—to defend his reputation or serve as spokesman for his peers. One of his fellow scouts recalled years later an early example of his emerging rhetorical powers. On an extended scouting trip to Haifa, Yigael and several of his friends left the camp without permission. Angry at this unauthorized adventure, Zion Ha-Shimshoni intended to send them back to Jerusalem at once. But when Yigael spoke up for the accused at a hastily called hearing, he was able to convince the scout leader to cancel the punishment. It was the first of many cases in which Yigael Sukenik would utilize his talent for expression as a weapon of self-defense.

By the fall of 1930, the Sukenik family had finally climbed the social ladder. After years of living in rented apartments in lower middle-class and often religious neighborhoods of Jerusalem, they at last moved into a house of their own. Even in Zionist Palestine, with its appeals to communal values, home ownership was a sure avenue to respectability. Despite the political developments on the horizon—including the in-

creasingly strident Arab opposition to Jewish immigration and land purchases—the Sukeniks' professional careers were going quite well. Eleazar
had finally achieved celebrity (among the general public, if not among
his colleagues) as the Yishuv's foremost archaeological expert, while
Chassiya had become a public leader as an elected member of the community council and an officer in the national Teachers' Union. The time
had come for them to end their wanderings among rented apartments
and establish themselves in a residence commensurate with their social
status. The 1929 riots motivated many middle-class Jewish families to
move to the new, wholly Jewish suburbs on the western side of the city.
Chassiya, as usual, took the initiative. She negotiated the purchase of a
lot, arranged for a mortgage, hired an architect, and supervised the contractors to build a family a house in the new garden suburb of Rechavia,
"God's Expanse."

The move to Rechavia placed the Sukeniks suddenly in a different
and not always easy social setting. The very idea of a garden suburb laid
out with aesthetically planned streets, public parks, and shaded walk-
ways was the inspiration of Dr. Arthur Ruppin, the German-born and
German-educated head of the settlement department of the Zionist Executive. The Ruppin family was joined in Rechavia by other members of
Jerusalem's Jewish aristocracy: Menachem Ussishkin, the veteran Russian Zionist leader and now the chairman of the National Committee
(the administrative council of the Palestinian Jewish Community) and
David Yellin, the venerable educator who had some twenty years before
led the War of the Languages and who was now a professor at the Hebrew University. Also among the homeowners were the city's most prosperous lawyers, bankers, and businessmen. In the next few years
continuing economic problems in Europe and the frightening rise of
Hitler in Germany would bring a flood of new settlers to Rechavia. They
were the doctors, lawyers, accountants, and investors of the so-called
Fifth Aliyah—cultured and largely assimilated German Jews who had
once scorned the poor Eastern European masses and their fervent belief
in Zionism. With strict immigration quotas now established in so many
other Western nations, Palestine became for the first time a viable alternative for them.

For Yigael and Yossi (Matti was still just a toddler), the move to
Rechavia meant that their days at the Deborah Kallen School were over.
The challenges of integrating themselves into the high school routines of
the Hebrew Gymnasium began. This was clearly a very different kind
of institution from the Kallen School's free-form projects, progressive
ideals, and strict discipline. What was now required of the boys was formal repetition, memorization, and intellectual conformity. No less chal-

lenging was the social environment, in which stylish fashions and quick wit took the place of playsuits and creativity. Indeed, an unembarrassed feeling of superiority was cultivated in the students by students and parents alike. "You could say that the gymnasium was the home of the aristocracy," wrote an anonymous eulogizer in the school's jubilee volume. "It's no exaggeration to say that within the school's walls played, sang, wrote, and read the children of the pioneers of the national resurrection living in Jerusalem." Yigael, even Yossi, wanted to be part of that world. On entering the gymnasium in the autumn of 1930, Yigael slowly began to reshape his identity, guided as much by the reactions of others as by his belief in any particular ideology.

Almost immediately, his self-confidence was challenged. He wanted at all costs to avoid the impression that he could not succeed among his teenage contemporaries, so he enrolled in the gymnasium's practical business course. The humanities course, he later recalled, attracted "mostly girls and the not very successful boys." But it was not long before his academic problems became obvious to both his classmates and his teachers. Sitting with a textbook in the rows of ordered desks facing a blackboard, Yigael was confronted with precisely the kind of educational exercises that he had been taught to avoid—and disdain—at the Deborah Kallen School. Some physical differences made the transition especially difficult; in contrast to the tiny classes of the Kallen School with six or seven pupils, the classes at the gymnasium often included more than thirty, especially after the children of the German refugees began to arrive. Despite his reputation as a leader of the scouts and the respect accorded him by many of the younger boys, Yigael's schoolwork suffered, and he developed a reputation as an evader. Still, Yigael was determined to deflect both his teachers' scorn and his classmates' ridicule, and one of his most distinctive talents emerged for the first time.

Some fifty years later, Yigael's friend and classmate Alex Ziloni described the surprise and delight of the students in a particularly tedious nature class, when Yigael showed them all what a perfect fool their strict and pedantic teacher was. "One day," Ziloni recalled, "he called Yigael to the blackboard to test him on a subject that Yigael clearly knew nothing about." The classmates must have smiled knowingly, getting ready for an embarrassing encounter, since "we all knew that he hadn't even opened the textbook to the right chapter." Somehow Yigael put on what would be the first of many convincing—and inspiring—performances. Striding confidently to the blackboard with chalk in hand, he looked the teacher squarely in the eye and gave a quarter-hour lecture, speaking in flowing, vivid language, embroidering on details that were evident in the question yet never dealing directly with the subject itself. It is easy to imagine the amusement of the class and the depth of their admiration for Yigael when at the end of the lesson, with the bell ringing and students gathering their books to rush off to the next period, the teacher nodded in approval and praised Yigael's firm grasp of the subject.

As his years at the gymnasium continued, Yigael distinguished himself as a slick talker without rival. Having exchanged Kallen's classes in drawing, sculpture, and carpentry for the mathematics, physics, and chemistry of the gymnasium, the art of rhetoric became his main creative outlet. Although few considered him a natural leader, he developed an increasingly powerful talent for standing out from the crowd. His native wit, long kept to himself, was now revealed to the public at parties, plays, and assemblies. His classmates later remembered his talent for twisting words and writing satirical poems, and as he matured into a good-looking young man with a sharp sense of humor, he turned the heads of even the most prominent, popular, and successful of his classmates. His background at the Kallen School, at first a handicap, now served him well. Kallen, after all, had stressed that children should be taught to be self-reliant and freely express themselves. This progressivist American sensibility was increasingly useful in an age when Jerusalem's developing urban culture of cafés, social clubs, and movie theaters made it possible for a younger generation to live a modern life, with a consciousness quite different from that of the grim ideological debates and dreams of socialist revolution that had motivated the generation of Zionist youth of twenty years before.

The cliques and clubs in Rechavia were also a world apart from the poorer neighborhoods of Yigael's early childhood, when he had played alone on the Street of the Prophets behind high garden walls. At high school parties in the homes of Jerusalem's rich and famous, at the afternoon tennis games at courts in the center of the quiet, ordered suburb, Yigael gained acceptance and a lifelong identity. He became, as his brother Yossi later recalled, "the aristocratic branch of the family." Though by no means one of the gymnasium's most brilliant students, he developed an ability to adapt skillfully to almost any situation; whether it was playing tennis with the sons and daughters of industrialists and public leaders; entertaining the crowd with a clever poem at the end of a party; or appearing smartly dressed as a youth leader, shepherding his band of admiring cubs. Compared with his rough-and-tumble friends from the scouts, Yigael was clearly not the strongest, the boldest, the handsomest, or the smartest. But all now had to give him at least grudging admiration for his ability to adapt to social situations with wit and elegance.

Yigael's success with girls of the gymnasium was a clear if superficial sign of his social triumph. As his delicate features now matured into a slender, more refined version of his father's, he offered the girls of the humanities course a sharp contrast to rougher, more impetuous teenagers like Zvi Spector and Abdu who would rather embark on an unplanned overnight hike out into the Judean desert than exchange pleasantries and quips with the girls. For years Yigael had maintained a special friendship with Hemda Feigenbaum, a warm, good-natured girl who had grown up with him at the Kallen School, but in Rechavia the girls were more concerned with status, fashion, and social events than she had been. Although the memories of his classmates were all embellished many years later in the retelling, everyone remembered Yigael in those days as something of a ladies' man. His own recollections clearly betrayed a false modesty about his romantic high school encounters, describing how some nights he would wander down with girls into the darkness of the secluded olive groves around the looming walled Georgian monastery in the Valley of the Cross.

At the same time, something troubling about his personality was developing, once the laughter at the clever jokes subsided, once the Saturday night parties broke up. More and more, Yigael seemed to be acting a role that had uncertain substance, a role from which his brothers Yossi and Matti diverged as they devoted themselves much more to the socialist youth groups and pioneering Zionist ideals of the times. While they would go off to soccer games or join in youthful political discussions, their older brother would prefer to be at the center of attention, surrounded by just the right clique of Rechavia boys and girls. While Yossi went on to establish his own youth movement and Matti, even as a young boy, dreamed of joining a kibbutz in the Jordan Valley, Yigael stubbornly steered clear of politics. It certainly was not that he lacked feelings for community commitment—like his brothers, he helped in his mother's election campaigns for the local council. It was rather that Yigael's naturally aristocratic and detached nature tended to disguise his own uncertainty about who he really was.

Lurking beneath the friendliness and the clever joking was a nervousness and sense of insecurity manifested in the habitual tense biting of his thick fingernails. Yigael had learned to succeed by being all things to all people. His personality encapsulated both the respectable idealism of his kindergarten-teacher mother and the skill at single-minded social maneuvering for which his ambitious scholar-father crudely strove but never was able to obtain. The painful, often divergent requirements of community idealism and personal social advancement would divide Yigael's energies and cloud the nature of his achievements for the rest of his life. His personality enabled him to lead a scouting field trip to Masada or a drawing room game of charades at a Saturday evening party with the same irrepressible charm. Like every other Jewish boy of his time and place, he would be soon called to make significant sacrifices for the sake of the larger community. But for Yigael, this was in no way a burden. In fact, he would finally be able to achieve the divergent aims of respectability, idealism, and social acceptance in the ranks of the underground Haganah.

Chapter Three

INTO THE
UNDERGROUND

n the candle-lit darkness of an apartment somewhere in Jewish Jerusalem, the solemn ceremony went on. Sixteen-year-old Yigael
Sukenik stood nervously, responding to sternly spoken questions,
facing initiation into a select and sacred fraternity. "Do you swear to
remain in the service of the Haganah all the days of your life, to take
upon yourself, without hesitation or question, the burden of its discipline? Do you swear, upon being called, to be ready to serve at any time
and place, to carry out all orders and to fulfill all commands?" Behind a
table sat three figures; before them lay an open Bible and a gun. After
ending the painful and even frightening silences between his answers to
the questions, Yigael stepped up to join the ranks of pioneers, of heroes
and doers, so different from the mild-mannered gentlemen who tipped
their hats to the ladies and children along the respectable streets of

Rechavia. In his pledge to undying secrecy and loyalty to his Haganah comrades, Yigael began to create a new identity for himself.

In a sense this initiation ceremony was a continuation of the underground politics that had begun in the workers' clubs, ghettos, and factories of Eastern Europe thirty years before. Yigael's father, now a phlegmatic middle-aged scholar, took rare pride in his teenage adventures in the self-defense corps of the young revolutionaries of Poalei Zion in Lithuania: telling his sons of smuggled pistols and secret meetings, defense plans, and code names in workers' basements and summer training camps. Indeed, Eleazar Sukenik's nostalgically recalled tales of violence and threats of pogroms, of fighting off hordes of rampaging Cossacks and peasants, flowed into a larger, shared tradition. In school and at scouting campfires, Yigael and his friends heard other romantic stories from their elders—how the young revolutionary guards of the ghettos of Eastern Europe transferred their armed struggle for Jewish independence to the fresh air and Oriental customs of the Middle East. The dashing mounted patrols of Ha-Shomer, "the Guardian," represented the next stage of development—the establishment of a secretive organization charged with guarding the property and persons of the newly established Jewish agricultural settlements throughout Ottoman Palestine. With the coming of World War I, many—like Lipa Sukenik—had received formal military training with the Jewish Battalions in the desert of northern Sinai. After the war the British were reluctant to sanction an exclusively Jewish security force in Palestine for fear of provoking violent confrontations with the Arab population. Yet veterans of both Ha-Shomer and the Jewish Battalions pressed on toward their ideal of an independent Jewish militia with the founding in 1920 of the Irgun ha-Haganah, the Organization of Defense.

For the Jewish boys of Jerusalem, the Haganah was a shadowy organization, made heroic by its members' defiance of the British authorities. There were rumors of secret agents dispatched to Vienna, Berlin, and Istanbul to buy guns and ammunition, of hidden arms caches placed in Jewish neighborhoods and settlements throughout the country, of special missions and harsh training regimes. Throughout the 1920s the rank and file of the Haganah had been, for the most part, tough young farm and construction workers, immigrants from Eastern Europe who were imbued with a revolutionary commitment to transform the country, an aggressive distrust of Arab intentions, and a healthy disdain for any Jew who would rely on a British policeman or soldier to provide for their defense. As an offshoot of the Histadrut, the Haganah was supervised by a national central council. Even though the local chapters were at first mostly concerned with local disputes, fistfights, petty crime, and insults

to the honor of Jewish women, the Haganah took on national significance in 1929. With the explosion of anti-Jewish violence by frustrated
and desperate Arab crowds all over the country—and with British forces
proving tragically impotent in their frantic attempts to restore order—
the Haganah came increasingly to be seen by ever wider segments of the
population as the only effective instrument of defense for the Jewish
community.

In the spring of 1930, as Yigael Sukenik was finishing his last term at
the Kallen School and his father was off digging, there were dangerous
rumblings of political dissension within the ranks of the Haganah. In the
period of reorganization after the 1929 riots, the command of the Jerusalem Haganah was given to Avraham Tehomi, an energetic young activist who launched recruitment drives among the adult Jewish population,
established courses in all phases of military activity, developed an intelligence network, and involved the Haganah in the defense plans of the
surrounding agricultural settlements. Tehomi had a fatal political flaw:
his dangerous sympathy for the rightist Revisionist party, which directly
challenged the Histadrut's control of the Jerusalem Haganah. Tehomi
was therefore soon deposed by the Haganah hierarchy, but he did not go
quietly. After a brief display of defiance, he took with him some of the
Jerusalem Haganah's best officers and a significant quantity of weapons
with which to establish a rival National Military Organization, one faction of which became the basis of the Revisionist Irgun.

For Yigael and other boys his age, the consequences of that defection were felt almost immediately. Tehomi's dissident officers, recognizing the advantage of attracting the youth of the city, stormed the Laemel
School courtyard, ejected the middle-of-the-road scouting organization,
and claimed the place as an exclusive training ground for the youth
movement that they intended to found. Not unexpectedly, the Haganah
leadership responded quickly. Histadrut general secretary David Ben-
Gurion, intervening for the first time in operational matters, dispatched
veteran Haifa commander Yaacov Patt to take control of events in Jerusalem. Patt immediately won back some of the defectors and recruited
new members, but the pool of available young workers was limited. Patt
found to his dismay that the organization was a shambles, with only 120
members and about 65 guns left behind by Tehomi and his men. With
the breakaway organization at the Laemel School attracting schoolboys
with its Revisionist-style appeal to strength, flag, and uniforms, Patt recognized that the Haganah, too, would have to widen its appeal.

Years later as aging men, the boys of Yigael Sukenik's generation
delighted in nostalgically recalling the mystery and wonder of their
induction into the secret organization. The process of selection—the

tapping—signaled a coming of age. One of the Jerusalem Haganah's most loyal members was none other than the scout leader and high school teacher Zion Ha-Shimshoni, who knew the potential recruits and their potential contributions. Discreetly calling aside the bravest and ablest of his charges after school or at scout meetings, he offered cryptic instructions that signified admission to a grown-up world. The expansion of the Haganah was, in fact, a rite of passage for the entire Jewish community, which was still shaken by the violence of the previous year. While a small core of intellectuals and civic leaders—Magnes, Ruppin, and Schwabe among them—still crusaded for Arab-Jewish peace and understanding, the majority quietly prepared for war. Even pale sidelocked yeshiva boys in the Jewish Quarter of the Old City were gradually brought into the Haganah. After an appeal by Chief Rabbi Avraham Kook to the Haganah leadership, their training sessions were shifted to Fridays rather than the Sabbath. They began to train with pistols and hand grenades, intent on averting a bloody replay of the events of August 1929.

As the British backtracked on their once-wholehearted support for the establishment of a Jewish homeland in Palestine and as the Arab nationalist leadership pressed for further British concessions, the Haganah steadily improved its ability to defend the Yishuv. It was not merely a matter of added firepower. Yaacov Patt, the newly appointed commander in Jerusalem, stressed training and efficient organization, established neighborhood watch committees throughout the Jewish parts of the city, and drew up a comprehensive plan of neighborhood defense. With the permission of the venerable educator David Yellin, he secured the use of a room in the new Teachers' College building in the western suburb of Beth Hakerem for instructing a new crop of officers. At the same time he initiated training classes for rank-and-file members in the various neighborhoods and even managed to appropriate funds to buy a few secondhand motorcycles so that the highest-ranking instructors could give lectures and lessons at several locations in a single night.

Yigael Sukenik, Zvi Spector, Abdu, and the other high school recruits were soon integrated into the larger system. Patt knew from his own experience in Haifa during the 1929 riots that important strategic advantage could be derived from the establishment and maintenance of efficient central command, and a notion of centralization guided the reorganization of the Haganah in Jerusalem. As commander of Haifa, Patt had used high school boys as messengers and runners to send orders and receive constant updates on the situation in the neighborhoods. Now, in Jerusalem, he instituted a training program in military communications for them. Yigael proudly recalled his growing skill in Morse code and semaphore signals, sending messages from point to point with a reflecting mirror called a heliograph. That was only the beginning. After learning the appropriate code words and code names of the various neighborhood commanders, they would take turns manning the phones at city headquarters, guarding training places to warn of the approach of British detectives, or carry arms and ammunition from one location to the next. On weekends the boys would go off under the cover of a scouting trip to participate in training sessions at the outlying settlements of Atarot and Kiryat Anavim.

Like a prophecy of violence that seemed inevitably self-fulfilling, tensions built to a new peak through the spring and summer of 1933. From Germany, where Adolf Hitler had been elected chancellor in January, was reported the suspension of constitutional rights, a national boycott of all Jewish businesses and professions, and the establishment of the National Socialists as the only legal political party. In Palestine, Arab nationalist leaders, seeing the problem of modern anti-Semitism as one created by and to be solved by Europeans, railed against continued Jewish immigration into Palestine and condemned the economic havoc and suffering wrought by the dispossession of Arab peasants and tenant farmers when absentee Arab landowners sold land to Jews. In March the mufti supported a boycott by Arabs of all "Zionist" products; mass meetings and angry demonstrations called for an immediate halt to Jewish immigration and spoke of resistance to the Mandatory government, which they felt was unfairly favoring the Jews. Within the Jewish community, too, there were growing tensions; Revisionists vied with socialists for control of the Zionist movement. The moderate Chaim Arlosoroff, director of the political department of the Jewish Agency—who was bitterly criticized by the Revisionists—was assassinated by two masked men as he strolled with his wife on the beach at Tel Aviv. At the World Zionist Congress held in Prague that summer, David Ben-Gurion finally captured the leadership of the Zionist movement. But there were more troubles to come. Throughout the autumn, Arab strikes and demonstrations in Jaffa, Haifa, and Jerusalem intensified into rioting, which the British forces put down with truncheons and gunfire.

In this atmosphere of growing violence, Yaacov Patt, the Jerusalem Haganah commander, took extraordinary precautions. Fearing an outbreak of violence on the order of the 1929 riots, he ordered that all members be mobilized, armed, and placed on the ready. At the same time he dispatched dozens of the younger messengers to circulate on foot and on bicycles to report what was going on in every neighborhood. Ammunition had to be smuggled secretly from the main arms cache to the defenders of the Jewish Quarter in case of an outbreak of fighting. Yet the means at his disposal for such a transfer on short notice were still primitive. As Abdu recalled years later, Patt gathered a few boys in his office, ordered them to take off their shoes, and instructed each to stuff a few bullets inside. "We did what we were ordered," Abdu wryly noted, remarking how oddly suspicious—and ridiculous—it must have seemed to the British sentries posted at the entrance to the Old City to see a stream of otherwise healthy-looking Jewish teenagers hobbling painfully through the Jaffa Gate.

———

Yigael Sukenik graduated from the Hebrew Gymnasium in 1934 with grades that were far from outstanding, giving no sign that he had a future in the scholarly world. Taking his long and tedious high school graduation examinations over a period of twelve weeks from May to July, he excelled in history and literature (for which he received final marks of 90) and did poorest in English, for which the government examiner gave him only a 50, an embarrassing failing grade. Generally his marks revealed him still to be an average student, with 70s and 80s in mathematics, physics, and chemistry. Yet Yigael Sukenik was never destined for conventional achievement. He stood out among his friends as a wit and as the object of attraction for many of the gymnasium girls. His self-confidence was boosted by his increasing responsibilities with the Haganah. His main interests continued to lie outside the classroom, and the year following his graduation, spent traveling around the country, moving from job to job, was a period of personal exploration and experimentation. He was determined to venture beyond the shade of the cypresses of Rechavia, its tennis courts, parties, and closed social circles, to see what life was like elsewhere in the Palestinian Jewish community. If it was not quite the heroic year of pioneering that he later described, it at least showed him that his career path lay surprisingly close at hand.

Since earliest childhood, Yigael had been influenced by heroic images of pioneering Jewish settlers. Like other children of the Yishuv he had been taught to regard the energetic, suntanned members of the kibbutzim of the Jezreel Valley and the Galilee and the workers in the citrus groves on the coastal plain as personifications of the Zionist dream. Like the pioneers on the frontiers of America, Australia, and southern Africa, they represented the outward movement of civilization into wasted or neglected land—clearing roads, planting fields, and making the desert green. In the months just before Yigael's graduation, however, the Hebrew pioneering ideal became the centerpoint of a bitter labor controversy. During the winter citrus harvest season of 1933–34 the Jewish grove owners of the coast brought in Arab workers to do the picking, complaining that most of the Jewish workers had gone off to earn higher wages at building projects in Tel Aviv. Zionist labor movement spokesmen, however, rejected that explanation. They angrily accused the grove owners of trying to cut costs at the expense of the workers, since the Arab workers were willing to accept far less pay than the going rate. The struggle to preserve the ideal of "Hebrew" labor—the principle of Jewish self-reliance in even the most menial or difficult tasks as a means to national independence—brought Jewish volunteers from all walks of life to work in the groves and give the lie to the owners' contention that no able-bodied Jewish workers could be found. The following summer, moved by this idealism, Yigael went down to the settlement of Ramat Hadar and worked in the groves for several months, receiving a paltry day wage (barely enough to pay for the cheap cigarettes he smoked) and living under difficult, often unpleasant physical conditions with thirty other workers in a shed. When he had proved to his own satisfaction that he could survive as a pioneering farm worker, Yigael returned home to Jerusalem. Never again would he feel the need to participate in the pioneering experience. Idealized pictures of healthy Jewish pioneers in children's textbooks and patriotic posters were one thing; as a seventeen-year-old he could—at least in some cases—distinguish myth from reality.

Indeed, for all but a few years of his life, Yigael Sukenik would be a Jerusalemite—an unembarrassed man of the city, far more comfortable in an office or living room than in an open field. Returning from the orange groves during the winter of 1934–35, he saw his city—its institutions and its structures of power—as an adult for the first time. In the mid-1930s, that city was expanding with suburbs, factories, and commercial centers, and although it was still no rival for the bursting metropolises of Tel Aviv and Haifa, as the national center of government and higher education it was no longer a small town, as it had been at the beginning of the century. From the perspective of the Zionist leadership, however, the growing Jewish neighborhoods of the city were islands surrounded by a potentially threatening sea of Arab villages. For years, the Jewish National Fund had been making serious efforts to establish Jewish agricultural settlements in the nearby hill country; it had succeeded at Kiryat Anavim on the west and at Atarot and Neveh Yaacov on the north. On the southern side of the city, private Jewish land investment companies were negotiating with village leaders and Arab middlemen to acquire land for new Jewish settlements between Jerusalem and Hebron. The newly purchased land had to be mapped and measured, and Yigael, having some experience in mapmaking from the scouts and from the Haganah, found a temporary job as a surveyor's assistant with the Jerusalem firm of Feitleson and Meyuhas. Sent south with the survey crews, he helped them mark the fields and boundaries of what would later be known as the Etzion Bloc, an outpost guarding the southern approaches of Jerusalem whose defense and resupply would one day be a matter of desperate concern. Yet this too was just a diversion. With his notorious weakness in math and hard science, Yigael never intended to make surveying or engineering his career.

Jerusalem was the center of the British administration, and more than a few bright young gymnasium graduates had found a secure future in the civil service ranks. Thus began Yigael's next brief incarnation, as a clerk in the government Immigration Department in the spring of 1935. In that year Jewish immigration reached unprecedented levels. The relentless persecution of Jews in Nazi Germany, the spread of anti-Semitism throughout the rest of Eastern Europe, and the absence of other refuges led more than 65,000 Jewish men, women, and children to seek a new life in Palestine. Assigned the task of filling out new passports and naturalization papers, the young Sukenik witnessed this massive historical movement firsthand. But his unconventional education betrayed him: This was precisely the kind of mindless bureaucratic work that he had been taught to loathe by Deborah Kallen and that he had largely evaded at the gymnasium. He proved an unwilling clerk, only grudgingly putting in hours behind the high desks with blotters and inkwells, misspelling so many names and mistaking so many birthdates that both he and the mandatory government finally came to the conclusion that it would be better for them to part ways. Never again would he be attracted to the prospect of bureaucratic advancement, in government offices or anywhere else.

As it turned out, his career path had already been marked out for him. He had never been directly encouraged to become an archaeologist, but only Yigael, of all the Sukenik boys, showed interest in his father's antiquarian enthusiasm. In the years after the frightened five-year-old visited William Albright's excavation, he had found growing interest in his father's discoveries and explorations. The trip to Beth Alpha was just the beginning of more serious involvement. By the time he was fourteen or fifteen, Yigael seemed well aware of the latest archaeological developments in dinner-table conversations with his father. In trips to Masada and other ancient sites, in school lectures about the antiquities of the country, he clearly felt himself on the inside track. Avraham Biran, a native of Rosh Pinna in the Galilee who returned to Palestine in 1935 with a Ph.D. from Johns Hopkins that he had earned under Albright, later recalled Yigael sitting among his high school friends at an informal evening lecture and responding to all of Biran's archaeological observations with a precocious, knowing nod. But it was only during the year following his graduation, when he accompanied Avigad and his father to an excavation on the coastal plain near Hadera, that Yigael realized that he might be able to pursue archaeology on his own.

Eleazar Sukenik had come a long way since his pioneering excavation at Beth Alpha, but his career had by this time settled into something of a routine. Despite the rising tensions after the 1929 riots, he and Avigad had undertaken a thorough survey of tombs in the Kidron Valley, further documenting unique Jewish burial customs of the Second Temple period, collecting many examples of Hebrew, Aramaic, and Greek scripts of the period, and gaining for Sukenik a seat on the government's Archaeological Advisory Board. Tirelessly traveling around the country, Sukenik maintained his special connection with ancient synagogues. In the spring of 1932, he supervised the clearance of a mosaic floor in the ancient synagogue at the site of el-Hammeh—known as Hammath Gader in the rabbinic sources—far to the north, at the confluence of the Jordan and the Yarmuk.

Unfortunately, Eleazar Sukenik could not find scholarly recognition as easily as he found mosaic floors. Despite his achievements and his even more considerable self-estimation, the brusque, self-taught former algebra teacher was still not accepted as an equal by scholars in the great archaeological institutions. At first, Sukenik attempted to raise his status by bureaucratic intervention, but this merely raised resentment against him. In 1931 a massive international expedition was mounted to continue the excavations of Roman and Israelite ruins at Samaria. The British Academy, the British School of Archaeology in Jerusalem, and Harvard University were among the main sponsors, and a substantial portion of the funding came from the well-known American Jewish philanthropist Mrs. Felix Warburg of New York. Through the intervention of President Judah Magnes and the insistence of Mrs. Warburg, the Hebrew University was also included as a sponsor of the dig. Eleazar Sukenik was named assistant field director. Taking Avigad along with him for the first season of digging, they were confronted with a distinctly unfriendly atmosphere. The other staff members were Americans, British, Scots, Australians—all professionals and postgraduates of proper archaeological schools. The workers were local Arabs watched over by stern Egyptian foremen. In this imperial atmosphere Sukenik's position was clearly a polite fiction. It was John W. Crowfoot, the director of the British School and formal field director of the expedition, who made all the decisions. His disdain for Sukenik was made continually and abundantly clear.

With the instinct for self-preservation that always distinguished him, Eleazar Sukenik decided that his archaeological future would be better served by concentrating less on digging and more on collecting.

He resurrected his idea for a national archaeological museum, for which he had tried to rouse interest in popular dailies years before, and began to comb the antiquities shops, private collections, and monasteries of the Old City. Sometimes alone, sometimes with Nahman Avigad, and sometimes with Yigael and Yossi, he spent innumerable hours and drank innumerable cups of black Turkish coffee coaxing out the best merchandise from the dealers or persuading the monks and nuns to let him into musty storerooms. During the course of these expeditions, he recognized artifacts whose value others had never appreciated. With a small fund provided by President Magnes he made purchases for a study collection for the university. His familiarity with ancient Jewish scripts, gained over the years in his tomb excavations, enabled him to recognize and decipher the first ancient inscription ever found bearing the name of a biblical character—a funerary plaque of Uzziah, king of Judah, dug up many years before and tucked away in a basement of the Russian monastery on the Mount of Olives.

Even greater discoveries were in store for Eleazar Sukenik among the city's antiquities dealers and collectors. But in September 1934, when, in recognition for his archaeological research, he was appointed "Lecturer in Archaeology of the Land of Israel from the Early Bronze Age to the Byzantine Period," his scholarly bluff was finally called. With no formal education to speak of, he was now asked to craft a course in advanced archaeological studies that would lead to masters' and doctoral degrees. The last time Sukenik had stood before students had been more than a decade before, in a high school algebra class. Sukenik was at least temporarily able to get by by working closely with Dr. Leo Arieh Mayer, an experienced orientalist who taught Islamic archaeology. In his early days at the university, he depended on others: Avigad to supervise his excavations and assemble all the technical details, Judah Magnes to help with administrative and financial matters, and senior colleagues in Jewish studies, history, and Talmud to advise him on the wider implications of his finds. But the next autumn he would be called upon to stand before a class of eager students—and there would be no one to help him with that.

In the summer of 1935, both father and son were preparing for new phases in their lives. Yigael had had his fill of odd jobs and roaming and realized that his future lay neither in a government bureau nor in the agricultural field. Whatever he may have known about the deeper meaning of archaeological exploration or its scholarly or political implications, he clearly wanted to come back into the fold. He informed his father that he intended to register as a student for the coming semester at the Hebrew University's department of archaeology.

"My father tried his best to dissuade me from going into archaeology," Yadin recalled of his announcement, remembering his father's unexpectedly discouraging words. "You just don't know what archaeology is all about," the elder Sukenik told him, with a rare insight into his own struggle, "how difficult it is, and how hard it is to make a living at it." Eleazar's distance and aloofness from his family was suddenly placed in mortal danger. After years of pushing and fighting for his own scholarly reputation, and often placing his pursuit of that reputation ahead of his family responsibilities, he would find it difficult to conceal his scholarly shortcomings from his admiring son. But nothing would stop Yigael from becoming an archaeologist. And in the coming years, he would learn, like his father, to mask his private insecurities with a respectable—if not entirely conventional—public identity.

Ranged across the barren ridge of Mount Scopus, with the low domes and minarets of the Old City spread out below it, the Hebrew University of Jerusalem was by 1935 the crown of the educational system of the Zionist movement. Established only ten years before, it now boasted hundreds of students in science, law, and humanities. The department of archaeology was one of the newest. Its facilities were limited, however; located in the basement of an old house that had come with the original property, its one room was filled with work tables and cases of the antiquities that Dr. Sukenik had dug up or purchased. Nahman Avigad, now over thirty, padded softly around in a white lab coat, suffering in silence while he carried out the unending instructions and demands of his boss. The few students who arrived for classes in November might have been disappointed to discover how poorly prepared Dr. Sukenik was to receive them. For years afterward he was remembered as one of the poorest, most painfully boring lecturers in the history of Western civilization—concealing antiquated German archaeology textbooks on his lectern, his eyes furtively darting down again and again. Yet the standards of the university were demanding: students were required to take one major and two secondary subjects, and the object of the study was not a bachelor's but a master's degree. Later in his career, Yigael always maintained that his father had been reluctant to serve as his teacher and thesis adviser for fear of appearing to favor him. Whatever the reason, Yigael became the student of the one other faculty member in the department, Dr. Mayer. And although he had come to the university ostensibly to study the Jewish antiquities of the country, Yigael enrolled for a master's degree in Islamic archaeology, choosing for his minors Hebrew philology and Arabic language and literature.

As much as he might have wanted to concentrate on his university studies, Yigael was soon called for further service in the Haganah. Ever since the disturbances in the autumn of 1933, political protests had continued in the country, as the newly founded National Defense party of the Nashashibis and the Palestine Arab party of the Husseinis continued to press unsuccessfully for a halt to Jewish immigration and land purchases. The leadership of the Haganah, expecting renewed and even more violent disturbances, stepped up its secret arms purchases, establishing a secure source of supply in Belgium and shipping large numbers of rifles and huge quantities of ammunition into Jaffa hidden in barrels of cement. In October 1935, in the course of unloading a shipment of more than five hundred barrels, one of them came loose from the crane and was smashed open; its contents of rifles, bullets, and white cement powder spilled out on the dock. The British police, hurriedly summoned to the scene, were unable to trace the source of the shipment, but news of it spread quickly through the Arab community. A general strike was declared and demonstrations were held in Jaffa, Haifa, and Jerusalem. The escalating tensions led Yaacov Patt, the Jerusalem Haganah commander, to begin training a new crop of officers.

Yigael Sukenik, Abdu, Zvi Spector, and Alex Ziloni were among the eighteen young men and women tapped to take on new responsibilities. Meeting for several hours every evening in the basement of the Teachers' College in Beth Hakerem, they listened to lectures and studied hastily translated pamphlets about English and German rifles and a favorite weapon for dispersing crowds in the city—hand grenades—which were known by the Haganah code word "eggs." The Haganah students underwent weapons training, dismantling and assembling rifles and light machine guns, and they drilled on Saturday mornings in a rocky field opposite the Teachers' College, without weapons lest the British police intervene. The tactics were designed to defend against rampaging urban masses, but in the spring of 1936, when the violence finally exploded, it engulfed the countryside as well.

The first stirrings of armed resistance in rural areas had been felt in the early 1930s in villages around Haifa, with the wide-ranging banditry of the Black Hand Band led by Sheikh Izz el-Din el-Qassam. The threat he posed seemed to have been eradicated when el-Qassam and some of his closest followers were cornered and killed by a British patrol in November 1935. But that encounter merely gave the Arab nationalist movement a martyr and was the sign of more trouble to come. On April 15, 1936, a band of armed Arabs killed three Jews traveling on the road between Tulkarm and Nablus, and the spiral of violence began. The next day, the separatist Irgun Zvai Leumi carried out a revenge killing against

Arabs in the workers' slums near Tel Aviv. On Sunday, April 19, groups of Arab port workers in Jaffa erupted in rage, beating Jews throughout the city; fighting, looting, and arson soon broke out in all the mixed neighborhoods. In Arab villages and towns throughout the country "national committees" were established, and an Arab Higher Committee headed by the Mufti of Jerusalem Haj Amin el-Husseini declared and coordinated protests and a general strike. In Jerusalem, Yaacov Patt prepared for the defense of the various neighborhoods. Since the Jerusalem command was now also responsible for the security of the outlying settlements, Patt hurriedly administered final exams to the officer trainees and dispatched them at once to what would soon become the front lines.

Yigael Sukenik was first sent to Kfar Etzion (close to the area south of Jerusalem that he had helped to map as a surveyor's assistant) to instruct the Jewish watchmen in the delicate art of tossing "eggs." But soon he received new orders when it became clear that a more vulnerable point was Kiryat Anavim. There at the site of so many fondly remembered summer scout encampments, Yigael and several of his closest friends were now to receive their baptism of fire. This kibbutz, nestled in a valley near the main road between Tel Aviv and Jerusalem, was faced with sniping and vandalism from the surrounding villages almost every night after dark. Reinforcements were needed immediately, so Yigael Sukenik was sent to assist the settlement's Haganah commander and hurriedly instruct the settlers in the use of a machine gun and in general rifle marksmanship. At the same time, Abdu, soon joined by Zvi Spector, was sent to man a concrete pillbox on a wooded ridge overlooking the settlement, to anticipate attacks from the surrounding hills.

The defensive situation was untenable. The model for Haganah training had been the earlier urban disturbances, but the defenders of Kiryat Anavim now faced a new situation. The young men of the neighboring villages, feeling a rage born of all the fears and misfortunes that the Jewish settlement had come to represent for them, would gather for action after sunset. Approaching Kiryat Anavim in the darkness, they would attack indirectly, sniping with whatever hunting rifles they had managed to lay their hands on, uproot fruit trees or set fire to crops, then return to their village at dawn. From within Kiryat Anavim's defensive perimeter it was difficult to stop these actions, and Abdu and Zvi Spector soon took matters into their own hands. They decided to mount an attack, to take the initiative. Without the permission or even the knowledge of their superiors, they crept through the darkness toward the neighboring village of Abu Ghosh, opened fire on some men working a field, and tossed an "egg" into the village coffee house.

In later years, "going beyond the fence" to preempt Arab attacks on Jewish settlements took on mythic dimensions in Israeli consciousness. But that only occurred with the arrival of Yitzhak Landsberg at Kiryat Anavim in May, a month or so after the disturbances began. Landsberg was a romantic figure, a burly former wrestler and former Red Army officer who was one of the founding members of the Haganah immediately after World War I. He made an indelible impression on the young men he gathered around him, convincing them that they had the power to control events and that it was the Arab villagers—not them—who should be afraid. At the beginning of the disturbances, Landsberg had volunteered his services to Commander Patt to defend some of Jerusalem's most vulnerable Jewish suburbs by mounting nighttime ambushes on arriving attackers—and to take the initiative in sniping at villages from which attacks had come. When Landsberg came to Kiryat Anavim to take charge of the faltering defenses, Abdu and Zvi Spector quickly became his eager protégés and set off with them on a series of late-night expeditions around the surrounding Arab villages. One night, their youthful enthusiasm was suddenly tested as they came face to face with a band of Arab villagers and faced a firefight at close range.

"That night's operation was a turning point for all our friends," Abdu later recalled, "for from that time onward Kiryat Anavim became both a battlefield and a school." Thus was born the Noddedet, Landsberg's impromptu mobile patrol. During the weeks that followed, he took groups of young Haganah members beyond Kiryat Anavim's protective fence almost nightly, relying on his memories of fighting in the Red Army during the Russian civil war among hostile peasant villages to perfect a distinctive brand of partisan warfare. Rousing the young men from their bunks in the middle of the night, he would gather them together with a few good-humored words of encouragement and lead them through the darkness over the rocky hills toward a village from which he suspected attackers had come. Sometimes firing toward the houses to make an impression, sometimes merely taking note of the layout for some future action, Landsberg had charismatic power over his boys. "Other older men would come and give orders," Yigael later remembered of the experience. "All of a sudden, this fellow comes, sort of crude, barbaric, and he goes out at night and he himself climbs on rocks and throws rocks and he comes with you." The casualties they caused to the other side in the darkness were never carefully counted. Their motivation was to exercise their own power to terrorize and intimidate to put an end to the attacks on Kiryat Anavim. "We learned a great deal," one of the Noddedet members later recalled. "We learned how to move in the darkness, what to wear, how to communicate with the other patrol members, how to whisper orders, how to fall and how to rise, how to shoot and how to hide, how to listen and what to listen to, how to establish a front line position and how to construct it—and above all how to anticipate the intentions of an armed attacker before he could mount his attack."

By the end of the summer of 1936, the British had finally begun to restore order throughout the country with massive army reinforcements, and the Haganah temporarily lowered its state of alert. The leader of the Arab Higher Committee, Mufti Haj Amin el-Husseini, silently acknowledged that the pain of the general strike and the violence had been borne mostly by the Arab population of the country, and he agreed to a face-saving gesture. On behalf of the Palestinian Arab people he acceded to the request of the kings of Iraq and Saudi Arabia and Emir Abdullah of Transjordan to suspend further acts of resistance and thenceforth rely on the goodwill of the British government for redress of their grievances. The Haganah, for its part, relied on the goodwill of no one. In the autumn Yigael Sukenik and his friends returned to Jerusalem, deeply and irreversibly changed. Assigned to the headquarters of the city commander, the young veterans of the Noddedet helped organize patrols through Jewish neighborhoods and at all the outlying settlements.

Within the city each of the young men was assigned a female companion and patrolled constantly on the lookout for trouble, with a pistol or hand grenade hidden handily yet probably uncomfortably under the Haganah girl's skirt. In the outlying settlements the maneuvers were more extensive, offering experience in the tactics of the battlefield. Each Haganah unit consisted of two squads, patterned after Landsberg's units. One of them would practice taking positions to intercept armed bands coming out of the nearby Arab villages while the other would block their way back. The irony of this for Yigael Sukenik's existence must have been obvious to him, even if it could never have been acknowledged publicly. Every few nights, he would patrol the area, all the while memorizing the topography of Arab villages, collecting information about them, and anticipating attacks. By day, he began his second year at the university, studying the development of Islamic art with Dr. Mayer and—despite his loathing for rote study—following others in Dr. David Baneth's Arabic classes in memorizing long, florid passages of pre-Islamic poetry.

Dr. Eleazar Sukenik was extraordinarily lucky. His career seemed to follow a sure if accidental pattern toward attaining the ideals he proclaimed. From his youthful studies in a Lithuanian yeshiva, he had been drawn to Zionist activism. During his early career as a teacher in Jerusalem, he had met William Albright and embarked on an archaeological career. Now stocky and approaching fifty, he sought to secure his archaeological reputation—not in teaching, which he loathed and avoided whenever possible—but in the establishment of a national museum. His efforts in soliciting funds from public leaders and the Jewish Agency were singularly unsuccessful. Few saw the advantage of such a museum at a time when there were much better causes to be supported; most treated the crude and bullish Sukenik with thinly veiled disdain. Then, like manna from heaven, came his salvation. Decades before in Bialystok, a young man named Gedaliah Kutscher had shared Lipa Sukenik's passion for the Zionist movement and fascination with Jewish antiquity. While Sukenik had gone off to Palestine, Kutscher became a tailor and left Lithuania for southern Africa. Over the years he had prospered, and though he never visited Palestine or participated in Zionist organizations, his youthful fascinations nonetheless endured. On January 10, 1936, Eleazar Sukenik was duly informed by a shocked university official that the University had just received a bequest of £40,000 "from an unknown person named Kutscher," with instructions the gift be used exclusively for the construction and maintenance of a Jewish national archaeological museum.

Yigael later recalled that the announcement was a turning point in his father's career. From then to the very end of his life, Eleazar Sukenik devoted most of his time and energy to planning, constructing, and filling the showcases of the national museum. In the summer of 1936, while Yigael was tromping through the darkness of the Jerusalem hills with Yitzhak Landsberg, Eleazar sailed for Greece. After visiting some important archaeological sites in the islands of the Aegean, he proceeded to Athens, where he purchased a collection of Greek vases for display in Jerusalem. Through the fall he continued his travels, with visits to Istanbul, Damascus, and Lebanon, all the while collecting coins, pottery, and other artifacts for his museum. The following summer, he undertook an exhausting tour through Europe, visiting archaeological sites, giving lectures on behalf of the Hebrew University, and negotiating with officials of the Louvre and the British Museum for specially made reproductions of inscriptions relating to biblical history. Sukenik's visit to Germany proved unexpectedly chilling, however, even though he was a corresponding member of the German Archaeological Institute and fancied himself a scholarly product of the University of Berlin. Since his last visit in 1931, Adolf Hitler and the National Socialists had come to power and imposed the Nuremberg Laws to distinguish Jews from "true" Germans—the ultimate and horrifying outcome of the teaching of dominant and subject races that he himself had heard from the classical scholars in Berlin. In one incident at the German border, he witnessed from the window of a train a Jewish couple and their baby being roughly escorted back to the border police post by several railroad officials. Their passports were apparently not completely in order. "Damn the Nazis!" Sukenik noted in his journal. "I felt as if I were escaping from a penitentiary."

Back in Palestine, despite a temporary lull in the fighting, the Haganah training intensified. In the spring of 1937, Yosef Avidar, a veteran Jerusalem officer, initiated a series of national courses based directly on the experience of the uprising of the previous year. Building on Landsberg's tactical innovations, exercises were now regularly held in night patrolling and in mock attacks on villages. In Jerusalem itself Commander Patt took advantage of the lull to retrain all the city's active Haganah members. In the summer of 1937, he designed an intensive three-day course for squad leaders that he conducted in the huge loft of the main barn in Kiryat Anavim. Yigael Sukenik was among the instructors, not only for the basic courses but, in light of his own experience in the Noddedet and the patrols, for new squad leaders as well.

In midsummer a diplomatic bombshell exploded that neither Jew nor Arab could ignore. In response to the uprising, the British government had dispatched a distinguished panel of elderly jurists called the Peel Commission, after the name of its chairman, to investigate the circumstances that had led to the widespread violence. Through the next several months the commission toured the country and took testimony from Jews, Arabs, and British administrators. The commission's conclusions were published on July 7, 1937, and suggested in true Solomonic fashion that if the rival claimants to a Palestinian birthright could not live together peacefully, the country should be partitioned between Englishman, Arab, and Jew. At the heart of the Peel Plan was the assumption that the rival parties were simply incapable of compromise since they represented different races, different mentalities. A Jewish state would be established along the coast northward from Tel Aviv and across to the Galilee. The British would maintain an enclave extending from Jaffa to Jerusalem. And the Arab State, consisting of the central hill country and the Negev, would be placed under the tutelage of the longtime British client, Emir Abdullah of Transjordan.

Reactions to the Peel Plan, as might be expected, were impassioned. David Ben-Gurion and longtime Zionist leader Chaim Weizmann came out as supporters, eager to gain even a small state that would allow free Jewish immigration from the Nazi nightmare. More radical Zionists— from both the left and the right of the political spectrum—angrily rejected anything less than the traditional biblical boundaries for their

Promised Land. In their bitter opposition to partition, they had an un-likely ally: Mufti Haj Amin el-Husseini, who also rejected the Peel Plan out of hand. Indeed, while the Emir Abdullah and the moderate National Defense party, led by the Nashashibi family of Jerusalem, were inclined at least to negotiate with the British, the mufti went on the attack. Address-ing a conference of four hundred pan-Arab, pro-Palestinian nationalist delegates that had hastily been convened in the Syrian resort town of Bludhan, the mufti condemned the mortal threat that he claimed parti-tion represented. It would create, in his estimation, nothing less than a British-protected enclave into which millions of European Jews would flow—endangering the dignity, freedom, and economy of the entire Arab world.

The spark for renewed violence was not long in coming. In Naza-reth, on Sunday evening September 26, 1937, Galilee District commis-sioner Louis Andrews was assassinated on his way home from church. In the face of that open act of resistance, the British government acted quickly; it disbanded the Arab Higher Committee, imposed censorship on the Arab press, arrested dozens of Arab political leaders, and igno-miniously deposed the mufti from his official post. Only with great diffi-culty did Haj Amin flee to Lebanon, where he hastily formed the Central Committee of the National Jihad in Palestine and called on the rural fighters of the previous summer to arise. Arise they did, all over the coun-try, now aiming their attacks at the British: railroads, roads, and the oil pipeline from Iraq to the Mediterranean Sea. As the months wore on, the loosely organized bands from the previous uprising (suggestively called *knufiot*, "gangs" in Hebrew, or *fasa'il,* "platoons or squadrons" in Ara-bic) became increasingly formalized under the command of charismatic leaders. Rallying to the banners of rebellion came idealistic villagers, re-gional patriots, hooligans, criminals, and soldiers of fortune who had filtered into the country across the mountainous, largely unguarded bor-ders with Syria and Lebanon.

The British were determined to liquidate this insurgency move-ment, which they considered a strategic threat to the very existence of their Middle Eastern empire. If Palestine was insecure, the Suez Canal and the overland approaches to the Persian Gulf would be in danger, a threat that could not be permitted, especially with the growing possi-bility of world war. Through the fall of 1937, as violence intensified throughout the country, emergency regulations were enacted, allowing the army and the police virtually unlimited search and seizure powers, sweeping rights of administrative detention, and the death penalty for terrorism. Counterinsurgency expert Sir Charles Tegart, who had waged a coolly murderous campaign against the anti-British terrorists of Bengal, was brought to Palestine as a special adviser and recommended the substantial expansion of the secret security services, the installation of a barbed-wire security fence along the Syrian and Lebanese border, and the construction of looming, turreted concrete fortresses at road junctions and strategic points throughout the country—the "Tegart fortresses" that still bear his name.

From the very beginning of the disturbances, the British government saw advantage in utilizing the young men of the Jewish community to maintain public order, and with the active support of the Jewish Agency (and the equally enthusiastic yet unspoken support of the Haganah leadership), they created a corps of auxiliary forces that eventually came to be called the Jewish Settlement Police. Equipped with pickup trucks and a few makeshift armored cars, the units became far more mobile than the Haganah foot patrols, ranging widely and responding to hit-and-run attacks immediately. Particularly in the rural areas of the country, the mobile troops, supported by salaries and equipment from the British administration, established permanent encampments and became full-time soldiers. Yitzhak Landsberg, still pushing hard for his policy of active response to Arab attacks, convinced the Haganah leadership to create its own permanent mobile patrols, establishing them all over the country and calling them by the Hebrew acronym Fosh, for *plugot sadeh,* or field companies. In fact, so committed was Landsberg to the idea of the field companies that he changed his own last name to Sadeh, signifying that he was, as Fosh commander, truly a man of the field.

In the spring of 1938, as Fosh units spread across the country under the cover of Jewish Settlement Police patrols and as the counterinsurgency efforts of the British army intensified, the small circle of young men from Jerusalem—many of them recent graduates of the Rechavia Gymnasium—were sent to take up command capacities. Zvi Spector and Abdu, always special favorites of Yitzhak Landsberg-Sadeh, led platoons on the "eastern" line, protecting the groves and Jewish settlements of the coastal plain from incursions from the nearby hill country. Under their guidance, based on their experience in the Noddedet patrols, they trained raw recruits by taking them along on night reconnaissance of Arab villages, sometimes engaging in close-quarter fire fights, planning revenge and preemptive strikes. Like the more closely controlled Special Night Squads led by British captain Charles Orde Wingate in the Galilee and Jezreel Valley, the Fosh units took the initiative, its young commanders having no hesitation in rousing the inhabitants of suspicious Arab villages in the middle of the night—or in dynamiting a few houses to leave a grim warning of further consequences if gang members were allowed to remain. These operations had different objectives for the British administration and for the Yishuv, but with the Haganah field companies and the Jewish Settlement Police largely composed of the same people performing the same actions, it might have been difficult for an independent observer to determine whether the Jewish Settlement Police was merely a cover for the Fosh units or whether the Fosh was merely a surrogate for the British army and police.

Back in Jerusalem, the security situation was no different. Abd el-Khader el-Husseini, nephew of the mufti, had gained supremacy in the region at the head of a loose confederation of bands that he called the Arab Army of the South. By August 1938, members of the Arab bands had taken over much of the Old City, boldly flying the flag of the rebellion over the Damascus Gate. The Jewish neighborhoods were well protected by constant Haganah patrols and police surveillance, but the situation in the surrounding countryside was far from secure. Traffic was subject to sniping; mines were laid along backroads and bridges blown up. Here, too, the British were determined to restore order, by reinforcing the army presence, staging searches and arrests of suspected Arab fighters, and substantially increasing the manpower of the Jewish Settlement Police.

Yigael Sukenik had chosen to remain at the university after many of his contemporaries left for service in other parts of the country, which made him an obvious candidate for advancement in the ranks of the Jerusalem Haganah. In the summer of 1938, after returning from a study trip to Greece and Turkey, he was summoned to the Jerusalem Haganah headquarters and informed that his name had been submitted to the mandatory government as a Jewish Agency candidate for command of the local mobile unit of the Jewish Settlement Police. Assigned the code name Haggai, to be used in confidential communications, he would also command the mobilized platoon of the Haganah's Jerusalem field company. Yigael willingly accepted this assignment. Taking a leave of absence from his studies, he spent his days and nights roving in an armored car with his platoon through the highways and back roads of the Jerusalem hills. As the months passed, it was hardly a secret to the British army company stationed in the area that Yigael was the "nightbird"— the Haganah liaison—of the Jewish police deputies. More than once they shared information and weapons and set nighttime ambushes, as much for diversion or training as for actual fighting, which except for occasional sniping never came. That hardly mattered to the Haganah leadership, for Sukenik had distinguished himself as one of its most dependable young officers. In December he was called with fifty other Fosh platoon leaders from all over the country to Kfar Vitkin, to attend the first national officers' training course.

Yigael Sukenik's military service was now becoming his profession; in it, he found a fulfilling sense of identity. Archaeology, at least for the time being, was less important. The change shocked even members of his own family, who had not been aware of the extent of his secret Haganah service until he arrived back at home one day with the surest sign of advancement in the underground. "When I learned of Yigael's position in the Haganah, I was really amazed," Yossi remembered. The familiar image of the high school playboy at the tennis courts, reading clever poems at parties, was now suddenly replaced by the self-confident figure of a mustachioed twenty-one-year-old wearing the uniform of a British auxiliary police sergeant, roaring through the quiet streets of Rechavia on a military motorcycle he had received from the Haganah.

Chapter   Four

THE INDIRECT
APPROACH

F rom the first time they met, the personalities of Yigael Sukenik
   and the tough young officer from Tel Aviv they called Fistuk,
   "Pistachio," were in head-on conflict. Though barely two years
older than Yigael, Shlomo Rabinowitz was a young man for whom the
Haganah was no recent avocation but a way of life. Born in Russia 1915,
he had come to Tel Aviv with his parents in 1925 and had entered the
Haganah while still in his teens as a full-time soldier. After working for a
while in the Haganah's secret Tel Aviv munitions workshops, he stood
guard over the property of the Jewish National Fund in the swamps of
the Huleh Valley, far to the north. With the outbreak of fighting
throughout the country in 1936, Fistuk moved frequently between assignments, supervising security in the citrus groves of Petah Tikva,
guarding convoys of Jewish workers at the quarries of Migdal Zedek,

then commanding a company of the Jewish Settlement Police assigned to protect the construction of the "Tegart Fence" along the borders with Syria and Lebanon. Though he was short and physically unimposing, Fistuk was fearless. Mastering the techniques of night patrolling and the use of high explosives, he eventually became one of the Haganah's main hand-grenade experts. In the course of time, he became one of the organization's most faithful commanders—and one of Yigael Sukenik's most dogged competitors.

In late 1938, when Fistuk was transferred to the Jerusalem Haganah district as training officer—and as a direct superior to Yigael Sukenik—he showed no respect whatsoever for Yigael's comfortable position as the local organization's rising star. For Fistuk, the armored-car patrols through the Jerusalem hills that Yigael had commanded were child's play. Fistuk was convinced that the Haganah would eventually be forced into combat, not mere police work, and he was determined to whip a new generation of Haganah recruits into shape. Thus, all the old security arrangements and working methods established by Yaacov Patt were now to be changed.

A new age was dawning for the Haganah as the long, violent Arab rebellion finally came to an end. Throughout the fall of 1938, massive reinforcements of the British army streamed into the country, and one by one the strongholds of the Arab resistance were surrounded and reduced. In a massive operation in October, the Old City of Jerusalem was surrounded and cleared of its rebel leaders. In the weeks that followed, checkpoints were set up at major road junctions, and unannounced searches and mass arrests were conducted in villages suspected of harboring terrorists. The pressure was relentless, and by the spring of 1939, all of the major rebel leaders had escaped from the country or been killed. But that was not the end of the story. With a great war now looming in Europe, the policy planners at Whitehall, not imperial soldiers, stepped forward to shape British Middle Eastern policy. Their perspective was on the entire region. They saw a hostile Islamic world—enraged by stubborn British support of Zionism—endangering Britain's imperial sea and overland route to the East. Lord Balfour's ambiguous promise became a dead letter as His Majesty's government sought to solve the "Palestine question" once and for all.

All the officers in the Haganah felt the change in British policy immediately. The underground force had grown used to official (if unspoken) backing; the salaries, uniforms, and freedom of action for the most aggressive of the field forces had been well integrated into the parallel structure of the Jewish Settlement Police. But through the spring of 1939, government support for the Jewish Settlement Police was gradually reduced, and the first official requests were submitted to the Jewish Agency—now that the Arab rebellion was largely over—that the Haganah give up its reported caches of illegal arms. The news from London was even more threatening. In January, delegations of Zionist and Palestinian Arab representatives had been summoned to a Round Table conference, an attempt at conciliation that failed miserably. When the rival delegations did little more than show their venom for each other, the British decided to take matters into their own hands. In a White Paper published in May 1939, His Majesty's government announced that all the obligations to the Jewish people incurred under the terms of the League of Nations Mandate should be considered paid in full. The Arab majority of Palestine, they asserted, would never accept partition. Therefore the British government announced that within ten years, a binational Palestinian state would be established, with a constitution that would insure the dominance of an Arab majority through restrictions on Jewish immigration and land sales from Arabs to Jews.

Violent, angry demonstrations erupted throughout the country with the news of the British decision. The movement toward Jewish autonomy in economic, political, and military affairs had come too far to be stopped. The Haganah increasingly came to be considered not merely a volunteer organization to guard orchards, factories, and outlying settlements, but the nucleus of an independent Jewish army that might someday be called upon to act alone. Even before the official publication of White Paper, two members of the Haganah national command had drafted a plan for restructuring Haganah forces, changing the very nature of the organization. The Haganah could no longer depend on committed volunteers and enthusiastic high school messengers. It had to become a broad-based militia drawn from the general population, divided into a static, regionally based home force and an aggressive, mobile field force, known in Hebrew as *hel sadeh,* or Hish. The transformation from Fosh to Hish was more than a matter of changed initials; physical trial and discipline, not youthful adventure, were now to characterize the Haganah experience.

Through the spring of 1939, Fistuk established an operational headquarters for the new formations in Jerusalem. He conscripted young men from working neighborhoods, construction sites, and factories; and he organized intensive, secret courses in the western suburbs on basic weapons training and the fundamentals of military life. Yigael Sukenik worked closely with him, though Fistuk rarely concealed his condescending view of him as a bright student but a military amateur. The Haganah still conducted regular night patrols in the Jerusalem region, but now their purpose was not only to discourage attacks but to collect information as well. Anticipating a time when Jews and Arabs might face each other in battle without the intervention of the British, Fistuk encouraged his squad leaders to compile files on every Arab village in their sector, including relevant details—and in some cases even photographs—of approach routes, population, and topography. There was also the matter of vital road connections. In the case of all-out fighting, the winding road through the hills from Jerusalem to Tel Aviv could be relatively easily blocked or captured, leaving Jewish Jerusalem under siege. So on many Saturdays, as Fistuk recalled years later, he and his most trusted young officers would go out on foot, in cars, and on motorcycles to search for alternative roads.

At the end of August, Fistuk put the best Haganah recruits to a test. These young men had not participated in the fighting during the Arab rebellion, and he wanted to assess their fitness for battle. Bringing together the best instructors in the Jerusalem region (Yigael Sukenik served as his deputy and chief weapons instructor), he put the recruits through their paces in weapons training, field drills, and basic tactics. Despite the danger of discovery by the increasingly hostile British forces, Fistuk concluded the course with a live fire exercise in one of the deep wadis north of Kiryat Anavim. But the most challenging trial took place after the course was over, when Fistuk staged a company march—with weapons—from Jerusalem through the wilderness to the Dead Sea. Stringent security precautions had to be taken: While the recruits were transported in open trucks from Kiryat Anavim to the starting point of the march at Kibbutz Ramat Rachel, their weapons—pistols, rifles, and submachine guns—were brought in a hidden arms cache welded to the underbody of an otherwise innocent-looking car.

Just after nightfall they set out through the Judean wilderness. Fistuk and Deputy Sukenik were in charge of the fully armed company, while Abdu and Zvi Spector, who had explored this country for years, moved ahead and served as guides. Ordered to march at full speed through the moonless darkness in order to reach the shore of the Dead Sea by daybreak, however, the fully armed Haganah company lost its way. With a growing apprehension that they might be spotted when daylight came by a border patrol of Emir Abdullah's Arab Legion, they groped for hours through the ravines and shepherds' paths of the Judean wilderness. Finally they regained their bearings and scrambled down to the Dead Sea shore near the fresh-water spring of Ein Feshka, soon after dawn. The summer heat, even in the early morning, was intense, and as many of the exhausted young men flung their weapons aside to drink their fill of the spring water, Fistuk had all he could do to maintain control. More drilling—more marching—would be needed before the Jerusalem field force was ready to fight.

For Yigael, the march to the Dead Sea was a personal trial that he survived with honor. Years later, even Fistuk had to admit that he had acquitted himself well. Within two weeks, an officers' course for another group of recruits got under way at Kiryat Anavim—and this time Yigael was in command. Once again he directed the standard weapons training, field drills, and basic tactics, but there was a difference: During the live fire exercise at the end of the course, Yigael placed much greater importance on the effective and speedy use of rifles and submachine guns. All over the country, as Hish units underwent such training, their fighting ability as formal military units steadily improved. Far to the north in the Yavneel Valley the Haganah national command established an even higher-level officers' course for platoon leaders, under the cover of a summer sports camp. The chance visit of a British officer destroyed their cover, however, and during a hurried overnight march across the Galilee to a new training site, forty-three fully armed Haganah cadets (among them Moshe Zelitsky, the Haifa commander, and a young Haganah activist named Moshe Dayan) were surrounded and arrested by hastily summoned British security forces.

The British were clearly prepared to invoke the emergency anti-terrorist regulations against the Haganah forces, so the organization members were compelled to go deeper underground. The trial of "the Forty-Three" in the military court in Acre became a public sensation, and long prison sentences were meted out to every one of the accused. The British army commander in Palestine, Lieutenant-General Evelyn Barker, had become convinced that the Yishuv was plotting an armed uprising. David Ben-Gurion, head of the Zionist Executive, requested an urgent meeting with General Barker and tried to calm him down, explaining that, after all, *haganah* was the Hebrew word for defense. "Men who carry bombs should not claim that they belong to the Defense," General Barker replied angrily. "They should call themselves the Attack—that's what they should call their underground." Through the fall, as government patrols against Haganah training centers and arms intensified and new regulations against land sales and Jewish immigration were strictly enforced, the British, as much as the Arabs, began to see themselves as the Haganah's enemy. The day of eye-winking between British officers and Haganah "nightbirds" was over. In order to survive, the Haganah now had to go deeper into the underground than ever before. Officers and rank-and-file members alike had to hide their allegiance and conceal their activities. In the fall of 1939, therefore, after an extended absence from his archaeological studies, Yigael Sukenik returned to the Hebrew University.

———

The world must have seemed mad in the autumn of 1939, as the academic year at the department of archaeology of the Hebrew University began. Overshadowing the tension between the British government and the Jewish community in Palestine, the war clouds that had been building for years in Europe exploded with unprecedented ferocity. Radio reports and newspaper headlines screamed of German tanks sweeping eastward across the Polish border and with the Polish defenses apparently helpless to stop them, it now seemed that the Jews of Eastern Europe would be subject to the ruthless violence of Nazi rule. The few first-year students who attended introductory lectures on "Jewish Antiquities from the Roman and Byzantine Periods" and "Islamic Miniatures and Medals" must have found it difficult not to be preoccupied by the military developments in Europe and the potentially frightening effects on their lives and those of their families. If they believed that quietly contemplating the achievements of ancient civilizations would bring them inner tranquillity in a modern time of trouble, they were soon roused to reality by the bizarre clash of personalities at the Hebrew University department of archaeology.

Eleazar Sukenik remained the dominant figure. He had been named a full professor in 1938, due in large measure to his directorship of the embryonic National Museum of Jewish Antiquities and his obsessive collection of museum-quality artifacts. Not political turmoil, not rising tensions, not even war could stop him. During the summer of 1939 he had taken a long trip through Syria and Lebanon, visiting ancient sites and antiquities dealers in Damascus, Baalbek, Qatna, Hama, and Aleppo, and after making his way across Turkey, he had arrived in Istanbul. At the outbreak of the war, he managed to return to home and family by finding passage on a Russian ship. Still his search for museum exhibits continued. At the end of November he successfully negotiated with the friars of the Dormition abbey to purchase their vast collection of ancient inscriptions, coins, ossuaries, weapons, and carved signet seals.

His students had a different perspective of the professor. His behavior at the university was imperious and vindictive to those who worked with him—except for the few young women so unfortunate as to have caught his eye. Their experience was often frightening. Among the first-year archaeology students in the fall of 1939 was a self-assured young woman from Tel Aviv named Hannah Rabinovich, soon to be disabused of all her romantic illusions about archaeology. Decades before, her own father had studied ancient Near Eastern languages and literature in tsarist Russia; the subject of antiquity had fascinated her from her earliest childhood. Despite her father's attempts to discourage her from concentrating on such an esoteric subject, she was determined to go to Jerusalem and enroll. After her initial interview with Dr. Sukenik, she learned from the other young women in the department that Sukenik loved to chase—if not always catch—the girls. Through the years, whenever they would go off on a bus for a field trip with the professor, each young woman would make sure that she had a partner to sit with, so that Sukenik wouldn't be able to sit next to them. The other teachers were hardly more alluring: a sour-faced Bible teacher named Dr. Gevariyahu, and Dr. Mayer, who always came to classes dressed in black.

In her first year of study, Hannah was overwhelmed by the challenge of learning facts and memorizing shapes and patterns of ancient artifacts without any real academic background. One of her first courses was Dr. Mayer's lecture on Islamic miniatures and medals. She suddenly found herself at a loss when the professor passed out Arabic coins to the students and requested that they read and translate the words inscribed on them. She squinted helplessly at the worn bronze coin, not having the faintest idea how to decipher it. The young man sitting beside her leaned over and reassured her in a whisper not to worry, just to rely on him. "Do you know Arabic?" she asked him. "Not very well," he answered wryly, revealing the key to success in this course. "But I've been here long enough to know what's written on the coins."

That was her first encounter with Yigael Sukenik, certainly the most popular student in the class and—at least to outsiders—the opposite of his father in almost every way. At twenty-two, Yigael had returned to his studies with a new sense of confidence and determination. His relationship with his father was also changing. Although Yigael would always maintain an outwardly respectful manner toward his father, he saw from his classmates' half-concealed ridicule and learned from overheard faculty gossip that his father was the butt of the other students' and teachers' jokes. Embarrassed by his father's peccadilloes and abrasive personal style, Yigael gradually distanced himself from him at the university and established ties with other faculty members—even with those considered to be the elder Sukenik's rivals. He eventually managed to rise to the top of the class, in spite of others' loathing for his father, because of a unique ability.

Whether in the classroom, in study sessions, or on field trips, he had—put simply—a genius for storytelling, for weaving convincing and entertaining tales. He could take a pottery sherd, a coin, or an arrowhead and elaborate on the bare details that the teachers had provided. He was clearly not the best or most brilliant of the students in the tedious work of memorization and study, but he had a genius for making fragmentary facts come alive. After two years as a part-time soldier, patrolling and exploring the Jerusalem region, he projected his vivid perceptions of the lives of modern villagers onto the remains of antiquity. "He put the *people* back into the picture," Hannah Rabinovich recalled many years later; "the woman who was limping, the girl who was beautiful." Yigael cut through the abstractions of artifact types and technical names; he saw the living people behind the dried olive pits and smashed pottery that they excavated from ancient graves.

In the spring of 1940 the whole class went off to the excavations of Tell Jerishe, a site on the outskirts of Tel Aviv where his father had been digging with Avigad and others on and off for years. Originally purchased and made available to the Hebrew University by a wealthy Tel Avivian, Yitzhak Leib Goldberg, with the hope that Jewish antiquities might be found there, Sukenik was disappointed with the meager gleanings of broken pottery and rough stone walls. Yet he continued, and in the spring of 1940, the team of students and temporarily hired workers uncovered a huge fortification rampart that extended down the steep slope of the tell. Now here was something for Yigael to conjure with—not a fragile glass bottle or worn Arabic coin. Here he could summon up visions of vast army attacks in the Bronze Age, of besieged Canaanite princes in their palaces, of invading Hyksos charioteers. Soon ancient warfare—meshing so neatly with his ongoing Haganah preoccupations—captured his imagination. He read widely about ancient armies and warfare, weapons, and tactics, their follies and victories. In contrast to his plodding, pedantic father, Yigael had a sense of drama, a talent that would also set him apart from other young officers of the Haganah.

Through the winter of 1939–40, the months of the "phony war" in Europe, the British forces were making large-scale preparations for hostilities in the Middle East. General Archibald Wavell, the British commander in Palestine who had extinguished the Arab rebellion, was transferred to Cairo and placed in command of all imperial forces in the region. Thousands of British, Australian, New Zealand, and Indian troops flooded into Palestine and Egypt, the bedrock of Britain's regional strategic defense. With the Nazis' lightning conquest of Holland and Belgium and their occupation of Paris, however, the strategic importance of the Middle East dropped suddenly in the overall British scheme of things. To the leadership of the Haganah, things appeared quite different. With the possibility of British preoccupation elsewhere and perhaps even defeat by the Axis, the Yishuv needed more than ever to be able to defend itself. At the outset of the war, Ben-Gurion declared that the

Jewish community in Palestine would continue to fight the White Paper as if there were no Hitler and would fight Hitler as if the White Paper did not exist. To fight either, more military leaders would be needed, and in the summer of 1940, Yigael Sukenik was called back into Haganah service to undergo higher officer training at a place called Juara in the Carmel range, near Kibbutz Ein Hashofet.

This training course was different from any that Yigael had ever taken. The emphasis was neither on weapons training nor on night patrolling, skills in which the hand-picked students were presumably already well versed. This course trained platoon leaders, and in slowly building up the scale of the Haganah units—from squad, to platoon, to company, to Hish battalion—battlefield tactics now came to the fore of the curriculum. First came theoretical sessions with a sand table, where platoons of toy soldiers were used to simulate deadly variations of defense and attack. Then, out on the hilly, wooded slopes around the cluster of buildings at Juara—isolated far from the prying eyes of the British security services—the students simulated the movements of a platoon in action; pursuit, retreat, and attack. Haganah veteran Yosef Avidar recalled that Yigael Sukenik quickly distinguished himself from the other students not by his strength or courage but by his wit. The other young Haganah officers were men of action who learned by practice and improvisation. Yigael Sukenik, the university scholar, had a different nature. He earned sudden, stunning advancement by learning from such distinctly non-Palestinian figures as Basil Liddell Hart, Erwin Rommel, and Karl von Clausewitz.

Years later, Yigael Yadin claimed that he had read the works of all of these great military thinkers on his own—and that of all of them, Liddell Hart exerted the most profound influence on his military thought. Historians of the development of Israeli doctrine were subsequently hard put to determine precisely what the young Sukenik had been reading and how far he had been able to influence others, but his adoption of the "strategy of the indirect approach" during these years became something of a taken-for-granted in Israeli military history. Liddell Hart's innovation—first expressed as a critique of the stodgy, passive British World War I commanders—was to insist that direct, head-on battle should be avoided at almost any cost. Through the use of rapid flanking movement, psychological warfare, and above all surprise, the successful commander should aim to knock the determined, defensive-minded enemy off-balance and destroy his will to resist. Liddell Hart—and for that matter, Rommel and Clausewitz—were names that meant nothing to Yigael Sukenik's fellow students or perhaps even to his instructors. But he was not merely a military pedant. Sukenik had the talent to explain various tactical theories as convincingly as if they were his own invention—and even more important, to sketch out scenarios that applied the tactics of daring German cavalry attacks or the Schlieffen Plan (to sweep around the Maginot line and encircle Paris) to situations that the Haganah might face one day.

Whatever the reaction of the other students, the instructors and officers at Juara began to pay attention. Sukenik distinguished himself, if not as a combat leader whom footsoldiers would follow, then certainly as a military thinker—a strategist more talented than any of them. He also possessed wit and charm; at the graduation ceremony for the training course, he rose before the assembled officers and his fellow students and read a clever satirical poem in which he jabbed fun at his comrades, himself, and his teachers, with sarcasm that, while stinging, was not meant to be taken too seriously. Present at the graduating ceremony was Yaacov Dostrovsky, the recently appointed chief of staff of the Haganah and longtime commander of the Haifa region, a shadowy figure whom most knew only as Dan. Dan saw something special in Yigael Sukenik. And soon after the graduation ceremony, he sent word that Sukenik should come to see him in his office in Tel Aviv.

———

Yaacov Dostrovsky, at first glance, was an unassuming presence. Short and frail of stature, balding, with thick wire-rimmed glasses, he looked less like the commander of an underground army than a veteran public works engineer. But beneath the appearance lay something of a legend. "He was a man whom I had heard of," Yigael recalled many years later of his first meeting with Dostrovsky, "but had never met face to face. He was a mysterious personality." Born in Russia in 1899 and brought to Haifa as a child, Dostrovsky had served in the Jewish Battalions during World War I and later was one of the founding members of the Haganah. His main interest was always in security matters. After studying engineering in Belgium in the 1920s, he returned to Haifa and served under Yaacov Patt, making his Haganah branch—with its efficient messenger system and policy of immediate retaliation—a model for Haganah branches all over Palestine. During the Arab rebellion of the late 1930s, he took resolute command of the Haganah in Haifa and assisted Orde Wingate in the organization and training of the Special Night Squads. In 1939, when the national Haganah leadership needed someone to coordinate the national training program, "Dan" was a natural candidate. And although he was reluctant to leave his security responsibilities in Haifa, he accepted the newly created post of chief of staff of the organization less than a week after the outbreak of the war.

Few rank-and-file members of the Haganah knew the extent of the far-reaching changes that were taking place in the upper echelons of the organization. By early in 1939, with the end of the Arab rebellion and the shift in British policy, it had become clear that the national command of the Haganah, based as it was on proportional representation by a group of civilian leaders, could not effectively respond to the ever-fluid security situation, in its haggling and endless debating over every operational detail. Two former high-ranking Jewish officers in the Austrian army, Raphael Lev and Sigmond von Friedman, had settled in Palestine and, as active Haganah members, stepped forward to propose that the organization adopt a proper military structure. There had to be, they insisted, a single commander who would receive the general strategic instructions from the civilian leadership and see that they were carried out. Like the chiefs of staff of conventional armies, this highest-ranking officer should be the final arbiter of all complaints and requests from local branches and mobilized units. He would coordinate the work of the various staff departments—operations and planning, technical, oversight, and training—to make sure that they effectively pursued the long-range strategic goals. In an organization riven by struggles between activists and moderates, socialists and conservatives, the mild-mannered Dostrovsky was an ideal compromise candidate. But his nature was more suited to acting alone than to choosing between alternatives proposed by others. "It was never easy for him to make a final decision," Yigael later observed.

Within a few days of his graduation at Juara, Sukenik had his first encounter with the confused reality of the Haganah general staff, headquartered in Tel Aviv. Although it had been formally in existence for almost a year, matters were still unsettled. The offices were cramped and, to maintain secrecy, were divided between two private apartments, one at 39 Ahad Haam Street and another on Lillienblum, a couple of blocks away. In these converted bedrooms, sitting rooms, and kitchens, Dostrovsky and the other department heads were trying their best to build an army where there had previously been only a voluntary organization. The transition was not accepted calmly by many of the regional commanders, who were used to making their own decisions and now, in response to every directive, flooded the Tel Aviv headquarters with protests, objections, and demands. Thus, the haggard, chain-smoking forty-year-old who sat across the desk was far different from the romantic character that Yigael Sukenik had always imagined Dan to be.

Even more surprising to Yigael was the reason he had been summoned to headquarters: Dostrovsky had selected him to become his personal aide. In contrast to the other young officers of the organization, who distinguished themselves by their daring or physical prowess, Sukenik impressed Dan as much more studious, diligent, and methodical. That was precisely the kind of person, Dostrovsky believed, whom headquarters needed to help get matters under control. The few full-time workers there were buried in a mountain of unanswered communications; files were in disorder, there was no administrative framework, and the chief of staff was simply unable to keep up with the work. Even though Yigael had always hated the routine and stifling formality of bureaucratic work, he quickly recognized that this job offered him some power and responsibility. In a 1981 interview he recalled his first encounter with Dostrovsky: "He said to me: 'Listen, I'm receiving endless amounts of material from regional commanders, instructors, and course commanders. As part of your job,' he told me, 'go over these things. Whatever you think you can respond to, answer in my name—I give you the authority.'" So twenty-three-year-old Yigael Sukenik—fresh from courses in light arms and the sand table—was now brought from the field to the headquarters, where he would remain for the rest of his military career. He was placed in the position of weighing and making judgments on routine pleas, requests, and demands from commanders across the country—and was instructed to respond with sufficient conviction that the commanders would assume that Dan himself had answered them.

Before he came to work at the Tel Aviv headquarters, Yigael had to select a new code name. His old code name, Haggai, which he had used in the Jerusalem district field force, was already taken in Tel Aviv. Without even asking Sukenik's opinion, Dan's secretary Hannah Yoselevitz quickly chose one for him. Since the young man was supposed to judge all Dan's problems, a biblical quotation fit perfectly. "Dan will judge his people," prophesied the patriarch Jacob on his deathbed in Genesis 49:16—in Hebrew, the poetic phrase was *"Dan yadin amo."* So *Yadin,* "he will judge," became Yigael Sukenik's official code name, as he prepared to leave his university studies again. A unique combination of circumstances, good luck, and quick thinking had placed the young man from Rechavia—scout leader, slick talker, platoon leader, and archaeology student—in a position to make history.

In the autumn of 1940 the code name *Yadin* appeared with increasing frequency on the internal communications and dispatches of the Haganah, and the reputation of the young man from Jerusalem began to grow. The inner circle of Haganah commanders began to recognize his talent. Yosef Avidar, who served as head of the technical department, noted that Yigael Sukenik grasped new concepts and information unbelievably quickly—and in those years rapid change and restructuring were essential. The world war got closer to Palestine with the entrance of Italy on the side of the Germans, and with several frightening Italian bombing raids on Haifa and Tel Aviv in September, the director of the planning department, Sigmund von Friedman, worked on a new plan to deal with the possibility of renewed rural violence. Yigael worked closely with Dostrovsky, reading, translating, and assimilating a wide range of military literature, to develop a uniform combat structure for Haganah units throughout the country. As he had always done so skillfully, Yigael could give life to otherwise lifeless material, vividly sketching out scenarios in which various western armies' squad, platoon, and company structures helped or hindered Haganah operations against a possible renewed Arab rebellion in Palestine.

Developments on the war fronts, however, brought a far more ominous possibility. The advance of the Nazis southward through Greece and eastward across the deserts of North Africa represented a direct threat to Palestine and sparked a flurry of new contingency plans. The advance of Rommel brought a renewed, if temporary, period of cooperation between the British forces and the Haganah. Ever since the dismantling of the field companies at the end of the Arab rebellion, Yitzhak Sadeh had been pressing the Haganah leadership to authorize and fund a new strike force. His opportunity came in the spring of 1941 with the establishment of assault companies, *plugot machatz*, better known by the Hebrew acronym Palmach. Unlike the rest of the Haganah forces, the Palmach consisted of specially selected and trained commando units, drawing to it some of the most daring and committed young officers in the organization, many from the leftist Kibbutz Meuhad movement.

With the pragmatic British search for every battlefield advantage, Palmach troops were incorporated into Allied Middle Eastern operations: an invasion of Syria (whose French colonial administrators had proclaimed their allegiance to the Vichy government) and a seaborne commando raid on the oil refineries at Tripoli. These operations marked the beginning of an independent military tradition within the Haganah, building on the aggressive daring championed by Yitzhak Sadeh and his enthusiastic protégés. They also provided a sudden, shocking reminder that military operations could be bloody. In the course of the Syrian invasion, Moshe Dayan, released from prison and newly recruited into the Palmach, lost his left eye in a fire fight with Syrian forces. The entire twenty-three-man commando unit sent to attack the refineries in Tripoli, commanded by Zvi Spector, disappeared mysteriously at sea.

Yigael Sukenik's attitude toward the Palmach was as ambivalent as his attitude toward the reckless yet daring night patrols through the Jerusalem hills with Yitzhak Sadeh had been. His city-bred nature never allowed him to mix easily with the rough-edged, maverick kibbutzniks who now flocked to Sadeh's encampments and campfires and saw themselves as a fighting, revolutionary elite. Many of the newly recruited Palmach members had grown up in close if uneasy contact with Arab neighbors on communal agricultural settlements. They had been taught from childhood that the only way to defend their families' farms, property, and honor was through constant demonstrations of strength. Sukenik's knowledge of the Arab population was always gained at a distance—in scouting hikes, Haganah patrols, and university Arabic classes. It is little wonder, then, that he saw the defense of the Yishuv in abstract, theoretical terms. His main emphasis continued to be on training techniques and tactics, to create a conventional fighting force like those about which he had taught himself. During the spring of 1941, while Abdu, Zvi Spector, Moshe Dayan, Yigal Allon, Yitzhak Rabin, and dozens of other young men were preparing to go into combat, Yigael divided his time between administrative work at the Tel Aviv headquarters and preparations for an intensive officers' course.

The grueling 1941 training sessions at Juara were unlike any that the Haganah had ever conducted. Lasting three full months, their goal was not merely routine training but the creation of an officer corps as the first step toward a coordinated national military strategy. Four years before, at the time of the Peel Plan, the Tel Aviv Haganah commander, Elimelech Avner, had hastily formulated a plan of perimeter defenses for the borders of the tiny proposed Jewish state. With the rejection of the Peel Plan, "Plan Avner" was also abandoned, but now, with the outcome of the war uncertain, the planning department of the Haganah began to formulate a detailed military contingency scheme. Based on the assumption that a future Arab rebellion would be very much like the earlier one, the plan (called Plan A, as the first of a series of strategic blueprints) called for the creation of a uniform system of defense, whose structure would rise in area and manpower from strongpoint, to sector, to settlement, to district, to region, and in which local residents would serve as the first line of defense against Arab attacks. Since Jewish settlements in many parts of the country were isolated, Plan A foresaw a heightened role for the mobile field force units: to keep vital roads between the settlements open and, if needed, to mount counterattacks.

Sukenik was among the select group of instructors—all veterans of the 1936–39 era—who were now called upon to train a new generation of Haganah officers. After a six-week review of basic weapons training, map reading, and military communications, the candidates were put through their paces in squad and platoon exercises, in full company marches at dawn and midday and after dark, simulating attack, defense, and retreat in urban and rural areas, ambushing vehicles and infantry units, coming to the assistance of besieged settlements, and (in accordance with the indirect approach) running rapid, sweeping, platoon-size patrols deep into enemy territory. Despite the seriousness of the training and the strenuousness of the drilling, however, they were still quite far from combat reality. The company-level war games were conducted against mock enemies, and because of the scarcity of firearms for training, flags of different colors and sizes took the place of submachine guns, rifles, mortars, and machine guns.

During the months that preceded the training course at Juara, the basic structure of Haganah forces remained a matter of bitter debate between the supporters of the Palmach and the supporters of a conventional army. Although it was agreed that a standard platoon would comprise three squads of twelve men armed with rifles and an automatic weapon, and that a company would comprise three platoons and an additional support platoon armed with machine guns and mortars, there was little agreement on what tactical role these various units would play. Zvi Gilat, one of the instructors at Juara in 1941, recalled that in these discussions examples from the experiences of the British, Russian, and German armies were introduced. It is likely that Yigael Sukenik's presentations contributed to the liveliness of these debates. At stake was the future shape of the Jewish forces: whether the roving platoon should be the basic unit of aggressive defense, or whether the platoon should be subordinate to the larger and less mobile company. As usual, the Haganah chief of staff found it hard to make a final decision. As a result, Dostrovsky left the bitter rift unresolved by determining that the standard Haganah platoon should be trained *both* as an independent unit *and* as part of a company.

During all his years of his university study and Haganah service, Yigael Sukenik had a faithful admirer. She was Carmella Ruppin, daughter of Dr. Arthur Ruppin, one of the founders of the modern Zionist settlement movement and one of the most respected leaders of the Yishuv. Since the Sukeniks moved to Rechavia in 1930, Carmella and Yigael had lived across the street from each other. He was four years older and at first paid little attention to the red-headed girl, known as Cari to her family. Yigael's female friends were girls from the Kallen School like Hemda Feigenbaum, and the smartly dressed daughters of the Jerusalem social elite. Carmella was different. Her background was aristocratic; her childhood was marked by travel and foreign connections, due to her father's meetings with public figures all over the world.

Carmella's mother, Hannah Ruppin, led the life of a Zionist empress, taking her children along on tours of Russia, Germany, England, and France. Despite their differences in family and social background, by the time Carmella was seventeen, acquaintances remember clearly, she had made up her mind to marry the young Haganah officer with the motorcycle, quick wit, and ready smile. Eventually, Yigael took notice of her as well. By the time she entered the university, a romance had developed. Nahman Avigad, faithful assistant to Dr. Sukenik, became an unlikely cupid, delivering sealed notes from one to the other as their relationship warmed.

Yigael's subsequent career and achievements would have been inconceivable without Carmella's constant support and help. As she had done for her father as his assistant in public projects and engagements, she was ready to devote all her considerable energy, determination, and intelligence to advancing Yigael (Ig, as she always called him) in his public and scholarly careers. When first informed of Carmella and Yigael's intention to marry, Hannah Ruppin voiced strenuous objections, considering the match beneath her daughter's social station: he was the son, after all, of a self-taught Lithuanian antiquarian and a kindergarten teacher with strange progressive ideas. Her husband's reaction was much calmer. On November 10, 1941, Arthur Ruppin recorded in his journal: "Cari informed me today that she and her boyfriend Yigael (the son of the archaeologist Professor Sukenik, twenty-five years old, employed by the Haganah (for £8 a month) want to get married." Carmella would later tell friends that her father gave his permission quickly, teasing her slightly about the chosen profession of her husband-to-be. "Very well," he told her as they talked in his study, "go ahead and marry this Hyksos and let me carry on with my work." The matter was quickly concluded, and despite the continuing German advance across North Africa toward Palestine, the wedding in the home of the Ruppins in Rechavia on December 21, 1941, was one of the social events of the year. Yigael Sukenik and Carmella Ruppin, once united in marriage in the presence of many of the Jewish community leaders in Palestine, began a tightly closed partnership of love, respect, and mutual emotional sustenance, into which no outsider would ever be allowed to pry.

In their first years of marriage, Yigael and Carmella were both occupied with military matters—he in the Haganah, she as a recruit in the Auxiliary Territorial Service, the women's corps of the British army in Palestine. The danger of an Axis invasion—with all its potentially terrible consequences for the Jewish community—was growing as the British and German armies tensely faced each other at el-Alamein.

With the German Afrika Korps poised to sweep over the Nile Delta, the British finally dropped their demand for numerical parity between Arab and Jewish enlistees in Palestine. As it had with the recruitment for the Jewish Settlement Police, the Haganah took pains to ensure that its own members assumed key positions so they could gain valuable experience in large-scale military operations. Yet by this time, Yigael Sukenik was a key figure in the Haganah headquarters, and enlistment was out of the question for him. Still, family legend has it that Yigael would visit Carmella on weekends and days off at the huge British base at Sarafand, outside Tel Aviv, driving an old margarine truck conscripted for secret service with the Haganah. They made an odd-looking couple, she in uniform and he in civilian clothes. More than once, according to stories their friends remembered, he was derisively called a "slacker" by young men who had volunteered to fight for the British Crown.

Sukenik was deeply involved in planning, however, despite his lack of a uniform. The edgy British commanders in Palestine began hastily planning for the evacuation of the country should Rommel overrun Egypt, an event that would leave the Haganah completely on its own. Plan A might be sufficient to deal with a rural rebellion mounted by irregular forces, but in their present state of training and armament, the squads and platoons of the local Haganah branches could do little against the tanks and strike forces of the Afrika Korps. Yaacov Yannai, another young officer in the Haganah headquarters, vividly recalled sitting with Yigael at a nightlong emergency meeting in which it was decided that, if necessary, the Haganah would make its last stand in the hills and forests of the Carmel range and Galilee. Palmach commander Yitzhak Sadeh sketched out a typically daring plan in which the entire Jewish population of Palestine would be concentrated in a compact, mountainous area; specially trained Palmach units would sabotage roads and bridges and carry out special missions against the invading forces; and every other able-bodied Jewish fighter would be armed. In this desperate contingency scheme hatched by Palmach stalwarts, images of ancient Jewish heroism were inescapable. In the Eretz Israel Plan, the Jews of Palestine would, if necessary, fight to the death. Fortunately the plan was never put into action. But even after the danger of Nazi invasion passed in October 1942, when British field marshal Montgomery smashed the German army at the Battle of el-Alamein, the special role of the Palmach as the Haganah's most concentrated force became a permanent part of the organization's arsenal.

Other challenges, too, faced the Yishuv apart from the purely logistic; political events were moving apace. The Zionist leadership began looking beyond the end of the fighting to a final resolution of the Palestine issue in a comprehensive postwar peace conference. While some Jewish leaders were still courting the gentlemen of Whitehall, Ben-Gurion turned his sights to America, where he hoped to muster support for political independence. In a dramatic announcement to an enthusiastic Zionist audience at the Biltmore Hotel in New York City in May 1942, he had laid out his explicit demand for the establishment of an independent Jewish "commonwealth" in Palestine after the war. At the same time, there were clear signs of the emergence of a Jewish army. In the autumn of 1944 the British finally agreed to the formation of a Jewish Brigade Group that would be sent as a unified Hebrew-speaking unit to northern Italy, where hundreds of thousands of Allied troops were being assembled and trained for the final assault on Nazi Germany. The men of the brigade would be fully trained in artillery, transport, support services, and communications. Secretly appointed to serve as the Haganah's chief liaison officer to the Jewish Brigade Group was none other than Shlomo Rabinowitz, Fistuk, former officer in the Jerusalem branch of the Haganah.

In the spring of 1945—as units of the Jewish Brigade Group pushed northward through the swamps and rivers of the Senio Valley in northern Italy pursuing the fleeing remnants of the Nazi Fifth Corps—the Haganah high command back in Palestine prepared for the challenges that it would likely face after the end of the war. Yigael Sukenik had by this time ascended to the highest ranks of the Haganah leadership. After briefly serving as deputy commander of the Tel Aviv region, he was given the command of the national officers' course in the autumn of 1945. Now twenty-eight, he had responsibility for training platoon commanders. Despite his high position, Yigael never regarded military service as a lifelong occupation; archaeology remained his main professional interest. Throughout his years of Haganah service, he had devoted most of his leisure time to his university studies. After completing his master's thesis on ancient Arabic inscriptions in Palestine in March 1944, he immediately began independent study for a doctoral degree. He genuinely enjoyed the escape and diversion that archaeology afforded him. With his sharp memory for details and his power of imagination, he naturally excelled and took great pride in sharing his expertise. Although his high rank and precise duties in the Haganah remained secret, Yigael Sukenik began to be known throughout the country as something of an archaeological authority, often publishing articles on recent digs and discoveries in the popular Hebrew press. Even in his Haganah courses, he offered the students his by-now characteristic mix of eloquence and imagination, of past and present, of Liddell Hart and ancient Canaan, in lectures on military tactics and strategy.

The 1945 course was, as usual, carefully prepared and highlighted problems of large military formations, their administration, and auxiliary weapons and communications service, which the Allies had used so effectively in the war. In this course, Sukenik continued to place emphasis on conventional battlefield tactics—the tightly disciplined maneuvers of squads working together as a platoon, and platoons working together as a company. But in the midst of the exercises in October 1945, an unexpected military operation rudely interrupted Sukenik's carefully planned training regime.

Ever since the previous spring, when the war in Europe had finally ended, there had been great hopes among Jews in Palestine and all over the world that the White Paper policy of the British would finally be abandoned and the establishment of a Jewish state would become a reality. The world's discovery of the horrifying extent of the Final Solution—with shocking newsreel footage of mass graves of millions of incinerated bodies and starving, haggard survivors fenced into displaced persons camps throughout Central and Eastern Europe—gave urgency to the contention of the Zionists that the time had come to allow free Jewish immigration into Palestine. Indeed, the British Labour party, vying to oust the Tories in the 1945 elections, enthusiastically adopted a plank in their party platform calling for an immediate end to the White Paper policy. Things looked different, however, when Labour got into power. With the overseas empire crumbling and the country badly in need of rebuilding, the new British government sought to maintain its international standing at the lowest possible cost. Fearing that a resumption of large-scale Jewish immigration into Palestine would spark an anti-British uprising throughout the Middle East and among the Muslims of India, the new foreign secretary, Ernest Bevin, remained firmly opposed to any change in British policy. This sudden disappointment drastically shifted Zionist tactics. Both Chaim Weizmann and David Ben-Gurion recognized that the time had come for the Jews to stage a graphic demonstration of their outrage. In the words of the civilian head of the Haganah national command, Moshe Sneh, the Jews of Palestine would have to show the British that "the cost of continuing the White Paper will be more than abolishing it."

That attitude was far from unanimous in high Haganah circles. By the autumn of 1945, the tension between "moderates" and "activists" was nearing the breaking point. In the months since the end of the war, Chief of Staff Dostrovsky had come into ever-increasing conflict with the Haganah's civilian head, Moshe Sneh, and other activist elements in the organization; a decision was finally taken at a meeting of the ruling Mapai central committee to replace Dostrovsky with Palmach commander Yitzhak Sadeh. As a face-saving measure Dostrovsky was given an overseas assignment, to direct the purchase of modern military equipment for the Haganah in the United States. According to some accounts, he asked Sukenik to join him, but Yigael was by then preparing for the annual officers' course. This year, however, Haganah training would not go on as usual. By October 1945, the political leaders in the Yishuv had finally decided to wage a war of action. The Palmach was ordered to stage a raid on a British internment camp for illegal Jewish immigrants at Athlit, on the Mediterranean coast.

It is uncertain to what extent Yigael participated in the planning for this raid, but it seems unlikely that he was deeply involved in light of his actions following the attack. With characteristically meticulous preparation, the Palmach forces surrounded the installation and sealed off the approach routes; in coordination with several members who had infiltrated into the compound as Hebrew teachers and sports instructors, they broke through the fence, overpowered the guards, and quickly led out the two hundred detainees to be dispersed among various Jewish settlements in the Galilee. The sudden mobilization of some of Sukenik's cadets for this action disrupted his carefully planned courses, but even more unsettling for him was the Palmach's great satisfaction in the operation's success. On their return to Juara the participants in the daring and successful mission loudly voiced their objections to what seemed to them to be antiquated, formalized military drills that Sukenik had them practice. They insisted that small-scale commando missions, directed to precise military and political objectives, were the wave of the future. The newly established chief of staff, Yitzhak Sadeh, certainly agreed.

Years later, Sukenik downplayed the personal significance of his sudden resignation from the Haganah headquarters in the autumn of 1945. It had all boiled down, he coolly explained, to a theoretical dispute with Yitzhak Sadeh about whether the smallest tactical unit, the squad, should be trained with a machine gun. Lurking behind that seemingly insignificant disagreement, however, was the lingering dispute over what the Jewish defense force should be. Sadeh's vision was of small units of highly trained, highly motivated commandos lurking through the darkness with submachine guns slung over their shoulders, ready with instant reflexes to respond. Sukenik's was of a conventional army, constructed of large hierarchically arranged units, based on discipline and teamwork more than on innovation, establishing their positions and, even in the squad, working with precise coordination to set up, load, and direct fire from a heavy and somewhat cumbersome machine gun. Sukenik's vivid scenarios had never particularly impressed the Palmach insiders, and now that Sadeh's boys were in control of the Haganah—able even to conscript his own students for an unorthodox mission—Sukenik found himself frustrated and enraged.

His brilliant military career, it seemed, had come to a dead end. After twelve years of faithful service, he had become, to his dismay, an outsider in the Haganah. He had previously rejected a role in the Jewish Brigade of the British army, and he had always made his distance clear from the close-knit circle of Sadeh's boys—young officers like Allon, Rabin, and Dayan. Within a few weeks of the 1945 training course at Juara, then, as the actions against the British forces by the secret Movement for Hebrew Revolt intensified, the familiar dispatches, orders, and informational messages sent from "Yadin" to the regional commanders of the Haganah suddenly stopped. For the next year and a half, Sadeh and the Palmach would rule the Haganah virtually unchallenged. Yigael Sukenik would seek self-esteem and professional fulfillment elsewhere—by leaving Tel Aviv with Carmella and returning, if only temporarily, to Jerusalem and the world of archaeology.

Chapter Five

PLAN D

B y the autumn of 1945, the rising stone walls of new villas on the
expanding southern fringes of Jerusalem symbolized the material prosperity that the world war had brought to both Arabs and
Jews. For three years after the threat of a German invasion had been
averted, Palestine experienced an unprecedented economic expansion, as
factories, stores, harbors, and skilled workers were called upon to feed,
clothe, and provide shelter for the massive British Army in the Middle
East. The wartime economic boom brought far-reaching material
changes, particularly in Jerusalem, where a new middle class was created
and sustained by modern innovations, modern lifestyles, and spendable
cash. Such was the case in the mixed Arab-Jewish neighborhoods in
southern Jerusalem—and certainly for Anton Daoud Kiraz, a Syrian Orthodox immigrant from Turkey in the 1920s. Kiraz had made a hand-

some living as a driving instructor in recent years. He was now, in September 1945, looking forward to building and moving his family into a new and more spacious home. But Jerusalem's past once again proved to be an unstable foundation. As his work crew detonated a dynamite charge to level the ground and begin construction, the dry earth gave way with a low rumble. A cloud of dust rose from beneath the surface to reveal the underground chambers of an ancient Jewish tomb.

Since the antiquities laws were strict and the penalties for a violation could be substantial, Kiraz halted the work and reported the find to the proper authorities. Within a few days, Dr. Eleazar Sukenik—duly alerted by an inspector from the Palestine Department of Antiquities—arrived on the scene to inspect the site. As usual, he left his assistant Avigad to conduct the excavation alone; Dr. Sukenik had other things on his mind than mere digging. Through the war years he had continued to search for a way to publicize his archaeological achievements, and in that regard the small excavation on the property of Anton Kiraz proved unexpectedly rich. The ossuaries in the tomb bore symbols that Sukenik believed were the earliest Christian crosses ever found, as well as Greek and Hebrew inscriptions that he interpreted as lamentations over Jesus' death. While other scholars disputed the readings, Sukenik briefly became the center of worldwide publicity. A local correspondent for *Life* magazine, well aware of the hunger of American audiences for material proof of the Bible, came to the site and persuaded Sukenik to explain his interpretations and pose for a few photographs. The story, "The First Sign of the Cross?" when finally published in the winter of 1946, created a minor sensation in America—and caused a certain embarrassment to Dr. Sukenik, who in his attempt to promote interest in ancient Jewish nationhood had become an unwitting instrument for evangelical Christian groups. Unfortunately, the archaeological discovery of the kind he had always dreamed—one that would secure his reputation forever—remained beyond his grasp.

For his son Yigael, however, social and academic acceptance would always come easily. Even before leaving full-time Haganah service, he had begun to pay increasing attention to his own scholarly advancement. In his 1944 master's thesis on ancient and medieval Arabic inscriptions, he had drawn out unexpected historical insights from the formalized and often fragmentary inscriptions, tossing out suggestions for thorny problems of Islamic history and commenting incisively on battles, kings, and conquests mentioned in some of the commemorative texts. His archaeological interest was increasingly turning to ancient warfare in the Land of the Bible as a base on which to build a scholarly career. For his doctoral dissertation, Yigael envisioned a compendium of ancient weapons, fortifications, and tactics gleaned from finds in Egypt, Greece, Syria, Asia Minor, and Mesopotamia in addition to Palestine. Unlike his father, he scorned the constraining rubric of "Jewish" archaeology. He would search for archaeological examples of ancient warfare throughout the region with the same restless energy with which he had combed modern military strategy books.

As he began his intensive graduate study, Yigael remained almost entirely cut off from modern military action. In the months after his departure from full-time Haganah service, Sadeh and the men of the Palmach had taken the organization even more deeply underground. In the intensified armed struggle against the White Paper policy, the inner circle of Haganah leaders included only those who were directly involved in commando actions against British army installations, bridges, and observation posts. Through the winter of 1946, as the British intensified their attempts to uncover Haganah arms caches and prevent further operations, life in the country grew increasingly difficult. Despite the imposition of curfews and the strict separation of the city into military districts, Yigael, having no active contact with the Haganah leadership, was able to evade arrest and even suspicion in his new scholar's identity. Single-mindedly combing the libraries of Jerusalem for published examples of ancient fortifications and weapons, he seemed to have wanted to escape the present by whatever means he could. Avraham Malamat, a fellow graduate student at the Hebrew University, recalled how surprised he was when Yigael confided in him—with a characteristic self-confidence that sometimes bordered on arrogance—that he had no intention of completing his doctorate in Jerusalem. He and Carmella were planning to go to the University of Chicago, he told Malamat, so that he could write his dissertation at the Oriental Institute.

If Carmella was planning to pack her bags and suddenly go off to America, it would have been hard to discern it from the regularity of her routines in Jerusalem. More and more, it was she who was determining the everyday structure of her and Yigael's life together, with tightly kept daily schedules for shopping, cleaning, letter-writing, and proofreading Yigael's scholarly articles. She was already beginning to devote herself completely to facilitating his professional advancement, not as a cold calculation for her own future but as total dedication to a cause. She carefully regimented their social life, alternating with almost mathematical precision between friends from the Rechavia Gymnasium, acquaintances from the university and the Haganah, and an elite circle of the best and the brightest of Jewish Jerusalem. Chaim Herzog, the chief rabbi's son, back from wartime service with the British army, recalled the gatherings of their shared social circle. Yigael and Carmella were among the

earnestly high-minded young couples of Rechavia who would get together for evening discussions, not parties, in which each member gave a
lecture in their field of expertise. Yigael was by then a devastatingly convincing speaker. In his capacity as a guide-lecturer at the Rockefeller or
Palestine Archaeological Museum, which served as the headquarters of
the government Department of Antiquities, he was always eager to make
his point and be admired by fellow students or to respond with authority
to visitors' questions. Hannah Rabinovich, who was then finishing her
master's degree and working in the museum library, recalled that whenever any of the archaeology students had a problem in their studies, they
would naturally go to Yigael Sukenik. "He'd give you the answer right
away. He never said 'I don't know,' 'I'll think about it,' or 'this is not my
field.' He'd give an answer right away."

Yet suddenly, in the spring of 1947, came questions for which there
were no easy answers. Amid his routine of study and museum lectures,
he received an unexpected message from a secretary at the Jewish
Agency: He had been requested to come for a private interview with
David Ben-Gurion. Sukenik had never met Ben-Gurion personally, but
over the previous two years he had, like everyone else in the Yishuv,
closely followed Ben-Gurion's speeches and political maneuvers. As director of the Zionist Executive, Ben-Gurion was taking an increasingly
militant stance toward the British government, demanding that the
White Paper policy be ended and that the way be paved for the establishment of a sovereign "Jewish commonwealth" at once. Making his way to
the tightly guarded Jewish Agency headquarters at the edge of Rechavia,
Yigael found himself sitting across from the fifty-eight-year-old Ben-
Gurion, with his square jaw, towering ego, and shock of gray hair. Suddenly, Sukenik was drawn from his study of the past back into the
present. "He asked me lots of questions about the Haganah and its structure," Yigael recalled in a 1976 interview, "on my own career in the
Haganah, what I did, and finally why I left and why I had a professional
dispute with Yitzhak Sadeh." The pace of the conversation, he remembered, was maddeningly slow, as Ben-Gurion conducted the interview
only as fast as he could scrawl down both the questions and answers in
his desk diary. The end of the meeting was inconclusive; Ben-Gurion's
interest had been piqued by the subject of Yigael's doctoral dissertation,
but they parted with Ben-Gurion offering only a vague promise that he
would be in touch again.

What Sukenik did not know was that Ben-Gurion was planning a
thorough purge of the Haganah. With an uncanny, not to say prophetic
vision of events unfolding in London, New York, and Washington, Ben-
Gurion was convinced that the Mandate would soon end and that Pales-

tine would be partitioned into independent Arab and Jewish states by the newly established United Nations—to which a frustrated and harried British government had finally transferred the whole affair. As early as the previous December, at the World Zionist Congress in Basel, Ben-Gurion had made his first, quiet preparations for the transformation, summoning Yaacov Dostrovsky back from America and conferring with Israel Galili, a young member of the national command. After taking over the shadow "defense portfolio" of the Zionist government-to-be, Ben-Gurion transformed himself into a field marshal with complete concentration and characteristic energy. His interview with Yigael Sukenik was one of dozens with Haganah veterans that proved to him beyond doubt that the voluntary underground organization could never stand against tanks, artillery, and fighter planes. He turned for advice to Jewish Palestinian veterans of the British army—among them Mordecai Makleff and Chaim Laskov, as well as Fistuk, Yigael's old rival who, fresh from war-ravaged Europe and its nightmarish visions of cities leveled and Jews herded to their deaths by the millions, had only contempt for the Haganah's tactics. They were "only good for blowing up bridges," another military adviser told Ben-Gurion. By early summer 1947, Ben-Gurion had come to the conclusion that he would have to build a new army. But he could not risk an open confrontation with the present Haganah leadership—at least, not right away; so as a first step he quietly relieved Sadeh of command of the Jewish forces and replaced him with the soft-spoken Dostrovsky, sending Fistuk to America in his place.

This was just when Yigael was making a significant impression in scholarly circles. Dr. Benjamin Maisler, a noted historian and longtime professional rival of his father, had hired Yigael as his administrative assistant at the first World Congress of Jewish Studies, which convened at the Hebrew University in July. Yigael was selected to be one of the speakers, and standing at the podium of the auditorium on Mount Scopus— backed by palm fronds and under the stern visages of Theodor Herzl and Hebrew poet Chaim Nahman Bialik—he made his academic debut with an ingenious and convincing reconstruction of King David's conquest of Jerusalem. By this time, Yigael's ability to evoke vivid military scenarios was admired in both scholarly and military circles—and within a week, he was recruited for service to the Jewish state-to-be.

The United Nations Special Committee on Palestine (UNSCOP) had come to Jerusalem to take testimony from Arabs, Jews, and British on the advisability of the partition. As expected, the British government and military witnesses continued to insist that in the face of determined, absolute Arab resistance to partition, the Jewish community would be unable to defend itself. Ben-Gurion was determined to counteract that impression, and a secret meeting was arranged in a safe house in the southern Jerusalem neighborhood of Talpiot between the UNSCOP chairman, Swedish judge Emil Sandström and representatives of the Haganah high command. Although Yigael no longer had a formal connection with the organization, Chief of Staff Dostrovsky insisted that his former aide be brought along.

Security precautions had to be stringent, lest the British authorities take advantage of the meeting to capture the Jewish underground leaders. After dark on July 13, Sandström and two of his assistants, Hu of the Republic of China and Ralph Bunche of the United States, were driven to a nondescript private apartment in separate cars by circuitous routes. Only after Haganah security officers were confident that they had not been followed did the Haganah representatives appear. Speaking passionately yet convincingly, the six unidentified officers allayed any doubts Sandström might have had about the Haganah's military capability, as Bunche faithfully recorded in detail. One of the Haganah men described the organization's capability to deal with an uprising of the Arab population on the model of the rebellion of 1936–39. Another spoke of the high morale of the Haganah troops and the rapidly developing arms industry. Another told of the tens of thousands of young Jewish refugees in displaced persons camps through Central and Eastern Europe ready to defend a Jewish state. Last, a slender young officer sketched out a particularly vivid military scenario: If the Arab states went beyond covert support for the Arabs of Palestine and staged an invasion with regular armies, the Haganah would respond quickly and decisively, though not with head-on counterattacks. It would adopt a strategy of indirect approach to stem the invasion, he told them, utilizing painful, direct strikes at vital naval and air bases deep behind enemy lines.

Hearing reports of this meeting, Ben-Gurion couldn't have helped but be satisfied with the man's performance, although he knew that it contained a large measure of bluster. Despite the Haganah's reputation as a daring, well-disciplined strike force, except for the few Palmach units its rank and file was untrained and disorganized. While the Haganah officers at the meeting with Sandström refused to divulge the number of artillery pieces and other heavy weapons they possessed "for security reasons," Ben-Gurion knew that apart from machine guns and mortars they had none. Machine guns, rifles, hand grenades, and mortars might be enough to defeat the armed resistance of Palestinian Arabs, but Ben-Gurion was now more convinced than ever that the main threat would come from the outside. At the end of August, when UNSCOP issued its final report recommending partition (as Ben-Gurion had expected), representatives of Egypt, Syria, Lebanon, Transjordan, Iraq, and Saudi Arabia reacted with public outrage. Insisting that the only solution to the Palestine question lay in immediate independence for a single state—ruled by its Arab majority—the political committee of the Arab League, meeting in Sofar, Lebanon, in September, threatened violence if their angry warnings went unheeded. That too was precisely what Ben-Gurion had expected, and he quickly stepped up the pace of the Haganah's heavy arms purchases in America and summoned back to active duty members of a new general staff for the Haganah.

None of Yigael Sukenik's classmates in the archaeology department of the Hebrew University could have anticipated his sudden departure. One day in the fall of 1947, Sukenik appeared in the library of the American School, impatiently summoned his friend Avraham Malamat, and announced to Malamat's utter amazement that he was leaving the university. "Yigael, that's impossible," Malamat recalled telling him. "You are at the very end of your doctorate—you have to finish it!" At that moment, Malamat saw the coldness that sometimes came to Yigael Sukenik in stressful moments. "I haven't come here to argue," Sukenik told him without even a word of reassurance or explanation. "The only reason I'm telling you is that I have decided that you will take over my tours and lectures at the Rockefeller Museum. Naturally you don't know archaeology as well as I do, but I'm sure that if you apply yourself, you'll be able to prepare the lectures and everything will be all right." With that, Yigael Sukenik left the library of the American School, not to return for many years. Despite all the effort he had devoted to his archaeological studies and his obvious satisfaction in his rising academic status, his reawakened feeling of responsibility to the Haganah took precedence. Once more he would devote himself to military exercises, planning, and tactics, but now with historical and human consequences that not even his fertile imagination could possibly have conjured at the time.

In the summer of 1947, Dr. Eleazar Sukenik returned to Jerusalem from a nine-month fund-raising expedition to the United States. He was tired, disheartened, and unsure of what lay ahead. The mood in the Yishuv was apprehensive; though UNSCOP gave every indication of being sympathetic to partition, the British authorities intensified their manhunts, curfews, and arms searches in a continuing attempt to end the dizzying spiral of anti-British, anti-Jewish, and anti-Arab violence. Sukenik's lecture tour had clearly been a disappointment; the audiences he had attracted at universities and civic and religious centers from Philadelphia to Los Angeles seemed less concerned with the past of the Holy Land than with its present. His plan to raise twenty-five thousand dollars for "a thorough and complete" archaeological examination of all the ancient synagogues in Palestine must have seemed frivolous to many at a time when Palestinian representatives of the Haganah and the Irgun were secretly soliciting many of the same people with impassioned pleas for contributions for ammunition and guns. Before leaving America, Dr. Sukenik wrote to President Abraham Neuman of Dropsie College, "I hope that through my lectures I was able to arouse interest in Jewish Archaeology and in our work in Palestine." But there is little realistic chance that Sukenik's halting, heavily accented monologues on ancient synagogue mosaics could have achieved that objective. Returning to Jerusalem in July after the World Congress of Jewish Studies, there was little for him to do but devote himself to the completion of several long-deferred excavation reports and continue to visit Jerusalem's antiquities shops.

By November 1947, even the most familiar routines of life in Jerusalem were being disrupted by rising tensions, violence, and the ever-stricter partition of the city into security sectors by the British authorities. Even though Jerusalem was to become an international enclave by the terms of the UNSCOP partition plan, the prospects for peace in the city were slim. Most Jerusalemites feared that the city would be swept up in a horrifying wave of destruction, fighting, and bloodshed if no compromise between Arabs and Jews could be found. Time was running out; no sudden turn toward reconciliation was evident among the population. A gradual chilling of Palestine's postwar economy had given rise to a wave of burglary, armed robbery, and violence in which the veneer of nationalist or religious motives was transparently thin. In the Arab villages of the hill country and along the coastal plain, armed bands were again forming, as they had in the mid-1930s, and local Haganah commanders ordered immediate retaliatory attacks. The rhetoric of the daily press became increasingly strident as, six thousand miles away in America, representatives to the UN General Assembly convened at Lake Success on Long Island to begin public debate and feverish backstage lobbying on the Palestine partition plan. Eleazar Sukenik continued to comb the antiquities shops of the Old City for unexpected treasures, even though he now had to obtain a military checkpoint pass for every trip through the Jaffa Gate. With the future so uncertain, Sukenik felt a sense of mission. He recorded in his diary on November 15 that he had visited the shop of an Armenian dealer named Ohan who showed him an inscribed Hebrew seal bearing the biblical name Hasdai Ben Ramalyahu. "Even though he wants a lot of money," Sukenik jotted down to himself in silent self-justification, "it will be necessary to buy it from him."

Just a week later, on Sunday, November 23, came a telephone call that changed Eleazar Sukenik's life. Arriving in his office on Mount Scopus, he found a message requesting that he contact Ohan immediately. It was an unusual request since on Sundays the shops and stores of the Armenian Quarter were usually closed. When Sukenik returned Ohan's call, he found him in a high state of agitation, speaking excitedly about some items that he wanted Sukenik to see at once. Sukenik impatiently asked for more details, but Ohan refused to reveal anything over the telephone. They had to meet early the next morning, he insisted, and since there would be no time for Sukenik to obtain a transit pass into the Old City, Ohan suggested that they meet at the Jaffa Gate checkpoint and talk through the barbed-wire security fence.

Sukenik's interest was piqued; he had dealt with Ohan for years and knew him as a canny businessman who never exposed his emotions in the course of a deal. But the next morning, when Sukenik made his way from Rechavia to the Jaffa Gate, where nervous British sentries checked the morning rush of workers from Bethlehem and the Hebron hills, he could see that Ohan was excited. Motioning Sukenik to come closer to the barbed-wire fence, he withdraw a large leather scrap from his briefcase, hurriedly explaining that it had been brought to him by an antiquities dealer in Bethlehem who claimed that it had been torn from a large scroll—one of several—recently found by Bedouin in a cave near the Dead Sea. This dealer was anxious to determine whether the scrolls were of any value and wondered if Ohan could help him find a buyer. At first the story seemed suspicious to Sukenik; for more than a century, gullible tourists in the Holy Land had been taken in by clever, often skillful forgeries of ancient inscriptions. But as he peered at the Hebrew letters on this piece of parchment, he could not dismiss its authenticity out of hand. Amazingly, the letters seemed to correspond to inscriptions of the Roman period—particularly on the ossuaries he and Avigad had found in dozens of first-century Jewish tombs. Could any forger have been skillful enough to reproduce the letters? Ohan was impatient. Was this scrap of any value? he asked. Would Sukenik be willing to purchase the complete scroll for the National Museum of Jewish Antiquities?

By Friday, Sukenik had obtained an official transit pass and made his way past the sentries at the Jaffa Gate, finally able to examine the manuscript fragments closely. His initial impression seemed justified, for the finely inscribed letters on the original fragment (and four more that Ohan had in the meantime been able to borrow from the antiquities dealer in Bethlehem) not only closely resembled those of the ossuary inscriptions but were written with a sure-handed consistency that no forger could likely achieve. As Ohan watched him intently, Sukenik stared down at the letters and attempted a quick translation. Though written in biblical Hebrew, they represented no texts with which he was familiar. The implications of this find were almost too much to ponder: here was an ancient, unknown Hebrew text, more ancient than any other known Hebrew manuscript by hundreds of years! Whether it proved to be an early version of a biblical book or a previously unknown work from the time of the Second Temple, these Dead Sea Scrolls were clearly the discovery that Sukenik had been searching for throughout his life. Determined to buy them as soon as possible, Sukenik arranged to travel with Ohan to Bethlehem to begin the negotiations the very next day.

Chassiya, however, exploded in anger when she heard of her husband's intention. Returning home from the Old City, Sukenik poured out his emotions in a tumble of words about scrolls, antiquities dealers, and a trip to Bethlehem, but Chassiya suddenly and rudely brought him back to reality. That night, November 28, the final vote was scheduled in the United Nations on Palestine partition. No matter what the outcome, a new wave of terrorism and perhaps even rioting was likely to begin. The trip to Bethlehem alone with Ohan, as Sukenik had planned for the next morning, would be foolhardy. In the previous months random terrorist attacks had become increasingly common against innocent Arab and Jewish civilians who had been so foolish as to wander unprotected into the other community's turf. Even now the Haganah was making preparations to counter a widespread outbreak of violence; on that very day Yigael was dispatched to Jerusalem from the Haganah headquarters to check on the defensive readiness in the Jewish neighborhoods. Stopping briefly in Rechavia to visit his parents, he heard the story of the scrolls and agreed with his mother. Before departing for Tel Aviv he warned his father that the trip to Bethlehem was too dangerous right now.

But Eleazar Sukenik had nothing to lose. Having weathered every political storm in the country since before World War I, his crowning archaeological achievement was now in his grasp. He would not allow external events to destroy this moment for him. Late in the evening, radio news reports from New York announced that the vote on Palestine partition would be delayed until the following day. Sukenik saw his opportunity and took it. Early the next morning, without informing Chassiya, Sukenik telephoned Ohan and told him, as he later recorded in his diary, that "I was coming over to see him right away." Sukenik passed through the Jaffa Gate with his pass and went straight to Ohan's shop, where he informed him that he was ready to go to Bethlehem. The Armenian antiquities dealer and the Jewish archaeologist quickly made their way to the open-air bus terminal outside the Old City and boarded a bus headed south, filled with Arab farmers, workers, and shopkeepers. Arriving in Bethlehem, Ohan led Sukenik to the home of Feidi el-Alami, the antiquities dealer in possession of the scrolls. Sukenik had never had much patience for gracious small talk with antiquities dealers, but this time he did not want anything to go wrong.

"Among the Arabs," Sukenik later wrote of this moment, "it is considered bad form to plunge immediately into business, and so, restraining my crude European behavior, I followed local custom and made polite inquiries about his health and the well-being of his family." After a half hour of sipping coffee and exchanging pleasantries, Ohan moved to the matter of the negotiations. On Sukenik's behalf, he asked el-Alami to relate the story of the bedouin's discovery of the scrolls. They then heard the tale that would in time become so famous—of a lost goat, a stone tossed by chance by one of the bedouin into a cave opening, and the unexpected sound of breaking pottery. Feidi then brought out for Sukenik's inspection two tall jars in which the leather bundles had been found in the cave, and then—finally—he brought out the two complete scrolls.

"My hands shook as I started to unwrap one of them," Sukenik later recalled. "I read a few sentences. It was written in beautiful biblical Hebrew. The language was like that of the Psalms, but the text was unknown to me." Sukenik wanted to take them back with to Jerusalem, but he knew that the negotiations for their purchase were liable to take time. He therefore appealed to el-Alami's sense of gentlemanly honor, announcing that he was deeply interested in purchasing these leathers on behalf of the Hebrew University but wanted to take them home for further study. He would, he assured el-Alami, inform Ohan of his final answer within two days. That arrangement was apparently satisfactory to el-Alami, who wrapped both the jars and the scrolls in paper and sent Ohan and Sukenik off with good wishes. They boarded a bus and rode back to Jerusalem, with Sukenik bearing a package under his arm, he later noted, that "must have looked like a bundle of market produce." Sukenik returned quickly to Rechavia and opened the precious package. Because of the brittleness of the parchment, it was not possible to unroll the scrolls, but he was able to examine at least the opening columns of the documents. After comparing their contents to known biblical and apocryphal texts, he realized that he had before him ancient religious texts that had been lost for two thousand years.

In the evening of November 29, 1947, the drama in New York was still unfolding. While Sukenik was absorbed by his ancient documents, Chassiya and their youngest son Matti listened intently to radio reports of the UN General Assembly debate. After midnight the result was announced: With thirty-three member states voting in favor, thirteen opposed, and ten abstaining, the United Nations had officially recommended that the British Mandate for Palestine be terminated and that two independent states, one Arab and one Jewish, be established within a year. The news was greeted with sullen resignation in the Arab sections of the city and with celebration in the Jewish neighborhoods. Eleazar Sukenik, dazed from the events of the last twenty-four hours, left his scrolls briefly to join the crowds gathered outside the Jewish Agency headquarters at the edge of Rechavia. Cars honked, young people danced, old friends embraced one another. The dream of an independent Jewish state was closer than ever to realization. Yet at this historic moment of communal celebration, Dr. Eleazar Sukenik, separated from his wife and son, wandered alone through the crowds, lost in thoughts of antiquity.

Yigael Sukenik was not in Jerusalem to share his father's greatest moment. By the time of the UN partition decision, his day-to-day responsibilities for the Haganah were consuming all his time and energy. Operating from a single, cramped office in the Jewish Agency building on Lillienblum Street in Tel Aviv, he had been given the title of Operations Officer, an ill-defined assignment that encompassed virtually every military action the Haganah would undertake in the months to come. He succeeded in establishing the organizational foundations of a functioning operations branch, which, with the supply and manpower branches, constituted the three main pillars of the rejuvenated Haganah. Though he had had no formal military training, Yigael relied on his instincts, his sense of order, and his hurried reading on the structure of headquarters of other armies to deal with the frighteningly wide range of operational matters he would soon be called upon to address.

Hiring a small staff of officers and instructors whom he knew from his earlier Haganah service, he created a department for fortifications; a technical department, composed of photographers and draftsmen; a foreign department, to draw up plans to repel a possible outside invasion; a domestic department, to deal with defensive preparations at individual settlements; a planning department, to draft operational plans for special missions; an intelligence department; and a general department, for the formulation of overall strategy. The means and manpower of the operations branch were severely limited; most of these seven departments were staffed by a single man. All of them faced an additional challenge: During Yitzhak Sadeh's tenure as chief of staff—with the

Haganah's emphasis on commando raids against the British—staff work had been seriously neglected. General membership lists and defense files for many individual settlements were either in disarray or destroyed.

Despite Yigael Sukenik's confident claims to UNSCOP chairman Sandström in midsummer, the general staff of the Haganah knew—even then—that the organization possessed no units capable of mounting large operations of extended duration. While local commanders could on occasion order punishing hit-and-run attacks on Arab villages and while Palmach units could mount well-planned operations to smuggle illegal Jewish immigrants into the country, the Haganah was incapable of meeting a regular army on the battlefield. Its helplessness in that regard was made plain in October, when Syrian infantry and artillery units massed on the northern border, briefly crossing into Palestinian territory. The several hundred hastily mobilized Haganah troops that were rushed to the Upper Galilee to confront the Syrian army provided an object lesson in logistical incompetence and military weakness. Shivering in the autumn cold without enough rifles or even blankets, coats, or winter provisions, the Haganah troops would have been no match for the Syrians. Recognizing this, leadership finally agreed that it would have to bring the Haganah out of the underground, to be fully capable of defending the boundaries of the Jewish state, whatever those boundaries might eventually be.

Through the fall, Ben-Gurion increasingly took on the role of supreme commander, listening to but often rejecting the advice of Chief of Staff Dostrovsky and Israel Galili, the head of the Haganah's civilian national command. Ben-Gurion's focus was still firmly set on the threat of an invasion by the armies of Syria, Lebanon, Iraq, Egypt, and Transjordan to make a last desperate effort to overturn the UN partition plan. After dispatching additional emissaries to America and Europe to step up the purchase of surplus tanks, artillery, and airplanes, he demanded that the Haganah leadership create a conventional army, not one tied to the static defense of Jewish neighborhoods and settlements, but an effective, mobile fighting force under the direct control of the chief of staff, with a clear chain of command, through brigades to battalions, companies, platoons, and squads. In fact, the National Command Order of November 1947 created that new army—at least on paper—establishing brigades in the north, center, south, and Jerusalem. These large military formations were to be to supported by a modern navy, air force, artillery, and armor corps.

Yigael Sukenik, a confirmed individualist by nature, was never particularly adept at teamwork. He was now forced into an intense and often uneasy working relationship with his Haganah colleagues, subordinates, and rivals, under the growing pressure of international events. His graduate-student self-confidence and lightning-fast grasp of facts and figures would now have to be applied to the task of organizing a modern army and determining its strategic doctrine—as quickly as possible. In order to establish realistic operational plans, he and his staff had to elicit accurate information on manpower and weapons from the newly appointed brigade commanders, who were suspicious of interference; he had to agree on shared goals with the other staff officers—among them, the ever-cautious Moshe Lehrer of the manpower branch and the aloof and correct Haganah veteran, Yosef Avidar, of supply. Tension also reigned between the veterans of the Jewish Brigade of the British army (who were convinced that they were the only competent ones to lead large formations into battle) and the Haganah old-timers (who looked on the preening formality of the British army with disdain). Sukenik managed to navigate this minefield of mutual suspicion partly because of his analytical brilliance, and partly because his own political and ideological allegiances were unclear.

In an era and society where one's career prospects were often brightened or dimmed by membership in certain political parties, military units, or ideological factions, Yigael Sukenik defied easy definition by stubbornly identifying himself as a student who had simply volunteered his services in defense of the state-to-be. Ben-Gurion, always apprehensive that his political foes were plotting against him, found reassurance in Yigael's neutrality. He also came to value Sukenik's ability to reduce an often dizzying hodgepodge of intelligence reports, equipment lists, aerial photographs, messages from brigade commanders, newspaper clippings, and passages from the Bible into a coherent, straightforward military analysis. Their relationship was often stormy, and there were many times when the thirty-one-year-old operations officer and the sixty-two-year-old Zionist leader would angrily disagree. "I was one of the few people who could tell him directly when I thought he was wrong," Yigael Yadin recalled years later, adding that "I was quite impulsive in those days—in what I'd dare to say to him, and also in the aggressiveness of my tone. But I was never afraid that I'd be fired because of what I'd said. On the contrary, I felt that it impressed him." By December 1947, Sukenik was included in most of the high-level strategy meetings at the new Haganah headquarters, a nondescript pink stucco apartment block on Yarkon Street, known simply as the Red House to the officers and men. Characteristically, he rarely hesitated to contradict his superiors with his own reading of the security situation. More than once, Ben-Gurion recorded in his diary extensive quotations from "Yadin's" clear, crisp monologues. Many times in the months that followed, Ben-Gurion would see in Yigael Sukenik's memoranda and briefing papers ingenious military elaborations of his own strategic master plan.

———

As a result of the growing civil disorder, the Hebrew University was gradually ceasing to function, and Dr. Eleazar Sukenik remained obsessed with his scrolls. In the days following the UN decision, Jerusalem was shaken by a wave of violence; first an attack by an angry Arab mob on Jerusalem's commercial center, and in the weeks that followed, increasingly frequent sniping between neighborhoods and the murder of innocent civilians on both sides. Personal safety, however, meant little to Eleazar Sukenik when there was the possibility of obtaining more scrolls. He remained in contact with Ohan by telephone, and on December 21 he met him again at the barbed-wire fence and purchased another scroll.

In the intensifying urban warfare, as the British concentrated on securing their own routes of evacuation, the city's neighborhoods were being raggedly and violently split along ethnic lines. Jewish families fled from mixed neighborhoods in the eastern part of the city, while Arab families fled from the west. Stranded in Rechavia, finding it increasingly difficult to visit the university on Mount Scopus and impossible to visit the Rockefeller Museum or the Old City, Sukenik was thoroughly absorbed in his ancient documents, even though he was unable to read more than a few lines. He came to the conclusion that the scrolls had been hidden away in antiquity in a cave used as a *geniza,* or place of deposit for worn or damaged religious texts, as required by traditional Jewish law. He therefore gave them the name *ha-Megillot ha-Genuzot,* "the Hidden Scrolls" (by which they are still known in Hebrew), though the rest of the world would come to know them as the Dead Sea Scrolls. The tightly rolled parchment was extremely brittle, and it snapped when Sukenik attempted to unroll them. He therefore contacted the only expert he could find in wartorn, besieged Jerusalem—Dr. James Biberkraut, a skillful German-born restorer of paintings and other objets d'art, who began unrolling them soon after the New Year. To his delight, Sukenik found that his texts included an unknown book of Psalms, a copy of the Book of Isaiah, and most intriguing of all, a vivid description of a violent war waged in the Holy Land at the end of times, which Sukenik named the "War of the Sons of Light Against the Sons of Darkness."

In early January no Jerusalemite was immune to the effects of the intensifying violence. In an effort to discourage attacks against Jewish neighborhoods, the Haganah dispatched armed patrols to Arab villages around the city, both as a show of strength and to distribute pamphlets calling for peace. Peace became increasingly elusive, however, as the cycle of strike and counterstrike claimed innocent victims simply because they were Arabs or Jews. On December 27 a convoy of Jewish workers returning to Jerusalem from the Dead Sea was attacked near the village of Silwan, and the following night the Haganah staged a raid on the village. The retaliation was not effective; it merely deepened the horror and provoked yet another act of retaliation. High explosives were soon employed in the deadly escalation. On the stormy night of January 5, Haganah sappers detonated a powerful explosion at the Semiramis Hotel in the Arab neighborhood of Qatamon, killing fourteen people, among them the Spanish consul in Jerusalem. The international outcry was immediate, and the Jewish Agency publicly condemned the action. But the explosion accelerated the panicked exodus of Arab families from the neighborhood to safer quarters in East Jerusalem.

Those who moved too freely between Arab and Jewish neighborhoods were in danger. Sniping at innocent passersby in the streets was a growing threat. Still, Eleazar Sukenik was willing to take great risks if there was a possibility of obtaining more scrolls. On January 13 he walked from Rechavia to meet Ohan near the main post office in downtown Jerusalem, but the Armenian dealer brought with him no scrolls, only the dubious promise that he would soon be in contact with Feidi el-Alami in Bethlehem. Bethlehem was now, for Sukenik, as distant as another planet. Sandbagged roadblocks manned by armed men made travel even from one section of Jerusalem to another impossible, while Bethlehem lay beyond the city's outskirts. Still, Sukenik's expanding involvement with the scrolls had not yet ended. Toward the end of January he received a letter that had miraculously passed through the barricades from Anton Kiraz, the Syrian Christian driving instructor on whose property he and Avigad had excavated in 1945. In the desperate handwritten message, Kiraz appealed to the professor to meet with him—to examine some ancient scrolls.

The meeting was arranged at the Jerusalem YMCA, a stately, stone building with a tall tower, manicured lawn, and porticoes that evoked memories of more placid colonial times. It was now in the heart of one of the most heavily guarded security sectors, across the street from the administrative offices of the British government at the King David Hotel. Anxious to avoid attracting attention as the only Jew at the YMCA, Sukenik made his way quickly into the library, where he was ushered into the office of the librarian, Malak Tannourji, also a member of the Syrian Orthodox community. In a matter of minutes, Kiraz appeared and produced several ancient scrolls. The story he told Sukenik was astonishing: Earlier in the summer of 1947 the Syrian Orthodox archbishop of Jerusalem, Athanasius Yeshue Samuel, an avid collector of old manuscripts, had purchased four scrolls from a group of Ta'amireh Bedouin. Only by a misunderstanding, a missed appointment, had another group taken *their* scrolls back to Bethlehem and sold them to Feidi el-Alami. The archbishop had subsequently heard of Dr. Sukenik through Anton Kiraz and sought the professor's opinion on the value of the scrolls. Dr. Sukenik had no doubt that they were genuine, and two of them were in far better condition than the scrolls he had already obtained. Seeking time to study them further and perhaps to confer with some colleagues, Sukenik received Kiraz's permission to keep them for a few days. With the archbishop's scrolls in a paper bag tucked carefully under his arm, Sukenik made his way back to Rechavia, determined to raise funds to acquire these scrolls for the National Museum.

Had life in Jerusalem been normal, Eleazar Sukenik could easily have raised an unprecedented sum to purchase these scrolls on behalf of the Hebrew University. To mobilize scholarly support for the purchase, he invited the noted biblical scholar Umberto Cassuto into his home and rolled out the first few columns of a magnificent—and apparently complete—copy of the Book of Isaiah. Emboldened by Cassuto's reassurance, he appealed directly to Hebrew University president Judah Magnes. Sukenik hoped that Magnes might be able to mobilize funds for the purchase—and offer a price high enough that the archbishop would not seek another bid. Magnes was impressed by Sukenik's presentation and by his intriguing suggestion that these ancient documents might be the work of the ascetic sect of the Essenes. But at a time when the inhabitants of the city were beginning to fear for their very existence and the overland links between Jewish Jerusalem and the outside world were slowly being cut off, philanthropic efforts and scholarly projects were understandably difficult to undertake. Magnes suggested that Sukenik turn to other sources. But time was running out. Sukenik had promised to return the scrolls to Kiraz at the YMCA on February 6 with a definite answer. But despite the obvious archaeological and biblical value of the manuscripts, Sukenik was unable to raise the needed funds. On February 6 he sadly returned to the YMCA with the scrolls.

In the privacy of the librarian's office he pleaded with Kiraz for just a few more days, but Kiraz was under strict instructions from Archbishop Samuel to bring the scrolls back to his residence at St. Mark's monastery. Desperate, Sukenik suggested that perhaps he could bring President Magnes to a meeting with the archbishop at the Yugoslav consulate. But in Jerusalem in February 1948 the future—even a week in the future—was dangerously uncertain. Just four days before, a massive car bomb had rocked downtown Jerusalem and leveled the *Palestine Post* building;

within a week another car bomb would demolish a wing of the Jewish Agency headquarters on the edge of Rechavia. Sukenik would never see the scrolls again. "Slowly I walked back toward my home," he noted in his journal. "The emptiness and depression of the streets perfectly fitted my mood." Unbeknownst to him, the archbishop had made contact on the other side of the city with some scholars at the American School.

At the beginning of February 1948, Operations Officer Yigael Sukenik assessed the unfolding situation in a memorandum to the other members of the general staff. His analysis was unsettling, concluding that "we have lost the strategic initiative and we still have not succeeded in regaining it." During the first weeks after the UN decision, the violence had spread slowly across the country, even as the political leaders of the Zionist movement—Ben-Gurion and Moshe Shertok among them—hoped that it could somehow be contained. Ben-Gurion and Shertok insisted that it was important to demonstrate that the partition plan could be implemented without much bloodshed. They hoped that once the resolve of the Yishuv and the international community was made clear to the Arabs of Palestine, the vast majority would accommodate themselves to the new reality. But they were mistaken. Through December, Arab-Jewish violence had intensified, beginning in the mixed neighborhoods of the large cities, slowly spreading to rural areas, and eventually endangering the free movement of traffic along the main roads. The two sides were pulled into a vicious circle of hatred and retaliation, usually initiated by a bloody act of criminal fanatics against civilians, to which the other side felt compelled to respond.

New threats had also appeared on the horizon. With the official British decision to terminate their Mandate over Palestine by May 15, British army units began withdrawing from many outlying regions of the country, often leaving Arabs and Jews to fight each other without hindrance. Across the northern border in Syria, a volunteer force mobilized and funded by the Arab League, the Jaysh el-Inqath, the Army of Liberation, was training for combat at a large camp at Qatna. At the same time, the legendary Abd el-Khader el-Husseini—the mufti's warrior nephew—had returned from self-imposed exile in Saudi Arabia and begun to mobilize *fasa'il* for action in the hills around Jerusalem. With a growing awareness of the scope of Arab military preparations, the Haganah leadership ordered harder and deeper attacks into the Arab neighborhoods and villages from which they suspected terrorist missions had been mounted, but their actions did little to quell the rising spiral of violence.

By mid-January, the arrival of the Arab volunteer forces had begun to shift the balance of terror. Full-scale battles erupted where once hit-and-run strikes were the norm. On January 9, Kibbutz Kfar Szold, near the Syrian border, was attacked by a force of Syrian irregulars; five days later, Abd el-Khader el-Husseini led several hundred fighters in an assault on Gush Etzion, to the south of Jerusalem; and on January 20, a force of approximately five hundred troops supported by automatic weapons and mortars, under the command of a Syrian officer named Adib Shishakli, attacked Kibbutz Yehiam, in western Galilee. None of the settlements were taken, and from the perspective of the Haganah headquarters, the defensive planning at each of the sites apparently proved itself. Yet there was certainly no reason for celebration. Serious casualties had been suffered in each battle, and a relief force of thirty-five of the Haganah's best fighters—sent at night through the hills to the south of Jerusalem to relieve the besieged defenders of Gush Etzion—had been detected by villagers in the area, surrounded by a hastily summoned force of Abd el-Khader's fighters, and wiped out to the last man. "The Enemy is freely choosing the place and intensity of action," Yigael Sukenik grimly reminded his colleagues in his February status report, noting that "our loss of strategic initiative at this stage of development will cause an extremely dangerous situation in the stages to come."

The stages to which he was referring was the increasing likelihood of military intervention by the neighboring Arab states. At an Arab League meeting in Cairo in early February, the representatives of Egypt, Syria, Lebanon, Transjordan, Iraq, and Saudi Arabia announced that the chiefs of staff of their armed forces would soon meet to coordinate operations to prevent the implementation of what was to them a Zionist-inspired partition plan. The operations branch of the Haganah was anticipating the forces it might face after May 15 and the final evacuation of the British, and in January, Yigael Sukenik and his staff formulated a new operative plan that they called Plan Joshua, in memory of Joshua Globerman, a general staff member who had been ambushed and killed on the Tel Aviv-to-Jerusalem road. Unlike the previous national defense plans—Plans Aleph, Beth, and Gimmel—which were based on static regional defense networks and had focused entirely on the threat to Jewish lives and property from local irregular forces, Plan Joshua directly addressed the possibility of invasion from outside. Still, its plan to stop the progress of the invading forces by blowing up bridges and by staging lightning raids across the borders against enemy troop concentrations far underestimated the power of conventional army units and overestimated the efficiency of commando tactics in conventional warfare.

The military challenge posed by the Arab armies was, in fact, unambiguous; they possessed the support of air power, armor, and artillery—weapons that the Haganah brigades would not receive until the end of the British Mandate and the lifting of the British blockade of Palestinian ports. Even though the Haganah forces were already overtaxed in repelling raids by the Arab volunteer forces, in mounting their own strikes on Arab villages suspected of harboring hostile forces, and in guarding vital supply convoys to isolated Jewish settlements and population centers, plans had to be made for the ominous prospects of even bloodier fighting after May 15. So during February and early March, Yigael Sukenik and his staff feverishly collected information, pored over maps, evaluated intelligence reports, and conferred with local commanders to formulate a complex operational document that would mark the beginning of a new stage in the history of the Haganah, the Zionist movement, and Palestine.

In early March, the new plan was ready. No document written by Yigael Sukenik was ever more viciously attacked, staunchly defended, condemned, and denied than Tochnit Dalet, or Plan D. Later characterized by critics as "the master plan for the conquest of Palestine," it was both the culmination of the long-range Haganah planning of the early 1940s and a coldly pragmatic operational plan to improve the Haganah's position on the ground. As early as December, Ben-Gurion himself had set the tone. "We should adopt a system of aggressive defense," he told senior Haganah officers Yohanan Rattner and Fritz Eisenstadt. "With every Arab attack, we should be ready to reply with a decisive blow, destroy the site or expel the inhabitants and take their place." With little more than a month remaining before the final British evacuation, the goal now was to formulate a plan that would establish a continuous strip of territory from which Haganah brigades would be able to mount an effective defense. Expulsions of civilians and the leveling of Arab villages were not the primary objectives. Yet the plan would result in a complete transformation of the human landscape in many parts of the country and the creation of a political and humanitarian problem whose solution would become more difficult with each passing year.

"The objective of this plan," Sukenik wrote in the introduction, "is to gain control of the territory of the Hebrew state and defend its borders. It also aims at gaining control of the areas of Jewish settlement and population outside the borders" of the territory allotted to the Jewish state by the UN partition plan. In the clear, unemotional discourse of military planning he listed the enemies to be confronted in this next stage of the fighting—local irregulars, the Arab League volunteer force, and the armies of the neighboring Arab states. Plan D was meant to take effect only after the evacuation of the British forces and on the assumption that no other international forces would have to be taken into account. It outlined eight major objectives in a spectrum of actions from purely defensive to aggressive, the details to be worked out by the commanders of the various brigades.

The fortifications of Jewish settlements and neighborhoods were to be strengthened. Enemy approach routes and lines of communication were to be blocked. Vital services and strategic points in the mixed cities were to be taken over, as were British police stations and army camps. Sieges were to be mounted against Arab cities such as Jaffa, Beth Shean, Acre, Bethlehem, Lod, and Ramleh in order to force the Arab forces to lift their siege of Jewish settlements and cities, primarily Jerusalem. The most far-reaching element in Plan D, however, was its instructions for the conquest of Arab towns and villages that were likely to serve as enemy bases, that were situated along vital routes of communication, or that occupied strategic points. Such villages were to be encircled by Haganah forces and searched for weapons, radios, motor vehicles, and political suspects. "In the case of resistance," the plan ordered the "destruction of the armed force and the expulsion of the population outside the borders of the state."

As the fighting intensified throughout the country during March, with the Arab volunteer forces concentrating their attacks on supply convoys to besieged Jewish settlements, Sukenik instructed the brigade commanders to select targets and train their units to swing into action on May 15. But toward the end of March, Sukenik's carefully drafted timetable was sabotaged by a chain of unexpected diplomatic and military events. On March 19, in a stunning reversal of policy, U.S. representative Warren Austin, in a session of the UN Security Council, declared that in light of the continuing bloodshed in Palestine, partition was no longer a viable option. His government believed, he said, that Palestine should be placed under UN control. In the growing international tensions of the postwar world, the Middle Eastern experts of the State Department, Defense Secretary James Forrestal, and Secretary of State George Marshall all feared that a war in Palestine would offer an ideal opportunity for the Soviet Union to extend its influence in the Middle East by coming to the aid of one of the warring sides. The overthrow of the Czech government in February and the continuing expansion of Soviet control across Eastern Europe aroused fears of Communist influence in the strategically vital Holy Land.

Ben-Gurion reacted in fury to the Americans' change of heart. "It is we who will decide the fate of Palestine," he announced at an angry press conference on March 20. "We cannot agree to any sort of trusteeship, permanent or temporary—the Jewish state exists because we defend it." In stubborn adherence to the terms of the UN partition resolution, Ben-Gurion drew up plans to establish a provisional government for the Jewish state. It would be a parliamentary democracy, led by a prime minister at the head of a coalition cabinet. The head of state would be a president, but the office would be largely ceremonial. The real power would lie in the hands of the prime minister. It was unthinkable that the first prime minister would be anyone but Ben-Gurion himself, and he would also serve as minister of defense. In that capacity he secretly dispatched urgent word to Haganah representatives in Europe that heavy arms should be sent to Palestine as quickly as possible. Ben-Gurion believed that the time had come to press ahead relentlessly toward independence, yet in the last week of March the Haganah suffered the most painful setbacks in its history. In the western Galilee, in the Negev, and in the Jerusalem region, hundreds of Haganah troops were killed and dozens of vehicles were destroyed or captured as the Arab Liberation Army and irregular forces virtually cut off all overland connection to a number of Jewish settlements—by far the most important of which was Jewish Jerusalem.

From Jerusalem came increasingly desperate pleas for food and reinforcements. With Arab forces ranged in the villages and high points along much of the winding road to the city—especially in the steep defile called Bab el-Wad, "the Gate to the Valley," just past the British police station at Latrun—even the most heavily armed and armored Jewish convoys were unable to get through. In worried telegrams to Ben-Gurion and the Haganah headquarters in Tel Aviv, the Jewish leaders of Jerusalem warned of open rebellion or surrender in many neighborhoods if relief supplies did not arrive soon. Ben-Gurion was desperate to avoid any reliance on international intervention to protect the Jewish population, and he hastily convened a meeting of the general staff at his Tel Aviv home on the evening of March 31. "There is now only one burning question," he lectured the assembled officers, "and that is the war for the road to Jerusalem." Anticipating Ben-Gurion's demand for action, Sukenik had with great effort managed to gather a reserve force of a few hundred men from several of the hard-pressed regional brigades, who were both fighting and training for the implementation of Plan D in just six weeks' time. Ben-Gurion waved off the number as far too puny to open the road. "The fall of Hebrew Jerusalem would be a death blow to the Yishuv, and the Arabs know this," he recorded in his journal, "and we have to take all the men who are not absolutely needed in the center, in Tel Aviv, and in the South—with their weapons" and send them to open the road to Jerusalem. According to the UN plan, Jerusalem was to remain an internationalized enclave. But Ben-Gurion would not leave its large Jewish population to the mercy of outsiders. The time for armed convoys had passed; it was now time to capture the vital route to Jerusalem—to implement the spirit of Plan D, if not yet all its details.

Sukenik and the other members of the general staff were at first horrified at this suggestion, but they proceeded to the Red House to start planning the operation at once. Ben-Gurion was insistent that they mount a brigade-size operation, marshaling not hundreds but more than a thousand fighters—even if it meant a calculated gamble in temporarily thinning the defense of other areas. Still more unsettling to the general staff was the fact that no operation with even battalion-size forces had ever been attempted. Haganah "brigades" had been primarily administrative formations since the previous fall. Yet the decision was made to go forward with Operation Nachshon (named for Nachshon ben Aminadav, who according to biblical tradition was the first of the Israelites fleeing from Egypt to dare to jump into the Red Sea). Diving into uncertain waters, "Yadin" quickly dispatched orders—not requests—to all the regional commanders to send their best men and equipment to the operation to mobilize a national brigade of three battalions, with sufficient force to conquer strategic points and villages and ensure the passage of relief convoys through the Jerusalem hills.

Superpower politics now entered the picture, for as Secretary of State Marshall had feared, the Soviet Union had a Middle Eastern card to play. It wanted the British imperialists out of the region and had approved some important shipments to make sure that the partition of Palestine was not delayed. On the night of the general staff's fateful decision to go ahead with Operation Nachshon, a DC-4 cargo plane from Czechoslovakia, bearing a cargo of two hundred Mauser rifles, forty machine guns, and 150,000 rounds of ammunition, landed in a small Haganah airstrip in southern Palestine. The next day, a Yugoslav freighter docked at Tel Aviv, and the Jewish stevedores there quickly unloaded five hundred rifles, two hundred machine guns, and more than five million rounds of ammunition hidden under a cargo of potatoes and onions. With this reserve of weaponry, the improvised Nachshon Brigade prepared to go on the offensive under the command of Shimon Avidan, official head of the Alexandroni Brigade. While Sukenik remained at the Red House, the brigade's units moved from Tel Aviv to the marshaling ground.

After patrols were sent to determine the disposition of hostile forces in the area and block the arrival of reinforcements, the operation was ready to begin. It followed the guidelines of Plan D closely: to stage a surprise raid against the heavily guarded headquarters of the Arab volunteers near Ramleh in the western area of operations and against the hill-top village of Kastel in the east. On April 6, Haganah units took up positions all along the road as the first convoy of sixty trucks passed safely, while other units of the Nachshon Brigade fanned out to capture villages from which previous attacks on the road had been staged. Abd el-Khader el-Husseini, hearing the news of the Haganah operation during a visit to Damascus, rushed back to the front and ordered an immediate counterattack. Kastel, now emptied of its inhabitants, passed back and forth between the competing armies several times. Finally, on April 8, Abd el-Khader was killed in the fighting, and after a humiliating rout of the Arab Liberation Army in a battle near Kibbutz Mishmar Haemek in the Jezreel Valley, the strategic initiative shifted back to the Haganah.

Operation Nachshon was by no means a conventional military operation, with perfect coordination and discipline between all units involved, once the immediate objective was achieved. The more radical Jewish underground groups—the Irgun and the Lehi, known also as the Stern Gang—had been instigators of much uncontrolled violence in Jerusalem, and only with the greatest difficulty was the Haganah able to keep them under control. During the fighting along the road to Jerusalem, Irgun and Lehi units were eager to take part in the action and fixed their sights on the village of Deir Yassin. Though the village leaders had signed a peace pact with their Jewish neighbors, Deir Yassin was the last concentrated enclave of Arab inhabitants on the western side of Jerusalem. The stories of what precisely happened at Deir Yassin are wildly contradictory, at least on the Jewish side. There is little dispute, however, that 245 of the village's men, women, and children were slaughtered by the frenzied Irgun and Lehi fighters. As the news of the Deir Yassin massacre spread, a panicked wave of refugees jammed the roads toward the main Arab centers, to join those who had elsewhere been forced from their villages by command.

The battle for the Jerusalem road was not yet over, for as soon as several convoys made their way up to Jerusalem and the Nachshon Brigade was disbanded, Arab troops once again descended on the steep slopes above the road to Jerusalem, choking off the passage of further convoys. Within Jerusalem itself, bloody revenge had become a horrifying commonplace of everyday life. On April 20 an ambulance convoy of Jewish doctors and nurses making their way up to Hadassah Hospital on Mount Scopus was ambushed in the Arab neighborhood of Sheikh Jarrah, and more than seventy of the passengers were killed. With the foreign consuls in the city calling for a ceasefire and the prospects of internationalized status for the city unsure, most of the inhabitants of the Jewish city had to concentrate simply on surviving the siege. In this situation, Chassiya and Eleazar Sukenik were no different. Although the professor had been the first scholar to recognize the significance of the greatest archaeological discovery of the century, he was now involuntarily reduced, like his fellow Jerusalemites, to a life of sacrifice and privation. Every morning in that terrible spring, Professor Sukenik could be seen slowly pushing a wheelbarrow filled with jerrycans of rationed water through the streets to his home in Rechavia.

Plan D was now being put into action. The British, long regarded as a potential threat to it, cared only to protect their evacuation routes. Elsewhere, the Haganah brigades were shifting to the offensive as the will to resist of Palestinian Arab villagers, townspeople, and resistance forces began to collapse. From the mountains of Galilee through the central hills, to the rolling plans of Philistia, roads filled with makeshift military vehicles, armed men, and frightened civilians—men, women, and children, dragging along suitcases, boxes, and prized personal possessions, hurrying toward what they believed was safety behind Arab lines. At the Haganah headquarters in Tel Aviv, Sukenik received constant reports of developments across the country, but from the closed, smoke-filled offices, there was no way he could comprehend the human dimension of the historical transformation he had helped bring about. On April 18, Haganah forces established control over Tiberias and witnessed the sudden, mass flight of the lakeside town's Arab inhabitants. Just three days later, an operation codenamed "Scissors" began in Haifa, and by the next day, with the sudden collapse of armed Arab resistance, an even larger-scale exodus began.

Like the massive migrations that Yigael Sukenik had imagined in remote epochs—of Amorites, Hyksos, Israelites, Arameans, and Arabs—he might have seen this migration as another inevitable stage of cultural development were it not for the direct effect that it would have on his life. Those other ancient migrations were abstractions—bold arrows slashing across maps of continents and oceans. None evoked the sound of lost children crying, the tragic shuffle of refugees' footsteps, the flash and crack of field artillery booming, or the flat, distant thud of stone buildings being demolished by TNT. The familiar world that Yigael had grown up with was now in the process of bloody reformation. The clusters of hilltop Arab villages, long seen as the "ancient" or "biblical" aspect of the landscape, were being destroyed. Plan D was no longer only a coldly precise plan of action but was a violent scenario for far-reaching change.

In Jerusalem at the beginning of May 1948 more of the plan's operational objectives were accomplished as Haganah forces consolidated their hold on the southern suburbs of the city, precipitating the flight of middle-class residents like Anton Kiraz and many members of the Syrian Orthodox community. In the Old City the bitter fighting continued as the residents and Haganah defenders of the besieged Jewish Quarter continued running gun battles with Arab irregulars from surrounding rooftops, determined to hold out as long as possible. Only a few hundred yards away, sheltered behind the thick walls of St. Mark's monastery, Archbishop Athanasius Yeshue Samuel debated his future. He had received confirmation from Dr. Sukenik that his scrolls were genuine and quiet assurance from several American biblical scholars that such a magnificent find would win him renown and perhaps a handsome reward in America. He had made up his mind to send the scrolls for temporary safekeeping to Beirut, then retrieve them soon afterward, in his own desperate flight from the war of light and darkness now engulfing the Holy Land.

Chapter Six

BEN-GURION'S SHADOW

W ith less than two weeks remaining until the end of the British
Mandate, Ben-Gurion moved quickly and decisively to steer
the Jews of Palestine toward statehood. His vision of the
future remained completely unshaken, even in the face of the intensifying violence. It was during this period that Yigael Sukenik underwent a
profound personal transformation, and it is impossible to understand its
depth and implications without emphasizing Ben-Gurion's role in it. David Ben-Gurion was a man utterly committed to achieving his strategic
objectives, and now more than ever he was contemptuous of his advisers'
military and political opinions when they clashed with his own. While
Yigael Sukenik was never afraid to clash angrily with him over operational planning matters and battlefield tactics, he never questioned the
Old Man's larger vision of the historical destiny of the Jewish people as

the battles of May 1948 got under way. Years later, Yigael would delight in retelling entertaining anecdotes about his stormy relationship with Ben-Gurion during the most critical moments of the war, but these anecdotes always involved disputes over details and never quite revealed how completely he submitted to Ben-Gurion's overall strategic plan. Despite occasional angry outbursts, sporadic and futile protests, and later claims to the contrary, Yigael Sukenik became an effective and conscientious instrument of Ben-Gurion's will.

In early May, Ben-Gurion took unchallenged control of the Haganah's military operations. Chief of Staff Dostrovsky, always frail, nervous, and high-strung, simply could not stand the stress of the unfolding battles. As early as midwinter, the pain of his increasingly frequent ulcer attacks was etched on the already sharp features of his face. Often absent from important meetings and planning sessions, Dostrovsky left Sukenik and the other branch heads to determine goals and priorities for themselves. In the middle of March, Dostrovsky was bedridden and would not return to full-time duty for several months. A potentially dangerous power vacuum was developing, in which there was no clear chain of command. Although Ben-Gurion met every day with the branch heads, jotting down his impatient evaluations of the achievements and problems, the young officers considered him an amateur in military affairs and turned increasingly for advice, arbitration, and encouragement to Israel Galili, head of the Haganah's civilian National Command.

Sukenik recalled that Galili, who had been active in the Haganah for more than a decade, "was so familiar with the structure of the Haganah, the development of that structure, operations, and officers, that he naturally seemed to us to be a person who was needed at the time." The officers depended upon him as an acting chief of staff, without the formal title, and they regarded his decisions as final in all headquarters disputes. Galili's fatal flaw, however, proved to be his political orientation. He was a leader of the newly established Mapam party, the outspoken rival to Ben-Gurion's Mapai within the Zionist left. Ben-Gurion therefore saw Galili's growing influence in the Haganah as a political danger. In the few days before the invasion of the Arab armies, Ben-Gurion concluded that political dissension—and even discussion—within the Haganah must come to an end.

Galili was no match for Ben-Gurion when it came to political cunning. Remembered fondly by his Haganah colleagues as a congenial and dedicated worker, with penetrating blue eyes and a thick mane of wavy blond hair, Galili was steadfast in his dedication to the ideals of pioneering Zionist socialism, as nurtured and elaborated in the kibbutz movement. Like earlier Zionist socialists, Galili thought the entire Land of

Israel would be liberated from British imperialists and corrupt Arab landowners through pioneering kibbutz socialism and aggressive defense. Mapam's international orientation was proudly pro-Soviet and anti-British. Its attitude toward the rural Arab population, forged over decades of constant and uneasy contact between kibbutzniks and villagers, rested on the belief that coexistence between Jews and Arabs could be based only on constant demonstrations of Jewish strength. That outlook was shared by the many Mapam members who held command positions in the Haganah brigades and who constituted virtually the entire leadership of the Palmach. Galili and his political allies had even challenged the right of the United Nations to partition Palestine. For Mapam, the boundaries of the Jewish state would not be dictated by outsiders but determined solely by the efforts of Jews.

Over the years, Ben-Gurion had bitterly denounced this schism in the Zionist labor movement, and he reacted to political criticism by the Mapam leaders as a personal affront. Yet the stubbornly independent Palmach, he knew, with its autonomous headquarters and constant political protection by Israel Galili, posed a potentially serious threat to his leadership of the war effort. As the Haganah's best-trained and most powerful fighting force, led by Yitzhak Sadeh's protégé Yigal Feikowitz, the Palmach played a central role in the implementation of Plan D, and it was likely to play an equally crucial role in the coming battles. In the few days remaining before the expected Arab invasion, Ben-Gurion attempted to bolster his authority over all units of the Haganah. Newly designated as the prime minister and defense minister of the provisional government, he abolished the civilian national command and thereby sealed the fate of Mapam's most influential voice in the Haganah. On May 2 he summoned Galili to his office to inform him that his services would no longer be needed. The following morning, Galili read Ben-Gurion's letter of termination aloud to the officers of the general staff.

Their shock was immediate and soon sparked a dangerous revolt in the Haganah high command. With only twelve days remaining before the end of the British Mandate, "Yadin" and his colleagues feared a total disruption of their routines and careful planning. For years, the tight circle of Haganah officers had been shielded from the interference of political leaders, but with the illness of Dostrovsky and the removal of Galili, they had no one to protect them from the whims of Ben-Gurion. The atmosphere in the general staff was poisoned by tension. Ben-Gurion had concluded from his frequent consultations with Jewish Brigade veterans that it was the Haganah officers—not he—who were the amateurs. In response to Ben-Gurion's demand that more mortars be sent to Jerusalem during Operation Nachshon, Yigael had sneered with youthful arrogance that he "was not ready to receive orders on where to send mortars—from a man who had never seen one in action, who didn't know how many we had, and didn't know what kind of terrain they were best suited for." Ben-Gurion had returned the sarcasm with a painful dig at Sukenik's pretended experience with mortars. "I've read books too," he had snapped. Yet now, when Yigael, Eliyahu Cohen, Zvi Letchener, and Moshe Lehrer appeared before him to appeal for Galili's reinstatement, Ben-Gurion reacted calmly. He patronizingly suggested that if they really felt the need for a deciding voice at their headquarters, perhaps Yigael Sukenik might accept the post of chief of staff temporarily.

The officers would not be put off so easily; nor did they accept Ben-Gurion's interference without a fight. All across the country, the chain of command had broken down almost completely: the brigades were carrying out missions with only occasional consultation with the headquarters, the training programs had come to a standstill, the refortification of outlying settlements was far behind schedule, and another desperate effort to open the road to Jerusalem had failed. Time was running out, and the headquarters was in chaos. Thus at noon on May 6, Sukenik and the others took a step that under other circumstances would have been unthinkable. In a terse letter to Ben-Gurion they demanded that Galili be restored as head of the National Command within twelve hours; if he were not, all would resign their commands and shut down the general staff. Containing his rage at this headquarters rebellion—later known as the First Revolt of the Generals—Ben-Gurion quickly summoned them for a private meeting and skillfully turned the tables on them. Instead of exploding in rage he offered a compromise, promising to allow Galili to continue to work in the headquarters—without defined functions—but insisting that abolishing the civilian national command was an essential part of the transition from an underground guerrilla organization to an army of a sovereign state.

The military power of the Haganah, which had been directed and controlled by a politically balanced (if cumbersome) civilian committee from the time of its establishment was now subject to the strategic vision of one man. Whether they recognized it or not, Yigael Sukenik and the others were being transformed from underground leaders to civil servants of the Jewish state. Whether that state would survive was another question. On May 11, with the return of Jewish Agency envoy Golda Meyerson from a secret meeting with King Abdullah of Transjordan, a war with the armies of Lebanon, Syria, Iraq, Transjordan, and Egypt became a virtual certainty. For months the political department of the Jewish Agency had been secretly negotiating with Abdullah to try to dissuade him from intervening in Palestine—and thereby short-circuit a united invasion. But Abdullah, under growing pressure from the Arab League and secretly ambitious to annex the area of the proposed Arab state to his own kingdom, offered Meyerson no assurances about the course he would take. It seemed fairly certain, however, that Abdullah's highly rated Arab Legion—armed, trained, and led by British officers—would enter the battle on May 15. Sukenik quickly convened a meeting of all the Haganah brigade commanders, and with only four days remaining before the fifteenth, he issued them a document entitled "Changes to Plan D," in which he assigned them the task of repelling five invading armies in addition to completing the objectives of Plan D.

There were already troubling signs that this new task might be beyond the Haganah's power. Ben-Gurion had laid down the general policy that the Haganah should defend not only the UN-defined boundaries of the Jewish state but all Jewish settlements, even those that lay within the area of the proposed Arab state. Through the preceding four months of fighting, no Jewish settlement had fallen, but they had not been attacked by a conventional army with armor and artillery. That was now happening for the first time at Gush Eztion, an isolated group of kibbutzim that straddled the road between Jerusalem and Hebron. At dawn on May 12 a large force of local irregulars, in coordination with units of the Arab Legion, launched an all-out attack. A few days earlier, the Haganah troops stationed there had been ordered to ambush Arab convoys headed to Jerusalem, and the Arab Legion was now anxious to wipe out that threat in preparation for the wider invasion that was soon to come. For the first time Haganah defenders were subject to intense and concentrated artillery bombardment. In radio dispatches throughout the day, "Yadin" urged them to continue fighting, although the chances of survival were slim. Gush Etzion seemed to test the ability of the entire Haganah framework, bolstered by its best-trained Palmach forces, to stand up to the heavy weapons of a conventional army.

Time was running out for further debate or speculation. Ben-Gurion summoned the members of the provisional council to a conference room at the Jewish National Fund building in northern Tel Aviv to consider a grave, last-minute political development. The United States was strongly urging that the warring parties agree to a three-month ceasefire. There was no guarantee that either the Arab League or the Palestinian Arab leadership would agree to the proposal. But several council members were hesitant to declare independence in direct defiance of American wishes, with the result that Ben-Gurion insisted on putting the matter to a vote.

But first, Golda Meyerson was brought in to describe her disappointing meeting with King Abdullah. Moshe Sharett, the provisional foreign minister, then soberly reported on his tense meetings with Secretary of State Marshall. An emotional debate began among the members, but before calling for a show of hands, Ben-Gurion hastily summoned Israel Galili and Yigael Sukenik from the Haganah headquarters to draw on their military expertise. It was a moment that Yadin later recalled as the most important of his career. "To you, there should be no political consideration," he recalled Ben-Gurion as saying. "The members want to know what will happen if we establish the state and the Arabs invade. Do we have any possibility of maintaining our position? You, Yadin, must give a purely military answer. Don't tell us what you want, or what you think might be desirable, but just if you think that there is a possibility for our forces to stand firm."

After so many months of planning, this was the moment of decision. Galili recalled that Sukenik at first expressed annoyance that he had been called away from the headquarters. But through the cigarette smoke, nervous coughing, and tense whispers, Yigael Sukenik spoke in a clear, firm voice on Ben-Gurion's cue. The impact of his words on the provisional council has been long debated. Some historians believe that they merely deepened apprehensions; others consider the speech to have been the professional reassurance the council needed to ensure the immediate establishment of the Jewish state. In either case he began with a sobering report on the attack taking place at that very moment on Gush Etzion, describing the devastating psychological effect on the defenders of the constant artillery pounding and the arrival of armored cars with heavy guns. The same situation, he said, could be expected on four other fronts as Haganah forces confronted the armies of Lebanon, Syria, Egypt, and Iraq. "The conventional forces of the neighboring states with their equipment and weapons have an advantage. But one must not make a purely military determination of weapon against weapon and unit against unit," Sukenik said. Noting that the Haganah presently lacked heavy armament, he pointed out that newly purchased artillery was expected shortly and that Haganah forces had been trained to attack armored vehicles with makeshift bombs.

"The question is," Sukenik continued, "to what extent our people will be able to prevail against that force, considering the morale and ability of the enemy and our own tactics plan. It's been proven many times that the numbers and the formations are not always decisive." Sukenik stressed the level of training and determination of the Haganah forces, then concluded with a brutally candid evaluation of their relative strength: "If I wanted to sum it all up and be cautious, I'd say that at this moment, our chances are about even. If I wanted to be more honest, I'd say that the other side has a significant edge."

Ben-Gurion was silently furious at the performance. "Yadin spoke with very great caution," he later recalled in his memoirs. "He did not say that we would be able to stand." Not surprisingly, it was Ben-Gurion, whose vision of the Jewish state never wavered, who finally convinced the provisional council. After Galili and Sukenik had finished, Ben-Gurion masterfully sketched out the dangers of suddenly calling a halt to their military preparations and depending on the mercy of others, especially when heavy arms were already acquired and a mass conscription was under way. He persuaded the members that they had to forge ahead with self-confidence and trust their destiny. "If we can increase our forces, widen training, and increase our weapons, we can resist and even win." With that, Sukenik and Galili were dismissed from the meeting. As chairman of the council, Ben-Gurion now called for a decision. By a vote of six raised hands to four, the American ceasefire proposal was rejected, signifying that the Jewish state would be established on the coming Friday afternoon, in two days. Sometime after midnight, at the conclusion of the historic meeting, the provisional council decided by a vote of seven to two that the official name of the new Jewish state would be Israel.

On the afternoon of May 14, 1948, as the world's attention was focused on the ceremony under way in the main exhibition hall of the Tel Aviv Art Museum, frantic activity and rising apprehension gripped the team of Haganah planners back at the Red House. Prime Minister-designate Ben-Gurion stood beneath a framed portrait of Theodor Herzl to read a parchment scroll declaring Israel's independence; at that moment Yigael Sukenik was sifting through piles of updated intelligence estimates on Arab intentions and ordering reinforcements of men and arms for sectors that seemed especially vulnerable. "We always said at the headquarters that any operation that was not fully planned, at least on the highest level, three or four days before its planned execution, was a plan whose chances of success were greatly lessened. In this case, the planning was not finished. But this was an entirely different situation. It wasn't the planning for a single operation." On the previous day the defenders of Gush Etzion had surrendered, marking the most important battlefield victory so far achieved by Arab forces in the war. According to the latest dispatches, the Jewish settlement of Kfar Darom, south of Gaza, was now coming under attack. These, the Haganah High Command knew, were preliminary skirmishes in what would be a much larger battle. President Truman had defied the advice of the State Department and issued a statement of recognition of the new State of Israel. All-out war was now a certainty. After midnight a squadron of Egyptian fighter planes flew unopposed over Tel Aviv, freely strafing and bombing the airport and municipal power plant. Ben-Gurion's last, terse diary entry of the day put the situation clearly: "At four o'clock this afternoon Jewish independence was declared and the state was founded," he wrote. "Its fate is now in the hands of the security forces."

But another element, no less important than the readiness of the Israeli forces, would determine the outcome of the battle: the utter disarray of the Arab League's invasion plans. Although Sukenik and his staff of planners had expected a large measure of coordination between the invading armies, they underestimated the depth of the mutual suspicions and divergent priorities among the member nations of the Arab League. In fact, for most of the neighboring governments, the impending joint military intervention in Palestine had been initially an instrument of political pressure rather than cause to coordinate a battle plan. In October 1947 the Arab League had appointed a military committee to study various avenues of joint military action, but not until March—at the height of the battles between the Haganah and the local and volunteer Arab forces—did the chiefs of staff of Egypt, Syria, Lebanon, Iraq, and Transjordan meet for the first time. Their governments still clung to the hope that the military pressure by the volunteer forces and their own diplomatic pressure on the superpowers would succeed in scuttling the UN partition plan. But with the dramatic Haganah turnaround in April and the beginning of the massive exodus from the rural villages and mixed towns, pressure for military intervention by the Arab armies heightened dramatically.

King Abdullah's announcement that he would dispatch his Arab Legion into Palestine on May 15 spurred the Egyptian government to assemble its own invasion force. But its motivation was as much suspicion of Abdullah's territorial ambitions as dedication to the Palestinian Arab cause. At this stage Transjordan and Egypt were acting independently, and it was not until May 12—the very day that Yigael Sukenik gave the provisional council his ominous assessment of Arab strength—that a joint military committee of the Arab League actually got down to the business of formulating an operational plan. Had that plan been carried out with the full cooperation of all the participating armies, it would have seriously, perhaps fatally challenged the still-crystallizing forces of the Haganah. Its initial strategic objective was well focused: the conquest of Haifa and the isolation of the Jewish settlements of Galilee. But the prime virtue of the plan was that it offered each Arab state a chance to obtain its specific national objectives, in addition to the shared goal of destroying the would-be Jewish state. From the north, the forces of Lebanon would cross the border and proceed toward Haifa, gaining control of additional coastal territory. The Syrians would push southward into the Huleh Valley, conquer the valuable water resources of the Upper Jordan and the Sea of Galilee, and press westward toward Nazareth.

At the same time, a combined Iraqi and Transjordanian force would cross the Jordan River and overrun the Jewish settlements of the Jezreel Valley, gaining control of the vital pipeline through which Iraqi crude oil flowed to refineries on the Mediterranean coast. In the south, the Egyptians would proceed across Sinai toward Gaza and then threaten Tel Aviv, both to gain control of territory and to draw off Haganah troops from the north. Once the invading armies had achieved these initial objectives, they would surround Haifa for a final assault. The key to this plan's success was speed and complete coordination. But on May 13, just two days before the projected invasion, King Abdullah decided that his kingdom's interest would be better served by a different plan. In a sudden, shocking announcement to the other Arab League members, Abdullah demanded that he be named the commander-in-chief of the combined Arab forces. Since he saw his most important objective as the rescue of Arab Jerusalem, he announced that he would concentrate his forces there. There was ample military reason for his change in planning: instead of facing the closely packed and heavily defended Jewish settlements of the Jezreel Valley, Abdullah's Arab Legion would cross the Jordan just north of the Dead Sea and make its way toward Jerusalem through uncontested Arab territory. But there was another factor, even more important in Abdullah's decision: in February, Abdullah had received a tacit green light from London to occupy and rule the area that would come to be known as the West Bank.

In a secret meeting with British foreign secretary Ernest Bevin, Abdullah's prime minister, Tawfiq Abul Huda, broached the possibility that after May 15 the Arab Legion might occupy the parts of Arab Palestine directly across the Transjordanian frontier. Bevin's reply both shocked and pleased Abul Huda: "It seems the obvious thing to do." So Commander in Chief Abdullah kept his own war aims secret and merely informed the Iraqis that they would be attacking the Jezreel Valley alone. Yet in order to help them, he instructed the Syrians to change their route of invasion—instead of attacking from the north, they should shift their troops all the way around the Sea of Galilee to attack on its southern side.

For Yigael Sukenik and the other officers in the Haganah headquarters, the situation unfolding on the five invasion fronts was both frightening and confusing. "I had the feeling that we had to be ready for any eventuality," Yadin later recalled, "and that we were not ready yet."

With reports of attacks unfolding all over the country, Yigael Sukenik's nail-biting and chain-smoking could not lessen the responsibility he felt on his shoulders—the frightening awareness of what could happen in the coming battle, without knowing exactly when, how, and where the enemy would strike. From the south came reconnaissance reports of an advancing Egyptian column and its first attacks on the Negev settlements of Kfar Darom and Nirim. From the north came news of fierce battles between the Yiftach Brigade of the Palmach and the Lebanese army and a head-on Iraqi attack on Gesher, a Jordan Valley kibbutz. At the same time, Haganah observers near the Dead Sea alerted headquarters that a line of Arab Legion vehicles were crossing the Jordan and heading for Jerusalem. Most confusing of all was the sudden movement of a Syrian column abandoning its original positions and making a difficult, last-minute move around the Sea of Galilee. During the first night of the war, the headlights of a large convoy could be seen making its way slowly southward along the ridge of the Golan Heights. And even though the Golani Brigade and the settlers in Deganiah and Kinneret at the southern end of the Sea of Galilee were fully alerted to the Syrian movement, it was there that the first serious crisis of the war broke out.

By sending planes ahead and shelling Israeli settlements in the vicinity, the Syrian forces took control of a former British army camp and launched an assault on the two communal settlements of Deganiah A and B, only a few kilometers away. After two days of intense fighting between Haganah and Syrian forces at the abandoned Arab town of Semakh, at the southern outlet of the Jordan, the Haganah defense fell back with heavy casualties. After dark the nearby kibbutzim of Massada and Shaar Ha-Golan were abandoned, and after the failure of a desperate counterattack by a Palmach company on May 19, there seemed little hope of stemming the Syrian advance. That night, with Haganah defensive arrangements on the verge of collapse, two of the most respected settlement members were sent southward on a personal mission. In the middle of the night, Yosef Baratz of Deganiah, a longtime activist in Mapai and Histadrut official, and Ben-Zion Yisraeli, one of the leaders of the nearby Kinneret commune, appeared at the Haganah headquarters to appeal to their longtime comrade Ben-Gurion for planes, artillery, and armored cars—weapons like those that were now endangering them. Ben-Gurion gave no reassurance. "We don't have enough artillery, enough airplanes," he told them sternly. "Every front needs reinforcements. The situation is extremely grave in the Negev, in the Jerusalem area, and in the Upper Galilee."

Baratz and Yisraeli were deeply shaken by this coldness. Yisraeli broke down in tears and pleaded for the lives of his family, of his community. At the sight of one of the movement's most respected pioneers "sobbing like a child," as Ben-Gurion recalled years later, he sent them to Yadin. But Yadin did not have much more to offer. On the previous day he had dispatched Moshe Dayan to take charge of their sector, but having no source of arms or reinforcements, he could offer only a cold military instructor's advice. "I don't know what Ben-Gurion can promise you," Yigael recalled telling Baratz and Yisraeli at this emotion-filled meeting. "But we are aware of the situation. There's no other way than to let the Arabs approach within twenty or thirty meters of the gates of Deganiah and then throw Molotov cocktails at them." The veterans exploded in anger, offended that the young headquarters officer, so far from the fighting, would condemn the young men of Deganiah to almost certain death at close range from the Syrian tanks. That much is in agreement in all the historical sources. But while Ben-Gurion's diary made no mention of any dispute between himself and Sukenik over the defense of Deganiah, Yadin repeatedly retold a story of confrontation and personal defiance as one of his most vivid memories of the war.

"I was suddenly shocked at that moment," he recalled almost twenty years later, "when I realized what the fall of Deganiah would mean, that the whole north of the country might be lost. In the south, the Egyptian army was advancing on Tel Aviv, Jerusalem was cut off, and the Iraqis were putting pressure on the middle of the country. This was a moment that I suddenly felt that the dream of generations was about to disintegrate." According to Yadin's version, he stormed into Ben-Gurion's office to demand that four field artillery pieces that had recently been offloaded at Tel Aviv and were intended for the Jerusalem road, be sent to the north. "The situation there was critical," Yadin continued. "Ben-Gurion was adamant. We sat together for three hours. Never have two men leading a war for the entire country sat for so long over so little." Their tempers soon flared to a confrontation. "In the heat of the discussion," Yadin remembered, "I pounded Ben-Gurion's glass-topped desk with my fist and the glass shattered." By such violence and determination, he reportedly forced Ben-Gurion to relent and to dispatch the artillery to the north.

The story of the smashed glass on Ben-Gurion's desk would in time become something of a legend, for the combination of Moshe Dayan's military leadership, Molotov cocktails, and the sudden arrival of the field guns allowed Deganiah to withstand and eventually repel the Syrian attack. The Syrian forces, weakened by the unexpected change in their invasion route and by heavy losses at Deganiah, retreated eastward toward the Golan Heights, never again to challenge the Israeli front lines south of the Sea of Galilee. Yadin long saw this defense as a personal triumph, even though Ben-Gurion's diary reveals no hint of disagreement between them. In fact, he recorded on May 19 that "Yigael said that the field pieces have already been sent to the Jordan Valley. Afterwards, it became clear that they had not yet been sent, but since it would be impossible to send them to Jerusalem before tomorrow night, they can in the meantime serve an important function in the Jordan Valley." That is not to say that the disagreement between them never happened. The Old Man often refused to acknowledge events that showed him in an unfavorable light. Whatever its historical reliability, however, the smashed glass on Ben-Gurion's desk became part of modern Israeli folklore. It was but the first of a series of vivid vignettes on which the Israeli public's profound admiration for Yadin was based.

After the first week of bitter fighting, it became clear that the operational plans of the Haganah would have to be changed. With the resources of the six Haganah brigades stretched to the limit, Yigael Sukenik realized that frantically shifting men and equipment from one breached sector to another was no way to mount a successful defense. Before the invasion, on May 8, Ben-Gurion had insisted that the Haganah organize an additional brigade unconnected to any particular region, for use as a mobile reserve force. Sukenik and Galili had agreed and urged that the new brigade be part of the Palmach. But Ben-Gurion, still determined to limit the power of that autonomous (and to his mind politically unreliable) force, was adamant that veterans of the British army finally be given important combat posts and insisted that Sukenik's old Haganah rival Fistuk—Shlomo Rabinowitz—have command of the new Seventh Brigade. Serious manpower problems, tensions, and mutual suspicions plagued the effort, however; while Rabinowitz appointed fellow British officers to lead the brigade's two infantry battalions, its armored battalion was led by officers from the Palmach. Making the Seventh Brigade's prospects for battlefield success even dimmer, its ranks were filled with wounded and infirm soldiers cast off by other brigades and several hundred recent immigrants, survivors of the Holocaust.

From the time of Operation Nachshon in April, Ben-Gurion never averted his eyes from Jerusalem. Again and again he stressed to the general staff the importance of the city, with its large Jewish population and enormous historical significance, to the overall Israeli military strategy. Although the UN partition plan had determined that Jerusalem would be an international enclave, the intense fighting in its streets and their virtual partition into Arab and Jewish sectors made the possibility of peaceful coexistence in Jerusalem seem remote. In the last days of the

British Mandate, the level of violence intensified further as the Haganah launched Operation Pitchfork to gain control of military and civilian installations evacuated by the British, to conquer the remaining Arab neighborhoods in the western side of the city, and to break the siege of the Jewish Quarter in the walled Old City. The Israeli offensive did not achieve all of its objectives: Two frontal attacks on the Jaffa Gate were repulsed with heavy losses, and fighting spread to other parts of the city as units of the Arab Legion arrived to prevent further Haganah gains. With the road from Tel Aviv still blocked by Arab forces, the Jewish civilian population was reduced to increasingly strict rations of food and water. Five days had passed since the establishment of the State of Israel, and Jewish Jerusalem remained cut off. On May 19, in a repeat of his decision for Operation Nachshon, Ben-Gurion ordered a massive military operation "to defeat the two generals threatening Jerusalem: Hunger and the Legion," as he noted in his diary. He ordered that the road to Jerusalem be smashed open by the new Seventh Brigade.

Sukenik, who always bridled at Ben-Gurion's intervention in operational matters, grudgingly agreed to transfer one battalion of the Seventh Brigade to a marshaling point near the Jerusalem road. But this was merely a delaying tactic. At a meeting of the general staff on the following day, May 20, Sukenik used all of his rhetorical skill to try to persuade Ben-Gurion that an operation could not be mounted immediately. The three battalions were insufficiently manned, he said, and the brigade's hastily collected weaponry was a confusing mixture of types. Since the Arab Legion was still threatening the northern suburbs of Jerusalem, everyone present at the meeting agreed that Yitzhak Rabin's battle-hardened Harel Brigade should return to Jerusalem while Rabinowitz's Seventh Brigade continued training for four or five more days. In fact, Ben-Gurion was persuaded at this meeting that the Seventh Brigade would not directly attack the Arab forces along the Jerusalem road but would undertake a diversionary attack against the Arab town of Ramallah. "Shlomo will carry out the operation," Ben-Gurion noted in his diary; "Yigael will plan."

As the Seventh Brigade began its redeployment, however, Sukenik received a steady stream of troubling reports about the men's low state of readiness. Most of the immigrant conscripts lacked even a rudimentary knowledge of Hebrew and certainly required much more practice in marksmanship and even standard military drills. Worse, the brigade possessed no field radios or other communications equipment—a factor that under the best of circumstances, with well-trained troops, would make battlefield coordination difficult. But Ben-Gurion had other worries. On the evening of May 22 all the fronts seemed to be in danger of collapsing. The battle in Jerusalem against the Arab Legion was going poorly, the relentless Egyptian advance was continuing, and the Iraqi forces, shifted to Nablus and Jenin, were threatening the Mediterranean coast. But Ben-Gurion had become fixated on the Jerusalem road, as appeals for reinforcements and grim reports on the food and fuel supplies in the city grew increasingly desperate. Convening a meeting of all the general staff branch heads, Ben-Gurion demanded action. He ordered that the Seventh Brigade launch an immediate frontal assault on the former British police post at Latrun and all the villages around it—to break the way open to Jerusalem "without any delay."

Sukenik rose in outrage. His temper flared as he told Ben-Gurion that his fears for the imminent fall of Jerusalem were dangerously overblown. "You don't have to explain the significance of Jerusalem to me," Yigael remembered insisting. "I was born there, and my whole family is there in the siege." He had great confidence in the strength and preparedness of Jerusalem's Haganah forces, he said, and the armored forces of the Arab Legion would likely encounter great difficulty in house-to-house combat. The Seventh Brigade was utterly unprepared to conquer the Latrun fortress, where occupying Arab forces were deeply dug in. Sending the Seventh Brigade into battle prematurely would likely be a catastrophe, Sukenik argued. With only two or three days of training, there was no way, he insisted, that those men would be able to open the road to Jerusalem. "I told him that it would be murder," he later recalled of that tense confrontation with the prime minister, "but that didn't help me. Nothing would help me because this was a matter of Jerusalem."

Impatiently dismissing Sukenik's objections, Ben-Gurion summoned Rabinowitz to ask him directly about the readiness of the Seventh Brigade. Within a couple of hours Rabinowitz arrived from the front. But before he went in to see Ben-Gurion, Sukenik pulled him aside and warned him frankly about the danger of a head-on attack against Latrun. "You have got a tremendous responsibility on your shoulders," he remembered telling the brigade commander. "If you tell him it's possible to carry out this operation, he'll order it immediately." Eight years before, Sukenik had been one of Fistuk's training instructors. Now, in the midst of an all-out war, Sukenik considered himself to be his superior. Rabinowitz refused, however, to be told what to do by an arrogant headquarters officer who had had no direct experience of combat. During his service with the Jewish Brigade in northern Italy he had seen a side of warfare that Sukenik, in his training courses and at the Haganah headquarters, had not. Rabinowitz was well aware of the difficulties of the attack on Latrun, and he described them to Ben-Gurion in detail. But he would not challenge Ben-Gurion's final decision. At the end of the meeting Ben-Gurion insisted that an attack against Latrun be launched within twenty-four hours; the commander of the Seventh Brigade responded with unquestioned obedience. According to Sukenik, Rabinowitz told Ben-Gurion that he would carry out the order. According to a more famous and probably apocryphal story of the meeting, Rabinowitz told Ben-Gurion, "Your wish is my command."

On Monday morning, May 24, only a few hours before the beginning of the battle to open the Jerusalem road, Sukenik left the Tel Aviv headquarters and flew out to the front to inspect the readiness of the troops. The chaos there was shocking. He had already known that the majority of the immigrants had little or no training, but now he saw how desperate the supply situation actually was. Uniforms and canteens had been issued to only a few of the soldiers; many of the immigrant conscripts were still wearing their civilian clothes. Even more ominous, many of the troops had been issued types of rifles that they had never seen before. There was also a serious logistical problem; the convoy that was supposed to carry supplies and reinforcements to Jerusalem as soon as the Latrun fortress was conquered had not yet arrived at the front. Sukenik dashed off an urgent telegram to Ben-Gurion requesting more time to organize the brigade for battle, but the brigade officers were determined to go ahead. At a final meeting with Rabinowitz, Sukenik announced that he still favored a postponement, but if he did not succeed in persuading Ben-Gurion, the operation would proceed as planned. By late afternoon no word had come from headquarters, and the Seventh Brigade commander announced that the breakthrough to Jerusalem would begin at twelve-thirty that night.

Sukenik had no success in changing the schedule; in fact, he began to feel the urgency himself since the military situation in Jerusalem was deteriorating. A force of Egyptians had attacked Kibbutz Ramat Rachel on the southern side of the city, and an armored unit of the Arab Legion had attempted to break through the Haganah forward positions at the pilgrims' hostel and convent of Notre Dame on the east. Commander Rabin of the Harel Brigade dashed off a desperate dispatch to headquarters: "Shlomo must break through with reinforcements tonight." Soon afterward came a report that the British consul was predicting an imminent surrender of the Jewish city. Down at the front, the Seventh Brigade officers were huddling over the plans, preparing for the capture of the Latrun fortress, which they believed was manned by Arab volunteers. At seven-thirty in the evening they received a stunning cable from "Yadin" that a large enemy force of armored cars and artillery trailers had been spotted moving along the road from Ramallah toward Latrun. Zero hour was accordingly moved up to ten o'clock. But the intelligence report proved to be worse than mistaken—it was late by a day. On the evening of May 24 the armor and artillery of the Arab Legion was already deeply dug into positions on the Latrun ridge, ready to direct a killing fire at the Seventh Brigade. Ben-Gurion assembled his ministers for a vote on the operation. At twenty minutes to nine, with less than an hour and a half to go before zero hour, Sukenik relayed the go-ahead to the Seventh Brigade, signifying his own resignation to the inevitability of the battle. "You must carry out your mission at all costs," he cabled to Fistuk.

After a final briefing by the commander and staff, platoon leaders dispersed to prepare the men of the Seventh Brigade for battle. They were told now for the first time that they were "going out to save Jerusalem." The battle plan consisted of two flanking movements to capture Latrun's village, police station, and strategic points overlooking the Jerusalem road. Rabinowitz and his officers were confident that their forces would succeed since they believed that the village was abandoned and that they would be able to surprise the irregular troops defending the police fortress. But the element of surprise was lost by sheer disorganization. It was already two o'clock in the morning by the time the troops were loaded into civilian buses to be taken to the front lines, and it was nearly four by the time they began their advance on foot toward Latrun. In command of one of the lead companies was a self-confident young officer named Ariel Sheinermann, later known to the world as Arik Sharon. Approaching Latrun, Sheinermann called for artillery support for the assault when he and his men were suddenly faced with a volley of intense, killing fire. The Arab Legion had been expecting the Israeli attack for hours. At five o'clock, with dawn breaking, Rabinowitz, unaware of what was unfolding on the battlefield, cabled Tel Aviv from his field headquarters, "The festivities have begun."

Needless to say, the attack was a disaster: Sheinermann's advancing troops were pinned down by continuous fire from the village. The immigrant soldiers of the Seventy-second Battalion met an even worse fate: having the grim misfortune of running into a reconnaissance patrol of the Arab Legion, they were caught in a brief fire fight in which most of their officers were wounded or killed. In their sheer panic of a first taste of deadly combat, uncomfortable with their newly acquired weapons, and exposed in open ground in broad daylight, their planned flanking movement turned into a living hell. The Arab Legion forces intensified their shelling, and local Arab snipers fired at the Israeli forces, who had become easy targets in the burning sun of that late spring day. Without canteens, many of the wounded lay prostrate in the high grass and thistles, begging for water in Yiddish, begging for help. Those who could stumbled back toward the Israeli front lines in horror and fear. Through the late morning and afternoon hours, Rabinowitz managed to reorganize his units to hold off an Arab Legion counterattack as armored cars and jeeps were sent to pull survivors from the battlefield. Black Tuesday was a day of infamy in the history of Israel, with more than eighty men killed or missing in action and a large quantity of equipment and weaponry discarded in the course of the fighting. Even more terrible was the conclusion reached on the afternoon of the same day of the disaster: The Seventh Brigade would have to attack again.

Late in the evening Sukenik accompanied Ben-Gurion to the Seventh Brigade field headquarters. Ben-Gurion's intention was to raise the morale of the men and to gain firsthand information on the reasons for the failure. What he found was a scene of mutual recrimination and sheer horror. Ben-Gurion did not want to see any of the wounded, Yigael later recalled, even though he was absolutely convinced that the attack had to be resumed as quickly as possible. To coordinate all Israeli forces operating in the area, Ben-Gurion called on David "Mickey" Marcus to take command of the Jerusalem front. This West Point graduate, American staff training officer, war hero, and presidential adviser had been recruited by Rabinowitz in America and had arrived in Palestine early in 1948. Sukenik had worked closely with him during February and March in establishing a training program for the Haganah forces and had conferred with him on tactics and strategy. Marcus avoided direct involvement in the fighting himself, however; now, in the wake of the defeat, there were to be some far-reaching changes. On May 26 the provisional government of Israel officially announced the establishment of the Israel Defense Forces (IDF)—formally replacing the Haganah with the regular army of the sovereign State of Israel. Two days later, Mickey Marcus was placed in command of all operations on the Jerusalem front and given the biblical rank of *aluf*.

Sukenik never got along particularly well with Marcus. He bridled at the American's annoying habit of calling him Eagle, an intentional, joking mispronunciation of his first name. Marcus was able to calm such personal tensions as he assembled a unified staff for operations on the Jerusalem front. The situation of Jerusalem was still critical, for in the aftermath of its victory in the First Battle of Latrun, the Arab Legion had gone on the offensive both in Jerusalem and in the Jerusalem hills. On May 28 the few surviving defenders of the Jewish Quarter finally surrendered, freeing the Arab Legion's Sixth Battalion to attack the outlying western settlements of Maale Hahamisha and Kiryat Anavim. In planning for a renewed attack on Latrun to break through to Jerusalem, the Haganah needed a quick and decisive victory, and it adopted a new strategy. Previous experience had shown clearly that a frontal attack on the police station without a serious diversion was doomed to failure. So Seventh Brigade commander Rabinowitz suggested that *two* simultaneous movements be coordinated to deceive and confuse the enemy. An infantry force (whose troops now had the benefit of a few more days' training and slightly better equipment) together with a veteran battalion from the Givati Brigade (hastily transferred from the south on Sukenik's orders) would sweep far to the east and conquer the villages and highpoints above Latrun. At the same time, on the western side of the action, the Seventh Brigade's own armored battalion, under the command of Jewish Brigade veteran Chaim Laskov and supported by infantry, would attack and conquer Latrun's police station, village, and nearby Trappist monastery.

The execution of such a coordinated two-pronged maneuver required extensive rehearsal, but there was little time to practice since the British government was now making intense diplomatic efforts to call a halt to the fighting and to salvage its position in the Middle East as best it could. Up to the very end of the Mandate, the British Foreign Office had done its best to sabotage the UN partition plan. It privately suggested to its counterpart in Washington that an independent Jewish state would not only be very bad for western relations with the Arabs but it might serve as a regional springboard for Soviet expansion—in light of the Zionist leaders' Eastern European backgrounds and socialist rhetoric. Yet President Harry Truman and his advisers, influenced by a genuine sympathy for the postwar plight of the Jewish people and by political consideration of the rapidly approaching 1948 presidential election, announced America's de facto recognition of the State of Israel a scant fifteen minutes after the official end of the British Mandate.

With that, Britain's hope of turning back the partition plan was ended, and from that moment forward all the hopes of the British Foreign Office were directed to limiting both the extent of the hostilities and the size of the Jewish state. On May 13, the day before the declaration of Israeli independence, UN Secretary General Trygve Lie had appointed Swedish Count Folke Bernadotte as the UN's official mediator for the Palestine question. Within just a few days of the start of the fighting, he set off with his American assistant Ralph Bunche (formerly secretary to UNSCOP) on the quixotic task of bringing about a ceasefire between Arabs and Jews. At the end of the month, with the initial force of the Arab invasion blunted, the British put forward a ceasefire plan of their own—that would bar the import of men and equipment while the fighting was halted and that would freeze the front lines of both sides. On

May 29 the Security Council adopted this ceasefire resolution. If it were to go into effect as scheduled on June 1, however, the territorial status quo would leave Jewish Jerusalem cut off from Israel.

Sukenik was apprehensive that the Egyptian invasion forces, still advancing along the coast, would attempt to link up with the Arab Legion. Under the mistaken impression that the forces at Latrun were now relatively weak, he recommended an attack "without delay." The Second Battle of Latrun—like the first—was a failure for the Israeli forces. Once again logistical problems caused a delay of the operation, and when it finally got under way on May 30, the advancing infantry faced a sudden, concentrated, killing volley of Arab Legion mortars, machine guns, and grenades. Although the Israeli armored vehicles blasted their way toward the main entrance of the police station, the support infantry, panicked by the explosion of land mines, turned and ran from the battlefield, leaving the armored forces in the fortress compound desperately calling for help. Front Commander Marcus saw no alternative but to order a general retreat. Immediately after the battle, he sent a cable to Ben-Gurion: "Plan good. Artillery good. Armor excellent. Infantry disgraceful."

The military action on this front was still not over. In early June, Ben-Gurion instructed Sukenik to transfer the Palmach's crack Yiftach Brigade from Galilee southward to undertake the conquest of Latrun. Despite Ben-Gurion's continuing misgivings about the Palmach's fabled independence, he had come to appreciate its fighting ability. Time was now, more than ever, a pressure. Although the Arab states had initially rejected the Security Council ceasefire resolution, Count Bernadotte had come to the Middle East and in a round of intensive personal diplomacy finally gained formal approval by both sides for a plan for a four-week ceasefire that would go into effect at ten o'clock in the morning on Friday, June 11. The Israel Defense Forces, like the Arab armies, were badly in need of a breather, but Ben-Gurion insisted on making one last attempt to capture Latrun. This attack, too, was a failure. The Arab Legion forces, now fully alerted to the likely direction of an Israeli advance, met the arriving Yiftach Brigade with intense fire. On the morning of June 9, with dawn breaking and no hope of reinforcement, the Israeli forces were ordered to break off the fighting and make an orderly retreat. In the wake of this defeat Ben-Gurion insisted on more military action, but no field commander was willing to undertake yet another doomed mission. Ben-Gurion impatiently suggested that Sukenik should himself take command of the forces, but Sukenik adamantly refused. Even though the third attack on Latrun had ended in another frustrating failure, the high command of the Israel Defense Forces had become aware of another way to break the siege of Jerusalem.

The discovery of an alternative route through the wooded hills of Judea has become a modern legend. In early May 1948, so the story goes, three soldiers were given leave from besieged Jerusalem and against all odds found a way back to Tel Aviv on foot through the enemy lines. Rumors soon spread about the discovery, and as early as May 28, other Palmach troops succeeded in carrying ammunition and mortars on their backs up to Jerusalem along the steep, twisting path. Even while planning for the second attack on Latrun was underway, Marcus and Rabinowitz went out to inspect the secret route themselves and determined that it might indeed be passable. Marcus immediately contacted Sukenik, who arranged for a bulldozer to clear the path. In the days that followed the second defeat at Latrun, Derekh Sheva, "Road Seven," became an increasingly attractive alternative. After hurried earth-moving operations, jeeps were soon able to traverse (though with considerable difficulty) even its steepest stretches. On the night of June 2 a convoy of fifteen jeeps carried military equipment, mortars, and shells up to Harel headquarters, and on the next night a detachment of wounded soldiers was brought down. On June 10, the day before the ceasefire was to go into effect, the leveling work on Derekh Sheva was finally completed. The alternative route was opened for the transport of arms, ammunition, food, fuel, and even cattle on the hoof. Late in the afternoon Rabinowitz cabled Sukenik to dispatch a UN official to certify that the road was open before the ceasefire began.

The battles for Latrun were episodes in a chaotic and largely improvised war. Yet in later debates on the battle Yigael Sukenik would always be remembered as the one who had warned Ben-Gurion against the consequences and had bitterly opposed the unquestioned obedience of Shlomo Rabinowitz to Ben-Gurion's command. The debates over the First Battle of Latrun ultimately took on political overtones as an expression of resentment toward Ben-Gurion's autocratic direction of the war. For the present, it had more immediate implications. Soon after the beginning of the ceasefire, Rabinowitz was relieved of the command of the Seventh Brigade and transferred to the general headquarters staff. His simmering personal conflict with Sukenik continued, made immeasurably more bitter by Sukenik's continuing, angry I-told-you-so's. The most tragic twist of fate connected with the Latrun front occurred just hours before the start of the ceasefire. In the middle of the night on June 11, Aluf Mickey Marcus rose from his bed in his headquarters, wrapped himself in a blanket, and stumbled outside the camp fence to relieve himself. A camp sentry, hearing the sound of footsteps, called out for the password. When the unidentified figure did not respond immediately in Hebrew, the sentry fired a warning shot in the air. Marcus, in all his months of service, still had not learned to speak Hebrew. Within a few seconds two more shots rang out in the predawn stillness. Mickey Marcus, aluf of the Israel Defense Forces and commander of the Jerusalem front, was dead.

There would be other battles in Israel's War of Independence far bloodier than Latrun. In some, particularly those against the Egyptians, Sukenik himself would order a battlefield commander to attack another strategic fortress—Iraq es-Sueidan, on the main road to the northern Negev—head-on, against seemingly impossible odds. Yet Latrun always remained a painful, unresolved national trauma. The clash of personalities in the tense triangle of Ben-Gurion, Sukenik, and Rabinowitz has always symbolized the misgivings and bad feelings that Latrun has evoked. For some, Latrun is the modern manifestation of heroic dedication—a latter-day Masada or Bar-Kokhba story played out in the fields of the Ayalon Valley by survivors of the Holocaust. For others, the desperate tactics employed in the direct, doomed assaults on the well-entrenched Arab Legion were a cold violation of Israel's fabled concern for the lives of its troops. The Battle of Latrun would be refought for years in veterans' memoirs, historical polemics, and after the Six Day War, in the transformation of the squat, shell-pocked police station overlooking the Jerusalem road into a national shrine. But for Yigael Sukenik, the historical significance of that battle, in its painful and unresolved tension between individual responsibility and unflinching dedication to duty, would always be "the greatest tragedy of the Independence War."

Through the difficult first three weeks of the fighting, Ben-Gurion could not have asked for a more eloquent or attractive spokesman than the IDF chief of operations. At times of crisis, setback, and victory, Sukenik was repeatedly asked to give background information and updates to the members of the international press. In the chaos of the early days there were no organized facilities for journalists in Israel. But as dozens of war correspondents, photographers, and newsreel cameramen arrived, eager to get close to the combat—and with the Israeli government recognizing the value of putting a favorable spin on battlefield reports and diplomatic developments—the Foreign Ministry initiated a system of press accreditation and press conferences. Twice a day, each morning and evening, at the Government Press Office in the Ritz Hotel in downtown Tel Aviv, journalists gathered for routine briefings from a bookish officer named Moshe Pearlman. On special occasions they would be treated to the performances of "Yadin."

Wearing a dark military beret and light khaki jacket, with his thin moustache and dramatic manner, Sukenik played the part of a dashing young army commander perfectly. Grasping a wooden pointer, he would stride confidently before a large map of Palestine marked with the UN partition lines, delivering entertaining lectures on the progress of the various fronts. Spicing his comments with wordplay and with archaeological and biblical allusions, he was instrumental in shaping the story of the war as it was covered in the world press. There is no question that he captured the journalists' imagination as a unique mixture of scholar and soldier, archaeologist and military leader, an attractive personification of a new nation with roots in the distant past. Sukenik, for his part, was becoming conscious of the power of the press and the importance of his performances. Avraham Harman, an early staff member at the Government Press Office, recalled Sukenik's military briefings with nostalgia; "There was a panache there, a charisma that was quite clear."

At the same time, however, behind the scenes there was a deep uncertainty about the way events were unfolding. By the end of May, Ben-Gurion no longer paid any heed whatsoever to Sukenik's plans for static defense aided by commando operations and had turned to a vision of an all-out offensive on all five fronts. In the days before the bitter defeats at Latrun, he had envisioned a sweeping conquest of Jerusalem and its surroundings, a leveling of the Arab towns of Lod and Ramleh with artillery, a conquest of Jenin and the Jordan Valley, painful attacks inflicted on the Syrians, the creation of a Christian state in Lebanon with a southern border at the Litani River—and even farther afield, the intensive bombing of the Arab capitals of Cairo, Damascus, and Amman. "And thus we'll end the war," Ben-Gurion noted in his diary, with his own biblical flourish, "and settle our ancestors' accounts with Egypt, Assyria, and Aram."

Subsequent developments on the battlefield belied Ben-Gurion's bold prophecy of victory. Every effort had to be made simply to stabilize the fronts. Sukenik had always warned Ben-Gurion that the Egyptians were Israel's most dangerous enemies; in the terrible days at the beginning of the invasion, as the Syrians were beaten back at Deganiah and the Lebanese and Iraqi offensives were blunted, the Egyptian invasion force had proceeded relentlessly northward, occupying Gaza and reorganizing its forces for a further advance toward Tel Aviv. On May 29 the Second Egyptian Brigade, under the command of General Mohammed Neguib, advanced northward in a column that included hundreds of vehicles as well as armor and field guns. Sukenik had been simultaneously coordinating offensives against Arab Legion at Latrun and against the Iraqis at Jenin, yet the progress of the Egyptian Brigade had to be stopped. Late in the afternoon of June 2, Sukenik sent word to the commander of the newly established Israeli air force to send his new Messerschmidt fighters (received just a few days before in a secret arms shipment from Czechoslovakia) into combat. After nightfall he ordered the reluctant commander of the Givati Brigade to send two companies against the advancing Egyptian Brigade in a seemingly futile and perhaps suicidal attack. Even as the battle near the Arab village of Isdud was raging, Ben-Gurion ordered Sukenik to meet with a hastily convened press conference of foreign journalists at the Ritz Hotel. "The reports we were receiving were not encouraging," he later remembered, "and at four in the morning in a Tel Aviv hotel, with all the stars of the world press corps gathered, I had no idea what to say."

Yigael Sukenik was rarely at a loss for words on any occasion. He announced to the assembled reporters that although the fighting around Isdud was bitter, he had just received a dispatch from the front that indicated that the bulk of the Egyptian invasion force, under continuous attack from the air and from artillery barrages, had been completely encircled by Israeli troops. "This was a complete bluff," he continued. "There was not a single word of truth to this at the time I gave this statement." But Sukenik was aware of the sheer power of the international news media. "The next morning," he recalled, "we intercepted a radio transmission between the high command in Cairo and the field commander. The high command was raging: 'What is your situation? Why are you not reporting?' And the commander responded: 'We're being attacked fiercely but we're holding our ground!' So they told him from Cairo: 'You don't even know your own situation! You're completely surrounded!' And that threw the Egyptian troops in the field into a panic. . . . It wasn't *me* that they believed. The foreign journalists reported it as a fact." The encounter with the Egyptians was still far from over, however. The Egyptian troops dug in deeply at Isdud and defended their position as Egyptian bombing raids on Tel Aviv intensified. At the same time several vessels of the Egyptian navy cruised northward.

Sukenik and his family would have a direct connection to the resulting naval battle, one that resulted in a deep personal tragedy. The battle against the Egyptian naval force would claim the life of Matti Sukenik, the youngest son, then eighteen years old. "Matti was charming, good hearted and intelligent," Yigael recalled of his brother, noting that he had been so determined to join the air force (despite his suffering from the Sukenik malady of color-blindness) that he had persuaded a gynecologist to certify that his eyesight was more than adequate for air service in the Haganah. Matti had always dreamed of flying. After high school, he spent time at Kibbutz En Gev, on the Sea of Galilee, and had spun utopian visions for his friends of building an airfield in the hot Jordan Valley and establishing a kibbutz of pilots there to deliver winter crops all over the world. Still, he never succeeded in becoming a pilot. During his early training in the Haganah air service, his color-blindness was discovered, and because it enabled him to distinguish camouflage better than those with normal vision, he was assigned to duty in light reconnaissance planes as an observer—or, as in the case of the desperate counterattack against the Egyptian navy, as a bombardier.

On Friday afternoon, June 4, Yossi and Matti met briefly in Tel Aviv. Yossi was by this time well established in his career as an actor and was serving in Tel Aviv with an army theatrical troupe. Matti vividly described for Yossi the intense fighting around Isdud that he had seen from the air on the previous night. It would be their last meeting. In midafternoon the Israeli frigate *Eilat* was sent out to meet them. Soon afterward, Yossi recalled, he saw several light planes take off from the Sde Dov airport in an apparent supporting action against the Egyptian fleet. By late afternoon, the intensity of the battle off the coast was obvious throughout Tel Aviv. In the midst of a meeting with a foreign visitor, Ben-Gurion noted in his diary, "we heard the thunder of cannons at sea—there was an encounter between three or four enemy ships with two of our ships and our planes." When given a report on the outcome of the battle, Ben-Gurion added the notation, "One airplane was apparently lost." In the evening the loss was made public. During a news broadcast that evening, the Kol Israel announcer described the action against the Egyptian warships, noting that while the Israeli navy, supported by the aircraft, had succeeded in turning back the enemy, one of the planes did not return to its base. Its two crew members, the announcer reported somberly, David Sprinzak, son of Histadrut secretary Joseph Sprinzak, and Mattatyahu Sukenik, had been lost at sea.

On receiving the news, Yigael was, to all outward appearances, stoic. His relationship with Matti, nine years his junior, had always been distant, if fond. As usual, he was fully preoccupied with professional matters. The last unsuccessful attack on Latrun was being mounted by the Yiftach Brigade, and Ben-Gurion was depending on him for the latest reports from the field. Yet the events of the day brought the stakes of the war home to him in a sudden, painful way. Yaacov Yannai, a fellow officer and close friend of Yigael and Carmella, recalled eating dinner in his apartment late that evening, as he, his wife Gila, Yigael, and Carmella sat in stony, shocked silence, Yigael unable either to cry or to articulate his feelings. Early the next morning, he and Carmella appeared at Yossi's apartment to share their grief.

In the Jewish neighborhoods of Jerusalem, daily life retained a surrealistic aspect. Since most of the younger generation were away in the service of the Israel Defense Forces, it had become an all-too-common ritual for the older generation—too old to serve as more than civil defense wardens or hospital volunteers—to pay condolence calls. Journalist Gershon Sweet recorded one such condolence call in the early evening of June 5: "Just before nightfall, my wife and I set out for the Sukenik home. We found the professor at his desk working, looking through a magnifying glass at photographs of ruins of ancient synagogues discovered in his excavations." The professor greeted his guests sadly, unable to speak. "Next to the photographs on the desk," Sweet continued, "was a letter, and without saying a word, he passed it to me to read."

The letter had arrived several hours earlier, brought from Tel Aviv by the light military plane that landed almost daily in a makeshift airstrip in the Valley of the Cross. Unable to leave the headquarters, Yigael sent his parents a simple, handwritten letter, a painful acknowledgement of his own shared sorrow at what the war had suddenly cost them all.

"Don't weep, don't grieve," the note said. Written in a stiffly formal Hebrew style, it did not quite conceal the emotion it contained. "When Matti took off yesterday to chase away the enemy ships from the shores of Tel Aviv, he knew very well what awaited him. He was not frightened by the risk. He was not terrified or deterred. He fulfilled his duty to his people and his country with bravery. So don't cry, because the danger did not shake him . . . with bravery he fulfilled his duty to the people and homeland. So don't cry. Just be proud that he was one of us. And let us all cherish his memory with the love and admiration he deserves. Yigael."

Chapter   Seven

TEN PLAGUES

Through the hours of daylight and darkness that followed the declaration of a temporary ceasefire and the sudden end to the fighting, the deep rumble and throaty roar of jeeps, trucks, and heavy tractors filled the rocky, winding road through the hills to western Jerusalem. On the first day came tons of flour, milk, cheese, and cigarettes. In the following days came ammunition, mortars, flour, gasoline, vegetables, and fruit. The discovery and construction of Derech Sheva had been a public relations triumph, a heroic story heralded in newspapers and newsreels all over the world. Renamed the Burma Road by *New York Times* correspondent Kenneth Bilby (for whom Sukenik had arranged a special nighttime tour while the fighting was still raging), it came to symbolize Israeli ingenuity and daring, fully equal to the proudest achievements of Allied forces during World War II. In a way, it was also the culmination of the secret Haganah training—the hikes and explorations in the Jerusalem hills and the teenage messengers hobbling into the Old City with bullets stuffed in their shoes.

The stakes were now enormous. With the main road past the Latrun fortress closed by the Arab Legion, the Burma Road was the only overland link to Jewish Jerusalem. On June 14, just three days after the end of the shooting, the roughly leveled road was opened to two-way traffic over its entire length. According to the UN partition plan, Jerusalem was to remain an international enclave. But the deep emotions and bitter fighting that the struggle for Jerusalem had engendered made that plan impractical. The possession of Jerusalem had always been the center point of Ben-Gurion's war strategy and the construction of the Burma Road—more even than the solemn proclamation Ben-Gurion had read one month before in the Tel Aviv Art Museum—marked a declaration of independence that would be defended and expanded by the force of arms.

The United Nations, for so long merely a passive time-keeper for the battles, now had to be taken into account by both sides as an active referee. After the successful ceasefire negotiations, Count Bernadotte had been directing operations from his comfortable headquarters on the Island of Rhodes, where "far from that uncomfortable corner of the world," he imperiously set about formulating a grand plan for the future of Arabs and Jews. Guided at every step by Ralph Bunche, his dedicated—and far more astute—assistant, Bernadotte first attended to practical matters, hastily dispatching a force of UN observers to monitor compliance with the truce. The presence of international forces in sensitive battlefield sectors, however, was not calmly accepted by the Israeli high command. When units along the Jerusalem road reported that the UN observers were instructing them to alter their forward positions, Sukenik issued strict orders that all Israeli units were to hold firm and be prepared to defend their positions by force if necessary.

The government of Israel was under no illusions that the United Nations was anything more than an instrument of superpower intervention. The busy diplomacy of the pompous Swedish count was merely a sideshow. Britain was eager to control events indirectly, now that it had failed to undermine partition. The struggle for Palestine was far from over. With the military situation at a stalemate and the Israeli forces exhausted and spread dangerously thin, Ben-Gurion wanted to take advantage of the scheduled four weeks' lull to institute far-reaching organizational changes. Training was to be intensified in all brigades, officers' courses, and special forces; conscription was to be widened to expand combat units and replace casualties. In order to improve the often chaotic communications between general staff and field units, Ben-Gurion became convinced that intermediate commanders were needed—to be placed in charge of the "fronts" in the north, center, and south and coordinate action between several brigades. In every way, he believed, the Israel Defense Forces, the IDF, had to come out of the underground and establish ranks, symbols, military courts, discipline, and regular pay. Now that Arab armies and British diplomatic pressure had been unable to end the plan for partition, the army of the State of Israel had to be made a more efficient instrument of the sovereign will.

The general staff, however, was still without a leader. Yaacov Dostrovsky remained bedridden at home in Haifa, and decision making at the headquarters was still subject to interminable wrangling and discussion. Since Sukenik had served as chief coordinator of all the branches during the first round of the fighting, Ben-Gurion—after consultation with Dostrovsky—offered him the position of acting chief of staff. Sukenik was reluctant to take the formal appointment, however, and Ben-Gurion did not conceal his displeasure with the young officer. "He doesn't see any one else to take over Operations," Ben-Gurion noted in his diary on June 13 in exasperation, "and he is worried about taking even greater responsibility on himself." On June 18, at a meeting of all the brigade commanders, Ben-Gurion realized that reorganizing the army would involve more than simply appointing a new nominal head. For the first time since the fighting began in December, the various commanders assembled in Tel Aviv and poured out their feelings. "It really was a soul-searching," Sukenik later recalled. "It was a very difficult meeting for Ben-Gurion, for me, and for all the participants." Each commander rose to blame the headquarters staff for the lack of arms, poor logistics, support services, and the lack of a coherent national strategy. For Ben-Gurion, all this criticism merely concealed a larger problem. "Of all the deficiencies of our army," he noted in his diary, "discipline is perhaps the most serious, especially in the highest ranks."

Ben-Gurion, as usual, reserved for himself the last word at the meeting, and it was he alone who thenceforth determined the time and place of operations, as well as overall strategy. If Sukenik would not serve as chief of staff, Ben-Gurion would be the supreme commander. He announced to the officers what they knew already—that with a resumption of fighting almost certain, they had to unify their efforts, not only to capture territory but to destroy the military power of the armies of Lebanon, Transjordan, Iraq, Egypt, and Syria. Over the centuries, Ben-Gurion told them, the conquest of carefully chosen strongholds had led to the sudden collapse of defending armies—in the ancient Egyptian victory over the Canaanite princes at Megiddo, the Roman conquest of

Jerusalem, and the triumph of Saladin over the crusaders at the Horns of Hattin. The fortress of Latrun was, to Ben-Gurion, still a primary target, and as the commanders' meeting adjourned and various structural suggestions were debated, he instructed Sukenik to supervise the development of a new operational plan. Total victory, not just defense, seemed possible. But suddenly a serious threat to Ben-Gurion's military planning came from an unexpected direction—the west, far out at sea.

The separatist National Military Organization, the Irgun Zvai Leumi, had its own, even more sweeping visions of conquest in the Land of Israel and had never been willing to abide by Ben-Gurion's judgments. After its separation from the Haganah in the wake of the 1929 riots, its members had come to believe fervently in the manifest destiny of the Jewish people, often without much concern for the subtleties of international politics or the possible cost in human lives. This tendency became even more marked with the Irgun's formal affiliation to the Revisionist movement and the rise to leadership of Menachem Begin. Now and then, the Irgun had cooperated with the Haganah, such as at the end of April, when Sukenik had been dispatched to the Irgun's headquarters to work out a joint operation in Jaffa with Begin and his operations officer, Gidi Paglin. On the big issues, however, the Irgun and the Haganah were opponents. The Irgun regarded the UN partition plan as a betrayal, not a triumph. During the winter of 1948, Irgun supporters in New York had purchased a war surplus landing craft that they renamed the *Altalena,* after the pen name of Vladimir Jabotinsky, the founder of the Revisionist movement. They intended to fill it with arms and volunteers bound for Palestine—and to liberate the areas of the Land of Israel that the United Nations had not seen fit to return to the Jews.

Despite an agreement that Begin signed on June 1 that all his troops would be inducted into the IDF, the *Altalena* sailed from France ten days later with a cargo of 865 fighters, five thousand rifles, three thousand bombs, hundreds of tons of explosives, and three million rounds of ammunition, as well as mortars, bazookas, and machine guns. When Begin objected to handing those weapons over unconditionally to the IDF, Ben-Gurion sensed a direct challenge to his political position and to the delicate, if temporary, ceasefire regime. At a time when the general staff was reorganizing and shifting units, the army was vulnerable. Even worse, an unauthorized attempt by newly armed Irgun units to conquer additional territory might spark a premature resumption of the fighting and bring down the wrath of the international community on Israel for an unprovoked violation of the truce. Now, with a shipload of arms and volunteers about to arrive and significantly augment the Irgun forces, Ben-Gurion called on Galili and Sukenik for consultations. Sukenik was instructed to proceed immediately to the *Altalena*'s landing place near Kfar Vitkin, between Haifa and Tel Aviv, make contact with the local brigade commander, Dan Even, and issue an ultimatum to Begin to surrender all the arms unconditionally. As he later would on other occasions, Begin deceived and humiliated Yadin. When negotiations bogged down and shooting broke out on the beach between IDF and Irgun forces, Begin escaped to the ship and ordered it to sail south toward Tel Aviv.

At dawn, as Irgun supporters streamed to the Tel Aviv beachfront to aid the *Altalena*, Ben-Gurion waited impatiently for Sukenik's return to IDF headquarters. He was now determined to sink the ship. As Irgun members were mutinying from IDF units all over the country and preparing to defend the autonomy of their organization, Ben-Gurion shouted out a shocking order to his operations officer: to prepare to commence hostilities against the Revisionists. Sukenik, ever cautious, demanded that Ben-Gurion put the order in writing. Ben-Gurion scribbled out: "You must make all the preparations—mobilization of forces, firepower (artillery, machine guns) flame throwers, and all the other means at our disposal to bring the ship to unconditional surrender." Later that day, fighting broke out between Irgun members and Palmach officers, bringing their longstanding ideological battles right into the streets of Tel Aviv—to the horror of onlookers and the astonishment of UN observers and the international press—to be fought now with automatic weapons and hand grenades. At four o'clock Ben-Gurion instructed Sukenik to order that the ship be shelled from a shore battery. Although the first round missed the *Altalena*, the second hit its target squarely. The ship, loaded with ammunition and volunteers for the Irgun Zvai Leumi, exploded, and sank just a few hundred yards off the beach at Tel Aviv. The independent military power of the Revisionist movement was soon broken. Even though Begin had managed to escape from the scene, many of his followers were rounded up and arrested in the following days.

A formal ceremony was held to mark the end of private militias. By the terms of the law establishing the IDF, an oath of allegiance was to be administered to all those serving in its ranks. The members of the general staff and the highest-ranking field commanders were to be the first to take the oath. On June 27, Ben-Gurion invited them to a festive lunch under the trees outside the Tel Aviv headquarters before the official swearing-in ceremony. Personal disputes and resentments were for the moment forgotten. Sukenik chatted affably with his colleagues and sometime detractors, who were seated around a table laden with grapes, cups of coffee, and bottles of wine. Palmach founder Yitzhak Sadeh and

Yigal Feikowitz, the current commander, chatted easily with the others. Israel Galili, the deposed head of the national command, wandered among the guests in good humor, his lingering resentment for Ben-Gurion's actions against him temporarily stilled. At the head of the table sat Ben-Gurion and his wife Paula, patriarch and matriarch of a warrior clan. After lunch, Ben-Gurion rose and administered the official oath of the Israel Defense Forces to the members of what had once been the Haganah high command.

The cherished secrecy of the Jewish underground, with its hushed, candlelit initiation rituals, was now to be replaced by the ceremonies and symbols of a sovereign army displayed proudly in broad daylight. As usual, Ben-Gurion's rhetoric included a biblical flourish. "With this oath you have sworn to," he said to the officers, "you have now been united with the long succession of Hebrew warriors from the times of Joshua Bin-Nun, the fighting and liberating Judges, the kings of Judah and Israel." At this moment nothing could disturb the power of those heroic ancient images—not the lingering tensions in the general staff, nor the diplomatic dangers of Count Bernadotte's intervention, nor the uncertainty of when the fighting would resume. Ben-Gurion had exercised his will over the officers in the moments just before the swearing-in ceremony. "He insisted that we all adopt Hebrew names and gave us ten minutes to select them," Yosef Avidar recalled of that historic moment, "and most of us chose our code names in the Haganah." Among the many quick changes, Yosef Rochel became Yosef Avidar; Zvi Letchener became Zvi Ayalon; Moshe Lehrer became Moshe Zadok; Fritz Eisenstadt became Shalom Eshet; Moshe Zelitsky became Moshe Carmel; Yigal Feikowitz became Yigal Allon; Shlomo Rabinowitz became Shlomo Shamir; and Yigael Sukenik became Yigael Yadin. Ben-Gurion insisted that they pose for a formal group portrait, so that the names and identities of the IDF high command might become generally known. And seated on the grass in the front row of the highest-ranking IDF officers as he squinted toward the camera in the bright sunlight, the young man now named Yigael Yadin was born again—to begin a far more public phase of his military career.

———

Count Folke Bernadotte belonged to that thin, decaying layer of European nobility that had been taught that they were born with a right to rule. As a nephew of King Gustav of Sweden, young Folke had spent most of his life in luxurious indolence—hunts, transoceanic cruises, and formal balls. Only in middle age, after the end of World War II, did he become involved in more important matters. His appointment as UN mediator in Palestine was a grand honor, even though, according to those who worked with him most closely, his knowledge of the region, its peoples, and its problems was "slight." On June 27, from his head-quarters in Rhodes—the same day Ben-Gurion swore in his general staff officers and invoked ancient Israel's greatest heroes—Count Bernadotte offered a plan in which the Jewish state would be asked to relinquish the Negev, strictly limit immigration, and agree to the annexation of Jerusalem to Abdullah's kingdom. Instead of trying to shore up the existing situation and build on it, the foolhardy Swedish count pleased only Abdullah and his British patrons and thus encouraged the ambitions of both sides for a resumption of the war.

The IDF had not been idle. Foreign arms had secretly been flowing into its arsenals, training had been stepped up, plans for a thorough reorganization were under way. To remedy some of the administrative defects so bitterly condemned at the officers' meeting, a front com-mander would be appointed for each major theater of war. Ben-Gurion requested that the staff officers prepare a list of candidates. Yigael Yadin's main criterion for the front commanders was their proven leadership and combat experience—and he believed that the best could be found in the Palmach. Galili and Ayalon, however, had an unspoken political motiva-tion: to preserve the primacy of Mapam-oriented Palmach officers in the highest ranks. As a result, the nominees that Yadin eventually presented to Ben-Gurion were striking in their political background. Four out of the five were Palmach commanders, including Yigal Allon, nominated for the critical Jerusalem front. Like the rest of the staff officers, Yadin had underestimated Ben-Gurion's suspicion of political plots against him since the sinking of the *Altalena*. They were all unprepared for the coming test of wills.

Ben-Gurion received the list from Yadin before leaving for a visit to Jerusalem and did not react immediately. He weighed his next step care-fully, for he was determined to bring more veterans of the British army into the service and to eliminate once and for all the privileged status of the Palmach. He wanted the IDF to be a conventional army with elite units dispersed throughout the various formations, shorn of all partisan political links. The appointment of the front commanders would be an opportunity for him to take a step in that direction. Without consulting the general staff, he chose Allon to be sent to the south (where, he be-lieved, Palmach-style guerrilla warfare would be most effective); Mordecai Makleff, the young commander of the Golani Brigade and a British army veteran, would take over the Jerusalem front; Moshe Dayan would replace David Shaltiel as military commander of Jerusalem; and Shlomo Rabinowitz, now Shamir, would head the manpower branch in the general staff. Reactions to these changes were angry. Yadin and Ayalon fumed at Ben-Gurion's interference in professional military matters. "They threatened me with the old threats of upheaval and destruction," Ben-Gurion noted in his diary on June 29. But this time Ben-Gurion was utterly unmoved.

On the following day, feeling that diplomacy was perhaps the best way to achieve his objective, Ben-Gurion invited Yadin into his office for a private chat. "I explained to him," Ben-Gurion dutifully noted, "that now that an army has been established, the structure of the general staff is awkward. . . . there isn't a single soldier in it. And that must be changed." After insisting that Yadin implement the new appointments, Ben-Gurion departed for Haifa to be present at the official takeover of the port from the last of the departing British troops. Unfortunately, his skill in persuading Yadin was lacking. On June 30 Ben-Gurion returned to Tel Aviv to find a mutiny. Waiting on his desk were four letters of resignation—from Yadin, Galili, Ayalon, and the head of the training branch, Eliyahu Ben-Hur. With only nine days before the end of the truce and the likely resumption of the fighting and with Bernadotte's distracting plans in the offing, they had declared an open rebellion. Their moment of truth in the long struggle with Ben-Gurion for operational control of the army had finally arrived. And while Ben-Gurion might have been happy to rid himself of political dissension within the general staff, there was one officer whom he did not want to dispense with.

"I summoned Yigael Yadin," Ben-Gurion recorded in his diary on July 1. "I said that the four letters I had received from him and from the three members of Mapam represent a kind of political revolt in the army and a matter of incomparable seriousness. It is liable to set the whole campaign in danger, a campaign of life and death." Ben-Gurion tried his best to explain to Yadin that this was a political struggle, not a military question, and that Yadin should not sacrifice all that he had worked for over the last six months for the sake of Mapam. If Yadin insisted on resigning, he would accept his resignation from the operations branch, "but it is my obligation to tell him that this seems to me to be grievous subversion. The war could go on," Ben-Gurion added ominously, "without me and without him." The next day, whether out of pride or out of loyalty to the other rebelling officers, Yadin refused to withdraw his resignation. With operational planning for the coming battles seriously disrupted, Ben-Gurion decided the dispute had become serious enough that the provisional government should discuss it. At that meeting, Ben-Gurion announced angrily—and with a measure of righteous exaggeration—that the rebellion was nothing less than the attempt of a certain political party to take over the army. This could not be tolerated. Then

Ben-Gurion tossed a bombshell: If his list of appointments were not approved in its entirety, and if Israel Galili were not removed from all future security functions, Ben-Gurion himself would resign as Prime Minister and Minister of Defense.

The government was shocked into action and quickly appointed a committee of five members, headed by Interior Minister Yitzhak Gruenbaum, to investigate the bitter conflict in the high command. It was clearly not to be an orderly judicial investigation; its very establishment was kept a closely guarded secret of state. Without even setting formal ground rules for its investigation, the Committee of Five held its first hearing on the next day—Saturday, July 3. Its members were more eager to resolve the command dispute quickly than to identify and punish guilty parties, and they summoned all the general staff members and several field commanders to discuss the tensions and mutual recriminations that were endangering IDF operations. With the strong personalities involved, however, and with both Ben-Gurion and Galili present at most sessions, flared tempers and sharp exchanges were unavoidable. Galili, called first, starkly described the increasingly chaotic state of the headquarters since he had been relieved of his official post in early May. To avert the chaos in the coming battles, he appealed for his own reinstatement and a restriction on Ben-Gurion's sweeping powers through the reestablishment of civilian oversight, on the model of the former National Command.

Yadin's objections to Ben-Gurion's behavior were more personal. Yet most of those present knew that Yadin himself was not a particularly easy person to get along with. Many years later, Galili remembered him in this period as a tense young man who had an annoying habit of breaking pencils during meetings. Now Yadin wanted to explain to the Committee of Five that this was not merely a clash of egos. "I know that there are those who say I have a very difficult personality"—Yadin spoke slowly and sharply—"that it is hard to work with me. I agree with that, but I just want to explain—as much as anyone can talk about his own character—that it's not true—that it has come from the sheer burden of work over the last several months." Speaking as logically and clearly as possible, he accused Ben-Gurion of using moments of crisis to make politically inspired and reckless changes in the command structure. The real problem, Yadin pointed out, was not the specific appointments but the relations of the general staff with the minister of defense. He insisted that there should be a full-time commander continuously involved in the work of the various staff departments, not a political leader who saw fit to intervene only on the operations that interested him. "I'm not ready to have someone say 'Send this to Jerusalem' and not say what will be in

Yigael, Matti, Chassiya, and Yossi Sukenik in a 1930 photograph.
Collection of Yossi Yadin.

Chassiya Feinsod-Sukenik (shown here as the second adult from left) with
her kindergarten class in Jerusalem, January 1915. Central Zionist
Archives.

A patrol of the Jewish Settlement Police at Kastel, 1938. Commander Yigael Sukenik (above) points out bullet marks on the side of his armored car. Haganah Archives.

The Haganah training course at Kiryat Anavim, summer 1939. Course commander Shlomo Rabinowitz ("Fistuk") is pictured at center. Yigael Sukenik stands on his right. Israel Ben-Yehuda ("Abdu") is third from right. Haganah Archives.

Tell Jerishe, 1940, with Avigad
and fellow student Ruth
Brandstetter-Amiran. Institute of
Archaeology, Hebrew University.

Yigael Sukenik as course
commander in the Haganah
company officers' course at Juara,
summer 1941. Haganah Archives.

The Haganah high command at national training exercises near
Mishmar Haemek, 1942. In the front row, left to right, are Yitzhak
Sadeh, Israel Galili, Yaacov Dostrovsky, Eliyahu Golomb, and Moshe
Sneh. Yigael Sukenik sits behind them with his hand raised to his face.
Haganah Archives.

Swearing-in ceremony of the commanders of the Israel Defense Forces in Tel Aviv, June 27, 1948. Yadin is seated on the ground, second from the right. Directly behind him are David and Paula Ben-Gurion, Israel Galili, Yohanan Rattner, and Yigal Allon. Standing in the back row, second from the left is Shlomo (Rabinowitz) Shamir. Yitzhak Sadeh stands behind Ben-Gurion. Haganah Archives.

Chief of Operations Yigael Yadin confers with Southern Front Commander Yigael Allon and his operations officer, Yitzhak Rabin, on November 28, 1948 in preparation for Operation Horev. Israel Government Press Office.

Yadin explains Operation Horev to foreign journalists during his last press wartime conference, January 7, 1949. Israel Government Press Office.

Yigael and Carmella Yadin. January 1949. Israel Government Press Office.

The Israeli delegation
departs for the
Rhodes armistice
talks, January 12,
1949. Walter Eytan
stands to Yadin's left.
Israel Government
Press Office.

Harkabi, Simon, Yadin,
and Rabin confer during
the Rhodes talks. Israel
Government Press
Office.

A formal session of the armistice negotiations, with Acting UN Mediator
Ralph Bunche presiding and the Israeli delegation seated at right. Israel
Government Press Office.

the Negev and the Galilee," Yadin insisted. What he and the other witnesses neglected to acknowledge, however, was that in Israel's uncertain military and political situation, a leader with vision was as important as a clear military chain of command.

Ben-Gurion indignantly rejected the committee's final recommendations, which addressed Galili's demand for reinstatement by calling for the creation of a small "war cabinet" to oversee general military matters and the appointment of a deputy defense minister—most likely Galili himself. To add insult to injury, the committee members declared that Ben-Gurion's list of appointments should be canceled and that the resigned officers should immediately return to their jobs. Stomping out of the commission meeting, Ben-Gurion returned to his home and dashed off an angry resignation letter. "The discussions that have taken place in the Committee of Five and the proposals that have been suggested by several of its members," he wrote, "have forced me from the Defense Ministry and the Provisional Government." Since late 1946, he had taken upon himself both the military and the political leadership of the Zionist movement; now he dared the bureaucrats and party activists to take both those responsibilities upon themselves.

With only two days remaining before the fighting would resume, Yadin took the initiative. Over the previous eight months—despite the angry outbursts and his claims to the contrary—he had managed to develop a close relationship with Ben-Gurion, the kind of affection that can sometimes develop between a tyrannical father and a headstrong, brilliant son. Ben-Gurion had never wanted this confrontation, but now, with neither prime minister nor chief of operations fully in control of the situation, Yadin appeared at the door of Ben-Gurion's house. After receiving a withering scolding for his irresponsible actions from Paula, Yadin insisted on talking directly with Ben-Gurion. "I went upstairs," he recalled of the late-night visit. "I opened the door. Ben-Gurion was lying in bed. When he saw me, he rolled over and turned his back to me in anger." Yadin had come with a compromise that might defuse the issue of the contested appointments: that Yigal Allon be named commander only of the *operation* planned to open the Jerusalem road, and that the permanent appointment of front commands for Jerusalem be deferred.

That broke the deadlock. "Ben-Gurion turned toward me and said: 'I accept. I accept,'" Yadin remembered, "and that's how it ended. I returned to my post and Ben-Gurion returned to his post as Defense Minister." That same evening, Israel Galili surrendered, offering to withdraw his demands and end his involvement with the general staff. The second and last War of the Generals was over. The following day the provisional government invited Ben-Gurion to return and assume his full responsibilities. The next day, July 8, battles resumed in the Negev, then in the Galilee, then on the Jerusalem front. Ben-Gurion was never again seriously challenged by the general staff officers. And in the next months he was free to show to Count Bernadotte that old-style European diplomacy was utterly irrelevant to the political and military future of Arabs and Jews.

———

Just as Operation Nachshon had turned the tide in April, Operations Dani, Dekel, Brosh, and An-Far (launched almost simultaneously against the Arab Legion, Fawzi Kaukji's force of volunteers and mercenaries in the Galilee, the Syrians, and the Egyptians) in early July seized the initiative for the Israeli side. From this point on in the war, the IDF would determine the place and timing of the fighting. UN pressure—rather than Arab military resistance—would determine when it would end. Despite the temporary disruption of headquarters work during the dispute with Ben-Gurion, Israeli operations were now far better planned and far more deliberate. Yadin and the other staff officers no longer remained tied to their desks in headquarters frantically reacting to unexpected events. They now visited combat units regularly, made on-the-scene assessments, and transmitted up-to-the-minute reports to Ben-Gurion on the bitter battles with the Egyptians and on Allon's two-pronged effort to surround and capture the Arab towns of Lod and Ramleh as the first stage of the general offensive toward Latrun.

Yadin's relations with Allon and the Palmach commanders, however, grew tense during this period. As the Palmach brigades continued their battlefield successes and their officers felt the effects of Ben-Gurion's campaign to lessen their influence, they developed a fierce pride in their independence on the battlefield. Years later, Yitzhak Rabin, still bearing the derisive air of a field commander toward mere headquarters officers, recalled that Yadin and his staff prepared a relatively unambitious plan for the conquest of Ramleh and Lod. He and Allon rejected it and instead carried out the two-pronged flanking attack, spearheaded by armor that the Arab Legion chose not to contest. In the north the Seventh Brigade, now reorganized and redeployed under the operational command of Chaim Laskov, mounted a lightning advance from Haifa that led to the conquest of Nazareth and Central Galilee. Despite failed attempts to dislodge the Syrians in the Huleh Valley and to capture the Jewish Quarter of the Old City, and despite yet another bitter defeat at Latrun against the Arab Legion, the dimensions of the Israeli victory were astonishing—so much so that they threatened to upset the balance of power in the Middle East.

On July 15 the United States, supported by Great Britain, brought a new ceasefire resolution before the UN Security Council. No longer were the rival sides asked for their approval. This ceasefire resolution demanded compliance, threatening painful international economic and military sanctions. Neither Israel nor the Arab states could afford to bear such sanctions, so at ten o'clock on the morning of July 18 the guns once again fell silent. The struggle for Palestine would continue, albeit on diplomatic, economic, military, and ideological fronts. Now more than ever, the opposing sides had to deal with the sensitive question of the civilian Arab population, which under the UN partition plan, would constitute almost 40 percent of the population of the Jewish state. In the battles in April, Haganah forces had occupied Arab villages along important roads and in areas of heavy fighting. In accordance with the directives of Plan D, the villages that were not immediately garrisoned were destroyed. Their civilian populations—who did not or could not prevent the spread of hostilities to their area—were sent away. By May 15, the once-mixed cities of Tiberias, Haifa, and Jaffa had been largely cleared of their Arab populations. The evacuation of rural villages that were considered to be in strategic locations or likely to present security risks continued—in regional plans authorized by the operations branch and in actions carried out on local commanders' initiative.

Even before the second round of fighting, Ben-Gurion had determined that under no conditions would the displaced Arab civilian population be allowed to return. His vision of historical change in the Land of Israel was so sweeping, so apocalyptic, that it admitted little room for humanitarian sentiments. In the passion of confrontation, in the unfolding total war between Jewish and Arab populations, he saw the rural Arab population as a probable economic burden and as a politically dangerous fifth column. Besides, land and housing would be needed for the expected massive flood of Jewish immigrants into Israel. So the flight of Arab civilians from areas of heavy fighting and their removal from sensitive sectors were not to be impeded. With the conquest of Lod and Ramleh, the exodus intensified. More than fifty thousand civilians, driven by fear and by the determination of the Operation Dani commanders to secure control of this territory, crossed the front lines to find an uncertain future under Transjordanian auspices. Farther north in Nazareth, a different scene was unfolding; most of that city's civilian population chose to remain. But in other parts of the Galilee—where the support for Kaukji's volunteer forces had been much stronger—tens of thousands of uprooted villagers now made their way across the Lebanese border or crowded into the hilltop villages of Central Galilee.

With the beginning of the open-ended truce on July 18, the State of Israel was no longer merely a political assertion but a continuous territorial entity stretching from the sources of the Jordan River down to the Sea of Galilee, across the Jezreel Valley, and southward along the coastal plain. Its military victories, won even as it was painfully transforming its military underground into a full-fledged army, were stunning. The sudden, sweeping transformation, achieved at the cost of thousands killed, tens of thousands wounded, and hundreds of thousands driven from their towns and villages, marked a unique turning point in the history of the country. On July 22, Ben-Gurion appeared before the provisional government and proudly spoke of the recent conquests mimicking the antique Hebrew style of the Book of Joshua. "With the end of the truce," he told the assembly, "the armies of Israel opened a great attack on the centers of Arab power in the country. They struck the kings of Lod and Ramleh, the kings of Beit Naballa and Deir Tarif, the kings of Kola and Migdal Zedek, the kings of Zora and Eshtaol, the kings of Artuv and Ein Kerem in the foothills, the kings of Hata and Hartia in the south, the kings of Shefaram and Sippori, the kings of Ein Mahal and Kfar Kana, Nazareth and Nimrin." Ben-Gurion's biblical images would be seared into the consciousness of an entire generation. The nightmarish fears of impending destruction, the successful counterattack against the invading Arab armies, and the mass exodus of much of the Arab civilian population—with whom they had uneasily coexisted since the beginning of the modern Zionist experience—were all subsumed in a powerful and unambiguous biblical image: the divinely ordained conquest of Canaan by Joshua, at the head of the tribes of Israel.

The atmosphere in Tel Aviv on July 27 was festive. Crowds of proud and cheering civilians—long tied to the spartan routines of rationing, air raids, and home guard service—massed along the city's sidewalks and public squares. A week before, Ben-Gurion, in a mood of celebration, had decided to stage the official victory parade. He entrusted the organization of the event to Shlomo Shamir, the recently transferred commander of the Seventh Brigade. The assignment suited Shamir's taste for ceremony and military discipline, and he carried it out perfectly. In the golden warmth of a summer afternoon, with the buildings along Allenby and Ben-Yehuda streets draped with Israeli flags and blue and white bunting, the triumphal parade got under way. Led by a military band, an honor guard, and flag bearer, the marchers passed smartly by the reviewing stand to receive the salute of recently returned Chief of Staff Yaacov Dori (formerly Dostrovsky). The lead units were followed by officer cadets, dressed in full battle gear, then by Palmach units, with men and women marching side by side. The Israel Police band came next, then a unit of women soldiers, then a formation of sailors marching before an amphibious vehicle, then members of the signal corps and a unit of the military police. Next came a detachment of mule drivers with heavy machine guns loaded on the backs of their animals, followed by the field artillery and the armored corps with its clanking, diesel-belching tanks. The wide array of military equipment made a significant impression. The cheers of the crowd rose noticeably toward the end of the parade, as marching units from each IDF combat brigade passed by the reviewing stand.

For Ben-Gurion, this ceremony represented not only Israel's triumph on the battlefield but his own triumph in establishing a formal army. When the parade finally wound its way through the streets and reached the Tel Aviv football stadium, filled with dignitaries and invited guests, formations of Israeli fighter planes, bombers, and reconnaissance craft flew overhead. Ben-Gurion was quick to point out both to the assembled throng and to the staff officers and brigade commanders gathered with him on the podium that the war was far from over. "We should not yet allow ourselves to celebrate our victory," he told them. "Only victory in the last and final battle will be decisive, and we cannot yet say that our triumphs in the recent campaigns were the final victories." Ben-Gurion did not have to explain to his audience the still-threatening military situation. Despite the considerable expansion of territory brought under Israeli control in the latest round of fighting, the Egyptians still occupied much of the northern Negev, the Iraqis still threatened to split the narrow coastal strip between Tel Aviv and Haifa; the remnants of Kaukji's volunteer units still roamed the Central Galilee freely; and Abdullah's Arab Legion still occupied most of the central hill country and all of East Jerusalem.

Even more threatening than the military situation was the continued strain that total mobilization placed on the economy of Israel. In order to ensure the transformation of the Jewish state into a viable political and economic entity, the hundreds of thousands of Jewish immigrants from the displaced persons camps of Europe—and the hundreds of thousands more that were expected to arrive from the neighboring Arab countries—had to be resettled and integrated into its civilian life. Ben-Gurion was confident that Israel would eventually be accepted by its enemies, once its viability was no longer in question. The issues that would later become complex problems in Israeli-Arab relations—reparations, refugees, boundaries, and mutual recognition—all seemed to Ben Gurion to be solvable once active hostilities had been brought to an end.

This had to be done as quickly as possible, so that the important work of state-building and colonizing conquered territory could get under way. In the days after the parade Ben-Gurion's aims were thus mainly military: He instructed to his staff officers to prepare operational plans for a stunning final victory.

Despite the busy shuttling of Count Bernadotte between his Rhodes headquarters and the various Middle Eastern capitals to formulate a new peace proposal, the IDF prepared for war. In August most of Ben-Gurion's earlier command appointments were effected with hardly a word of objection. Yadin (who was now given the rank of aluf, as were all the other staff officers and brigade commanders) was assigned to oversee the reorganization and intensified training of the army and the planning of operations on each front. In Ben-Gurion's strategic conception the UN partition plan was dead. Although he was not yet ready to set as his goal a conquest of all of Palestine (as his opponents on both the left and the right never tired of urging), he was convinced that certain territorial advances still had to be made. In this respect, Yadin was sometimes too cautious. Early in September, noting the weakness of the defenses at some of the more isolated settlements, Yadin suggested that the government declare a "week of fortifications" to enlist volunteers to dig trenches and fill sandbags. Ben-Gurion rejected this idea as a waste of time and effort, since the front line was certainly going to move. "If the war starts again," he told Yadin, "either we will move the enemies from their positions or they will move us." The planning continued, with Ben-Gurion and his officers debating which front—Iraqi, Syrian, Transjordanian, or Egyptian—should be attacked first. But at the end of September, in the midst of these preparations, Count Bernadotte regained the attention of the Israeli leadership—and the world—in an unexpectedly horrifying way.

Bernadotte still believed in his own diplomatic prowess, even if others had little confidence in him. A colleague at the United Nations later recalled that the count appeared like "a man who is lost in a labyrinth, yet who continues walking with great speed and decision as if he knew exactly where he is going." Bernadotte's first sweeping blueprint for a solution to the Palestine problem, in June, had been a complete failure; his unilateral decision to bestow the territory of the projected Arab state and the city of Jerusalem on King Abdullah was rightly regarded by Israel and most of the Arab states as a diplomatic ploy by the British to bolster the power of their most docile Middle Eastern ally. That summer, the Swedish count and his faithful American assistant had gone back to the drawing board. After secret consultations with officials of the U.S. State Department and the British Foreign Office, Bernadotte issued a new peace plan—just in time to be put on the agenda of the General Assembly session scheduled for Paris in the fall. Still proposing that Israel give up its claims to the Negev in return for the entire Galilee, Bernadotte offered a few important changes: the city of Jerusalem was to be international, not Transjordanian; and the right of return (or suitable compensation) for all Arab refugees from Palestine should be guaranteed.

Bernadotte himself would not be able to debate this new proposal. In his frequent visits to Jerusalem he had faced boisterous protests from members of Lehi, the radical separatist organization known to the world as the Stern Gang that still operated freely in Jerusalem since it was not technically part of the Jewish state. "Stockholm is Yours. Jerusalem is Ours," their placards proclaimed. "Your Work is in Vain. *We* are Here." The political activism of Lehi, under the leadership of Nathan Yellin-Mor, Israel Eldar, and Yitzhak Shamir, was not limited to angry picketing. On September 17, the day after the mediator's new proposal was issued, a unit of masked Lehi members ambushed Bernadotte's car in the streets of western Jerusalem and shot the Swedish count and his French military adviser, Colonel André Serot, to death.

The international community reacted in horror. But even as Ralph Bunche called for the immediate implementation of Bernadotte's peace plan as a memorial to the late mediator, Ben-Gurion moved quickly to consolidate his power in Jerusalem before considering Israel's response. On the day after the assassination, Ben-Gurion ordered army troops to seize the Lehi headquarters in Jerusalem and arrest all Lehi leaders. Since a small contingent of the Irgun was also still operating in Jerusalem, Ben-Gurion instructed Yadin to incorporate this last remnant of Revisionist military power into the IDF and confiscate its arms. By this time, the Irgun commanders, headed by Menachem Begin, were ready to surrender, but after years of bombastic saber-rattling, they needed a face-saving gesture to comply. They therefore quietly transmitted a plea to Yadin that because of the internal politics of their organization, they needed an official ultimatum from the government. With Ben-Gurion's approval Yadin duly issued that ultimatum, and by the end of the month, all the Jewish separatist organizations were finally broken up. But serious damage had been done to Israel's diplomatic position. With the UN General Assembly session about to convene in Paris, Ben-Gurion came to the conclusion that Israeli actions on the battlefield would have to prevent the implementation of the Bernadotte plan.

While Yadin and other members of the general staff preferred to launch a preemptive attack against the Iraqis, Ben-Gurion ordered that plans be drawn up for still another assault on Latrun. This time, the goal was not simply to open the Jerusalem road; the reduction of that stubborn fortress was to be an opening movement in the conquest of all territory west of the Jordan still under Arab control. In a battle plan that fully conformed to Ben-Gurion's biblical visions, one Israeli strike force would sweep over the Latrun fortress and press on to the Jordan River, where it would join with another that had swept in a wide arc from the south to encircle Jerusalem and the Judean hills. The presence of a large civilian Arab population in those areas should not, in Ben-Gurion's opinion, be seen as a deterrent. "I assumed," he later recalled, "that most of the Arabs of Jerusalem, Bethlehem, and Hebron would flee, as had the Arabs of Lod, Jaffa, Haifa, Tiberias, and Safed, and we would control the full expanse of the country north and south of Jericho and the entire western shore of the Dead Sea would be in our hands."

Ben-Gurion's colleagues in the provisional government were reluctant to challenge international public opinion so brazenly. Foreign Minister Moshe Sharett, briefly back from the General Assembly meeting in Paris, reported that Ralph Bunche had succeeded in portraying Bernadotte as a fallen martyr and was actively marshaling support for the Bernadotte plan. In fear of arousing even greater outrage, the Israeli cabinet voted against authorizing the campaign to conquer the West Bank. It was unwilling to break the truce so openly and to conquer so much territory not allotted to Israel by the UN partition plan. Ben-Gurion called that rejection a source of "lamentation for generations," since he believed that a golden opportunity to seize most of the Land of Israel from Abdullah had been lost. But the prime minister's attention was soon diverted southward. He had always seen the Negev as a desert wilderness that could be developed and, eventually, thickly populated with Israeli settlers. To prevent the Bernadotte "swap" of the Negev, he decided that the Israeli army should launch an all-out attack against the heavily dug-in and defended Egyptian invasion force.

All through the summer, both Yadin and Allon had been insisting that Israel's most dangerous enemy was Egypt. Even after the renewed round of fighting, the Egyptian force still blocked the main road to the Negev, maintaining a siege on the scattered Israeli settlements there. With overland communications disrupted, the IDF had been forced to mount a massive airlift of supplies and reinforcements to hastily built desert airstrips, but toward the end of September, even that link was challenged. Front-line Egyptian units mounted an offensive against the airfields, one action of which was led by a thirty-year-old major named Gamal Abdul Nasser, whose confrontations with the IDF had only just begun. Yadin and Allon knew nothing as yet of Nasser, but they recognized that the time had come to engage the Egyptian forces head-on. This time, the government had no objection to the operation. In close coordination with Southern Front Commander Allon and his operations officer Yitzhak Rabin, Yadin and his staff planned an all-out offensive against the Egyptians that he gave the ironic biblical code name Operation Ten Plagues.

This plan was to be different from previous operations in the South. Instead of merely blasting a corridor through the Egyptian lines to resupply Negev settlements, Ten Plagues was meant to annihilate the Egyptian invading force. Thus on October 15, an Israel supply convoy was intentionally sent southward along the contested road and when it was fired upon, and the renewed hostilities began. Operation Ten Plagues was the first Israeli operation in which armor, air support, and proper artillery batteries were effectively used to support coordinated infantry attacks. Despite continuing angry flare-ups between Yadin and Rabin over last-minute changes in the carefully detailed battle plan, the simultaneous lightning attacks by the IDF in several sectors ultimately succeeded in destroying the military effectiveness of the Egyptian invasion force. Some units surrendered, some fled back toward Sinai, and some— like the entire brigade in what came to be known as the Faluja Pocket— were surrounded and trapped. With rapid Israeli advances the main road to Negev was opened, and the desert town of Beersheva came under Israeli control. No other Arab state chose to come to the aid of the Egyptians, who now agreed to accept help from the United Nations.

Even though a ceasefire began on October 22, this phase of the fighting was not over. Yadin coordinated operations as the Israeli forces mopped up resistance in areas captured from the Egyptians and, far to the north in a separate action (named Operation Hiram after an ancient king of Phoenicia), routed the last of Fawzi Kaukji's volunteer forces in the Central Galilee and captured fourteen villages in southern Lebanon.

No longer would the United Nations be able to impose a territorial swap on Israel, since both the Galilee and the Negev were now substantially under its control. Domestic American politics also played a role in scuttling the Bernadotte plan. Thomas Dewey and Harry Truman were running neck and neck in the 1948 presidential campaign; with the establishment of the State of Israel being an emotionally charged issue for many voters, both candidates quickly affirmed that Israelis should not be obliged to give up territory they had won at great sacrifice. Ben-Gurion's gamble had paid off handsomely. The battered remnants of the Arab invasion forces were now desperate to prevent further fighting. They had suffered heavy losses of men and equipment and had utterly failed to prevent the implementation of the UN partition plan. They now faced the question of how to deal with hundreds of thousands of Palestinian

Arab refugees. The IDF, under Ben-Gurion's strategic guidance, was on the verge of complete victory. Yadin had by now become a faithful follower of the prime minister. No military objective seemed impossible. On October 31, in a strategy session with Ben-Gurion and Dori, Yadin asked a simple and obvious question of his commander: "Where do we go from here?"

———

Ernest Bevin, the British foreign secretary, was not a man to give up easily. Soon after assuming office in the summer of 1945, he had made a determination that the strategic interests of Great Britain in the Middle East would be best served by abandoning official support for Zionism and cultivating a close relationship with the emerging states of the Arab League. That decision—and Bevin's stubborn adherence to it—had led to a violent and costly confrontation with the Jews of Palestine; it had done nothing to further the cause of Palestinian Arab independence; and it had utterly failed to gain the unquestioned support of the leaders of the other Arab nations. In late October, Ben-Gurion wondered when the British would finally accept the new reality. "If Bevin were able to act strictly in a rational manner," he noted in his diary, "he would have to come to the conclusion that the Arab Army isn't worth anything, that we are the only military power in the Middle East, and that he should find efficient means either to destroy us—or reconcile himself with us as with any important power." For the time being, however, Bevin adopted a different strategy: He would exert intense diplomatic pressure to strip Israel of its recent military gains.

Accordingly, on November 4, the UN Security Council passed a resolution introduced by Great Britain and China that called for a return of Egyptian and Israeli forces to the positions they held on October 14—before the last round of fighting—under the threat of sanctions if they refused. Naturally, the Egyptians would have been only too happy to do so, for their military progress had been only backward. Not unexpectedly, Ben-Gurion refused to accept it and even contemplated additional military moves. Yadin was dispatched on a secret mission to Paris to convince Foreign Minister Sharett of the advisability of action, but once there, he discovered a complex and confusing situation at the United Nations. Each of the major powers and players had its own idea about the future of the country. Ralph Bunche, now officially designated as Acting Mediator, suggested that both sides withdraw to the October 14 lines and leave a demilitarized zone between them. Yet the British were still urging the implementation of the Bernadotte plan, with its swap of the Galilee and Negev; and the Soviets insisted on resurrecting the partition plan idea of establishing both a Jewish and an independent Arab State. On November 16 an additional element was added when Bunche called for the two sides to open peace negotiations. But the Egyptians, despite their untenable military position, rejected the idea.

By early December, Ben-Gurion was feeling increasing pressure to deal a final coup de grâce to Egypt. Yadin agreed that the time was ripe. "Yigael has the impression that the Egyptians want to leave the country," Ben-Gurion noted in his diary. "It's clear that they want to end this miserable adventure, but they don't know how." The IDF would soon offer them a solution. Operation Horev, as finally planned in the operations branch by Yadin and his staff and elaborated in the field by Yigal Allon and Yitzhak Rabin, was a masterpiece of surprise and rapid movement that effectively ended the 1948 war. On December 22 the Golani Brigade mounted a diversionary attack against Gaza, while the Negev, Harel, and Eighth brigades pushed south along the route of an ancient Roman road, through sand dunes and a driving rainstorm, to mount a surprise attack on the Egyptian forces at the border outpost of Auja el-Hafir. For years afterward, the choice of that forgotten ancient caravan route was popularly ascribed to Yadin's archaeological background, but where the credit for the discovery lies is much less clear. What is indisputable, however, is that the arriving Israeli troops emerged suddenly from the desert and fought a bitter battle at the heavily fortified border post of Auja. And when the Egyptian defenses collapsed and the forces retreated into Sinai, the Israelis unhesitatingly crossed the international border to pursue the fleeing troops.

The Israeli forces, under Allon's command, drove deep into Sinai without significant resistance. They conquered the oasis of Abu Ageilah, and while some units were dispatched westward toward the Suez Canal in pursuit of retreating Egyptians, the main force turned north to encircle the Gaza strip. With the Egyptian army on the verge of total collapse, the northern Sinai airfield and military base at el-Arish became a tempting target. Indeed, the stunning Israeli advance seriously threatened the delicate balance of political power in the region. Rumors of the Egyptian rout in Sinai reached Cairo, and demonstrations exploded in the streets. Islamic fundamentalist forces condemned the Egyptian government for its ineptness and wildly accused the British of treachery in facilitating a Zionist victory. On December 28, Prime Minister Nuqrashi was gunned down by Muslim Brotherhood terrorists. British foreign minister Bevin demanded that something be done. The Security Council hastily convened on the next day and passed a resolution calling for an immediate ceasefire. But as the Israeli forces ignored the order and continued to roam freely in Sinai, the British government decided it had no alternative but to intervene.

In a sobering announcement on December 30, the British warned that should any Israeli forces be found in Egyptian territory, they would invoke the 1936 Anglo-Egyptian mutual defense pact to justify repelling the hostile attack. This was a possibility that Ben-Gurion had not expected, but he refused to be intimidated. At a meeting with Dori, Yadin, and Southern Front Commander Allon, he decided that the IDF would gradually reconcentrate its operations against Gaza but carry out a few more diversionary actions in Sinai. "If the English come," Ben-Gurion instructed the officers, "we will withdraw to our border, to Auja. If they come to Auja, we'll fight them there." Content that his war aims were being achieved and that final victory was just around the corner, Ben-Gurion left Tel Aviv with Paula to spend New Year's Eve in a favorite hotel by the Sea of Galilee.

Late on New Year's Eve, however, the U.S. envoy to Israel, James MacDonald, traveled north to Tiberias to underline the seriousness of the situation to Ben-Gurion. Great Britain had appealed to the United States to help put an end to the fighting. Both superpowers now acted in unison. Shortly before midnight, in a small room off the lobby of the Galei Kinneret Hotel, MacDonald read the text of a stern warning from President Truman that Israel's relations with the United States and its application for UN membership would be gravely endangered if its troops did not immediately evacuate Sinai. Ben-Gurion reacted calmly, assuring MacDonald that the order had already been given to withdraw. What he did not know was at that moment Yadin was having difficulty confirming that the order had been received at the front. The first of his dispatches to Allon went unanswered, for Allon was determined that the last and greatest victories of the War of Independence not be taken from him. He was on the verge of destroying the entire Egyptian army, units that remained in Gaza and all the units in Sinai as well.

Allon was, in fact, unwilling to accept Yadin's instructions. He commandeered a military plane and flew back to Tel Aviv to plead his case. Confronting Yadin and Foreign Minister Sharett, he asked for one more day. If he could conquer el-Arish and *then* withdraw across the border, the isolated defenders of Gaza, he believed, would be much easier to overcome. He rejected Yadin's arguments and insisted that Sharett telephone Ben-Gurion directly, even though it was the middle of the night. Ben-Gurion, roused from a deep sleep and in a bad humor, was in no mood to play games with superpowers, no matter what ingenious battle plan the independent-minded Palmach commander proposed. He angrily instructed Sharett to tell Allon "that he should get used to receiving orders—and that he should carry out the withdrawal as we planned."

There was one more surprise to come in Operation Horev. Staging a calculatedly slow withdrawal from Sinai, Allon gained approval for one last foray into Sinai along a road that skirted the international border—in order to sever communications between the Egyptian forces in Gaza and those in Sinai. The operation achieved its objective, and on January 5, 1949, the Egyptian government, with its invasion force surrounded, finally dropped its objections to negotiating an armistice with Israel under UN auspices. On January 7, even though the fighting had ended, the British Middle East Command dispatched a squadron of RAF fighters from the Suez Canal Zone to make sure that the Israelis had fully withdrawn from Sinai. Four of the aircraft were shot down by Israeli fighters and one by Israeli antiaircraft fire. For a few tense hours it seemed that an Anglo-Israeli war was in the offing as the British garrison in Aqaba was reinforced and the Royal Navy put on alert. But with the direct intervention of President Truman, tempers cooled quickly. Foreign Secretary Ernest Bevin was finally convinced of Israel's military power. Unable to destroy it, he would at last come to terms with the existence of the Jewish state.

For one last time, Yigael Yadin appeared before the foreign correspondents at the Ritz Hotel, and his performance on January 8 was his most relaxed, dramatic, and witty of the war. Unofficial rumors had spread of the sweeping Israeli victories in Sinai and the Anglo-Israeli confrontation, and Yadin was now authorized to give the official version of the events. Describing the two Egyptian columns that surrounded the Jewish settlements in the Negev, Yadin quipped that "they were trying to embrace us, out of love perhaps." He went on to describe the planning of Operation Horev, the feint toward Gaza, the surprise advance down the Roman road toward Auja, and the virtual destruction of the entire Egyptian First Brigade. "They ran like hell and it seems that they did not know where the frontier was," Yadin joked, to deflect the tense issue of Israel's advance into Sinai. "Some of them, we have learned from their own sources, have succeeded in reaching Ismailia," he went on, conjuring up an image of frightened Egyptians racing all the way to the Suez Canal. As always, Yadin was able to offer an elegant and unexpected juxtaposition of present and past. Speaking of the Israeli army's controversial sweep through Sinai, he noted, "While we were there, we thought it was a good opportunity to do as much damage as possible. It is not every day we are in Egypt—the last time we were there was 3,400 years ago." With a wave of his pointer across a large map, Yadin lectured the assembled journalists on the theories of Liddell Hart, military movement, and the indirect approach. "This was one of the most successful movement wars in the history of the country," he boasted, rivaling perhaps even General Edmund Allenby's sweep thirty-one years earlier that had led to the British conquest of Palestine.

In magazines, newspapers, and newsreels across Europe and America, Colonel Yigael Yadin was depicted as a central figure in the astounding military victories of the State of Israel. As coordinator and spokesman for the victorious Israeli army, Yadin now stepped ahead of the front commanders in public recognition and acclaim. Ben-Gurion, well aware of Yadin's personal shortcomings, prized his quick wit and intellect. A visiting American journalist and military expert, Fred Harris, conveyed the same impression: "Yigael Yadin—brilliant, but relies too much on his own improvisations and he doesn't think things through enough to the end." Still, Yadin was the only high-ranking officer whom Ben-Gurion would trust completely as military representative to the delicate armistice negotiations with Egypt, scheduled to begin under UN auspices on Rhodes the following week.

———

Back in Jerusalem, Professor Eleazar Sukenik was preparing for a long-delayed journey. Now that the war was over, he was finally able to contemplate a triumphant lecture tour to England and America to present the Dead Sea Scrolls to the scholarly world. Throughout the summer and autumn of 1948 he had devoted himself entirely to their decipherment and translation, with the invaluable assistance (as usual) of his assistant, Avigad. In December he had learned that Archbishop Samuel had fled to America with the other batch of manuscripts, and he went to see Ben-Gurion to gain official help in preventing their sale and perhaps even gain permission to search the wadis and canyons of the Dead Sea region for more scrolls. Ben-Gurion, deeply preoccupied with the secret planning for his last and greatest military campaign, did not act on either suggestion. But Dr. Sukenik was riding an unprecedented wave of public acclaim as the first scholar to recognize the importance of the Dead Sea Scrolls. He had indeed found what he had been searching for throughout his archaeological career. The lecture tour of America, England, and Europe he was now planning was meant to raise funds for the Hebrew University and spread positive publicity for the State of Israel. On his return trip through Italy, he would be received for a personal audience by Pope Pius XII. Thus, on New Year's Eve, December 31, 1948,

Sukenik jotted in his journal, "The most historic year in the annals of our people has ended. It was a difficult year—with the loss of Matti, may his memory be blessed. If it hadn't been for the scrolls," he concluded, "it would have been a very, very hard year for me."

Three days before, when the Israeli forces were in hot pursuit of the Egyptians across Sinai, Professor Sukenik had addressed more than three hundred members of the Israel Exploration Society (formerly the Jewish Palestine Exploration Society), convened for their annual meeting in the Histadrut auditorium in Jerusalem. This was the first large event to be held in the city since the World Congress of Jewish Studies in the summer of 1947. Jerusalem was now a divided city. In September the city's Israeli military commander, Moshe Dayan, and his Arab Legion counterpart, Abdullah et-Tell, had agreed to a permanent ceasefire line that cut the city in two. Now the Old City and the Rockefeller Museum were beyond the reach of the citizens of Israel; the university buildings on Mount Scopus were virtually cut off, linked only by occasional UN-supervised convoys. But a new Jerusalem—a new Israel—was under construction. After welcoming speeches of Dr. Mayer, Minister of Transport David Remez, Governor Dov Joseph, and UN ambassador Abba Eban, Professor Eleazar Sukenik rose to sound what would become something of a national creed.

"Ten years ago," he recalled, "there was a popular saying: every new discovery of antiquities in the country gives strength to our claims and our rights to the Land of Israel. Today there is no need for such proof." In his words was a devotion to the political value of archaeology to the new Jewish state. "Here in the East," he noted, "there is only one people, the Jewish people, that has a connection to the past and to the antiquities that are being discovered every day. The archaeological reality instills a feeling in the heart of the individual and the public that every inch of this country is ours and it is our obligation to defend and to fight for it. This science is our spiritual weapon and an important buttress for the State in its path to the future." Lecturing on the scroll that he called "The War of the Sons of Light Against the Sons of Darkness," Sukenik reached the crowning achievement of his career. In the presence of the assembled scholars, archaeologists, and enthusiastic amateurs, however, his great moment was soon to be eclipsed by a display of honor and respect for his son.

After the society held its internal elections, Moshe Schwabe, classics professor and former scoutmaster, announced with obvious pride that Aluf Yigael Yadin had been elected to the governing board of the Israel Exploration Society. Yadin was no longer just a promising archaeology student, no longer merely the son of Professor Sukenik, but an admired military hero and national celebrity. Yadin was unfortunately unable to be present at the congress to deliver his lecture on the ancient roads to Jerusalem, Schwabe said. Yadin's role in the battles along the Jerusalem road the previous spring was by now widely known. He was becoming comfortable with his role as a national leader, eager to inspire his people for the present and future, no longer only concerned with the past. From IDF headquarters, Yadin conveyed his heartfelt wishes for the success of the society's meeting. With a Ben-Gurionesque biblical flourish, he noted that of all the roads to the Holy City, "the love of Jerusalem is one of the most important paths."

Chapter   Eight

THREATS AND
PERSUASIONS

The island of Rhodes looked deceptively peaceful from the window of the UN DC-3 Dakota carrying the Israeli delegation to the armistice talks. Even in midwinter, the port city of Rhodes, jutting sharply north into the Aegean, with its picturesque Crusader walls, Greek ruins, and lush gardens, offered just the kind of tranquil asylum from Middle Eastern hatred and killing that the late Count Bernadotte had sought. Ben-Gurion had initially suggested that the armistice talks with Egypt be held on the international border between Sinai and the Negev, or perhaps even on an American battleship. But in his eagerness to move from a military to a diplomatic offensive, he gave way to Bunche's suggestion. Separate floors were reserved at the Hôtel des Roses for the Israeli and Egyptian negotiators.

The Israeli delegation was headed by the astute and often acerbic director-general of the Foreign Ministry, Walter Eytan. Aluf Yigael Yadin (whose rank was now equated with that of colonel for diplomatic purposes) led the military contingent and shared responsibility with Eytan for the overall negotiating strategy. In the few hurried days before their departure, Ben-Gurion, Chief of Staff Dori, and Foreign Minister Sharett had given them some basic guidelines. Egyptian forces should not be allowed to remain anywhere within the borders of Palestine, and the IDF should not withdraw from any positions it currently held. Although this position stood in sharp contradiction to Security Council resolutions demanding a return to positions held *before* the last two rounds of fighting, Yadin was prepared to stand fast. As he and Eytan and the rest of the Israeli delegation arrived at the Hotel des Roses, greeted by the popping of flashbulbs and shouted questions from reporters, they began the unexpectedly complex task of establishing a new diplomatic reality in the postwar Middle East.

The Egyptian delegates, who had arrived in Rhodes several hours earlier, were wary. They protested strenuously to Bunche about the annoying presence of journalists and photographers in the hotel lobby and insisted that even the ceremonial meetings of the two delegations be closed to the press. The composition of the Egyptian delegation reflected the tense, three-cornered nature of Egyptian politics in the wake of the Palestine debacle. Neither army, the court, nor the parliament wanted to be blamed for the humiliating defeat. At the delegation's head was a career officer, Colonel Muhammed Ibrahim Seif el-Din, who was watched closely by Ismail Sherinne, King Farouk's confidant and brother-in-law-to-be. Two high-ranking members of the Egyptian Foreign Ministry, though not official members of the delegation, were present and active behind the scenes.

On the afternoon of January 13, 1949, Bunche convened the two delegations for their first formal meeting in the hotel's Yellow Room. Eytan and Seif el-Din shook hands and gave brief opening statements. Bunche was unanimously appointed chairman, and an agenda was agreed upon within half an hour. The atmosphere was surprisingly cordial. That evening, Eytan cabled Foreign Minister Sharett in Tel Aviv with a positive report that "the Egyptians were pleasantly surprised at our appearance; they had apparently expected fierce, warlike persons to come exultantly to the table, with grim expressions on their faces." Prospects now seemed good for an early, successful conclusion of the negotiations, though Eytan added, "The Egyptians were visibly nervous, never quite sure that they were doing the right thing."

That afternoon, Ralph Bunche sat in the middle, at least officially Count Bernadotte's successor but certainly acting in the interests of his nation as well. The postwar Middle Eastern situation was unformed and chaotic. With a cold war looming in Europe and the power of Great Britain obviously declining, it was important for the United States to step in and limit hostilities in this vital region—to prevent the defection of either Israel or its Arab neighbors into the Communist camp. Bunche therefore adopted the goal of achieving only interim agreements, not the sweeping peace plan favored by the late count. "The lives of many people, and indeed the peace of the Near East, hang in the balance while you meet," he told the assembled delegations. "The decisions you will be called upon to make in achieving agreement, therefore, are momentous. You cannot afford to fail. You must succeed." In an effort to create an atmosphere of mutual trust and good humor, Bunche did his best to add a comic touch. As Eytan recalled, he revealed to the delegations that he had ordered hand-painted plates for each member, bearing the inscription "Rhodes Armistice Talks 1949" in the distinctive Rhodian pottery style. "If you reach an agreement," Bunche told them, "each one of you will get one to take home. If you don't, I'll break them over your heads!"

But there was nothing comic about Bunche's subsequent tactic of keeping the two sides as far apart as possible, masking their differences and largely keeping them in the dark. Despite the increasing friendliness of hallway encounters between Israelis and Egyptians and their shared meals in the hotel dining room, neither delegation knew how far apart they really were. The Egyptians interpreted Bunche's continuing optimism as a sign that the Israelis were about to accede to the Security Council resolutions and agree to Egypt's resumed military occupation of much of southern Palestine. The Israelis, for their part, believed that the Egyptians were indeed ready to end their Palestinian adventure. "We have no hint what the Egyptians have in mind regarding armistice lines, withdrawal, and reduction of forces," Eytan reported to Sharett after three days of indirect negotiations, "but it is perfectly clear that they have orders to reach agreement and to reach it quickly." Expectations were so high that the Israelis allowed the evacuation of an Egyptian brigade trapped in the Faluja Pocket within seven days, since it seemed almost certain that the armistice would be concluded by then. But on January 21, just three days before the scheduled evacuation, the cooperative atmosphere was suddenly poisoned when both delegations discovered that Bunche had been hiding the truth.

As the delegations faced each other across the ballroom and prepared to present their positions, the Israelis fully expected to hear an

Egyptian timetable for complete withdrawal from Palestine. The Egyptians, on the other hand, believed that the Israelis had come to their senses. Ismail Sherinne, King Farouk's representative, therefore rose to acknowledge Egypt's claim to the Negev, to request that Egyptian forces be permitted to return to their earlier positions, and to ask that an Egyptian governor be dispatched to Beersheva as soon as possible. Yadin, never one to react calmly to unpleasant surprises, now exploded in rage. "Before we give you Beersheva," he shouted over to the king's representative, "we'll give you back the sun and the stars!" His nervous habit of fiddling with pencils during meetings now betrayed him. As he pounded angrily on the conference table, the pencil he was holding flew out of his hand and—in one of those miraculously horrifying accidents—struck Colonel Seif el-Din square in the forehead. As everyone gasped, Seif el-Din rose in fury at such an indignity from the arrogant Israeli officer. A quick-thinking member of the Egyptian delegation suddenly broke the tension and quipped, "Why don't you give us back the moon too?"

The situation was salvaged for the moment, but there was still a serious problem. With the date for the evacuation of the Faluja Pocket quickly approaching but no possibility of an early agreement in sight, the Israeli delegation announced that it would not permit the withdrawal of the trapped brigade. Bunche tried with every means at his disposal to convince the Israeli delegation to relent. He pleaded that a failure of the talks at this stage would have disastrous consequences for the participation of the other Arab states in subsequent armistice talks—and for the larger process of ending the war. The Israelis stood firm on their refusal. On January 24, Foreign Minister Sharett cabled Eytan that "Bunche has to understand that the Egyptians are paying for their criminal invasion and its failure," and he practically dared them to break up the talks. But the Egyptians received instructions from Cairo to continue the negotiations. In return for an Israeli agreement to allow food and medicine into the besieged Faluja Pocket, they agreed to take at least a small step forward by signing an official ceasefire agreement.

The hard bargaining for the formal armistice agreement, signifying that the two nations had agreed to terminate their military conflict, still lay ahead, before even the possibility of a peace treaty could be discussed. Bunche wisely adjourned the talks for a few days to clear the air and await the results of the first Knesset election, held on January 25. In that election Israeli voters offered Ben-Gurion some room to maneuver; his centrist Mapai party was able to form a ruling coalition without the hardliners of either Mapam on the left or Menachem Begin's newly established Herut, or "Freedom party," on the right. Ben-Gurion easily persuaded the new government to approve a territorial concession: the continued Egyptian occupation of the Gaza Strip (whose population was now dangerously swollen by refugees from the villages of southern Palestine). Back at the resumed talks, however, Bunche urged the Israelis to go further—especially with regard to the crucial road junction and border fortress of Auja el-Hafir. Since this border area had been allotted to the Arab state in the UN partition plan, it belonged to neither Israel nor Egypt. Bunche's suggestion was to place the Auja border area under UN jurisdiction—and leave other Egyptian territorial claims open, to be raised in the final negotiations for a permanent peace treaty.

To the Egyptians, ever anxious to end this messy business, this seemed a perfectly reasonable solution. But to Yadin it seemed a dangerous threat to the military security of the State of Israel. In his first diplomatic assignment Yadin proved to be a shrewd and unrelenting bargainer, gaining Egyptian approval for his suggestions about postwar troop levels, the thinning of forces in certain areas, and the creation of demilitarized zones. Having successfully fended off attempts to restore Egyptian control of Beersheva, however, he would not yield now on the even more sensitive question of Auja el-Hafir. The Israeli forces had been able to conquer it only after a seemingly impossible advance down the desert road and after a bloody battle. There was no way that he could ever ask the men of the combat brigades to muster the courage and make the sacrifices to conquer it again. There was no question in Yadin's mind—if not in Eytan's—that the Israeli forces must remain in strongpoints around Auja and on the Egyptian border. He urgently returned to Tel Aviv to persuade Chief of Staff Dori, Foreign Minister Sharett, and Ben-Gurion that Israeli withdrawal from the hard-won border posts and their reoccupation by the United Nations would set a dangerous precedent for armistice negotiations on the other fronts.

With the other Arab states already signaling their impatience to join the negotiating process, Bunche applied serious pressure to force the Israelis into an agreement. He was convinced that the pale blue UN flag fluttering over the largely ruined stone buildings of Auja would be sufficient protection against a future invasion. Behind the scenes he quietly contacted U.S. State Department officials to apply friendly pressure on both Egypt and Israel. At the same time, he encouraged what he considered to be the more moderate influences in the Israeli delegation. In a series of long letters to Eytan he pointedly criticized Yadin's unyielding negotiating stance. "Colonel Yadin," he wrote, "seems to feel that a question of inequality of treatment is involved whenever it is suggested that Israeli troops should be withdrawn from a particular locality," Implicit in Bunche's pressure on the Israeli delegation was the threat that if the talks failed, the Security Council would impose an even less acceptable solution on Israel. Eytan urged Ben-Gurion and Sharett to consider the consequences before they rejected Bunche's suggestion, and eventually Yadin was overruled. At the last moment Eytan came up with an ingenious alternative that satisfied Yadin: an area on *both* sides of the border around Auja would be demilitarized, without a UN presence. The Egyptians snapped up this recommendation, and after six tiring weeks in the Aegean, the deal was finally struck.

On February 24, 1949, the Israeli-Egyptian armistice was signed in a festive ceremony in the Yellow Room of the Hôtel des Roses. Both delegations were relieved that the long negotiations were over. As he had promised, Bunche distributed hand-painted plates to all the delegates, and in a gesture of extravagant celebration the Egyptian delegation flew in sweets and pastries from Cairo's famous Groppi's Cafe. Back in Tel Aviv, Ben-Gurion exulted in the diplomatic achievement. "After the establishment of the state and our victories on the battlefield," he noted in his diary, "it is the greatest event in a year of momentous events." On the following day another UN DC-3 charter carried the Israeli delegation back to Tel Aviv, where they were greeted on the tarmac by Foreign Minister Sharett. Yadin had gotten his first taste of international negotiations and carried out his mission, in Ben-Gurion's opinion, "with patience, talent, and success." His diplomatic career was just beginning; in less than a month, he and Walter Eytan would be given an even more challenging task.

The painstakingly surveyed maps of the Land of the Bible, produced by nineteenth-century explorers and antiquarians in search of biblical ruins and landmarks had served as the blueprints for territorial redistribution for European diplomats after World War I. The old Ottoman boundaries were redrawn to create new entities: Syria, Lebanon, Palestine, and Transjordan—each one a combined expression of antiquarian imagination and imperial will. Now that independent nation-states had arisen from the earlier colonial order, a new generation of soldiers and statesmen attempted to shift the boundaries again. Soon after the successful armistice talks with Egypt, another team of Israeli negotiators met under UN auspices with representatives of the Republic of Lebanon. These talks were held on the Mediterranean coast at two sites on the border between the two nations: the Lebanese custom house at Ras en-Naqura and the Israeli police station at Rosh Haniqra.

The Israeli-Lebanese talks should have been relatively quick and painless. From the start, the Lebanese delegation, led by Chief of Staff Tewfik Selim, was eager to agree to a return to the international border—especially since Israeli forces still held fourteen villages in Lebanese territory. Though Yadin was not personally involved in these negotiations, he was adamantly opposed to abandoning any forward positions conquered in battle. He urged the Israeli military representative, Mordecai Makleff, to take a hard line and insist that Israeli withdrawal on the Lebanese border be linked with Syrian withdrawal on the east. His argument was that since the boundary from the Sea of Galilee to the Mediterranean was a single, indivisible geographical line (drawn by the British and French in 1920, before the separation of Lebanon from Syria), it must not be changed in only one place. Ralph Bunche, however, quickly intervened to support the Lebanese position. The issue of the Syrian border, he assured the Israeli government, would be addressed in due time. Since Ben-Gurion was eager to maintain the diplomatic momentum, he overruled the objections of Yadin and Makleff, and a formal armistice agreement was signed with Lebanon on March 23.

Next came the turn of Transjordan. In these highly unorthodox negotiations, however, the old imperial boundaries were completely irrelevant. For years Abdullah had been the only Arab leader willing to contemplate far-reaching economic and political cooperation with the Zionist movement. In the spring of 1948 there had even been hopes in Tel Aviv that Abdullah might be persuaded to stay out of the war. But the Transjordanian monarch had skillfully seized control of the invasion, and while the Syrian, Iraqi, and Egyptian armies had faced bloody battles and painful military reverses, Abdullah's Arab Legion had accomplished a relatively unchallenged occupation of the Jerusalem and Hebron Hills. Except for the bitter fighting at Latrun, the loss of Lod and Ramleh, and the battles for Jerusalem, Abdullah had emerged from the war with his military forces intact. At the end of November he and Ben-Gurion had both concluded that they should partition Jerusalem between them, and they instructed two trusted young officers—Moshe Dayan and Abdullah et-Tell—to seal the deal. At the end of the year, with the Arab League coalition disintegrating, Abdullah sought a comprehensive agreement. Acting without the knowledge of his ministers, the king initiated secret negotiations to achieve a comprehensive peace treaty with Israel.

Yadin's behind-the-scenes role in these negotiations was that of an outspoken advocate of military power. In meetings with Foreign Ministry officials and political leaders, he opposed making any territorial concessions in the hope of achieving diplomatic or political gains in return. For Yadin, the possession of territory was immeasurably more valuable than the uncertain prospects of goodwill with neighboring Arab states or international guarantees. The last major area that the UN partition plan allotted to the Jewish state that remained unconquered was the southern

Negev, that slender triangle of desolate desert mountains jutting southward between Transjordan and Egypt toward the Gulf of Aqaba. Ben-Gurion, whose attention was turned increasingly toward Israel's economic development, was intent on gaining full control of this direct passage to the Indian Ocean and the Far East. Since Abdullah made no secret of his own desire to control this area, Yadin and Yitzhak Rabin drew up plans for a lightning military offensive—named Operation Uvdah, or "Fact"—to create new facts on the ground. On March 5, the day after the opening of formal Israeli-Jordanian armistice negotiations on Rhodes (with none other than Moshe Dayan heading the Israeli delegation), the Negev and Golani Brigades left Beersheva and in less than a week arrived at the seaside village of Umm Rashrash, raising a hastily made, ink-colored Israeli flag over what would become the Israeli port of Eilat. There was little Abdullah could do to change this new situation; he decided to cut his losses and dutifully instructed his representatives at Rhodes to sign an official ceasefire agreement on March 11.

Unfortunately for Abdullah, he could not cut his losses completely. The Iraqis had occupied the northern sector of the West Bank around Nablus since the time of the invasion, and in response to Israeli complaints about continuing ceasefire violations, Abdullah had undertaken to replace the Iraqi forces with his own Arab Legion troops. But the Israeli general staff, sensing the possibility of further, relatively easy conquest as the Arab forces were shifting, moved three brigades into position to conquer the West Bank. At the same time the Israeli Foreign Ministry issued a formal protest to the United Nations, insisting that Abdullah's replacement of the Iraqi troops with the Arab Legion constituted a serious breach of the current ceasefire. Abdullah felt betrayed, but he was eager to defuse the situation and arranged an urgent secret meeting between Dayan and et-Tell.

At that meeting Dayan presented what amounted to an ultimatum: In return for allowing the replacement of the Iraqis with the Arab Legion, Israel demanded significant territorial concessions all along the Iraqi front. In particular, Israel sought control of Wadi Ara, an important overland connection between the coastal plain and the Jezreel Valley. Despite the angry objections of his ministers, Abdullah had no choice but to give up the disputed territory, for he had been informed by John Glubb, the British-born commander of the Arab Legion, that there was no way he could hold the present line if the Israelis launched an all-out attack. Abdullah therefore accepted the Israeli demand, reportedly insisting, "I am ready to give up my throne before renewing battle with the Jews." As the Israeli-Jordanian armistice talks in Rhodes droned on inconclusively, Abdullah turned to secret diplomacy. He asked that an

Israeli delegation be dispatched to his winter palace at Shuneh in the eastern Jordan Valley. For this delicate mission, Ben-Gurion and Foreign Minister Sharett selected Walter Eytan and Yigael Yadin.

For the rest of his life Yadin would delight in recounting vivid and colorful details of his three nights as a guest of the Hashemite monarch. After dark on March 22, he and Eytan and a young officer named Yehoshafat Harkabi picked their way through the rubble and barbed wire of No Man's Land near the Mandelbaum Gate in Jerusalem and crossed to the other side, where Abdullah et-Tell was waiting for them. After a high-speed drive down to Jericho and across the Allenby Bridge over the Jordan River, they arrived at the king's winter "palace," which proved to be little more than a modest country house. Eytan was both surprised and amused by the furnishings of the main reception room, which included preposterously ornate chairs and end tables and an oversized oil painting of the Battle of Trafalgar that, he later learned, had been given to His Majesty by King George V. King Abdullah, they were informed, would not be present that evening. They were to conduct their negotiations with Colonel et-Tell, His Excellency Falah el-Madadhah, the Transjordanian minister of justice, and Hussein Siraj, the undersecretary of state. After exchanging polite speeches, the two delegations got to work. Eytan later reported to Foreign Minister Sharett that "His Excellency, who asked to be remembered to various Jewish acquaintances of his (mainly of the trading class), and the Under Secretary of State, who told me that he had once been the basketball champion of Amman, took no very active part in the proceedings which centered chiefly around the line that had to be drawn on the map."

In fact, there were no real negotiations. Yadin had prepared a map, with the approval of Ben-Gurion, showing a new line that would transfer approximately four hundred square kilometers and thirty villages to Israel. On seeing the map, Abdullah et-Tell expressed his concern that the king would object to the extent of this territorial transaction, but for the Israelis it was a take-it-or-leave-it affair. Yadin made clear that if the offer were rejected, the IDF was prepared to capture all the territory in question—and perhaps even more—by force of arms. At one o'clock that morning the first working session at Shuneh concluded, and et-Tell drove his guests back to Jerusalem, parting with the understanding that he would confer with the king and inform his Israeli counterparts of the king's answer on the following day.

In midafternoon on March 23, Abdullah et-Tell relayed His Majesty's agreement to the Israeli suggestions and conveyed an invitation to a festive dinner and signing ceremony at the Shuneh palace that night. Once again, Yadin and Eytan made their way after nightfall across No

Man's Land, accompanied by Harkabi and Moshe Dayan, who had just returned from Rhodes. Once again, Abdullah et-Tell greeted them on the other side and drove them to Shuneh. This time, since the king was to be present, Yadin and Eytan had brought what they believed were appropriate gifts: a Bible encased in a silver binding and a pair of silver candlesticks. Soon after their arrival the king entered the reception room and greeted the Israelis warmly, accepting their tokens of friendship and bestowing upon Eytan what he later described as a "murderous looking dagger" in return. Only in retrospect was the next moment amusing: Yadin recalled that when the king opened the Bible, his face suddenly tightened. As a frontispiece it had a colorful map of the Kingdom of Solomon, with vast borders extending from the Euphrates to the Nile.

A few hurried words of explanation quickly smoothed the matter over, and the party proceeded to the dining room, where Yadin was seated on the king's left and Eytan on his right. One of the many unusual details that Eytan later reported to Sharett was that the king's plate was surrounded by a semicircle of medicine bottles, from which His Majesty took pills at regular intervals. The conversation, in English, was difficult, "but whenever it failed," Eytan recalled, "the King put things right by extending his hands and grasping me and Yadin by the arm, apparently as a silent gesture of friendship." An even stranger connection was made when Abdullah turned to Yadin and mentioned the comfort that ancient Arabic poetry gave him in troubled times. Yadin suddenly remembered a passage of pre-Islamic poetry that he had been forced to memorize in one of Professor Baneth's courses at the university. He recited it flawlessly, to the Hashemite monarch's amazement. "Naturally," Yadin later recalled with good-humored smugness, "my stock rose with the king."

Yadin, Eytan, and Dayan had not come to trade gifts and listen to poetry, however, but to preside over what amounted to a surrender ceremony. After dinner the party retired to the main reception room, where the king gave a long and flowery speech. According to Eytan, he spoke of "the friendship between our two countries, the past (including Deir Yassin), the future (naturally not so specific), his relations with the British and the United States, as well as what he thought of the mufti and solicitous inquiries after the health of Mr. Ben-Gurion, Mr. Sharett, Mrs. Meyerson." As Yadin later remembered, Abdullah made pointed use of a traditional bedouin parable. Recalling his misgivings about entering the war against the Israelis, he concluded his speech with a proverb: "If you are fleeing from your enemy with your tent and all your possessions are loaded on your horse, and you see that the enemy is getting closer, you have two alternatives: either to fall into your enemy's hands with all your goods or to try to escape by throwing off your possessions one by one.

And I want you to know," Abdullah said, turning directly to his ministers, "that I have invited our Israeli friends here in order to throw bundles to them."

As the king withdrew to await the final draft of the secret Israeli-Jordanian agreement, Lieutenant Colonel Charles Coaker, a British officer of the Arab Legion, was brought into the discussions. He pored over the map that Yadin had previously marked, closely discussing with him each territorial change. While the major alterations in the northern sector were accepted without question, Coaker pressed Yadin to make a cosmetic shift in the Hebron region so that the king might claim at least some territorial gain. As usual, the most important element for Abdullah was the retention of villages; the farmland from which those villages subsisted was readily dispensable. Yadin agreed to turn over the relatively minor village of Tell Beit Mirsim—while retaining for Israel the village's fields and a famous archaeological site. After additional agreements that Israel would protect the rights of the civilian populations in the transferred villages and compensate the Arab Legion for the construction of a new road, the negotiations were concluded and the secret agreement was signed. Sometime after two in the morning, the king reappeared to congratulate all those present and to distribute roses to the Israelis. Once more, Abdullah et-Tell drove them back from Shuneh to Jerusalem, and at dawn they were in Tel Aviv to report their success to Ben-Gurion.

The agreement was, according to Eytan, "too good to be true and I shall not believe in its reality completely until the time comes for it to be implemented." But an additional condition remained: The agreement was subject to the final ratification of Prime Minister Tawfiq Abul Huda, who had been in Beirut during the negotiations. Abul Huda was aghast at the terms Abdullah had agreed to and was determined to try to get the Israelis to alter them. Accordingly, on the evening of March 30, the Israeli delegation returned to Shuneh and were met by a much more determined Jordanian delegation, led by Abul Huda and Fawzi el-Mulki, the minister of defense. Abul Huda and el-Mulki urged the Israelis to consider the political implications of their agreement; they argued that the king would face dangerous criticism for giving up so many villages and leaving their inhabitants to an uncertain future, without receiving anything meaningful in return. The king, in the meantime, was determined to conclude the agreement and repeatedly came into the negotiating room to check on its progress, dressed in a long white nightgown. Yadin later remembered a particularly uncomfortable conversation at the very end of the negotiations, a desperate appeal for just one well-known village, Beit Jibrin, burial place of one of Muhammed's closest followers, Tamim Abu Ruqayya. "When we were about to sign the agreement,"

Yadin recalled, "Abdullah came in, put his hand on my shoulder, hugged me, and almost begged, 'O Yadin, give me Beit Jibrin. Tomorrow is my birthday. Give me Beit Jibrin as a birthday present!' " But Yadin had his orders and could not yield, not even to a royal request. "I said to the king," Yadin continued, " 'Who am I? You're a king and I'm a dog. Even if I said I'd give Beit Jibrin to you, they'd fire me tomorrow and wouldn't give you anything.' " Abdullah and his ministers resigned themselves to the inevitable, and shortly before four in the morning the agreement was signed. The Israeli victory was total—so total, in fact, that both Eytan and Yadin had silent second thoughts.

"Both Yadin and I were acutely conscious of the Transjordanians' right to take up the positions they did," Eytan admitted in a long letter to Sharett. "We were, after all, discussing the future of villages that were wholly Arab in population and situated in territory under Arab control. In spite of all guarantees and fine phrases, it was as clear to the Transjordanians as to us that the people of these villages were likely to become refugees as soon as the Iraqis withdrew, and possibly even before." But all that mattered now was strategic advantage. The agreement at Shuneh soon became the basis of an agreement at Rhodes. The talks there had been stalled for weeks, but suddenly—miraculously, it must have seemed to the international press corps lounging in the lobby of the Hôtel des Roses—the deadlock broke. On April 3, at a joint meeting of the Jordanian and Israeli delegations, the text of the Shuneh agreement—rewritten by Bunche in suitable UN language—officially adjusted the ceasefire line to Israel's advantage in Samaria and tacitly ratified Jordan's annexation of much of the West Bank. Despite bitter criticism of the agreement from hard-liners in both Jordan and Israel (Begin angrily called for a no-confidence vote in the Knesset for the abandonment of such a large part of the Land of Israel), the agreement satisfied policy-makers in Washington and London, and that was enough. Yigael Yadin had once more helped shape the modern history of the region. With the de facto partition of the country between Israel and the Hashemite kingdom of Jordan, the 1947 UN partition plan—with its provisions for an independent Arab state in Palestine—was dead.

―――――

Driving back across the Allenby Bridge in the predawn darkness, Abdullah et-Tell was in high spirits. As a young military man with great ambitions and a court favorite of King Abdullah, he harbored heroic visions of leading a Transjordanian conquest of Syria. On several occasions Tell had revealed his thinking to Yadin and the other Israeli representatives; he claimed that an attack on Syria would be an easy military undertaking.

He boasted that he had learned that there was only one company defending Damascus—and that he could conquer the entire country with a single battalion. But this evening, he seemed more eager for action than ever. Earlier in the day word had come that the Syrian chief of staff, Husni el-Zaim, had toppled the civilian government in a sudden, violent coup d'état. Now that an Israeli-Jordanian agreement had been concluded, Tell asked his guests what their attitude would be if Abdullah marched on Damascus. More to the point, he wanted to know if the government of Israel would help. "Lend us a few planes for a single night," Tell suggested. "We'll paint them with Jordanian colors; we'll make an impression on the Syrians; and then we'll return all the planes to you." The idea was too dangerous and too absurd for the Israelis to take seriously, since the Syrians were the next on the Israelis' negotiating list.

Of all of Israel's military enemies, Syria alone occupied territory that had been allotted to the Jewish state by the 1947 UN partition plan. Although the Syrian invasion force had been beaten back from the gates of Deganiah in the first week of the war, it had regrouped and attacked another sector and had conquered three small tracts of Palestinian territory: near the headwaters of the Jordan River; near the southeast coast of the Sea of Galilee; and on the west side of the Huleh Valley, overrunning the Israeli settlement of Mishmar Hayarden. More was at stake here between Israel and Syria than national honor; the contested areas included rich water resources, which in the Middle East had a value beyond reckoning. Ten days before the coup that deposed him, Syrian president Shukri el-Quwwatli informed Ralph Bunche of Syria's readiness to open direct armistice negotiations with Israel. Syria was determined to negotiate at its own speed and on its own terms. Refusing to meet the Israelis at the Hôtel des Roses in the distant Aegean, the Syrians insisted that the talks be held in a tent at Khirbet Yarda, set up between opposing front lines. And even after President el-Quwwatli's precipitous fall from power, their decision to open negotiations with the Israelis was not reversed.

The new Syrian leader, General Husni el-Zaim, had greater ambitions for his country than self-defeating rhetorical supremacy in inter-Arab politics. He recognized the disastrous consequences of further fighting with Israel and looked forward to a new era of altered power alignments in the Middle East. As he confided to American diplomats in Damascus, he hoped to forge a military and economic alliance with the United States, which he recognized as the rising superpower in the region. There were certainly some indications that the new Syrian leader might be open to compromise with Israel. As a member of Syria's Kurdish minority, el-Zaim was not bound to pan-Arabism's political imperatives. As a would-be domestic reformer, he needed a period of lessened military tension with Israel, particularly since Israel had already reached agreements with Egypt, Lebanon, and Jordan.

On April 5, when the first meeting between Israelis and Syrians was held under the mediation of Bunche's deputy Henri Vigier, it was clear that much hard bargaining lay ahead. On the Israeli side was the same team that had successfully concluded the armistice talks with Lebanon—Yehoshua Palmon of the Foreign Ministry and Colonel Mordecai Makleff. On the Syrian side were Colonel Selo Fawzi and Commander Muhammad Nasser, the latter an outspoken protégé of General el-Zaim. While Israel demanded complete Syrian withdrawal to the former international boundary east of the Jordan, the Syrians—like the Israelis in their negotiations with Egypt and Jordan—insisted that only the current military positions could be the basis for the official armistice lines. At the increasingly tense confrontations the two delegations merely restated their positions, and Vigier seemed at a loss to bridge the gap. Then came an unexpected personal initiative: in a private conversation with Palmon and Makleff one of the Syrian representatives suggested that the two sides might dispense with these tiresome armistice talks and go directly to a peace treaty—including an immediate exchange of ambassadors, economic ties, and even a military alliance between Syria and Israel—if only Israel would agree to share the Huleh, the Upper Jordan, and the Sea of Galilee.

Though informed of el-Zaim's offer, Ben-Gurion insisted on a total Syrian withdrawal; once that was accomplished, he promised, the wider terms of peace could be addressed. The Syrians were eager to come to an agreement despite their adamant public position, and after one of the formal sessions Colonel Nasser quietly approached Palmon and suggested that the deadlock be broken in a face-to-face meeting between el-Zaim and Ben-Gurion. Though Ben-Gurion was still skeptical of el-Zaim's ulterior motives, he agreed to a secret meeting at a lower level. Thus, on May 5, Yigael Yadin and Reuven Shiloah were dispatched to Rosh Pinna, where they met for several hours with Colonel Nasser, but the position of neither side changed. International pressure began to mount against Israel, and American officials unsubtly let it be known that they favored some boundary alteration between Syria and Israel. But the deadlock continued. On May 17, when the Syrian and Israeli positions were once again presented with no significant changes, Vigier adjourned the talks indefinitely. By this time the Syrians were considering some unconventional options. El-Zaim's protégé, Colonel Nasser, secretly approached one of the junior Israeli delegates and suggested a Syrian-style conspiracy. He promised arms, trained troops, and financial support in the "millions" if the officer could buy Makleff and Yadin's cooperation in assassinating Ben-Gurion and backing their rise to power in Israel by military coup d'état. This bizarre idea had no takers. And it was months before an acceptable armistice arrangement between Israel and Syria was finally worked out.

Eventually, Ralph Bunche stepped forward, proposing a characteristically ingenious compromise. The armistice line, he suggested, would be along the lines of the current miltiary positions (as the Syrians demanded), but the area between it and the international boundary would be demilitarized and resettled by its civilian population (requiring the withdrawal of the Syrian troops, as the Israelis demanded). Leaving the question of sovereignty intentionally open, the proposal was accepted and signed by both delegations on July 20, bringing the last of the 1949 armistice talks to a successful conclusion. Though serious conflicts over water rights in the Upper Jordan Valley would continue, the negotiations with Syria had at least ended the threat of imminent hostilities. The territorial shape of Israel had now been at least tacitly ratified in signed agreements with all the neighboring Arab states. But the talks with Syria taught an important lesson: Direct deals with Arab leaders would have to be made with the utmost caution. On August 14, less than a month after the conclusion of the armistice agreement, Syrian president Husni el-Zaim was overthrown.

In the meantime, however, Yadin was dispatched on another diplomatic assignment—to accompany Walter Eytan to the meeting of the UN Palestine Conciliation Commission (PCC) in Lausanne, Switzerland. This meeting was doomed to failure. In sharp contrast to Ralph Bunche's technique of mediating bilateral armistice agreements, the PCC convened a single megaconference to settle all outstanding diplomatic problems in one fell swoop. To save time and effort, the PCC decided to consult the Arab nations *together,* forcing Egypt, Lebanon, Syria, and Jordan to abandon their individual interests, at least publicly. Under the umbrella of the Arab League they clung to the same kind of pan-Arab position that had led them to a disastrous war in Palestine. Their joint position was that all the Palestinian Arab refugees would have to be repatriated before any peace talks with Israel could possibly begin. When the PCC solicited the opening position of the State of Israel, Ben-Gurion and Sharett both insisted that a secure peace would have to be established before the issue of the refugees could be addressed. A vicious cycle of recriminations was begun—and continued long after. With the progress achieved in the armistice talks now frozen, Israel found itself suspended in a state of no-peace-no-war, as were the hundreds of thousands of Palestinian Arab refugees crowded into temporary camps in the West Bank and Gaza Strip. In September the Lausanne conference adjourned, having achieved nothing. In the following months hopes for peace quickly faded. More and more it seemed to Yadin and the other Israeli military planners that the Arab world had every intention of resuming the armed struggle—and that Israel too would have to prepare for war.

In early June 1949, during a break from the Lausanne conference, Yadin quietly visited Prague as an official guest of the Czech government. The self-proclaimed foreign policy orientation of the State of Israel was neutral in the cold war. Jewish immigration and arms shipments from Eastern Europe were continuing without interruption, and the Israeli leadership was unwilling to do anything to alienate the Soviet Union. During his Prague visit Yadin first experienced the trappings of power—mixing easily with the generals of the Czech armed forces, visiting major bases, and reviewing troops. Back in Switzerland he received similar treatment. Intrigued by the reserve system of the Swiss army as a possible model for the IDF, he contacted the army's general staff and, after a detailed briefing, was invited to lecture on the campaigns of the recent Arab-Israeli war. By the time he returned to Israel in August, he had completely abandoned the old egalitarian Haganah ethos and was ready to take an active role in reorganizing and streamlining the Israeli army. And by that time, Ben-Gurion had decided to entrust the future of the IDF to Yigael Yadin.

Among the biblical images and desert legends spawned by the first all-out war between Arabs and Israelis, the stereotype of the dashing young sabra officer at the head of a victorious Jewish army became a standard of pulp novels and action movies for decades. Idealism, ingenuity, and dedication were his weapons; mindless Middle Eastern radicalism, fanaticism, and violence were his foes. Naturally the line between Israeli and Arab, between West and East, between Light and Darkness was drawn far too sharply to provide any understanding of the conflict. Like most literary creations, it fulfilled a political and ideological function; it became an active element in waging the war by other means. For in the early months of 1949, Israel faced a difficult challenge. Its leaders were convinced that the Arab world was unrelentingly hostile to the existence of a Jewish State and that continuing warfare was likely. They were determined to maintain military power that could be unleashed on command against their defeated but uncowed neighbors—and at the same time to reduce substantially the dangerous economic burden of a fully mobilized army that had swollen to almost 100,000 in a total civilian population of little more than 600,000.

Ben-Gurion, as usual, had a clear vision of the future. "If the war ends tomorrow and peace emerges," he had told the general staff officers on the eve of Yadin's departure for the Rhodes armistice talks, "and we can break up the army, that will all be fine with me. But the possibility is unlikely. We have to assume that there will be other wars—and even if we win them—there will still not be peace and an army will be necessary." It was already clear to Ben-Gurion that the Arab states could effectively fight Israel through means other than battlefield offensives: by an economic boycott and a steady war of economic attrition, and by forcing Israel to keep its troops fully mobilized. "If we don't find a way to make significant cuts," Ben-Gurion continued, "we might win the battle and also suffer a decisive defeat. The existing economy is being destroyed, because we can't bear the present financial burden; there are no workers for the citrus harvest, for the farms, for the building trades, or for civilian industry." His solution was to streamline the administrative and service units of the army that had been built with such great effort during the later stages of the war.

The first major round of discharges was planned for the end of December 1948, but the process bogged down and the only soldiers released in early January were those in low ranks, the sick, wounded, the oldest, and those with pressing family responsibilities. Ben-Gurion was intent on reducing troop levels by 10,000 as soon as possible, but Yadin emerged as an outspoken opponent, considering that cut to be far too drastic. If Ben-Gurion's proposal were adopted, Yadin insisted, it would be impossible to maintain proper garrisons throughout the territory that had come under Israeli control. And if that were the case, there would be no point holding on to all of it. Yet at this time, Ben-Gurion and Chief of Staff Dori overruled Yadin.

The cuts were only just beginning. After armistice agreements were signed with Egypt, Lebanon, Jordan, and Syria, the likelihood of renewed conflict faded at least for the immediate future, and Chief of Staff Dori proposed to cut the standing army by half again, down to 45,000 men. Yadin, by this time, was largely left out of the planning. Since he steadfastly clung to his earlier objections, the reorganization was entrusted to a special committee of other members of the general staff. In fact, the long and close relationship between Dori and Yadin suffered as Yadin continued to object to the far-reaching cuts. The tension between them grew to the point that early in April, Yadin tendered his resignation to Ben-Gurion. Even though Dori would have been perfectly happy to replace Yadin with the up-and-coming Mordecai Makleff, Ben-Gurion was not ready to dispense with Yigael Yadin quite yet.

The growing conflict between Yadin and his superiors was not limited to administrative matters. During the war, while Dori had been in his sickbed and Ben-Gurion had paid attention only to grand strategy, the operations branch had enjoyed almost unlimited autonomy in planning small, impromptu combat actions and communicating them to field commanders. Through the spring of 1949, Yadin continued to exercise this prerogative, ordering occasional retaliatory forays against the Syrian front lines. But in the midst of delicate armistice negotiations and the ever-present threat of UN condemnation, Ben-Gurion acted quickly to rein in the chief of operations. After one particularly provocative foray Ben-Gurion issued instructions that Yadin was no longer authorized to order attacks across the international border without the explicit approval of both the defense minister and the chief of staff. To head off Yadin's renewed threat of resignation, Ben-Gurion had appointed him to join Walter Eytan at the PCC conference in Lausanne.

During the summer, while Yadin was away at the Lausanne conference and touring the bases of the Swiss and Czech armies, it was Dori who began to disappoint Ben-Gurion. On June 1 a major army reorganization got under way, aimed at an eventual reduction from sixteen to three brigades and active manpower levels down to 20,000. This would entail a massive demobilization of soldiers, the transfer of units from one end of the country to the other, and a nightmarish logistical and bureaucratic effort to keep it all under control. By September, little progress had been made in the vast operation. The troop level still stood at 40,000—double the number demanded by the economists and budget planners of the Finance Ministry. Even more troubling to Ben-Gurion were indications that this was not just a matter of slow implementation. Operational plans were still being drawn up for a total force of 30,000, even though no formal approval had been sought for this level from either the Finance or the Defense Ministry.

Finally at the end of the summer Ben-Gurion made up his mind that the army needed a more energetic and aggressive chief of staff. Dori had always been a gray if reliable presence. The reforms that now had to be accomplished, however, required a younger man's energy and skills. The popular choice of the field commanders was thirty-one-year-old Yigal Allon, who had demonstrated his leadership skills in battle and who, more than any other single officer, was responsible for Israel's victorious campaigns on the northern, central, and southern fronts. Allon's long association with the Palmach and his unembarrassed political association with the left-wing Mapam party, however, disqualified him from promotion in Ben-Gurion's wary eyes. He scanned the list of other possibilities and conferred with officers who had gained his trust during the war.

Chaim Laskov and Mordecai Makleff were among his favorite advisers, and they urged him to give the command to Yadin, so long as "he will take it upon himself to execute faithfully the government plan." Despite Yadin's bitter opposition to the extent of the planned cuts, they were confident that Ben-Gurion would be able to exercise a guiding influence over him.

On August 26, Yadin arrived at Ben-Gurion's office for a private chat about the future. He seemed pleased with the prospect of succeeding Dori as the chief of staff, and instead of offering angry objections to Ben-Gurion's planned changes in the army's structure, he quickly demonstrated his loyalty. Ben-Gurion described what he believed should be the future foundations of the IDF: administrative and professional efficiency (on a standard fully equal to the best armies in the world); a spirit of pioneering self-sacrifice; and the absolute absence of partisan politics. The last principle was of crucial importance to Ben-Gurion, since he had recently ordered the dismantling of the Palmach and had been bitterly attacked for carrying out a political purge. Yadin now had no objections to these three principles and announced his readiness to take on the responsibilities of chief of staff. He requested only that Ben-Gurion carry out the last of his personnel changes—the abrupt replacement of Yigal Allon with Moshe Dayan on the southern front—before his appointment was formalized.

In a quiet ceremony in Jerusalem on November 9, 1949, the transition was made from one generation to another. The rancor of the previous spring had been forgotten as Yadin chatted casually with Dori in an anteroom to the prime minister's office, glasses of orange juice in hand. The physical contrast between Dori, wearing a somber formal uniform with dark, baggy jacket, and Yadin in a open-necked khaki military shirt with sleeves rolled up, was startling. It was a contrast between age and youth, between exhaustion and energy. Soon the new members of the general staff arrived, hand-picked by Yadin from among his colleagues (and occasional detractors) during the course of the war. There was Shlomo Shamir, now dressed in the white uniform of a naval commander, assigned to bring the navy under disciplined control. There was Mordecai Makleff, Ben-Gurion's secret favorite, entrusted with the dual titles of chief of operations and deputy chief of staff. There was Chaim Laskov as new head of the training department, and Chaim Herzog as head of military intelligence. Most recognizable of all was the new southern front commander, Moshe Dayan, with the black eyepatch that had already become his trademark.

Yadin, seated next to Ben-Gurion for the formal group portrait, turned to the camera with a confident smile. His first order of the day revealed decisiveness and confrontation. "Soldiers of the Israel Defense Forces, on land, in the air, and at sea," he announced, "in recognition of the great responsibility that has been placed on me, I turn to you to intensify your efforts to achieve your mission and fulfill the great tasks and challenges placed on us today. The leaders of the Arab states and their advisers are even now rattling their swords for a second round. Our faces are turned toward peace, but we are ready for war." Chief of Staff with the IDF's highest rank of rav aluf, Yadin would soon be subject to intense pressure not only from the Arab states but from the changing tides of East-West confrontation, and from domestic political struggles as well. At thirty-two Yadin had reached the top of the military establishment, and many forces and many individuals would soon be eager to see him fall. His most powerful potential adversary was even then sitting right next to him, with a smile even broader and more confident than his own. Prime Minister and Defense Minister David Ben-Gurion was now at the height of his power. He was prepared to give full backing to Yigael Yadin as chief of staff only so long as he did not threaten his own control over military affairs.

Chapter Nine

CHIEF OF STAFF

Frightening visions of billowing mushroom clouds, Russian tanks sweeping westward across Europe, and a Red Menace spreading in East Asia kept diplomats and policy planners sleepless in London and Washington through the autumn of 1949. One by one, the nations of Eastern Europe receded behind what Churchill had called an iron curtain. In the Far East a bamboo curtain had risen as well. In preparation for what seemed an imminent superpower conflict, Western military commanders hurriedly mobilized forces, forged new military alliances, and drafted plans for regional defense. Washington and Whitehall considered the Middle East, with its oil resources and vital shipping lanes through Suez, to be an obvious target for Soviet expansion, but old policies and attitudes had to be changed. In late 1949 the military capability of Britain's traditional Arab allies was badly damaged and the Israel Defense Forces was the most significant military factor in the area. Therein lay the problem. The continuing flow of arms and immigrants from the Soviet bloc into Israel made its allegiance in the East-West conflict dangerously suspect. It therefore must have been something of a relief to U.S. ambassador James G. McDonald when he paid his first courtesy call on the newly appointed IDF chief of staff to find "a tall, slim, handsome figure" who offered a welcome reassuring image to the conservative cold warriors of the Western world.

"We were greeted at the door by Mrs. Yadin," McDonald recorded in his diary on November 15, 1949, noting that the twenty-eight-year-old woman, clad casually in slacks and not in the pearls and prim dress of the wives of high-ranking American officers, "looked like a high school girl." The tall, white-haired, patrician McDonald was quickly ushered into the living room of the Yadins' modest Tel Aviv apartment, where "after tea," McDonald noted, "Yadin launched into approximately an hour's talk about the military situation in the Middle East." The American diplomat was eager to sound out the new Israeli commander on Israel's role in the East-West conflict, but Yadin concentrated on Israel's place in the Middle East. He warned McDonald that the intensive British rearmament of Jordan, Iraq, and Egypt—not Soviet expansionism—was the gravest threat facing Israel. If war were to break out again, Yadin assured his visitor, "Israeli forces would seek to drive deep into enemy territory." This was meant to be a clear warning to McDonald, to his superiors in Washington, and to their colleagues in London that Israel was determined to maintain unquestioned military dominance in the area—even if that meant toppling the delicate balance of power and perhaps even driving some of the Arab states into the Soviet Union's warm socialist embrace.

Though his rhetoric was uncompromising, something about Yadin's background and manner seemed reassuring to the American diplomat. After their grim political discussion, Yadin led McDonald and the American military attaché who accompanied him "out onto the balcony," where, McDonald noted, "the family clothesline was stretched above our heads." Expounding on the history and ancient landscape of the country in terms as definitive as those of his earlier monologue on tanks, airplanes, and artillery, Yadin pointed into the distance toward the ancient mound of Tell Qasile. There, he explained, Dr. Benjamin Mazar (formerly Maisler) and a group of Hebrew University students were now uncovering the remains of a Philistine city that had become a part of the Israelite kingdom in the later Iron Age. This mix of past and present, too, offered seductive reassurance for the rise of a modern Jewish state. Israel's image so long linked with the socialist rhetoric of Labor Zionism and with the revolutionary ideals of the Palmach and the kibbutz movement became more acceptable in conservative Western eyes in the hands of archaeologist-soldier Rav Aluf Yigael Yadin. "Thus the talk and thus the man," McDonald concluded in admiration for the thirty-five-year-old commander; "informal, quiet, studious, Yadin remained for me the professor rather than the general."

That professor would soon apply his talents primarily to organization and administration. In his first few months as chief of staff Yadin's task was to oversee a far-reaching reorganization of the IDF that would allow it simultaneously to confront Arab hostility, lessen its burden on the domestic economy, and maintain its image of strength and efficiency in the eyes of the world. Now that Allon and many of the outspoken Palmach officers had returned to their kibbutzim or to civilian careers, internal political tensions within the officers' corps had greatly lessened. Ben-Gurion's long-standing goal of purging the army of overt political opponents had finally been achieved. Yadin's challenge was now to reshape the command structure so as to clearly subordinate all field commands and special services to the general staff. To this end he recruited experienced British veterans—for the most part colorless but hard-working headquarters officers—to establish schedules, routines, and standards for the general staff's painstaking bureaucratic work. After a tense head-to-head confrontation with Air Force Commander Aharon Remez (in a secret meeting arranged by Ben-Gurion on a battleship off Haifa), Yadin stripped the air force of its independent command structure and brought it under the direct control of the general staff.

Once the supremacy of the general staff was established and the standing army reduced to acceptable levels, the most pressing objective was the creation of a reserve system for the rapid mobilization of forces. To Yadin a "second round" in the Arab-Israeli conflict seemed inevitable, and now that the standing army consisted of only three brigades, the border police, and a small air force and navy, it could not possibly defend the long armistice lines against concerted attack by Lebanon, Syria, Jordan, and Egypt, much less mount a counterattack. During the War of Independence all economic and social considerations had been put aside as the nation mobilized against local and volunteer Arab forces, then against the invading Arab states. Never again would such a haphazard, emotion-driven mobilization be possible; it was Yadin's task to lay the foundations of a system that could be activated quickly and efficiently. Here his quick grasp of concepts and his ability to envision their application on a massive scale could be seen. During his visit to Lausanne, touring Swiss army bases and lecturing to the generals, Yadin had been deeply impressed with the Swiss reserve system, in which civilian reserve units were not merely auxiliaries for the mobilized troops but formed the core of the army. In the IDF reserve system, as in the Swiss, the standing army would become an intensive training program to produce future soldiers for the reserves. There was in this system also an unspoken similarity to the methods of the Haganah in its underground days, when intensive officer training courses had provided a high standard of leadership for the reserve units mobilized in towns and settlements.

This far-reaching organizational development did not take place in a vacuum. As Yadin and his staff were drafting plans and debating the size and composition of the reserve units, the cold war was affecting the general tenor of military activity in the Middle East. Israel had continued to protest the British rearmament of Iraq, Egypt, and Jordan—and implicitly threatened to take action against those nations. As a result, on May 25, 1950, the governments of the United States, Great Britain, and France issued a Tripartite Declaration that, to keep both Israelis and Arabs from seeking an alliance with the Soviet Union, guaranteed the present armistice lines and promised to maintain (through regulated arms sales) a balance of military power in the region. Israel's neutrality in the East-West conflict was quickly giving way to a pro-Western position, expressed unambiguously and openly for the first time in its announcement of support for UN (essentially American) intervention in the Korean war. The British were already hedging their bets in the Middle East, and after de jure recognition of Israel in April, arms sales to the IDF were officially approved by the British Cabinet. In October, Yadin conferred with the visiting British secretary of state for air on a subject that would have been unthinkable just a year before: the establishment of British bases on Israeli territory in time of war. Israel's military power was increasingly recognized in Western circles. Yadin's carefully crafted reserve system—now ready to be put into action—offered an impressive display of military strength to the West.

On October 15, 1950, precisely two years after the beginning of Operation Ten Plagues against the Egyptian army, an even more massive maneuver called Operation First Fruits began. Shortly before midnight, in a surprise national mobilization, call-up orders for all reserve units were dispatched to the nation's newspapers for immediate publication; other orders were transmitted by messenger and word of mouth. It was an experiment in mobilizing all available manpower for a military operation; more than 75,000 civilians were roused out of their beds, summoned from schools, shops, farms, and factories, to participate in extensive maneuvers. At dawn on the first day of the exercise the country's roads were filled with trucks, private cars, and taxis that had been expropriated for national service and were now driven by army personnel to designated deployment sites. Special government regulations gave mobilized soldiers priority on all means of public transport, and detachments of military police were sent to apprehend citizens who knowingly disregarded the call to arms. "We must not slacken our efforts in the defense of the State," Chief of Staff Yadin announced to the nation, "in view of the fact that our enemies who are arming themselves have not yet made peace. All the work and the effort that have been put into the organization of the army—the regular and reserve forces and all its branches—will now be put to the test."

Nine days later, at the successful conclusion of the air, naval, and ground force exercises, Ben-Gurion expressed satisfaction at Operation First Fruits. "The maneuvers proved that we have something we can rely on," he told reporters. While he denied that the exercise had been intended as a provocative show of power, he added pointedly that if it "proved that a force existed—we can only be glad of it." Indeed, Israel was determined to show that it would not peacefully be integrated into a regional defense alliance without first looking out for itself. Despite continuing British and American efforts to facilitate a more permanent peace settlement between Israel and Jordan, negotiations had broken down in a tangle of disagreements about Israeli access to the Dead Sea and East Jerusalem, and Jordanian hopes for territorial control of the Negev and free passage to the Mediterranean Sea. Moshe Dayan, the southern front commander, was active in these negotiations. With Yadin's continuing support (and experience gained in the earlier round of negotiations with Abdullah), Dayan opposed significant compromise with Transjordan, insisting that Israel had the power to obtain its objectives by force.

In many places along the arbitrary armistice line between Israel and Jordan, unauthorized and in some cases hostile border crossings became sites of tension. Some of the infiltrators from Jordan were clearly motivated by military objectives, laying explosives or opening fire on Israeli settlers. In many cases, however, they were neither criminals nor commandos but civilian refugees who had simply crossed into Israel to visit their homes and property, retrieve hidden money or possessions, or gather crops from their former orchards and fields. Yadin ordered sharp, stinging reprisal raids to discourage these infiltrations and instructed the field commanders to defend Israel's other territorial claims by force. At the end of August 1950, Israeli and Jordanian forces clashed briefly over disputed lands in the northern Jordan valley. A far more serious incident took place in the south in December. A detachment of the Arab Legion, claiming that Israel had appropriated Jordanian territory in the Arava Valley, blocked a four-kilometer stretch of the new road to Eilat. After receiving Dayan's initial report, Yadin quickly dispatched his deputy Makleff to confer with Ben-Gurion, who was then vacationing in Greece. Yadin received authorization to clear the Jordanian obstruction, by force if necessary. After an Israeli ultimatum and a brief exchange of fire at Kilometer 78 of the Arava Road, the Arab Legion retreated. It apparently did not matter to the Israeli military and political leadership that the Jordanian contention was later found to be correct by UN surveyors, or that this demonstration of power caused a further weakening and isolation of King Abdullah, the only Arab ruler willing even to contemplate a peace treaty with Israel. Power seemed far more persuasive than diplomacy; even Abdullah's longtime British patrons were now enamored of Israel's image of military strength.

With the intensification of fighting in Korea and heightened East-West tensions in Europe, the British Foreign Office decided to move decisively toward a closer alliance with Israel. Early in 1951, British and American military commanders met on Malta and determined that NATO's southern, Mediterranean flank was dangerously vulnerable and that the Israeli forces would have to be integrated into Western defensive preparations. American authorities inquired of the Israeli government whether it would provide facilities for strategic stockpiles, and the British commander of Middle Eastern forces, Sir Brian Robertson, visited Israel to discuss urgent military matters with Chief of Staff Yadin.

For the Arab nations and the world, the visit of General Robertson was a symbolic validation that the Israeli army had come of age. For Yadin and his staff, it was a first encounter in the subtleties of military protocol. In the days before Robertson's arrival, the British military attaché in Tel Aviv duly presented Yadin's aide-de-camp, Captain Netanel Lorch, with a list of the various dress uniforms that the British commander would wear at each scheduled event. Up to that point the Israeli army had only one variation of uniform—"with the khaki sleeve either rolled up or down," Lorch recalled—so Yadin quickly called in a local tailor to design and create impromptu dress uniforms for the eleven highest-ranking IDF officers. Despite loud and angry demonstrations that Mapam and the Israeli Communist party organized to protest the arrival of the British commander, Yadin clearly relished the opportunity to accompany Robertson on extensive tours of IDF facilities and reviews of Israeli troops. Ben-Gurion, however, was not seduced by ritual as easily as Yadin. During a meeting attended by Ben-Gurion, Foreign Minister Sharett, Yadin, and Robertson, the prime minister asked the British commander point-blank what his government intended to do if a war with the Soviet Union broke out in the Middle East. Robertson explained that the latest intelligence reports predicted a rapid drive southward by Soviet forces toward Iraq and the Persian Gulf; in response, NATO forces would launch a counterattack from British bases in Egypt, by way of Israel and Jordan, toward Iraq.

Ben-Gurion exploded in fury. "How can you talk in that way?" he reprimanded the British commander like a schoolboy. "Do you think you have Israel in your pocket? Do you think we are a British colony?" The State of Israel was not willing to serve an international coalition unquestioningly, without guarantees of its own freedom of action or enhancements of its own security position. "Israel is a small country," Ben-Gurion continued, "but it is an independent state. And before you decide to use it as transit route for your armies, you're going to have to negotiate with us." Robertson was suitably chastened, but in the coming years the potentially explosive tension between the superpowers, the continuing hostility of the Arab states toward Israel, and Israel's unhesitating use of military force as an instrument of political persuasion created a dangerous and delicate balance of power in the Middle East.

———

Ben-Gurion's grand strategy for the establishment of Israeli independence was not based on military power alone. His defense of the sovereignty of the State of Israel against superpower encroachment was also based on his notion of Israel's future economic role in the Middle East. In his far-reaching, largely desocialized Zionist vision, the prime minister saw the Jewish people emerging from economic dependence to take their place at last as a sovereign economy—a respected and prosperous participant in the world's international marketplace. Just as British military officials had come to the conclusion that the IDF was a potentially powerful ally, so did British political advisers see a clear advantage in economic cooperation with the Jewish state. In December 1950, Sir Thomas Rapp, the new head of the Middle East Office of the British Foreign Ministry, concluded after a brief visit that the people of Israel—in contrast to the Arab nations of the region—possessed "superabundant energy applied with a fixity of purpose transcending all sectional differences to the creation of a highly-organized state." Ben-Gurion's almost messianic vision of futuristic cities, blooming deserts, and a cultural renaissance born of scientific achievement would be realized only later. First, a complex tangle of pressing social and fiscal problems had to be overcome.

Never in the history of the Zionist movement was the scale of Jewish immigration so overwhelming as now. Within the first three years of Israel's existence, its Jewish population almost doubled, as more than half a million immigrants arrived from Eastern Europe, North Africa,

Yemen, Iraq, and Iran. The country's human landscape—not to speak of its physical appearance—was dramatically changing. As towns and agricultural settlements were established and the sites of former Arab villages were bulldozed, fenced off, or converted to new uses, the State of Israel became a progressively more rooted reality. The economic consequences for the citizens, however, were painful. The economy had hardly recovered from the devastating expense of the war and the damage caused to roads, factories, and water and electric systems; at the same time large amounts of capital were required to provide housing, employment, education, and health services for the hundreds of thousands of immigrants. In the spring of 1949, the government embarked on a strict austerity plan, the Tzena, to reduce public consumption by strict price controls and food rationing. By the summer of 1950, despite patriotic exhortations and rousing folksongs (among them "Tzena, Tzena, Tzena," later to become a standard in the American folk repertoire), the austerity plan aroused anger, evasion, strikes, and black marketeering. Rationing and price controls were extended to clothing and footwear, even as wage levels continued to drop.

During this period the army's role in civilian life was expanding. The Security Service Law of 1949 widened conscription to include virtually all young men and women reaching eighteen—with a one-year basic training and service period for women, two years for men, and continuing service in reserve units for yearly exercises and emergency call-ups until age forty-five. The ideals of pioneering agricultural work and army service were eventually institutionalized in the army branch known as Nahal, an acronym for the Hebrew words for "Fighting, Pioneering Youth." Yadin was an energetic advocate of widened educational and cultural activities in the army. He established an army radio station and monthly magazine and conferred with RCA chairman David Sarnoff, then visiting Israel, about the possibility of setting up an army television broadcasting facility. To answer the common complaints of mobilized soldiers whose families were suffering economic hardships, Yadin approved the establishment of a chain of army stores that sold nonrationed items to military families at a significant discount.

But these were all mere institutional improvements. Yadin had a far more sweeping vision of the IDF's role in Israeli society. He took enormous pride in the Nahal units, which established communal settlements and worked the land in thinly settled border areas, characterizing this force of farmer-fighters as "an army that grows tomatoes," an original creation of the State of Israel without parallel in the world. Pointing to the success of the reserve system and the wholehearted dedication of the general public to it, he characterized the Israeli citizen as "a soldier on eleven months' leave." Speaking before an audience of high school teachers in March 1950, Yadin suggested that a revolution had to take place in the nation's educational system in order to prepare students for army service. He urged them to stress mathematical and scientific subjects that might have immediate utility for the IDF special branches. Suggesting a change in the style if not the substance of Israeli education, he urged, for example, that high school mathematics teachers end the standard algebra exercises that calculated the profit and loss of anonymous shopkeepers and replace them with calculations of the relative speed of air force planes flying from Base A to Base B. "When young people get used to thinking about this type of problem," he added, "they will serve the nation more effectively and they will be ready for active duty in a shorter time."

Objections were quick in coming. An editorial writer for *The Jerusalem Post,* openly hostile to Yadin's algebra suggestions, argued that Israel's fighting spirit had not been established and would not be maintained "through such superficialities." Other commentators denounced Yadin's apparent intention to transform Israel into a modern Sparta, with the citizens' identity shaped primarily by the military experience. Other critics came from within the political establishment, unwilling to share Yadin's vision of a modern technocratic state. Years later, Yadin delighted in repeating the objections of a leader of the Orthodox party Agudat Israel to his proposal to introduce television broadcasting. "I am shocked that the Chief of Staff would propose such a thing," the party leader reportedly announced in outrage, "If we were to have television, all our enemies could see what was going on here." Ben-Gurion repeatedly came to Yadin's defense, attacking "the insipid prattle of the critics of the military." For while the army had successfully carried out massive reserve exercises and had gained the attention of the world for its competence and efficiency, the government bureaucracy and private sector were proving pitifully unequal to the challenges they faced.

By late summer 1950, the government's austerity plan was clearly failing. Shopkeepers began a general strike to protest mounting price controls, bureaucratic restrictions, and the scarcity of many consumer goods. In even the most respectable neighborhoods, black-market transactions were common, and unrest developed in the temporary immigrants' camps as well. To house the hundreds of thousands of immigrants streaming into the country, transit camps called *ma'abarot* had been established, with makeshift water and sanitary systems, and providing only tents and tin sheds. The Ministry of Education vied with private religious organizations for the right to educate the immigrants' children. At the same time, the work of other ministries—Labor, Housing, Welfare, and the officials of the Jewish Agency—became bogged down in bureaucratic conflicts and budgetary battles. Many new immigrants from Europe, Asia, and Africa therefore remained stuck in remote, unfamiliar, and uncomfortable surroundings, losing hope that they would ever be assimilated into Israeli society. With the coming of autumn and a steady drop in temperature, life in the *ma'abarot* became progressively less comfortable. By winter, when the government ministries were still unable to offer either employment or permanent shelter, dissatisfaction among the immigrants mounted. Unusually severe winter storms, floods, and freezing temperatures caused the physical suffering in the camps to be so severe—in many cases life-threatening—that the IDF had to be called in.

Yadin was not one to suffer the foolishness of incompetence of others lightly. Bursting with energy and a sense of righteous mission—fortified with the continuing support of Ben-Gurion—he had little fear of lesser ministers and bureaucrats. In fact, his aide Netanel Lorch recalled, "he got into fights with practically all the cabinet ministers, who were older and who thought that they deserved to be treated with more respect than they usually got from Yadin." A clash with Labor Minister Golda Meir (who had Hebraicized her original name Meyerson) was particularly serious, coming as it did during the rescue effort in the immigrant camps. As the army medical, supply, and engineering corps were preparing to swing into action, Yadin impatiently demanded answers from Meir, head of a ministerial coordinating committee to deal with the problems of the *ma'abarot*. Yadin wanted to know why the army was not informed earlier of the impending crisis, why the government waited until all services had completely broken down. He accused her ministry of complete incompetence in causing so much needless suffering. Worse yet, as his tirade continued, he charged her with personal irresponsibility. This angry encounter would have political ramifications far in the future. As Lorch recalled, Golda Meir never forgave Yadin for this outburst. Despite the success of the army's rescue effort, her memory of the impertinence of the young chief of staff affected their relationship to the end of her life.

In the meantime, Yadin was fully occupied with the operational details of the relief mission. "The speed with which the army organized to get food and clothing and housing to the various *ma'abarot* was really quite a feat," Lorch recalled. "It was done at such great speed that no lives were lost." Within the first four months of the operation Yadin headed an effort that accomplished what the civilian authorities had failed to do: building more permanent housing, schools, and community centers; installing functioning water and sanitation systems; and providing effective medical and supply services to almost a hundred *ma'abarot* throughout the country. In an address to the troops broadcast on Galei Zahal, the army radio station, at the end of April, Yadin proudly announced that in this operation the IDF "appeared as a national instrument for the execution of missions of the highest importance for the advancement of the State—and not necessarily those in the purely military sphere." Even after the official conclusion of the rescue effort, the IDF remained active in immigrant relief. During the following winter, another massive operation was mounted, in which Yadin placed special emphasis on "raising the morale, organization, discipline, and internal solidarity" of the inhabitants of the *ma'abarot*; and ordered special medical care for infants and the transfer of more than a thousand school children to more permanent quarters on military bases during the winter.

For the first time in his life, Yadin now had the power to implement a progressive vision of social improvement, of a superficially nonpartisan political type. By improving standards of living and cultivating good citizenship, it preserved faint echoes of earlier lessons Yadin had learned as a scout, as a student at the Deborah Kallen School, and as the son of Chassiya Feinsod-Sukenik. This was not the Yadin of wartime press conferences, the dashing young operations officer pointing to the battlefield map and tossing off biblical quotes. Here was a national figure attempting to transform diverse communities into a disciplined, uniform society. Although Yadin's vision was initially identical to Ben-Gurion's, their ideas about the role of the army within society gradually diverged. As his public stature mounted, Yadin focused increasingly on expanding the scope of IDF activities, spending ever more of its annual budget on training, salaries, and services in the belief that only a large army in a constant state of readiness could adequately protect and aid the economic development of the state. Ben-Gurion, however, gradually recognized political and economic dangers in that ambitious vision of the IDF. To make matters worse, the IDF's readiness for battle was soon brought into doubt.

The Arab Republic of Syria had always been Israel's most persistent opponent. After the 1949 armistice agreement the demilitarized areas between the two nations remained the sites of confrontation over property ownership, boundaries, and water rights. By the terms of the armistice normal civilian life was to be restored in the demilitarized zones between the two nations (in the far north near the sources of the Jordan; in the Huleh Valley; on the southeastern coast of the Sea of Galilee; and at el-Hammeh, at the confluence of the Yarmuk and Jordan rivers). Yet restoring normal life in these areas was nearly impossible, owing to conflicting claims to sovereignty and continuing, indirect attempts by both parties to gain territorial control. Time and again the UN Mixed Armistice Commission was forced to arbitrate disputes between Israeli settlements and Arab villages and over the areas of jurisdiction of Israel and Arab police patrols. The most serious and ultimately most explosive crisis occurred at the beginning of 1951, over an ambitious Israeli development project just north of the central demilitarized zone.

There was no question that the project would provide an enormous boost to the Israeli economy. The drainage of the vast Huleh swamps and the rechanneling of their water resources would reclaim about 45,000 acres of rich agricultural land and ultimately provide irrigation water for agricultural settlements as far south as the Negev. While the Huleh swamps themselves lay outside the demilitarized zone, much of the important earth-moving work had to be done within it, and in February 1951, when Israeli bulldozers arrived to begin widening and deepening the channel of the Upper Jordan River, the Syrians objected strongly to the expropriation of about a hundred acres of Arab land (after the owners had refused repeated Israeli offers to purchase) and contended that the draining of the Huleh was, in any case, an unacceptable alteration of the status quo. In late March, even after the United Nations had tacitly confirmed Israel's right to undertake the project, tensions rose as the earth-moving work continued and the Arab landowners refused to negotiate. Small-arms fire from the Syrian side was soon opened on the Israeli bulldozers. Despite secret negotiations between Deputy Chief of Staff Mordecai Makleff and his Syrian counterpart, Adib Shishakli, no agreement on the lease or purchase of Arab land was reached. Syrian sniping and Israeli earth-moving continued until finally, at the end of March, Ben-Gurion decided to establish unquestioned Israeli sovereignty over this portion of the demilitarized zone. On March 31, Israeli police transferred the 785 inhabitants of the Arab villages of Kirad el-Baqqara and Kirad el-Ghannama to the Western Galilee, destroyed their village houses, and intensified patrols along the Syrian border.

Further attempts at UN mediation failed, and the Syrians moved to assert *their* sovereignty in the southernmost demilitarized sector, at the village of el-Hammeh southeast of the Sea of Galilee. (It was also the site of an ancient synagogue excavated by Eleazar Sukenik nineteen years before.) Even though it was situated on a narrow finger of land between Jordan and Syria and its population was entirely Arab, the village and its famous hot baths were included within the international boundaries of Israel. On April 3 the Israeli general staff received report that a squad of Syrian troops had entered el-Hammeh, and Yadin dispatched an Israeli patrol there "to demonstrate that in this demilitarized zone, the sovereignty is that of the State of Israel, and there should be no debate about it." Ironically, the Syrian and Israeli representatives to a meeting of Mixed Armistice Commission had been close to agreement when the shocking news came later that day that the Syrian troops at el-Hammeh had fired on the arriving Israeli patrol, killing seven of its members. Events were moving toward armed conflict. The same afternoon Yadin was summoned to a meeting of the Israeli cabinet and received authorization to order the first tactical air strike of the Israeli air force since the end of the war. Early the next morning, April 5, he traveled to the headquarters of the Northern Command.

In an operation that staff officer Yitzhak Rabin later termed as "only a reaction, not a solution," a force of Israeli Mustangs and Spitfires attacked the Syrian positions and police station at el-Hammeh, leading to a sharp rebuke by the UN Security Council and the eventual Israeli loss of control over the village. Not for another fifteen years would Israeli troops attempt to enforce their claims on the area. But the fighting was far from over. Less than a month later, on May 2, an early-morning patrol of Israeli reservists in the hills northwest of the Sea of Galilee encountered a Syrian force that had crossed from the demilitarized zone into Israeli territory. After a brief firefight the Syrians established positions on Tell el-Mutilla and two other nearby hills. Even though a company from the Golani Brigade recaptured Tell el-Mutilla, reinforcements from both sides streamed to the area, and throughout the next three days—with the brief interruption of a ceasefire—the battle continued with the support of airplanes and artillery. On May 4, Yadin arrived at the scene of the fighting and urged the field commanders to go on the attack. But it was not until two days later, after several unsuccessful assaults and unexpectedly heavy casualties, that Israeli ground forces, supported by air force Spitfires, finally forced the Syrian troops to withdraw.

For the Israelis, who were by now taking their military superiority for granted, this battle had not gone as expected. The casualties to the Golani Brigade had been heavy—twenty-seven killed in a relatively small-scale action—and some of the field commanders were seriously shocked at how difficult the operation had been. "We were still reorganizing," recalled Meir Amit, then commander of the Golani Brigade, "and the problem was that the great fighters of 1948 had gone home. In their place came new immigrants." After the battle Yadin assembled all the field commanders for a day of debriefing at the Golani headquarters. It was a day of frank discussion of the army's unexpected level of performance and lack of combat discipline. "All of them came with all kinds of stories and excuses," Amit recalled. "But Yadin attacked them and offered an incisive analysis of the things that had gone wrong in the battle. On that day he was brilliant and very eloquent, and spoke very convincingly." The battle of Tell el-Mutilla was a watershed, for it convinced Yadin that the army's level of training had to be heightened. For that year's annual exercises, scheduled to take place in less than four months, he planned an unprecedentedly large-scale military lesson to show how a surprise attack could be effectively repelled.

Ever since the nationwide test of the efficiency of the reserve system the previous autumn, Yadin had struggled with the Defense Ministry to gain sufficient funds for another full-scale exercise. Because the cost of mobilizing the reserves was high and the economy damaged by so many lost workdays, civilian officials were reluctant to appropriate the sums needed for war games. Yadin succeeded in convincing Ben-Gurion that this training was necessary, especially in light of the poor performance of the troops at Tell el-Mutilla. He planned the maneuvers with characteristic imagination: In a simulation of a surprise attack against Israel, the forces of the Southern Command under Moshe Dayan (the "Greens" in this maneuver) would play the invaders and be pitted against the "Blues" of the Central Command, led by Zvi Ayalon. Yadin carefully choreographed the movements to provide the combat troops with as many military lessons as possible; The Greens were to mount a surprise advance into Blue territory; the Blues were then to assume a defensive deployment; and once the front had stabilized, they were to mount a counterattack. It was all to be accomplished within thirty-six hours—far shorter than their exercises the previous year. Yadin came south to observe the operation. All would have gone perfectly according to schedule, had it not been for Moshe Dayan.

Yadin's relationship with Dayan had been problematic from the time they first met in the Haganah in 1940. "He was already a lone wolf then," Yadin recalled, "and everyone—Dori, the British, and me—knew that for certain functions, to communicate with the Arabs and for all kinds of dirty work and ruses, Dayan was the best." Their paths crossed frequently over the years—in the training courses at Juara, in the defense of the Jordan Valley against the initial Syrian invasion, in Jerusalem, during the negotiations with Abdullah, and now in the Southern Command. But Dayan could never tolerate Yadin's ideas of proper order, and he gleefully flouted Yadin's attempts to instill discipline in the officer corps. Yadin's aide-de-camp Netanel Lorch recalled the day he spotted Dayan lounging in the shade on the grass in front of the chief of staff's office at army headquarters. "I went out and told him, listen, you know that this is prohibited. Our soldiers are not even allowed to walk on the

grass. And if any officer would catch them, he'd fine them half a pound."
Dayan, refusing to be roused from his afternoon relaxation, lazily
reached into his shirt pocket and tossed a half-pound note at Lorch.
"Take it. It's worth it," he said.

But now in the 1951 exercises the stakes were much higher. Instead
of wasting time waiting for the exercise to get under way at the precise,
predetermined hour, Dayan ordered the Seventh Brigade (now under his
command and transformed into a formal armored brigade) to make a
sudden sweep around the southern flank of the Blue forces. A full forty-
eight hours before the exercises were supposed to get under way, Dayan
had demonstrated the art of surprise in a way that utterly infuriated
Yadin. Dayan, as usual, was unrepentant. At the hurriedly convened debriefing session Dayan disparaged the formalism of the high command.
Yadin, for his part, recalled that "in the discussion after the exercise I
wanted to reprimand him, but I didn't mention his name. What I said
then has since become famous: 'Someone here is not playing according
to the rules of the game and if he continues to act this way, I'm going to
have to put out his other eye.'"

During the summer of 1951 the military status quo on other fronts
was collapsing. Repeated violent incursions were mounted across the
border from Jordan, and the IDF responded with its usual retaliatory
raids. The hope that an accord with King Abdullah might someday be
reached was quickly fading. Revived national self-confidence in the Arab
world made it unlikely and even dangerous for the Hashemite monarch
to contemplate a separate deal with the Jewish state. But whatever the
hopes, however faint, for negotiations with Jordan, the assassination of
Abdullah at the entrance to the el-Aqsa mosque in Jerusalem on Friday,
July 20, 1951, brought them to a sudden definitive end. On the same day
Yadin instructed Makleff to review and update the operational plans for
the conquest of the West Bank. Yosef Avidar, then northern front commander, recalled that when they received word that Abdullah had been
assassinated, everything was ready and in place. "If I had received the
order," Avidar recalled, "I could have put the plan into action in two
hours and have conquered the entire West Bank in forty-eight." But the
plan was not put into action. As Israel's economic problems mounted
and quick international intervention could be expected to prevent
lengthy operations, a new battlefield doctrine emerged. Small-scale,
stinging commando operations offered a cost-effective alternative to
Yadin's meticulously planned battlefield stratagems. Dayan's eye for action—far more than both of Yadin's—was already firmly fixed on the
tactical approach that the IDF would rely on for years to come. Dayan

was clearly the rising star in Ben-Gurion's circle, and as he ascended through the levels of command, he helped create an army and a society very different from Yadin's tomato-growing ideal.

Through five exhausting years of fighting and state-building, Yigael Yadin and David Ben-Gurion established a personal relationship whose intensity was often obscured by the self-confident, independent public image that each of them cultivated. From their first meeting at the Jewish Agency headquarters in the spring of 1947 through the bloody battles of 1948, they shared a tacit understanding of the enormity of the historical changes under way. Neither was a soldier, hardened in battle to the sight of men dying, to the numbing, all-encompassing grip of fear. Beneath their strategic calculations, cold operational planning, and smashed glass and angry exchanges, they shared private moments of uneasiness and horror. Yadin long remembered the night they traveled together to Latrun and how Ben-Gurion had not wanted to see the wounded men from the battle—or their trip south to the front during Operation Horev, when the thirty-one-year-old operations officer and the sixty-two-year-old prime minister had wandered innocently through the abandoned Arab village of Kawkaba, not knowing that it was thickly strewn with mines. During a training exercise in Galilee in 1951, during his tenure as chief of staff, Yadin recalled, he and Ben-Gurion had sat together in a jeep and watched two paratroopers fall to their deaths. "We were the first on the scene," Yadin remembered, "and the bodies were still warm. Ben-Gurion looked and looked, and said to me in amazement, 'You know, they look just like they're alive.'" It was the first time Ben-Gurion had ever seen dead bodies. Yadin was a headquarters officer, not much more battle-hardened than the prime minister, and he never forgot the profound effect that these two dead men—as horribly twisted and motionless flesh, not statistics—had on Ben-Gurion.

In his own way the prime minister had come to depend on Yadin for reliable information and incisive analysis. Quite apart from larger strategic questions, he deeply admired Yadin's powers of abstraction and memory for detail that always enabled him to spin off a dizzying flow of opinions, perspectives, and ideas. Those who worked close to both men recalled the importance of Yadin's and Ben-Gurion's frequent private meetings. Netanel Lorch recalled that Yadin would prepare intensively for his confidential sessions with the prime minister, carefully reviewing raw intelligence data and the latest military statistics so that he would be able to make concrete recommendations. Yitzhak Navon, who became the director of the prime minister's office in late 1952, recalled the intensity and uniqueness of their relationship. Their meetings would often begin, he recalled, with a discussion of biblical, historical, or archaeological issues. While Ben-Gurion discussed biblical history to alleviate the tedium of dreary meetings with bureaucrats, politicians, and foreign visitors, he also seemed genuinely interested in what Yadin had to say. Both men shared a love of books, and fascination with antiquity, and a talent for using historical imagery.

Even to some of its closest observers, however, the nature of this relationship remained a mystery. "Yigael would bite his fingernails and angrily throw files on the floor," Pinchas Sapir (director-general of the Defense Ministry and later finance minister) told Michael Bar-Zohar, Ben-Gurion's biographer. "But Ben-Gurion accepted all that. I don't know who Ben-Gurion appreciated more—those who weren't afraid to confront him or those who meekly submitted to him. But he respected Yigael, even though he gave him constant problems." What Sapir failed to recognize was that the angry outbursts and the "problems" were only the most visible part of the relationship. On the level of day-to-day operational details, administrative planning, and tactical options, Yadin was always a confident and sometimes aggressive challenger of many of Ben-Gurion's ideas. On that level of army command and operations, Ben-Gurion respected Yadin's analytical powers and quick grasp of facts and figures. But on the longer-range strategic and philosophical levels, Ben-Gurion was Yadin's unquestioned mentor. They had bitter arguments about the deployment of particular units or the cost of fortifications at a particular base, but Yadin rarely questioned Ben-Gurion's vision of the future or his political analyses of Israel's role in the world. Indeed, over the years, Yadin came to adopt Ben-Gurion's understanding of Jewish history through the ages—a chronicle of military conquest, exile, migration, and territorial destiny—and would, in time, become one of its most eloquent exponents.

By the summer of 1951, in the aftermath of the fighting at Tell el-Mutilla, the tensions and pressures of the army command were taking their toll on Yadin. To those around him, he was even more difficult to work with than usual. Relations in the headquarters deteriorated to the point that, on June 16, Ben-Gurion noted in his journal, Deputy Chief of Staff Mordecai Makleff was seriously considering resignation because of increasingly strained relations with Yadin. During the following week, the prime minister spoke at length to Yadin, who mused aloud about the advisability of his leaving the army, apparently at the urging of his wife. Ben-Gurion then summoned Carmella, who explained that the pressures of the army command on Yigael were affecting their relationship and having a damaging effect on Yigael's personality. General staff meetings became progressively more acrimonious. Ben-Gurion recorded in his diary that Yadin was determined to resign because he was "tired and nervous and feels that he often does not act in a proper way with his colleagues." At the end of the month, after one particularly unpleasant encounter, Ben-Gurion noted that "it is sad to see this talented young man behaving so badly. Is there any way to deal with this worrisome flaw?"

During 1952, serious political, economic, and budgetary problems were added to the existing pressures. In early January, Yadin was called upon to be a policeman, to put army forces on alert in case of riots in Jerusalem and Tel Aviv. The issue was the painful question of German reparations to survivors of the Holocaust. After Chancellor Konrad Adenauer made a public declaration in the Bundestag of German responsibility and contrition for the crimes of the Nazis, long, complex negotiations between the Federal Republic of Germany and the State of Israel began, on behalf of individual Holocaust survivors and the Israeli government. There was widespread, outraged opposition within certain sectors of the Israeli public to accepting any monetary payments and to forgiving the German people for their willing participation in genocide, which such acceptance would imply. Menachem Begin, head of the opposition Herut party, took the lead in whipping up emotions against Ben-Gurion and the government. After delivering an emotional speech to a large crowd in downtown Jerusalem, he led a violent demonstration outside the Knesset that disrupted the reparations debate. Several weeks later, rumors spread that Begin was planning to instigate even more violent disturbances in Tel Aviv, and Yadin was called to put army troops on a state of high alert.

This was not to be another *Altalena* affair, however. Reparations to individuals and to the State of Israel for lost property and for resettling Jewish refugees from Eastern and Central Europe were eventually approved, and further violence was averted. From a strictly economic standpoint, the German payments helped to keep the Israeli economy afloat. With a steadily worsening foreign trade imbalance (despite intensive fund-raising among Jewish communities in Europe and America), Israel's foreign currency reserves were completely exhausted by the end of 1951. Moreover, foreign banks and oil companies threatened to suspend all relations with Israel, so that a catastrophic economic crisis loomed and radical steps had to be taken. In early 1952 the government announced a "New Economic Policy" of relaxed price controls and the drastic devaluation of the Israeli lira to stimulate exports. As expected, these moves had a far-reaching impact on the domestic economy. Prices for goods and services soared, and Ben-Gurion insisted that the army, like every other branch of the government, slash its budget. He informed Yadin where he believed that significant annual expenditures could be cut. As usual, Yadin bridled at Ben-Gurion's direct interference in military administration. Clearly annoyed, he responded that he and his staff had already done all that was possible to reduce the standing army and its civilian employees and to keep the training days for the reserves down to a bare minimum.

"I do not disparage the value of your efforts," the prime minister responded in a stern letter on February 29, 1952, "in economizing and cutting back to make the structure of the army and its budget more in accord with the general needs of the State. It's natural—and in my mind desirable—that you should always have the needs of the army in mind. But I have to consider everything. And I see a need for cuts." Far more was at stake in this intensifying confrontation than mere numbers. Ben-Gurion was convinced that the continuing state of war and Israel's fragile economy meant that the IDF should concentrate on utilizing small, elite units and advanced weapons—not on expanding the citizen army and the wide range of civilian services that Yadin had long championed. Yadin, however, was not ready to give up his vision without a fight. He was convinced that Israel's national security depended both on battlefield readiness and on the army's ability to undertake important civilian tasks like constructing roads and housing, absorbing new immigrants, administering medical services, and providing efficient transport services on land and sea. While he accepted in principle the necessity for overall budget reduction, he rejected what seemed to him to be Ben-Gurion's arbitrary and specific demand that almost 20 percent be slashed from the annual defense budget and that six thousand career soldiers and civilian employees be laid off.

Yadin had devoted great effort to encouraging the most talented career officers to stay in the army and to developing the IDF's wide range of social services; he now believed that he alone should determine where the cuts should be made. But Ben-Gurion showed no signs of budging, and by early autumn 1952, Yadin's personal anxieties and budgetary worries flowed together. Suspecting that the prime minister had lost confidence in him, he spoke against the cuts in nonnegotiable terms. "If you think—despite my explanation," Yadin wrote to Ben-Gurion on September 3, "that your recommendations should be adopted, don't hesitate for a moment in requesting that I be relieved of my post." The prime minister immediately acknowledged Yadin's great dedication and his natural feeling for the sanctity of the army—but he rejected Yadin's threat of resignation out of hand. "I believe in your ability and your good intentions," he wrote, "and if changes have to be made—and they certainly do have to be made—I'm sure that you'll be able to carry them out." A final showdown was approaching, since there was no sign that Yadin would compromise. At the end of October, Finance Minister Levi Eshkol sent an urgent message to Ben-Gurion: "It is with great anxiety that I must point out that the implementation of the promised cuts in the structure of the IDF are very much behind schedule." Eshkol implored Ben-Gurion "to take every measure to accelerate the implementation of the cuts."

In Ben-Gurion's eyes, the vision of the citizen army "growing tomatoes" was neither desirable nor even feasible under the present economic circumstances. He therefore had few alternatives but to replace or reassign the chief of staff. Not wanting to lose Yadin's talent, however, he even considered reshuffling his cabinet; perhaps he could more easily persuade Yadin to radically downsize the army if he were named to the civilian post of minister of defense. Ben-Gurion expected a great future in public service from Yadin and came to the conclusion that "his being in the government will offer him a more encompassing knowledge about the needs of the state—and that in the final analysis, security is not dependent on the army but on the overall potential of the state and its standing in the world." By this time, however, Yadin had made a critical decision. He would submit his resignation as chief of staff—finally and irrevocably.

In a private meeting on November 11, Yadin refused Ben-Gurion's offer of the Defense portfolio on the grounds that he was not a politician and had never belonged to any party. Naturally, there were far deeper reasons for Yadin's reluctance to enter political life. For months, Carmella had seen Yigael's behavior take a destructive turn with the constant jealousies, animosities, and confrontations with other high-ranking IDF officers. The prospect of a political career was hardly more appealing; Carmella knew as the daughter of Arthur Ruppin the toll that professional political activity could take on family life. More to the point, she felt that her husband was far too sensitive and intelligent to spend his life among the government bureaucrats and party hacks who were now ensconced in key positions of power in the Jewish State. She believed—rightly—that Yadin did not have the temperament of a politician and that he should return to the academic world.

Yigael and Carmella now had a family to think of. In April 1949, their first daughter, Orly, had been born. An appointment for Yigael in the faculty of the Hebrew University could afford them a comfortable and respectable lifestyle and allow him to resume his beloved archaeological research. Despite the demands placed on his time and attention as chief of staff, Yadin had never lost his archaeological fascination. Through his years of army service he had kept up with the latest discoveries, visited excavations and exhibitions, and faithfully read current scholarly publications. In tours of the country with high-ranking officers he had often gone out of his way to visit archaeological sites and point out sites of historical significance. At thirty-five, it was not too late to resume his archaeological career. The prospect of solitary study of ancient military strategy, fortifications, and technology—without the meddling interference of politicians and bureaucrats—was clearly appealing. He had tired of constant public attention and army politics and looked forward to reentering the academic community. In only a year or two he could update and complete his doctoral dissertation on ancient warfare (which he had left unfinished in 1947), and with his high public standing he could almost certainly expect a faculty appointment at the university. While Yadin insisted that his resignation as chief of staff was connected to the current budgetary debate, there were personal motives as well. As in his bitter dispute seven years before with Yitzhak Sadeh over Haganah doctrine, Yadin chose to retreat to the more secure realm of antiquity when serious political opposition arose. Announcing his final opposition to Ben-Gurion's budget cutting suggestions, he submitted his letter of resignation on November 23, 1952.

In one of his last meetings with Yadin as chief of staff, the prime minister could barely conceal his disappointment. His journal for November 26 contained the evocative entry: "In the morning, an extended conversation with Yigael—actually almost a monologue by Yigael. The standing army should not be touched, nor should the technical structure of the reserves. He sees a strengthening among the Arabs—and yet he is leaving. He intends to finish his doctorate on the history of the army and warfare in the Bible. He'll do the work abroad. He is ready to accept a fellowship, but I said that it's not proper for someone who has served as chief of staff to receive support from foreigners—so he should go with army support." There is no question that Ben-Gurion had hoped to retain Yadin in ruling circles, and over the coming years he would appeal to him again and again to return to public life. Yet on another level Ben-Gurion quietly admired Yadin's decision to devote himself to the study of ancient history.

Years later, Yadin recalled Ben-Gurion's devotion to his valuable collection of books on archaeological, historical, and biblical subjects. Often when Yadin was at Ben-Gurion's house on official business, the prime minister would take him into the library, to the high shelves of first editions and obscure historical reference books, many of them specially bound with Ben-Gurion's initials impressed in gold leaf on the spine. This collection was not merely for show; Ben-Gurion was a self-taught scholar who was widely read and could understand the complexity of the historical questions—"that was something I often saw for myself," Yadin remembered, "even during the fury of the war." This fascination for the study of antiquity was something that Yadin and Ben-Gurion could never fully share with the politicians of Mapai or the professional soldiers of the general staff. Unfortunately, their close working relationship was now coming to an end.

On December 12, 1952, in a ceremony almost identical to the one that had ushered Yadin into office, he handed over the command of the Israel Defense Forces to his deputy, Mordecai Makleff. Under Makleff, control over the general staff and the regional commands would be shifted to officers who had none of Yadin's polish or intellectual brilliance. Moshe Dayan would serve as Makleff's deputy and chief of operations—a sure stepping-stone to appointment as chief of staff himself someday. The budgetary recommendations would be approved and accepted, placing increasing emphasis on highly trained paratroop and commando units that could strike quickly and decisively.

By the end of 1952, hopes of including Israel in a western regional alliance had all but evaporated. The United States would now be governed by a Republican administration under Eisenhower and a stern secretary of state, John Foster Dulles; it would abandon its attempts to facilitate reconciliation between Israel and the Arab states. In the meantime the balance of power in the Middle East was changing, as Yadin had warned Ben-Gurion. The death of Abdullah made the future of the Hashemite kingdom and its intentions toward Israel uncertain; in Egypt, King Farouk had been ousted by an army coup in July 1952. In the next years Israel would turn decidedly away from diplomatic initiatives, preferring to create facts on the ground and maintain its military position through constant, punishing retaliatory attacks.

Yadin did not participate in that policy change, and he had few regrets. He looked forward to his return to the academic world. Yet there was some sadness in the parting, especially from Ben-Gurion, with whom he had worked so closely and so intensely for five years. "One of the things that really moved me, when I left the army," Yadin told interviewer Yoav Gelber in 1978, was that "despite all our disagreements, all the arrogance I had shown toward him . . . I still held the greatest respect for him . . . and I also felt that he felt the same about me." Yadin recalled with some emotion how Ben-Gurion called him into his library on the day after his resignation and took down from a shelf two volumes of Josephus Flavius' histories in Greek, bound in leather, with the letters

BG embossed in gold leaf on the spine. This edition of the works of the first-century Jewish historian—clearly a rare and valuable one—was Ben-Gurion's parting gift. "And because I knew how precious his books were to him," Yadin recalled, "it was the most meaningful thing he could possibly have done." Ben-Gurion opened the first volume, took out his fountain pen, and wrote out an inscription in the same tightly formed Hebrew letters that filled his diaries. Yadin had often noted that Ben-Gurion's compulsive diary-writing was also a process of refining and crystallizing his thoughts. And now, with his handwritten inscription, Ben-Gurion acknowledged that an important era in the history of the State of Israel had finally come to an end. It read:

To Yigael Yadin
a memento
of faithful comradeship in arms
in the War of Liberation and the formation of the IDF
in the sorrow of parting and with the love of a brother
from
D. Ben-Gurion

SONS OF LIGHT, SONS OF DARKNESS

A t a gala dinner in London on June 17, 1953, Yigael Yadin basked in the pomp, ceremony, and status of the new life he had chosen for himself. Seated with Carmella at a long dining table in the refectory of University College, he was surrounded by some of the most famous dignitaries of the archaeological world. The occasion was the centenary of the birth of Sir William Matthew Flinders Petrie, acknowledged by many—certainly by all those present—as the founding father of modern Egyptian and Palestinian archaeology. Before dinner, Yadin and Carmella had taken their place in the receiving line of Petrie's colleagues, students, and admirers to offer good wishes to Lady Hilda Petrie, the great man's eighty-two-year-old widow. They had listened to speeches and warm words of appreciation from representatives of museums, universities, and archaeological societies all over the world. They had laughed at stories of Sir Flinders's adventures and had raised their glasses to join in a toast. Yadin had met the Petries years before, when they were residing at the American in Jerusalem and he was a beginning archaeology student. Now, as the official representative of the Israel Exploration Society and the Hebrew University to the Petrie Centenary celebration, Yadin was making his debut as a respected member of the international archaeological community.

The dinner at University College was but one event in a dizzying whirl of scholarly lectures, receptions, and meetings the Yadins attended in the spring of 1953. In the sudden flush of postwar digging and discovery, London had become the hub of a revolution in classical, biblical, and Near Eastern archaeology. At the Institute of Archaeology at St. John's Lodge, Sir Mortimer Wheeler—always flamboyantly playing to the crowd—delighted his listeners with colorful anecdotes and discoveries from his recent digs at Mohenjo-Daro, Verulaminium, and Stanwick; Max Mallowan presented his spectacular finds from Nimrud; Gordon Childe wheezed out his sweeping theories of the origins of European civilization; A. J. B. Wace reported on his important new discoveries at the citadel of Mycenae; and a young architect named Michael Ventris astounded the scholarly world with his brilliant decipherment of the Bronze Age Linear B script, identifying it as a form of Homeric Greek. It was a time of intense excitement and enthusiasm in archaeological circles, a time of great change in the ways the Western world looked at the past. And like his father at the University of Berlin in the early 1920s, Yadin was intent on reshaping his public and professional identity.

More than six months had passed since the bittersweet resignation ceremony in the prime minister's office. During that time he had returned to archaeological study with the same intensity that he had applied to operational and organizational tasks. He had received a two-year research fellowship from the Hebrew University (on the urging of President Benjamin Mazar and despite Ben-Gurion's preference for army funding) and planned to spend his time at the British Museum and the Institute of Archaeology completing his dissertation. During his days of study in Jerusalem in 1946–47, he had combed the libraries of the Rockefeller Museum, the American School, and the École Biblique and collected hundreds of published examples of ancient weapons, battle depictions, and fortifications. But now, with access to the vast collections and photographic archives of the British Museum and the Institute of Archaeology, he could examine artifacts and drawings from Greece, Asia Minor, Egypt, Syria, and Iraq. Yadin's challenge was to use archaeological finds to trace advances and innovations in military technology, tactics, and strategy during the first six thousand years of settled life in the Near East.

A dissertation so ambitious would have been a full-time undertaking for any graduate student—even one possessed of Yadin's modern military background and fabled memory for details. But Yadin brought another assignment with him to London—one that would have kept most scholars working for years. Among the ancient Dead Sea Scrolls that his father had purchased from Feidi el-Alami on the day of the UN partition decision was a nine-foot-long, fairly well-preserved document that Sukenik had called "The War of the Sons of Light Against the Sons of Darkness." The elder Sukenik had worked on it briefly in the summer of 1948 and had published two short passages, but because of the detailed military terminology employed in its description of an apocalyptic war between the forces of Good and Evil, he had entrusted the final translation of the "War Scroll" to his militarily oriented son. The world of biblical scholarship was buzzing about the implications of the still unpublished Hebrew documents from ancient Judea and their possible theological or historical connection to early Christianity. This offered Yadin a unique opportunity. But to take full advantage of it, he had to immerse himself in transcribing the tightly written columns of scribal writing and searching biblical, rabbinic, and classical literature for parallels to the literary and military motifs. This was an entirely different challenge from arranging and classifying battle axes, mace heads, and broadswords, but Yadin, inspired and excited by his scholarly surroundings, undertook both projects with confidence and enthusiasm.

The new life that unfolded for himself and Carmella and four-year-old Orly was carefully organized and ordered. Carmella budgeted their time and funds precisely, tended to housekeeping and the care, feeding, and schooling of Orly; and as always paid special attention to the advancement of Yigael's academic and social career. Early in 1953 the Yadins moved into a small apartment in Hampstead Garden, so small, in fact, that Yigael had to work at a desk tucked into a corner of the living room. With his exceptional powers of concentration (which he always attributed to the chaotic conditions of the headquarters during wartime) he was able to block out even a four-year-old's singing and playing and Carmella's polite conversations with a steady stream of guests. But he was by no means a recluse. When his allotted work time was over, Yigael proved to be exceptionally good company for a rapidly growing circle of London friends. His ready wit and conversational skill—not to speak of his fame from Israel's War of Independence—put him at the center of an eclectic social circle, one carefully arranged and coordinated by Carmella to include a pleasing collection of soldiers, scholars, and businessmen.

The Yadins quickly became sought-after dinner guests among the young Jewish executives of the department store chain Marks and Spenser (a number of whom had served as volunteer officers in the War of Independence), and he delighted them with his amusing anecdotes of middle-of-the-night dinners with King Abdullah and behind-the-scenes confrontations with Ben-Gurion. Carmella, as usual, zealously protected Yigael from every annoyance, imagined or real. Invited to dinner at the home of Leon and Lilly Shalit soon after their arrival in London, Carmella coldly informed her hostess as she served the main course that "Yigael does not eat spinach." The insult was soon forgotten, and the Shalits and the Yadins grew to be close friends. And right away, this association offered a tangible benefit to Yigael's work. He had collected hundreds of examples of ancient weapons and fortifications for his dissertation and dozens of linguistic parallels to phrases that appeared in the War Scroll. Leon Shalit, director of Marks and Spenser's buying departments, offered him a practical suggestion: Why not utilize the system that the huge department store chain employed to keep its inventory and accounts?

Carmella, never one to overlook an innovation that could make Yigael's work more efficient, accompanied him to the Marks and Spenser headquarters to learn about the Manual Power system that Shalit had so highly praised. Shalit arranged a tutorial for them in the firm's accounting department; among the rows of desks and towering file cabinets, one of the accounting clerks instructed Carmella in the use of long metal rods with variously shaped cross-sections to separate and sort specially punched account or inventory cards. The Marks and Spenser Manual Power System proved essential to Yigael's work as Carmella carefully registered ancient weapons and biblical phrases on punched inventory cards. Indeed, her ability to retrieve certain classes of information for her husband with this system proved useful for years to come, not only in the study of archaeological artifacts but in the logistical organization of his ambitious excavations.

Although Carmella undertook the raw data processing (in that era long before digitized data bases), she left the analysis to him. Yigael's capacity for retaining facts and figures about troop displacements and ammunition supplies served him well in his imaginative reconstruction of the armies and defensive systems of the ancient Near Eastern civilizations. Determined to make order out of the confusing variety of city gates, fortification walls, assault weapons, and personal armor that archaeologists had dug up from the Nile to the Euphrates, he imposed the same logic of standardization and uniformity that he had used in reorganizing the IDF. If a certain phenomenon or innovation were observed in several localities, he would ascribe it to a similar tactical motivation—in the same way that during Haganah training in the 1930s, similar conditions of rural uprisings had led to the uniform fortification of all outlying Jewish settlements. Yadin mobilized his modern military experience for his antiquarian study, and in his frequent mixing of past and present it often became difficult to disentangle the two.

In 1953, Yadin was honored to be asked to contribute an article on the recent Arab-Israeli war to Basil Liddell Hart's new edition of *The Strategy of the Indirect Approach*. He could hardly refrain in his article from evoking ancient images to substantiate the timelessness of warfare in this part of the world. At the same time his archaeological analysis of ancient warfare subtly integrated Liddell Hart's fierce critique of the static defenses of World War I with eras of New Kingdom Egypt, David, Ahab, and Sennacherib. One side's advances, he (like Liddell Hart) argued, were answered by the other side's countermeasures, in a process that knew no limit or end. From the huge ramparts of Bronze Age Canaan, to the battle tactics of the Israelite tribes under Joshua, to the fortifications of the Crusaders, to the jet planes of the Israeli air force, the deadly progress of innovation and counterinnovation had inexorably proceeded over millennia.

For Yadin, this historical process was more than a philosophical abstraction. It was the motive force in all of biblical and Jewish history. Never one to dwell on complex sociological analyses or theological speculations, Yadin tended to see the past as clear-cut and unambiguous and the course of events as driven by national will and technological skill. For Yadin, archaeology would always be a powerful tool to apply—without questioning—this lesson to his own people and land. He offered stunning, innovative suggestions about the dating or use of particular artifacts and he explained puzzling biblical passages through archaeological discoveries, but he never questioned or altered his basic concepts of nationhood and national will. He never considered that he might be unfairly imposing modern concepts on the peoples of antiquity.

The nature of biblical and classical archaeology in those days was such that its practitioners possessed a subtle yet pervasive imperial outlook. It is no coincidence that Yadin's professional model was in London, not Jerusalem. In the reception rooms and lecture halls of University College, he observed the genius of Sir Mortimer Wheeler and gained an invaluable lesson in how modern military concepts, archaeological finds, and patriotic rhetoric might be powerfully woven together. In Yadin's eyes, Wheeler was no mere antiquarian pedant but a man of action. After service as an artillery officer in France during World War I, he had brought stirring episodes of British history to life at the Romano-British town of Verulaminium at the modern site of St. Albans, and at the Dorset hillfort of Maiden Castle. There he had skillfully juxtaposed archaeology with ancient annals to bring imaginative and persuasive (if highly speculative) "proof" of some of the most melodramatic incidents in the wars between the Roman invaders and the early British kings and queens. The summer before Yadin's arrival in London, Wheeler completed an excavation at the Stanwick hillfort in North Yorkshire, where he had neatly (far too neatly, according to his critics) matched the three rebuilding phases at the site to the main incidents in the bitter first-century conflict between the pro-Roman British queen Cartimandua, her liberty-loving consort Venutius, and the Roman general Cerialus.

It all made for high drama—and was strongly reminiscent of the florid descriptions of Josephus Flavius of battles in Jerusalem and Masada. In the face of Wheeler's well-honed skill as a storyteller, who was to quibble over the difference between imagination and demonstrable fact? Describing the last moments of British resistance against the Romans at the Stanwick hillfort, Wheeler noted that the rebel leader Venutius, "fighting as he doubtless did to the end, was pitting an embattled mob in unwonted conditions against an army engaged upon a normal manoeuvre. Stanwick is at the same time," he concluded, "a very notable memorial to a heroic episode of British resistance and a monument to its futility." This didactic, moralistic approach to history was clearly echoed in Yadin's later work. But Sir Mortimer based his stirring reconstruction solely on inferences he drew from the ambiguous evidence of buried stonework and pottery sherds. These became the oracular talismans of an archaeologically based national myth. Such a moving patriotic version, he knew, would not easily be challenged. As the secretary of the British Academy and a popular national television celebrity, Sir Mortimer was enjoying unprecedented national prestige.

Every week, as Yadin and Carmella and other young couples crowded around flickering television sets to watch the popular game show *Animal, Vegetable, Mineral?* they relished the quick wit and graceful banter of the pipe-smoking Wheeler as he vied with the other panelists to identify obscure and mysterious artifacts. This was a brilliant and elegant scholar who avoided involvement in tawdry party politics, yet was nevertheless regarded as something of a national sage. Wheeler's self-confident knowledge of the minutiae of ancient cultures, his sharp sense of humor, and his conviction that lessons from the past might help shape Britain's future offered Yadin a personal example and a course of action outside academia. As a former public figure himself, Yadin would never be satisfied to pursue his archaeological research in isolation—he needed the attention of the press and the applause of large audiences.

And just as Sir Mortimer had used archaeological discovery to create stirring national sagas of the British people, Yadin would, in his own distinctive way, draw enormous patriotic power from archaeological finds.

———

In late 1952, Dr. Eleazar Sukenik's health was failing. He had suffered a series of paralyzing strokes over the previous few months, was bedridden, and was physically unable to continue working on his precious scrolls. His National Museum of Jewish Antiquities on Mount Scopus was virtually inaccessible (in a besieged enclave in Jordanian-held East Jerusalem) and four of the scrolls were still in the possession of the Syrian archbishop. But during the five years since he had first glimpsed the precious Dead Sea manuscript fragments through the barbed wire, his life had undergone a far-reaching transformation. He was now praised by scholars all over the world as the first to recognize the antiquity of the scrolls and their possible connection to the first-century Essenes. Sukenik zealously guarded the exclusive privilege of studying and publishing the scrolls that he had acquired for the Hebrew University. Although colleagues on the faculty—particularly those with far greater linguistic and literary expertise—objected to Sukenik's scholarly monopoly, he stubbornly refused to share his treasure. In 1948 and 1951 he published preliminary reports on the unique Thanksgiving Hymns Scroll, on the early Book of Isaiah manuscript, and on the War Scroll. Although he had entrusted the final publication of the War Scroll to Yigael when it became clear that he would return to academia, Sukenik's own work on the other two scrolls was suspended. So it remained when he died on February 28, 1953.

Sukenik's death could not have come as a surprise to Yigael and Carmella, since they had seen him deteriorate during his long, painful months of infirmity. Many of their colleagues and friends were nonetheless surprised that they chose not to return from London for the funeral. As usual, their coldly dispassionate logic and practical calculations took precedence over emotion and dutiful family ties. Since they had adjusted to life in London and established a strict schedule for the completion of Yigael's dissertation, they offered Chassiya their words of condolence by telephone and letter and relied on brother Yossi to take care of the details. So Eleazar Sukenik's funeral went on without them. It soon became clear, however, that Yadin could not defer or ignore the issue of the Dead Sea Scrolls.

Within a week of Sukenik's death Yadin received an urgent letter from Dr. Mazar at the Hebrew University informing him that the faculty had appointed a committee to facilitate the publication of the scrolls and urging him to come back to Israel at once. Although there was no question that Yadin would be permitted to complete the publication of the War Scroll, decisions had to be made on the disposition of the other two scrolls that his father had purchased and the unfinished excavation reports, scholarly articles, and unpublished discoveries that Sukenik had accumulated over twenty-five years.

With travel funds provided by the university, the Yadins returned to Israel in April to visit Chassiya and to confer with the faculty committee. It was decided that Sukenik's unfinished excavation reports and articles on ancient synagogues would be edited (but not substantially changed) by a colleague, Michael Avi-Yonah; that Yadin, Nahman Avigad, and another colleague, Jacob Licht, would prepare a posthumous edition of Sukenik's translation of and commentary on the Isaiah and Thanksgiving Hymns scrolls; and that Yadin should complete his work on the War Scroll as soon as possible.

Therein lay a problem. For upon his return to London, as Yadin became more deeply immersed in researching the manuscript, he recognized that he had bitten off far more scholarly work than he could (at least for now) comfortably chew. The scholarly debate over the dating and religious meaning of the Dead Sea Scrolls had recently intensified greatly with the discovery of important new manuscripts in the Jordanian caves of the Dead Sea region and with the beginning of excavations at nearby Khirbet Qumran. It was becoming clear that the Dead Sea Scrolls were not merely imaginative theological writings that had been hidden in the caves during an emergency but were closely connected to the life of a reclusive wilderness community that had apparently been destroyed at the time of the Jewish revolt against Rome, near the end of the first century A.D. The War Scroll, with its detailed descriptions of tactics and weapons and its battlefield liturgy, was simultaneously an apocalyptic vision and an operational plan.

Yadin had been mistaken if he thought that he could complete a translation of the War Scroll and move quickly on to the more important challenge of his dissertation. In May, soon after his return to London from Jerusalem, he wrote Mazar that he was working on the War Scroll "day and night," but that "the subject is much more complicated than I had thought, since the subjects I must deal with are numerous and complex." Although his father had transliterated most of the scroll before his death and had published two poetic passages from the document, he had not attempted to make sense of the document as a whole. As Yadin was to discover, the War Scroll was not merely a straightforward account of a holy war but a ritual manual for combat that included specific instructions on the construction and decoration of the army's weapons, trumpets, and banners; strict purity laws for the camp; prayers to be recited at various stages of the fighting; and the crucial roles that various angels would play in the war. This document therefore had to be analyzed in light of both military and religious thought. Yadin hoped that if he devoted all his energy to this project, he would be able to finish it by October. But even meeting that self-imposed deadline would leave him too little time to complete his dissertation. Might it be possible, he now asked Mazar, for him to submit his translation and commentary on the War Scroll as his doctoral dissertation instead of his compilation on biblical weapons and warfare?

Dr. Mazar responded that the university would certainly accept the War Scroll dissertation and requested only that Yadin send him a full outline. Mazar's primary object, he himself recalled years later, was to facilitate Yadin's return to the university as a member of the faculty. Time, not Yadin's obvious talent, was the most pressing element, and despite Yadin's obvious enthusiasm for his subject, Mazar warned him not to expand the dissertation beyond what he could complete by January at the latest. Clearly there was no chance Yadin's dissertation would be rejected. Dr. Mazar and Dr. Tur-Sinai of the department of Hebrew philology (who had been Yadin's Bible teacher at the Rechavia Gymnasium) were to be the judges. Yadin's text and commentary had already been accepted—sight unseen—for publication by the Bialik Institute.

Working through the summer and fall of 1953 in London, Yadin progressed methodically through the long transcription. He produced a meticulous linguistic commentary (drawing upon biblical and rabbinic parallels) on the nineteen surviving columns of tightly inscribed Hebrew characters, as well as a wide-ranging essay on the Qumran sect's military plan for the conquest of the world. Few scholars could have expected that the former chief of staff, whose earlier archaeological studies had concentrated on ancient fortifications and weapons, would be able to tackle complex theological issues of angelology, messianic expectation, and religious ritual with such thoroughness and authority. After completing the transcription and offering restorations for lost words and phrases, Yadin composed a general introduction in which he described the phases of the war and the sequence of enemies to be defeated by the Sons of Light, the precise dimensions and construction of the banners and trumpets to be held by the leaders of the congregation, and the text of the appropriate battlefield prayers. In the course of forty years of fighting, the Sons of Light were to defeat in divinely ordered succession the traditional foreign enemies of the people of Israel (Edomites, Moabites, Ammonites, and Philistines); Israelites who had joined the Sons of Darkness; and the "Kittim" of Assyria and Egypt. In the final phase they would defeat all the remaining foreign nations known to the Israelites, to the farthest reaches of the world.

All other scholars had based their dating of the Dead Sea Scrolls on the forms of letters or on vague historical allusions. Yadin based his on his familiarity with ancient military practice. Far from seeing this scroll as the Qumran community's religious delusion about the imminent End of the World, he interpreted its highly detailed rules for conscripting fighting forces and dividing the men into units and its intricate battle-field movements as evidence of its author's experience—or at least famil-iarity—with contemporary military affairs. The War Scroll, he later wrote "was not essentially written for the purpose of consolation and description of the splendid future at the End of Days. *Its purpose was to supply an urgent and immediate need,* a guide for the problems of the long predicted war, which according to the sect would take place in the near future." Yadin, the former chief of staff, went even further. The sequence in which the information was presented—a description of the rival forces followed by the general aims of the operation, its principal phases, and the assignment of tasks to the various forces—"expresses the logical thought process of the military commander and is still in practice in most armies. It enables the 'recipient of the directive' appointed to carry it out to realize the intention of the Supreme Commander and to under-stand his own duties in the framework of the general plan."

Yadin's reputation as a military leader lent authority to his opinions as a military historian. For university-bound scholars who had never been within miles of a front line or inside a war room, Yadin's long service with the Haganah and in the 1948 War of Independence seemed auto-matically to add weight to his judgments about warfare (in even the most remote historical periods). But it was his implicit understanding of mili-tary logic—not his battlefield experience—that enabled him to discern ancient parallels to the tactics to be employed by the Sons of Light. Few other scholars were both competent to translate the War Scroll and widely read enough in military history to recognize the combat forma-tions it described. The technical terms used for various infantry and cavalry maneuvers—even the Hebrew word for "wings," in a sense equivalent to the Latin military term *alae*—suggested to Yadin a unique Jewish parallel to the structure and battlefield doctrine of the Roman legion in the early imperial period. Thus he was able to hypothesize that the text of the War Scroll was composed in the late first century B.C.

In the spring of 1954, as Yadin neared the end of his work on the War Scroll, he turned from military matters to a detailed commentary on the intricate religious rituals and prayers of the Sons of Light. On April 24 he wrote to Dr. Mazar that his dissertation was finally completed, but because of his imminent departure on a trip to America with Carmella, he had time to proofread the typescript only very hurriedly, and he feared that it might contain a number of typographical errors—far more than the normal doctoral candidate would have been allowed. He regretfully informed Mazar that time pressures had been such that he had not had a chance to compose a proper preface or acknowledgments, but he assured Mazar that he would include them in the published version. As there was little question in Yadin's mind that the dissertation *would* be published, he sent a copy of the manuscript directly to the director of the Bialik Institute, with detailed instructions on how the index should be prepared. As a former chief of staff—not an average graduate student— Yadin was naturally accustomed to the perquisites of power; he sent the manuscript to Mazar by diplomatic pouch—in care of Teddy Kollek, then serving as director-general of the prime minister's office.

The political landscape in Israel had changed dramatically in the year and a half that Yadin had been away. During the summer of 1953, Ben-Gurion had grown weary of the constant bickering and back-biting within the Mapai party. He announced that he intended to take a three-month leave of absence and recommended to the ruling council of the Mapai party that Foreign Minister Moshe Sharett be chosen to serve as acting prime minister. Ben-Gurion's influence was still so great that his recommendation was accepted without question, as was his selection of minister-without-portfolio Pinchas Lavon to serve as acting minister of defense. But three months proved too short a vacation for Ben-Gurion; in the fall of 1953 he announced that he would live for the next two years in the remote Negev kibbutz of Sde Boker—and fulfill personally the pioneering ideal that he had preached from the comfort of Tel Aviv for so long. Sharett and Lavon remained in their posts; at about the same time Chief of Staff Makleff concluded his one-year term, to be succeeded in office by Moshe Dayan. Yigael Yadin was drifting farther and farther from the center of power. Archaeology—not politics—would be the stage on which he fashioned his public career. His self-imposed seclusion in London was ending. His starring performance as soldier, scholar, and goodwill ambassador would debut during his first triumphant lecture tour in America.

The Archbishop Athanasius Yeshue Samuel was tired of American biblical scholars' empty promises. Ever since he had purchased the four ancient scrolls from Ta'amireh bedouin in the summer of 1947, he had been courted, fawned over, and sweet-talked. But few of the scholars whom he consulted had done anything to help him benefit from his discovery. Though the first few experts who saw the scrolls at St. Mark's monastery in the Old City in the fall of 1947 declared them to be of little value, the intense interest of Professor Sukenik (in the course of his abortive negotiations with Anton Kiraz) had led the archbishop to seek the advice of scholars at the American School of Oriental Research. America was then the very symbol of prosperity, from the perspective of war-torn Palestine. But instead of offering to buy the scrolls outright as Sukenik had done, the American scholars promised him that far greater riches would come to him and his community if he would let them photograph, publish, and publicize his scrolls. So it was Millar Burrows of Yale who issued the first press release to the world about the great discovery, and it was his student Dr. John Trever who painstakingly photographed the large scroll of the Book of Isaiah, the commentary on the Book of Habakkuk, and a previously unknown religious composition that Burrows suggestively named "The Manual of Discipline" after the title of the theological rule book of the Methodist Church.

The fourth and last of the archbishop's scrolls was too fragile and decomposed to be photographed immediately, but when the archbishop arrived in America in January 1949 with his precious ancient manuscripts, Dr. Burrows persuaded him to come to New Haven to supervise the opening and photographing of the fourth scroll. Despite vague promises that Yale might purchase the scrolls, no concrete offers were forthcoming; nor were there any during the highly publicized exhibitions of the scrolls at the Library of Congress, the Walters Art Gallery in Baltimore, Duke University, and the Oriental Institute of the University of Chicago. In the meantime serious questions about the archbishop's legal title to the documents were raised by the Department of Antiquities of the Hashemite Kingdom of Jordan, which charged the Syrian Orthodox prelate with illegally exporting those valuable antiquities. No respectable institution or collector in the United States was willing to risk a large sum (a quarter-million dollars or more) on scrolls that might be claimed as the national property of the Kingdom of Jordan. At the same time the Archbishop Samuel, appointed spiritual head of the newly-formed archdiocese of the United States and Canada, was becoming increasingly impatient to gain funds to support himself and to expand the activities of his Church. Dr. Burrows of the American School was unwilling to offer further assistance, even though he published two large volumes containing photographs and transcriptions of the scrolls. By the end of 1951, the archbishop had run out of patience and terminated his relationship with the Americans. But as two more years passed, with Jordanian legal action against any potential buyer a virtual certainty, the chances of his concluding a satisfactory deal must have seemed slim.

In the late spring of 1954, Carmella and Yigael arrived in America. As a unique combination of soldier, scholar, and venerator of the Bible, Yadin proved a near-perfect fund-raising attraction for the Friends of the Hebrew University, Israel Bonds, the United Jewish Appeal, and the America-Israel Society. Among the sponsors and enthusiastic supporters of Yadin's lecture tour were celebrities from show business, business, and politics spanning the political, ethnic, and cultural spectrum from Eleanor Roosevelt to Leonard Bernstein to Thomas Dewey to Thurgood Marshall to Norman Vincent Peale. The toast of postwar American high society, Yadin arrived bearing good news of an ancient testament from the shores of the Dead Sea. In response to public fascination with the Qumran documents, he prepared a series of lectures based on his own research and that of his late father, titled "New Light on the Dead Sea Scrolls." At one of those lectures, on May 27 at Johns Hopkins University, Yadin's interest was unexpectedly turned to the scrolls still in the possession of Archbishop Samuel.

The Yadins' host at Johns Hopkins was Dr. William Foxwell Albright, the undisputed doyen of American biblical archaeology and a close friend of the Sukenik family for almost thirty-five years. Yadin and his father admired the kindly, bookish, and indisputably brilliant American scholar whose sympathy for Zionism and the State of Israel was well known. Now, in a relaxed and nostalgic conversation after Yadin's lecture, they spoke of Albright's recent trip to Israel and his memories of Sukenik from many years before. The subject shifted to the four scrolls that Eleazar Sukenik had long sought but failed to obtain. Albright was well aware of the acrimonious break between Archbishop Samuel and Dr. Burrows and suggested that Yadin might be able to purchase the scrolls for the State of Israel if he contacted the archbishop directly and offered a reasonable price. Yadin followed Albright's advice and wrote to the archbishop, who was then living with a friend in Worcester, Massachusetts, but he received no reply.

Yadin and Carmella moved on to New York and were soon occupied with a whirl of social events, meetings, and lectures. But the archbishop apparently realized that the time had come to make a deal for the scrolls. After five years in the United States he knew that he had sorely tested the hospitality of the struggling Syrian Orthodox communities, and he needed an independent source of support. The persisting Jordanian accusations against him and the political orientation of most of his parishioners had made him unwilling to reply directly to Yadin's offer. Fortunately, the archbishop's host and confidant in Worcester, Charles Manoog, had another idea. As a successful wholesale plumbing supply dealer with experience in dealing with national distributors, he suggested that they place an advertisement in a periodical where it might attract the right kind of clientele. Thus with the archbishop's blessing Manoog placed the following ad on the front page of *The Wall Street Journal* of June 1, 1954:

The Four Dead Sea Scrolls

Biblical Manuscripts dating back to at least 200 BC are for sale. This would be an ideal gift to an educational or religious Institution by an individual or group. Box F 206 The Wall Street Journal.

Yigael Yadin and his scholarly colleagues did not usually read *The Wall Street Journal* but a curious grapevine of journalists and American supporters of Israel alerted Yadin to the unusual ad. William Cohen, a businessman and American public relations director for the Haifa Technion, telephoned Charles Roth of *The National Jewish Post and Opinion* with the idea that the sale of the Dead Sea Scrolls might make a good story; Roth contacted Monty Jacobs of the London *Jewish Chronicle* on the hunch that together they might find out more about the proposed sale. Monty Jacobs then contacted Avraham Harman, the Israeli consul-general in New York and Harmon lost no time in alerting Yadin, who was staying at the St. Moritz Hotel. Needless to say, Yadin was eager to jump at the opportunity, but unlike his father's situation in war-torn Jerusalem, this transaction could now be conducted with businesslike discretion and efficiency. Harman suggested that they utilize the services of New York attorney Maurice Bookstein, who was the legal adviser of the Israeli consulate, but Carmella rightly pointed out that any overt connection to Israel or Israelis might sabotage the deal. Instead they contacted Carmella's cousin Theo Bennahum, a New York financier with international contacts who had experience in the purchase and sale of works of art. Following the customary practice of anonymous buyers, Bennahum instructed his banker, an officer of the Chemical Bank, to reply to the advertisement. Contact was thus established within a few days with Charles Manoog.

At the end of the following week Manoog came to New York to begin the secret negotiations. Whether he knew or suspected the identity of the buyer that Chemical Bank represented, Manoog slowly lowered his million-dollar asking price for the four scrolls to $250,000—the value that independent appraisers had determined several years before. On June 11 Manoog concluded the negotiations and quickly transmitted the good news to the archbishop, who was then staying with parishioners in Jacksonville, Florida. Yadin was ecstatic. "I felt for the first time that our object was really in reach," he later recalled. But the matter of money was now pressing. Although Yadin had privately contacted some prominent New York donors about the possibility of financing the purchase of the scrolls, a quarter-million dollars would take time to raise. He turned to his government for assistance, cabling Teddy Kollek in the prime minister's office. "An unexpected miracle has happened," he wrote Kollek. "The four Dead Sea Scrolls, including Isaiah, brought to the U.S. by the Syrian Metropolitan, are offered for sale. They can be bought at once for 250,000 dollars. No need to stress the importance of the scrolls and the unrepeatable opportunity. Any delay may ruin our chance. Have already probed several important donors, and consider it certain that the sum may be collected within a year. A guarantee from the Treasury for the whole sum is imperative. Request your immediate intervention with the PM and Minister of Finance. Harman who is near me, doing his best to help. I rely on you and expect a positive answer. Secrecy imperative. Yigael."

That positive answer was quickly forthcoming. Since the purchase price was now guaranteed by the government of Israel, Harman was able to arrange an interim loan of $250,000 from the New York–based Fund for Israel Institutions to execute the deal. Further delays were unavoidable, however. The two sides' lawyers took several days to arrive at the precise wording of the sale contract, and since the archbishop wanted to be present at the signing, the conclusion of the deal was deferred further. In the meantime Theo Bennahum had to leave New York, and his business partner Sidney Estridge became Yadin's representative. With increasing apprehension they waited a full ten days for further word from Manoog. Although they had agreed on the sale price and Yadin had secured the sources of funding, they feared that if the Israeli connection were too blatant, the archbishop might cancel the deal. On June 28 word finally came from Worcester that the archbishop, Manoog, and their lawyer would arrive in New York to consummate the sale in a few days. On July 1, they sent word to Sidney Estridge to meet with them at their suite at the Waldorf Astoria to conclude the negotiations, sign the contract, and transfer the scrolls.

It remained only to verify the scrolls' authenticity—a point Yadin's lawyers insisted upon before they would allow the deal to go through. This caused a last-minute complication, for the scholar whom Yadin had contacted several days before to undertake the assignment had to leave New York. Even as Sidney Estridge was concluding the negotiations, Yadin had to find an expert to certify the authenticity of the scrolls. After a morning of frantic telephoning and becoming aware that most scholars were already away for the July 4 weekend, he managed to reach Dr. Harry Orlinsky of Hebrew Union College, who was about to leave for vacation himself. Yadin implored Orlinsky to come to the Israeli consulate as soon as possible—on a matter of the utmost importance and urgency. Only when Orlinsky arrived at Harman's office did he learn of his assignment. Armed with a copy of Dr. Burrows' publication of the scrolls, Orlinsky was to take a taxi to the Waldorf and meet Sidney Estridge (who would be wearing a flower in his lapel) at the Lexington Avenue entrance, then proceed with him to the vault of the Chemical Bank branch where the archbishop's representatives would show him their scrolls. He was to carefully compare each manuscript with the published photographs to make sure that they were genuine and complete. In an added security precaution Yadin instructed Orlinsky to identify himself only as "Mr. Green."

The cloak-and-dagger trappings were probably not really necessary. The archbishop had by this time apparently concluded that this was the best offer he was ever likely to get. Years later, both Harman and Orlinsky recalled feeling at the time that the archbishop and Charles Manoog knew very well with whom they were dealing, yet the business arrangement went on precisely as planned. Orlinsky duly examined the scrolls in the stuffy bank vault and declared them to be genuine; upon leaving the vault with Estridge, he proceeded to a phone booth where he called Yadin and Harman and used the prearranged Hebrew code word *le-Chaim*, "to life," to signify that everything was fine. After returning to the consulate and signing an affidavit, Orlinsky and his wife finally went off on their vacation. The next morning, the funds were transferred to the archbishop, and Yadin took possession of the scrolls. Together with Carmella and Sidney Estridge, he went to the Chemical Bank vault and supervised the transport of the trunk containing the scrolls to the Israeli consulate. And over the next several weeks the four scrolls were dispatched by separate couriers to Israel. Total secrecy about the transaction was still strictly maintained.

In the meantime Yadin and Carmella resumed their tour across America as if nothing had happened. Large audiences continued to attend Yadin's lectures, and he continued to enjoy celebrity status. While stopping for a few days at the University of Chicago, the Yadins were official guests of the Oriental Institute. Avraham Malamat, Yadin's longtime acquaintance who was then at the Institute as a visiting research fellow, recalled that the entire faculty turned out to listen to the lecture of the Israeli soldier-scholar and meet him at a small reception afterward. Seven years before, Yadin had secretly planned to come to America and study at the Oriental Institute, but that had been before Ben-Gurion called him back to service. Even though, as Malamat recalled, Yadin now played humble in the presence of the distinguished archaeologists and Near Eastern scholars, he no longer needed the Oriental Institute. Having completed his dissertation and just acquired four more Dead Sea Scrolls for Israel, far greater career horizons were opening up for him.

Beneath the Gothic spires and university towers of Cambridge, England, at the Twenty-third International Congress of Orientalists held in the late summer of 1954, Yigael Yadin was a shining star. At this international convocation of scholars in ancient Near Eastern studies, Far Eastern literature, linguistics, history, and the ethnography of "non-Western" cultures, Israeli scholars had an opportunity to demonstrate that the intellectual standards of their nation were fully equal to the best of the Western world. Included in the Israeli delegation were some of the Hebrew University's best and brightest young scholars: the Egyptologist Chaim Polotsky, the geographer David Amiran, the Islamicist David Ayalon, the historian Avraham Malamat (on his way back from Chicago), and Yadin. But Yadin's position was quite different from the others'. For Yadin, an appearance at a congress or public meeting was never merely the reading of a scholarly article. It was an opportunity to shape his public image, and his appearance at the congress in Cambridge allowed him to demonstrate his intellectual versatility. As former head of the military delegation that had concluded an armistice with Egypt, his lecture "Military Contacts between Palestine and Egypt in the Third Millennium B.C." had fascinating modern overtones.

With his rare combination of photographic memory, military logic, and creative intuition, Yadin brought together an unlikely mélange of archaeological evidence to weave a vivid story of one of Egypt's first foreign military campaigns. The key to his interpretation was the Narmer Palette—a carved gray slate tablet that Egyptologists had been studying for more than fifty years. Not unexpectedly, Yadin was confident that he could do better than the earlier scholars. While they saw the palette as a visual depiction of the unification of Upper and Lower Egypt by King Narmer, Yadin went much farther afield. He identified two of the figures of captives as a Canaanite city dweller and a Transjordanian pastoralist (not Egyptians!) and suggested that Narmer, once securely in power in Egypt, had claimed conquests in the lands to the north and east. Yadin remained skeptical whether the Egyptian king had indeed achieved what he claimed. "In the typically boasting manner encountered later in many Egyptian documents," Yadin noted ironically, based on his knowledge of other hieroglyphic inscriptions and in unspoken acknowledgment of his own wartime experience, "it might echo only a short penetration, a military expedition, or perhaps an even less conspicuous event." Yadin was indeed the star of his own scholarly performance. Malamat recalled that in Yadin's audience there were about two hundred people, while most scholars attracted no more than twenty. Most significant of all, the Egyptian delegation attended. Even though they scrupulously avoided contact with the other Israeli scholars, they too were curious about the famous Israeli scholar-general.

Back in Israel, some of those in power naturally assumed that Yadin would want to return to public life after his two-year fling with academia. But as early as February 1954, acting Prime Minister Sharett expressed concern about Yadin's future. In his journal he noted that, in order "to use him in a way that is best for the country and to prevent him from going astray," perhaps Yadin should be named Israel's ambassador in the United States. In March, Sharett received a disturbing report that Yadin had no intention of returning to public life in the immediate future. Moshe Zadok, Yadin's former colleague on the general staff, had just returned from England and reported to Sharett that Yadin expected to be in England for another year and begin teaching at the Hebrew University the year after that. Sharett also noted Zadok's observation that Yadin seemed "sure he was headed for big things in the service of the State, but is unsure of what other people think of him." The acting prime minister therefore brought up his name in April as a possibility for the Washington ambassadorial post. But Yadin was not interested. During the course of their trip to America and with Yigael's growing reputation as a scholar, Yigael and Carmella finally decided that there would now be no return to the world of politics.

At the end of August, Yadin received a warm letter of praise and congratulation from Dr. Mazar, who had been told of the scroll purchase by Abe Harman in New York. Dr. Mazar was also unstinting in his praise for Yadin's dissertation on the War Scroll and saw no reason why it would not be accepted at the first meeting of the humanities faculty in the fall. But he had an even more pressing matter to present to Yadin. The Israel Department of Antiquities and the Israel Exploration Society were planning a truly massive undertaking—the excavation of the ancient fortress of Masada in the Judean wilderness. The importance of the site was known to every Israeli; the tragic story of its siege by the Romans and the mass suicide of its defenders had become a well-known patriotic motif. Dr. Mazar was convinced that only Yadin could successfully direct such large-scale and highly publicized excavations, and he appealed to him to consider taking them on. But Yadin and Carmella had already chosen a site to excavate and formulated a plan that would highlight one of the Jewish people's great victories, not one of its most bitter defeats. What was more, they had secured an independent source of funding for the project that would allow Yigael to work with a free hand.

As the Yadins' social status rose in London and their social connections expanded, they had developed a special relationship with James and Dorothy de Rothschild, the uncrowned heads of Anglo-Jewish aristocracy. The English Rothschilds were not run-of-the-mill industrialists who had made recent fortunes in business and enjoyed seeing their names mentioned in *The Jewish Chronicle* and inscribed on brass donors' plaques in synagogues, hospitals, and schools. The Rothschilds were the highest nobility among the Jewish people. At the beginning of the Zionist movement, Baron Edmond de Rothschild (scorning publicity and allowing himself to be mentioned in the Zionist press only as *ha-nadiv ha-yadua,* "the well-known benefactor") had underwritten vast colonization schemes, educational projects, and commercial ventures in the Land of Israel. His son James had inherited something of the baron's reputation in Jewish circles; he had served as a military liaison with the first official delegation of Zionist leaders to Palestine after World War I and remained active in support of the Palestine Jewish Colonization Association and the Hebrew University. Though born in France, James became a naturalized British subject in 1919 and later served as a Liberal member of Parliament. Educated at Cambridge, he adopted a monocle as his personal trademark and delighted in fine racehorses and his seventy-room Waddesdon Manor in Buckinghamshire. James de Rothschild was immediately impressed with Yigael and Carmella. And before long, Yadin's engaging conversations about archaeology and his anecdotes about modern combat became regular features of weekend outings and dinners at Waddesdon.

The thirty-seven-year-old former chief of staff had something valuable to offer the Rothschilds. Sponsorship of an archaeological dig in the East, like horses or a fine manor, was still a symbol of only the highest reaches of the British aristocracy. The excavation that Yadin was proposing had an object far more alluring than mere treasure. This articulate and elegant young Jewish soldier-scholar offered the Rothschilds the opportunity, indeed the privilege, to underwrite the discovery of the palaces and fortresses of their own noble forefathers, Joshua and Solomon. The site he had chosen for an ambitious new archaeological project was the mound of Tell el-Qedah, situated near the Syrian border in the Upper Galilee. This site was confidently identified by many scholars as the biblical city of Hazor. Hazor, Yadin explained to the Rothschilds and the circle of supporters that gathered around him, was an ideal place to investigate Canaanite and Israelite history. Hazor was, after all, one of the mighty Canaanite cities mentioned in the biblical narratives of Joshua's conquest, and it played an important part in the reigns of Solomon and the later Israelite kings. The very ambitiousness of Israeli excavations at Hazor would challenge the authority and dominance of foreign archaeologists in the country. Most important of all, the Rothschilds could provide the means to implement Yadin's archaeological vision on a previously unimaginable scale.

The rediscovery of Hazor's royal citadels, fortification walls, and city gates would enable Yadin to present the Israeli public with the grandeur and power of biblical history. Never before had an Israeli expedition tackled such a huge Near Eastern site, fully equal in importance to Megiddo (excavated by the Oriental Institute in the late 1920s and 1930s) and Jericho, where excavations were even now under way. Since 1952, British archaeologist Kathleen Kenyon (a longtime protégé of Mortimer Wheeler) had been excavating the site of ancient Jericho under the auspices of the Jordanian Department of Antiquities. Her preliminary analysis of the superimposed city levels had tended to cast doubt on the historical accuracy of the Book of Joshua. Yadin listened carefully to Kenyon's presentations at the Institute of Archaeology in London, where he had come to know her, if not like her. He was eager to provide an alternative version. In August he had confided his plans to Avraham Malamat, who had come to England for the Orientalists' Congress. Malamat recalled that Yadin "took me into a room in the Institute of Archaeology and he sat on the desk—he liked to sit on the desk, with his legs swinging—and he said I want to tell you a secret, a great secret." Malamat was convinced that Yadin had already told many others, but he went along with the pretense of secrecy. "I am going to excavate Hazor," Yadin told him with characteristic drama. "I must know about Joshua. I must know if he really conquered it."

In the meantime, another mission was being prepared for Yadin. During the two years when he was fully occupied in London with ancient scrolls and visions of biblical kings and battles, the Israeli leaders and the IDF commanders were becoming increasingly concerned with a growing threat from the south. An Anglo-Egyptian agreement had been concluded in the summer of 1954, paving the way for the withdrawal of British forces from the Suez Canal Zone and thereby removing the military buffer between Israel and Egypt. Many in the Israeli defense establishment—including acting Defense Minister Pinchas Lavon and Chief of Staff Moshe Dayan—urged a policy of aggressive defense on the southern border. Others, like Prime Minister Sharett, sought a quiet diplomatic understanding with Gamal Abdul Nasser, the leader of the Revolutionary Command Council that had deposed King Farouk. Through secret contacts Sharett gained Nasser's agreement to meet an Israeli representative in Cairo as a first step toward wide-ranging diplomatic talks. Despite the arrest of a ring of Israeli agents in Cairo and Alexandria in December 1954, Sharett was still intent on the secret negotiations. On January 21, 1955, he decided that the secret Israeli envoy should be Yigael Yadin.

As one of the few Israelis who had experience in direct negotiations with the Egyptians, Yadin was the obvious candidate for this delicate assignment. He received a confidential cable in London from Teddy Kollek on January 26 detailing the secret mission and the objectives. On the following day Egypt announced that two of the accused Israeli agents would be executed, and hard-liners within the Israeli government applied intense pressure on Sharett. Fearing that the secret contacts with Nasser might damage his political standing, Sharett called off Yadin's secret mission to Egypt. Tensions with Egypt escalated through the spring; with the growing regional tension, Ben-Gurion agreed to end his self-imposed Negev exile and return to office as minister of defense. Yadin apparently had no desire to help shape Israeli policy toward Egypt, once his mission to meet Nasser was called off. The plan that he and Carmella had worked out for their future was coming to fruition. His doctoral dissertation had been approved by the humanities faculty of the Hebrew University, and he had been formally appointed a research fellow; and the Rothschild funding for the Hazor excavations was in place.

One more triumph crowned his personal transformation from chief of staff to world-famous archaeologist; it concerned the Dead Sea Scrolls. In the months since his secret negotiations with Archbishop Samuel, Yadin had worked hard to secure funds to underwrite the purchase. He found a willing benefactor in Samuel Gottesman, a prominent New York industrialist and philanthropist. The Gottesman family was to play a crucial role in the preservation and exhibition of the scrolls in the coming years. With the financing arranged and the scrolls safely transported back to Israel, the veil of secrecy over the transaction could finally be lifted. On February 13, 1955, at a hastily called press conference in his office in Jerusalem, Prime Minister Sharett officially announced Israel's acquisition of the four famous Dead Sea Scrolls. The nation was fascinated not only by ancient Hebrew and Aramaic documents themselves but by the daring, ingenious way they had been recovered. Kollek cabled Yadin in London: "At this memorable moment the Prime Minister is telling the country and the world about the homecoming of the scrolls. Excitement and joy are great." Reporters in London eagerly descended on Yadin for interviews and additional details; his celebrity status rose. While his former colleagues in the IDF grimly faced the prospect of renewed fighting with Egypt, Yadin achieved the status of national hero, through the medium of archaeology.

In the late winter of 1955, with their glorious time in London ending, Yigael and Carmella invited two of their closest friends from Israel, Yaacov and Gila Yannai, to join them on a European tour. The friendship between the two couples dated back to when Yigael and "Jan" were officers in the Haganah headquarters. The two couples had been married on the same day in December 1941, and for years they had celebrated their anniversaries together. When the Yannais arrived in London, however, it must have been clear how much had changed in just two years. Yadin was no longer a military officer dreaming of regimenting Israeli society through discipline and pioneering. He had become a scholar and celebrity, comfortable with the genteel affectations of high society and the academic world. They set off for a two-week auto trip on the Continent, and Jan recalled with wry nostalgia that Yadin was "a terrible driver." One can almost imagine the scene on that memorable tour: Yadin, with a pipe in his mouth and tweed cap on his head, behind the wheel of a roadster; next to him Carmella with sunglasses and a kerchief; and Jan and Gila in the back seat. Wherever he went, Yadin was always a confident guide and a congenial traveling companion. But now, as he grandly pointed out the historical sights and cultural highlights along the winding country roads of France, Belgium, and Holland, he must have seemed the perfect British gentleman.

Chapter Eleven

HEAD OF ALL THOSE KINGDOMS

S tanding on the summit of Tell el-Qedah, Yadin felt the power. Plodding across the soft, spongy ground still soaked by the late-winter rains, he paced out the distances between excavation areas, accompanied by the newly recruited staff members of his James A. de Rothschild Expedition to Hazor. As the buried ruins of the ancient city stretched out before them, Yadin discussed with his colleagues the most promising locations to dig for palaces, citadels, temples, and main entrance gates on the upper plateau. Then he guided them down the slope to the vast lower city, a two-hundred-acre rectangular area enclosed by high earthen ramparts, where building stones, smashed pottery, and stone altars lay scattered among the weeds. Yadin had been away from field archaeology for almost a decade (and admittedly lacked the excavation experience of most of his staff members), but he was confident and enthusiastic about the prospects for the dig. The excavation of Hazor, even more than his recovery of the Dead Sea Scrolls, offered him an opportunity to establish his scholarly credentials. With the city described in the Book of Joshua as "the head of all those kingdoms" and mentioned prominently in ancient Egyptian and Mesopotamian sources, he would make his debut as a practicing archaeologist. No less important—and this was almost certainly among his conscious intentions—Yadin was determined to use the Hazor excavations as a testing ground on which to invent, create, and shape the distinctive national endeavor that would eventually be known as Israeli archaeology.

He intended Hazor, in fact, to be Israel's declaration of archaeological independence. During the British Mandate, the pioneers of Jewish archaeology in Palestine—Eleazar Sukenik and Benjamin Mazar among them—had carried out only small excavations, concentrating for the most part on tombs and synagogues in small trial digs. They had neither sufficient financial means nor manpower to compete with the foreign schools in excavating the largest and most famous biblical sites. This situation changed with the establishment of the State of Israel. The influence of the foreign schools vanished, as most were now located across the border in East Jerusalem and operating exclusively in Jordanian territory. Even though dozens of excavations and surveys were conducted every year by the Israel Department of Antiquities, however, only Yadin had the foresight, energy, and connections to mount an expedition on the scale of those of the British, American, and French. In that achievement, Yadin fulfilled an ambition of which Eleazar Sukenik could only have dreamed: The Hazor dig, with its staff of forty-five supervisors and students; its full complement of surveyors, photographers, pottery restorers, and registrars; its modern excavation equipment; and its workforce of more than two hundred laborers would be the largest and most ambitious excavation ever undertaken in the Holy Land.

In the meantime, the political landscape in Israel was shifting again. Ben-Gurion had returned from Sde Boker to reassume office as minister of defense, and by the summer of 1955 he had retaken the office of prime minister as well. Moshe Sharett offered no serious objection; as the unchallenged leader of Mapai, Ben-Gurion could assume any office he chose. Ben-Gurion was eager to bring new people and talent into the government. Soon after Yadin's return to Israel in April 1955, he had summoned Yadin for a chat about his future and suggested that he accept the specially created post of minister of the South and the Negev to lend his organizational talents to Israel's economy and society. But Yadin firmly rejected this offer and Ben-Gurion's other repeated appeals. Yadin saw the Hazor project as his own contribution to the state, far transcending the bounds of pure archaeology. The Eastern Galilee and Huleh Valley, where Hazor was located, were areas that Yadin knew well from his many inspection tours of the Syrian front, and their strategic importance for Israel's future was clear. In the early 1950s the government had been only partially successful in developing this region's economy, settling it with immigrants from the Jewish communities of North Africa. High unemployment and a sense of alienation were rampant. Yadin therefore believed that a large-scale project at Hazor could offer material and cultural benefits to the region—a source of steady employment for workers and an impressive historical monument to link this far northern region with the mainstream of Israelite history.

With typical thoroughness and energy, Yadin launched the project as if it were a military operation. In contrast to the directors of earlier, small-scale Israeli excavations who had been saddled with endless administrative and financial tasks in addition to their archaeological responsibilities, Yadin knew how to delegate authority. In England he had hired a retired Israeli army officer, Lieutenant Colonel Joseph Pelz, to take over budgetary and administrative matters so that Yadin himself would be "free to concentrate on the archaeological aspects of the work." During the spring, Pelz conducted negotiations with nearby Kibbutz Ayyelet Hashahar for staff accommodations, and he directed the construction of prefabricated barracks, offices, storerooms, and laboratories across the road from the tell. The local branch of the Government labor exchange at Rosh Pinna willingly arranged for the daily transport of immigrant workers. In the meantime a treasure trove of crated excavation equipment began to arrive at Haifa port. Back in London, Yadin's friend Leon Shalit at Marks and Spenser served as the dig's purchasing agent, and he budgeted, ordered, and shipped to Israel the items Yadin had requested—from typewriters to wheelbarrows, to darkroom equipment, to pens, pencils, picks, and shovels, to a miniature railway (complete with locomotive) to dump the thousands of tons of earth that were expected to be dug from the site.

The generous support of the Rothschilds was not the only factor setting this dig apart from earlier ones. In sharp contrast to Eleazar Sukenik, who had surrounded himself with submissive scholars and unimaginative technicians, Yadin chose for the Hazor staff the strongest and most competent personalities he could find. Benjamin Mazar suggested three of Israel's most promising young archaeologists, Yohanan Aharoni, Ruth Amiran, and Trude Dothan, for permanent area supervisors and senior specialists. Immanuel "Munya" Dunnayevsky, an insightful and experienced architect who had worked with Dr. Mazar at his earlier excavations joined Yadin to help in architectural and engineering matters and to supervise the drawing of plans. To add an international touch to the expedition, Yadin recruited Jean Perrot, director of the French Research Center in Israel, an elegant, cosmopolitan scholar with many years of excavation experience both in Israel and in Iran. By the middle of July, the staff of forty-five was completed and assembled in the camp at Hazor.

With the first excavation season due to begin on August 1, the surveyors laid down a grid of hundred-meter squares over the entire tell, and other staff members devised new forms of registration tags, diaries, and logbooks for the use of the area supervisors and the pottery specialists at the base camp. Workmen were dispatched to set up field telephones at each of the excavation areas and lay tracks for the dump train across the surface of the tell. With the logistical preparations nearly completed, Yadin made the final determinations about the excavation strategy. Almost thirty years before, the British archaeologist John Garstang had briefly explored Tell el-Qedah, and his sketchy excavation report now provided some indication of what the Israeli expedition was likely to find. Garstang described "a palatial building or temple" on the west end of the upper city and the ruins of a pillared "stable" of the Solomonic period in its center. Yadin entrusted Yohanan Aharoni with Area A, the area around Garstang's stable, and he assigned Ruth Amiran to oversee Area B, the "palatial building" on the west. After a preliminary investigation of the lower city, Yadin assigned Jean Perrot and his team to Area C, at the southwest of the enclosure, to dig a trench through the earthen ramparts to determine their construction and destruction date. Area D in the lower city was entrusted to Claire Epstein, an experienced archaeologist and staff member. Trude Dothan would supervise the registration of all excavated pottery.

Only when the project was under way were Yadin and his staff confronted with the enormity and complexity of what they had undertaken. Their challenge was not merely to excavate an entire ancient city, one of the largest in ancient Canaan, but to create a working atmosphere in which the senior archaeologists—all used to working independently— would accommodate themselves to working under Yadin's command. Yadin was careful to cultivate the good feelings of the workers and encourage the students and field assistants, but his relations with his closest colleagues were sometimes strained. From the army Yadin was used to barking out orders to his highest subordinates and assuming that they would silently carry out his will. This was an entirely different situation. While Lieutenant Colonel Pelz instinctively accepted the discipline, Ruth Amiran and Trude Dothan, who had both known Yadin in Rechavia and at the university and considered him their peer, rebelled.

"There was a dramatic meeting early in the summer," Trude Dothan recalled, "where we confronted him about the military discipline. He was giving us orders and we simply went to talk to him about team-work—about how we thought the work should be done." Yadin re-sponded angrily at first to this challenge; shouted words were exchanged. "But the meeting ended very well," Dothan continued. "He finally agreed to change his attitude toward us, and he apologized for his tem-per by telling us an anecdote about an angry outburst that he had against an Egyptian general during the armistice talks at Rhodes."

Only one staff member remained unsatisfied: Yohanan Aharoni. An officer of the Department of Antiquities, he had not known Yadin before joining the Hazor excavations and would remain something of an odd man out. He had arrived at Hazor with his wife and family in July, and little by little, they separated themselves from the rest of the staff by insisting on sitting at a separate table in the kibbutz dining hall. At least at the beginning Yadin had nothing against Aharoni; he respected him as an experienced excavator, and a scholar who had received Dr. Mazar's highest recommendation. Yet no sooner had Yadin and Aharoni estab-lished a working relationship than tension arose between them: Aharoni questioned Yadin's judgment at every turn. Aharoni's background and motivations were different than Yadin's. He had come to Israel as a teen-age refugee from Nazi Germany in 1933, and after nine years on Kibbutz Allonim he had entered the university to study archaeology and histori-cal geography. Aharoni's archaeological theories were indisputably inno-vative; during his studies and early years as an inspector with the Department of Antiquities, he had pioneered the exploration of the Ju-dean Wilderness and the Upper Galilee. For Aharoni, archaeology was not only a scholarly pursuit but a medium through which he could exer-cise his personal ambition, in a continuing struggle to advance profes-sionally. In that respect he resembled Eleazar Sukenik. Whenever he saw an opening he would take it, no matter whom he offended or pushed out of the way. Aharoni's distaste for Yadin's British affectations and imperi-ous manner—and Yadin's angry reaction to him—became a long-running clash of wills.

For now, this simmering personal conflict was still in the back-ground. The finds from the first season of digging justified and even surpassed the most optimistic hopes of the team. In Area A in the upper city, Aharoni uncovered a fascinating sequence of superimposed Israel-ite strata, offering a unique glimpse at the life and wars of the Kingdom of Israel under the shadow of conquest by the Assyrian Empire. Beneath a level of modest houses, Aharoni's workers uncovered a prosperous, well-built city that had been suddenly and violently destroyed. Roofs had collapsed onto ground-floor rooms with all their contents; all were covered by a thick layer of ash. The distinctive pottery dated this level to the late eighth century B.C. This neatly matched the date of the destruction of Hazor by the Assyrian king Tiglath-Pileser, an event recorded in II Kings 15:29 as having taken place "In the days of Pekah, King of Israel." In Area B, in the meanwhile, Ruth Amiran and her team discovered that Garstang's "palatial building" was really a heavily fortified Israelite citadel that had guarded the western side of the acropolis. But the most exciting and unexpected finds from the first season came from Area C in the lower city, directed at first by Jean Perrot and subsequently by Trude Dothan.

Yadin had two reasons for investigating the huge rectangular area. As a longtime student of ancient warfare, he knew that similarly shaped fortified enclosures in Egypt and Syria had been interpreted as armed camps for Hyksos charioteers. This was the only such occurrence in Israel, a sure sign of the city's importance; he was determined to discover its date and method of its construction. No less important was the date of its final destruction, for according to the Bible, Joshua and the Israelites had conquered Hazor. John Garstang, after examining finds from the lower city, had suggested that Hazor's conquest by the Israelites took place around 1400 B.C. Dr. Albright, on the other hand and on other grounds, insisted that the conquest took place around 1250 B.C. At the start of the excavations, Yadin had no particular preconception. Although he did not doubt the historical reality of Joshua's conquest, he was ready to accept evidence for either date. In fact, evidence for the date of the lower city's destruction came quickly. Just one meter beneath the surface, Perrot and his team uncovered the remains of a densely packed and apparently prosperous city, not an open-air enclosure. Signs of destruction were everywhere—charred beams, smashed pottery, and collapsed walls—and scattered on the floors were fragments of Mycenaean ceramic vessels, imported from Greece around 1250 B.C.

This discovery created a sensation—and not in scholarly circles alone. Newspaper reporters from Tel Aviv flocked north, eager for a story on an ancient Israelite triumph uncovered by a modern Israeli chief of staff. "I do not imply that we have here as yet any proof that this city was destroyed by Joshua," Yadin cautioned a correspondent for *The Jerusalem Post*. "Such an assumption can only be tested by future excavations." At the same time he reinforced the image of conquering Israelites by his dramatic description of what he called "the most important discovery of the season." As the team was digging into the inner face of the rampart to check the construction of that massive line of fortifications, they came upon a small headless statue of a Canaanite king or god carved of black basalt. As they expanded the excavation area here they uncovered a small Canaanite shrine whose central features were an offering table and ten upright stone tablets arranged in a niche in the back wall. The fact that the head of the statue was found nearby suggested that it had been desecrated intentionally by "a blow at the neck with a sharp instrument." The evidence seemed to be accumulating that Hazor was indeed conquered by the Israelites, who set fire to the city and threw down their enemies' idols around 1250 B.C.

An important transformation was taking place in that first season of digging at Hazor, far more important than any specific hypothesis or find. In drawing the attention of the nation to archeological evidence, new visual images of the "ancient" and the "biblical" landscape became impressed upon Israeli popular consciousness. For decades the school-children of the Yishuv had imagined that biblical villages and towns resembled rural Arab villages of low stone buildings, with outdoor clay ovens, grazing flocks of sheep and goats, braying donkeys, and stone threshing floors. The rural Arab population, seen from a distance and with romantic exaggeration, came to be the present-day physical embodiment of all that was ancient and biblical in artworks, school pageants, and history books. Biblical scholars and historians—not to mention countless school groups, scout troops, and amateur explorers dedicated to the patriotic pastime of *yediat ha-aretz,* "knowledge of the land"— devoted great energy throughout the Mandate period to attempting to match contemporary Arab villages with biblical sites.

But all that had changed with the earth-shaking violence of 1948. The traditional Arab village culture was now largely removed from the landscape of Israel. Hundreds of thousands of Palestinian Arabs were now refugees in Syria, Jordan, and the Gaza Strip. Scores of their abandoned hilltop clusters of stone houses were dynamited, bulldozed, fenced off, or repopulated with Jewish immigrants. The process that had begun with Plan D, written by the Haganah operations branch under Yadin's supervision, had succeeded in creating a geographically contiguous Jewish state. The plight of the Arab refugees could be put out of mind, be militarily justified, or balanced against the long sufferings of the Jewish people. But there was a subtle yet pervasive aftereffect of the 1948 war that could not be ignored. Simply put, much of what the Jewish community had long identified as "ancient" had vanished. To replace the familiar, psychically reassuring symbols of biblical antiquity, a new physical connection with the past had to be made.

The excavations at Hazor therefore continued on a symbolic level the process that Plan D had begun. Archaeology became a means by which the historical landscape could be remolded. Tells, not Arab vil-

lages, became focal points of popular attention. Ancient pottery and fig-
urines, not romantic sketches of Arab shepherds and farmers, became
icons for biblical antiquity. Photographs and drawings of ancient buildings and artifacts uncovered at Hazor and elsewhere, widely published in
newspapers and magazines and eventually in history books, helped reshape the common images of ancient Israel. The effect was not only to
provide more accurate illustrations, but also, unconciously, to sever the
longstanding visual connection between modern Arabs and the biblical
past. It was a past that in many ways reflected the self-perception of the
young State of Israel, in its preoccupations with warfare and territorial
conquest, fortifications, ethnic divisions, and migrations to a promised
land. The epic of biblical Israel now found expression in Yadin's massive,
well-coordinated archaeological excavations, in which modern Israeli archaeologists played a starring role.

Thus, returning to Jerusalem after the first season of digging, Yadin
had much to attend to. Carmella had remained at home and in May
1956 gave birth to a second daughter, Littal. Almost immediately Yadin
began planning for the next season at Hazor, but he also found time to
work with Nahman Avigad on the translation of the last of the recently
purchased Dead Sea Scrolls. Yadin did not need a political office to remain in the public eye. Just a year after his return to Israel from England,
he received an honor that came to few Israeli scholars in their lifetimes:
the Israel Prize in Jewish Studies, awarded to him by President Yitzhak
Ben-Zvi in an official ceremony on Independence Day 1956.

In the late autumn of 1955, after the first season of the Hazor excavations, Yadin finally began his teaching career. He had been appointed to
the Hebrew University faculty as lecturer in the archaeology of Israel in
April, but only in November, with the beginning of a new academic year,
did he face students for the first time. The physical conditions under
which he had to work were far different from those at the Institute of
Archaeology in London, and even from those of his own student days.
The original building of the National Museum of Jewish Antiquities on
Mount Scopus had been besieged, sandbagged, and garrisoned with soldiers since the 1948 War of Independence, so the department of archaeology (like all the other university departments) had been forced to shift
its activities to West Jerusalem. In the converted parlor and bedrooms of
a cramped apartment on Jabotinsky Street, Yadin joined Dr. Mayer, Michael Avi-Yonah, and Nahman Avigad (who had earned a Ph.D. in 1952)
in conducting classes on the archaeology of Israel, the Mediterranean
world, and the ancient Near East.

Yadin was by this time an experienced public speaker. As chief of staff, he had continually been called upon to speak to soldiers and civilians, and later, as Israel's goodwill ambassador in England and America, he had given dozens of archaeological lectures, after-dinner speeches, and fund-raising appeals. Now in the 1955–56 academic year, he would be required to guide students through a four-year course of study, prepare and grade their examinations, and supervise their independent work. He approached the task with energy and enthusiasm, immediately capturing the attention—and imagination—of the dozen or so students. "Suddenly Yadin arrived, and Yadin certainly gave the whole thing a new impetus and a new energy," recalled David Ussishkin, who began his university studies in the fall of 1955. "He was a very fine lecturer and very enthusiastic about the subjects he taught." In his first course on ancient warfare and weapons, Yadin offered his students a sweeping saga of ancient kingdoms in conflict—of chariot forces, siege tactics, archers, cavalry, and battering rams. In contrast to the often tedious lectures of Avigad and other teachers, who often got bogged down in details and pedantic distinctions, Yadin adopted the technique of an expert storyteller, never allowing ambiguity or unnecessary complexity to blunt the emotional impact of his tale.

Through the winter and spring of 1956, as Yadin lectured to his students about Hyksos chariot forces sweeping southward from Syria, northward invasions of Egyptian pharaohs, and victories of the Israelite tribes over Canaanite cities, military tensions were mounting all along the borders of modern Israel. The current chief of staff, Moshe Dayan, was committed to the doctrine of immediate and painful retaliation for every border incursion. Yet the number of violent incidents with Egypt, Jordan, and Syria continued to mount. President Nasser of Egypt had emerged as one of the leaders of the nonaligned movement and had concluded a massive arms pact with Czechoslovakia; his influence continued to rise throughout the Arab world. In July 1956, to the horror and outrage of the Western powers, Nasser nationalized the Suez Canal. Yet back in Israel, despite the darkening security situation, Yadin prepared for a second season of excavation at Hazor. As in the first, the digging was scheduled to continue for three full months, beginning on August 1, under the supervision of an expedition staff that now included undergraduates. And once again the finds continued to be impressive; Aharoni and Amiran uncovered the buildings of the Israelite kings in the upper city, and Trude Dothan and Jean Perrot uncovered a wealth of Bronze Age Canaanite finds in the lower city.

The rising international tensions, however, cut short the digging. Raids and counterraids across the Israel-Jordan armistice line had intensified through the summer, and in the wake of a massive IDF operation against the Jordanian town of Qalqiliya on October 11, the Hashemite kingdom entered a military alliance with Egypt and Syria. Despite official British warnings to Israel about further military actions against Jordan, Prime Minister Ben-Gurion and Chief of Staff Dayan appeared unwilling to back away from a direct confrontation. A national mobilization of IDF reserve forces was announced, and many of the students and staff members at the Hazor excavations received orders to report to their units at once. Aviva Rosen, the administrative secretary of the excavations, recalled that Yadin occasionally conferred with members of the general staff who came to visit, but he was tight-lipped about the unfolding military situation. Suddenly, on Monday, October 29, he was called to the headquarters of the northern command.

Though only a few more days remained in the digging season, Aviva Rosen and the other senior staff members expected to stay at the site for several more weeks to complete the registration and packing of the season's finds. But that afternoon, Rosen received an urgent message from Yadin to pack up and prepare to leave the site immediately. Since there was no way they could transport the hundreds of boxes of artifacts on such short notice, Yadin instructed them to bury all the important finds that the could not take with them. Soon after dark, Yadin returned to the expedition compound and gathered the remaining staff members in the photographer's makeshift studio. He somberly announced that a war was under way and asked for volunteers to remain at the site—Munya Dunnayevsky, his assistant Ehud Netzer, and Ruth Amiran stepped forward. He directed all the others to pack up their cars and follow him in a convoy back to Jerusalem. They drove all night and were allowed to pass quickly through the many military roadblocks once Yadin—driving his station wagon at the head of the caravan—identified himself. Yadin refused to give his colleagues further details about the military situation, and while everyone else assumed that a war with Jordan was beginning, all the military vehicles and tank transports they saw on the road that night were moving south. Only the next morning, after they arrived back in Jerusalem, did they learn from the radio and newspapers that the threat of war against Jordan had only been a diversion. A lightning Israeli campaign in Sinai against Egypt had begun.

In the days that followed, as Yadin's old IDF colleagues and former subordinates achieved impressive victories in their conquest of the Sinai peninsula, it became painfully clear that Yadin was neither informed nor consulted about the military events. To his colleagues on the Hazor staff he seemed vaguely embarrassed to have been excluded from a more active role by the current army high command.

Yet public relations—not military planning—was to be his func-tion. The opening of the academic year was delayed by the fighting, so he agreed to go abroad on a hastily arranged lecture tour to mobilize public support for Israel in England and the United States. Returning in early January, he reported a disturbing development to Ben-Gurion. "Yigael lectured at several universities," the prime minister recorded in his diary, "and of course for the United Jewish Appeal and for Israel Bonds. He hardly saw any young people at any of the meetings. The younger gener-ation knew practically nothing about Israel. And the masses don't know anything either because they invite only the biggest contributors to the banquets." Yadin would be instrumental in changing that situation, and he would be sent abroad on goodwill missions with increasing frequency during the coming years—often with little regard for his teaching sched-ule at the university.

Other faculty members at the Hebrew University carped and grum-bled about Yadin's special treatment. Despite all the publicity he had garnered for the university—or because of it—many scholars never con-sidered Yadin really to be one of them. More than a few eyebrows were raised at the speed with which his doctoral dissertation had been ac-cepted and his faculty appointment awarded, especially at a university where academic advancement was often achieved only after decades, not years. Some resented the fact that Yadin had been appointed to the ar-chaeology faculty because of the prestige he had gained in military af-fairs. Philosopher Gershon Scholem, the Hebrew University's most revered faculty member, viewed Yadin's quick flip from soldier to scholar with cynical amusement. "That's not scholarship, that's acrobatics," he reportedly quipped.

Yadin, for his part, did not make things any easier. He was con-vinced that he had received only what he deserved. There clearly was a difference in the way he was accepted in comparison to most scholars. In April 1955, when his doctoral dissertation was officially accepted and he was called upon to deliver the traditional public presentation, photogra-phers from all the major newspapers came. While most new Ph.D.s deliv-ered their inaugural lecture to no more than twenty or twenty-five friends and family, Yadin's lecture attracted a standing-room-only audi-ence at the university's largest auditorium. Dr. Mazar, who was both Yadin's dissertation adviser and president of the university, understood from the beginning how Yadin could advance Israeli archaeology, the finances of the University, and the international image of Israel. As his reputation grew far beyond the department of archaeology—and even the Hebrew University—Yadin planned an ambitious fund-raising tour abroad before the final season of digging at Hazor. A special exhibition of finds from the excavations was planned for the British Museum in May, and he accepted invitations to lecture in Leiden, Amsterdam, Vienna, and Stockholm. The culmination of this tour would be Yadin's personal appearance at the Israel pavilion at the 1958 Brussels world's fair on Israel's Independence Day.

In consultation with Mazar, Yadin intended to use all these events to promote the cause of Israel and raise money for the department of archaeology. The Hebrew University was about to dedicate a modern new campus in west Jerusalem, so he told President Mazar that he was willing to raise money for the university general fund as well. But the standing committee of the faculty was not so ready to allow Yadin to dump all his spring classes in the lap of the long-suffering Dr. Avigad. In an unmistakable rebuke the faculty's academic secretary sternly informed Yadin of the faculty's "uneasiness" at his proposed travel plans and, in barely disguised terms, accused him of shirking his teaching responsibilities. If the professors had expected Yadin to bow his head and submit quietly to their wishes, however, they were mistaken. The former chief of staff dashed off an angry letter, fuming in self-righteous indignation and making serious threats. "In my opinion," Yadin informed the academic secretary, "the work of a member of the university is not expressed in teaching alone, and judging from the many requests I have received from the university authorities to supply them with information about the excavations, finds for exhibitions, and tours for guests of the university, I would have concluded that the Hazor project is one of the most important activities of the university.

"Perhaps the standing committee is not aware," Yadin disdainfully emphasized to the scholars in their ivory tower, "that the obtaining of funds for these excavations—which has cost the university almost nothing—is not an easy undertaking." He lectured them on the prestige to be gained for Israeli archaeology from the special exhibition at the British Museum, and on the funds to be raised for the university from his scheduled lectures in Belgium, Holland, Austria, England, and Scandinavia. He also pointedly noted that the idea for his appearance at the Brussels world's fair had come directly from the office of Prime Minister Ben-Gurion. "I have done everything," Yadin concluded, "in the belief that I was working as a dedicated academic employee of the university, but there is surely no point in going on a mission that is not to the liking of those who would send me. Therefore I will immediately contact all of those institutions in an attempt to see if it is still possible to cancel all preparations made for my arrival. As soon as I receive their answers I will inform you, and it may be possible that I will not have to cancel the spring semester after all."

A flurry of frantic correspondence soon arrived at the university administration offices, informing the faculty of the seriousness of their error. One particularly outraged letter came from the chairman of the official government committee in charge of organizing Israel's participation at the 1958 world's fair. "I hereby request that the officials of the university reconsider their decision in this matter, since Dr. Yadin is scheduled to be the main speaker at the gathering that is to be the main event of Israel Day at the fair. It will be difficult for us to explain to the Belgian committee and to the directors of the fair the reason for the change," he continued, pointing out that Yadin's inability to come because of his teaching responsibilities "will seem to them a very strange reason, in light of the fact that many of the world's greatest scholars will be assembled in the other pavilions and assemblies held at the same time." The writer of this letter, the chairman of the government committee, was none other than Yaacov Yannai, Yadin's closest friend from Haganah days.

Needless to say, Yadin got his way and the press release issued by the Hebrew University on June 19, 1958, told the end of the story. Portraying Yadin's triumphant European tour in glowing terms, it noted that "everywhere, deans and rectors spoke highly of the Hebrew University." It went on to describe Yadin's audience in Stockholm with King Gustav, "who as an archaeologist himself, was interested in discussing with the Hebrew University's Lecturer in Archaeology aspects of the Dead Sea Scrolls and the Hazor excavations." The Hazor exhibition at the British Museum, the press release further noted, "aroused considerable interest in England" and "received wide publicity in the press, on the radio and television." This might be acrobatics, but the Hebrew University, now opening its new Givat Ram campus, could hardly exist without it. "Independence Day found Dr. Yadin in Brussels," the release proudly concluded, "where he addressed a special meeting of Jewish youth on the occasion." Later on the same day, he delivered a lecture on the Dead Sea Scrolls "at a meeting organized by the Friends of the Hebrew University under the patronage of Her Majesty Queen Elizabeth, after whom the Archaeology Building on the University campus was named."

Despite Yadin's foreign triumphs, in Israel the archaeological battle over Joshua's conquest of Hazor was just beginning. Yohanan Aharoni, supervisor of the excavations in Area A in the upper city, was determined to challenge Yadin's widely acclaimed reconstruction of biblical events. At the end of the 1957 digging season he mounted his counterattack. Aharoni had a vested interest in his particular historical theory. Several years earlier, as field research for his doctoral dissertation, he had conducted a pioneering archaeological survey of the hilly areas of Upper Galilee. There he had discovered a group of small, unfortified hilltop settlements far from major Canaanite centers like Hazor. Those small settlements, he suggested, were evidence of the quiet and peaceful arrival of an early wave of Israelites. Following the theories of German biblical scholars Albrecht Alt and Martin Noth, Aharoni suggested in his dissertation that the entry of the Israelites into Canaan had been a social process, not a military campaign. He argued that it was only after the arriving Israelite pastoralists had settled down to become farmers that they came into violent conflict with the Canaanites. For those who believed in the literal truth of the Bible and the divinely directed triumphs of Joshua, this was a disturbingly radical theory. Even though Yadin felt confident that he had produced convincing evidence that the destruction of Hazor had taken place in 1250 B.C., *before* the establishment of the remote Israelite settlements, Aharoni was not prepared to budge an inch from his reconstruction of the events.

These were more than dispassionate scholarly alternatives; in their differing reconstructions of the Israelite conquest, Yadin and Aharoni both implicitly expressed their own understanding of modern processes of territorial conquest and nationhood. For Yadin, the importance of unified military action for territorial conquest was obvious. As a former operations officer and student of classical battlefield tactics, he would never abandon his unspoken conviction that the Israelite conquest of Canaan—like the modern Israeli victory in 1948—was possible only through innovative leadership and unified command.

Aharoni's attachment to the gradual-immigration theory was more subtle. As usual, he took satisfaction in rebelling against conventional wisdom, and as a native German speaker, he was far more familiar with the writings of Alt and Noth than Yadin. But there was also a philosophical attachment. As a former kibbutz member and sympathizer of the Achdut Avodah movement, Aharoni was deeply influenced by the pre-1948 belief that the entire Land of Israel would gradually come into the possession of the Jewish people not through political declarations or formal statehood but through hard work, pioneering, and steadily expanding settlement. That was the reason that the leftist Zionist opposition had opposed the partition of Palestine throughout the British Mandate period. They believed that the Yishuv should not settle for only part of their sacred inheritance, when, in the fullness of time, the whole land might be won by "practical" Zionism. Indeed, the gradual-immigration theory of the ancient Israelite conquest of Canaan strikingly paralleled the modern leftist Zionist ideology of territorial maximalism. In both versions, conquest of the Promised Land was made possible by the steady reclamation of sparsely settled hillsides and desert fringes, combined with Palmach-style partisan warfare. The plodding movements of opposing armies played only a minor role in this timeless scenario. Thus, between the lines of Yadin and Aharoni's archaeological dispute at Hazor—quite apart from the archaeological facts and their bitter personality conflict—lay a metaphorical debate over the sensitive issues of land and power in Zionist ideology.

Their first acrimonious showdown took place at an otherwise festive occasion, the 1957 annual convention of the Israel Exploration Society. On the afternoon of October 2, archaeological enthusiasts from all over the country descended on Kibbutz Ayyelet Hashahar in cars, trucks, and buses to tour the nearby Hazor excavations and enjoy an evening of lectures in the kibbutz amphitheater. The members of Ayyelet Hashahar were by now accustomed to the expedition and its steady flow of VIP visitors, but they had never seen anything like this. The annual convention of the Israel Exploration Society was quickly becoming a national celebration. Under the guidance of Joseph Aviram, the society's indefatigable and enthusiastic secretary, a distinctive popular archeology was being produced, shaped, and merchandised. Here was a national pastime perfectly suited to the emerging Israeli temperament, in which stirring stories of Canaanite kings, Bronze Age armies, and Israelite heroes found material expression in the landscape, and in which excavated remains offered a physical connection to the land. By Israeli standards, the growth of the society was explosive. "In 1948 there might have been three hundred people at our convention," Aviram recalled, "and that was huge for the time. But after that, there was really an awakening. There were fifteen hundred people at Ayyelet Hashahar, when Yadin was in all his glory. And it was then that people started to speak of us as an Archaeology Movement—not just a small society." In recalling that famous evening at the Ayyelet Hashahar amphitheater, Aviram noted with the self-satisfaction of a successful impresario that it was then that "the whole business between Yadin and Aharoni over Joshua's conquest really started to heat up."

The stage was decked with flowers and welcoming banners, and after obligatory greetings from the society's officers, local politicians, and the secretary of the kibbutz, the real business of the evening began. Yadin rose to the podium with self-assurance and charisma and offered a masterful recap of the progress of the excavations. He wove together evidence from the Book of Joshua, the presence of Mycenaean pottery in the prosperous lower city, and the presence of crude huts and storage pits in the ruins above them to bring the Israelite conquest of Canaan to life. As he had done so often in staff meetings at the IDF headquarters—and in his classes at the university—he reduced a complex tangle of facts and possible perceptions to a single unambiguous reality. He did not doubt for a moment that it was the Israelites who had destroyed the mighty Canaanite city, or that the Israelite settlement in Hazor's ruins had been established in the wake of that great victory. Later generations of archeologists would seriously question both the dating and the sequence of events. But for the moment, on that chilly October evening in Upper Galilee, Yadin's vivid descriptions and down-to-earth logic allowed the audience to imagine Joshua and his people smashing the idols and setting fire to the fine houses of the Canaanite nobility on the summit of the nearby tell.

Aharoni then rose to offer his interpretation of the archaeological evidence, but he proved to be but a poor showman compared with Yadin. His was a competent if not completely convincing attempt to redate the pottery forms found at his Israelite settlements and explain why his own theory of the Israelite conquest was correct. Aharoni had originally dated the isolated hilltop settlements to the twelfth century B.C. (and a similar settlement, he knew, was established *above* the ruins of thirteenth-century Hazor). But he now argued that certain pottery types could perhaps be dated a full century before that. It was painfully clear what he was doing: In order for his theory of gradual immigration or "peaceful infiltration," to work, isolated Israelite settlements in the surrounding hills would have had to be established *before* the destruction of Hazor. He now arbitrarily set their date back into the thirteenth century B.C., despite his earlier insistence that their pottery dated to the twelfth century B.C.

Aharoni was proud to be the first archaeologist to put forward evidence for the "peaceful infiltration theory"; his doctoral dissertation was a long elaboration of that point. But there was more at stake in this debate with Yadin than merely dating a level or revising a theory or even defending a conception of history and territory. It galled him to see the attention that Yadin was getting without having paid his professional dues. It was painful for Aharoni to realize that even though he had pioneered the exploration of the Upper Galilee, walking on foot over hills and into rugged valleys to gain material for his dissertation, Yadin, newly arrived from London and backed by Rothschild money, had gained so much positive publicity. For Yadin everything seemed to come easy. For Aharoni everything seemed to come hard. Even though the Hazor excavations seemed to undermine his earlier theory, he pressed on with it, determined to fight to the bitter end. Other scholars might have acknowledged the new evidence and altered their theories, but not Yohanan Aharoni. That was what thoroughly infuriated Yadin.

Suddenly breaking the polite decorum of the evening lecture program, Yadin rose from his place on the dais and loudly attacked his colleague for refusing to acknowledge the facts. It wasn't simply that Yadin couldn't bear the idea of someone challenging him (he had never been a particularly gracious interlocutor in his bitter debates with Yitzhak Sadeh, Shlomo Shamir, or Ben-Gurion). It was rather that Yadin still innocently believed that the academic world was a place of honor, where personal motives and attachments should never be allowed to dim the transcendent power of scientific facts. Though he now gave his wholehearted support to the historical reliability of Joshua's conquest, some of his students believed that he had originally come to Hazor with an open mind, eager to investigate problems in the Israelite conquest and let the facts speak for themselves. If he had suspected that this was not going to be a fair fight—that Aharoni would refuse to abandon his theory under any conditions—Yadin would certainly never have invited him along. Now locked in a contest of wills, Aharoni resolved to stand firm in the face of Yadin's attacks, no matter how public and painful they were. Yadin, for his part, was determined to force Aharoni to acknowledge that the facts uncovered by the Hazor excavations discredited his theory—in as sharp and humiliating a way as possible.

The convention at Ayyelet Hashahar was just the opening volley in a longrunning feud; the next public confrontation took place soon after the end of the 1958 digging season, in the presence of the prime minister. Like two prizefighters, Yadin and Aharoni were brought together to show their mettle. But only in Ben-Gurion's Israel could such a bitter personal contest be waged and won over an issue of biblical history. The prime minister was always eager to use biblical imagery to portray Israel's modern victories and its path to the future, so it was only fitting that he hosted a biweekly Bible Circle to discuss the latest biblical scholarship. In the late fall of 1958 the subject was the Book of Joshua, no doubt because of the recent findings and debate at Hazor. Yadin and Aharoni were invited, as were a group of prominent scholars from the university, including Dr. Mazar and historian Avraham Malamat. Malamat immediately perceived the farcical aspects of the gathering. "There were really three groups in this circle," he recalled. "There were the leaders of the Bible Society, headed by Dr. Gevariyahu, which had thousands of members all over the country. There was a small group of invited scholars from the university. And there were all of Ben-Gurion's physicians, the medical specialists who took care of him from his head to his toes. When Yadin introduced me to Paula," Malamat noted of his first meeting with Mrs. Ben-Gurion, "Paula asked him what *my* specialty was." Yadin smiled and pointed to his head. "She probably thought I was a neurologist," Malamat said.

With the niceties concluded, Yadin presented a rhetorical master-piece to the Bible Circle. He simultaneously explored the techniques of ancient warfare, implicitly compared the conquest of Canaan to the 1948 War of Independence, and—most pointedly—attacked his oppo-nent's manliness. "It's interesting and perhaps amusing," Yadin said at the beginning of his remarks, with a knowing glance toward Aharoni, "that certain 'civilized' individuals cast doubt on the credibility of the events described in the Book of Joshua on the basis of military principles that they themselves have no experience with. In contrast are military leaders, who, almost without exception, accept the reliability of the mili-tary descriptions of the Book of Joshua." Yadin went on to present a masterful résumé of what he considered to be the facts: the various meth-ods by which ancient armies conquered walled cities (scaling, ramming, tunneling, siege, and deception) and the arms they used (the sword and composite bow were the most common). Describing the political and military situation at the time of Joshua, Yadin offered images that would have been unmistakably familiar to the members of the generation that had lived through the Arab rebellion of the 1930s and the first few months of the 1948 war.

In the sedate surroundings of the prime minister's Bible Circle, the former chief of staff quoted passages from the Book of Joshua and spoke with authority about the value of superior intelligence, the effectiveness of surprise attacks on the enemy, and how a burning determination to defeat a demoralized civil population could enable a small force to defeat a much larger foe. There was no archaeological or military reason, Yadin insisted, to doubt that events had indeed taken place much as described in the Book of Joshua. The Hazor excavations had shown that Israelites had completely leveled and resettled the Canaanite city. In the face of this vivid and tangible scenario, Aharoni's chronological quibbles seemed pointless, at least to many of the assembled scholars, Bible Soci-ety members, and physicians who politely nodded their heads. To sug-gest that a unified military force of Israelites, motivated by deep national feeling and a sense of divine guidance, had been *unable* to plan and exe-cute a campaign of conquest against Hazor and the other great Canaan-ite cities would have been tantamount to challenging both modern experience and common sense.

When Aharoni addressed the Bible Circle several weeks later, he quickly fell into Yadin's trap. He stressed that the conquest stories in the Bible must be seen as unreliable heroic legends and attempted to depict

the true course of events as a gradual transformation of Israelite shepherds and herders from pastoralism to settled life. His historical conclusion echoed the credo of leftist pioneering Zionism in its steadfast
rejection of political arrangements as a substitute for facts on the
ground. "The transformation of the Land of Canaan to the Land of
Israel," Aharoni concluded, "was not the result of a one-time conquest
of an inhabited country. It was first and foremost the result of the initial
occupation and settlement of territory." The implication of that statement must have been clear to all of those present and galling to many in
light of Aharoni's political background and longtime association with
Achdut Avodah. Aharoni's alternative scenario of "peaceful immigration," however, conspicuously avoided any mention of Hazor. And at
the conclusion of the lecture Yadin rose to attack what he believed was
Aharoni's Achilles' heel.

"The time has come, I believe, for Aharoni to muster up the courage and acknowledge the facts that were discovered in the excavations of
Hazor, in which he was a most active participant." Yadin quoted at
length from Aharoni's articles and doctoral dissertation in which he
suggested that the culmination of the process of Israelite settlement and
the final, violent confrontation with the king of Hazor occurred only at
the end of the twelfth century B.C. Yadin pointed out that the excavations at Hazor showed that the city was destroyed a full hundred years
before that. How could the Israelite tribes have conquered a city that no
longer existed? He pressed Aharoni to admit once and for all that the
conquest of Hazor was the opening act in the historical drama, just as
the Book of Joshua had said, and that only after the Canaanites had
been defeated in battle did the process of Israelite settlement begin.

But Aharoni would not surrender. Once more he equivocated on
issues of pottery dating and stratigraphy, unwilling to concede that he
might have been wrong. It didn't matter that later archaeologists redated
the Hazor destruction level and questioned whether it had anything to
do with Israelites at all. Archaeological facts were only the medium, not
the motivation for the growing hatred between Aharoni and Yadin.
Yadin considered his adversary to be intellectually dishonest, motivated
by personal ambition, and willing to ignore data that did not serve his
purposes. Aharoni's allies accused Yadin of the very same sins, but none
could deny that Yadin committed them far more elegantly. The more
Yadin attacked Aharoni at congresses, in scholarly papers, and in newspaper interviews, the more stubbornly Aharoni resisted. The long-running
conflict between Yadin and Aharoni forced an entire generation of Israeli
archaeologists to choose sides. The increasingly hateful personal conflict

flared up over virtually every major archaeological question on the Israeli scene; the feud continued for decades—to the day of Aharoni's death, and even beyond.

———

Through the four digging seasons of the Hazor excavations and during his first years on the university faculty, Yadin maintained regular contact with his former colleagues in the army. He and Carmella still shared their wedding anniversary celebrations with Jan and Gila Yannai; they were often invited to general staff receptions and state dinners; and at least once during each digging season high-ranking army officers like Meir Amit, Meir Zorea, Chief of Staff Moshe Dayan, and his successor Chaim Laskov came to visit Yadin at Hazor. Yadin kept his own public activities to a minimum, accepting appointments only to such innocuous government committees as the Advisory Committee for the Improvement of the Landscape, the Defense Fund Public Committee, and the Commission for Higher Education for IDF Officers. With the publicity from his recovery of the Dead Sea Scrolls and from the Hazor excavations and the bitter debate over Joshua's conquest, Yadin had become a national celebrity. Under his influence and the tireless promotional activity of Joseph Aviram of the Israel Exploration Society, archaeology reached a new height of popularity, while school trips to archaeological sites, participation in archaeological excavations, and collecting antiquities (carried to an extreme in Chief of Staff Dayan's plundering expeditions) became fashionable. More than ever, Yadin was seen as the personification of the sabra soldier-scholar. In late 1958, Prime Minister Ben-Gurion, eager to strengthen his ruling coalition in the upcoming elections, once more tried to persuade Yadin to renew his political career.

Ben-Gurion had always hoped that Yadin would lend his talent to shaping the future, not only the past. The prime minister had been deeply disappointed in 1958, when Yadin had turned down an appointment to become minister of the South and the Negev, and in the years that followed Ben-Gurion rarely lost an opportunity to gently remind Yadin of his unfulfilled public responsibility. "I have heard great things about the excavations at Hazor," he wrote to Yadin on October 10, 1957, "and even though I would prefer to see you in another position, I wish you continued success." In September 1958, Ben-Gurion paid his first visit to the Hazor excavations, arriving on the tell by army helicopter with a large entourage. He listened patiently to Yadin's explanations of the Bronze and Iron Age ruins, but clearly he had other things on his mind. Elections for the Knesset were now only a few months away, and his ruling Mapai party had to improve its image with the voters. The political landscape of Israel was studded with activist parties that attracted young people, but Mapai was seen as the party of aging socialist bureaucrats. On the left were Achdut Avodah and Mapam, with their idealistic kibbutz image and popular leaders like Israel Galili and Yigal Allon. On the right was Menachem Begin's Herut party, led by the hardline heroes of the Irgun underground. In late 1958, Ben-Gurion had come to the conclusion that the Mapai old guard should be gradually augmented by a new generation of energetic young men—*bitzuistim,* or "doers." A few weeks after his visit to Hazor, Ben-Gurion summoned Yadin to his office in Jerusalem for a three-hour chat.

Yadin listened impatiently and uncomfortably as Ben-Gurion revealed his plan for the elections. He wanted Yadin to run for the Knesset on the Mapai list along with two other rising stars of the party, Abba Eban, the diplomat, and Moshe Dayan, recently retired as chief of staff. Yadin had always prided himself on his political neutrality, however, and he rejected the idea that he would ever feel comfortable as a leading member of Mapai. Yadin was also unwilling to abandon his academic career. By this time, he and Carmella and their two daughters, Orly and Littal, had settled into a comfortable existence as a professor's family in Jerusalem. At forty, Yadin was unwilling to make a radical change in this lifestyle. He was content with his work routines, dividing his time between excavations, teaching, and traveling abroad. At home, Carmella, an efficient and dedicated partner, edited and typed his speeches and articles, arranged his files, maintained his appointment calendar, and made sure that his public persona was sufficiently respectable. In the spring he was to be appointed associate professor at the Hebrew University, another important step in his academic career. Carmella was unwilling to see Yigael give all this up for an uncertain future in the smoky back rooms of Israeli party politics.

Ben-Gurion was not interested in Yadin's comfort or his and Carmella's ideas about respectability. He was determined to convince him to return to politics. Just a few days after their first meeting, he summoned Yadin for another private talk. "Most of the discussion concerned his immediate future in this country," Ben-Gurion noted in his diary on December 11, "whether it will be only in archaeology or in a public career." Yadin once again objected to having to join a party whose platform he might not fully accept. Ben-Gurion recognized that this was merely an evasion. "I told him that I saw only two sound reasons for his refusal: if he sees archaeology as his main mission in life, rather than the improvement of the state . . . or if he does not see the possibility of effective partnership with the group in which he has been called to serve."

Even as Yadin was resisting Ben-Gurion's pressure tactics, he was having a hard time saying no. He asked about the specific post he would be given in the government; he made it clear that he would serve as a shaper of policy, not merely as an adviser or expert. Ben-Gurion was eager to reassure him. "There's no need to have experts as cabinet members," Ben-Gurion noted. "And that's why the specific portfolio he's given isn't important; his participation in the government is the main thing." But Ben-Gurion saw that his arguments weren't working. "He was still uncertain when he left," Ben-Gurion added. "He still hasn't given the final word."

That final word came ten days later, in a polite and neatly typed letter to Ben-Gurion. "I would like to thank you," Yadin wrote, "for the faith you placed in me in inviting me to a conversation about the possibility of my accepting a political post in the future. I have seriously thought about the subjects we discussed, and since I do not want to continue to waste your precious time, I have decided to answer in writing." The tone of refusal was already clear in the opening sentences, but Yadin went further. "My decision to engage in scholarship was made neither by chance nor from any external circumstances, and as long as the matter remains in my hands, it is my desire to continue in this path." In a tone that contrasted sharply with his decisive public image, Yadin argued weakly and unconvincingly that joining Mapai was out of the question. "Up to now," he insisted, "my reluctance to join any party was due to a recognition that my opinions about various matters of state are not identical with the policies of any one particular party. In some issues my opinions are the same as one party; on others, with other parties. Therefore my joining a party—and becoming one of its active members—is something to which I could never agree."

Needless to say, Ben-Gurion was deeply disappointed. In the prime minister's eyes, Yadin valued his comfort and respectability more than service to the state. Ben-Gurion eventually appealed to Yadin's public spirit and convinced him to join a committee to reform the electoral system, but a post for him in Ben-Gurion's next cabinet was not to be. As the prime minister had planned, three newcomers were indeed included on the Mapai list for the 1959 elections: Abba Eban, Moshe Dayan, and another young "doer" named Shimon Peres. Yadin remained outside the circles of highest power, preferring to fight his battles at archaeological congresses and in the pages of scholarly periodicals.

Yadin had other kingdoms to conquer. After his fourth digging season at Hazor, he turned his sights toward Megiddo—Armageddon of the New Testament—one of the most important Canaanite cities and an administrative center of King Solomon. During the late 1920s and 1930s the site had been partially excavated by the Oriental Institute. But in January 1960 it was Yadin's to explore. Assembling a small group of students to serve as his workers and field assistants, he organized a small study dig sponsored by the Hebrew University Institute of Archaeology (its change in status had accompanied the opening of its new building on the Givat Ram campus). His object at Megiddo was to dig in a few carefully selected areas to clarify the plan of the fortification system in the Solomonic period and to confirm a hypothesis about the centralized military planning of the Israelite kingdom. According to the First Book of Kings 9:15, Solomon rebuilt the walls of Jerusalem, Gezer, Hazor, and Megiddo. At Hazor, Yadin had discovered an impressive city gate from that period, linked to a distinctive double wall. A turn-of-the-century British report on the excavations at Gezer had provided evidence for a similar situation. As a modern military planner who had improved the efficiency of the IDF by making units, defense systems, and regional command structures uniform and interchangeable, he expected no less from the officers of King Solomon. Indeed, his excavations at Megiddo uncovered evidence of similar central planning and the impressiveness of Solomon's administrative center at the site. Even though later scholars questioned his conclusions and dating, Yadin's excavation once more captured the public imagination: in the city gates of Hazor, Megiddo, and Gezer was tangible proof of the great public works of King Solomon.

This was the kind of insight for which Yadin would become famous: fitting together a well-known biblical passage with an impressive archaeological discovery. Even as his critics carped within the closed world of academia, he entranced students, potential donors, and the general public by bringing the past to life. At Hazor and at Megiddo he gave the Israeli public tangible monuments of Joshua and Solomon that tourists and schoolchildren could visit. He made secular shrines of the tumbled foundations of palaces, citadels, and fortification walls. His neat, methodical reconstructions of ancient Israelite history often left much of the uncertainty and complexity of life out of the picture, but that was his storyteller's genius—to highlight only those elements that were essential to his tale. Palaces, city gates, and storehouses were symbols of order and authority. Destruction levels, smashed pottery, and toppled statues were signs of ancient territorial conquests. In the world of archaeology—if not in modern politics—Yadin could rule many kingdoms. And in discovering ruined palaces, temples, and fortifications, he had the power to conjure up for modern Israel an heroic, self-justifying past.

Chapter   Twelve

THE CAVE
OF LETTERS

B y late 1959, as Dr. Yigael Yadin's international reputation rose,
his schedule of public speeches, lectures, and fund-raising trips
grew ever more hectic. The previous summer, he had been
awarded an honorary doctorate at Brandeis University (it was but the
first of many academic honors that he would receive in coming years),
and he was already making plans to lead the Israeli delegation to the
International Congress of Orientalists to be held in Moscow in the
spring. As usual, the university administration requested his presence at
dinners and receptions for important benefactors. Ben-Gurion, who still
had not given up the idea of drawing him back into politics, persuaded
him to address public gatherings on the pressing issue of electoral reform. As social, political, and professional pressures came from so many
directions, Carmella played an increasingly important role in keeping

them from overwhelming Yadin. But his archaeological career was still
the most important part of his life. He had all he could do to keep up
with teaching, writing, and supervising the final report of the Hazor dig.
The first massive volume appeared in 1958, but the conflict with
Aharoni made further progress increasingly difficult.

Carmella did everything possible to ease the burden. She took complete control of the household, its accounts, and its problems, and she
supervised the raising and the education of the girls (now three and ten).
But Carmella was not only a devoted homemaker and strict mother; she
was dedicated to the advancement of Yigael's career. He, in turn, respected her advice and allowed her free rein in shaping his public image.
He seems to have enjoyed the protective cocoon she spun around him,
allowing him to work alone at home in his study without the clamoring
distractions of the outside world. Friends and colleagues recalled that
Carmella closely controlled access to Yigael, politely but firmly fending
off telephone calls if she judged them not worth his time. She regularly
used Yigael's stationery to write letters of gracious refusal for the steady
flow of invitations and requests. And she signed many of them herself,
with an uncanny imitation of his signature.

At the university Yadin's personal impact continued to be overwhelming. Within the boxlike modern Institute of Archaeology, named
after Belgium's Queen Elizabeth and sited incongruously at the edge of a
large parking lot outside the Givat Ram campus, Yadin was rightly regarded by incoming classes less as a faculty member than as a celebrity.
His incisive, witty, and polished introductory lectures on the archaeology of Israel implanted his historical theories in the minds of first-year
archaeology students. His skill as a storyteller provided a tidy, highly
logical saga of ancient peoples (each with its appropriate gods, art forms,
and military technology) waging wars with one another over thousands
of years. In seminars and advanced courses Yadin attracted a small circle
of favorite students; one of the first was David Ussishkin, grandson of
the great Zionist leader Menachem Ussishkin and a boyhood neighbor of
the Sukenik family in Rechavia. Another was Amnon Ben-Tor, who had
abandoned an earlier ambition to become an architect for an archaeological career. Yigal Shiloh, from Haifa, would soon join this close circle of
protégés.

Ironically, the nationwide interest in archaeology and the growing
number of students at the institute created the need for more faculty,
and Yohanan Aharoni was appointed to the teaching staff. Now ostensibly colleagues, barely a word was ever passed between Yadin and Aharoni
in the hallways of the institute. The personal tension between them grew
as each suspected the other of plotting against him; Aharoni was ever

wary that Yadin would attempt to steal glory from him. Since the Hazor excavations, their professional paths had parted. As Yadin conducted the study dig at Megiddo, Aharoni directed excavations at the Judean fortress of Ramat Rachel, on the southern outskirts of Jerusalem. He had had no choice but to concede his claim to have pioneered the modern exploration of the Galilee after Yadin's massive Hazor excavations, but he remained protective of his exclusive right to the rugged, arid Judean Wilderness, by the western shore of the Dead Sea. As early as January 1953, when he learned that bedouin were plundering ancient manuscripts from caves in the border area between Israel and Jordan, Aharoni and a team of volunteers set out to explore the caves within Israeli territory along the steep ravines of Nahal Hever and Nahal Arugot.

Scholars in Jordan had in the meantime made an astounding discovery. Had this discovery "been made earlier," Yadin later noted, "or had it been the only find in the Dead Sea area, it would have excited the scholarly world as much as the discovery of the scrolls." It was a large collection of ancient documents recovered by Ta'amireh bedouin in a ravine called Wadi Murrabat, southwest of Qumran. It included legal documents, religious texts, and, most important of all, military dispatches written to local commanders by the leader of an ill-fated Jewish revolt against Rome some sixty years after the destruction of the Temple, in A.D. 132–135. Until the 1950s this ancient Jewish rebel had been largely a figure of folklore, less of historical substance than of myth. Even his actual name was uncertain. Rabbinic tradition had always been ambivalent about him, praising his superhuman strength and unwavering courage but bitterly condemning his messianic pretensions (for which the rabbis derisively called him Bar-Kosiba, "Son of a Liar"). His fervent supporters and the early Christian and Roman historians who preserved accounts of his desperate battle with the Romans knew him as Bar-Kokhba, or "Son of a Star." Bar-Kokhba had also become an heroic figure in modern Zionist literature, and now the discoveries along the rugged border revealed his true name and brought him to life. A number of dispatches published by scholars in Jordan were signed with the confident salutation: Shimeon Bar-Kosiba, Prince of Israel.

The find created a sensation in the scholarly world and spurred Aharoni to undertake repeated explorations of the ravines on the Israeli side of the border in 1953, 1956, 1957, and 1958. One cave in Nahal Hever—soon to be called the Cave of Horrors by Aharoni—revealed the ultimate cost of the Bar-Kokhba revolt. There Aharoni and his team discovered dozens of skeletons of men, women, and children—apparently Jewish rebels who had fled the fighting and had met their grisly death in the Judean Wilderness.

Yadin kept his distance, content to pursue his interest in earlier biblical periods and to keep up with his public responsibilities. He did not even intervene toward the end of 1959, when a new rumor from Jordan told of a disturbing development. A visiting American scholar reported to Aharoni that a number of the important Bar-Kokhba manuscripts that the bedouin had sold to the scholars in Jordan had reportedly come from a ravine called Wadi Seyyal (Nahal Zeelim, in Hebrew) on the Israeli side of the border, in the Judean Wilderness. Aharoni immediately assembled a new expedition to examine the caves in Nahal Zeelim. He located one small cave that the bedouin had apparently not noticed, but it seemed clear that unless an intensive archaeological rescue effort were mounted quickly, the Ta'amireh would soon thoroughly plunder most of the caves in the area.

Aharoni was not looking for partners, but Prime Minister Ben-Gurion soon intervened. During a chance meeting between Ben-Gurion and Yadin in early February 1960, Yadin had drawn the prime minister's attention to the bedouin incursions and Aharoni's rather meager findings. Ben-Gurion thereupon ordered Chief of Staff Chaim Laskov to intensify border patrols. Though sympathetic, Laskov had far more serious security problems on his hands in the spring of 1960 than bedouin antiquities robbers. Tensions were again rising with the Syrians over rights to the headwaters of the Jordan; in the south, the Egyptians were deploying large troop formations in the Sinai for the first time since the 1956 war. Laskov was prepared to discourage further bedouin incursions along the Jordanian border, but he preferred a quick and decisive operation, not a permanent patrol. In a subsequent conversation with Yadin (under whom Laskov had served in the general staff), Laskov suggested an all-out archaeological offensive: Why not gather all of Israel's best archaeologists and mount an intensive, large-scale expedition with the full logistical support of the army to systematically search and excavate every cave in the area?

The idea was certainly intriguing, but Yadin was unwilling to be accused of edging into Aharoni's turf. He therefore suggested that Laskov directly contact Hebrew University president Mazar and Israel Exploration Society secretary Aviram about the plan. Needless to say, Mazar and Aviram were enthusiastic about the prospect of a national search for the remains and documents of the Bar-Kokhba rebels. They even convinced Aharoni of the advisability of including Yadin and Avigad in a large expedition to the Judean Wilderness caves. Aharoni considered himself the most experienced explorer of this region and drew up a list of needed equipment, while Yadin and Aviram met with Chief of Staff Laskov, his deputy Yitzhak Rabin, and Southern Commander

Avraham Yoffe to formulate the operation's broad outlines. It was agreed that IDF overland transport, helicopters, field communications, base camps, and personnel specially trained for scaling cliff faces would aid the expedition in exploring four major ravines. But there was a serious time restriction: the expedition would have to complete its work within two weeks.

The tension between Yadin and Aharoni finally surfaced in discussions of tactics. With four separate ravines to explore, it was decided that Aharoni, Yadin, Avigad, and Pesach Bar-Adon, a longtime employee of the Department of Antiquities, would each direct operations in one of them. Once again, Yadin stressed that he had no intention of edging in on Aharoni's province, and he proposed that the work in all the ravines be considered part of a single large expedition, with all discoveries to be published jointly by the four leaders of the teams. Aharoni angrily objected, so it was decided that the expedition would comprise four independent groups, each working in a defined sector and each to have sole scholarly control over its discoveries. The next question was territorial selection. Aharoni, who had most recently explored the area, was given priority and chose the northern bank of Nahal Zeelim, where the bedouin digging seemed spottiest and chances of discoveries the best. Avigad chose the southern bank of Zeelim, close to Masada. Bar-Adon chose the small ravines of Nahal Mishmar and Nahal Asael. Yadin, calmly puffing on his pipe, seemed content to accept the last and shortest straw, the northernmost sector, Nahal Arugot, and the northern bank of Nahal Hever, whose largest cave Aharoni had thoroughly explored in 1953.

These decisions made, Aharoni looked forward to besting his rival, and preparations got under way. On the morning of March 13 the four team leaders met in Beersheva, to be taken on an extensive aerial reconnaissance of their sectors. Boarding air force helicopters, they were ferried to the Dead Sea shore kibbutz of En Geddi and each taken on a harrowing ride up one of the twisting, steep ravines. Yadin had hoped that the helicopter inspection would reveal previously overlooked crevices or crannies along the northern bank of Nahal Hever, but this hope was not fulfilled. An air force photographer helped Yadin document the entire northern face of the ravine, but the only new feature he spotted was a small opening filled by a vulture's nest, several hundred feet above the ravine floor. Yadin returned to Jerusalem and went through the motions of organizing his team. He chose David Ussishkin, who had worked with him at Megiddo, to be his chief assistant. The two of them went over the air force photographs and regretfully concluded that except for the Cave of the Vulture, the most likely place to search was the large cave that Aharoni had explored seven years before.

Aharoni's published report of that earlier expedition underlined the difficulties of further exploration there. The cave was accessible only by a steep, narrow footpath from the top of the cliff down to a narrow ledge, more than six hundred feet up on the cliff face. The main opening of the cave was more than thirty feet above that ledge. That was just the start of the logistical problems. The cave's main chamber was covered with boulders that had fallen from its ceiling. Aharoni's team had recovered some artifacts from the crevices between these fallen stones, but he had concluded uncovering any more finds from the Bar-Kokhba period would require breaking up those boulders with pneumatic hammers, to get to the levels below. With these uninviting prospects it is little wonder that Yadin seemed aloof and detached, content to leave most of the preparations to others. Joseph Aviram recruited volunteers for all the expedition teams; Ussishkin submitted his list of equipment to the army (pneumatic jackhammers, a few hand digging tools, and a small number of artifact boxes for the unlikely event that they found anything). In fact, Ussishkin remembered years later, the prospects in Nahal Hever seemed hopeless. "Yadin really didn't have any expectations," he recalled of the preparations. Yadin was apparently eager for a brief respite from his hectic routine and commitments. "He just went along as if it were a kind of picnic," Ussishkin concluded, "to spend two weeks in the desert looking at the view."

The expedition soon proved to be anything but a picnic. The four teams set out from Jerusalem early on Wednesday morning, March 23. With Joseph Aviram serving as an overall coordinator, the team leaders stopped for a brief conference in Beersheva. Then they and their staffs all boarded heavy army vehicles for the journey over rough tracks and natural valleys toward their camps in the wilderness. Yadin brought along four students, in addition to David Ussishkin. At Beersheva they were joined by a dozen or so eager volunteers from kibbutzim across the country whom Aviram had recruited for the two-week enterprise. Part of Aviram's genius was to recognize that Israeli archaeology had to be based on enthusiastic public participation by young people, not just on lectures and annual dues for the Israel Exploration Society. He had lured volunteers with the mystique of Bar-Kokhba. The experience proved unpleasant at first; a week of heavy rains had washed out the main routes to the Judean Wilderness and had flooded gullies that were usually passable. The trip was slow and halting, and expedition members were repeatedly forced to help push the trucks out of the thick mud. It was after nightfall when they reached the first of the base camps, and not until eight o'clock did Yadin and his team finally arrive at the base camp for their own Sector D. Liaison officer Yosef Kastel of the Golani Brigade greeted them with all the preparations completed—tents for sleeping, tents for excavation workrooms, and a field kitchen in full working order. The rain had abated, yet Yadin still felt uneasy. He confided to Ussishkin that he always had an unpleasant, disoriented feeling when he arrived after dark at an unfamiliar place.

That sense of foreboding continued the next morning as the team members rose from their tents, ate a quick army breakfast, and began their work. In the hope that some caves might still be found by direct inspection, Yadin sent off several small groups to examine every possible nook and cranny in the surrounding area, and he personally accompanied the team that went to investigate the Cave of the Vulture, the most promising new lead. But with its opening on the sheer cliff face a full one hundred yards beneath them, gaining access was a dangerous task. Captain Kastel volunteered for the assignment. Wearing a combat helmet to protect against falling stones and arming himself with a pistol (lest the vulture return to the nest or attack), he was slowly lowered by rope. But stuck on a ledge, he failed to gain access to the cave. Perhaps believing that there had been easier means of approach to this cave in antiquity, the team tried again the next day. Another soldier agreed to be lowered by a parachute harness secured to a rope that was slowly unwound on the axle of a jeep. He managed to swing into the small opening, but he found the cave empty except for the nest. In the meantime the other teams had no better success, marking every empty small cave or crevice with a large blue chalk T. Within a few days, all hope of finding new caves was exhausted. Yadin had no alternative but to devote all his team's efforts to the large cave on the northern face of Nahal Hever that Aharoni had already explored.

Again, establishing safe access was a priority but that was easier said than done. From the team's base camp a narrow, steep path descended down the cliff face, forming a ledge that was in some places only a foot or two wide. Erosion and collapse of stones had created gaps in the narrow pathway, which made walking along it, even without having to carry heavy excavation equipment, a test of courage. Yadin therefore sent a veteran of Aharoni's earlier excavation to widen the path, lay a walkway over the largest gap, and fasten a rope ladder to the main entrance— which was presumably the means that the Bar-Kokhba rebels had used to enter the cave. But when Yadin's first group of diggers edged down the narrow path and scaled the rope ladder, they saw how difficult this excavation would be. Crawling through a dark entrance corridor about twenty-five feet long, lit only by flashlights, they climbed over a tumble of boulders to enter a huge chamber about forty yards wide and twenty yards high. In its center was a high mound of dirt and more fallen boulders, whose illumination by flashlight cast eerie, jagged silhouettes on the far walls. An undulating blanket of bats clung screeching to the uneven dome of the ceiling. A thick layer of bat droppings blanketed the boulders below. And the pitch-black openings of additional tunnels led to chambers farther inside.

On the following day Yadin ordered that excavations begin in earnest. Twelve of the workers went down the path this time carrying picks, digging hoes, baskets, record books, and hurricane lamps. One of Yadin's students, Menachem Magen, was to set up lamps in various parts of the cave and keep them burning—which proved to be an unexpectedly difficult challenge because of the lack of oxygen. Ussishkin directed the others to begin digging in the main chamber near a scatter of ancient pottery sherds. In the darkness and uncertainty of the first work day, it was difficult to keep track of all the people on the team, and one of them, a kibbutznik named Pinchas Porath, wandered off. Apparently bored by his assigned work and motivated by reckless curiosity, he crawled alone with his flashlight through a back passage of the cave and made his way through a second chamber, then into a third. There—somehow—he noticed a wide crevice. Sticking his head and his flashlight into it, he was confronted by a horrible sight.

Porath scrambled back to the main chamber, almost speechless, and motioned to Ussishkin to follow him. Ussishkin crawled with him back to the large fissure, where he saw Porath's ghastly discovery: a pile of straw baskets filled with skulls—all missing their jaws—surrounded by a jumbled mass of cloth, clothing, tufts of hair, straw mats, and other human bones. In the days that followed hurricane lamps were brought there and Yadin and Ussishkin supervised the removal and registration of the bones of three men, six women, and eight children, as well as an unprecedented collection of Roman-period tunics, mantels, scarves, woven spreads, linen sacks, and straw baskets almost perfectly preserved by the dry air of the Judean Wilderness. Up to this point Yadin had virtually conceded the glory of this expedition to Aharoni, but the sudden discovery of the mass burials in the back of the cave altered everyone's expectations. Meanwhile, in Nahal Zeelim, Aharoni's team had found very little, which made the situation even more uncomfortable. "We hardly had enough packing material," Ussishkin recalled, "and I had to go over to Aharoni's camp to ask for more packing material, boxes and so on. It was very unpleasant. I was given the things grudgingly, and I saw the looks in the eyes of Aharoni and his team."

After that first unexpected discovery, however, work in the Nahal Hever cave settled down to a routine. Once a quick surface examination of all the chambers was completed, Yadin ordered that the pneumatic drills be brought down and the stone-breaking begin. But the lack of oxygen caused the drills to cough out after stirring up thick, acrid clouds of dust from the bat dung that covered the cave floor. Work became nearly impossible; the hurricane lamps were impossible to keep lighted. At one point Menachem Magen climbed down from the cave and walked out onto the ledge to breathe some fresh air. And there, standing on the ledge, Magen spotted a glimmer of tarnished metal. He reached down and picked up a bronze coin of the Bar-Kokhba period. Yadin and the other team members were excited by this find, but it was soon to lead to even more important discoveries.

On the same day the southern IDF commander and a longtime Yadin colleague, Avraham Yoffe, paid a visit to the cave in Nahal Hever. A brusque, boastful combat veteran, Yoffe took good-natured delight in providing Yadin's team with supplies. Yadin had mentioned several days before that he needed a better pair of work shoes; Yoffe made sure that a brand-new pair of paratrooper's boots was sent by helicopter to the Sector D base camp immediately. During Yoffe's visit, Yadin requested an electric generator so that the interior of the cave could be lighted more efficiently. When Yadin showed Yoffe the coin that Magen picked up from the ledge, Yoffe made his own suggestion: Why not look for more coins inside the cave with the help of a battlefield mine detector?

The next day, as Yaffe had promised, a mine detector and two army technicians were ferried by helicopter to Yadin's base camp, and a heavy gasoline-powered generator arrived soon afterward by military truck. The generator was set up on the plateau above the cave entrance, and a heavy electrical cable was led down to it. The next day, as word was shouted from soldier to soldier that the cable connections were secure, the generator current was switched on. The blazing, blinding glare of dozens of light bulbs instantly dispelled the ominous darkness in the cave's halls and innermost passages. No longer would the team have to feel their way slowly across the collapsed boulders lit only by the glow of field lamps. The mine-detector crew was then brought down the path, and they briefly scanned the dusty surface of the ledge where Magen had picked up the Bar-Kokhba coin. Finding nothing, they hoisted the mine-sweeper up the rope ladder into the cave entrance and took a few minutes to check the floor of the entrance corridor. Again they found nothing, and they proceeded into the main hall.

When the disc-shaped sensor passed between two of the boulders, the metal detector emitted a loud and steady hum. Yadin instructed the nearby workers to move all their metal digging tools out of the area, but the hum continued. He therefore instructed the team members to begin digging through the layer of bat droppings, and under just a few inches of the accumulation, they uncovered the outer surface of a straw basket that was bulging with artifacts. Yadin had the honor of lifting this unexpectedly heavy prize from its finding place. The handles were tied tightly together with rope. Yadin gently loosened the knot and drew out a set of tarnished bronze vessels: two large bowls, eleven jugs, three incense shovels, and an open pan known to archaeologists as a *patera,* with a fluted handle that ended in a ram's head. These were Roman-made vessels used for pagan ritual, to sacrifice to military standards or to appeal for good fortune from the gods. Yet the carefully cast human and animal figures on their handles would have been abominations—idolatrous graven images—to the religious purists of the Bar-Kokhba revolt.

Yadin closely examined the treasure trove of well-preserved vessels and noticed that the human faces on some of the handles had been intentionally sanded off or scratched out. In response to a reporter's question after the end of the expedition, Yadin theorized "that the rebels, who were active to the very end, might have launched a sorties against a Roman camp, probably at night, and taken the vessels as booty." Thus the intentional disfigurement was apparently the work of the Jewish rebels who were eager to keep their war trophies but were strict in their abhorrence of idolatrous pagan motifs. These unique bronze vessels were another treasure that Aharoni and his team had missed in their earlier search of the cave. If this was luck, Yadin had more than his share. But in Yadin's case, luck meant being able to mobilize assistance unavailable to others. It also meant having the talent for correctly analyzing a situation, then making the most of it.

Yadin soon realized that the boulders in the cave had apparently collapsed onto the floor well *before* the time of Bar-Kokhba. Now, with constant electrical illumination and the escape of most of the bats, Yadin and the members of his team could see the smudges of soot from ancient cooking fires on the *present* ceiling of the cave. The refugees who had taken refuge there in the Bar-Kokhba period would therefore have hidden away their most precious possessions between the fallen rocks. Yadin was confident that the key to finding more of their personal effects was simply a matter of dividing the cave into sections and searching each one thoroughly. So the search continued, slowly and methodically. The team members carefully examined the area surrounding the cache of the bronze vessels and the first discovery of a written document came suddenly and unexpectedly. As one of the soldiers reached between a gap in the stones, he grasped a small, leaflike tatter of parchment that bore parts of seven lines of finely written Hebrew script. It proved to be a fragment of the Book of Psalms, close in style to (though slightly later in date than) the Qumran manuscripts.

Electric lights strung all the way to the innermost chamber created the conditions to continue exploring around the crevice where Pinchas Porath had found the baskets of skulls. Three kibbutzniks eagerly volunteered for the assignment, and they soon located a narrow gap between the collapsed boulders and the cave's natural wall. Removing a medium-size covering stone, they discovered one of the most important caches in the cave. One of them hurried off to summon Yadin to the spot, and when he arrived he found that one of the workers, Yoram Vites of Kibbutz Dalia, had squirmed down to the bottom of the crevice, which extended about ten feet beneath the surface of the cave. Yadin climbed partway down, and Vites showed him a long leather bag lying on the bottom. But the bag seemed too delicate and too stuffed with artifacts to be lifted up to the surface intact. Yadin therefore instructed Vites to open the bag and lift the objects up to him, one by one.

As news of the discovery spread through the cave, other members of the team gathered around and peered over the edge of the crevice. Vites handed the artifacts up to Yadin, who in turn passed them onto the team members above him, to be registered and placed in separate boxes for transport to the base camp. Yadin kept up a running commentary as he passed each object along. First came balls of wool, dyed purple and orange; then a string of colorful beads of quartz, agate, amethyst, and glass. Next came perfume bottles, a wooden box filled with rouge, a hand mirror in a wooden case, some clothes including a baby's tunic, an iron key, a bone spoon, and a knife. These seemed to be a woman's possessions, hurriedly gathered, packed into a goathide waterskin, and taken along with her to this desert refuge. The last find that Vites handed up to Yadin was by far the most precious: a thick bundle of inscribed papyrus documents, neatly folded and tied with string.

Beneath the forced laughter and light banter of the closing-night party of all the expeditions, the tension was unmistakable. Aharoni and his team members could barely conceal their frustration. For two weeks they had combed every visible crevice of Nahal Zeelim but had come up with only a pitiful collection of papyrus scraps, pottery sherds, and empty cigarette packages tossed away by the bedouin. Even though the organization of the expedition had been stacked in Aharoni's favor and he had gambled on keeping the expeditions separate, he and his team had apparently lost. In contrast, Yadin's team proudly regaled the others with excited descriptions of their many discoveries among the boulders in the cave in Nahal Hever. Yadin, sitting off to the side and calmly smoking his pipe, was already pondering his next move. Soon after daybreak the next morning, the teams loaded their finds onto the army trucks and returned to Jerusalem. In the late afternoon they unloaded the artifacts at a laboratory used by the Department of Antiquities, and Yadin returned to his wife and daughters in Rechavia. Yet he was not yet ready to put his recent expedition out of mind: He had brought home with him the small cardboard box containing the bundle of ancient papyrus documents.

The fragile state of the papyrus fibers made Yadin reluctant to handle the documents, despite his intense curiosity. During the course of the excavation, he had offered some preliminary speculations. Since the goatskin that held the documents also contained a mirror, beads, perfume bottles, cosmetic instruments, and textiles, Yadin assumed that the contents were the private effects of a woman and he therefore suspected that the bundle of papyri included her personal papers, perhaps her marriage contract or property deeds. But he could not risk damaging the documents. He wanted Dr. James Biberkraut, the preservation expert he most trusted, to open the bundle under the proper conditions and with the proper tools. Twelve years earlier, at the time of the siege of Jerusalem, Eleazar Sukenik had also depended on Biberkraut's skilled touch and surgical instruments to unroll his brittle parchment scrolls. In 1955, Yadin had called upon Biberkraut once more to peel open and flatten the badly decomposed fourth scroll that he had purchased from the Archbishop Samuel. Yadin intended to be patient, but the next morning his repeated telephone calls to Biberkraut went unanswered. He could no longer restrain himself. He opened the bundle, and he noticed several thin wooden slats that bore signs of writing wedged in the middle. Slowly pulling them out, he found that they fitted together and were neither a deed nor a contract, but a letter. And its sender was none other than "Shimeon Bar-Kosiba, Prince of Israel."

The next few weeks were a blur of excitement and intense study. Dr. Biberkraut, soon contacted and informed of the discovery, got to work on the documents, slowly separating and unfolding fifteen separate letters (Yadin preferred to call them dispatches) from the commander-in-chief of the Jewish revolt. Yadin's work with the Dead Sea Scrolls had given him considerable experience in deciphering the handwriting of the scribes of the Qumran community; he had strained his eyes for months over the tightly written columns of the War Scroll and the Genesis Apocryphon. But the documents from Nahal Hever posed an even greater challenge. They were written in hurried, cursive script by several camp secretaries (whose handwriting markedly varied), and although the language of most of them was Aramaic, there were also some in Hebrew and Greek. Most of the letters were addressed to Yehonathan son of Be'aya and Masabala son of Shimeon (identified as the commanders of the En Geddi settlement) and dealt with a wide range of military problems: the confiscation of privately owned wheat for military purposes; a stern warning against providing shelter to collaborationists; requests for safe conduct for certain officers and for the immediate arrest of others; and—in a unique demonstration of the religious observance of the rebels even at a time of desperate battles—an urgent request from Bar-Kokhba for the immediate dispatch of ethrogs and lulavs from En Geddi for the celebration of the Festival of Tabernacles.

The historical significance of the letters discovered in caves across the border in Jordan could only now be fully appreciated in light of Yadin's finds. Many of the letters from the caves of Wadi Murrabat were addressed to Yeshua Ben Galgoula, who was enigmatically identified as "Chief of the Camp." They contained the same kinds of orders, threats, and directives and served as evidence that as the tide of war turned against the rebels, Jewish commanders and civilians from all over Judea fled their homes and military encampments and sought shelter wherever they could. Rabbinic sources had hinted at the desperation of the rebels and even mentioned that some took refuge in caves, but until these archaeological discoveries, the gruesome stories of mass starvation and massacres seemed more like folklore than historical fact. The documents from the Judean Wilderness therefore had a direct, emotional impact on Yadin, with his own experience in military dispatches, mass mobilization, and the terror of civilian populations. And he knew that they would have a stunning effect on the general public in Israel, not only his archaeological colleagues. But rather than share the news immediately, he kept the contents of the documents a secret, taking into his confidence—besides Carmella—only a few of his closest associates.

To Joseph Aviram, in his tireless efforts on behalf of the Israel Exploration Society, Yadin's discovery offered a unique opportunity for a spectacular media event. He had already arranged for an evening of lectures at the President's Residence on the recent expedition to the Judean Wilderness. That was not in itself unusual; the office of president of Israel is largely ceremonial, and President Yitzhak Ben-Zvi was a scholar and historian who often sponsored archaeological lectures and symposia. Yet this was now to be something out of the ordinary. With Yadin's cooperation and carefully prepared presentation, Aviram planned to stage-manage a stunning demonstration of the continuity of the modern State of Israel with the ancient Jewish past. Invitations were sent out to members of the Knesset, high-ranking army officers, scholars, and celebrities.

And although the results of the recent expedition had not yet fully been made public, interest was high.

Ironically, during the spring of 1960, Ben-Gurion was creating a national commotion with one of his own daring historical assertions. At a Tel Aviv press conference he questioned the historical reliability of the Bible's account of the Exodus, suggesting that only six hundred families, not six hundred thousand warriors, had left Egypt on their way to the Promised Land. Ben-Gurion was eager to prove that the majority of the early Israelites who fought under Joshua were natives of Canaan, not intruders. But his nationalistic point was lost in the outraged reactions of the religious right at such blasphemous biblical revisionism. Yadin, however, was about to step forward with a new historical image that all could agree on: the heroic, religiously observant warriors of Bar-Kokhba, fighting against a massive Gentile army. The heroism and religious faith of the rebel army would perhaps outweigh even the fact of their defeat.

On the evening of May 11, 1960, the politicians, academics, and IDF officers gathered for an evening of uplifting diversion from the everyday controversies, challenges, and uncertainties of life in the Jewish state. Joseph Aviram mounted the podium and offered his almost ritualized words of welcome and thanks to all who had supported the work of the Israel Exploration Society. One by one, the leaders of the individual teams rose from their places to deliver reports to the president and his guests. Each had his distinctive style. Nahman Avigad, who for years had languished in the shadow of Eleazar Sukenik, described his team's meager finds in low monotone and had little to offer except a single Roman arrowhead embedded in the wall of one of the caves he had explored. Aharoni, never much of a public speaker either, spent most of his time describing his previous explorations and the evidence of bedouin robbing in his area. The only new archaeological evidence he produced was a collection of flint blades from the Chalcolithic period, left by cave dwellers in this area around 3000 B.C. Pesach Bar-Adon, a salty and colorful character who had spent years exploring this area, had, at least, uncovered clear evidence of occupation during the Bar-Kokhba period: small fragments of pottery and glass, the dried remains of dates and olives, and a very fragmentary papyrus document in Greek.

The audience waited expectantly for the last of the speakers. In a short press release several weeks before Yadin had announced his discovery of the baskets of bones, the bronze vessels, and the fragment from the Book of Psalms, so the audience knew that he would have far more to say than his colleagues. Yadin did not disappoint them. His lecture was characteristically clear and compelling. He recounted his team's adventures, intentionally stressing his low expectations and describing the frustrating failure to find any previously unexplored caves. As he told of his team's spectacular discoveries, he drew admiring gasps from the audience, showing slides of the bronze vessels, goatskin bag, cosmetic bottles and mirror, textiles, and finally the grisly human remains. Quoting rabbinic, Roman, and early Christian references to the violence and brutality of the Bar-Kokhba rebellion, he was able to transform the archaeological artifacts into people whose desperation and fear for their lives had led them into the dark recesses of the cave.

Finally he told the story of the mysterious bundle of papyrus documents, conveying it with intentional suspense. He recounted the circumstances of the discovery and the painstaking challenge of opening the fragile bundle. But this was mere prologue. When he projected a slide of the first letter he had deciphered, he paused, then read aloud its opening line, which contained the real name of the legendary Bar-Kokhba, Shimeon Bar-Kosiba. "Your Excellency," he said, turning toward President Ben-Zvi with a dramatic flourish, "I am honored to be able to tell you that we have discovered fifteen dispatches written or dictated by the *last* president of Israel eighteen hundred years ago."

Years later, Joseph Aviram recalled this moment with relish and described it as one of the high points of Yadin's career. Based on the objects and documents discovered in Nahal Hever, Yadin told a heroic and tragic story of an ancient Jewish community paying the ultimate price for its struggle for independence. Here was no mere scholarly listing of artifact types and linguistic esoterica but a flesh-and-blood epic of men, women, and children declaring war on the Romans and ultimately sacrificing their lives. The audience of dignitaries was clearly moved by the documents. They listened in silence as Yadin, his face illuminated only by the reading lamp on the podium, dramatically read out the names of the ancient Jewish officers, towns, and villages that had played a role in the last desperate days of the revolt. In the end he suggested that it was the wife of Yehonathan son of Be'aya, the commander of the rebel forces in nearby En Geddi, who had saved her husband's correspondence with the national leader and would-be messiah Bar-Kokhba and had packed the cherished letters with the rest of her personal possessions when she sought refuge in the cave. "It was an incredible moment," Aviram remembered years later, "but naturally afterward the jealousy against him began to get more intense."

Yohanan Aharoni and the other expedition leaders were no less stunned then the rest of the audience. They had had no idea of the enormity of Yadin's discovery. Even David Ussishkin, his chief assistant who had worked with him so closely in organizing the expedition and registering the artifacts, had been kept in the dark. Some of the assembled politicians viewed Yadin's dramatic presentation as grandstanding. Yitzhak Navon, then director-general of the prime minister's office, admitted to being slightly disappointed that the documents Yadin had unveiled with such high-flown rhetorical flourish were little more than mundane military orders and petulant threats to subordinates. But for the nation there was no such disappointment. Yadin had done something miraculous: he had brought a legendary character to life. It was as if a Swiss scholar had suddenly located the private papers of William Tell, or as if a British archaeologist had stumbled upon Robin Hood's personal correspondence. The earlier discoveries in Jordan paled by comparison with Yadin's rich finds and the tale he told about them. Soon after the official announcement in the President's Residence, Kol Israel broadcast news of the great discovery, and the next day's newspapers carried headlines and detailed feature stories about the "Cave of Letters" in the Judean Wilderness. Once again Yadin had shown the power of the past on the present. In his career as a national figure, that evening was a turning point.

Just a few hours after Yadin's announcement, a real-life drama took place thousands of miles away, on a quiet residential street in Buenos Aires. After a long and intensive manhunt for one of the most notorious architects of the Final Solution, agents of the Mossad—Israel's international intelligence network—captured Nazi fugitive Adolf Eichmann and hustled him back to Israel to stand trial for crimes against the Jewish people and against humanity. For the next two years, in the wrenching and cathartic public trial of the unrepentant man in the glass booth, the people of Israel relived nightmarish feelings of impending destruction. Witness after witness recounted the unspeakable horrors of the death camps. Frightening images of extermination reinforced the nation's resentment against a cruel and hatefully calculating outside world. Israel's national self-perception was changing. In the twelve years since independence, the population of the state had more than doubled; its culture was increasingly fragmented by the distinct communities of Jewish immigrants from Asia, Africa, and Europe who had arrived since 1948. Perceptions of external threat and fears of internal divisions roused attempts by the government to create a new, homogenous national culture. And in this respect Dr. Yigael Yadin embodied the high-minded, nonpartisan leadership demanded by the times.

As chairman of the Society for Electoral Reform (the post he had accepted on Ben-Gurion's urging) and in his vivid evocations of Joshua and Bar-Kokhba, Yadin was increasingly regarded as a national symbol, no less attractive than the fictional sabra hero of Leon Uris' 1958 world-wide best seller *Exodus.* A correspondent for *The Jerusalem Post* interviewed Yadin on the need to streamline the Israeli party system and make the government more responsive to the public; Yadin clearly captivated him. "Tall and sparse," correspondent Philip Gillon wrote of the professor, "he talks softly but incisively, selecting his words with precision and testing the implications of every idea before accepting it. A humanitarian in the broadest sense of the term, he is a far better symbol of the 'new Jew' born in the Land of Israel than any mythical hero like Ari Ben-Canaan."

Yadin was still unwilling to leave his academic surroundings to enter the political arena. He rejected yet another appeal by Ben-Gurion in the summer of 1960 (this time to fill the post of education minister, in the wake of a minor government crisis) and devoted himself to teaching, overseeing the compilation of the Hazor report, and writing scholarly articles on a wide variety of archaeological problems. His interests, as ever, were wide-ranging. Other scholars based their careers on the ever-more-minute study of a certain period or artifact type, but Yadin took delight in stirring up new questions and challenging conventional scholarly wisdom whenever his curiosity or interest was piqued. There was hardly a field of study in the history and literature of the Land of the Bible that escaped his attention or comment. His ingenious, elegantly presented ideas on subjects as diverse as the administrative division of the Judean kingdom, anomalies in biblical texts from Qumran, the economic significance of Judean weights and measures, and his variant interpretation of inscribed potsherds found at the Israelite capital of Samaria, promoted new ideas and active discussion in scholarly circles whose hallmark had often been lifeless pedantry.

Few other scholars with such an eclectic approach to archaeological and historical study would have been taken seriously, but Yadin was different. Even those who envied his celebrity status or contested the validity of his theories could not help but be amused by his elegant, witty presentations at archaeological congresses and his power to articulate ideas simply and logically. There was clearly something unique about Yadin's talent and self-confidence in tackling subjects whose complexity would have intimidated most of his colleagues. This was certainly the case with the Cave of Letters. Although he had been drawn into the Judean Wilderness expedition by circumstances not entirely of his own choosing, he became increasingly fascinated by the historical and archaeological problems of the Bar-Kokhba period. With his skill in grasping new information, he immersed himself in rabbinic purity laws to understand better the design and composition of the garments, leatherwork, and woven mats in the Cave of Letters, and in a private visit to Italy during the summer, he was able to locate exact parallels to the bronze vessels in the museums of Herculaneum and Pompeii.

Yadin insisted on thoroughness in any task he undertook, and by the autumn of 1960, he was convinced that there was more to find in the Nahal Hever cave. While going over the excavation records, he realized that there were many areas that had not been searched thoroughly, and a detailed ground plan of the cave still had to be drawn. Other scholars would have been content with the rich haul of artifacts (and would have spent years completing slow and reflective studies on them), but Yadin was determined to find more. At the Israel Exploration Society annual convention in October, Yadin described his latest conclusions about the historical significance of the artifacts, and Joseph Aviram announced plans to mount a second expedition to the the Judean Wilderness, during the coming spring. Needless to say, the general public was excited about the prospect of more discoveries in Nahal Hever. But when Yadin and Aviram appealed for additional logistical assistance from the new IDF chief of staff, they were unexpectedly met with something less than wholehearted enthusiasm.

The previous chief of staff, Chaim Laskov, had resigned his command on January 1, 1961, after months of tension with Ben-Gurion and his immediate circle of political protégés. Yadin had been a close friend of Laskov since the War of Independence; their ideas about the desirability of formal discipline in the Israeli army and about the respect that should be accorded its high-ranking officers were essentially the same. This contrasted sharply with the Moshe Dayan doctrine of informality and impetuous battlefield bravado. Yadin made no secret of his sympathy with Laskov and had benefited from his wholehearted, unquestioning backing for the IDF for the expedition to the Judean Wilderness. But the new chief of staff—Zvi Zur, a well-known Dayan partisan—gave Yadin a much less sympathetic hearing. Bedouin incursions across the border from Jordan no longer posed a significant security problem, and while Zur was willing to provide some logistical assistance to a new expedition, he insisted that the Israel Exploration Society, the Hebrew University, and the Department of Antiquities underwrite a large part of the cost. If Yadin felt slighted by this suggestion, he was hardly deterred. During January 1961, Joseph Aviram organized lectures and fund-raising gatherings all over the country, and with Yadin's presentations attracting continued public interest and wealthy contributors, the Israel Exploration Society succeeded in raising the funds needed to send the teams headed by Yadin, Aharoni, Avigad, and Bar-Adon back into the field.

The 1961 expedition to the Judean wilderness heralded some important developments in the character of Israeli archaeology. Yadin's Bar-Kokhba finds had gained publicity far beyond the borders of Israel, and for the renewed expedition a sizable group of youthful volunteers from the United States, Canada, Germany, and Norway were recruited as participants. Yadin had invited some foreign archaeology students to participate in the Hazor project, but never before had foreigners with no special academic training been encouraged to join an expedition—as much for the adventure and the uplifting experience as for the archaeology. The other element that distinguished the second expedition was the thoroughness of the logistical preparations. During the previous season Yadin had been content to allow the army engineers to establish the camp without his direct supervision—he had only arrived on the night before the excavation. But this time he dispatched David Ussishkin several days in advance of the start of the expedition to direct the preliminary work. Confidently expecting more discoveries—and a steady stream of VIP visitors, Yadin wanted the access to the cave to be easier and less harrowing. On Yadin's instructions, the army engineers sited the expedition camp much closer to the Cave of Letters and considerably widened and leveled the path down to it. By the time the team began work on the morning of March 15, a field telephone had been installed to facilitate communication with the base camp and all its interior chambers were fully illuminated with electric lights.

The other team leaders moved to new areas in hope of better luck in the second season, but Yadin knew exactly what he had to do. He assigned some of his workers to excavate the Roman camp on the cliff edge above the Cave of Letters, and he directed the rest to carefully go over the cave's unexplored areas, with the knowledge that more hiding places were likely to be discovered in crevices or gaps between the collapsed boulders. In the two weeks that followed, Yadin's team uncovered a collection of personal effects no less stunning than the finds of the first season. On the very first day of renewed exploration, Sefi Porath, a volunteer from the settlement of Kfar Vitkin, located another treasure trove in the innermost chamber. Yadin once again supervised the slow removal of the contents of a bulging straw basket: wooden bowls, iron knives, a mirror, a frying pan, bronze jugs, and a pair of leather sandals, all amazingly well preserved. Even more stunning were the documents. Beneath the basket, mixed in a pile of rumpled textiles, Yadin and the team discovered six folded papyrus documents that had apparently been enclosed in a small leather purse. Nearby, inside the remains of a large goatskin bag, was a small bundle wrapped in cloth that contained dozens more folded papyrus documents, which were tied together, as Yadin would later describe them, "like a bunch of asparagus."

The news of the finds spread quickly, and as expected, a procession of VIP visitors began. On the first weekend of the expedition, Carmella came down to the camp by helicopter in the company of Washington columnist Art Buchwald, wearing a baseball cap and chomping on his trademark cigar. Despite his fabled cynicism, he made his way down to the cave and had only wide-eyed amazement for the team's spectacular finds. The discoveries continued—more knives, another Bar-Kokhba coin, a fowling net, iron keys, clay cooking pots, and a precious set of glass dishes carefully wrapped in palm fronds. The stream of visitors also continued. Chief of Staff Zvi Zur came with an entourage of high-ranking officers, and on the last day of work in the cave, March 27, Prime Minister Ben-Gurion came with his large staff and with Paula for a personal tour and explanation of the finds by Yadin.

Ben-Gurion had not been much impressed by Yadin's previous discoveries from the time of Bar-Kokhba. That would-be messiah was, after all, a political and military failure who had gone to his death fighting for a lost cause. Ben-Gurion had always been far more interested in the saga of Joshua and the conquest of Canaan, a story with a happy ending as far as the Israelites were concerned. During the previous spring Yadin had revealed to Ben-Gurion privately the contents of the Aramaic letters bearing the name of Shimeon Bar-Kosiba, but the prime minister reacted with disappointment and apparent annoyance that the ancient nationalist leader had not written in Hebrew. Yadin later recalled that Ben-Gurion had acted as if "the scribes had been members of his staff." But Ben-Gurion's visit to the Cave of Letters was an acknowledgment of Yadin's achievement, grudging as it still might have been. David Ussishkin recalled the prime minister's arrival in vivid detail; the elderly Ben-Gurion was unable to make his way down to the cave but sat in a tent in the base camp, surrounded by his obsequious aides and assistants, intently discussing the significance of the finds with Yadin. Ussishkin recalled that Yadin's explanations were interrupted only by Paula's occasional insistent whispering to her husband that it was time for him to take his medicine.

Yadin made the most of the visits of the dignitaries. The pattern that began at Hazor was now transformed into something of a ritual. When someone important was expected, Yadin would make his way to the helicopter landing pad and receive the visitor personally. He never played the aloof or indifferent scholar to any of the invited guests. As Ussishkin recalled, Yadin would lead the visitor down the path to the cave and up the rope ladder into the eerily illuminated chambers, all the while offering a firsthand account of the work under way and the challenges that lay ahead. Yadin made every effort to involve and interest the visitor in the reality of archaeological work. After the visit to the cave, he would lead the visitor back to the base camp for a personal explanation of the objects discovered. Ussishkin would stand close by, ready to open appropriate boxes and display the various artifacts of the Bar-Kokhba rebels as Yadin related his tale.

Yadin returned to Jerusalem at the conclusion of the two-week expedition and immersed himself in a study of the latest finds. Carmella had already taken the large collection of papyrus documents back to Jerusalem so that Dr. Biberkraut could open and unfold them. Although they were not dispatches from Bar-Kokhba but private documents—deeds, legal writs, and affidavits—of two of the refugees in the cave, Yadin became fascinated with reconstructing their lives through this fragmentary evidence. Particularly evocative for him was the personal story to be gleaned from the bundle of papyri wrapped in cloth and tied with string. Those documents revealed what he would later call "the life and trials" of Babata, a Jewish widow from the town of Mahoza on the other side of the Dead Sea, who had made her way to En Geddi at about the time of the outbreak of Bar-Kokhba's revolt.

It would take years for Yadin to disentangle the complex web of family relationships, inheritance claims, and legal battles over real estate and the custody of children that could be gleaned from the Aramaic, Nabatean, and Greek documents. During the spring and summer of 1961 the past (even a past as tragic as the ill-fated Bar-Kokhba revolt) must have had its attractions for Yadin, for modern developments were ominous and threatening. Only a few days after Yadin's return from the Judean Wilderness expedition, the government arrested his former aide in the Haganah operations branch, Yisrael Beer, on charges of espionage for the Soviet Union. The announcement did not come as a complete surprise to Yadin, for he had long distrusted Beer. Yadin had reacted in outrage in 1955 when Beer published a series of articles criticizing Yadin's behavior at Latrun, and he had tried unsuccessfully to block Beer's appointment at Tel Aviv University. The specter of treason at home now reinforced the menace of continuing Soviet hostility. Added to that, the ongoing proceedings of the Eichmann trial brought daily reenactments of horror and dread.

During the next academic year, Yadin and his family enjoyed a welcome respite. That summer he persuaded the university authorities that his first sabbatical should be moved up by one year, owing to the fact that he had given up all his normal vacation time to direct university-sponsored excavations at Megiddo and Hazor. In the fall of 1961 he and

Carmella and the girls departed for London. James de Rothschild had died in 1957, but Yadin could still depend on his generous support for his research, now almost entirely concerned with the Bar-Kokhba finds. Another of his British philanthropist patrons, Charles Clore of London, established a Bar-Kokhba Foundation to underwrite the publication of a full report on the Cave of Letters, and Lord Marks offered him the free use of the Marks and Spenser photographic laboratory to prepare color plates of the unique ancient textiles. Even more than his finds from the early Israelite period at Hazor, the message of Bar Kokhba far transcended strictly archaeological questions. In an address to the British Association for the Advancement of Science in the winter of 1962, suggestively entitled "The Past Communicates with the Present," Yadin underlined the importance of archaeology in modern Israeli society.

The expeditions to the Judean wilderness were a turning point in Yadin's career in that they provided him with a means of remaining in the public spotlight and exerting his influence on the nation while simultaneously pursuing his archaeological career. Few archaeologists had the skill to depict themselves so convincingly as heroes of their own research. Fewer still have been able to craft a tale of archaeological adventure that expressed a powerful political point. Israel's modern existence, Yadin argued with complete conviction, was poetically validated by his own archaeological discoveries. In his later popular account of the Bar-Kokhba expedition, he made the link between past and present explicit. "Descending daily over the precipice," he wrote of Nahal Hever, "crossing the dangerous ledge to the caves, working all day long in the stench of the bats, confronted from time to time with the tragic remains of those besieged and trapped—we found that our emotions were a mixture of tension and awe, yet astonishment and pride at being part of the reborn State of Israel after a Diaspora of 1,800 years. Here were we, living in tents erected by the Israel Defense Forces, walking every day through the ruins of a Roman camp which caused the death of our forefathers. Nothing remains here today of the Romans save a heap of stones on the face of the desert, but here the descendants of the besieged were returning to salvage their ancestors' precious belongings." Here was also the constellation of assertions and emotions that Yadin would utilize with such telling force in the coming years.

In the meantime, Ben-Gurion's political opponents were combining their forces to challenge his continuing autocratic rule over the nation. The Ben-Gurion era was clearly coming to an end. At the end of May 1962, Adolf Eichmann's final appeal for clemency was rejected by President Yitzhak Ben-Zvi, and the death sentence decreed by the Jerusalem district court and upheld by the Supreme Court of Israel was carried out.

But fears of a new Holocaust were by no means silenced. In July the Egyptian army unveiled its el-Zafir missile, reportedly manufactured under the supervision of German scientists; President Nasser proudly claimed it could strike any target south of Beirut. At this time of crisis and foreboding Yigael Yadin returned to Israel from his sabbatical. In London, he and Carmella had formulated plans to embark on an ambitious new archaeological project. And even though Yadin was still adamant that his career was in archaeology and not in politics, his upcoming expedition to the remote mountain of Masada would be interpreted by many as a profound and powerful political act.

Chapter   Thirteen

MASADA

On that Friday afternoon in mid-June 1963, the Old Man
seemed unusually placid. During this last appointment before
the Sabbath, David Ben-Gurion sat behind his desk quietly listening to the ambitious plans of Joseph Aviram and Dr. Yigael Yadin.
They had come to the prime minister's office in Tel Aviv to describe the
objectives of their proposed excavation of Masada—the largest and most
challenging archaeological project ever attempted in Israel. From a
purely logistical standpoint, the excavation would be far more difficult
than even that of the caves of the Judean Wilderness. Masada was a remote and isolated plateau, an enormous boat-shaped butte or mesa, located on the arid western shore of the Dead Sea. Since Masada was cut off
on all sides by deep ravines and there was no paved road in the immediate vicinity, all food, water, and excavation supplies would have to be

brought to the site by heavy four-wheel-drive vehicles. In addition, cranes and a cable transport system would have to be devised, for the excavations were to be undertaken on the summit and steep slopes of the mountain, hundreds of feet above the surrounding terrain. The climate too was difficult—dry and hot in summer and subject to high winds and driving rains in winter—but Yadin was undaunted. His excavation force of two hundred staff members and volunteer diggers would attempt to uncover and restore the remains of King Herod's desert pleasure palaces. Perhaps they would even be able to identify evidence of Masada's desperate and ultimately futile defense by Jewish rebels who had occupied the mountain during the first revolt against Rome in A.D. 66–74.

Ten years before, when Yadin resigned as chief of staff, Ben-Gurion had given him his own copy of the works of the first-century historian Josephus Flavius. And it was Josephus who provided the main source of knowledge about Masada's history. According to his account, King Herod chose the remote mountain as a secure place of refuge in case of domestic rebellion or dynastic intrigue. Building on the foundations of a fortress established by the Hasmonean kings of Judea earlier in the first century B.C., he spared no expense in equipping Masada with lavish bathhouses, colonnades, and living quarters as well as storerooms and water cisterns that would permit him and his entourage to live comfortably and securely in otherwise impossible terrain. But nearly seventy years after Herod's death, Masada became the scene of the siege that would make it famous. In A.D. 66, at the time of a popular uprising in Judea against Roman rule, a small group of Jewish rebels known as the *sicarii,* or "knife men," captured Masada from the legionary garrison stationed there. Josephus went on to describe how they continued to hold it even after the Romans crushed the Jewish insurrection everywhere else in the country and sacked and destroyed the Temple in Jerusalem. But because Masada was a self-sustaining fortress far out in the wilderness, at least as difficult of access in the first century as in the twentieth, it was the last pocket of Jewish resistance to stand.

Josephus' account of the Roman conquest of Masada had gained some archaeological verification in the years since Yadin had visited the site as a boy. Modern explorers to the Masada region had mapped the layout of the Roman camps at the foot of the mountain, traced the line of the low siege wall that was constructed around the mountain to prevent the rebels from escaping, and identified the massive earthen ramp on the western side where the Romans' battering ram was pushed into position and finally broke through the fortification wall. Yet Josephus' story of how the 960 Jewish men, women, and children holding out on Masada chose to take their own lives rather than suffer the fate of Roman captivity was yet to be verified by scholars. Book Seven of Josephus' *Jewish War* told how Eleazar Ben-Yair, the leader of the Masada zealots, assembled his comrades in Herod's once-magnificent palace when it became clear that the Roman siege forces could no longer be held back. He attempted, according to Josephus, to convince his rebel followers that God had apparently forsaken their cause and that death was preferable to Roman slavery. Convinced that they were taking the only honorable course available to them, the Jewish defenders of Masada went off to slay their own families, then set fire to all their supplies and possessions. They then chose ten men by a grim lottery to slay all the others, and one of those ten to slay the other nine and himself.

The following morning, Josephus related, the Romans stormed the fortress expecting fierce resistance but encountered only the silence of death. Two women and five children had hidden themselves in an underground cistern and now came out to surrender; they told the arriving Romans what had happened the previous night. According to Josephus, the Romans could not gloat over their victory. They put out the fires set the previous night by the defenders, made their way into the ruins of Herod's once-magnificent palace, and discovered a horrible sight. "Here encountering the mass of slain, instead of exulting as over enemies, they admired the nobility of their resolve and the contempt of death displayed by so many in carrying it, unwavering, into execution." So, according to Josephus ended the last episode of the great revolt.

In other times, Prime Minister Ben-Gurion would have viewed the plans to excavate Masada and search for the remains of the zealots with indifference or perhaps even with hostility. Like the story of Bar-Kokhba, the epic of Masada offered only the grim image of national disaster and defeat. Ben-Gurion had always preferred the historical imagery of Moses and Joshua, leading the Jewish people from slavery in Egypt to triumph in the Promised Land. But times were changing, and so were his political perceptions. The previous year's pressures seemed to have caused Ben-Gurion to lose his clear vision of both the future and the past. In growing anxiety about a hostile new federation of Egypt, Syria, and Iraq, he had swallowed his pride and appealed for diplomatic and military protection for Israel from the heads of state of England, France, the Soviet Union, and the United States. As news reports described the work of German scientists in Egypt, his political opponents on both left and right pressed him to act more forcefully. In the summer of 1963, when Israel was seemingly encircled and beset by external threats, the image of besieged Jewish freedom fighters—rather than a triumphant Israelite army of conquest—suddenly assumed, even for Ben-Gurion, a vivid and compelling reality.

Yadin was himself only a recent convert to the idea of excavating the site. Like Ben-Gurion, he had long distanced himself from the epic imagery of defeat on the mountain. In 1954, while in England completing his doctoral dissertation, he had respectfully declined Dr. Mazar's suggestion that he lead an archaeological expedition to Masada as his first scholarly undertaking. He had already set his sights on Hazor, where he could continue to study military technology in the biblical period and the historical reliability of the Book of Joshua. By that time, Masada had become a partisan political symbol whose overtones Yadin was apparently reluctant to embrace. In the late 1920s the young Yigael had visited Masada during scouting hikes and outings; but it was mainly in later years that the kibbutz and Zionist labor movement increasingly venerated the site. In 1927, Yitzhak Lamdan's poem "Masada" captured the public imagination with its final image of young Jewish pioneers dancing around a bonfire at the top of the mountain proclaiming "Masada Shall Not Fall Again."

During the underground struggle against the British Masada adopted with particular fervor by the Palmach and its supporters as a model of heroic partisan resistance against the forces of a great world empire. During the early 1940s, when the Palmach held training exercises in the Judean Wilderness, the ascent to the summit of Masada, with its spectacular view of the Dead Sea and the desert and its associations with ancient heroism, became a rite of passage for Palmach recruits. During Hanukkah 1941 a kibbutz movement activist named Shmaryahu Guttman led a small group in an exploration of the ruins on the summit and proposed to the Jewish Agency that it purchase the site and transform it into a national shrine. Early in 1942 a much larger group scaled the steep mountain and cleared the "snake path" to its summit.

Indeed, no image seemed more suited to the spirit of Yitzhak Sadeh's partisan fighters than Masada. In 1942, when Rommel seemed about to advance into Palestine, Sadeh's Eretz Israel Plan prepared for Masada-style resistance to the Nazi invaders. Even after the War of Independence and the disbanding of the Palmach, Masada remained a spiritual attraction. In 1953, Guttman led a kibbutz group on a thorough archaeological survey of the ruin-covered plateau and massive underground cisterns. Their detailed descriptions and photographs of the tumbled stones and once-ornate porticoes encouraged many to contemplate a much larger project. That was the context in which Dr. Mazar had first broached the idea to Yadin. While Yadin went on with his Hazor excavations, the Hebrew University, the Israel Exploration Society, and the Department of Antiquities organized a survey and preliminary excavation of Masada in March 1955.

This was Joseph Aviram's first major administrative undertaking, and in many ways it paved the way for the later expedition to the Judean Wilderness. Ten days' work on the mountain revealed to the team—jointly headed by Michael Avi-Yonah, Nahman Avigad, Immanuel Dunnayevsky, Yohanan Aharoni, and Shmaryahu Guttman (who was by now famous all over the country as "the man of Masada")—just how rich were Masada's remains. Even the brief 1955 excavations seemed to substantiate Josephus' description of the splendor of Herod's palaces, the extent of his storehouses, and the sophistication of his water system. The architectural remains were still fairly well-preserved, and the bases of some of the walls still bore molded and painted plaster decoration. There were rows of long, narrow storerooms, just as Josephus described. Clear signs of burning and destruction were observed in many of the ruined buildings, which the archaeologists believed were evidence of the final Roman conquest of the mountain. And while these preliminary finds were certainly suggestive, it would clearly take a much larger and longer expedition to reconstruct the history of the site and determine whether there was any truth to the story of the mass suicide.

During the 1955 Masada expedition Yadin had been preparing for the first season of digging at Hazor, and two members of the Masada survey team, Aharoni and Dunnayevsky, joined him there. In fact, the Masada project was soon abandoned. Except for another brief season of digging by Aharoni in the spring of 1956, further efforts were given up due to lack of funds and sufficient logistical support. The situation changed, however, with the great public excitement over the finds from the Bar-Kokhba period. At this time Yadin reconsidered his earlier reluctance to lead a large-scale expedition to Masada. The idea's attractions grew during his sabbatical in London in the winter of 1962. His fame there was on the rise—the 1958 Hazor exhibition at the British Museum had won him great publicity, while in 1961 the *Illustrated London News* had featured an admiring story about his adventures in the Judean Wilderness. Once again he turned to his wealthy and influential social connections, confident that he would be able to mobilize public support throughout Israel as well. Yet it was another factor that transformed the Masada project into something much larger and more important than the expedition to the Judean Wilderness.

At an elegant dinner party at the home of Lord Marks in London, Yadin was introduced to David Astor, editor of *The Observer*. Astor listened intently to Yadin's dramatic retelling of the story of the ancient Jewish zealots on the mountain stronghold and the idea of modern Israeli archaeologists mounting a massive expedition to uncover the site. Astor was fascinated and pledged to provide a substantial proportion of the expedition budget, in return for exclusive newspaper, magazine, photographic, and television rights to the story of the dig. Thus was born the notion of a massive, highly publicized archaeological undertaking, in which the modern discovery story was no less important than the finds themselves. Yadin's archaeological career was becoming a larger-than-life public spectacle, in which an intense search for heroic chapters of the Jewish past was followed with obsessive fascination by the general public all over the world. The Masada excavation would be by far his greatest production and would become—next to the discovery of the tomb of Tutankhamen in the Valley of the Kings—the most celebrated archaeological undertaking of the twentieth century.

At a press conference in Jerusalem on August 11, Yadin proudly announced his plans. Flanked by Joseph Aviram of the Israel Exploration Society and his old friend Yaacov Yannai (now head of the National Parks Authority), Yadin declared his intention to excavate the site and simultaneously to restore it, uncovering the lavish palaces of Herod and possible evidence of the zealots' last stand. Describing the excavation of Masada as the "big dream of archaeologists and the Yishuv," Yadin said that the IDF would be called upon to assist in the difficult logistical arrangements. A dirt road would have to be cleared from the town of Arad (about fifteen miles to the west), and a large base camp would be established on the western side of the mountain, "alongside the camp of the commander of the Roman forces." Yadin announced that in addition to the professional staff and work groups recruited from Israeli settlements, youth movements, and army units, able-bodied volunteers from all over the world would be permitted to participate in the dig.

The modern symbolism of Masada was compelling, and in an effort to underline the significance of his project, Yadin attended a solemn military ceremony on the summit of the mountain in the summer of 1963. Since the days of Moshe Dayan's tenure as chief of staff, new recruits of the armored corps of the Israel Defense Forces had hiked up the steep path to the plateau of Masada and taken their oath of allegiance in that dramatic setting, so resonant with heroic images from ancient Jewish history. Now Yadin lent the weight of his own authority to the proceedings. Standing in the flickering torchlight, the chief-of-staff-turned-professor declared to newly sworn Israeli soldiers that "when Napoleon stood among his troops next to the pyramids of Egypt, he declared that 'four thousand years of history look down upon you.' But what would he not have given to be able to say to his men: four thousand years of *your own* history look down upon you . . . ' The echo of your oath this night," Yadin concluded, "will resound throughout the encampments of our foes. Its significance is not less powerful than all our armaments!"

The martial tone was surprising in light of Yadin's long absence from military affairs. It marked a style of expression he had not used since his days as chief of staff. But in the summer of 1963 dramatic changes had become common. On June 16, just two days after Yadin and Aviram met with Ben-Gurion to unveil their ambitious plans, the Old Man shocked the nation with his decision to leave public life. This time it was not a gambit or political maneuver. The father of the nation retired to Sde Boker, and the leadership of the State of Israel passed to others. And the symbolism of Masada, resurrected through Yadin's archaeological efforts, would become one of the new era's hallmarks.

On October 13, 1963, the great national project began in the chill and rain of early winter, as a stream of eager volunteers arrived at the assembly point in Arad. During the previous few months, enthusiastic stories about the upcoming Masada excavations had been carried in the London *Observer* and syndicated to newspapers all over the world. Thousands of applications from twenty-eight countries had soon flooded the offices of the Israel Exploration Society. Carmella was instrumental in organizing the expedition. In addition to keeping up with the general correspondence and administrative arrangements, she took responsibility for selecting the foreign volunteers. Using her "power sword" system, she transferred all the information on the applications to punch cards, which she sorted to maintain an even distribution of age, physical condition, and professional experience. By early autumn, she had selected fourteen two-week teams of volunteer workers, who along with Israeli youth groups and military units would constitute the primary labor force.

The scene at Arad on opening day was remarkable. "They started coming at six in the morning," wrote *Jerusalem Post* reporter Daniel Gavron of the scene. "They arrived by bus, or hitchhiked, with rucksacks, suitcases, banjos, and typewriters, in shorts, jeans, slacks, and skirts. Bearded and bespectacled, clean-shaven and clear-eyed, they came from all over Israel and all over the world." Also present was a correspondent from *The Observer*, Patrick O'Donovan, whose employers had a sizable investment in the newsworthiness of the dig. In a dispatch filed from Beersheva, O'Donovan indulged in breathless prose of a sort that would always be used to describe the Masada expedition. "For Israel, then, this expedition is more than an archaeological dig," O'Donovan informed his British readers. "It is an act of piety. In its own terrible right, Masada presents a challenge to the present that Israel could not refuse."

Yadin and his large staff had completed the complex logistical preparations on schedule, and they bore an unmistakable military quality.

Unlike the Judean Wilderness expedition, where a small number of participants carried out the work quickly, or the excavations of Hazor, where nearby kibbutz residents provided essential services, the isolated base camp of the Masada Excavation Project possessed all the characteristics of a large army unit in the field. It must certainly have looked that way to the foreign volunteers. To one side were evenly spaced rows of tents for the workers; in the center were a field kitchen and dining tents; off to the south, at a respectable distance from all the others, were living quarters, offices, and workrooms for the professional staff. The first season was planned to last seven months, and the work schedules would have to be strictly upheld if the ambitious objectives of the expedition were to be achieved. To accomplish the simultaneous excavation and reconstruction of Masada's extensive palaces, storehouses, and administrative buildings, Yadin recruited a staff of three groups of professionals, each with a clearly defined area of responsibility.

To oversee the camp administration, security, food, water, mechanical maintenance, and field communications, Yadin obtained the services of a team of army officers, some of whom, like Captain Yoske Yefet, had participated in the Judean Wilderness expedition. Another group, under the supervision of Yaacov Yannai, director of the newly organized National Parks Authority, consisted of experienced stonemasons, crane operators, and construction engineers. Their job would be to rebuild the collapsed walls and crumbled foundations of Masada's ancient structures and to install stairways and pathways for the influx of visitors expected after the dig. Last and certainly not least were the archaeologists. In contrast to Hazor, for which Yadin had recruited Israel's most experienced and prominent archaeologists (and as a result had suffered the fate of being first among equals), for Masada he assembled a team of his own graduate students from the university—and recruited Shmaryahu Guttman, "the man of Masada"—over all of whom Yadin would be a figure of unquestioned authority.

As always, Yadin quickly grasped the essential points of archaeological interest. Never allowing himself to become bogged down in details or overwhelmed by the undertaking, he kept track of the ongoing excavations at many locations on the plateau, monitored the mapping and excavation of the double fortification wall around the summit, and directed the exploration of huge water cisterns and natural caves discovered just below the upper plateau. Before the excavation began, he had appointed an administrative assistant, Gideon Foerster, to assemble all the information that had been collected and published by previous explorers of Masada, to have as precise an idea of the extent and condition of the remains as possible. Masada's ruins were not buried under deep layers of accumulation but had collapsed and lay strewn on the surface. Aerial photographs and the maps of earlier explorers clearly delineated the ruins of a lavish, three-tiered palace extending down the nearly vertical northern "prow" of the boat-shaped mountain. It was on the lowest terrace that one of the expedition's first and most important discoveries was made.

As other supervisors began work in the various buildings on the summit, Amnon Ben-Tor was given the harrowing assignment of excavating the lowest levels of Herod's northern palace, accessible only by a rickety, makeshift wooden stairway that army engineers installed on the northern face, hundreds of feet above the surrounding terrain. The effort and risk proved to be justified; the lower level was rich in finds beyond all expectation. Ben-Tor's team cleared the main portico and uncovered elaborate wall paintings, then discovered off to the side a small private bathhouse, with cold pool, heated chamber, and dressing rooms, all constructed according to standard Roman technique. It seemed clear from the level of debris that had accumulated on the floors of that luxurious structure, however, that the small bathhouse, and indeed the rest of the palace, had fallen into disrepair by the time of the revolt against Rome, more than sixty years after Herod's death. And there in the rubble of destruction the Masada story began to take on a life of its own. As Ben-Tor's volunteer workers cleared the debris of the bathhouse, they came upon a scatter of silver-plated armor scales, dozens of iron-tipped arrows, remains of clothing, several pairs of sandals, and human bones.

Ben-Tor quickly summoned Yadin to the area, as the diggers continued to clear away the ash and rubble from the cold water pool of the bathhouse. They eventually distinguished the fragmentary skeletons of three individuals. On the surface of the plastered stairs they found a dark stain that resembled blood and, nearby, the long plaits of a woman's hair, grotesquely preserved in Masada's arid soil for almost two thousand years. With this and other such discoveries, Yadin and others felt that they had established a direct and powerful link to the legendary heroes of the Jewish past. The leaders of the 1955–56 expedition had had difficulty connecting specific artifacts and structures with the Jewish rebels, but slowly Yadin and his staff realized that the zealots had not constructed their own buildings but had merely reoccupied the Herodian complex. Soon after the discovery of the human remains in the northern palace, other teams found evidence of what seemed to be zealot occupation in the interior chambers of the casemate wall around the plateau. In dozens of individual rooms they found small handmade ovens and humble personal possessions, in many places covered with a destruction layer of tumbled stones and ash. In the rooms of the royal palace and administrative buildings, they also uncovered signs of squatters' occupation. Crude mud and stone partition walls had been fashioned that divided the once-opulent royal reception rooms into makeshift cubicles.

Evidence of the zealots now appeared throughout the excavations. In one chamber of the casemate wall that the victorious Roman soldiers had apparently used as a refuse dump, Guttman's team uncovered hundreds of rounded catapult stones that the rebels had collected but not used, a hoard of silver shekels minted during the revolt (and apparently overlooked by the Romans), textiles, baskets, keys, arrows, sandals and—to Yadin's great satisfaction—large fragments of seven ancient Hebrew manuscripts. This was the first time that parchment documents of a type nearly identical to the Dead Sea Scrolls had been discovered in a controlled excavation, and Yadin made the find public in a press conference held at the end of the week. Terming the discovery one of "extreme importance," he announced the find of the bodies in the northern palace, the apparent living quarters of the zealots, and a large hall attached to the casemate, which he identified as the earliest synagogue ever found. Although the excavation had been under way for only six weeks, Yadin's fabled luck had admirably proved itself. In fact, Yadin hoped that this press conference would electrify the nation and spark excitement around the world. Once more he had produced tangible evidence for ancient historical legends. At Masada he believed that his team had found the very bones of the Jewish rebels who had taken their own lives. Unfortunately, modern events betrayed him. The world's attention soon shifted westward to Dallas, Texas. It was November 22, 1963.

Even as public attention was diverted to the funeral of John F. Kennedy and the transition to the Johnson administration in Washington, and as tension was renewed on Israel's border with Syria, Yadin pressed on relentlessly with his plan to uncover all of the main structures at Masada. After completing the excavation of the northern palace, Amnon Ben-Tor and his team began work in the even larger palace on the west. Another area supervisor, Dan Bahat, cleared a large bathhouse and then began to excavate the rows of storerooms that had once made Masada a self-contained refuge. Each evening, Yadin would convene the senior staff members for a meeting, with tape recorder running, to review that day's developments and to plan the strategy for the next. It was as if Yadin were back in charge of the general staff in the midst of an ongoing campaign, with thousands of pieces of information flowing into the headquarters and decisions to be made every day. The undisputed commander, Yadin led the discussions, asked probing questions, and suggested ingenious comparisons between finds in the various areas.

Although he was admittedly not a specialist in Roman architecture, physical anthropology, or pottery analysis, he had a vision of the overall significance of the discoveries. Although he would often accept factual or technical input from senior staff members, it was Yadin who was "navigating the ship quite well," Gideon Foerster recalled in admiration, "and the people followed him."

During these nightly meetings Yadin gradually orchestrated a vision of Masada's remains that closely paralleled Josephus' account. As at Hazor, where he defended the historical accuracy of the Israelite conquest, he was reluctant to challenge a tradition that was not clearly *disproved* by the archaeological evidence. In that regard the human remains at Masada were central. In addition to the three skeletons discovered in the northern palace, a team led by Yoram Tsafrir located a grotesque jumble of human bones in a cave just below the mountain's southern edge. Were these the remains of the zealots? A physical anthropologist found that the bones in the southern cave represented the bodies of twenty-four individuals: fourteen men, six women, and four children, one of them apparently an unborn child. The wide age range and the presence of so many women and children seemed to preclude the connection with the Roman soldiers or the Byzantine monks who later occupied the site. Indeed, their physical characteristics (at least in the estimation of Dr. Niko Haas of the Hebrew University–Hadassah Medical School) seemed identical to those of the bodies found in the Bar-Kokhba caves. Mixed among the human remains were the bones not only of cattle, sheep, and goats but also—unthinkable for Jewish zealots—a significant number of pigs. Yet the pig bones could perhaps be explained by the presence of the Roman garrison at Masada after the fall of the fortress, when the legionnaires could have used the cave as a garbage dump.

There was little doubt in Yadin's mind that the human remains found on the lowest level of the northern palace were evidence of the zealots' final, bloody defense of Masada. Here, too, he could use archaeological data (however tenuous) to verify the familiar story. Dr. Haas identified the three very fragmentary skeletal remains uncovered in the ruins as belonging to a young woman aged sixteen or seventeen, a boy aged eleven or twelve, and a man aged twenty to twenty-two. Clearly influenced by Josephus' emotional descriptions of the deaths of the family groups at Masada, Yadin seemed intent on making some sort of family out of these remains. During a staff meeting in late November he suggested that, with the adjustment of a year or two in Dr. Haas's age estimates, the boy could perhaps have been the son of the young man.

Since the young man and the young woman were the right ages to be a married couple, he concluded that the boy was the man's son by another wife, or perhaps even a brother of the young woman or man. All this was just speculation, but Yadin was never content with equivocation. He had to tell a vivid, lifelike story. And before long, the unambiguous image of a Jewish rebel family dying in the ruins of the northern palace, just as Josephus had described it, would become a central element in the modern legend of Masada's archaeological rediscovery.

If anyone had expected David Ben-Gurion to drift softly into political twilight after leaving office, they were sadly mistaken. Through the fall and winter, as the Masada excavations got under way, Ben-Gurion waged a bitter public campaign against his successor, Levi Eshkol. Eshkol, for his part, had given Ben-Gurion ample reason. Instead of furthering the careers of Ben-Gurion's protégés like Dayan and Peres, Eshkol had turned to the leftist opposition to expand his power base. In late 1963, Eshkol concluded a coalition negotiation with the left-wing Achdut Avodah party and brought into the cabinet a group of young leaders— Yigal Allon, Israel Galili, and Moshe Carmel, among them—who were smarting from their treatment by Ben-Gurion during and immediately after the 1948 war. Further moves cemented the political changes of the post–Ben-Gurion era. On the insistence of the relatively small Achdut Avodah party, Eshkol agreed to shelve Ben-Gurion's plan for electoral reform. At the end of 1963, Chief of Staff Zvi Zur, Dayan's faithful assistant, was replaced by Yitzhak Rabin, Allon's longtime lieutenant. It was another sign (as if another were needed) of the growing alliance between Levi Eshkol and the old-boy Palmach network.

Yadin at this time was fully involved in the Masada excavations and tried his best to remain aloof and neutral, refusing to be drawn into the political quarrel since he had friends and former adversaries on both sides. "There were many telephone calls for him at the dig," Foerster recalled, from politicians and public leaders, "but it seemed as if he couldn't care less." In fact, Yadin tried to play the part of a disinterested but patriotic scholar who rose above all partisan strife. Early in the season he led Prime Minister Eshkol on a brief tour of the excavations, and a few weeks later, he did the same for Ben-Gurion. But by early spring, Yadin had become a pawn in the political battle. At the end of February, Ben-Gurion returned from his annual vacation in Tiberias and, taking a slap at Eshkol, announced his intention to renew the fight for a change in the electoral system by meeting with Yadin in his capacity as chairman of the Public

Committee for Constituency Elections. Yadin refused to be drawn into this maneuver, but he could not contain his displeasure when the former prime minister extended his political battle into the realm of history.

One of Ben-Gurion's avowed intentions in his retirement was to publish his memoirs, and as an experienced political tactician he was fully aware of the power of the past. His interest lay neither in Joshua nor in Masada but in the commanders, heroes, and battles of the Independence War of 1948. In an interview in the daily newspaper *Haboker,* the former prime minister pointedly remarked—surely intending to make headlines—that if he had known Moshe Dayan at the beginning of the war, "the frontiers of Israel would have been different now." This amounted to accusing the other 1948 commanders of failure. And Ben-Gurion wanted to leave little doubt about that. Accusing "some forces" of keeping Dayan away from him during the opening phase of the fighting, Ben-Gurion went on to lavish praise on Dayan's 1948 commando assault on Lod (which he characterized as "one of the most daring feats in our military history"), his tactical plan for the 1956 Sinai campaign, and his entire tenure as chief of staff. Despite the ill wishes of Dayan's detractors Ben-Gurion proudly asserted, "I succeeded in pulling him up, and I am glad that I have not been disappointed."

That Moshe Dayan was one of Ben-Gurion's closest political allies and leader of the faction that the Old Man hoped would soon take over the party was lost on no one. The daily newspapers, eager to agitate the already-choppy political waters, asked the other heroes of the war for a response. Former chief of staff Dori tactfully refrained from comment, but Yigal Allon, now minister of labor in the Eshkol government, angrily went on the offensive, true to his 1948 form. "The country has remained dismembered not because of any failure of strategy or fighting ability," he insisted, "but because the Government, for which Mr. Ben-Gurion was responsible, ordered a withdrawal." The partition of Jerusalem occurred "because the political authorities refused to subscribe to operational plans that would have changed that state of affairs."

Yadin fired a salvo of his own from Masada. "If the war did not achieve complete liberation," he told *The Jerusalem Post,* it was due to necessary political calculations and to unsuccessful operations like the battles for Latrun. That failure, Yadin asserted, was due to "the unwise intervention of Mr. Ben-Gurion himself." Yadin's unassailable national prestige became particularly clear at the end of June, when he was awarded the annual Rothschild Science Prize, in a public ceremony filled with political symbolism. The chairman of the panel of judges was none other than Rav Aluf Yaacov Dori, Yadin's old Haganah patron, now president of Israel's foremost technical and scientific institution, the Technion. In announcing the award Dori indirectly responded to the former prime minister when he praised Yadin for his "dynamism and brilliance, his indefatigable archaeological research and ability to inspire his assistants to work as one team." In times of increasing political conflict within Israel, heroic ancient images from Masada and idealized memories of the War of Independence made Yigael Yadin an actor in the public arena whether he desired it or not.

At Masada, the military discipline that Yadin imposed on the excavation contrasted sharply with the much-touted sabra ideal of individualism and informality. At Hazor strong objections from the senior staff had quickly forced Yadin to abandon his martial manner, but at Masada, with a much younger and more compliant staff, there was no such protest. Every morning at five, precisely as Yadin instructed, Captain Yoske Yefet played a recording of reveille over the camp loudspeaker system. The blaring bugle cadence, followed by Yefet's booming encouragement to rise and shine, get dressed, and move quickly to breakfast, echoed in the looming mountains and ravines eerily and, for most of the volunteers and staff members, painfully. Work was to be in full swing by six o'clock, and Yadin stood at the top of the path to the summit at the start of every working day. "If someone was late," recalled Leon Shalit, who visited Masada frequently, "Yadin looked at his watch and looked at the person and that person was never late again." The hierarchy was clear and uncompromising; the volunteers' tents were separated from those of the staff, and Yadin had a tent of his own. "He was not very sensitive to human problems," Foerster recalled of the occasional poor provisions and living conditions in the winter cold. "There was some resentment, but no one dared say anything."

To many of the young archaeologists on the Masada expedition, Yadin's personality seemed paradoxical. He could be cold and imperious, puffing his pipe in silence, as he watched the volunteers and staff file in and out of the dining tent or climb up to the site. At other times he could be an engaging, even charming conversationalist, readily showing flashes of brilliance and wit, especially in relaxed conversations after the evening meetings. An offhand reference to a historical event or a famous personality would remind him of a colorful story, which he would relate with vivid and always entertaining detail. Most of the senior staff had been children at the time of the 1948 war and had grown up hearing stories about the siege of Jerusalem, the battles of Latrun, and the defense of Deganiah. Yadin was a direct link to a heroic period that was quickly becoming part of Israeli folklore, and they listened with great interest to his stories about

King Abdullah, the Rhodes peace talks, the battle for Jerusalem, and Ben-Gurion. His stories had become highly stylized anecdotes whose direct relationship to the truth lessened as the years went on, but their power to fascinate was enormous. No less than Yadin's visions of death and heroism at Masada, they were part of an idealized and unchanging past.

Yadin's genius was his ability to draw people into a web of myth-making, into a deeply felt communal consciousness. During Ben-Gurion's tenure as prime minister, history had often been used as a weapon to challenge outmoded notions and religious fundamentalism—and to craft a secular Israeli nationalism. Thus the stories of Joshua downplayed divine inspiration and stressed military prowess. The orthodox religious population had often reacted in outrage, skeptical of the hidden agenda of modern archaeology. But now Yadin reached out to every sector of the Israeli public. In a small news report during the first season of digging, he announced the discovery of a *mikveh* or ritual bath used by the zealots and quickly transformed the find into a public relations coup. In a gesture of little archaeological significance but great symbolism, he invited two elderly rabbis from Jerusalem, David Muntzburg and Eliezer Alter, to Masada to examine the *mikveh* and determine whether it conformed to modern Jewish ritual law. Naturally, they came—pilgrims like all the others—along with an entourage of shuffling, black-garbed followers from the synagogues and yeshivas of Meah Shearim into the brilliant light of the Judean wilderness. Guided by Yadin to the southeastern sector of the casemate wall at the edge of the summit, they measured the *mikveh* and closely examined its shape and construction. Their confident determination that this ritual bath was "among the finest of the finest" gave Yadin a vivid symbol of the uniting power of his work.

After the first digging season ended in April and through the summer of 1964, the high-minded "spirit of Masada" rose in direct proportion to the growing acrimony on the national political scene. At the end of July, Yadin publicly announced that the second season of excavations beginning at the end of November, once again supported by *The Observer* and with the participation of army units, school groups, and foreign volunteers. There was to be even wider public participation this season: at a press conference in Tel Aviv on November 22, Yadin announced a national fund-raising drive to reconstruct the ruins of Masada, so that they could be opened to the public sometime the next year. "Masada certificates" went on sale at banks, schools, and factories, signifying that the purchaser had subscribed to the reconstruction fund. When President Zalman Shazar (who had been elected to the ceremonial post in the summer of 1963, after the death of Ben-Zvi) arrived at the site by helicopter to open the second season, Yadin presented him with the very first certificate of the Masada Preservation Fund. The excavation's patriotic overtones were gradually obscuring its more scholarly aspects. "At this time when we are trying to renew the heroic period of our nation's history," Shazar stated for the journalists, "the story of Masada should penetrate into every home in the country." Taking the podium to press the political significance of the project further, Yadin declared that "Masada was the symbol of our refusal to live as slaves."

The VIPs present for the ceremony included a number of prominent representatives from the Eshkol government. There was more than a little irony in Yadin's tacit—and certainly unplanned—boost to the prestige of the ruling coalition, but in those days the Masada expedition was attracting enormous positive publicity for Israel all over the world. At the same time, Eshkol's political fortunes were rising on the international stage. In June 1964 he became the first Israeli prime minister to be officially invited to the White House; he returned to Israel triumphant, with President Lyndon Johnson's firm commitment to support Israel in the international arena and more quiet promises of arms supplies. The transformation of Israel's international image from the time of Ben-Gurion was already striking: the Jewish state was losing its revolutionary fervor and was gradually becoming a bourgeois, docile ally run by a kindly Jewish grandfather. Ben-Gurion, still in the wings, tried at every turn to undermine Eshkol's authority. Just as Yadin was getting ready for the second season with Masada certificates, Ben-Gurion and his allies went on the attack. In October 1964, Moshe Dayan resigned from his post as minister of agriculture in Eshkol's government, loudly protesting that he had been locked out of security affairs. An open split in the ruling Mapai party was quickly approaching.

From the Olympian heights of Masada, Yadin directed the second digging season, intending to finish the excavations of the western palace, the casemate wall, and the remaining storerooms. The rich finds continued; during the first two months, workers uncovered more manuscript fragments, an extremely rare group of shekels minted near the end of the revolt against the Romans, and continuing evidence of the zealots' occupation of rooms in the casemate wall. The mass suicide story, although central to the symbolism of Masada, had been hinted at in the two, widely separated discoveries of human bones the previous year. Far more suggestive finds were now made in an area near the storehouses, supervised by Dan Bahat. During the previous season they had uncovered hundreds of *ostraca,* or inscribed potsherds, marked with letters, num-

bers, and symbols. With these, according to Yadin, the zealots had distributed their provisions and other supplies. But a group of eleven
ostraca found together on the ground between the storerooms and a
large administrative building seemed different; they bore the nicknames
or first names of eleven men, as well as names like "The man from the
valley," "The son of the baker," and "The one with curly hair." As Bahat
recalled, Yadin was greatly interested in the inscribed sherds, and his
interest turned to excitement when he read the name "Ben-Yair" on one
of the potsherds—for that was the name of the zealot commander at
Masada in Josephus' account.

When all the area supervisors sat down that evening to examine the
potsherds and discuss their significance, Yadin quickly pulled out a copy
of Josephus. Quoting the story of the Eleazar Ben-Yair's passionate
speech and the mass suicide that followed, he read aloud the passage
in which the zealots "chose ten men by lot out of them, to slay all the
rest . . . and when these ten had, without fear, slain them all, they made
the same rule for casting lots themselves, that he whose lot it was to first
kill the other nine, and after all, should kill himself." As Bahat recalled,
Yadin made an explicit connection between the *ostraca* and the mass
suicide in this staff meeting. He suggested that they had perhaps found
the very lots cast by the last surviving zealots; the appearance of the name
Ben-Yair seemed to clinch the case for him. "The interesting thing was
that when he first started talking about this, none of us were very impressed. We all thought the idea was pretty far-fetched. But Yadin stuck
with the idea to the very end and that's how it was published. He had
already made up his mind about it."

The digging continued through early April, but for Yadin the main
outline of the traditional Masada story had already been confirmed. The
splendor of the Roman-style Herodian palaces and bathhouses contrasted sharply with the piety and determination of the zealot defenders
at the end of the revolt. On March 26, Yadin gave his final press conference at Masada before a large contingent of local journalists. Summariz-
ing the results of two seasons of digging with mathematical precision,
Yadin itemized twelve ancient manuscript fragments, 750 *ostraca* (including the group that he said "might have been the very lots drawn by
the commanders at the time of the mass suicide"), nearly four thousand
coins, and a million and a half pottery shreds. "While the dig answered a
number of questions," *Jerusalem Post* correspondent Daniel Gavron
noted, "several mysteries remained unsolved. The most important of
these was what had happened to the 960 bodies of the defenders who
committed suicide. Only 28 skeletons had been found, several belonging
to women and children, probably Zealots." But Yadin had a ready expla-

nation: "He thought it possible that the remainder had been burned and the ashes scattered." Still, the richness of the finds was undeniable. Once again Yadin had successfully undertaken a challenging archaeological mission. Certainly no other scholar in the world could have conveyed the story of Masada with such skill and conviction, or carried it out on such a grand scale. Even though his speculations about the fall of Masada were based only on intuitive assumptions, the mass suicide story was now given the outward appearance of final confirmation by modern archaeology.

International acclaim was quickly forthcoming. During the excavations Yadin received word that he had been made a member of the Israel Academy of Sciences and of the French Académie des Inscriptions et Belles-Lettres; at the end of July 1966 he was named a corresponding fellow of the British Academy. The most significant nomination of all, however, was the one he rejected. During the spring of 1965, Ben-Gurion and his political allies were planning to challenge Eshkol's leadership of the Mapai, but by their best estimates they would have the support of only forty percent of the membership in any head-to-head vote. At a party congress in February, Ben-Gurion gave a fiery speech accusing Eshkol of being unfit for leadership due to his shameless courtship of the left and his refusal to implement electoral reform. Ben-Gurion became embroiled in a renewed controversy over the role of former defense minister Pinchas Lavon in the 1950s intelligence scandal in Egypt. When his other stratagems failed to work, Ben-Gurion turned to Masada. Despite all Yadin's earlier demurrals, Ben-Gurion believed that the former chief of staff was now his man. He therefore sent Yadin a confidential handwritten letter suggesting that he accept the leading position on an alternative Mapai list.

Yadin was enjoying his lofty public image far too much to enter a nasty political fight. Not unexpectedly, after conferring with Carmella, Yadin politely turned down the offer. Nonetheless rumors quickly spread. Some newspapers suggested that Yadin's candidacy was a foregone conclusion; others began predicting the result. Reuven Barkatt, the Mapai secretary-general, arranged a secret meeting with Yadin at the Masmiya junction on the road from Jerusalem to Masada. As Yadin later recalled, Barkatt was nervous and wanted to avoid a public conflict that would tear the party apart. "If you said yes to Ben-Gurion, that's your business," Barkatt reportedly told Yadin. "But if you said no, I beg you not to reveal it publicly." Yadin, as usual, remained discreet about his political intentions, maintaining absolute neutrality. But had Yadin accepted Ben-Gurion's proposal and ridden the wave of popularity he had gained at Masada, the modern history of Israel might have been different. In the next months Eshkol prepared for a head-to-head showdown, since Ben-Gurion now had no alternative but to challenge Eshkol himself. The results of the internal Mapai election held in early June 1965 were definitive: Eshkol received 179 votes to Ben-Gurion's 103. No longer was there room for compromise between the two factions. An acrimonious split in the governing Mapai party was now all but inevitable.

———

The drama of the Masada excavations and the virtuoso brilliance with which Yadin conveyed the discoveries to the public made the project as much an exercise in patriotic inspiration as in scientific research. Soon after the digging was completed and as the staff began the process of analysis, study, and eventual publication (which would take nearly thirty years and be finished only after Yadin's death), he was besieged by requests for public appearances, both in Israel and the United States. With his classic sense of drama Yadin traveled directly from Masada to Tel Aviv on the last day of the excavations to a special gathering of the Friends of the Hebrew University. During the following autumn, he was the starring attraction in a highly publicized lecture tour across the United States to celebrate the university's fortieth anniversary. Enthusiastic crowds and generous donors delighted in Yadin's tales of the Judean Wilderness at black-tie dinners from New York City to Beverly Hills. Yadin, eager to reach an even broader audience now that the digging was over and the exclusive arrangement with *The Observer* had ended, signed a lucrative book contract with Random House. Summoning his old friend Moshe Pearlman, an experienced journalist, diplomat, and government adviser, they worked together through the spring of 1966 to prepare a lavishly illustrated popular account of the dig. Based loosely on the *Observer* articles, personal memories and anecdotes, and color slides that Yadin himself had taken at important moments, this archaeological book carried a message in which the present was as important as the past. Whether by intention or unconscious osmosis, the book's message was surprisingly in tune with the times.

Israel's military stance, under Prime Minister Eshkol and Chief of Staff Rabin, was swinging back to the idea of a large conventional army, basing deterrence on extensive training for all units and on the acquisition of large numbers of tanks, artillery pieces, and airplanes. This vision was strikingly similar to the one Yadin had held as chief of staff in the early 1950s and was a striking departure from the doctrine of Ben-Gurion, Dayan, and Peres—of secret nuclear development and covert commando raids. The warming of relations with the United States made this possible. The Johnson administration, increasingly bogged down in its Vietnamese morass, was eager to cultivate dependable military allies in other world trouble spots. For the first time Israel acquired large quantities of American weapons, including tanks and Skyhawk jets. Despite the continuing protests of Ben-Gurion, Dayan, Peres, and their allies, the battle to expand Israel's conventional military capability, rather than the nonconventional, was gradually won. From March through July 1965, in response to Syrian attempts to divert the headwaters of the Jordan, the Israel Defense Forces destroyed the Syrians' heavy earth-moving equipment through intensive artillery bombardment, not through a daring commando raid.

In a strange way, Masada became a highly adaptable symbol, useful to both sides in the ongoing military debate. During his lecture tour and in his writing about the excavations, Yadin emphasized emotional motifs pregnant with modern meaning, but he never precisely defined their significance. The Masada story could be used to justify unconventional tactics, with which a brave few held out against the many; on the other hand, the very fact of the conquest of the zealots' fortress by the Roman army could be used as metaphor to justify conventional military strength. Yadin's talent was in crystallizing vivid images, never in philosophy. As he refined and sharpened his public lectures about Masada over time, he downplayed the natural ambiguity of archaeological evidence in order to make the Masada story a better tale. That is not to say that he knowingly concealed or manufactured evidence, but as a skilled storyteller he merely strung together a series of narrative assumptions that led his audience to the inevitable and satisfying conclusion that Josephus' story about the mass suicide of the zealots was true.

When Yadin described the cave on the southern side of the mountain with the jumble of human bones of men, women, and children, he noted that "most of the skulls belong to the same type as those we discovered in the caves of Bar-Kokhba in Nahal Hever. It seems to me that those facts conclusively rule out the possibility that the skeletons are either those of the Roman garrison or of the monks." He apparently saw no need to mention the presence of types that did not conform to Nahal Hever, or the presence of pig bones. "They can be only those of the defenders of Masada," Yadin concluded with an air of scientific certainty. So it went with the other great discoveries of the zealots' resistance—the eleven *ostraca* inscribed with the names of individuals and the human remains in the lowest terrace of the northern palace.

Indeed, based on the three highly fragmentary skeletons of uncertain age and family relations, Yadin crafted a touching scene worthy of Josephus Flavius himself: "When we came to clear the formidable pile of debris which covered the chambers of the small bathhouse," he wrote, "we were arrested by a find which it is difficult to consider in archaeological terms, for such an experience is not normal in archaeological excavations. Even the veterans and the more cynical among us stood frozen, gazing in awe at what had been uncovered; for as we gazed, we relived the final and most tragic moments of the drama of Masada. Upon the steps leading to the cold water pool and on the ground nearby were the remains of three skeletons. One was that of a man of about twenty— perhaps one of the commanders of Masada. Next to it we found hundreds of silvered scales of armour, scores of arrows, fragments of a prayer shawl (talith) and also an ostracon (an inscribed potsherd) with Hebrew letters. Not far off, also on the steps, was the skeleton of a young woman, with her scalp preserved intact because of the extreme dryness of the atmosphere. Her dark hair, beautifully plaited, looked as if it had been freshly coiffured. Next to it the plaster was stained with what looked like blood. By her side were delicately fashioned ladies' sandals, styled in the traditional pattern of the period. The third skeleton was that of a child. There could be no doubt, that what our eyes beheld were the remains of some of the defenders of Masada."

That, in itself, was a reasonable assumption based on the archaeological evidence. That the Romans had besieged the mountain fortress was certain and its defenders were Jewish zealots seemed likely, but their behavior at the moment of conquest was beyond the power of archaeology to determine. In fact, historian Shaye Cohen would later question the historical basis for Josephus' stirring suicide story, citing strikingly similar incidents of collective heroism recorded by such prominent classical authors as Herodotus, Pliny, Appian, Plutarch, Xenophon, and Polybius. From the sixth to the first century B.C., these ancient authors (most of whom would have been familiar to Josephus Flavius) described how in desperate circumstances of imminent defeat such diverse peoples as Lydians, Phocians, Taochians, Sidonians, Cappadocians, Isaurians, Spaniards, Greeks, Gauls, and Illyrians sacrificed their lives and their property rather than allow them to fall into the hands of their victorious enemies. While it is possible, perhaps even probable, that some of the rebels holding out on Masada would have taken their own lives as *individuals* rather than fall into the hands of the Romans, it remains questionable whether Eleazar Ben-Yair's passionate speech to his followers, the grim lottery, and the orderly execution of the family groups ever took place. The neat and stirring climax of the Masada story might simply have been Josephus Flavius' skillful use of a then-familiar and acceptable literary motif.

Far more significant than the truth or fiction of the suicide story was Yadin's reluctance or inability to define precisely its modern significance. Emphasizing again and again that Masada was an important symbol for modern Israel, he failed to articulate its meaning and thereby unleashed a powerful image that took on a life of its own. With an implicit (if perhaps unintended) allusion to the heroic myths of the Alamo and George Armstrong Custer for American readers, Yadin's book, *Masada: Herod's Fortress and the Zealots' Last Stand,* published first in English by Random House in 1966, was quickly translated into French, German, Italian, and Hebrew and became a best seller all over the world. The book's climactic paragraph attempted to make some sense of the importance of the excavations, but every one of its phrases could have been written before the digging began. "It is thanks to Ben-Yair and his comrades," Yadin's story concluded, "to their heroic stand, to their choice of death over slavery, and to the burning of their humble chattels as a final act of defiance to the enemy, that they elevated Masada to an undying symbol of desperate courage, a symbol which has stirred hearts throughout the last nineteen centuries. It is this which moved scholars and laymen to make the ascent to Masada. It is this which moved the modern Hebrew poet to cry: Masada shall not fall again! It is this which has drawn the Jewish youth of our generation in their thousands to climb to its summit in a solemn pilgrimage. And it is this which brings the recruits of the armoured units of the Defense Forces of modern Israel to swear the oath of allegiance on Masada's heights: Masada shall not fall again."

The popular tale thus ended with a martial, national call to arms that might have seemed like saber-rattling were it applied to the antiquities of Cambodia, Croatia, Mexico, or Iran. In time, voices of criticism began to be heard about the implicit message as well as the archaeological facts. "There is a large and interesting book to be written about the politics of modern archaeology," wrote British historian Moses I. Finley in his 1966 review of Yadin's book in *The New Statesman,* "in which Masada will be a centrepiece." After reviewing Yadin's achievement in the sheer scale and results of the excavation, Finley suggested that Yadin could not "resist making historical judgments in a way that conceals how controversial and uncertain they are." Yadin, he contended, had adopted "the mythmaker's approach." But with the growing fame and popularity of the Masada story, such comments came increasingly to be seen as politically inspired; by the early 1970s, Masada had gained an almost mystical significance in the Israeli consciousness. The American columnist Stewart Alsop popularized the term "the Masada complex" to describe what he saw as Israel's emerging diplomatic inflexibility. Writing at a time of diplomatic and military deadlock in the Middle East, Alsop observed that national acceptance of the image of suicide (even as something to be avoided) might someday become a tragically self-fulfilling prophecy. But his observation was not accepted as constructive criticism. Golda Meir, on a visit to Washington in 1973, confronted Alsop directly about it at a luncheon at the National Press Club. "And you, Mr. Alsop," she said from the podium with righteous indignation, "you say we have a Masada complex. It is true. We do have a Masada complex. We have a pogrom complex. We have a Hitler complex." Alsop and the other critics were, for the time being, silenced. To question the significance of the Masada story as revealed by Yadin's excavations was seen as a challenge to Israel's right and reason for existence in the modern world.

Masada had become a part of modern Israeli history, but where that history was heading was increasingly unclear after the Masada dig. At the end of June 1965, Ben-Gurion and his followers officially withdrew from the ruling Mapai party, forming their own Israel Workers' List, known by its Hebrew acronym as Rafi. Knesset elections were scheduled for November, and the leaders of Rafi embarked on an energetic campaign to attract voters, evoking themes of efficiency and technological progress, and the transformation of Israel into a modern society through reform of its social services and its electoral system. These were causes that Yadin had long supported, but he remained scrupulously neutral in the bitter 1965 campaign. When the Rafi rebellion proved to be a disastrous political failure (its members gained only ten seats in the 120-member Knesset), Yadin's reputation remained unscathed. He accepted appointments by Prime Minister Eshkol to public commissions, such as panels on the advisability of oil prospecting in the Dead Sea region and on the future of the National Defense College. And as he occasionally spoke out on nonpartisan public issues, such as religious discrimination by the chief rabbinate against the Bene Israel Jews of India, the image of Yigael Yadin as a potential future candidate for national leadership grew.

He was not unaware of that public perception. In the fall of 1966, before leaving for a lecture tour that would bring the message of Masada to audiences in Teheran, New Delhi, Bombay, Bangkok, Hong Kong, Tokyo, Honolulu, Los Angeles, Chicago, New York, London, and Rome (where he would be granted a private audience with Pope Paul), Yadin granted a long and revealing interview to correspondent Moshe Kohn of *The Jerusalem Post*. He spoke of his upbringing, his father, his experiences in the Haganah and in the War of Independence, his feelings about present Israeli society, and his archaeological hopes. It was all presented in the tone of an elder, spiritual statesman, even though he had not yet reached his fiftieth year. Public speculation about his political future had become so widespread that Kohn asked him point-blank if there was any truth to rumors that he was secretly planning a grand entry into politics. Yadin, apparently expecting the question, made a nonpartisan disclaimer; at time of continuing, unseemly bickering between the old-timers of Mapai and the Young Turks of Rafi, it made him even more attractive than before.

"From time to time I hear that people think my aim and tactic is to wait and then come riding in on a white horse," Yadin replied condescendingly. "It's no use trying to explain, but I think it's most ridiculous. I think it usually comes from people who have no academic or scholarly training, and they can't understand how a man who was chief of staff can possibly find fulfillment in research. But I have no political ambitions. For me archaeology is not a Sde Boker or an asylum; it's my main life." The denial, however heartfelt, was naïve. There was a price to be paid for fame and respectful attention, even if Yadin was unable or unwilling to understand the realities of modern political life. His own political philosophy was vague and, on many issues, uncertain. But from the time of the Masada excavations onward, whether or not he intended or even desired it, Yigael Yadin's continuing public proclamations, newspaper interviews, and stirring archaeological lessons were interpreted by many observers as acts of considerable political significance.

Chapter Fourteen

PREPARING FOR
BATTLE

F luttering flags, cheering crowds, and mounting political tension
marked Israel's Independence Day parade in Jerusalem on
May 15, 1967. Nineteen years before, many of the aging politicians and retired military leaders who were now seated as honored guests
in the grandstand of the Hebrew University stadium had faced the frightening prospect of simultaneous invasion by Egypt, Transjordan, Iraq,
Syria, and Lebanon. And they had faced that invasion with far less impressive military formations than the marching and motorized units that
now passed before them in review. But in the spring of 1967 the size and
scale of the parade was a matter of public discussion. Israel now possessed an impressive arsenal of armored forces, advanced artillery, and jet
fighters, but none of them were on display. Some, like former prime
minister Ben-Gurion, angrily boycotted the celebration, derisively call-

ing it "Eshkol's miniparade," and insisted that at a time of rising tensions with Syria, Egypt, and Jordan, Israel's sovereignty should not be limited in any way. But Prime Minister Eshkol refused to rattle any of Israel's high-tech sabers; he was reluctant to violate the terms of the 1949 armistice agreement with Jordan, which permitted only light infantry on either side of the barbed-wire boundary dividing Jerusalem. Far more was at stake here than the character of Israel's 1967 Independence Day celebrations. The real issue was Eshkol himself. Ben-Gurion and his Rafi supporters maintained that the present government was leading the nation toward disaster, and that the fainthearted and indecisive prime minister must be removed from office as quickly as possible.

Yadin, as usual, avoided taking sides. Such intraparty struggles did not concern him; they were, in fact, the ostensible reason for his remaining above party politics. But never before were the implications so serious for Israel's national security. During the autumn of 1966, when he and Carmella had gone to the Far East, America, and Europe on a triumphant lecture tour, the Eshkol government had allowed itself to be drawn into a cycle of intensifying violence. While Eshkol had sought to open secret negotiations with Arab leaders and while his grandiloquent foreign minister Abba Eban toured foreign capitals giving speeches and turning elegant phrases, the IDF commanders embarked on a quite different policy course. As Israeli border settlements suffered repeated attacks by a shadowy guerrilla group called Fatah (under the command of the newly established Palestine Liberation Organization), the IDF resorted to ever more overt and violent retaliatory acts. In September 1966, Chief of Staff Yitzhak Rabin publicly threatened the government of Syria that Israel would hold it responsible for all terrorist attacks that emanated from its borders. In early November, in response to a mine explosion near Beersheva, IDF forces mounted a massive daylight retaliatory raid on the village of Samu (considered to be a staging base for terrorist missions) in the Jordanian-controlled West Bank. This was no surgical strike across the border. An Israeli armored force entered the village soon after dawn on November 13, roused the entire population, and blew up more than a hundred houses as well as the village clinic and school. Fifteen Jordanian troops and three Jordanian civilians were killed in the operation, as was one Israeli soldier. As an act of pure revenge and a demonstration of fearsome military power, the attack may have achieved its planners' objectives. But as a means of permanently ending the tension and cross-border violence, it clearly failed. Worse, it highlighted the dangerous and widening gap between the avowed diplomatic objectives of the Eshkol government and the hard-line tactics of the independent-minded military leadership.

In the days of Ben-Gurion, retaliatory raids had been, for the most part, conducted under the cover of darkness by elite commando units. They were meant to convey quiet, succinct, and often bloody lessons to the various Arab leaders about the cost of confrontation with Israel. But with the extensive use of armored forces, infantry units, and air strikes in broad daylight—reported extensively by the international press through television and instant communications—the cycle of violence steadily rose as Arab leaders felt the need to respond to Israeli actions with public acts of their own. In January a new round of hostilities began between Israel and Syria over the issue of Israeli cultivation of lands in the demilitarized zone in the Huleh Valley. In early April a Syrian artillery barrage into Israel from the Golan Heights was met with return fire and air strikes. When brand-new Syrian MiGs rose up to meet the Israeli jet fighters, six of the MiGs were quickly shot down. Many in Israel greeted this action with pride and satisfaction, but Ben-Gurion and even Moshe Dayan accused the general staff of recklessness in leading the country to war. Even more troubling, the mild-mannered Eshkol (who was so scrupulous about observing the armistice agreements in Jerusalem and sending off Foreign Minister Abba Eban on far-flung diplomatic missions) seemed not to be in total control of his own generals.

By mid-May, the complex web of inter-Arab relations, further complicated by the Soviet Union's eagerness to expand its influence in the region, suddenly brought matters to a head. Yadin was among the first in Israel to learn of troubling new developments, during the parade in Jerusalem on Independence Day. Seated in the reviewing stand next to the current chief of staff and the prime minister, periodically rising to salute the elite paratroopers, navy, air force, and Nahal units, Yadin overheard Rabin's words of concern about sudden Egyptian troop movements into Sinai. The Soviets had warned the Egyptians that an imminent Israeli attack on Syria was likely, and Nasser, as self-styled leader of the Arab world, felt the need to respond in some way. But in Israel, at least for the time being, the movement of Egyptian troops into Sinai was seen merely as a political gesture, devoid of military significance. "To tell the truth," Yadin later admitted, "it really didn't make an impression on me." Indeed, on the following morning, when all the former chiefs of staff were called to IDF headquarters for consultations, only Moshe Dayan expressed serious concern about the Egyptian troop movement—and took the opportunity to condemn Rabin and his staff officers for heightening tensions and bringing about the present state of affairs. Dayan was right about Nasser's intentions. On the next day, May 17, the Egyptian president responded to his detractors in the Arab world who jeered that his army was merely hiding behind the "blue hats" of the UN peacekeeping forces in Sinai, unwilling to confront the Zionist enemy head-on. He formally requested from Secretary General U Thant that the UN forces be withdrawn immediately.

Thus began the period of *hamtanah,* or "waiting," that would lead to the third Arab-Israeli war. As Egyptian troops streamed into Sinai and the UN forces withdrew on U Thant's instructions, Chief of Staff Rabin received authorization from Prime Minister and Defense Minister Eshkol to mobilize the reserves. A war room was established in the general headquarters, and operational planning got under way. In contrast to all of Israel's major campaigns, however, the strategic leadership was reacting to unfolding events rather than orchestrating them. Although the general staff was convinced that war was inevitable, pressures were building on the Eshkol government to delay opening any hostilities. Even after Nasser announced that he was closing the Straits of Tiran to Israeli shipping, the U.S. government, wary of possible Soviet intervention, warned Israel against precipitous action. Ben-Gurion, contemptuous of Eshkol's ability to lead, likewise spoke out against the possibly disastrous consequences of a war waged without the support of at least one of the superpowers. The building tension and uncertainty eventually took their toll on Chief of Staff Rabin, who suffered a physical collapse from frayed nerves and complete exhaustion and had to be temporarily replaced by his chief of operations, Ezer Weizman. At this moment of confusion and conflicting pressures, Prime Minister Eshkol, finding himself besieged, isolated, and pressured from all directions, requested that Yigael Yadin return to active service as his special adviser on security affairs.

Caught up in the atmosphere of crisis, Yadin accepted. And for Yadin, this appointment was an occasion for considerable self-satisfaction. He had been entirely excluded from the strategic planning at the time of the 1956 Sinai campaign and was left innocently directing the excavations at Hazor while Moshe Dayan achieved his great victory. Now the tables would be turned, with Yadin back in uniform and Dayan a civilian critic on the outside. In his initial visits to the "Pit" (as the subterranean situation room and communications center in the Tel Aviv headquarters was known), Yadin learned of the current operational plans. In a sense they represented the conclusion of the 1948 war against Egypt, cut short by the British-sponsored ceasefire: After a sharp and devastating surprise air attack on Egyptian air bases, the IDF would finally conquer the Gaza Strip. Yet even though the reserves were mobilized and the generals were ready for action, Prime Minister Eshkol insisted on a further delay. He dispatched Abba Eban to gauge sentiment in Paris, London, and Washington, but that act merely made him seem indecisive and encouraged the public clamor for Ben-Gurion to return to national leadership. A dangerous deadlock developed as Eshkol refused to give up power and Ben-Gurion refused to enter any government in which Eshkol remained. In the meantime Eban received only discouragement in the foreign capitals, and the Soviet Union warned Israel against starting a war. Rav Aluf Yigael Yadin was trapped, like the others, in a flow of events that seemed to have a pace and intensity of its own.

With Ben-Gurion adamant about remaining on the sidelines, Moshe Dayan suddenly was seen as a possible national savior, a man who might be able to take control. The swashbuckling professional soldier-adventurer with the eyepatch, so long associated with Israel's greatest victories (due in no small measure to Ben-Gurion's controversial memoirs), became a reassuring symbol for both hawks and doves. At the beginning of the crisis he had toured army bases in the south of the country and had provided a sounding board for the headstrong generals who wanted to go to war immediately. Pressure was steadily building on Eshkol to give up at least his role as defense minister to a more experienced soldier, perhaps Labor Minister Yigal Allon or former chief of staff Yigael Yadin. With the reserves fully mobilized and nation on a war footing, Levi Eshkol was losing his grip on power. When he stammered out a confused and inconclusive address to the nation on May 28—offering no clear indication when or how the present crisis could be ended—it was clear that he was no Ben-Gurion. He could not continue to be both prime minister and minister of defense; a change had to be made.

At this point, Yadin stepped forward with a recommendation. On May 30 developments in the region were especially ominous: King Hussein of Jordan had flown to Cairo and concluded a mutual defense pact with Egypt, at least technically placing the Jordanian armed forces under Egyptian control. If war broke out, military action could therefore be expected not only in the Sinai but also in the West Bank. At a chance meeting that day with Allon in the corridor outside the prime minister's office, Yadin revealed his own unexpected solution to the crisis that Israel faced. "It's true that either one of us is qualified to serve as minister of defense," Yadin recalled telling Allon, his colleague and sometime rival in the War of Independence, "but under the present circumstances, Dayan is the only one who can raise the nation's morale." In Yadin's opinion, the public clamor for Dayan could no longer be ignored. Despite Yadin's long and tense relationship with Dayan and his steadfast refusal to associate himself with Rafi, he soon conveyed the same opinion directly to Prime Minister Eshkol.

Eshkol could not accuse Yadin of harboring partisan political motivations, and he clearly had to accommodate Dayan in some way. At first, in an effort to minimize the political influence of Rafi within his cabinet, Eshkol suggested that Dayan be placed on active duty in the army as head of the southern command. This, Yadin pointed out, was utterly impractical because it would require a dangerous reshuffling of personnel at the highest levels of command. Dayan had been an outspoken critic of Rabin for months, and it seemed unlikely that he would obediently carry out Rabin's instructions if war were to break out. Pressure was building on Eshkol to expand his ruling coalition and form a national unity government that would include both Rafi and Menachem Begin's Herut party, and the leaders of both those parties would settle for nothing less than Dayan's appointment as minister of defense. Yadin later claimed a large share of the credit for Dayan's appointment, but many factors were pushing Eshkol toward that decision. On May 31, Yigal Allon withdrew his name from consideration, assuring the return of Moshe Dayan to the military leadership of Israel. But Yadin was destined to play a role in the final negotiations. Eshkol called him into his office on June 1, he recalled, and announced his decision with one condition. "You know this 'Arab' as well as I do," the prime minister jokingly confided in Yiddish, "and I want you to delineate the powers of the prime minister and the defense minister in a written document, and I want you to be my personal military adviser, to coordinate and supervise what's going on over there at the Ministry of Defense." Dayan had long been identified with Ben-Gurion's public position that counseled against war in the immediate future, but Eshkol knew that Dayan was never one to meet conventional expectations. As prime minister, he wanted to protect himself against unpleasant surprises.

So on the following day, Friday, June 2, after preparing a draft document on the separation of powers between the two ministries with Yaacov Herzog, director-general of the prime minister's office, Yadin made his way to the Jordan Restaurant in downtown Tel Aviv. Waiting for him there was certainly the most recognizable man in Israel, Moshe Dayan, seated at a table with Zvi Zur, the former chief of staff having agreed to serve as Dayan's assistant. In the quiet of the nearly deserted restaurant, Yadin, as Eshkol's official representative, read the letter from the prime minister to Dayan. It stipulated that the new minister of defense must seek the approval of the prime minister before beginning hostilities, opening new fronts, bombing Arab cities, or staging retaliatory raids. The terms were acceptable, but Dayan insisted that the document be changed from a letter of instruction to an agreement between peers. A few slight changes were made in the wording, and only then did Dayan let Yadin in on his secret. Despite his previous public statements, he did not believe the country should wait any longer. In just three days' time—on the coming Monday morning—war would begin.

In the first days of June, the activity at the Israel Museum and the Institute of Archaeology at the Hebrew University reflected the general uncertainty about the future. With most young men mobilized in reserve units and the prospect of war frighteningly close, normal routines were abandoned. Basic precautions had to be taken to prepare for violence. Aviva Rosen, then the academic administrator of the university department, later recalled taking some of the most precious artifacts from the university study collection to the underground storerooms of the Israel Museum and then, with the help of the librarian, decided to move the card catalogue to a safer place.

While she was clearing a space for it in an office closet, a small, dusty notebook fell off one of the shelves. "I opened it," she recalled, "and I recognized the handwriting. It was the handwriting of Eleazar Sukenik, and it was his journal of travels in the country when he was interested in synagogues." She remembered one passage in particular, inscribed almost forty years before in Sukenik's antique hand. "It read: 'Today we crossed the Jordan on the backs of Arabs.' We laughed at the time," she remembered, "and it seemed so strange to us that he should record such a detail." But now, at a time of national emergency and mobilization, with Arab armies threatening to come back across the borders, it was nervous laughter at the strange sensibilities of a bygone age.

Avraham Biran, then director of the Department of Antiquities, later recalled that the hurried transfer of ancient artifacts to safer storage quarters continued throughout Sunday, June 4. At the Shrine of the Book at the Israel Museum, the scrolls that had been purchased by Eleazar Sukenik and Yigael Yadin—and the documents Yadin had found at the Cave of Letters—were taken from their display cases and placed in secure underground rooms.

The official announcement of Dayan's appointment as minister of defense on Friday had eased some of the tension. On Saturday, after three weeks of total mobilization, leaves were granted to thousands of reserve soldiers at bases in the south, and it seemed as if the crisis were about to pass. Moshe Dayan appeared at a Tel Aviv press conference to reassure the journalists that they should expect no sudden change in the situation "in a month, two months, or six months," and he emphasized that the government was still seeking a diplomatic solution to the present military standoff. On Sunday, the first day of the Israeli work week, the government held its usual formal meeting. The dull press statement on the meeting reported only that the ministers had briefly reviewed the current military situation, then turned to domestic matters. The chances of imminent war seemed remote.

But the following morning, shortly after eight o'clock, the people of Israel were informed by an official news bulletin that heavy fighting was under way between Israeli forces and advancing Egyptian units. At ten-thirty Dayan spoke to the nation, reporting that Egyptian and Israeli ground and air forces were engaged in battle and that he had every confidence in an eventual Israeli victory. Around eleven, Jordanian artillery and mortars opened a barrage on western Jerusalem, and civil defense sirens began blaring. A few shells dropped near the Knesset and the Israel Museum. But the situation was quite different than it appeared, especially in Jerusalem. The archaeological grapevine was humming: Avraham Malamat received a surprising telephone call from Joseph Aviram just as the Jordanian shells began to fall. Carmella Yadin, Aviram reported, had just spoken with Yigael in the situation room at IDF headquarters. His mood had been buoyant. Although he could not yet reveal precise details about the war that had just started, Yadin had suggested that she prepare a bottle of champagne.

Yadin later recalled the morning of June 5, 1967, with considerable personal satisfaction. He was present in the Pit with the IDF high command when the word came in that nearly three-quarters of the Egyptian air force had been destroyed. During the previous weekend he had been present at a series of meetings where Defense Minister Dayan approved a sweeping offensive in which Israeli forces would overrun the Sinai peninsula in an expanded replay of the 1956 campaign. On Monday morning waves of Israeli jet fighters and bombers strafed, bombed, and efficiently obliterated runways, hangars, radar installations, and planes of the Egyptian air force, taking the Egyptians by complete surprise. Soon after midday the same treatment was applied to air bases in Jordan and Syria, and to an Iraqi air base near the Jordanian border. Israel had gained air supremacy in the opening hours of the conflict, and land victory seemed to be a foregone conclusion. Before he telephoned Carmella in Jerusalem, Yadin called Prime Minister Eshkol with the good news.

Eshkol requested permission to convey the news to the public, but when Yadin relayed the request to the defense minister and chief of staff, they brusquely turned it down. "Yadin believed that it would be good for the morale of the people," Rabin recalled years later. "But we believed that it was better that the Egyptians not know the truth, because we believed that Nasser himself didn't know the truth." During the afternoon it became clear that Rabin was right; intercepted radio communications from the Egyptian forces in Sinai indicated that headquarters in Cairo were still promising them air support—even though the Egyptian air force no longer existed as an effective combat element. Yet there was another important reason for disagreement between Yadin and Dayan over the advisability of a public statement. "I wanted to prevent the entry of Jordan into the war," Yadin later told a reporter, in his recollection of Dayan's reaction, "and he secretly wanted Hussein to go in—and for us to smash him. My advice was not accepted, and looking back, maybe Dayan was right."

Now, in June 1967 the closing act of the 1948 war was about to be concluded. King Hussein had transferred substantial armored and infantry forces to the West Bank and Jerusalem under the command of Field Marshal Habis el-Majali, a Jordanian hero of the Battles of Latrun. But the fighting on the West Bank would have a dramatically different outcome, in large measure due to the confusion and self-deception of the Arab leadership. On the morning of June 5, Nasser urged King Hussein, by telephone to join the attack against the Israelis, since—he boasted— the initial Israeli air attack had failed miserably, Egyptian armored forces had gone on the offensive and an Arab victory was near. At the same time, completely baseless reports were coming from Baghdad claiming that the Iraqi air force had bombed Tel Aviv and had caused heavy damage. Whether or not Hussein believed these reports from his erstwhile allies, he—like his grandfather Abdullah—could not afford to appear as a traitor to the pan-Arab cause. Ignoring a message from the Israeli government (transferred via the United Nations) that Israel had no immediate plans to initiate operations against Jordan, Hussein ordered his forces in Jerusalem to cross into no man's land and take possession of UN headquarters. The battle for Jerusalem and the West Bank had begun.

In earlier years, Yadin had helped plan many operations to conquer the West Bank, but none of them had ever been approved. In the fall of 1948 he and Allon had worked on an operational plan for an Israeli advance to the Jordan River; it had been briefly reconsidered when King Abdullah was assassinated in the summer of 1951. But now a campaign was developing in which the field tactics and strategic objectives were to be formulated piecemeal, closely following the course of events. And Yadin was now just an observer, watching the maps and listening to the battle reports streaming into the Pit. By late afternoon, Israeli forces had driven the Jordanians from their positions around the UN headquarters and moved southward to cut off the main road to Bethlehem and Hebron. At the same time in the Judean hills northwest of Jerusalem, an

Yadin in conference with Ben-Gurion, shortly before assuming the post of chief of staff, November 9, 1949. Army spokesman Moshe Pearlman stands nearby. Israel Government Press Office.

After the swearing-in ceremony. Seated, left to right: Foreign Minister Sharett; Chief of Staff Yadin; Prime Minister David Ben-Gurion; former chief of staff Dori; and Shaul Avigur, secretary to the Ministry of Defense. Standing directly behind Yadin and Ben-Gurion are, left to right: Aluf Chaim Laskov; Air Force Commander Aharon Remez; Navy Commander Shlomo Shamir; unidentified; Deputy Chief of Staff Mordecai Makleff; and Aluf Moshe Dayan. Israel Government Press Office.

Prime Minister Ben-Gurion and his entourage tour the Hazor excavations, September 1958. Israel Government Press Office.

Yadin shows the newly discovered glass plates from the Cave of Letters to an uninterested Ben-Gurion. Shimon Peres, deputy minister of defense, is seated at left. March 27, 1961. Photo by Werner Braun.

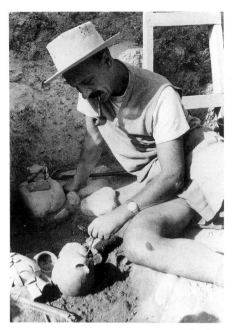

Excavating at Hazor, summer 1968.
Photo by Zeev Radovan.

The state funeral at Masada for
the excavated human remains,
July 7, 1969. Israel Government
Press Office.

Yadin in his study,
with a photographic
facsimile of the
Temple Scroll. Photo
by David Rubinger.

The Agranat Commission (left to right): Yadin; Supreme Court justice
Moshe Landau; Supreme Court chief justice Shimon Agranat; State
Comptroller Yitzhak Nebenzahl; former chief of staff Chaim Laskov.
Israel Press and Photo Agency, Tel Aviv.

Yadin announces at a Tel Aviv press conference the Dash candidate list for
the upcoming Knesset elections, March 18, 1977. Seated (from left to
right): Dr. Amnon Rubinstein, Meir Zorea ("Zaro"), and Shmuel Tamir.
Israel Press and Photo Agency, Tel Aviv.

Yadin and Begin soon after signing the Dash-Likud coalition agreement, October 1977. Israel Press and Photo Agency, Tel Aviv.

Deputy Prime Minister Yadin makes a public appearance at the Maimouna Festival in Jerusalem. Photo by David Harris.

In the Knesset during the debate on the Camp David accords, March 20, 1979. Israel Press and Photo Agency, Tel Aviv.

With Sadat in Alexandria, June 1979. Collection of Joseph Aviram.

Deputy Prime Minister Yigael Yadin. Israel Government Press Office.

Israeli armored column smashed across the armistice line toward Ramallah. The chief of staff gave his approval for an attack later that night against the fortress of Latrun. At two that morning an Israeli tank force concentrated its fire on the old British police station. But no fire was returned, and the tank crews broke through the perimeter fence to find the fort over which so much blood had been spilled empty, abandoned by Arab Legion troops. Once again the roads leading toward Ramallah were filled with civilian refugees and retreating Jordanian soldiers. After nineteen years of frustration and recrimination, the goals of the 1948 campaigns to conquer Latrun were finally realized.

The afternoon of June 5, Eshkol's cabinet remained convened for continuous consultations. Israeli progress into Sinai was proceeding according to schedule, and with operations against the Jordanians beginning, certain of the ministers—particularly Allon and the newly appointed minister-without-portfolio Menachem Begin—exerted considerable pressure for the IDF to capture the Old City of Jerusalem. During the night the decision was taken. An Israeli paratroop brigade under the command of Colonel Mordecai "Motta" Gur launched an attack against heavily fortified Jordanian positions to the north of the Old City under the cover of an intensive artillery barrage. By dawn on June 6, Gur's battalions had opened a secure route to the original campus of the Hebrew University on Mount Scopus and had fought their way through the streets of East Jerusalem. One of the battalions had reached the Rockefeller Museum, overlooking the Old City walls. At this point Yadin was once more brought back into active planning, because the capture of the Rockefeller Museum (still officially known in Jordan as the Palestine Archaeological Museum) was a significant and sensitive political development. The museum, nationalized by the Jordanian government the previous summer, was the main repository and study center for the tens of thousands of Dead Sea Scroll fragments that had been retrieved during the 1950s by archaeologists and bedouin from caves along the western shore of the Dead Sea.

Yadin immediately called Carmella. He was impatient to discover whether the Jordanian authorities had removed the precious ancient documents from the museum before the start of the fighting. If the scroll fragments were still there, he was determined to make sure that they were not stolen or destroyed. He instructed Carmella to contact Avraham Biran, director of the Department of Antiquities; Nahman Avigad of the Hebrew University; and Joseph Aviram of the Israel Exploration Society. She was to tell them to proceed immediately to the combat headquarters of the paratroop brigade and obtain an escort to the Rockefeller Museum. The three men assembled at Gur's headquarters (temporarily in the Tnuva milk plant in northern Jerusalem) and were taken in a military convoy across the front lines. When they arrived at the museum, shots were still being exchanged between Israeli forces and Jordanian defenders ranged in parapets in the nearby city walls. The archaeologists scrambled into the fortresslike building through a back entrance, and with the help of some soldiers and a museum watchman, they were led into the laboratories where the preserved scroll fragments were kept. Most of the fragments, mounted between glass plates, were packed in wooden crates, apparently for transfer to Amman. Biran, Avigad, and Aviram soon left and reported back to Yadin. On the following morning, June 7, Gur's paratroop forces made the final assault on the Old City, entering through the Lions' Gate. By afternoon, all of Jerusalem and its outlying suburbs as far south as Bethlehem were under Israeli control.

At this point Yadin realized that he might be able to gain yet another great treasure, both for himself and for the State of Israel. For seven years he had been engaged in inconclusive, secret negotiations with a middleman of questionable credentials for the purchase of a complete—and so far unknown—Dead Sea Scroll. In the summer of 1960, after his first triumphant campaign in the Judean wilderness, he had received a letter from a Virginia minister named Joseph Uhrig, who explained that he was in a position to facilitate the sale of "important, authentic discoveries of Dead Sea Scrolls." Reverend Uhrig claimed to be acting as the exclusive agent for a Bethlehem antiquities dealer named Khalil Iskander Shahin, better known as Kando, who was well known for his ties to the Ta'amireh bedouin. In fact, it was common knowledge among scholars that Kando had facilitated the sale of most of the Dead Sea Scroll material now stored in the Rockefeller Museum. Uhrig now claimed that Kando was in possession of ten scrolls of gazelle and goatskin, one of bronze, and one of pure gold. The asking price was as outlandish as the description: a million dollars for each. Yadin was unwilling to disregard this offer, however, and after an exchange of letters in the autumn of 1960, he was shocked to receive from Uhrig a large and beautiful manuscript fragment that had been wrapped in a napkin and stuck between two pieces of cardboard, then sent in a plain manila envelope by regular mail.

This fragment proved to be a part of an otherwise complete Dead Sea Psalms Scroll in the Rockefeller Museum, so clearly Reverend Uhrig's claims were not pure fantasy. Yadin agreed to a purchase price of $7,000 for the fragment, but he cautioned Uhrig that the price of any complete document had to be reasonable—Yadin had, after all paid only $250,000 for four complete scrolls in 1954. The correspondence continued through the spring of 1961, and after Uhrig's repeated trips to Jordan and meetings with Kando, it became clear that there was only one scroll for sale and that the asking price was $100,000 in cash. Feeling that the purchase was now possible, Yadin solicited contributions from his philanthropic contacts in England and the United States. The negotiations continued while Yadin was in London after the final season of the Bar-Kokhba expedition; there he received another fragment in the mail from Reverend Uhrig, this one supposedly detached from the scroll that was for sale. Yadin had no question about the authenticity of this document. The handwriting was similar to that of other Qumran manuscripts, and the broken lines of text contained intriguing references to sacrifices and to a high priest. Yadin contacted an American lawyer-acquaintance to draw up a contract, hoping to conclude the matter during his lecture tour of the United States in the fall of 1961. But Uhrig proved unable to make good on his commitment. After Yadin expressed his sincere interest in making the purchase, the asking price suddenly skyrocketed to an incredible $750,000. Angrily, Yadin threatened to terminate all negotiations; a new purchase price was then agreed upon—$130,000, with $10,000 to be paid as an immediate advance. Uhrig, in his capacity as Kando's exclusive agent, signed a contract in November. But this legal document proved worthless. When Yadin met Uhrig face to face in New York, the reverend offered only excuses, claiming that Kando was now demanding $200,000. To make a sad story shorter, Yadin soon lost all contact with Uhrig and was unable to recover his $10,000 deposit. The scroll remained in the hands of Kando in Bethlehem.

But on June 8, 1967, the boundary between Yadin and Kando had fallen. As the personal military adviser to the prime minister of Israel, Yadin had unique means at his disposal to persuade the Bethlehem antiquities dealer to part with his scroll. He briefly explained the situation to Eshkol, Dayan, and Rabin and received permission to direct an unorthodox mission: to send a small detachment of intelligence officers to locate Kando and recover the ancient document. Despite confusion about Kando's real name, the officers eventually located Kando's home in Bethlehem. At first Kando denied knowing anything about ancient scrolls, even when the officers repeatedly reassured him that he would receive a fair price. But Kando had not made his fortune in the antiquities trade by being forthright or unnecessarily talkative. Only after a lengthy and increasingly unpleasant interrogation of both Kando and his son Anton at a military installation did they eventually understand how serious the Israelis were. On the evening of June 8 the officers accompanied Kando and his son back to Bethlehem and retrieved the scroll, which was wrapped in cellophane and kept in a shoebox, from a specially constructed hiding place under the floor tiles of Kando's bedroom. Wasting no time, they made their way to the IDF headquarters to inform Yadin of their success.

Yadin was by this time involved in a more pressing matter. The Ministerial Committee on Defense convened late on Thursday night to make one of the most crucial decisions of the war. Tensions with Syria the previous winter and spring had been one of the causes of the confrontation. Even though Egypt had been militarily humiliated and Jordan stripped of its control of the West Bank, the Syrian leadership—for all its bombastic, radical rhetoric—had yet to enter the war. Emergency discussions were under way at that very moment in New York at the UN Security Council. With Egypt and Jordan both having agreed to a ceasefire, time was running out. General David Elazar, head of the northern command, was strongly in favor of taking offensive action against Syria. So were the representatives of a number of northern settlements who had endured Syrian shelling from positions on the Golan Heights. So were Allon and Eshkol. "There was extraordinary pressure to conquer the Golan," Yadin recalled of that meeting. "But Dayan had two considerations against it: the fear of a Soviet reaction . . . and also a fear of the operation itself, that perhaps it would be extraordinarily difficult." Dayan, adamant, effectively vetoed any offensive operations, and the meeting was adjourned around midnight. During these discussions Yadin was summoned to the corridor, where he was presented with the shoebox from Bethlehem. Even though he went to bed that night secure in the knowledge that he had at last obtained his ancient treasure, Yadin—and Prime Minister Eshkol and Chief of Staff Rabin—awoke on the following morning to an unpleasant surprise.

During the night Dayan had flagrantly violated the agreement signed seven days before in the Jordan Restaurant—in the presence of Yigael Yadin. Without consulting either Eshkol or Rabin, Dayan had telephoned General Elazar directly, ordering him to open a new front against the Syrians. Eshkol was shocked; Rabin was outraged. Yadin would later characterize it as "a typical move for Dayan." But luck in war was still with him. On the following evening, June 10, after nearly twenty-four hours of fierce fighting against the Syrians, the Six Day War was finally over, with Israel in possession of the Golan Heights.

———

At the end of July 1967, Yadin's brief return to active military service ended. "As soon as I saw that the thing was more or less over, I left," he later recalled. "I had absolutely no desire to stay on in the government." All of the West Bank, Sinai, and the Golan Heights were now under

Israeli control and the armies of Egypt, Jordan, and Syria were publicly humiliated; it seemed only a matter of time, as Defense Minister Dayan publicly speculated, before the Arab nations would sue for peace. In the meantime the new territorial situation afforded Israelis an exhilarating situation. The state of siege and a frightening uncertainty about the future was replaced by a new national self-confidence. Tens of thousands of Israelis crowded into the Old City, excitedly revisiting the Western Wall and the Jewish Quarter and exploring the nearby—and long inaccessible—towns of Bethlehem, Hebron, and Ramallah, avidly buying souvenirs, patronizing restaurants, and creating a tourist boom. The Six Day War had sparked a flow of refugees across the river into the Hashemite Kingdom, but the lives of many of those Palestinians who remained underwent a profound transformation. In hopes of gaining a higher material standard of living, many West Bank inhabitants gradually abandoned traditional village farming for wage labor in the farms, factories, and construction sites of the industrialized Israeli economy.

Biblical archaeology also underwent a realignment in those heady days of victory. For nineteen years, excavations in Israel and Jordan had been conducted in isolation from each other, each under the auspices of a separate department of antiquities. The closed borders and state of war between Israel and Jordan had hindered the flow of information between scholars working at sites sometimes only a few miles apart. But now Yadin and his Israeli colleagues had the chance to visit sites they had only read about in archaeological publications, or heard about from their British and American counterparts. In July and August, Yadin visited for the first time the sites of Kathleen Kenyon's excavations at Jericho and East Jerusalem and the American digs at the biblical cities of Shechem and Taanach. Indeed, those sites were now—at least temporarily—under the control of a "staff officer for archaeology" of the new Israeli military government. Yadin also visited the scroll caves and site of Qumran at the northwest shore of the Dead Sea. Yet by the late summer Yadin was back at home in Jerusalem, hard at work unrolling and transcribing his newly acquired Dead Sea Scroll.

His first concern was its immediate physical preservation; the ancient parchment scroll, while hidden beneath the floor of Kando's bedroom, had been damaged by dampness. One of its ends was intact and well preserved, but the other end (which had apparently rested on the concrete floor of the secret compartment) had absorbed moisture and was blackened into a gooey mass of rotting leather. Something had to be done to stop the deterioration right away. Then the entire scroll would have to be carefully unrolled under the proper temperature and humidity conditions, and the already detached pieces (which Kando had thoughtfully handed over to the intelligence officers in a cigar box) would have to be photographed and fitted into their proper places in the body of the scroll. For years Yadin and his father had depended on James Biberkraut to undertake this delicate work of preservation and restoration, but Biberkraut was now too old and infirm to undertake the task. Sending the scroll to a foreign laboratory or even revealing its existence to foreign scholars was out of the question in light of the unconventional method by which it had been acquired. In fact, Kando had already retained an Israeli lawyer to challenge the confiscation and at the very least demand a substantial purchase price. Yadin therefore determined that the scroll would have to be opened in secrecy, by a technician he could trust. He turned to Joseph Shenhav, head of the restoration laboratories at the Israel Museum, who had participated in the expeditions to Hazor and Masada. And as soon as Shenhav was released from his reserve army unit in late summer, the work on the scrolls began.

Shenhav's home life was completely disrupted by Yadin's impatience. With his usual talent for persuasion, Yadin convinced him to take a vacation from the museum and devote himself completely to unrolling the scroll. To keep the entire process secret, Yadin suggested that Shenhav do the work at home—an apartment in a hundred-year-old stone house in Jerusalem's German colony. "I turned the whole apartment into a lab." Shenhav later recalled, "and I sent the wife and kids to her mother for three weeks." Shenhav was not specifically trained in the techniques of preserving or unrolling ancient manuscripts ("Biberkraut never worked with anyone else and kept his secrets to himself," Shenhav later admitted), but he was familiar with a method that had been first successfully used at the British Museum: to subject the brittle ancient parchment to intense humidification to restore its pliability. As an experiment, Shenhav dissected several compressed wads of parchment that had broken off the tightly wound scroll. Eventually, working in his kitchen with a steaming kettle on the stove and a gauge to monitor the humidity level, Shenhav was able to moisten the fused parchment layers and separate them with a scalpel.

The parchment was so thin that the inscribed letters were sometimes preserved only in mirror image on the back of the layer against which they had been pressed for so long. With the help of photographer Arieh Volk, who had also worked with Yadin at Hazor and Masada, Shenhav provided Yadin with facsimiles of these chunks of original text. Photographs of the text of the main scroll came after it was slowly humidified and unrolled to its full length of more than twenty-six feet. This project took more than three weeks of intensive, delicate work, in which Shenhav was helped by a colleague, Ruth Yekutieli of the Israel Museum.

Yadin frequently checked on the progress of the work, but "he really didn't mix in or care how I did it," Shenhav recalled, "as long as progress was being made." The undamaged scroll, fully opened, was impressive. Joseph Aviram recalled coming into Shenhav's apartment toward the end of the unrolling process and seeing Yadin and Shenhav down on the floor examining the full-length document. "It ran from the shower to the living room to the kitchen," Shenhav recalled. Photographs were taken of all the remaining text, and the scroll was then carefully rerolled and deposited for safekeeping at the Israel Museum.

As he studied the photographed text, Yadin became more and more convinced that it was of enormous importance in understanding the historical, religious, and political conceptions of at least one of the sects of ancient Judaism. This was the most complete and most beautiful of the nine intact Qumran scrolls so far discovered, inscribed with a sure hand on nineteen separate sheets of parchment sewn together with thread. In 1956, the nearly complete Psalms Scroll had been found in a cave near Qumran and had been sold to the Rockefeller Museum by Kando; Yadin suspected that *this* scroll had come from the same cave. He recognized two distinct styles of handwriting in the document, one slightly earlier, that enabled him to place date this copy (if not its original composition) in the first century B.C. This document did not contain religious poetry like the Psalms Scroll; as Yadin transcribed and translated the tightly written columns of ancient Hebrew, he came upon passages of laws pertaining to such diverse topics as city planning, religious architecture, royal powers, and military matters. He came to believe that this was not simply another of the Qumran community's unique apocalyptic documents but a scripture fully equal in authority to the five books of Moses—a book of the Bible that had been lost for two thousand years.

Yadin's presentation at the annual Israel Exploration Society convention in Jerusalem in October was another unforgettable performance. At this festive Saturday-night session Dr. Benjamin Mazar offered his theories on the establishment of the city of Jerusalem in the biblical period, and Chief of Staff Yitzhak Rabin gave new details about the battle for the Old City in the recent war. Yadin, as usual, provided a dramatic climax to the evening. He revealed that he had come into the possession of a complete Dead Sea Scroll that had been "kept illegally and under extremely bad conditions," but that contained fascinating new material of a religious nature that might transform modern understanding of the sacred law of ancient Judea. Yadin recited from passages relating to the proper observance of Rosh Hashanah, Yom Kippur, Succoth, Passover, and Shavuot. The scroll also included laws pertaining to two heretofore unknown celebrations: the Feast of Oil and the Feast of

Wine. Other sections of the scroll dealt with purity laws quite different from those in the Bible, including in a series of laws about the conduct of the king, his court, and his army that were not explicitly addressed in the traditional biblical text. Most astonishing, it described the layout, architecture, and sacred ceremonies of the Temple in Jerusalem, which the authors of the scroll presented as a detailed divine building plan. Since almost half the text dealt with the Temple's sacred gates, courts, altars, vessels, sacrifices, and inner sanctuary, Yadin decided to call this manuscript the Temple Scroll.

"Only Yadin could have done it," Avraham Malamat later observed, "from finding it, to unrolling it, to deciphering it." Although Yadin was not a trained biblical scholar or a Talmudist, he was a scholar with an amazing capacity to absorb new material if it served his purposes. The dense legal subject matter of this scroll required that he immerse himself in rabbinic literature and in matters of purity and religious observance. In a strange reversion to the feverish studies of his father in the yeshiva in Lithuania, Yadin consulted noted religious scholars and pored over Talmudic tractates and commentaries to see where the contents of the Temple Scroll diverged or agreed with traditional rabbinic rulings. The scroll delineated a biblical world with new sets of sacrifices and offerings, new festivals, and a detailed description of the Temple, with a symmetrical and symbolic arrangement of courts and gates and sacred areas. It provided a plan for the surrounding city of Jerusalem, in which the strictest standards of purity would be demanded; among other prohibitions, sexual intercourse would be absolutely forbidden and bodily functions would have to be performed at a specially constructed area for privies far outside the city walls. And it provided the laws by which a wise king would rule the people of Israel, conscripting and mobilizing a citizen army in case of attack by external enemies.

In a sense, Yadin believed that this scroll completed the apocalyptic vision of the Qumran community that his father had first suggested twenty years before. The various surviving examples of their literature contained biblical interpretation, unique psalms and other religious compositions, and strict rules for members' conduct. The War Scroll presented the saga of a world-encompassing battle in which the community members would fight with the angels to defeat the forces of evil. Yet what would happen after that final victory? How would holiness finally be established upon the earth? Yadin believed that the Temple Scroll provided the answer. Over the next ten years he immersed himself in preparing a detailed translation and commentary on this long and complex document. In time, the political complications about its acquisition were eventually resolved. Although Yadin initially favored the Israel government's confiscation of the scroll—an ironic call for the enforcement of the Jordanian antiquities law that permitted government seizure of any artifacts that were discovered, concealed, or otherwise held without notifying the proper authorities—he eventually agreed to a settlement of $105,000 with Kando. Most of that sum was provided by British industrialist Leonard Wolfson, one of Yadin's closest London friends and faithful archaeological patrons.

The ideal realm of the Temple Scroll, however, contrasted sharply with the reality Israel faced after the Six Day War. Dayan's optimistic prediction of the imminent beginning of a peace process soon proved badly mistaken. Within just a few weeks of the end of the war, both Syria and Egypt were being massively resupplied by the Soviet Union, and at an Arab summit conference at Khartoum in August, the Arab nations announced three uncompromising postwar positions: no peace with Israel, no recognition of Israel, no negotiation with Israel. The armed struggle—whose object was now the restoration of the rights of the Palestinian Arab people—must go on. In Israel most people resigned themselves to an indefinite continuation of the status quo. Levi Eshkol became a mere figurehead, while Yigael Allon, who proposed territorial compromise with the Arabs, clashed with Moshe Dayan, who refused to speak of withdrawal as long as the Arabs refused to come to the peace table. A growing segment of the Israeli population grew used to the idea that the entire Land of Israel, as won by force of arms in the Six Day War, should never, under any conditions, be returned.

Yadin was among the first to caution the public about what was threatening to become an idolatrous relationship with the land. After the end of the war, the Ministry of Religious Affairs—long a preserve of the rigidly conservative National Religious Party—began building an empire for itself in the West Bank. It assumed jurisdiction over such sites of Jewish folk pilgrimage as the Tomb of Rachel just outside Bethlehem and the Tombs of the Patriarchs (also a Muslim religious shrine) in Hebron. These monuments suddenly became popular among the Israeli public. Yet when Yadin expressed his considered opinion that no archaeological evidence confirmed these as actual sites of the tombs they purported to be, his comments—much to Yadin's surprise and dismay—created something of a storm, and not in religious circles alone. On the opening day of the Israel Exploration Society convention, a well-known tour guide and veteran archaeological enthusiast, Zeev Vilnay, was conducting a walking tour to the Jewish Quarter and Western Wall in the Old City, during which he launched a thinly veiled attack on Yadin. Calling upon an unnamed fellow archaeologist to "stop de-sanctifying the holy places," he suggested that such statements "undermine the claim which has sustained the nation up to now." Soon afterward, the director-general of the Religious Affairs Ministry, S. Z. Cahane, joined in with a public rebuke to Yadin. "What concern have you with the holy places and Rachel's tomb?" Cahane asked Yadin rhetorically in an angry press statement. "You take care of the archaeological sites and leave the holy places to me."

This time Yadin refrained from escalating the argument. He seems to have felt a sting of public disapproval and instead of repeating or further explaining his cautionary words against religio-territorial euphoria, he became one of the most eloquent advocates of the idea of the religious sanctity of the land. In an interview with *The Jerusalem Post* in April 1968 he himself blurred the boundary between religious faith and archaeological fact. "This generation has created a new religion, the religion of history, a belief in the history of its people as a religious faith. It has been said that our boys have often fought with a sense of 'no alternative.' I submit this doesn't explain why the paratroopers fought the way they did in order to get to the Western Wall as quickly as possible. Boys who may never have been in a synagogue went to the Wall together with boys who pray three times daily. For the boy who goes to the synagogue three times daily, the Wall may have a more formalistic significance. For the other kind of boy, the Wall represents his people's history.

"I say that we created this," Yadin continued, in a reversal of his earlier caution. Now he actually claimed some of the credit for the rise of religious consciousness. "For the generation of the State, the State and history have acquired a religious quality. It would not be an exaggeration to say that they fought with verses from the Bible. Through archaeology these people discover their 'religious' values; in archaeology they find their religion, they learn that their forefathers were in this country three thousand years ago. This is a value. By this they fought and by this they live. What a vast difference there is between digging up Masada with 20 students of the sort that I have and doing it with 20 professional archaeologists. Our boys are digging up their own past, their own history."

Yadin's unfortunate tendency to retreat into the platitudes of patriotic devotion whenever challenged in serious debate reflected a troubling weakness, a lack of conviction about the ideals or ideas in which he claimed to believe. He often seemed more concerned with maintaining a positive image, with the applause of an admiring public, than with challenging the consensus, even when he felt his dissenting view was correct. In avoiding political confrontation he revealed an insecurity about his ability to champion a valid if unpopular cause. Thus he retreated into patriotic platitudes rather than accept the mantle of spiritual leadership.

In fact, by the summer of 1969, he merely echoed the public feelings about the sanctity of the past rather than guiding its expression in any way.

On July 6 he appeared with his former adversary, S. Z. Cahane, at a press conference to announce that on the next day, twenty-seven skeletons that had been discovered during the Masada excavations would be buried with full military honors on a low hill (now officially called Givat Hameginim, "Hill of the Defenders") at the southern base of the mountain. As for the identity of the human remains, Yadin dismissed all doubters, saying that "it was possible that most, if not all, were Jewish, although it was not absolutely certain. However, even if some were Roman, Jewish tradition on this matter was very humane and commands that enemy dead on the battlefield be buried with honor." Thus he gave his scientific imprimatur to one of the final acts of the modern drama of Masada. The following day, precisely as planned by a government committee, an army vehicle left Jerusalem carrying two coffins draped in Israeli flags to the gravesite in the Judean wilderness. IDF pallbearers and an honor guard brought the two coffins to their final resting places. In attendance were a few prominent politicians, among them Zerah Warhaftig of the National Religious party and Menachem Begin of Herut. Chief IDF chaplain Shlomo Goren recited Kaddish and "a special prayer he had composed for the occasion." Yadin read from the speech of Eleazar Ben-Yair as recorded by Josephus. As a final sanctification of the solemn proceedings, an IDF honor guard fired three volleys over the graves.

By the spring of 1968, Yadin was an acclaimed international figure. He accepted an honorary doctorate from Witwatersrand University in South Africa with renowned paleontologist Mary Leakey, which placed him in the first rank of the world's archaeologists. At the same time, his fame and the folklore about him were reaching new heights within Israel and among staunch supporters of Israel elsewhere. In 1966 an American author, Shane Miller, interviewed Yadin for a children's book; the result was a wildly romanticized hero biography published in New York in 1967 entitled *Desert Fighter: The Story of General Yigael Yadin and the Dead Sea Scrolls*. Miller's book followed Yadin's life from his boyhood in the Haganah through the Masada dig; he spiced it with anecdotes about meeting Yaacov Dori, arguing with Ben-Gurion, and digging up archaeological evidence of Joshua, Bar-Kokhba, and the zealots of Masada, all with breathless, admiring description and self-consciously heroic dialogue. "Today Yigael Yadin is a busy man," the biography concluded. "As a world authority on archaeological exploration in the Holy Land, his time is spent in lecturing, travel, and fieldwork that brings him back to the sites he continues to explore. Dr. Yadin's service to his country as a military man has not been forgotten, nor his part in the UN Mission at Rhodes, as a negotiator of Israel's War of Independence. There are many who feel that his greatest days of service to his country may still be before him." Yadin couldn't have asked for a more adoring portrait. At a time when his standard lecture fee was $4,000 plus expenses ($3,000 as a contribution to one of his research funds and $1,000 as a personal fee), clubs, civic groups, universities, and philanthropic organizations from Tokyo to Cincinnati were eager to have him as their guest speaker and to bask in the presence of one of modern Israel's most charming celebrities.

James Michener may have had something to do with Yadin's new status. His 1965 best-selling novel *The Source* was a gripping poolside page-turner that provided more than a thousand pages of vicarious archaeological thrills for readers all over the world. Setting the scene at the fictional archaeological site of "Makor," Michener diced, chopped, and pureed vast quantities of archaeological facts and presumptions to create an easily digestible literary casserole of the history of Israel from the Neolithic period to the War of Independence, with a dash of modern-day romance thrown in. The story was filled with a cast of romanticized, stereotyped archaeologists like the sultry sabra Vered Bar-el ("Israel's top expert in dating pottery sherds") and the handsome, strong-jawed American Archaeologist John Cullinane (from the "Biblical Museum in Chicago"). Yet there was little question who had served as inspiration for the pipe-smoking Israeli archaeologist Dr. Ilan Eliav, "who had been both a soldier and a scholar" and "whose political skill had been found to be so valuable to the government that he was rarely allowed out in the field." *The Source* ended when the romantic rivalry between Cullinane and Eliav for the hand of Israel's top pottery expert was cut short by Eliav's sudden, dramatic departure to become a government minister. The reality of Israeli archaeology (and Yadin's life) in those days was somewhat more prosaic. In July 1968 the pipe-smoking soldier-scholar announced the resumption of the Hazor excavations after a ten-year hiatus. His goal was not to romance, but to locate the ancient city's water system and, if possible, the Bronze Age palace and royal archives of Hazor.

Too bad Jim Michener wasn't around to chronicle this distinctly unromantic story. By the summer of 1968, Yadin was the undisputed lord of the Hebrew University Institute of Archaeology, and he was not reluctant to exercise his archaeological power. His longtime critic

Yohanan Aharoni had left to establish a rival institute at Tel Aviv University. From this point on, their feud was conducted at a distance, abetted by each man's loyal faculty allies and undergraduates. The renewed Hazor excavations were to be an entirely in-house operation, with a senior staff composed of Yadin's favorite students, among them Yigal Shiloh, Avi Eitan, Malka Batyevsky, Amihai Mazar, and Amnon Ben-Tor. The results were, as usual, impressive. By the end of the three-month digging season, the team had cleared Hazor's enormous subterranean water tunnel and uncovered an early Israelite highplace and a magnificent Canaanite temple of the Bronze Age. The fabled archives of the city, however, remained hidden, awaiting yet another dig. But for most of the participants the most significant discovery was the disturbing change that had taken place in Yadin's behavior and personality.

"The 1968 season at Hazor was a horror," one of the participants recalled—in contrast to the mood and physical conditions of the previous decade. In the first four seasons of digging at Hazor in the mid-1950s there had been a semblance of teamwork and at least some attempt to embody a communal ideal. But now Yadin treated Hazor as if it were his private possession. After all the archaeological triumphs he had experienced, he considered himself a special person who deserved special rights. While the staff were housed atrociously in abandoned and rundown immigrants' barracks in Rosh Pinna, Yadin hired a private apartment for himself. "There at Hazor," another staff member recalled, "you could really see how selfish he was." While the staff was served cheap and often indigestible food, Yadin was given steak—and ate it unashamedly in the presence of the others, claiming that his doctor had designed a special diet for him. This haughty aristocratic behavior clearly annoyed the young men and women who supervised the excavations. Having thrown in their lot with Yadin at the Hebrew University, however, there was little they could do but go down to a nearby roadside cafe after meals. During working hours they had to make do with the shoddy trowels, buckets, hoes, shovels, and wheelbarrows that Yadin's administrator had scraped together at minimum cost for the dig. "Never have I seen an excavation with poorer food and poorer equipment," Amihai Mazar recalled of the experience. In many ways, this Hazor dig resembled the often haphazard excavations of his father more than the romantic nonsense of *The Source* or the spectacular logistical triumphs of Masada and the Judean Wilderness.

More and more, Yadin was retreating from reality into the shielded environment of his home and the university. Although he was only fifty-one years old, he was feeling his age. His mother died in early 1968, and from that time he was increasingly concerned for his own health. As always, Carmella remained in control of the household and the administrative aspects of Yigael's career, tending to the family finances, professional correspondence, editing and typing of manuscripts, travel schedules, social commitments, and even auto repair ("I only *break* the car," Yadin once told a reporter). Ever since the early days of their marriage she and Yigael had been full partners in the construction of his public image. In his professional life Yadin depended on Carmella as a talented performer or artist depends on agents, editors, and business managers. Yadin found all of these roles admirably filled by the single confidante and partner of his life. While he had the luxury of devoting his full attention to the Temple Scroll and his thousand and one other archaeological interests, Carmella worked tirelessly to maintain his reputation and public visibility through carefully scheduled lectures and public appearances. In her systematic way, she still ordered their social life by arranging dinner parties with just the right number and right mix of guests from business, politics, the army, and academia. "She could work all day, get home at five o'clock, and have twenty people for dinner at seven o'clock and nothing would be missing," recalled Hannah Barag, who with her husband Dan rented a small apartment in the Yadins' home in Rechavia. Yadin always acknowledged his debt to Carmella in his lectures and books, and in his complete devotion. "Carmella was involved in every decision of his life," recalled friends Lilly and Leon Shalit, "but not in the way of dictating. She was his most trusted adviser. They were a complete couple in every way."

Home life at the Yadins' on Ramban Street in Rechavia, though orderly, was neither relaxed nor idyllic. Daughters Orly and Littal were held to a standard of behavior far higher than most of their classmates. Family acquaintances remember Carmella as abrupt and sometimes shorttempered with the girls; raised in the Ruppin household, in an atmosphere of strict Germanic discipline, she became an exceptionally demanding mother herself. Both Yadin daughters were expected to be models of behavior. Though their parents were often away on overseas trips and lecture tours (frequently leaving them in the care of grandmother Chassiya or family housekeepers), Orly and Littal were brought up to fulfill their parents' cultural ideals. Many visitors to the Yadin home were struck by the fact that both Yigael and Carmella spoke English to the girls (despite the patriotic significance of the Hebrew language in Israel). This was perhaps characteristic of Carmella and Yigael's coldly utilitarian outlook, even on a decision as basic and as personal as the language spoken at home. Although neither Yigael nor Carmella were native Englishspeakers, they apparently assumed that since Orly and Littal would learn

Hebrew in school and at play with their friends, complete fluency in English would be of substantial benefit to them in later life.

———

In the fall of 1969, Yadin left Israel for a year's visiting professorship at Brown University, and the year spent amid American campus turmoil had a gradual but profound effect on him. He returned to the Hebrew University with enthusiastic ideas about educational innovation and reshaping the course of study at the Institute of Archaeology. Even more important, both he and Carmella began to show growing interest in public issues and political reform. Over the years, both of them had occasionally participated in petition drives and protest meetings against the excessive power of the religious parties. Yadin and Carmella, like many other liberal, nonreligious Israelis, had long been critical of the system of backroom government coalition negotiations that enabled the small religious parties to dictate religious restrictions on the entire population, on matters like the legality of autopsies, the permissibility of abortions, and the criteria by which the state determined who was a Jew. The shortcomings of the Israeli parliamentary system were becoming ever more glaring. Since the Six Day War, the power of behind-the-scenes party politics had eroded the influence of the electorate. Secretly negotiated coalition agreements between the major parties, repeatedly made, changed, and broken between general elections, were now a major factor in determining Israel's domestic and international policies.

Early in 1968 the long rift in the main labor parties (between Ben-Gurion's Rafi supporters and the old-timers of Mapai) began to be mended with the creation of a single Israel Labour Party that included most of the feuding factions. Levi Eshkol had been steadily losing political power ever since he appointed Dayan as defense minister; his worsening health, though kept secret from the Israeli public, also had something to do with it. On February 26, 1969, news of Eshkol's death from cancer took the nation by surprise. With Eshkol's passing, the Labour Party council elected longtime Mapai functionary Golda Meir as its candidate for the prime minister. Yadin remained, as usual, on the sidelines, but he could not have been happy with the selection. His resentment of Meir as an arrogant party functionary dated back to the early 1950s, when he had come into direct conflict with her over emergency aid to the temporary immigrants' camps. In the summer of 1970, Menachem Begin and his political allies left the national unity government, pressing for a more militant Israel stance toward the peace pressure of the United States and for the retention of the occupied territories at all costs. As backroom politics went on as usual and the country fell into a dangerous malaise, Yadin felt compelled to speak out on public issues, even if it sparked new rumors about his personal political ambitions.

In a revealing interview published in *Maariv* in the spring of 1973, just before Israel's twenty-fifth Independence Day celebration, Yadin reflected on the need for far-reaching social and religious reform, in terms more explicit than he had ever used before. Looking back on the establishment of Israel and the development of its society, he emphasized that his "ideal has always been that the state would be both Jewish and democratic. And I place equal emphasis on both." His continuing work on the Temple Scroll had deeply immersed him in the complexity of Jewish ritual law and religious history, and he clearly placed modern Israel's moral and political problems in that spiritual context. "In two thousand years of exile we never had to face the actuality of questions of sovereignty," Yadin told reporter Dov Goldstein. "Only three times in history have the Jews had to accommodate themselves to independence: in the time of David, during which a real revolution occurred and ways of life were determined that would last for hundreds of years of monarchical independence; when the Jews returned from Babylon, it was Ezra and Nehemiah who altered the religion and the religious way of life of the First Temple, in order to make the change. . . . And the third time—when the Maccabees achieved independence—Judaism changed the character of Torah in the greatest revolution that has ever taken place in Jewish history." What was needed now, Yadin believed, was a far-reaching reform of Jewish beliefs, values, and everyday practices that would bring the people of Israel into accord with the changed circumstances of independence in the twentieth century. What was needed, Yadin contended, was a "new" torah "to help us lead our lives."

These professorial ruminations were expressed in a characteristically emotionless and analytical manner, yet there was something heartfelt in Yadin's call for a renewed commitment to social justice within Israeli society. "A democratic-Jewish state," Yadin continued, "can arise only when everyone has the feeling that opportunities are equal for everyone. That wasn't up to us in 1949 and 1950. But we have not learned in the twenty-five years of the state to give the weaker and disadvantaged strata of society a feeling of equal worth. This is no less important than matters of national defense. In this area we have failed." At a time when most Israelis were preparing to celebrate Independence Day with a massive parade in Jerusalem (this time with a full complement of tanks, heavy artillery, and roaring jet fighters), Yadin stressed the challenge that remained. "A catastrophe is likely to befall us if we don't see the seriousness of the situation and give it some impetus," he continued. "It's written in the Bible: 'On the Lord's returning to Zion, we were as if dreaming.' Our challenge is how to keep dreaming. To continue to deal with problems of everyday reality—and not to forget the larger dream."

Not unexpectedly, these eloquent reflections on Israel's future— coming from the sage of Masada, Hazor, and Bar-Kokhba—drew a re- newed round of speculation about Yadin assuming a position of national leadership. Knesset elections were scheduled for the coming October, so he would soon be compelled to act upon his idealistic calls for social rebuilding and economic reform. In the summer of 1973 he began by renewing his crusade for electoral reform. As chairman of yet another public committee for this purpose, he appeared at a press conference and presented a plan for a regional system of representation, in which each Knesset member would be dependent not on party status for advance- ment but on the voters of a particular constituency. With an eye on the upcoming Knesset elections, Yadin urged all the major parties to place this issue on their platforms. "As a means of exerting this pressure," Yadin suggested in an uncharacteristically combative proposal "voters should threaten to withhold their support."

Representatives of both the Labour Party and the newly formed rightist Likud (composed of Begin's Herut and its allies) sensed which way the wind was blowing and dutifully sent messages of support to Yadin. Ariel Sharon, recently retired from the army and contemplating a political future, told reporters at the same press conference that he agreed with the basic aims of Yadin's group. Once again Yadin had dis- tinguished himself as a committed nonpartisan who had only the best interests of the nation at heart. He represented a refreshing contrast to the backroom politics-as-usual of both the Labour Party and the Likud. But Yadin stubbornly denied that he had personal political ambitions and insisted that he would never abandon archaeology for politics. That, however, was before the Day of Atonement. On Yom Kippur 1973 a military and political earthquake shook the Holy Land with horrifying violence and suddenness. The painful aftershocks in the following months would profoundly alter the course of Yadin's career and his place in the modern history of Israel.

Chapter Fifteen

WAR OF ATONEMENT

J ust before two o'clock on Saturday afternoon, October 6, 1973—a day doubly sacred as the Sabbath and the Day of Atonement—the whine of air raid sirens and the ominous, repeated broadcast of mobilization code words on a day when the radio was normally silent roused the people of Israel from their slumber and their prayers. Since around four o'clock that morning, the high command of the Israel Defense Forces had known for certain that an attack by both Egypt and Syria was imminent. But through the early morning hours, Defense Minister Dayan and Chief of Staff David "Dado" Elazar wasted precious time in arguments over the tactical steps the IDF should take and on the number of reserve troops that should be mobilized. By the time Dayan summoned Yadin and the other former chiefs of staff to the Pit for consultations, Prime Minister Golda Meir had personally authorized a call-up of 100,000 reserve troops. By early afternoon, when Yadin left his home in Rechavia for Tel Aviv, the war was already raging. The powerful position and unshakable self-confidence that Israel had gained in 1967 was to be severely challenged. By late afternoon, as the former chiefs of staff—Yadin, Dayan, Zur, Laskov, Rabin, and Bar-Lev—assembled in the war room, they faced a situation unparalleled in Israeli history.

This hurried summoning of the old soldiers without warning was symptomatic of the chaos unfolding on the battlefield. In the aftermath of the Six Day War, the IDF commanders had based their planning on three badly mistaken assumptions, for which they would now dearly pay. First was the assumption that the Golan Heights, Sinai, and the West Bank provided Israel with enough strategic depth that it could respond effectively to any invasion by its neighbors; a successful Arab surprise attack was not even considered as a possibility. Second was the assumption that because of its experience in 1967, Egypt would not go to war again until its air force rivaled that of Israel—an achievement that, despite massive Egyptian rearmament, was still many years away. The third mistaken assumption was that Syria would not go to war without Egypt. Accordingly, the assessment of the head of Israel's military intelligence as late as the previous day, October 5, was that the likelihood of war breaking out anytime soon was "low probability." That is not to say that there were no warning signs. Since the 1967 war both Egypt and Syria had been bolstering their air defenses with thick concentrations of Soviet surface-to-air missiles. In late September, Egypt brought reinforcements and heavy equipment to its side of the Suez Canal. These developments were noted by Israeli military intelligence, but the seductive power of the three mistaken assumptions blinded the IDF to what was happening. When the armies of Egypt and Syria attacked around two o'clock on Yom Kippur, Israeli forces were in only an early stage of mobilization— yet Defense Minister Dayan was still confident that the IDF could blunt the Arab attack. That evening, in a televised address to the nation, he reassured the families of the hastily mobilized soldiers that a punishing Israeli counterattack would soon be mounted and that the war "will end with victory in the coming few days."

Yadin tended to agree with that assessment when he arrived at the Pit. Hearing of only minimal Egyptian forays across the Suez Canal and only limited Syrian incursions on the Golan Heights, he urged Chief of Staff Elazar to announce the good news to the public at once. As he had been in 1967, Yadin was concerned to maintain the morale of the civilian population, but once again, Yitzhak Rabin strongly objected. As Rabin later recalled, he warned Elazar against making premature public statements. In the light of the utter unpreparedness of the few Israeli forces on the Golan Heights and the Suez Canal, Rabin considered the news "too good to be true." And so it was. During the evening and first night of fighting, nearly 100,000 Egyptian troops crossed the canal in boats and on pontoon bridges, overwhelmed the approximately five hundred Israeli front-line defenders, and easily established secure bridgeheads in Sinai. On the Golan Heights a massive Syrian armored force supported by helicopter-borne commandos overran large areas of the Israeli-held territory, in some places arriving within only a few kilometers of the Sea of Galilee. By the morning of October 7, it was clear that the initial reports from the front-line commanders had been either mistaken or intentionally misleading. "The army had really been caught with its pants down," Yadin later recalled. Enormous logistical problems now complicated the IDF response to the simultaneous Egyptian and Syrian invasions. To counterattack, the IDF had to organize and equip the arriving reserve forces and move entire divisions, brigades, and battalions to the Sinai and Golan.

"What happened to us in those days was something like a Greek tragedy," Yadin later remembered. "On the one hand, we tried to save the people at the front-line outposts. On the other hand, this was a strategic mistake because it caused the thinning out and destruction of all the tanks we had there." No less disturbing to those in the headquarters was the panic and despair that suddenly seemed to grip Defense Minister Dayan, who had appeared confident only hours before. Realizing that this would not be an easy victory—that the Arab armies would not turn and run as they had in 1956 and 1967—Dayan shocked the other officers by recommending deep strategic withdrawals and even urging that Israel turn to the United Nations and seek an immediate ceasefire. When his advice was rejected by "Dado" Elazar and the others, he asked Prime Minister Meir to accept his resignation. But by this time, others had taken over direction of the war. "It was then that I saw Dado as a field commander in all his strength," Yadin recalled of Chief of Staff Elazar's determination to regain the upper hand. A counterattack at the Suez Canal on Monday October 8 failed, but the Israeli forces slowly recovered the initiative. By Wednesday, October 10, they had driven the Syrians back beyond the ceasefire lines of 1967 and had finally stopped the momentum of the Egyptian advance in Sinai.

Yadin remained in the Pit throughout the first days of the fighting. Only after the momentum had shifted did he agree to leave headquarters late in the evenings to catch some sleep at the home of his friend Yaacov Yannai in the Tel Aviv suburb of Zahala. But for almost two weeks he remained in the war room, experiencing (as he had done in 1948 and again in 1967 in very different circumstances) the tension and excitement of being present at the highest levels of the army command. Whatever the other officers might have thought of Yadin's presence, he believed himself to be a valuable liaison between the various front-line commanders and the officers of the general staff. "I was there as an independent adviser," he later explained to an interviewer, claiming that as the senior of all the former chiefs of staff he had been a nonpartisan coordinator, sitting in on all the meetings and on occasion offering suggestions and opinions to the defense minister, the chief of staff, and his deputy, Israel Tal. He sometimes also willingly served as a go-between. "Several of the highest officers knew that I had access to Dado, to Tal, to Dayan," Yadin recalled, "and they openly expressed their complaints against the commanders and brought me all kinds of suggestions." Yadin also renewed his close contact with old army colleagues like Meir Amit and Meir Zorea, who had—like him—been summoned for advice and consultation with the general staff.

The fighting in the Golan Heights was all but over by Friday, October 12, leaving Israel in control of Syrian territory even beyond the 1967 lines, and the attention of the IDF general staff now shifted to the south. The Egyptians held a twenty-kilometer-wide strip of western Sinai. Over the next few days, massive tank battles raged as the Egyptians attempted to proceed farther inland, and most of Egypt's armored forces were transferred to the east bank of the canal. But the IDF high command detected a glaring weakness in the enemy deployment. On the night of October 15, an Israeli armored division under the command of Ariel Sharon mounted a daring canal crossing, thrusting westward through a gap in the Egyptian lines. After several days of bloody fighting the Israeli force succeeded in destroying the surface-to-air missile batteries and occupied considerable territory in Egypt itself. By this time, international pressure was mounting to end the fighting. OPEC declared an oil embargo on shipments to Western Europe and America, causing oil shortages and skyrocketing prices that posed a serious threat to Western economies. The Soviets were concerned about the impending military collapse of their Egyptian and Syrian allies, and on October 22 the UN Security Council called for an immediate ceasefire. Despite unsuccessful last-minute Israeli attempts to liquidate the surrounded and vulnerable Egyptian Third Army in Sinai—and avoid a nuclear confrontation between the United States and the Soviet Union over the Soviets' threat of direct intervention—the War of Atonement was at an end.

Yadin left the Pit and returned to Jerusalem on October 18, even before the ceasefire, but during the final days of fighting he kept in constant contact with the general staff. The results of the war for Israel were numbing in terms of human losses; nearly 2,500 had been killed, 5,000 were wounded, and more than three hundred were held in Syria and Egypt as prisoners of war. Israel still held virtually all the territory it had gained in 1967, but public confidence in the military and political leadership had been shattered. All across the country there was a deep feeling that the leadership had been both arrogant and ineffective. Even more unsettling, the generation of Israel's founding fathers was quickly passing from the scene, leaving a vacuum in moral leadership. On December 18, 1973, just a few weeks after the war, David Ben-Gurion died, and his passing symbolized the loss of direction that Israel now felt. In the aftermath of the war the people of Israel were thrust into a new era with no sure guidance, no clear vision of where the nation was to go.

Israel had achieved a striking military triumph after the initial surprise attacks and chaotic first days of fighting. But the diplomatic situation was now dangerous and delicate. A portion of the Egyptian invasion force remained fatally trapped in Sinai but was protected by UN intervention; both superpowers were, at the same time, intent on increasing their influence in the region through a postwar political settlement. As Henry Kissinger sought to bolster American leverage in both Egypt and Syria, it seemed clear that serious Arab-Israeli negotiations would soon get under way. Yadin was eager to play a role in these diplomatic maneuvers. As a veteran of the 1948 negotiations with Egypt, Jordan, and Syria, he felt himself uniquely qualified. It was not that he possessed any particular negotiating position or any particularly passionate conviction about the future of the Middle East. It was rather that he had finally come to believe what people always said about him: that he was a man destined to lead. His generation was now fully in power, and in heartfelt discussions with Carmella, they both came to the conclusion that the time had come for him to enter public life.

Impatient to get off the sidelines and into the action, Yadin telephoned General Israel Lior, a longtime acquaintance from the Haganah and the 1948 war and who now served as the chief military aide to Prime Minister Meir. Meir's relations with Yadin had never been friendly, but Yadin, convinced that his time had come, thought she and the other veteran Mapai leaders would welcome him with open arms. He asked Lior to convey to the prime minister his willingness to serve in her government in any capacity she deemed useful. In light of his experience at Rhodes and Shuneh, Yadin suggested—with no unnecessary modesty— he might best serve to coordinate the upcoming peace talks. He apparently did not recognize that such an appointment would conflict with the ministerial responsibilities of Foreign Minister Eban, Defense Minister Dayan, and the prime minister herself. But Yadin pressed ahead with every expectation that he would again enter the highest circles of power.

Writing in *Maariv* on November 1, he forcefully opposed a proposed official investigation to apportion blame and punish the politicians and military leaders responsible for the utter unpreparedness of the nation. Yadin instead stressed the need for national unity. "We must emphatically demand of all our political leaders, of all public bodies, of ourselves, to close ranks and put aside everything that divides us," he asserted. "We have a common position—to stand firm at the gates, against both military and political dangers."

Unfortunately, Yadin's eagerness to help was met with stony silence from Meir, who well understood the political implications and consequences of such a move. Her government was now besieged by the nation's rage and mourning. Many Israelis thought its criminal incompetence had been the main cause of the battlefield deaths of so many loved ones. For the first time in the history of modern Israel, tens of thousands of civilians and demobilized reserve soldiers massed in angry protests against the national leadership, holding Meir and her ministers personally and criminally responsible for the *mechdal*—the great "blunder"—that led to the Yom Kippur War. Signs and placards called for the immediate resignation of Defense Minister Dayan. Meir, however, ever stubborn and self-righteous, refused to acknowledge that her government was in any way responsible for what had occurred. Knesset elections (delayed by the war from October to the end of December) were now fast approaching, and she was unwilling to make any change in the composition of her cabinet that might acknowledge wrongdoing or guilt. She therefore declined Yadin's offer of service. Yet her refusal to bring Yadin into the government—even in a ceremonial position— proved a costly error, with enormous political significance.

Yadin would no longer be content to return quietly to scrolls and potsherds. On November 18, 1973, he received a telephone call from Supreme Court chief justice Shimon Agranat that would profoundly change the course of Israel's political history. On that day, Agranat had been officially asked by the government to set up a public commission to investigate the conduct of the political and military leadership in the months leading up to the Yom Kippur War. The public pressure for such a commission had been relentless. Despite the political dangers, Meir now saw that it might also temporarily divert public attention during the election campaign. Rumors had been circulating for several days about possible members for the commission, and Yadin's name had been mentioned prominently. According to an anonymous source in *The Jerusalem Post,* Yadin was "said to be unacceptable to most of the Labour Party leadership, who regard him as too independent." As the rumors continued, Yadin's initial doubts about the advisability of the commission suddenly vanished. In an interview with Israel Radio on November 17, he urged that such a commission be established immediately—and threw in an unsubtle jab at the government's election campaign. "If they simply go back to the old slogans in their platforms," Yadin warned, "they are likely to generate a dangerous frustration with the democratic process." For the first time in many years Yadin was engaging in public debate as an active participant, not as a nonpartisan sage. When Chief Justice Agranat called on November 18 to ask him to become a member of the commission (ignoring the rumored Labour Party opposition), Yadin readily agreed. He would lend his time, his talents, and his judgment to the nation. His first task would be to help apportion blame and suggest punishment for those responsible for the great blunders of the Yom Kippur War.

At the Hebrew University Institute of Archaeology, the 1973–74 academic year was severely disrupted by the mobilization of virtually all the male students and faculty. Before the outbreak of the war, Yadin had been continuing his work on the Temple Scroll, overseeing research on finds from his various excavations, and impatiently dealing with endless administrative details as head of the Institute of Archaeology. He had established a close working relationship with a promising graduate student named Shulamit Geva, who soon efficiently and devotedly took over much of his burden at the university. Indeed, many of his colleagues slowly came to resent the power and independence he gave her, the prerogative to decide and act in his name. When he returned to public life, Yadin seemingly turned his back, at least for the time being, on his academic responsibilities. He did it with the same coldness and lack of emotion with which he had always shifted his attention from one subject to another, from one identity to the next. It was as if, in accepting the new public position, he could suddenly break off human contact with those he had worked with for years, with hardly a word of good-bye. He simply disappeared from the world of archaeology, and only Shulamit Geva was permitted to serve as a link, when it was absolutely necessary. For more than a year from the time he accepted Agranat's invitation to join the commission, Yadin immersed himself in an intense study of Israeli military preparations and actions. He apparently never stopped to consider the effect that this work would have on his relationship with others or on his hitherto untarnished image with the people of Israel.

For some critics, Yadin's membership on the Agranat Commission brought up troubling ethical questions. In asking Yadin to join, Chief Justice Agranat had been willing to overlook the fact that Yadin had close personal ties and long professional connections with many of the military commanders likely to come under scrutiny. An even more serious blot on his ability to be impartial was the fact that he had been present in the Pit and had attended, if not always participated in, many crucial general staff meetings in the first few days of the war. Yadin raised these issues with Agranat during their first conversations, but in his eagerness to recruit a distinguished panel member with professional military expertise, Agranat did not find them a serious obstacle. Agranat explained to Yadin that the commission's objective was to investigate primarily the events *leading up to* the war's outbreak and how they influenced the first three days. In that case, he said, Yadin's involvement should not present a problem. "I didn't ask any questions in the Pit," Yadin later noted—a bit ingenuously—in reference to this question, "and I really didn't ask anyone what really had happened up to the outbreak of the war."

Yadin's advice proved decisive in the recruitment of another military man to serve on the five-man commission. Agranat had already selected three civilians: in addition to himself, there would be his Supreme Court colleague Moshe Landau, and the legendarily incorruptible state comptroller, Yitzhak Nebenzahl. Since much of the testimony and evidence to be presented would likely be of a technical military nature, Agranat solicited Yadin's suggestions for another military candidate. Because of the importance of the investigation, Agranat thought the fifth member should be another former chief of staff. But Dayan was one of those to be closely examined, and Zvi Zur had long and close relations with Dayan; both were immediately rejected. Chaim Bar-Lev and Yitzhak Rabin were longtime Palmach comrades of Chief of Staff Elazar, who also was likely to come under scrutiny. That left only Chaim Laskov and Mordecai Makleff. Since Yadin had never been particularly fond of Makleff, he urged Chief Justice Agranat to appoint Laskov.

As the Agranat Commission began its investigation in late November 1973, a thick veil of secrecy descended over its deliberations. Though it was not a proper judicial proceeding, as a fact-finding panel it was to be given unrestricted access to the most sensitive and secret workings of the Israel Defense Forces—and the authority to request personal testimony from any official or officer it saw fit. Tight security was therefore essential. The Agranat Commission established its headquarters on two sealed floors of a Ministry of Justice building in downtown Jerusalem. The upper floor contained the hearing halls and the offices for the commission members. The lower floor held the commission files and archives, a room for stenographers who listened to the proceedings through earphones (and were rotated every ten minutes for security reasons), a small dining room for members to use during the often-marathon sessions, and a desk near the elevators occupied by security men. Dr. Yoav Gelber, a historian and reserve lieutenant-colonel, was hired by the commission to catalogue, arrange, and provide access to the transcript and mass of documents. In the coming months the commission would hold 140 sessions and take testimony from 58 witnesses who held posts in varying levels of the political and military hierarchy. The staff would assemble on most mornings at seven; the commission members would arrive by nine o'clock. Interrogation of witnesses would begin precisely at ten-thirty and would often continue through the afternoon. The commission members would confer privately about the day's testimony late into the evening, often requesting specific documents and newly typed excerpts from the day's transcripts.

Try as they might to insulate themselves from the ongoing political realities in Israel, however, the commission members could not ignore the public controversies in the wake of the Yom Kippur War. On December 31 the delayed national elections were held, and the Labour Party lost almost ten percent of its strength in the Knesset; its task of putting together a ruling coalition would be even more delicate than before. Despite public rage and protest, Prime Minister Golda Meir reappointed Moshe Dayan as defense minister. And for the next two months, she courted, threatened, bargained, and otherwise cajoled would-be coalition partners in an attempt to put together even a slim parliamentary majority. This was precisely the unresponsiveness to public pressure and the backroom deal-making that Yadin condemned in his repeated campaigns for electoral reform. But as a member of the Agranat Commission, he had become an effective instrument in the perpetuation of this process. Meir contended that any significant shuffle of ministers while the Agranat Commission was still meeting would be recklessly premature. Thus while the nation impatiently waited for even a preliminary report, Meir presented her new government in the Knesset in early March. It was destined to be the shortest-lived government in the modern history of Israel.

Through the winter and into the spring, the Agranat Commission summoned dozens of witnesses and dispatched staff members to gather documents and depositions. Before long, a division of duties emerged among the panel members as they discussed each day's testimony. Agranat ruled on most of the procedural matters. Landau took the lead in defining and sharpening the legal questions. Laskov was most concerned with practical, logistical problems of troop deployments and readiness. And Yadin, with his great talent for analysis and his intelligence experience, became dominant in strategic and tactical matters and played an important role in apportioning personal responsibility. What emerged from the testimony and documentation was not only a grim picture of an enemy buildup unnoticed by Israeli military intelligence. Far more troubling was the evidence of a complete breakdown of the fabled IDF training and planning. The Israeli forces in Sinai seemed to have been utterly ill-equipped and unprepared for the Egyptian offensive. When that offensive came, the front-line troops underwent a stunning, bloody collapse. In one of his few public statements on his commission work, Yadin later recalled his uncomfortable position as potential judge-executioner of Israel's highest political and military leadership. "You think it was easy to cross-examine Golda Meir for hours on end? To question her about documents, decisions, and why she said this or that, and why she thought this and not that? . . . We had all the material," he continued, "including transcripts of government meetings, the inner cabinet, the general staff . . . we saw everything—and we had to ask all the witnesses difficult and unpleasant questions. So even though the physical effort was difficult, the psychological and human side was many times harder, especially when it was clear to us that the majority of the public, like the woman knitting in the shadow of the guillotine, was looking forward to our verdict against Dayan and Golda. The public wanted their heads to roll, and we knew that if we didn't come up with that verdict, it would be very unpopular."

But it is unlikely that the commission members fully anticipated the depth of the public reaction. On April 1, 1973, the Agranat Commission submitted a forty-page interim report to the government; the following day, the published summary struck the Israeli public like a bombshell. The Agranat Commission ascribed the IDF's appalling lack of readiness to the mistaken assumptions and overconfidence of its commanders. It proposed that a special committee of ministers be appointed to monitor security affairs more closely and (as Yadin had recommended during his service with an earlier commission in 1963) that the prime minister appoint a special adviser for intelligence affairs. The most serious and shocking findings regarded personal responsibility. The commission recommended that Chief of Staff David Elazar, Intelligence Chief Eli Zeira, Deputy Intelligence Chief Arieh Shalev, and Southern Commander Shmuel Gonen be relieved of their commands immediately. In a nation that prided itself on the character and heroism of its military leadership, many saw this verdict against four distinguished career soldiers (especially "Dado" Elazar, whose career had begun in the Palmach and whose reputation had been gained in the 1948 battles for Jerusalem) as a travesty of justice, especially since neither Prime Minister Meir nor Defense Minister Dayan was to bear any of the responsibility.

From a strictly legal perspective, the commission's ruling had some justification, since in the Israeli system of government the legal relationship between the minister of defense and the chief of staff was hazy. Although the minister of defense was the government's representative in military matters, he was regarded primarily as a civilian, dependent on the professional advice and assessments of the general staff. Ironically the Agranat Commission was rehashing the point at issue in the 1948 War of the Generals, when Ben-Gurion, as defense minister, had overruled the officers of the high command. In that case, the defense minister would clearly have been responsible for a disastrous outcome. But in the Yom Kippur War, Defense Minister Dayan had *accepted* the opinion of his professional military advisers that war was a *remote* possibility. Although Dayan had a military background, the commission ruled that his service as defense minister had been as a political leader, not as a professional soldier. "Why should Dayan have known more than the chief of staff and the chief of intelligence, when they told him that there wasn't going to be a war?" Yadin later indignantly responded to an interviewer on this painful issue. "Why should he have known better than they? Because he was a former chief of staff?" Dayan was then serving in a purely political capacity as minister of defense. "From this standpoint," Yadin continued, "he did not bear personal responsibility, even if people were calling for his head."

Such coldly analytical explanations did little to quiet the public furor. "The reaction of the press was really politically inspired," Yoav Gelber noted of the uproar. "Everybody wanted the commission to validate their own feelings about the war. But those feelings were not based on facts, because no one else had the facts." The Agranat Commission had sincerely attempted to rise above partisan perspectives and find out what really happened. But the public's anger and frustration were soon turned against the investigators themselves. Yitzhak Rabin, a longtime comrade of Chief of Staff Elazar who was then serving as minister of labor, expressed the general feeling that the commission's procedures were unfair. "Dado didn't even know what he was being accused of," Rabin later insisted. "He didn't have the opportunity to counter the witnesses against him . . . there had to be a principle of political responsibility and Dado didn't do anything without approval. I told him 'You're going to be blamed,' and he accepted it. But he shouldn't have been the only one."

Yadin, by far the most famous of the commission members, became the object of much of the criticism. Newspaper columnists and political commentators questioned not only his military judgment but his impartiality. They recounted his close ties with Dayan from the earliest days of the

IDF, and they reminded the public that Yadin was, after all, the man who had facilitated Dayan's appointment as defense minister before the Six Day War. Yadin was deeply wounded by such accusations. He insisted that he had joined the Agranat Commission without overt political motives—certainly not to absolve Dayan of responsibility—and for years afterward he remained convinced of the correctness of the commission's findings on ministerial responsibility. But the ultimate effects of the Agranat Commission's interim report *were* political, whether Yadin and his colleagues intended it or not. When Chief of Staff Elazar and the other accused officers resigned, massive public demonstrations erupted outside the Knesset angrily calling for Golda Meir and Moshe Dayan to step down as well.

The legalistic distinctions of the commission's report could not still the general outrage, and on April 11, Prime Minister Golda Meir succumbed to the pressure and resigned, bringing her short-lived coalition government to an end. Golda's retirement from public life marked the end of the era dominated by the veteran Mapai leadership. Moshe Dayan's political exile also began as he was rudely toppled from his pedestal of military leadership. A Labour Party election was soon held to find a successor to Meir, and a new generation of leaders emerged. In the bitterly fought internal election at the end of April, Yitzhak Rabin narrowly defeated Shimon Peres for the leadership of the party. On June 3, Rabin (the first sabra prime minister) presented his new government in the Knesset, with Shimon Peres as defense minister and Yigal Allon as minister of foreign affairs.

The Yom Kippur War and the Agranat Commission investigation had together accomplished a revolution in Israel's political life. But as a member of the commission, Yadin became increasingly dissatisfied with the political state of affairs that he—ironically—had been instrumental in bringing about. He had never held much respect for Yitzhak Rabin, from the Independence War onward, and he resented the back-room negotiations that had elevated Rabin to national leadership. The time would soon come for Yadin to make an even greater commitment to political life of the nation. In just a few months he would lend his support and reputation to a direct challenge to the new Labour government.

───

The Agranat Commission continued to work for nearly nine months after the publication of its interim findings. As the Rabin government took office and embarked on a new round of intensive diplomatic activity, the commission members, sequestered in their headquarters, took testimony and reviewed documents to complete their exhaustive evaluation of Israeli conduct in the war. "After the publication of the interim report, the nature of the work changed," Yoav Gelber remembered. "The interim report was about the facts leading up to the war. It almost didn't deal with the war itself. In the later stage, they had to begin a study of the battles and at this point there were fewer questions of responsibility. They were more concerned with trying to understand what happened— deciding which version was right." Through the late spring and summer, the commission relied increasingly on the documentary evidence (the hundreds of written orders, records, and transcripts of battlefield communications), which often contradicted the oral testimony. An archaeologist and historian like Yadin found this research an important case study in historical investigation; official accounts written or sworn to by the high-ranking officers often did not square with the documentary evidence. Yadin took the lead in piecing together a convincing historical reconstruction, and his version of the events in Sinai became the official account. In July the commission issued a second report of four hundred pages, and in January 1975 it ended its work with a final report of fifteen hundred pages. Virtually all the collected material remained classified; only the general introduction was released to the press.

With the work of the Agranat Commission ending, Yadin briefly returned to his archaeological career. His translation and commentary on the Temple Scroll remained unfinished, as did the final reports on the Hazor and Masada excavations and the translation of documents from the Bar-Kokhba period. In addition to resuming work on these projects, he also resumed his teaching responsibilities. Once more he found himself at the Institute of Archaeology, now shifted to quarters in the rebuilt campus on Mount Scopus, conducting graduate seminars and presenting his masterful "Introduction to the Archaeology of the Land of Israel" to enthusiastic first-year students. But his return was not that of a serene or mellow scholar coming back to his life's true calling. He no longer had patience for administrative meetings or planning sessions. He preferred to appear at the institute only when his classes were scheduled and to spend the rest of his time secluded in his study at home.

In the years since Aharoni left for Tel Aviv University, moreover, Yadin's feud with him had grown increasingly bitter. So pervasive was the conflict, in fact, that the Israeli archaeological community was split into two rival camps; no one could remain completely neutral, even though there was no coherent principle at stake in the Yadin-Aharoni feud, only a simmering clash of personalities. Yadin still saw Aharoni as motivated primarily by personal ambition, willing to do or say anything to get ahead in the academic world. Aharoni, for his part, despised Yadin as a pampered product of the Rechavia aristocracy, but he also took advantage of Yadin's celebrity to boost his own public visibility. By 1975,

Yadin and Aharoni could not even bear to speak to each other but conducted their bickering through surrogates. The effects of their feud were destructive. They had little sense of a shared participation in formulating a new historical understanding for Israel in the post-1973 period. Like disciples of rival rabbis, Aharoni's and Yadin's students distinguished themselves and advanced their careers by demonstrating their skill in defending dogma, not in challenging it. Archaeology in Israel, though it continued to attract international attention, was becoming bogged down in institutional and ideological inertia. Despite the ever-expanding scale of digging and bitter debates over specifics of dates and stratigraphic minutiae, the implicit messages both Yadin and Aharoni conveyed were nearly identical. Ethnic movements and conflicts, innovations in warfare, settlement patterns, and monuments of civil administration were the landmarks of an imagined ancient landscape that uncannily reflected the preoccupations of modern Israel.

In the spring of 1975, modern questions of ethnic coexistence, of peaceful and gradual social transformation, and of economic inequality, all largely absent from Yadin's archaeological reconstructions, were taking up an increasing proportion of his time. Even before the Yom Kippur War, his political involvement had been steadily growing. In the summer of 1973 a number of politicians, civic leaders, and former army colleagues had urged him to take a leading role in a national movement. In July he agreed to serve as chairman of another committee for electoral reform, to attempt once again to establish a system of regional representation in place of the traditional party lists. Even more important was Carmella's increasing interest in political issues. Through most of her life, she had participated mainly in philanthropic and volunteer organizations, but in August 1973 her longtime acquaintance Shulamit Aloni founded the Movement for Civil Rights and Peace in a highly publicized break from the Labour Party. Carmella had always supported Aloni's liberal positions on social and international issues, applauding her efforts to combat the coercive power of the religious parties, her defense of the rights of women in Israeli society, and her moderate foreign policy stand based on the principle of territorial compromise. The Yom Kippur War and the behavior of the Meir government pushed both Yadin and Carmella even further. Shulamit Aloni became a member of the new Rabin cabinet, and political change finally seemed possible. "Whenever Yigael would come home fuming about some political development," their friend Leon Shalit remembered of this turbulent period, "Carmella would tell him that he had to act if he wanted to change anything."

After years of evasion and rejection of political offers, then, Yadin seemed headed toward political activism, though it was still highly uncertain what form it would take. He remained adamant that he would not under any circumstances join the Labour Party, but in the spring of 1975, after he completed his work with the Agranat Commission, his fellow panel member Chaim Laskov offered him an alternative. Their mutual friend and former general staff colleague, Meir Zorea, had been holding informal discussions with various public figures about establishing a new political movement in Israel that would directly challenge the Labour Party establishment. Elections were still more than two years away (scheduled for November 1977), but Zorea's rage was building against what he saw as dangerous weakness of the Rabin government. Zorea, a plain-spoken kibbutznik with hawkish views about Israel's need for territorial security, had been a founding member of the Greater Israel Movement, which opposed any withdrawal from lands occupied in the 1967 war. Zorea, still known by his Haganah code name Zaro, was also deeply committed to a thorough reform of Israel's domestic political system. "At that time I was convinced that the Labour Party had destroyed political life in the country," Zaro recalled, "and we thought that Yadin would be the best person to stand at the head of a completely new party that was unconnected to any particular interest."

Yadin was at first reluctant to move forward with this idea, but Carmella had decided that the time was right. In fact, as Yadin later recalled, she actively encouraged him. The political situation within Israel was troubling on both the international and the domestic fronts. Prime Minister Rabin, seeking to expand his parliamentary majority, had brought the National Religious Party into his coalition after acceding to its demands. In angry protest, Aloni and her Civil Rights Movement resigned from the government, and it seemed that Israeli politics were back to business as usual. Yadin later repeated Carmella's reaction to his entering politics: " 'If I knew that you really want to do it and are ready to invest all your energy in it, I'm for it,' " she reportedly said. In June 1975, before he left with Carmella for a trip to Mexico and the United States, Yadin contacted Laskov and Zaro and told them that he was ready to explore the possibility of leading a new political movement. He suggested that they assemble a small group of like-minded people to begin serious discussions when he returned to Israel in the fall.

It was in Mexico that Carmella first felt the symptoms. As she and Yigael toured the Mayan temples and climbed the famous stepped pyramids of the Yucatán, she suddenly felt the sharp, painful signs of what seemed at the time a heart attack. Never before had health been a concern to Carmella, but after initial medical consultations in Mexico, she and

Yigael flew to New York, where they were urged to seek more extensive diagnostic testing. At the Mayo Clinic they learned the gravity of her medical situation. Carmella was suffering from a rare degenerative disease of the heart, whose effects were almost always fatal. The only hope she had, the doctors insisted, was complete bedrest for at least six months, on the slim chance that the progressive deterioration of her heart might be slowed. To Carmella, this sudden restriction of all physical activity seemed unduly severe, but the specialists they consulted in London on their way back to Israel could offer no alternative. Yigael returned to Israel in October for the beginning of the academic year and hired a nurse to care for Carmella for the hours he would not be at home. For the first time in his life, he had to run the household. His inclination was to suspend the political plans he had formulated with Laskov and Zaro the previous June.

But Carmella was not willing to have Yigael abandon his public commitment so easily. Although she acceded to the doctors' demands that she remain immobile, she continued to make lists of chores and errands for the housekeeper to run, and she still kept track of Yigael's research and publishing accounts. As she followed the news, she was determined that Yigael speak out on the most pressing issues of the day. The political scene was more turbulent than ever. During the previous August and September, U.S. secretary of state Kissinger had concluded an intense round of shuttle diplomacy between Egypt and Israel, resulting in an Israeli agreement to pull its forces back into the heart of Sinai. This agreement sharpened Israel's internal conflicts. In noisy and angry demonstrations against the Rabin government, a group of young people associated with the National Religious Party calling themselves Gush Emunim, or "Bloc of the Faithful," linked Orthodox Judaism with territorial maximalism. At the same time, Israel's economy was faltering under the burden of the enormous cost of the Yom Kippur War. Huge government deficits, raging inflation, and stringent price controls led to bitter and sometimes violent labor disputes. Carmella had always been primarily concerned with domestic political issues, and Yadin now expressed similar concerns publicly. In an interview with Israel Radio on November 22, 1975, he called on the Rabin government to appoint a deputy prime minister to coordinate domestic policy. Referring to the members of the Labour government who seemed preoccupied with foreign and security affairs, Yadin warned that "if they do not grasp the idea of leadership by the horns and grapple with the country's basic problems, they will lose the trust they enjoy, and that would be a tragedy."

Soon after Yadin had returned to Israel, Laskov and Zorea contacted him again. Both were eager to establish the new political movement they had discussed in June. They gained Yadin's agreement that each should invite an additional participant and gather for a series of political discussions at Yadin's home. Laskov's and Zorea's main interests were concentrated on foreign policy, maintaining a tough stand against both the United States and the Arab states. Laskov brought into the group Dan Tolkovsky, a former air force commander and member of the Greater Israel Movement, while Zaro invited Yuval Ne'eman, the hawkish security adviser of Defense Minister Shimon Peres. Yadin, more concerned with domestic issues, invited Dr. Mordecai Abir of the Hebrew University and Ernst Yephet, director-general of Bank Leumi. Carmella strongly supported widening the political circle, and Yadin continued to rely on her judgment. This brought up a logistical problem, since she could not leave her bed. "She said that if I wanted her to be able to express her opinion, she would have to hear all the discussions," Yadin recalled some years later. So with the approval of the other members of the discussion group, Yadin installed an intercom system between Carmella's bedroom and the living room, where the discussions were held.

In the first meetings, held in December, it quickly became clear that the participants' priorities were distressingly diverse. Yadin felt uncomfortable with the hawkish stands of Ne'eman and Tolkovsky toward the Palestinians and negotiations with Egypt—his own inclinations were somewhat more conciliatory. But Laskov and Zaro persuaded him that matters of territorial compromise were, at least at this stage, purely hypothetical, and that all decisions about Israel's ultimate borders should be deferred until the Arabs were willing to come to the negotiating table, which might be years away. Domestic reform, Laskov reportedly insisted, should be their main priority, suggesting that "the problem is with us, the Jews." In meetings in December and January, Yadin would often interrupt the discussion to confer with Carmella upstairs. "He would sometimes come up in the middle of the meeting to ask her opinion," Carmella's nurse recalled, "and if there was something she thought was wrong or that needed a reply, she would call him to tell him what she thought." In mid-January the group was no closer than it had been before to agreeing on a specific platform, beyond vague general statements about the need for Israel to present a united front to the world. Rumors nonetheless spread about secret meetings at Yadin's house of the "Party of the Generals," and he received nervous courtesy calls from representatives of both the Labour Party and the Likud. He brusquely rejected all offers to join any of the existing political parties. If he entered politics—and Yadin repeatedly stressed to his visitors that he had not definitely decided to do so—he would do it in his own way, on his own terms.

In the meantime Yadin was increasingly preoccupied with Carmella's deteriorating condition, and he made it clear to the discussion group that he could not make a further commitment of his time and energy as long as Carmella was ill. Except for the discussion group, he discouraged all visitors to the house, suggesting that well-wishers and relatives telephone instead. Friends recalled Yadin as being very protective of Carmella's weakened state and concerned that everything be quiet and peaceful in the house. She eventually was forced to reduce her physical activity. In early February, when even the smallest movement was becoming painful, she could no longer sit up in bed. During the day a nurse would sit in Carmella's bedroom, and Yadin would permit himself a few hours of work in his study. But in midafternoon he would come up to make sure that Carmella was not alone. Their elder daughter, Orly, was living in London, and Littal was serving in the army, so Yadin often shouldered the emotional and physical burden of caring for Carmella alone. He was deeply shaken that their love, their thirty-four-year marriage, and their total partnership was coming to an end.

In later years, friends and adversaries alike would claim that Carmella had always—wisely—prevented Yadin from entering politics, knowing that he was utterly unsuited to the naked opportunism, brutal deal-making, and willingness to compromise that are often keys to political success. It was only after her death, so the standard explanation went, that he succumbed to temptation and sought out the national spotlight. This version of the events was far off the mark. Up until her final days, Carmella was a full partner in Yadin's career decisions. It was she who helped him formulate his public positions and select his political strategy. Yadin later dismissed any suggestion that she had shielded him from the public. "She didn't protect me from exposure," Yadin insisted in a 1981 interview with journalist Tom Segev; "she just protected me from all kinds of nudniks who wanted to waste my time." Yadin always benefited from Carmella's skill in weighing career alternatives and judging the motives of the many people who sought his support for their organizations or political causes. Indeed, the real tragedy of Yadin's political involvement was not that he acted against Carmella's wishes; it was rather that he followed her advice and finally entered the political arena. For when she died on February 18, 1976, she left her lifelong partner suddenly alone and deeply involved in a snowballing political process whose ultimate ramifications he was unable to foresee.

The political discussion group was, by that time, ready for action. Its members were in the process of choosing between three distinct modes of political activity, each of which would take advantage of

Yadin's public image and reputation to achieve specific results. Dan Tolkovsky wanted the group to become part of the Labour Party and challenge that party's present leadership. Laskov was strongly opposed to any such partisan activity; he wanted the group to be seen as a circle of concerned, high-minded citizens who could put pressure on the government through lectures, public meetings, and newspaper columns. Their goal should be to remain aloof and above the electoral process—to propose new ideas and new administrative structures and rouse public opinion to force the government to implement them. Zaro was by far the most aggressively eager to wage political warfare against what he considered a corrupt and ineffective government; he could not be content with drawing up idealistic position papers and hoping for the best. "It became clear soon enough that the idea of changing the Labour Party from inside was unrealistic," he later recalled. "I really felt that if we collected enough strength, we could topple the walls." In early February that strength was quickly rising. A group of important, longtime Labour Party loyalists headed by former Mossad director Meir Amit contacted Zorea about joining the movement. So did the general-turned-politician Ariel Sharon.

After Carmella's death and an informal period of mourning, Yadin became the focus of increasing attention. Newspaper columns and radio commentators renewed their speculation on the possibility of his entering public life. But without his helpmate and closest adviser, he was surrounded by ambitious and energetic men who did not have—as Carmella always had—his best interests in mind. Zaro was eager for Yadin to give his final commitment to lead the new movement so that he could issue a public announcement and begin organizing. But Yadin refused to be rushed. Carmella had planned an overseas lecture tour for him in late March and April, and he was intent on carrying it out. A stage in his life was clearly ending; his longtime adversary Yohanan Aharoni had died in early February, and continuing the feud with Aharoni's successors had little appeal. Political activity seemed destined to claim all his energies in the coming years. Yadin assured Zaro that he would have a definite answer about his political future when he returned to Israel. But his mind was already made up. Shortly before his departure, Yadin was contacted by Eli Ayyal, a political commentator for Israel Television who had pestered and prodded him for an exclusive interview for months. Yadin had always refused to be questioned about his political beliefs on live television, but in March 1976, when Ayyal once again invited Yadin to appear on the popular *Moked* interview program, Yadin did not reject the offer out of hand. "Call me when I get back," he reportedly told him, a clear indication that his time had indeed arrived.

When Yadin returned to Israel several weeks later, rumors and excitement were rampant. The man who had for so long stayed out of the public limelight now seemed headed toward national leadership. As promised, Ayyal contacted Yadin, and he readily agreed to an interview. A prime-time television appearance was scheduled for May 25. The people of Israel eagerly awaited his message. No one could have possibly predicted the outcome in those days of hope and anticipation, but Yadin's decision to enter active politics would prove to be the most tragic mistake of his life.

Chapter Sixteen

THE RISE AND FALL OF DASH

I n the air-conditioned darkness of the studio at Television House in Jerusalem, Yadin had only a few moments to prepare himself. Ever since word had leaked out that he was to appear on *Moked*—the country's most avidly watched interview program—many Israelis waited expectantly for his words of rescue and reassurance, for the announcement that he would indeed offer himself as a candidate for national leadership. It was a measure of the public's dissatisfaction with the current Labour government—bogged down in economic malaise and under increasing international pressure—that the voters were so eager to follow a leader about whom they actually knew so little. But that was becoming a common phenomenon in the television age. At that very moment in America an obscure politician named Jimmy Carter was poised to capture his party's presidential nomination. With enough prime-time exposure, anything seemed possible. In a candid interview four years later, Yadin described the dangerous power of the image that launched his own career in politics. "What did the people who believed in me really know about me?" he rhetorically asked journalist Tom Segev. "They knew that I had been chief of staff. That I was with Ben-Gurion and that I was one of the only ones who dared to stand up to him. That I was young then and not yet completely bald. They admired me as an archaeologist, because I'm an excellent lecturer. I'm the only person in the country who can fill the Hall of Culture for a lecture on Masada. *That* was what my image was built on. But did the people really ask themselves what kind of a person I was? How I really was? As a leader, as an administrator, how I was in relations with other people? People," he concluded sadly, much wiser in the fickle ways of the electorate, "just didn't ask."

On May 25, 1976, at nine-thirty p.m., Yigael Yadin enjoyed his first intoxicating moment in that dangerously uncritical public spotlight. Over the years he had gained on-camera experience as the host of a popular program called *News about Antiquities,* in which he had presented the latest archaeological discoveries to the Israeli viewing public with elegance and wit. For twenty-five years Yadin had enjoyed the luxury of only occasionally speaking out about public issues, then being able to retreat to his study at any time he wished. Carmella had always been there to schedule his public appearances, to select his shirt and tie, and to help him tailor his message. But now under the glare of the studio's klieg lights, as the stage manager counted down the last ten seconds before air time, as the red light blinked on the main camera, and as correspondent Eli Ayyal began his introduction, Yadin was alone. During the next thirty minutes he put on a competent if not overwhelmingly charismatic performance, answering Ayyal's questions about domestic and international affairs smoothly and confidently. He offered no new solutions to the country's problems but gave the people what they wanted to hear. Yadin's was the voice not of Masada but of reason, underlining the social problems of the nation, the need for domestic reform, and the need for territorial concessions to the Arabs in order to achieve a just and lasting peace. He refused to answer Ayyal's point-blank question about his political intentions ("I'm considering it," he replied coyly, "but first I intend to travel the length and breadth of this country to investigate the whole subject."), but Yadin's full-time political career had nevertheless begun.

Yadin's appearance on *Moked* would long be remembered as a historic event, marking the beginning of a serious challenge to the static constellation of Zionist parties founded in the prestate period. After his appearance he was besieged by well-wishers and obsequious political figures who could not afford to ignore the potential threat that he posed. As he had promised, he toured the country and in lectures and impromptu stump speeches he began to articulate a vision reminiscent of the national social mobilization that he had tried to implement many years before as chief of staff. In an address to the Tel Aviv Press Club in July, he strongly urged the IDF to assign units to rebuild Israel's inner cities. It was crucial, he believed, that the army "carry out other goals in addition to security." His opinions on the occupied territories and relations with the Arabs remained vague and more or less identical with the position of the Labour Party, but there was one point about which Yadin remained absolutely clear. The elections scheduled for November 1977 were still more than a year away, but he promised that if he *did* decide to establish a new political movement and if that movement gained enough Knesset seats to be included in the next government, its central demand would be the complete reform of the electoral system and new elections within six months.

Through the summer and into the autumn, many of the early members of Yadin's discussion circle feared they were losing control of the movement. Most of them had been initially motivated by frustration at what they saw as the Rabin government's surrender to U.S. pressure in its withdrawal in Sinai, and by fear of a likely additional withdrawal from the West Bank and Golan Heights. To their dismay, they now found that Yadin favored territorial concessions, a position he made public in his first *Moked* interview. Since then, domestic reform had become his main focus, and he refused to be further pinned down on questions of territory, repeating that any discussion would be purely hypothetical and perhaps even counterproductive until the Arab states were ready to negotiate. Yadin wanted to broaden the scope of movement beyond retired generals and public figures, and so he began private discussions with the leaders of Oded, a political group formed by North African immigrant activists to improve social conditions and expand economic opportunities for Israel's Sephardim. Yadin also established contact with the liberal political movement known as Shinui or "Change," which had been formed by a prominent group of intellectuals, industrialists, and private citizens during the political protests that immediately followed the Yom Kippur War. Its most prominent spokesman was Dr. Amnon Rubinstein of Tel Aviv University, a legal scholar and journalist who had been an unstinting critic of the Agranat Commission. At the time, Yadin had been deeply offended by Rubinstein's criticism, but now the leader of Shinui had something tangible to offer him.

On the surface Rubinstein's political positions seemed strikingly close to Yadin's. Both sought a liberal, centrist political bloc that would shoulder aside the traditional parties and modernize Israeli society and political life. In close accord with Yadin's public proclamations, the goal of Shinui was to reform Israel's economy, social services, and electoral system on the model of progressive Western democracies. Thus from Yadin's first interview on *Moked* and in his subsequent tour Amnon Rubinstein realized that Yadin was an ideal public personality to head this movement. "Give me a general and a million dollars," he recalled telling Shulamit Aloni, "and I can change the nation." Shinui already had the million thanks to the generosity of liberal donors and members' contributions; it also had party offices, committees, and membership lists. But it lacked a high-visibility leader. Rubinstein's challenge was therefore to forge a political alliance with General Yadin. Despite the misgivings of some of Yadin's closest advisers, Yadin and his circle held secret negotiations with the leadership of Shinui through October and early November. And on November 22, 1976, at a festive press conference in Jerusalem, Yadin announced the formation of a new grassroots political organization called Hatenuah Hademocratit, the "Democratic Movement." Within a few days, the leaders of Shinui voted to merge with it, and the name was slightly altered to Hatenuah Hademocratit le-Shinui, the "Democratic Movement for Change."

The new composite party, known to the public by the acronym Dash, quickly gained political momentum. Events in early December made the need to reform the political system far clearer than Yadin's speeches could ever have done. On December 10, Prime Minister Yitzhak Rabin proudly hosted a VIP ceremony at Ben-Gurion Airport to welcome the first F-15 Phantoms that Israel had obtained in a recent arms agreement with the United States. Rabin had always been an advocate of expanding Israel's conventional military power, but it was the timing of the ceremony—rather than the military purchase it celebrated—that ultimately brought his government down. For the welcoming ceremony was held late on a Friday afternoon in midwinter, with the onset of the Sabbath dangerously close. By the time the jets landed, the speeches were delivered, and the invited guests were dispersing, darkness had already fallen. Two days later, the outraged religious parties introduced a no-confidence motion in the Knesset against the government for its shameless violation of the sanctity of the Sabbath. Even the leaders of the National Religious Party who were members of Rabin's coalition felt compelled to vote against the government for its disregard of religious sensibilities. But Rabin was ready, and he responded with a clever and surprising political move. Sensing the growing public interest in Yadin's reformist party and the sentiment against the exaggerated power of the religious parties in Israeli society, he fired the religious ministers who had voted against him, resigned as prime minister, and called for early elections the coming spring.

The leaders of Dash had not expected elections to be held until November; now their full-time activity had to move into high gear. Taking over the former Shinui offices in Tel Aviv, the interim ruling council of Dash appointed Zaro to establish and coordinate local branches throughout the country. He quickly took charge with his blunt, no-nonsense manner: He scheduled regular meetings of volunteers in the Tel Aviv headquarters and closely monitored party recruitment in the regional offices. Zaro lacked the elegance of Yadin and the intellectual airs of the Shinui faction, but he was determined to see Dash accomplish an electoral revolution. The necessary work of chairing meetings, overseeing administration, hand-shaking would-be voters, and backslapping loyal supporters was nothing that Yadin could have taken on.

Prospects seemed promising for a political upheaval. The internal councils of the Labour party descended into internal squabbling, primarily between Rabin and Peres, who were fighting for the top position on the Labour list for the coming elections. In contrast to Labour, Dash emerged as a serious element on the political scene. Yadin, though not particularly active in day-to-day party operations, was a powerful symbol to Israelis. It seemed probable that his Dash list could attract enough votes to win a place in the next government coalition. Not surprisingly, some prominent politicians jumped onto the Dash bandwagon as it gained momentum, bringing into Yadin's inner circle a discordant mixture of personalities and political views.

From the beginning Yadin was insistent that Dash members disavow allegiance to any other political organization. He believed that reforming the Israeli governmental system should be a shared, nonpartisan goal. For that reason, Yadin avoided demanding unity on foreign policy questions. Because the members of his movement differed widely in their views on the future boundaries of Israel and on the political rights of the Palestinian Arabs, Yadin asked only that his group unify around ideals of domestic change, economic growth, and electoral reform. That was enough to attract Shmuel Tamir, head of the small Knesset faction called the Free Center, as well as a breakaway faction of longtime Labour Party activists headed by Meir Amit. Another stringent precondition for admission to the party was that all new members' political resources (campaign funds, membership lists, and local organizations) were to be transferred to Dash; current Knesset members who wanted to join had to resign their seats. With his typical idealism Yadin sought to create something entirely new on the Israeli political landscape: a unified, reform-minded grassroots movement with no internal factions fighting among themselves.

Here Yadin was not in touch with reality. He had lived a sheltered and pampered existence for so long that he failed to see that the struggle for power is an inevitable part of political life. So instead of confronting that reality and viewing his new allies within Dash as potential competitors or even enemies, he remained aloof and passive at the head of the organization, with the aristocratic demeanor of someone who believed that he had been born to rule. Unquestionably his reformist political ideas and calls for spiritual and economic rebirth struck a responsive chord with the public. But unbeknownst to the public, he was losing control of the Dash party machinery. The Knesset elections were set for May 17, so the Dash central committee scheduled internal elections on March 15 to select party officers and to nominate a list of Knesset candidates. In this internal election Yadin's laudable reformist instincts were steamrolled by hard political realities. Dash adopted the principle of the grassroots primary (in sharp contrast to the closed-door nominating committees of the established parties), opening its selection process to every member, Jewish and non-Jewish alike. Dash had previously decided that membership should be available to every Israeli citizen, and appeals went out now to minority voters, particularly the Druze communities of the Carmel and the Galilee. The forthcoming Dash primary elections, to be held at branches all over the country, were hailed in the press as the dawn of a bright, new democratic era for Israel. But as Zaro later put it with characteristic bluntness, "everyone started running after the Druze for votes."

Although there were no longer supposed to be any factions within Dash, the main political figures—Rubinstein, Tamir, Amit, and even those most loyal to Yadin—campaigned intensively among the Druze villages, where large blocs of voters could be gained through the right contacts with village leaders. As a result of a complex statistical system that Dash adopted to analyze the voting results, its Knesset list seemed strangely unbalanced. Yadin was in the top position, followed by Rubinstein, Amit, Tamir, and Zorea. But the former members of Oded, who were expected to attract Sephardic voters in the coming national elections, did poorly; the proportion of Dash members from the small Druze minority was relatively insignificant, but there were two Druze candidates among the top thirteen names on the Dash list. In the weeks that followed, the sorry spectacle of charges and counter charges of corruption and voting irregularities did little to raise the prestige of Dash in the eyes of the public. But the Labour Party had no reason for celebration either. In addition to its potential problems with Dash, there was the threat of the Likud. Despite Begin's recent heart attack, the Likud's up-and-coming leader Ezer Weizman was running an exceptionally aggressive campaign. Unpleasant challenges continued to shake the Rabin government. During a March 1977 visit to Washington to meet the newly inaugurated president Jimmy Carter, Rabin learned of American intentions to force a complete Israeli withdrawal from the occupied territories in order to achieve a comprehensive Middle Eastern peace agreement. Soon after his return to Israel, an investigative journalist revealed that, in direct violation of Israel's stringent foreign currency restrictions, the prime minister's wife, Leah, maintained a small personal account in U.S. dollars in a Washington bank. That was enough to topple Rabin's already-teetering leadership of the Labour Party. Thus with only a few weeks remaining before the election, Shimon Peres assumed the leadership of the badly shaken Labour Party campaign.

The impossible suddenly seemed about to happen. Despite the negative publicity over the primaries and Yadin's sometimes indecisive leadership, it seemed probable that Dash would receive enough votes to force the Labour Party to accept it as a coalition partner—and would thereby be able to impose its reformist demands. In the last two weeks of the campaign, in stump speeches, radio interviews, and published manifestos, Yadin continually emphasized Dash's seven inviolable principles for joining the next government:

- A strict limit on the number of ministers, and the formation of a special ministerial committee with joint responsibility for economic and social reform.
- Adoption of an emergency economic program to reduce inflation, slash government expenditures, and encourage the development of export industries.
- A special government effort to establish and maintain fair contracts with workers in the public sector, to avoid disruptive strikes and labor unrest.
- Formulation of a high-priority plan for rebuilding inner cities and disadvantaged neighborhoods.
- Immediate drafting and passage of an electoral reform bill, and elections to be held under the new system within two years.
- New legislation to regulate the campaign financing and internal administrative procedures of all political parties.
- Adoption of a foreign policy that did not diverge from Dash's previously stated principles of territorial compromise in return for a secure and lasting peace.

On the evening of May 17, 1977, hopes were high in the Dash head-quarters that the new political movement was about to make history. Voter turnout was heavy, and Dash was expected to gain enough "mandates" or Knesset seats to implement far-reaching change. The bottles of champagne were ready, and the party was about to begin. But at eleven o'clock, when the official results were broadcast over Israel Television, Yadin and his colleagues were struck dumb by the electoral mathematics. Labour had received thirty-two mandates, and Dash had received fifteen. The long dominance of Labour Zionism was indeed over, due at least in part to Dash's uncompromising calls for reform. The political predominance of Socialist Zionism had been seriously challenged for the first time since the 1930s. But Yadin and most Dash activists had overlooked the possibility that their relentless campaign against the corruption and impotence of the Labour Party would bolster the fortunes of the conservative Likud. For decades, Jabotinsky's Revisionists and Begin's post-1948 Herut party had been outside the political mainstream, strident critics of the socialist ideal. During the War of Independence, Yadin—as a member of Ben-Gurion's inner circle—had himself helped curb their power in the sinking of the Irgun ship *Altalena*, in the days following Bernadotte's assassination, and in the German reparation riots of 1952. Under the leadership of Ben-Gurion, Sharett, Eshkol, and Meir, Mapai institutions had become fixtures in Israel. But now, due in part to Yadin's Dash, the office of prime minister lay within Menachem Begin's grasp. For in this election the Likud had received forty-three mandates. With the twenty that the religious and far right-wing parties had gained, Likud would be able to command a narrow majority in the 120-seat Knesset. Yadin had helped make history, but instead of becoming Israel's political redeemer, he was now powerless to direct the course of events. The Zionist right had finally gained a position of political supremacy, and there was little that either Labour or Dash could do. "We didn't hold the balance of power, and it was possible for them to get along without us," Yadin later painfully remembered. "That was the real tragedy. And from there all the troubles began."

Even as late as the 1970s, Menachem Begin, with his fastidious manners, tie, handkerchief, and slickly combed hair, was still regarded as a symbol and spokesman for the hundreds of thousands of Eastern European clerks, shopkeepers, and professionals who had come to Palestine as refugees but who had found no attraction in the socialist bureaucracy of Mapai. Begin had emerged as the archenemy and constant critic of Ben-

Gurion and had eventually shared his antisocialist, ultranationalist message to the inhabitants of Israel's slums and poor neighborhoods who had grown tired of Mapai paternalism. He was also in a position to forge an alliance with the religious parties, especially the young activists of Gush Emunim, "the Bloc of the Faithful," who were determined to expand Jewish settlements throughout the biblical Land of Israel. Now Begin had lived to see his hour of triumph. In one of his first public acts after the election, he demonstrated his devotion to Greater Israel: together with arch-hawk Ariel Sharon and Yosef Burg of the National Religious Party, he visited a newly established Gush Emunim settlement near Nablus, named Elon Moreh.

At this time of nationalistic euphoria for the victorious Likud and its allies, the leadership of Dash had to decide what to do. Their challenge was to serve the nation and to uphold the "seven principles" on which they had based their campaign. Although Begin's parliamentary majority seemed secure, Likud officials soon made contact with the Dash leadership, and a tentative, cautious round of negotiations began. Begin's delicate health was a question and the sixty-three-member coalition was too narrow for comfort, so the inclusion of Dash in the Begin government would considerably improve its durability. But Yadin insisted on remaining true to his convictions in the negotiations. At first, it seemed as if an agreement would be possible. The Likud negotiators were willing to discuss the immediate drafting of an electoral reform bill. As for future of the occupied territories, they were even willing to propose that no move to annexation be made while diplomatic negotiations with any Arab states were under way. Yadin and other Dash leaders came to believe that they might have a moderating influence if they were to join the Begin government. The post of defense minister had already been allotted to Ezer Weizman, but the foreign ministry was still open, and Yadin was an obvious candidate. All indications pointed toward an early Dash-Likud agreement, until an audacious political maneuver by Menachem Begin suddenly brought the negotiations to a halt.

On Sunday morning, May 22, just five days after the elections, one of Begin's spokesmen announced the appointment of a foreign minister for the new government. The nominee possessed considerable diplomatic and military experience, and though he was not a member of the Likud, the spokesman explained, Mr. Begin believed that he could offer the new government considerable international credibility. Moshe Dayan, who had resigned from the defense ministry under a cloud, was now making a comeback as Israel's highest-ranking diplomat, thanks to a politician even more coldly pragmatic than he. When Yadin learned of this appointment, he was outraged and immediately suspended negotiations.

Begin went ahead without him, and presented his new government in the Knesset on June 20, confident that he would eventually lure Dash into his cabinet. Begin recognized that the Dash leaders were just beginners; he was the ultimate professional. Rather than fill all the ministerial posts and thereby burn all his bridges, Begin announced that he was leaving open the ministries of justice, labor, welfare, and transportation (as well as the post of deputy prime minister) just in case Dash decided to reconsider joining the government.

With the bait dangling before them, the Dash leaders were deeply divided. Throughout the summer the negotiations went on in fits and starts, and a serious rift developed between those who preferred to remain in the opposition and those who insisted that political reform could be effected only from *within* the government. As the months dragged on and Dash appeared less and less certain of its role in the new political landscape, Begin sensed its weakness. He appealed directly to Yadin to fulfill his responsibility to the Dash voters and accept a position that Yadin himself had proposed during the campaign: the post of deputy prime minister, with special responsibility to coordinate the administration of national social services and supervise the reconstruction of the country's poor neighborhoods. Yadin, however, replied that Dash was less concerned with governmental positions than with ethical obligations. Its seven principles all had to be adopted, without horse-trading or compromise. At the beginning of August, Yadin held a press conference in Tel Aviv to announce that Dash had decided to remain in the opposition. But this did not stop pressure from building within Dash between those who adamantly refused to join the government and those who wanted to snap at the still-dangling bait.

One of the most eager to join the government was Shmuel Tamir, a talented trial lawyer and experienced politician who had resigned his Knesset seat to join Dash and had established a special relationship with Yadin. Tamir was born and raised in Rechavia and had attended Chassiya Sukenik's kindergarten, but later in life his political path had diverged from Yadin's. Long associated with the Revisionist movement, he had eventually dared to challenge Begin's leadership of Herut. In recent years he had led a small Knesset faction called the Free Center but had found a common language with Yadin. In fact, he had provided Yadin with the kind of support that no one else in Dash had been willing to provide. "Yadin never felt at home in the political arena," recalled Maya Bailey, Yadin's secretary and administrative assistant, "and Tamir was the one who did the work for him." For so many years Yadin had been relieved of direct contact "with all kinds of nudniks," but now kissing babies, handshaking, and backslapping were part of the political game. "Tamir did all that," Maya Bailey continued, "and he gave the impression that he was doing it all for Yadin. Yadin respected him as being bright, but the only problem was that Tamir was brilliant in anything that did not have to do with his own political career." Tamir was determined to crown his legal career by becoming minister of justice. Yadin eventually became so dependent on Tamir's constant practical advice and assistance—perhaps as a replacement for the help he had always received from Carmella—that he allowed himself to be seduced into joining the Begin government without achieving any of his political goals.

The pace of events sped up in early October, soon after the United States and the Soviet Union issued a joint communiqué announcing their sponsorship of Middle East peace talks in Geneva and hinting that they were prepared to impose a solution if the warring sides could not settle their problems themselves. Begin was in the meantime laying the groundwork for far more daring diplomacy with the help of Foreign Minister Dayan. To succeed, he knew he had to broaden his coalition, and he began to turn the pressure on Dash, by announcing that he would soon fill the four vacant ministries. Shmuel Tamir began to get nervous. When Yadin was temporarily out of the country, Tamir secretly and single-handedly revived the coalition negotiations that had been suspended for months. Defense Minister Weizman put on more pressure when he met Tamir by chance at a Tel Aviv social function; he taunted Tamir about Yadin's self-righteousness and reluctance to act like a normal politician. "This Sukenik of yours," Weizman teased—using Yadin's former surname in its literal meaning of "cloth peddler"—"hasn't done a damn thing since he found Bar-Kokhba's sandal, and now he thinks he's discovered America. I'm warning you—if you don't join the government, you'll fall apart."

Tamir sensed that he had only limited time. Begin was threatening to fill the positions, and the Shinui faction's opposition to joining Begin's coalition was strong. So Tamir went to work intensively on Yadin—at first in daily telephone calls to him in hotels across America, then in person upon his return. Tamir suggested that the coming Geneva conference and threat of superpower pressure required that the nation be united—which meant as broad a government coalition as possible. Another argument was Dash's debt to its voters—it could never get anything done as a mere protest group on the outside. Last and most intriguing were the rumors that Begin's health was failing; if Yadin accepted the appointment as deputy prime minister, he would be in a perfect position to succeed Begin at a time of national emergency. "Yadin knew he was being manipulated, yet he let it happen," Maya Bailey observed. "He had the feeling that Tamir knew what he was doing—that he was a very experienced politician—and Yadin was very, very naive."

On October 20 Dash formally joined the government of Menachem Begin, having gained nothing more than the official government positions that they had always claimed to scorn. Not one of their seven principles was accepted or even discussed. It was now all a matter of position: Yadin became deputy prime minister, Meir Amit became minister of transport, Israel Katz became minister of labor, and Shmuel Tamir became minister of justice, just as he had always hoped. Amnon Rubinstein and many of the Shinui faction members bitterly opposed the development and quickly grew disillusioned with Dash's emasculated public image and Yadin's pitifully weak leadership. "If Yadin had stayed out of the government," Rubinstein later suggested, "Dash would have prospered." But this assessment overlooks the effects of Yadin's personal insecurities. Joining the government was just the beginning of an even more unfortunate political adventure. "From that point on," Maya Bailey recalled, "what happened was that instead of Tamir manipulating Yadin, it was Begin who started manipulating him."

During much of his adult life, Yigael Yadin had been a participant in some of the most decisive moments in the history of the State of Israel. But serving as deputy prime minister from 1977 to 1981, he played an increasingly marginal role. During the long months of off-and-on coalition negotiations, Moshe Dayan had carried out a series of secret diplomatic missions to India, to Iran, to meet with King Hussein in London, and with King Hassan of Morocco in Rabat. His goal was to create an alternative to the superpower-sponsored conference: direct diplomacy. President Anwar el-Sadat of Egypt, equally afraid of what the Americans and Soviets might choose to impose on his country, took the dramatic step of flying to Israel on November 19, 1977. Of all the members of the Israeli cabinet, only Yadin had had experience in direct negotiations with Egypt, but this was Begin, Weizman, and Dayan's shining moment and Yadin was shunted to the side. His participation in Sadat's visit was strictly ceremonial. Still, Sadat had been thoroughly briefed on the political leaders he was likely to meet in the receiving line at the airport, and he interrupted Begin's introduction of his new deputy prime minister. "I know," Sadat reportedly said with mistaken confidence, "this is the head of the Progressive Movement for Change."

Yadin was never invited to join the inner working group of Weizman, Dayan, and Begin, the architects of the evolving Israeli policy toward Egypt. His subsequent meetings with Sadat were brief and entirely formal. Paired by protocol with the Egyptian deputy prime minister, Hassan Tehomi, he was never consulted and rarely informed about

diplomatic intentions and strategies. Here, too, his failing was political
rather than intellectual, for Yadin's understanding of ancient, medieval,
and modern Egypt was far more sophisticated than the brutal realpolitik
of Begin and Dayan. Although he had innovative ideas on the peace
process, he never managed to present them aggressively or fight for them
with total conviction. Dayan and Weizman's ideas were not in essence or
in principle more acceptable, but they played the game of international
politics with gusto, while Yadin preferred to wait his turn and speak
softly and reasonably. As a result, he always took a back seat. Yadin was
conspicuously excluded from the talks at Camp David. Although he was
regularly briefed on the progress of the negotiations in the Maryland
mountains, it was more of a matter of courtesy than of meaningful consultation. It was Yadin's function as acting prime minister merely to brief
the other minor cabinet ministers on the status of the peace talks. It was
an obvious slight and a painful loss of status for a man who hardly
needed the trappings of office of the deputy prime minister to consider
himself a success in life.

What was it that caused Yadin to accept public humiliation and
abandon all of his proclaimed political ideals? Colleagues recall that
Yadin's admiration for Begin was nearly boundless—an ironic reversal of
the view of Begin as archenemy during all the years of Yadin's service
with the Haganah. "The Begin that I knew as prime minister," Yadin
recalled at the end of his government service, using words usually reserved for saints and other holy figures, "was incredibly tolerant. I admire him and honor him. And I admire him because I was a direct
witness to the incredible strength of will he showed in overcoming his
illnesses and carrying out his mission to the best of his ability." Yadin's
admiration was not repaid adequately by any standard, for it was clear
that Begin held Yadin in his power by manipulating Yadin's sense of duty
and playing on his exaggerated sense of loyalty. Throughout the Dash
campaign Yadin had proclaimed his determination to bring about a renewal of the Israeli social fabric. He had strived for the same ideal even
during his tenure of chief of staff and in his periodic campaigns for electoral reform. But Begin, a canny and experienced politician, was able to
keep Yadin content and loyal without having to expend any political
capital. Begin made Yadin feel that he had been entrusted with responsibility for solving pressing social problems, even as the budgets for social
programs were slashed. He had appointed Yadin deputy prime minister
but kept him in the dark on diplomatic plans and security strategies.
Bailey recalled that one of Begin's favorite tactics was to summon Yadin
to his office for urgent one-on-one consultations. The subject would not
be important, nor would its practical outcome. These private meetings

were opportunities for Begin to reassure Yadin that despite the criticism of the press and the public, his role in the government *was* crucial to the betterment of Israeli society. Unfortunately, because Yadin had long left administrative affairs to others, he had never developed the ability to distinguish between an ideal and the likelihood of its being attained. All that was important to him was that he remained faithful to his mission— his destiny—in political life, and Begin assured him that he was. "Yadin was always euphoric after these meetings," Bailey remembered. "Begin made him eat out of the palm of his hand in a way that was undignified.

"It was insulting how he was treated," she continued, "and the sad part of it was that he never considered resigning. Yadin had lots of other reasons to resign, because Dash did not achieve any of its aims in joining the government." But Yadin was unable to recognize what was happening to him as long as he believed that he was serving Israel's best interests. Once he had arrived at a decision about where those interests lay, he would not be moved. When Begin requested that Yadin delay discussion of an electoral reform plan for an indeterminate period (so as not to upset Israel's delicate international position), Yadin acceded, thereby subjecting his Dash colleagues to public scorn. In October 1977, in an effort to humiliate Dash, Gad Yaakobi of Labour proposed legislation that was strikingly similar to Dash's electoral reform plan. The Begin government officially announced its opposition to the legislation, and Yadin called the Dash Knesset faction together to persuade them either to vote against Yaakobi's bill or to abstain. The loyal Yadin could not conceive of violating his solemn personal allegiance to the prime minister as a member of the government. As a result, he participated in defeating a cause he had actively championed for twenty years.

Within less than a year of joining the Begin government, the Democratic Movement for Change was on the verge of an open split. Zaro, an early supporter of joining the government, was among the first to declare his disgust at Dash's pitiful political impotence, and he resigned his Knesset seat. "I wanted to bring about a change in the country," Zaro remembered, "and Yadin bothered me because he seemed to be completely seduced by Begin at this time." His hopes that Dash could serve as a moderating influence or even implement some of its promised reforms from within the government were all now shown to be chimerical. During the debate over the Camp David accords, the split became open and official. The Dash members and ministers in the government coalition thenceforth called themselves the Democratic Movement, while those who opposed continued compromise and stalemate (Amnon Rubinstein and Meir Amit among them) went over to the opposition as a faction that they pointedly called *Shinui ve-Yozma*, or "Change and Initiative." Political scientist Allen E. Shapiro, writing in *The Jerusalem Post* at this time of crushed dreams and lost hopes, called Yadin "not a false Messiah, but an irrelevant one."

The truth of this assessment became especially evident in the cabinet debate over the West Bank, another issue on which Dash had promised its voters it would remain firmly committed to principle. Although Yadin had obtained an assurance from Begin before joining the government that he could appeal cabinet decisions relating to the establishment of new Jewish settlements on the West Bank, that concession had no practical effect. For the most part, these decisions were left entirely up to Agriculture Minister Ariel Sharon and Defense Minister Ezer Weizman. Their classification of new settlements as "expansions" of existing ones struck Yadin as a shameless deception and his verbal clashes on this subject with Sharon in particular grew increasingly intense. Sometimes Yadin threatened to resign if he were not granted the right of appeal he had been promised, but his threat carried little weight. The Democratic Movement dwindled to four members, leaving Yadin little power to defend its opposition to the establishment of new Jewish settlements in densely populated Arab areas.

The breakup of Dash directly affected Yadin's standing in the cabinet. In January 1979 the National Religious Party, always looking for an opening, demanded more representation in the government and rejected out of hand Yadin's meek proposal that he take a NRP representative as deputy in his own ministry. Yadin's fatal political flaw was that he was unwilling to interact with people—friends, colleagues, adversaries, and enemies—either to impose his will on them or to compromise. "Yadin was really a loner," Bailey noted, confirming what his colleagues in the army and archaeology already knew. "He was not at all a social person. Even though he was charming at social gatherings, he put it on. He put it on because he had the talent for it, but it was never from the heart. He really liked to be alone and he was happiest not being bothered by anyone." Begin understood how to deal with him and was not taken in by Yadin's personal myth. Slowly it became clear that Yadin was not the leader the people had hoped for. Despite his eloquent dissenting speeches, he never did anything against the government, or to stop the settlements, or to change the direction of the peace process.

Even before Dash joined the coalition, Begin had announced the "vital national challenge" of reshaping the country's neighborhoods. This national call to action at least superficially fulfilled one of Yadin's most important social objectives. And eager to gain legitimation for his participation in the government, Yadin had enthusiastically accepted the task of chairing a ministerial committee on social welfare. Sadly, this task force proved not to be an efficient working group dedicated to address-ing complex social problems but an arbitrary assemblage of powerful politicians, each with interests to defend. In August 1978, Yadin an-nounced the initiation of a wide-ranging program he called Project Re-newal, dedicated to the physical and spiritual revitalization of many of Israel's poorest neighborhoods. He called on his many philanthropic contacts to invest in Israel's future and succeeded not only in raising funds but in rousing the donors' enthusiasm for the enormous task. Yadin intended Project Renewal to encourage young people to take the lead in rebuilding their communities while the government helped re-construct sewers, sidewalks, and water systems. His goal and his vision were to create a core of people who would help shape the future of their neighborhoods. But as an archaeologist, Yadin had become accustomed to dealing with social forces as abstractions. And as an aristocrat by nature, he had little real understanding of or even contact with the kinds of people he was now eager to help.

Hopes quickly faded for Project Renewal, which Yadin had focused on as his main effort. Bogged down by bureaucratic inefficiency, ob-structed by his own cold, analytical approach to human problems and by continual budget cutting, it had little possibility of effectively dealing with Israel's pressing urban problems. In 1979 important American and Cana-dian donors began withdrawing their support from the project, claiming "everything was so disorganized. The bureaucracy is a cruel joke." At the end of November 1980 a newly appointed finance minister, Yigal Hurvitz (who in any case preferred to allocate funds to West Bank settlements rather than inner-city slums), declared Project Renewal a dangerously in-flationary undertaking and froze all funds that had been earmarked for it. For the first time in his tenure in the government, Yadin refused to be ignored or stampeded. Asserting that Project Renewal was the only mean-ingful social program the Begin government had undertaken, he issued an ultimatum: If the funds remained frozen, he would have no alternative but to resign. Unlike the young Sukenik who had bitterly disputed Ben-Gurion over the 1952 military budget, Yadin now, twenty-seven years older and politically far weaker, lacked the power to carry through on his convictions. Hurvitz remained firm on eliminating the social welfare as-pects of the Project Renewal budget, retaining only the construction con-tracts. The hopes that Yadin himself had raised among young people in big-city slums were disappointed. Despite his noble intentions, Yadin failed to convince or compel other political actors to accept his priorities. In June 1980 even Mordecai Virshubski, a member of the original Dash list for the Knesset and a strong supporter of social reform, attacked Proj-ect Renewal as an "administrative monster" and "complete failure." Few remaining in power—except perhaps Yadin himself—would now disagree.

If one moment in Yadin's government service can be pointed to as a pleasure, it was his state visit to Egypt in the summer of 1979. At least briefly, Yadin was again at his best. Taking along his younger daughter Littal, his friend Joseph Aviram, and his secretary Maya Bailey, he was given a VIP archaeological tour conducted by the director of the Egyptian Antiquities Service. At the head of an official delegation and accompanied by a large press entourage, Yadin was treated royally; he could escape the endless criticism and questions about coalition politics, his relationship to Begin, and Project Renewal. His schedule was filled with ceremonial, scholarly, and diplomatic assignments. After laying a wreath at Egypt's Tomb of the Unknown Soldier, he visited a Cairo synagogue, then proceeded on to the Cairo Museum, where he had a chance to see artifacts and inscriptions he had studied and written about only through drawings and photographs. Clearly he was being cultivated as a "dovish" member of the Israeli cabinet, in highly publicized meetings with Foreign Minister Butros Butros Ghali and as the guest of honor at a state dinner hosted by Defense Minister Kamal Ali. But for Yadin, the high point of the journey was his trip to Upper Egypt to view the monuments of Luxor, Aswan, and Abu Simbel. During his visit to the massive Temple of Karnak, an organized welcoming demonstration of schoolchildren brought him back—if briefly, humorously, and unintentionally—to the internal rivalries and struggles of Israeli politics. Upon arriving at the temple, they greeted him with a shouted smiling chorus: "Dayan! Dayan! Dayan!" An embarrassed member of the official Egyptian entourage quickly corrected the error, and the welcoming crowd began the chant again: "Yadin! Yadin! Yadin!"

He returned home to serious problems, to what Maya Bailey recalled as a grim and increasingly untenable situation that faced them both. "I stayed with him for two years, and already during the second year, I literally sat at an empty desk," she recalled, "At first there were constantly calls and papers and problems, and slowly it diminished to practically no calls, no papers, nothing was happening." There was little for Yadin to do for Project Renewal; most of the work was being carried out by the ministries of housing, labor, education, and social welfare. "I couldn't take it," Bailey recalled. "It was so insulting and I said to him, 'Even if you don't care about your own reputation . . . there is a certain responsibility we have to the people that voted for you, that gave you their complete confidence. Don't you feel that you owe it to them to leave the government?' He said, 'No, you don't understand, I have to go with this to the bitter end.'"

Most of Yadin's colleagues from this period simply shook their heads, unable to fathom how such a dramatic change could have come over a man like Yadin, but Bailey placed his political performance in a broader perspective. "There was a certain weakness in him, and it had to do with his upbringing or his education," she observed years later. "It had to do with his totally distorted view of loyalty—loyalty to the government—loyalty to the court. He still tried to pretend that what he was doing was having some kind of an impact on the poor masses out there in those development towns and neighborhoods. But he was kidding himself that he was doing a job and that he had to carry it out to the bitter end. His loyalty was completely distorted—because it finally served Begin to the utmost and totally destroyed Dash."

———

Dr. Elizabeth Podkaminer had met Yadin many years before, when he came to see her as a cardiac patient; their patient-doctor relationship had expanded into a deeper friendship as she and her husband got to know Yigael and Carmella on a social basis. Yadin trusted her medical judgment completely, and Dr. Podkaminer recalled that even if Yigael was traveling outside the country when he took sick or felt unwell, he wouldn't hesitate to telephone her for advice. After Carmella died, Yigael visited Dr. Podkaminer more frequently (her husband had died in July 1976). "He must have been lonely because an important part of his life was gone," she remembered. "His home was always his closed realm—and that was what brought him slowly to me. He started coming around simply to have someone to talk to, to find a warm home. That was how it started. He needed someone who would listen to him—anxious to find out how he was, how he appeared." In time they established a life together, in which Yigael turned to her for warmth and reassurance in the safe closed world that he blocked off from increasingly threatening and unpleasant political realities.

By late 1979, Yadin's political and physical health was collapsing. In October, just when Moshe Dayan angrily resigned as foreign minister in protest over Begin's handling of the Palestinian autonomy talks, Yadin was hospitalized for a mild heart attack. A reshuffle of the cabinet was necessary, but Yadin was by then just a figurehead. Nonetheless, Begin felt the need to go through the motions of offering Yadin the position, and Yadin docilely agreed to cooperate with the public relations performance. At a photo opportunity in the intensive care unit of Hadassah Hospital, Begin announced to the assembled reporters that the ailing Yadin had declined his offer of the foreign ministry. This was the post Yadin had first sought in the hope of achieving territorial compromise on the West Bank as the possible key to a lasting peace. Yadin now issued a polite and utterly feeble statement that "it would be somewhat unethical for me to criticize the government's foreign policy and at the same time also defend it. . . . Furthermore, I am interested in Project Renewal for the country's slums, especially as we have finally brought it to a takeoff position." It was a far cry from his earlier angry refusal to consider joining the Begin government unless it immediately and unconditionally accepted Dash's principles.

Yadin's public reputation had been all but ruined. About a year after joining the government, he felt the pain of public ridicule. The jokes and satirical sketches on television about the ridiculously impotent pipe-smoking professor out to save the nation were deeply humiliating. The once-respected chief of staff and once-venerated sage of Masada was the butt of cruel political cartoons that mocked his seeming subservience to Begin. But still convinced that he was the leader of an idealistic national movement, Yadin refused either to attack his critics or to act on their recommendations. "I understand that people want this government to fall," he explained to a reporter, "and therefore they now focus most of their attention and attacks on us—on me—because they know we can bring it down. . . . But I cannot behave in accordance with that vox populi—if indeed that's what it is. I have to act according to my conscience, my responsibility," which, as he saw it, was to serve as a moderating influence on the Begin government. But with the plan for electoral reform discarded, the party system as corrupt as ever, and Project Renewal bogged down in red tape and funding problems, all he could do was meekly protest the steadily growing number of Jewish settlements being established on the West Bank, whose size and geographical distribution would make future territorial compromise all but impossible. Scorned by the public and ignored by his fellow ministers, Yadin's health deteriorated further. In January 1981 he collapsed in a Jerusalem restaurant and was rushed to Hadassah Hospital. His condition was not serious, and he was released after only a few days. But it must have come as a relief when he finally saw the end of his nightmare approaching. On January 18 the Begin government announced that Knesset elections would be held earlier than planned—at the beginning of July.

Just one month after that announcement, Yadin's political career ended with a whimper—televised to the nation in prime time. In a final reflective interview on *Moked*, where he had announced his political intentions just five years before, Yadin said that he would not seek reelection. He expressed his regret that he had been unable to reform the political system in Israel, in a sad summing-up of his political experience. "I don't regard it as a personal tragedy that I failed in politics because of naïveté and refusing to work by other people's rules. After all, I'm not a professional politician. I have somewhere to go, and I'll resume my archaeological work at the Hebrew University with a clear conscience," he said. Amnon Rubinstein had indeed found a general to lead a new political movement, but it turned out to be a poor choice for his purposes.

On April 2, 1981, the executive council of the Democratic Movement met for the last time. After rejecting a proposal that Yadin be replaced as the movement's leader, the members voted to disband. Some joined Moshe Dayan's new Telem party; others, like Shmuel Tamir, returned to the Likud. The remaining funds in the Democratic Movement's coffers were divided accordingly, though Yadin had no part in the negotiations. He had been physically and emotionally drained by the experience. Later, when journalist Tom Segev asked him why the personal criticism of him had been so bitter, he spoke with rare honesty and perceptiveness. "I destroyed a myth for the people," he conceded, "And they'll never forgive me for that. They wanted the Yigael Yadin that had grown up in their imaginations over the last twenty-five years. And it became clear that the myth did not match the reality. And that's why they're so angry—angry in a completely irrational way. It's because it became clear to them that the *real* Yigael Yadin is not the man that they were so eager to invest all their hopes in."

Chapter   Seventeen

THE BURDEN
OF HISTORY

T he last sad drama of Yigael Yadin's political career unfolded in
the very same office which he entered with such high hopes and
ambitions less than four years before. But now, on August 13,
1981, his earlier energy and optimism had vanished. His office was
empty, and all his framed photographs and memorabilia were packed up
in cardboard boxes ready to be carted away. In the presence of the usual
gaggle of press photographers, he posed stiffly and uncomfortably with a
beaming David Levy, minister of housing in the newly formed Begin
government. The recent Knesset elections had resulted in a virtual tie
between the Likud and Labour, and in order to piece together a razor-
thin coalition, Begin had been forced to trade away every available political asset. Project Renewal, with its large budget and promise of lucrative
reconstruction contracts, was the price demanded for participation by

David Levy, an ambitious Herut party leader, eager to increase his own public visibility and political clout. Yadin was, of course, left entirely out of the process. Although he claimed to some reporters that Begin had offered him a post in the new cabinet (which he said he declined), his powerlessness was painfully obvious. Exhausted, discouraged, and tired of political maneuvering, he now quietly warned Levy that the transfer of Project Renewal to the Housing Ministry might lead to an excessive emphasis on "physical reconstruction" and not enough attention to the social and economic conditions that were the real causes of inequality. But by August 1981, no one was listening. Project Renewal had become just another political plum, and Dash was a shattered dream. Yadin had come to the sad realization that despite his noblest intentions it was beyond his power to implement his idealized vision of redeeming and rebuilding Jewish society in the Land of Israel.

So Yadin returned to the world of archaeology, sadder and considerably wiser about his personal limits, no longer a rising political star but an aging and humbled professor who had been scarred by a misguided adventure in a dangerous political realm. In a way, his failure and success seemed the reverse of his father's. While Eleazar Sukenik had been forced to struggle and push to achieve anything in his professional career, his life had ended with the miraculous discovery of the Dead Sea Scrolls and (whatever his colleagues and students might have thought) a respectable place in the annals of archaeology. Yadin, in contrast, had lived a charmed life from infancy, and praise, respect, and recognition had always come effortlessly to him. Yet now the debacle of his political career near the end of his life cast a tragic shadow over his place in Israeli history.

In a candid 1983 interview with Hershel Shanks, editor of *Biblical Archaeology Review*, Yadin expressed his personal disappointment. "I couldn't play the game, by the rules of the game of the politicians. That was, I think, my greatest weakness. I suddenly found myself in the jungle . . . and in the jungle there are the rules of the jungle. And if you can't play by the rules of the jungle, then you are prey for other animals." If Yadin believed that he could escape those prowling beasts by withdrawing into academia's ivory tower, however, he had not fully learned his political lesson. For in the wake of the 1981 elections the jockeying between special political interests for partisan advantage had only intensified. If anything, the rise and fall of Dash had created an even more chaotic competition between special interests and small political parties, and a violent political power struggle soon erupted over—of all things—an archaeological dig.

For years, the ultraorthodox Agudat Israel party, which insisted above all on the strict observance of ritual law, had dogged the steps of many Israeli archaeologists, protesting what they saw as their callous violation of the sanctity of Jewish burials no matter what research objectives the scholars proclaimed. Yadin had always been careful to avoid offending religious sensibilities at his excavations, and he had even invited rabbinical authorities to officiate at the burial of Masada's human remains. For most of his career, Yadin had been too powerful a personality for the religious parties to openly challenge. Indeed, as long as Agudat Israel remained a small fringe party in the era of Mapai and Labour party dominance, its demands on archaeologists were little more than an annoyance—perhaps given occasional lip-service by the government but certainly not allowed to interfere with Israeli archaeology. But Yadin had unwittingly participated in their rise to power. Agudat Israel joined the government coalition in the aftermath of the Begin victory in 1977. Now the Likud needed the support of all the religious parties to maintain its parliamentary majority, and a sudden uproar and political test of strength arose over the ongoing excavations at the traditional site of the "City of David" in Jerusalem. Yadin had been one of the most vocal supporters of that important investigation of Jerusalem in the Bronze and Iron Ages, directed by his student and colleague, Yigal Shiloh. In the summer of 1981, during Begin's delicate coalition negotiations with the religious parties, noisy demonstrations were organized in Jerusalem's religious Meah Shearim quarter, claiming that part of the site that archaeologists identified as the City of David was actually a medieval Jewish cemetery—and its excavation should be halted at once.

Hundreds of black-coated protesters massed outside the Education Ministry (which had authority over the Department of Antiquities) and threw rocks and bottles and overturned trash cans. Riot police quickly arrived, fully armed for battle, and dispersed the crowd with truncheons and tear gas. Yadin, in his new capacity as private citizen, visited the excavations the very next day as a sign of solidarity with Shiloh, and he called on Prime Minister Begin to lay down the law. For Yadin, archaeological research was a pillar of Israeli society, one of the most meaningful links between the people and the land. But he underestimated the Begin government's need to conciliate the religious parties and the political competition between the religious leaders themselves. Ashkenazi chief rabbi Shlomo Goren urged that the dig be stopped at once and bombastically announced (without producing definitive documentation) that the City of David was not located where the archaeologists suggested and that the site was indeed a cemetery. "The archaeologists have to learn once and for all that it is forbidden to violate cemeteries," Goren proclaimed to the press, adding cynically that "there is nothing in the Ten Commandments about archaeological excavations." Education Minister

Zevulun Hammer of the National Religious Party, whose ministry included the Department of Antiquities, could hardly reject the ruling of the chief rabbi. As the pressure built to open conflict, Yadin shied away from confrontation and made an appeal to patriotism.

"I'm personally surprised at Rabbi Goren," Yadin noted, "because Rabbi Goren is, as far as I know, a very extreme nationalist, and he should know that these excavations especially help strengthen the people's roots in the land." In what must have seemed an utterly empty threat to the ringleaders of the religious demonstrations, Yadin warned that he would exert personal pressure on the prime minister. He intended to let Begin know that the campaign against the excavations was "harming archaeology, the state, the Jewish people, and the capital of Israel." Rabbi Goren remained adamant in his demand that the excavations be halted immediately, and despite the attempts of Minister Hammer, he refused to negotiate or even speak with the archaeologists. A deadlock seemed inevitable, especially when other archaeological figures stepped forward, determined not to be cowed. "The rabbinate has no legal standing with respect to archaeological excavations," announced Joseph Aviram, speaking for the Institute of Archaeology and the Israel Exploration Society. He insisted that it would set a dangerous precedent to require rabbinical approval for every excavation permit. The City of David excavations had a valid excavation license. "The moment that license is curtailed or revoked," Aviram threatened, "we will immediately appeal to the Supreme Court against the government." The dispute eventually reached the Supreme Court, where the justices ruled *against* intervention by religious authorities in a legally authorized dig. But both sides knew this was merely a highly publicized skirmish in a continuing campaign.

In the autumn of 1981 the Knesset members of the Agudat Israel party continued the political maneuvers by introducing an amendment to the Antiquities Law. By the terms of the "bone bill," as the archaeologists and their supporters derisively called it, a representative of the chief rabbinate would have to be summoned to any excavation where human remains were discovered, and the Chief Rabbinate, in consultation with other religious bodies, would decide whether that particular dig should proceed. In the struggle over the "bone bill," which amounted to all-out cultural war, Yadin was at the forefront. "This regressive law would bring an end to the golden age of archaeology in Israel," he announced at a public protest meeting. Despite all that Yadin's career had done to crystallize a unifying national message, the religious radicals understood the tactics of national power politics far better than he. During the next two years, as the debate continued in the Knesset, they verbally and physically assaulted not only Yigal Shiloh, but in a particularly painful way Yigael Yadin. In the summer of 1983, when discussion of the bone bill in the Knesset was renewed, anonymous vandals desecrated the gravestones of Eleazar and Chassiya Sukenik in Jerusalem's Sanhedria cemetery. The spraypainted graffiti read: "It hurts . . . and is a shame . . . just like in the City of David . . . these are the results of Yigal Shiloh."

In perhaps the most effective political maneuver in the battle, Chief Rabbi Goren brought up a matter that had been almost forgotten for more than twenty years: the bones recovered from the Cave of Letters in the Judean Wilderness expedition—the baskets of skulls, leg bones, and other skeletal fragments whose discovery in a crevice was one of the highlights of Yadin's oft-told tale. "Those bones were taken for examination and till today we don't know where they are," Rabbi Goren announced in the summer of 1981. "I demand that Yadin clear this up." Yadin was conciliatory, and within two weeks of that announcement he agreed to submit to Rabbi Goren's ultimatum and hand over the bones for proper Jewish burial.

It is unlikely that Yadin suspected what the chief rabbi was up to. Shortly after he received the remains, Rabbi Goren contacted Prime Minister Begin directly and proposed that "Bar-Kokhba's fighters and people" be given a state funeral of unprecedented pomp and scale. Begin was deeply influenced by the image of Jews desperately fighting for their lives against the gentile forces of darkness—in the Warsaw ghetto no less than in the Judean Wilderness. Having declared the coming year Israel's "Year of Heroism," he recognized that a Bar-Kokhba funeral near Nahal Hever, jointly performed by the chief rabbi and the prime minister, would perfectly symbolize the unity of Israel's religious parties and political right wing. That winter, plans for the state funeral went forward with gusto—with the Ministerial Committee on Symbols and Ceremonies working closely with the office of the chief rabbi to plan the ideological extravaganza down to the smallest detail. And with Begin's wholehearted support and with lavish government funding, the government committee supervised the bulldozing of helicopter pads near the edge of Nahal Hever, the construction of grandstands, and the selection of a large tombstone to mark the final resting place of ancient heroes, whose remains would be brought by helicopter from Tel Aviv. The earlier reburial of the Masada remains would pale by comparison. *The Jerusalem Post* reported that Goren's plan called "for large detachments of Gadna paramilitary youth groups and three or four IDF companies, representing all services, to attend the interment." In a personal letter, Begin wrote to the chief rabbi that he was looking forward to the funeral with "awe and reverence."

As additional details of the plans were gradually made public, local authorities and environmental groups objected to the damage that all the proposed bulldozing, road construction, and the arrival of dozens of VIP guests were likely to have on the delicate desert ecology. Yossi Sarid, an outspoken member of the Knesset opposition, called the ceremony a "dubious and wasteful spectacle." The archaeologists, most closely connected with the bones and their analysis, reacted with horror and disbelief. Dr. Patricia Smith of the Hebrew University–Hadassah Medical School, who had examined the remains, pointed out that Begin's and Goren's plans for a military burial of the ancient Jewish warrior-heroes was rather excessive, since "of the nineteen specimens, only three are of adult males . . . the majority were children under the age of six." Yadin, disgusted with the entire event, announced that he would have nothing to do with it. While he had participated in the reburial of the remains from Masada in 1969, he now accused Rabbi Goren of utilizing the event to rebuke "the grave-robbing archaeologists." Still, Yadin's absence was hardly noticed by the dozens of politicians, army officers, and religious leaders who arrived at Nahal Hever on the newly leveled access road on May 11, 1982 (the Festival of Lag B'Omer, a traditional day of commemoration of the revolt against the Romans). Precisely as planned, the helicopters bearing the coffins arrived, and the appropriate prayers were chanted by Rabbi Goren, the chief IDF chaplain, and the Sephardic chief rabbi, Ovadiah Yosef.

Israel Television broadcast the ceremony live to the nation, and the eulogy delivered by Prime Minister Begin conveyed a political message that was implicitly about the future as much as the past. "Our glorious fathers," Begin proclaimed (not knowing or not caring that the remains were mostly refugee women and children), "we have a message for you: We have returned to the place from whence we came. The people of Israel live, and will live in its homeland of Eretz Israel for generations upon generations. Glorious fathers, we are back and will not budge from here." The Masada complex had suddenly been shouldered aside by what Yehoshafat Harkabi would soon call the Bar-Kokhba syndrome: the irrational celebration of a suicidal military defeat. Yet Rabbi Goren was quite explicit in his hopes for the effect that this ceremony would have on the nation. In addition to creating a "new symbol of national heroism," he hoped that interest in the ceremony would encourage intensified Jewish settlement. Yadin, as usual, refused to engage in public polemics, merely insisting that politics and archaeology should never mix. But they did mix—powerfully—and in refusing to speak out more forcefully, Yadin could not completely evade moral responsibility. For despite his best intentions and sincerest objections, the symbolic exploitation of his archaeological finds had an enormous political impact. In less than a month the Israel Defense Forces were ordered to begin the bloody and disastrous war in Lebanon, and the finds from the Cave of Letters, hijacked and given a new political meaning by the Begin government and the religious establishment, took on a life of their own. Yadin had lost control even over his own Bar-Kokhba myth.

Returning to the world of scholarship, Yadin refrained from commenting publicly about the war in Lebanon, though he was clearly not in sympathy with it. During his final months as a cabinet minister, he had repeatedly come into conflict with Ariel Sharon over the establishment of new West Bank settlements. Sharon was now defense minister, and with the sudden massive invasion and armored sweep northward toward Beirut in June 1982, his frightening strategic master plan began to be revealed. Despite Yadin's reputation as an authority in military strategy and his eagerness to comment on all of Israel's previous wars, he now kept his thoughts largely to himself, revealing his misgivings only to those closest to him. He reportedly confided to his brother Yossi his distrust of Sharon and his disapproval of his actions. "If I had not been in the cabinet, he would have gone into Lebanon a few years earlier than he did. He managed to twist them around his little finger; he had all his plans ready," Yadin supposedly claimed. Months after the massacres at Sabra and Shatilla, and the Kahan Commission's judgment that Sharon should resign as defense minister, Yadin repeated his long-held contention that the prime minister needed a special intelligence adviser to evaluate the often-contradictory assessments of the defense minister and the chief of staff. "If Begin had such an adviser who would be free from administrative responsibilities and close to the prime minister, then this wouldn't have happened," he told a radio interviewer. It was the closest he came to entering the public debate about the Lebanon war. At the same time, it represented a subtle reminder of his earlier career as the trusted confidant and military adviser of Ben-Gurion and Levi Eshkol.

After his disastrous political experience, however, Yadin was viewed less as a serious public figure than as a valuable historical resource. A new generation of Israeli historians had began to probe the Haganah and the War of Independence, and Yadin proved to be a willing—even enthusiastic—participant in the compilation of oral histories. Over the years he had granted newspaper interviews filled with entertaining anecdotes about his fights with Ben-Gurion, his talks with King Abdullah, and his occasional rivalries with Yigal Allon and Moshe Dayan. But now the researchers came to him with more probing questions as British, American, and Israeli archives were gradually being opened and the War of Independence approached its thirty-fifth anniversary. Historian Yoav Gelber interviewed him at length about tensions within the Haganah high command and its eventual transformation to a regular army; Benny Morris recorded his recollections of the causes of the Palestinian exodus and the formulation of Plan D. Avi Shlaim interviewed him about the secret negotiations between Israel and the Hashemite kingdom, and Anita Shapira of Tel Aviv University sought to gain his perspective on Ben-Gurion's tense relationship with the Palmach and the War of the Generals.

Shapira vividly recalled her 1983 meeting with Yadin in the living room of his Jerusalem home. When she first contacted him for the interview, he had been immediately receptive. He was familiar with her works on the modern history of Israel (her biography of Zionist activist and philosopher Berl Katznelson had just been published), and he knew that she was working on a biography of Yigal Allon. But she was particularly interested now in Yadin's memories of the July 1948 crisis over Ben-Gurion's military appointments that resulted in the mass resignations of most of the general staff and the top-secret hearings before the Committee of Five. Shapira had an invaluable resource for the study of this episode; she had obtained a full transcript of the tense and angry hearings and she asked Yadin to read through the transcript before they sat down to go over the details. He readily assented. "He was very willing to talk to me," she recalled of the initial phone call. "I think it reflected his loneliness . . . his wife was no longer living . . . he was looking for someone to talk to about past times, about better times."

Shapira found the house on Ramban Street in Rechavia eerily cold and quiet. As she and Yadin went over the transcript and discussed the events, she recalled that "he was clearly scarred by the Dash experience." In the course of their discussion "he was constantly making asides about his recent political experience that were very disconcerting. He made some remarks that left the impression that he was bitterly disappointed." His comments on the events they discussed were at least in part dictated by the nostalgia of a sixty-six-year-old man looking back at his youth. According to Shapira, he had forgotten many of the details of the War of the Generals, but when he reread the transcript, he was astonished by his aggressive testimony and open defiance of Ben-Gurion. "I'm amazed at how brave I was," he said.

Their conversation ranged widely as Shapira's tape recorder ran. They talked about Latrun and the painful decision to send untrained troops against the Arab Legion. They spoke of Ben-Gurion's leadership and Yadin's relationship to Israel Galili, who had always considered

Yadin skillful in formulating operations, but annoyingly high-strung. Galili had previously described for Shapira how the young chief of operations had the annoying and distracting habit of breaking pencils during headquarter meetings to dispel the tension that he felt. The man who sat before Shapira now was no longer a young and impetuous officer but a tired and sickly professor. Although Yadin impressed her as being very intelligent, he was unwilling to delve too deeply into the wider implications of the events. "What interested him and what he found to be of importance were political things, power things. He never moved from the level of operations and army politics to anything more elevated like ideas and general views." In his discussion of the War of Independence, Yadin was particularly critical of Rabin, reflecting their long and acrimonious relationship over the years. While Yigal Allon, as Palmach commander, possessed strong leadership qualities, Yadin thought, Rabin was only effective as a second-in-command and got panicky the moment he was left on his own.

The end of the interview was particularly unsettling for Shapira. After their formal discussion Yadin insisted on getting out a journal he had kept in 1967 and reading aloud a long, handwritten passage, making sure that she included it in her tape recording of the interview. Over the years, in repeated newspaper interviews and after dinner stories, Yadin had proudly claimed responsibility for convincing Prime Minister Eshkol to appoint Moshe Dayan as defense minister in the tense days before the Six Day War. But now, inexplicably, Yadin related an entirely different version. Loosening his belt as he sat on the sofa, Yadin read from his diary that Allon—not Dayan—had been offered the defense ministry by Eshkol and that the objection of the religious parties had caused Eshkol to go back on his word. Eshkol then asked Allon to relinquish his place to Dayan, and he diplomatically acceded. Yadin had insisted on reading the entire passage into her tape recorder, Shapira said, even though she was by that time clearly eager to go home. After the Yom Kippur War, the Agranat Commission, and the disappointment of being shunted aside in the Begin cabinet, Yadin wanted to distance himself from his longtime competitor and colleague. "It was if he somehow wanted to prove that *he* was not the one who had brought up Dayan," Shapira recalled.

Yadin was a man of regular habits. Returning to the Institute of Archaeology in 1983 and 1984, he divided his time between teaching, digging, traveling, and working in blissful solitude in the book-lined downstairs study in his home. He spent much of his free time with Elizabeth

Podkaminer at her home in the nearby Talbieh neighborhood. Almost every morning, after having breakfast and reading the newspaper, he would return to Rechavia to work on his many still-unfinished articles and excavation reports. A housekeeper kept things in order there, and she prepared lunch for him every day. As Podkaminer recalled he enjoyed being alone again with his research; he would sit at his desk with the radio constantly playing in the background and would hum or sing along with the latest popular songs. He clearly worked best in isolation. There in his study he had completed his work on the Temple Scroll and carried on his other archaeological research. Occasionally, he would have to go up to the Institute of Archaeology on Mount Scopus for meetings and planning sessions, but more and more he left those to his research assistant, Shulamit Geva—to the resentment of many of his colleagues. "It's not that he didn't like people," Podkaminer recalled. "He just needed a special place that he could never let other people share."

His archaeological interests continued to range widely. While most of his colleagues concentrated on a particular period or culture, Yadin's work typically spanned millennia, from the dating of Bronze Age rampart fortifications, to the organization of the Israelite kingdoms, to the military technology of the Assyrian armies in their eighth-century-B.C. invasion of Judea, to the theological complexities of the Dead Sea Scrolls. In 1983 the English translation of his commentary on the Temple Scroll was published to nearly universal scholarly praise and tribute; after forty years of work on the manuscripts from Qumran, Masada, and the Cave of Letters, he was now justifiably regarded as one of the foremost authorities on the Dead Sea literature. But he was not yet ready to bring his career to an end. In the spring of 1983 he left Jerusalem for a two-week excavation at Tell Beth Shean in the northern Jordan Valley, in collaboration with Geva and a small group of graduate students. The main object of this dig was to examine the site's early Iron Age levels, for Yadin had returned to the question of the Israelite conquest with renewed interest. During the last year of his life, he would again be preoccupied with the question of Joshua's conquest of the Promised Land.

Two years before, while Yadin was still in the government, Avraham Malamat had come to him with the idea for an intensive reexamination of the problem of the Israelite conquest of Canaan. Yadin had already announced his intentions to return to academia, and Malamat assured him that he would have "the best year of his life." Malamat planned to form an advanced seminar on biblical history and archaeology at the Institute for Advanced Study of the Hebrew University. It would be composed of hand-picked scholars from Europe, America, and Israel who would discuss the latest finds and exchange views on the emergence of the Israelite nation. This subject, after all, was central to understanding the country's history. Yadin initially hesitated (perhaps at working so closely with a group of colleagues), but eventually agreed to serve as co-chairman. He knew that in the years since he had finished his last season at Hazor in 1968, the scholarly consensus had dramatically shifted to a position much closer to Aharoni's than his own. A new generation of archaeologists, most of them trained at the Tel Aviv Institute of Archaeology, had adopted the technique of wide-ranging surface survey rather than intensive excavation as a primary means of archaeological exploration. Throughout the West Bank—in the traditional tribal territories (and new Israeli administrative districts) of Manasseh, Ephraim, Benjamin, and Judah—these archaeologists had located remains of hundreds of early Iron Age herdsmen's enclosures, hilltop hamlets, and unfortified villages far from the major cities, with pottery and artifacts clearly adapted from Canaanite prototypes.

This geographical distribution suggested to many scholars that the Israelite "conquest" might have been more of a social transformation than a violent invasion. Some even suggested that it took place entirely *within* Canaanite society; changes in economic and political conditions, they argued, forced Canaanite pastoralists who had roamed the hillcountry for centuries to settle down as farmers and thus—at least metaphorically—inherit their promised land. During the academic year 1983–84, Yadin traveled throughout the country with his colleagues, visiting sites of newly discovered early Israelite settlements, discussing modern pastoralism with cultural anthropologists, and examining the emergence of the Israelite nation from perspectives he had never seriously considered before. One participant in the Institute for Advanced Studies seminar, Israel Finkelstein of Tel Aviv University, recalled that Yadin seemed to be softening and perhaps even changing his ideas about the nature of the Israelite conquest. Yadin listened intently to the evidence of early Iron Age social transformation, but he was still not ready to express a new opinion openly.

Many of the participants in this seminar—Malamat, Finkelstein, Amihai Mazar from the Hebrew University, Baruch Halpern from York University, and Lawrence Stager from Harvard, among them—recalled with special fondness Yadin's wit, perceptiveness, and skill at weaving entertaining stories, especially during their working lunches and on the many field trips they took. A glimmer of the old spark came back as he dominated the group's discussion and gossip. As he had at staff meetings at Masada more than two decades before, he charmed the participants with his stylized anecdotes about Ben-Gurion, King Abdullah, and the 1949 armistice conference at Rhodes. But for Yadin, these memories were not entertainment. The concepts he had derived from his experiences during the War of Independence had deeply shaped his larger perception of the world. The young scholars at the seminar may not have recognized how deeply *their* personal experiences in the rapidly industrializing post–World War II world had influenced their scholarly concentration on such issues as ecological adaptation, agricultural efficiency, and social transformation. But Yadin still felt the power of the traditional stories of the Israelite conquest, and he faithfully adhered to them.

Writing in defense of the historical basis of the story of Joshua's invasion, Yadin had noted several years before that the scholars who doubted the scriptural accounts were motivated "by a reluctance—conscious or unconscious—to envisage the Israelites as warriors of the calibre required to overcome heavily fortified Canaanite cities." As usual, Yadin came up with an ingenious solution that accommodated all the apparently contradictory archaeological evidence. Noting that the fortifications of most of Canaanite cities had been originally constructed in the Middle Bronze Age, he suggested that most were rundown and dilapidated by the time the Israelites first appeared in the Early Iron Age. Ultimately, Yadin could never reject the inevitability of enmity and warfare between Israelites and Canaanites (or even question the ethnic distinction between them). Having reshaped and refined his image of the Israelite conquest to accommodate some of the new insights, Yadin was still able to paint a picture of daring, independent, and highly motivated pastoralists overcoming a corrupt and degenerate urban society.

"What was needed, and brought into play," Yadin insisted, "was not technical skill, but courage." Yadin still saw in the wars of the ancient Israelites an image of the conflicts he experienced in his own lifetime. While the younger generation of scholars, raised in the 1960s and 1970s, preferred to describe the settlement of the ancient Israelites in Canaan in terms of environmental adaptation and social change, Yadin remained firmly attached to the ideals of his youth and early adulthood—physical daring, tactical ingenuity, and selfless patriotism—as key to understanding the establishment of the people of Israel in their Promised Land.

By 1984, Yadin was determined to return to Hazor to search for more evidence of the Canaanites' downfall and the Israelites' triumph by finding the city's royal archive. He had resumed the excavations there in 1968 to find the city's royal palace, where such an archive would undoubtedly be kept. Other major Bronze Age cities in the region—Mari, Ugarit, and Ebla—had contained vast libraries of cuneiform tablets that provided their excavators with direct insight into the wars and invasions faced by those cities' kings and princes. At Hazor the discovery of an

elaborate private temple—presumably attached to a much larger structure—strengthened Yadin's confidence that he was on the right track.
But in the intervening years, the study and publication of the Temple
Scroll, the Yom Kippur War, the Agranat Commission, and his years as
deputy prime minister had diverted him from Hazor. Now, after the
year-long seminar at the Institute for Advanced Studies, he was ready to
undertake the challenge again. With his many philanthropic supporters
in America and Europe, fund-raising was not a major problem. He
hoped to begin the excavations in the coming winter, under a specially
constructed shelter. And in the spring of 1984 he began planning the
logistics of the dig.

Yadin had always been particularly interested in fostering American
participation in Israeli archaeology. He venerated the memory of William Foxwell Albright, the dean of American Biblical Archaeology who
had done so much to further Eleazar Sukenik's early career and who had
exerted a profound effect on Yadin's own archaeological thinking. Yadin
now sought to raise funds to establish professorships at American universities, specifically earmarked for the study of the archaeology of the
Land of Israel. Some of Yadin's most ardent American admirers were
conservative Christians who had been deeply impressed by his vivid, material illustration of biblical events and localities. With the hope of mobilizing financial support and perhaps volunteer workers for the upcoming
Hazor excavations, he turned to Dr. Paige Patterson, president of Cris-
well College in Dallas, some of whose students were then working with
Amnon Ben-Tor at a biblical site near Megiddo called Yokneam. Patterson later recalled a conversation in which Yadin explained that the search
for the archive had become "something of a consuming desire." Yadin
indicated that the discovery of an archive at Hazor "might be the last
great project of his life and, indeed, in the comprehension of history, the
most valuable." A new source of *written* information about the early
history of the Israelites, independent of the biblical narrative, would,
without question, be Yadin's greatest discovery.

But Yadin's plans never came to fruition. He had hoped that Amnon
Ben-Tor would join him at Hazor, but Ben-Tor was reluctant to return at
this stage of his career to the status of second-in-command. In the
meantime, Yadin became busy with other matters. In April 1984, he,
Benjamin Mazar, and Joseph Aviram organized an ambitious International Congress on Biblical Archaeology in Jerusalem, and Yadin agreed
to give a keynote address. He also set aside time to visit the sites of
ongoing excavations like those of Israel Finkelstein at the site of biblical
Shiloh, where Finkelstein had uncovered remains of an early Israelite

settlement. There was more than a little irony in the visit, since Yadin, as a minister in Begin's cabinet, had strenuously protested Gush Emunim's establishment of a modern Jewish settlement in the vicinity of the archaeological site. But the modern settlement of Shiloh was now a hard reality, and the excavations an accomplished fact. So in the spring of 1984, Yadin accompanied Finkelstein on a journey through the hills to the north of Jerusalem in a landscape where past and present were ever more closely intertwined.

Finkelstein recalled the unease with which Yadin viewed the surroundings, as they drove along the narrow, winding highway more than twenty miles north of Jerusalem. The landscape was dotted with Arab towns and villages, Israel army installations, and new Jewish settlements. Even in those days before the intifada, acts of violence between Israelis and Palestinian Arabs were not uncommon. Yadin, always cautious, brought along a large pistol for his personal protection (it "looked like it was from the 1940s," Finkelstein recalled). As the two archaeologists arrived at the main gate of the modern settlement of Shiloh, an armed watchman mistook them for building contractors who had come to check on the progress of some government-funded construction work. Once the confusion was cleared up with the watchman, Finkelstein parked his car inside the settlement compound and walked with Yadin out toward the open trenches and exposed walls of his dig.

Yadin had always been a scholar and a headquarters officer, not a fighter, not a combat officer ready to lead an attack. In the midst of this biblical landscape he saw the Arab villages as potentially dangerous presences, and considered the gruff, suspicious settlers of Shiloh with their mystical territorial attachments no less threatening to the future of Israel. Yadin was lost in an alien landscape, one whose transformation, ironically, he had helped to make possible as a military officer, historical mythmaker, and cabinet minister. After touring the excavations, Yadin and Finkelstein returned to the modern settlement compound. Once there, Yadin, for no particular reason, raised and pointed his pistol toward a nearby hillside. The antique gun's booming explosion echoed emptily and eerily through Valley of Shiloh.

The high-pitched screech of the cicadas cut through the heat of a summer morning along the coastal highway from Haifa to Tel Aviv. At the end of a narrow road lay Michmoret, a quiet seaside hideaway village for vacationers and pensioners, and a popular weekend retreat for artists and businessmen from Tel Aviv. In 1961, Yadin had purchased a house there next to his brother Yossi's, and over the years he and Carmella and the children had spent many weekends and holidays there. Yadin spent even more time there after his forced retirement from politics, and for the first time in many years, he and Yossi—an active and well-known performer in Tel Aviv's Cameri Theater—had the opportunity to spend time together, to tend their adjoining gardens, and to speak of the past. Yadin's relationship to his younger brother had always been somewhat distant, but now he sought his companionship.

Yadin had maintained only a few close friendships in his life, and loneliness now afflicted him as it never had before. Yossi recalled how much of a toll the unfortunate political experience had taken on his brother. As he had gotten older, Yigael became more and more concerned about his health problems, especially after his heart attack in 1979. He felt betrayed by his erstwhile political allies and was upset that his achievements in initiating Project Renewal had not been fully appreciated. He did have plans for the future: he was spending most of his leisure time with Elizabeth Podkaminer; he was busy completing his Masada, Bar-Kokhba, and Hazor publications; and he was still hoping to convince Ben-Tor to join him at Hazor. But there was no denying the lingering sense of sadness. The disaster of Lebanon hung over the country; Menachem Begin became mired in a deep depression and in September 1983 resigned as prime minister, handing over the office to Yitzhak Shamir, a pugnacious career politician who had once served as a leader of the rightist Stern Gang. This was not the political change that Yadin had envisioned when he entered public life in 1976. "In his last years he suffered a deep disappointment," Yossi remembered. "If Carmella were alive, it would have helped him a great deal."

On Thursday, June 28, Yossi was surprised to see Yigael at Michmoret. Yigael had attended an academic function at the University of Haifa on the previous evening and hadn't felt like driving all the way back to Jerusalem. He would begin his weekend a day ahead of time. Early in the morning, Yossi remembered hearing Yigael shout to him from the garden—something about not feeling well. Just then, Yossi's wife Hedy was leaving the house to visit a neighbor who had taken ill. As she opened her car door, she saw Yigael approaching. He was pale, and his steps were halting. "Hedy," he said, "I don't feel well." She moved toward him quickly, and as she approached him, he collapsed. The village doctor was quickly summoned, and an ambulance arrived to take him to the hospital. But it was already too late.

By late afternoon, the news of Yigael Yadin's sudden death had spread across the country. Kol Israel broadcast the somber announcement with word that a state funeral would be held for him the following day. His death came as a shock to all the people who had worked with him, fought with him, and admired him over the years. Joseph Aviram, his longtime confidant and promoter, had just been getting up from his customary afternoon nap when he heard the announcement. Avraham Malamat received a shocked phone call from a colleague in England, who had heard the news over the BBC. Maya Bailey was at the home of Yosef Avidar, Yadin's longtime colleague in the Haganah and the IDF general staff. For each of them, the death of Yigael Yadin meant the passing of an era. And at the memorial service the next day in Jerusalem's *Binyanei Ha-Uma*, the "Halls of the People," an unlikely melange of politicians, generals, and scholars came together, if only briefly, to pay formal tribute.

———

The Israel that Yigael Yadin left behind was suffering from the painful fragmentation that he had tried so hard to overcome. The Likud had attempted to institute an Israeli brand of supply-side economics, abolishing customs duties on luxury goods and consumer electronics; this had resulted in a national spending spree that drove the nation's trade deficit upward into dangerously unchartered territory. By mid-1984, the national inflation rate was zooming past 300 percent per annum, with no prospect of relief in sight. At the time of Yadin's death another raucous, contentious campaign for the Knesset was under way, in which the Labour Party, under the leadership of Shimon Peres, was hoping for a comeback. Even as new splinter parties appeared at the right end of the political spectrum, the Likud (even without Begin) managed to maintain a tentative grip on power. The election produced an evenly split electoral vote and the ultimate back-room arrangement—the idea of "rotation," in which Shimon Peres of Labour would serve as prime minister for the first two years of the government term, and Yitzhak Shamir of Likud would serve the final two. Dash's loud demands to change the electoral system had had no effect whatsoever. Worse yet, according to some observers, the utter, humiliating failure of the grassroots party to reform the obviously moribund party system could well discourage would-be reformers from ever trying it again.

Yigael Yadin's true legacy was in the study of the past, not in the reform of the present. Under the energetic and insistent encouragement of Joseph Aviram, the scholarly publications of the manuscripts from the Cave of Letters and the excavation reports from Masada were finally completed, putting an end to fears that the vast and valuable information obtained from those excavations would never be available to scholars in detailed, technical form. The renewed excavations of Hazor finally got under way in the summer of 1987, when Amnon Ben-Tor began the "Hazor Excavations in Memory of Yigael Yadin" with a brief exploratory season; large-scale digging began in 1990. Some of Yadin's most famous theories about the city's fortifications were called into question by the new excavations, but his prophecy about the archive seemed to be coming true. In the summer of 1991 the first cuneiform tablet came to light (it was an administrative tablet listing payments of silver to individuals), and in the following year Ben-Tor announced the discovery of another cuneiform document—this one containing an apparent reference to the king of Hazor. The king's name, Ibni Addu, was known from the archives of the ancient city of Mari in the Euphrates Valley. The name, several scholars had pointed out, was linguistically identical with the name *Yabin*, who was mentioned as the king of Hazor at the time of Joshua. But this tablet was dated to the Middle Bronze Age, some six hundred years before the accepted date of the Israelite conquest. The name *Yabin* was apparently famous—or notorious—among the people of Canaan long before the Bible was written. This tablet and tablets to come from Hazor's buried archive might in time provide evidence that the story of Joshua's conquest was neither wholly true nor completely false but a single epic weaving together heroic stories of the battles and conquests of many peoples, clans, and tribal groupings who fought for millennia over the same promised land.

Yadin's personal story had itself grown larger than life over the decades. The colorful tales of his participation in the Haganah and his adventures in the War of Independence, his organization of the reserve system, and his legendary archaeological triumphs all formed a myth of their own. It remained to be seen, however, whether they could ever block out the bitter memories of his disastrous political career. "The tragedy of Yigael Yadin," noted Aviva Rosen, longtime administrative secretary of the Institute of Archaeology, "is that he didn't finish his life as a professor emeritus, with his reputation intact." Teddy Kollek recalled that "he was a good soldier, and excellent archaeologist, but a lousy politician." Yadin's friends, colleagues, and admirers repeatedly stressed the contradiction between the strength and charisma of Yadin the army commander and explorer and the pitiful weakness of Yadin the deputy prime minister. Even his longtime political adversary Yitzhak Rabin, who had ample reason to be bitter, recalled Yadin's organizational and archaeological achievements with admiration and dismissed Yadin's political experience as "a tragic end to a magnificent career."

But is it possible to separate the phases of Yadin's life without finding a common thread? His life was played out against the background of the rise of the Zionist movement, a centurylong transformation of a significant part the Jewish people from economic and social segregation to sovereignty in a modern nation-state. The pain of that transformation was blunted at least partially by the creation of a new tradition in which fascination with the antiquities of the Land of Israel forged a tangible link between the people and the land they claimed as their patrimony. The role played by archaeology in an era of nation-building was to be far more powerful than could ever have been imagined by the turn-of-the-century Zionist romantics, fighting for the rebirth of Hebrew culture and dreaming of ancient Jewish heroism. From the late 1920s archaeology helped to shape the landscape of modern Israel and mold its image of itself. Yigael Yadin did not invent Israeli archaeology—his gruff and ambitious father has a much better claim to that honor. Yadin was, rather, its personification: a sabra soldier and scholar in search of his past. His genius lay in the very eloquence and persuasiveness with which he could convey his people's connection to the land.

Yet a nation's vision of its past can also serve as a blueprint for its future. And Yadin offered his nation ancient visions without always fully comprehending the ideological message they contained. The military power, ethnic enmity, and ever-escalating armament that were the main themes of many of his archaeological scenarios had a far-reaching effect on the formation of the modern Israeli consciousness. Yadin's stories of Joshua, Masada, and Bar-Kokhba, vividly conveyed in lectures and books, and in tourist sites visited every year by millions, were political essays as much as historical works. Unfortunately, as times changed and Israel faced new challenges, Yadin could not bring himself to fight for his emerging vision of a peaceful, rational future with the same conviction and total dedication that he had devoted to his well-received, patriotic stories about the past. The mythic visions he crafted were too often exploited by others. And his forceful, martial tales of Joshua, Masada, and Bar-Kokhba ultimately—and tragically—proved far more persuasive than his soft-spoken appeals for democracy and change.

BIBLIOGRAPHIC NOTES

PROLOGUE: THE VIEW FROM MASADA

The account of the discovery of the human remains in the northern palace at Masada is based on an interview with Amnon Ben-Tor and on the transcripts of the evening meeting for November 14, 1963. A full listing of sources consulted for Masada and Yadin's 1963–65 excavations can be found in the bibliographical notes for Chapter 13.

For some important general studies of the transformation of Jewish cultural consciousness in the late nineteenth and early twentieth centuries, see Cohen, *Zion and State*; Even-Zohar, "The Emergence of a Native Hebrew Culture in Palestine: 1882–1948"; Shenfeld, *From King Messiah to Messiah of Flesh and Blood*; Elon, *The Israelis*; Shapira, *Land and Power*; and Liebman and Don-Yehiya, *Civil Religion in Israel*.

CHAPTER 1: LOST IN THE RUINS

My reconstruction of the home life of the Sukenik family is based on an interview with Yossi Yadin; on Ben-Porath, "Conversations"; Yuval, "Archaeological Exploration"; and on file material in the Yediot Aharonot Archives.

For the family background of Chassiya Feinsod-Sukenik in Bialystok, I have used her own account in *Pirkey Gan*; file material in the Yediot Aharonot Archives; an interview by Uri Avneri in *Ha-Olam Hazeh*, January 10, 1968, and July 7, 1984. On the early life of Eleazar Lipa Sukenik, I have relied primarily on Yadin, "Biographical Outline"; material in the archives of the Ben-Zvi Institute in Jerusalem; and an unpublished autobiographical sketch written by Sukenik and dated October 28, 1946, in the Dropsie College Archives of the Annenberg Research Institute in Philadelphia.

On archaeological activity in Palestine during the first decade of British rule, see Moorey, *A Century of Biblical Archaeology*, and King, *American Archaeology in the Mideast*. On the early history of Jewish interest in archaeology, see Brawer, *Memoirs* and "From the Early Days of the Israel Exploration Society"; Shavit, "'Truth Shall Spring Out of the Earth'"; Broshi, "Religion, Ideology, and Politics"; and Kempinski, "The Impact of Archaeology on Israeli Society and Culture."

Details on Sukenik's first archaeological explorations were drawn from Yadin "Biographical Outline," and from Sukenik's article published in *Journal of the Palestine Oriental Society* in 1920. His frequent visits to the American School from February 18, 1921, to September 21, 1922, are recorded in his own handwriting in the school's guestbook. On Sukenik's decision to study in Berlin, see Press, *A Hundred Years of Jerusalem*.

The anecdotes from Yadin's childhood were based on Ben-Porath, "Conversations"; an interview with Yossi Yadin; conversations with Yadin recalled by Elizabeth Podkaminer; and conversations with Chassiya Feinsod-Sukenik recalled by Hannah and Dan Barag.

For Chassiya Feinsod-Sukenik's career in education, see her *Pirkey Gan*. For the history of Hebrew kindergarten teaching, see Rinott, *Hilfsverein*, and Elboim-Dror, *Hebrew Education*. For the general context of kindergarten education in this period, see Cavallo, "The Politics of Latency."

The account of Yadin's years in the Kallen School is based on interviews with Yossi Yadin, Hava Magnes, Trude Dothan, Havah Ya'ari, and Rita Arnon. Other sources include Yuval, "Archaeological Exploration"; Efrat, *Deborah Kallen; Her Life and Work*; and material from the Ben-Zvi Institute Archives.

On Sukenik's year in Berlin, see Yadin "Biographical Outline," and Loewinger, "Prof. E. L. Sukenik." For the intellectual history of archaeology in Berlin in that period, see Solmsen, "Classical Scholarship." A full bibliography of Sukenik's early archaeological works can be found in Ben-Horin, "The Writings of E. L. Sukenik." On his early experiences at Hebrew University, see Sukenik, "Twenty-Five Years of Archaeology."

CHAPTER 2: FATHER AND SON

My account of the Beth Alpha excavations is based on interviews with Yossi Yadin and Nahman Avigad and on material in the files of the Israel Antiquities

Authority. Published sources include Sukenik, *The Ancient Synagogue of Beth Alpha*, and his remarks at the Fifth Archaeological Conference of the Jewish Palestine Exploration Society. News of Sukenik's discoveries at Beth Alpha and their possible significance appeared in *The New York Times*, January 23, March 4, and April 29, 1929.

On the growing tensions in Jerusalem in 1928 and 1929, see Rosenthal, *The Jewish Community in Palestine*; Taggar, *The Mufti of Jerusalem*; Mattar, *The Mufti of Jerusalem*; Cohen, *The Year after the Riots*; Slutzky, *Haganah*; and Yanait et al., *The Haganah in Jerusalem*. The effect on the children of the Kallen School was described for me in interviews with Havah Ya'ari and Hava Magnes. Yigael Sukenik's composition is printed in Efrat, *Deborah Kallen; Her Life and Work*, p. 87.

The account of the Jewish scouting movement in Jerusalem and Yadin's involvement in it is based on Hemda Allon, "The Scouting Movement from its Beginnings"; Yuval "Archaeological Exploration"; and interviews with Yossi Yadin and Eliyahu Carmel. On the early commemoration of Masada, see Shapira, *Land and Power*, and Dan Bitan, "Masada: The Symbol and the Myth."

The establishment of Rechavia, its gymnasium, and its community life is documented in interviews with Yossi Yadin, Trude Dothan, and Hava Magnes, and in interviews published in Yuval, "Archaeological Exploration"; *Hebrew Gymnasium Anniversary Volume*; and material in the Ben-Zvi Institute and Jerusalem Municipality archives.

CHAPTER 3: INTO THE UNDERGROUND

The basic source for the early history of the Haganah is Slutzky, *Haganah*. Other sources for the Haganah's organization in 1929–39 are Yanait, *The Haganah in Jerusalem*; Avidar, *On the Way to Tzahal*; and Pa'il, *The Emergence of Zahal*.

The account of Yadin's early experiences in the Haganah is based on his own testimony in Yanait, *The Haganah in Jerusalem*; an interview with Yosef Avidar; and the unpublished testimonies of Yaacov Patt and Israel Ben-Yehuda in the Haganah Archives.

Yadin's graduating grades are preserved in the Rechavia Gymnasium papers in the Jerusalem Municipality Archives. I have based this reconstruction of his postgraduation year on an interview with Yossi Yadin and on Ben-Porath, "Conversations." For the background of the labor unrest in the Sharon Valley, see Naor, "The Struggle for 'Jewish Labor'"; for the acquisition of the lands of Gush Etzion, see Katz, "Purchase of JNF Land."

Yossi Yadin, Avraham Biran, and the late Dr. Avigad provided details on Yadin's early interest in archaeology. On Eleazar Sukenik's archaeological activity, see Yadin, "Biographical Outline," and Sukenik, "Twenty-Five Years." Yadin provided additional details on his decision to study archaeology in Ben-Porath, "Conversations," and in a recorded interview for the Hebrew University, November 24, 1983. For a description of the faculty and course offerings in the late 1930s, see Barshai, "The Hebrew University," and the 1939 edition of *The Hebrew University: Its History and Development*.

The political and economic background to the 1936–39 Arab rebellion is provided by Bowden, "The Politics of the Arab Rebellion"; Abboushi, "The Road to Rebellion"; Arnon-Ohanna, "The Bands in the Palestinian Arab Revolt"; Stein, "Rural Change and Peasant Destitution"; Hurewitz, *The Struggle for Palestine*; Black, *Zionism and the Arabs*; and Bethell, *The Palestine Triangle*.

Details of the 1935–36 Haganah officers' course are drawn from Slutzky, *Haganah*; Yanait, *The Haganah in Jerusalem*; and a report by Hadassah (Rabinovitz) Berlinsky in the Haganah Archives. Yadin's career at Kfar Etzion and Kiryat Anavim was described by him in Yanait, *The Haganah in Jerusalem*, and by Abdu in testimony in the Haganah Archives. On Yitzhak Sadeh's creation of the mobile patrol in the Jerusalem hills, see Slutzky, *Haganah*; Sadeh, *What Did the Palmach Introduce?*; and generally, Shapira, *Land and Power*. The 1937 course at Kiryat Anavim is described in Slutzky, *Haganah*, and in the testimony of Lukik Gershonovitch in the Haganah Archives.

On the donation that established the National Museum, see Sukenik, "Twenty-Five Years." On his collecting expeditions and travels through prewar Europe, see Yadin, "Biographical Outline."

For details and chronology of the British response to the Arab revolt, see, among others, Slutzky, *Haganah*, and Bowden, *The Breakdown of Public Security*. On the establishment of FOSH and its organization, see Pa'il, *The Emergence of Zahal*, and Slutzky, *Haganah*. For Yadin's first code name and those of his friends, see Rivlin and Rivlin, *The Stranger Cannot Understand*.

CHAPTER 4: THE INDIRECT APPROACH

My description of activities in the Jerusalem Haganah branch in 1939 and 1940 is based on interviews with Shlomo Shamir amd Yosef Avidar; material in the Haganah Archives; Slutzky, *Haganah*; and Yanait, *The Haganah in Jerusalem*. For the transformation of the Haganah, see also Pa'il, *The Emergence of Zahal*, and Avidar, *On the Way to Tzahal*.

On the change in British policy toward Zionism and the Haganah and on the arrest of the "forty-three," see, in addition to the works cited above, Zweig, "Britain, the Haganah," and Shefer, "Principles of British Pragmatism"; for a personal account, see Dayan, *The Story of My Life*.

The description of academic life at the Hebrew University department of archaeology is based on the 1939 university catalogue; Sukenik, "Twenty-Five Years"; Yadin, "Biographical Outline"; Yadin's recollections in his 1983 interview for Hebrew University; and interviews with Nahman Avigad and Hannah (Rabinovich) Gordon.

On the Haganah training courses, see Slutzky, *Haganah*; Avidar, *On the Way to Tzahal*; and an interview with Yosef Avidar. On Liddell Hart's influence on the young Sukenik's military thinking, see Bond, *Liddell Hart*, pp. 244–46, and Ben-Moshe, "Liddell Hart and the Israel Defense Forces," pp. 373–76.

Yadin recalled his first impressions of Dostrovsky in Ben-Porath, "Conversations," and in a eulogy he delivered on March 8, 1973. The text is preserved in the Haganah Archives. On the wartime activities of the Haganah and the establishment of the Palmach, see Bauer, *From Diplomacy to Resistance*. On Plan A and the 1941 national training course at Juara, see Slutzky, *Haganah*, and a detailed interview with Zvi Gilat in the Haganah Archives.

For Carmella's childhood and her father's reaction to her courtship with Yigael Sukenik, see Ruppin, *Memoirs*. Additional information on their early acquaintance came from interviews with Yossi Yadin, Nahman Avigad, Hannah Gordon, Hava Magnes, Nahum Hacohen, Leon and Lily Shalit, and Yaacov Yannai.

On the Haganah's response to the threatened German invasion, see Gelber, *Masada*. On the establishment of the Jewish Brigade Group, see Gelber, *Jewish Palestinian Volunteering*. For Fistuk's own account of his wartime experience, see Rabinowitz, "Lessons."

Yadin later published an excerpt from his master's thesis in Yadin, "Arabic Inscriptions." From 1943, he served as archaeological correspondent for the newspaper *Al Hamishmar* and also published articles on archaeological subjects in *Teva ve-Aretz*.

On the move toward activism within the Haganah and for details on the Athlit operation, see Slutzky, *Haganah*. Additional details on the 1945 training course were provided in a report in the Haganah Archives. The circumstances of Yadin's disagreement with Sadeh were recalled by him in Ben-Porath, "Conversations," and in more colorful and vivid detail in an article in *Haolam Hazeh* on January 19, 1977.

CHAPTER 5: PLAN D

The excavation on the property of Anton Kiraz is described in Meltzer, "The First Sign of the Cross?" and in Sukenik, "The Earliest Records of Christianity."

My account of Yadin's return to full-time university study is based on interviews with Benjamin Mazar, Avraham Malamat, Trude Dothan, Moshe Dothan, and Hannah Gordon. Details of the social activities of Yigael and Carmella came from interviews with Chaim Herzog and Hava Magnes.

Yadin recalled his first interview with Ben-Gurion in an interview with Shlomo Sneh on December 20, 1976; a transcript is in the Ben-Gurion Archives. For Ben-Gurion's early efforts to institute changes in the Haganah, see Gelber, *Emergence*, pp. 20–33. On the secret meeting with the UNSCOP members, see Avidar, *On the Way to Tzahal*, pp. 260–61.

My account of Eleazar Sukenik's fundraising trip to America is based on documents and correspondence in the Sukenik file in the Dropsie College Archives of the Annenberg Research Institute. For Sukenik's dealings with Ohan in the autumn of 1947 and his acquisition of the first Dead Sea Scrolls, see Yadin, "Biographical Outline," and Yadin, *Message of the Scrolls*. Although both Yadin and Sukenik recorded the name of the Bethlehem dealer as Feidi Salahi, it seems that his correct name was Feidi el-Alami. See Brownlee, "Edh-Deeb's Story," pp. 491–92.

On Yadin's work as head of the operations branch in the autumn of 1947, see Gelber, *Emergence*, pp. 449–50. Yadin's own recollections are included in the 1976 Sneh interview; Ben-Porath, "Conversations"; and in an article by Dov Goldstein in *Maariv* on April 4, 1983. For the general diplomatic and military situation, see Bar-Zohar, *Ben-Gurion*. Additional details about the atmosphere in the general staff at this time were provided in an interview with Yosef Avidar. Yadin's quote on his aggressive manner with Ben-Gurion comes from a 1976 interview by Shlomo Sneh for the Department of Oral History of the Ben-Gurion Institute of Sde Boker.

For Sukenik's negotiations with Kiraz in the late winter of 1948, see Yadin, "Biographical Outline," and *Message of the Scrolls*. For the participation of President Judah Magnes, see Goren, *Dissenter in Zion*, pp. 54–56.

On Yadin's February assessment of the Haganah's loss of initiative, see Pa'il, *The Emergence of Zahal*; Gelber, *Emergence*; and Avidar, "Plan D." The text of the general guidelines of Plan D was published in Slutzky, *Haganah*, pp. 1955–1959. See also Khalidi, "Plan Dalet."

For the diplomatic and military events of March 1948 and Ben-Gurion's decisive reaction to them, see Bar-Zohar, *Ben-Gurion*. The most detailed history of the battle for the road to Jerusalem is Yitzhaki, *Latrun*. For a readable popular account, see Collins and Lapierre, *O Jerusalem*.

My account of the March 31 meeting at Ben-Gurion's home is based on Ben-Gurion, *War Diary*; Bar-Zohar, *Ben-Gurion*, p. 695; Yadin's recollections in the 1976 interview with Shlomo Sneh; Ben-Porath, "Conversations"; and an interview with Yosef Avidar.

For Operation Nachshon and the subsequent events, see, for example, Slutzky, *Haganah*; Yitzhaki, *Latrun*; Morris, *Birth of the Palestinian Refugee Problem*, pp. 61–131; and Khalaf, *Politics in Palestine*, pp. 199–230.

CHAPTER 6: BEN-GURION'S SHADOW

The main recent sources for the first War of the Generals are Gelber, *Why Did They Break Up the Palmach?*; Shapira, *Army Controversy 1948*; and Pa'il and Ronen, *Rift in 1948*. I have also used the description in Bar-Zohar, *Ben-Gurion*; Yadin's recollections in his many published interviews; Ben-Gurion, *War Diary*; and an interview with Yosef Avidar.

For the secret negotiations with Abdullah and the question of a tacit agreement, see Shlaim, *Collusion*. The description of the famous meeting of the provisional government on May 13 is based on Bar-Zohar, *Ben-Gurion*, pp. 736–37, and on Yadin's somewhat idealized recollections in Goldstein, "Interview"; his 1976 interview with Shlomo Sneh; and Ben-Porath, "Conversations."

Additional details on the day of the official establishment of the State of Israel and the preparations of the Haganah are drawn from interviews with Yosef Avidar and Yaacov Yannai; Goldstein, "Interview"; and Gelber's 1978 interview with Yadin for the Department of Oral History of the Ben-Gurion Institute of Sde Boker. On the movements and disposition of the Arab armies, see Yitzhaki, *Latrun*, pp. 131–44, and Shlaim, *Collusion*.

The reported dispute over the dispatch of the artillery pieces to Deganiah is described in Bar-Zohar, *Ben-Gurion*, pp. 756–57, and by Yadin in virtually all of his published interviews on the War of Independence. I have quoted from Bashan, "Yigael Yadin," and Goldstein, "Interview."

The battle for Latrun and the controversy and recriminations surrounding the repeated failure to open the main road to Jerusalem is the subject of an enormous body of historical analysis and polemic. In addition to the accounts in Gelber, *Emergence*; Bar-Zohar, *Ben-Gurion*; Yitzhaki, *Latrun*; and the 1948 testimony in Shapira, *Army Controversy*, I have benefited from discussions with Professors Shapira and Gelber and from interviews with Chaim Herzog, Yitzhak Rabin, and Shlomo Shamir. For Yadin's own version of the events, I have quoted his recollections from Bashan, "Yigael Yadin"; Goldstein, "Interview"; and Ben-Porath, "Conversations." On Marcus's tense, teasing relationship with Yadin, see Berkman, *Cast a Giant Shadow*, p. 74 and throughout.

An interview with Avraham Harman supplied general background on Yadin's appearance and performance at wartime press conferences. Yadin recalled his intentionally deceptive report about the progress of the battle with the Egyptians in Goldstein, "Interview."

Yossi Yadin shared with me his recollections of his brother Matti and his last meeting with him. Yadin's memories are quoted in Ben-Porath, "Conversation." Details of Yadin's reaction were provided in interviews with Yossi Yadin and Yaacov Yannai. Yadin's letter of condolence to his parents is quoted in Sweet, "Yadin."

CHAPTER 7: TEN PLAGUES

On the construction and expansion of Derekh Sheva and the resupply of Jerusalem, see Yitzhaki, *Latrun*, pp. 333–51. For the reorganization of the high command during the first truce, see Gelber, *Emergence*, pp. 472–80. Yadin's recollection of the daylong officers' meeting is quoted in Goldstein, "Interview." For Ben-Gurion's perspective, see the extensive entry in his *War Diary* for June 18.

Yadin's role in the *Altalena* affair is described at length in Bar-Zohar, *Ben-Gurion*, pp. 783–92. On the official swearing-in of the IDF high command, see Ben-Gurion, *The Renewed State*, pp. 207–208. My account is also based on an interview with Yosef Avidar.

On the second War of the Generals, see Gelber, *Why Did They Break Up the Palmach?*; Shapira, *Army Controversy 1948*; and Pa'il and Ronen, *Rift in 1948*. A transcript of the proceedings of the Committee of Five is appended to the text of Shapira's book; Yadin's main testimony begins on p. 103. For the explosive culmination of the hearings, see Bar-Zohar, *Ben-Gurion*. For Yadin's version of the compromise resolution, see Goldstein, "Interview."

For an extensive account of the resumption of the fighting, especially in the area of Lod and Ramleh, see Oren, *Operation Danni*. Additional details on the tensions between Yadin and the Palmach were provided in an interview with Yitzhak Rabin. On the conquest of Lod and Ramleh and the resulting exodus of Arab inhabitants, see Morris, *The Birth*, pp. 203–12.

For a detailed description of the Tel Aviv victory parade, see Ben-Gurion, *The Renewed State*, pp. 242–46. The reorganization and redeployment of the IDF for renewed fighting is documented in Gelber, *Emergence*, pp. 477–80. On the activities of Bernadotte and the circumstances of his assassination, see Amitzur, *Bernadotte in Palestine*, and Tzameret, "The Affair of the Mediation."

For Ben-Gurion's strategic planning in September 1948, see Shlaim, *Collusion*, and Bar-Zohar, *Ben-Gurion*, pp. 819–25. My account of Operation Ten

Plagues is based on Lorch, *Israel's War* , with additional details from interviews with Yitzhak Rabin and Chaim Herzog. On the attempt of the British government to influence the territorial outcome of the 1948 war, see Pappé, *Britain and the Arab-Israeli Conflict*. On the threat of British intervention and the American ultimatum, see McDonald, *My Mission in Israel*. The events are described from the Israeli perspective in Bar-Zohar, *Ben-Gurion*. Yadin's memories of the successful operations against the Egyptians are quoted in Ben-Porath, "Conversations," and Evron, "The Operation."

The quotations from Yadin's January 8 press conference were published in a lengthy news report in *The Jerusalem Post* on the following day. Ben-Gurion noted Fred Harris's evaluation of Yadin in his journal on January 4, 1949.

For Eleazar Sukenik's activities in late 1948, see Yadin, "Biographical Outline." His remarks about the role of archaeology in the new state of Israel are in the *Bulletin of the Jewish Palestine Exploration Society* 15 (1949), p. 49. Schwabe's announcement of Yadin's election to the governing board of the society appears on p. 57; his greeting to the assembled members, on p. 55.

CHAPTER 8: THREATS AND PERSUASIONS

The basic published source for the 1949 armistice negotiations is Rosenthal, ed., *Israel State Archives, Documents on the Foreign Policy of the State of Israel, Armistice Negotiations with the Arab States, December 1948–July 1949*. Most of the diplomatic dispatches and communications quoted in this chapter are derived from this source. Also important are Eytan, *The First Ten Years*; Berger, *The Covenant*; and Rabinovich, *The Road Not Taken*.

Additional details on the negotiations with Egypt at Rhodes have been drawn from interviews with Walter Eytan and Yitzhak Rabin and from contemporary press reports. Yadin's recollections of the negotiations are quoted in Bashan, "Yigael Yadin," and in Ben-Porath, "Conversations." Ben-Gurion's expressions of satisfaction with the conclusion of an agreement with Egypt and with Yadin's negotiating skill appear in his *War Diary* on February 24 and 25, 1949.

My account of the secret negotiations with King Abdullah is based on the general sources cited above, as well as on an interview with Walter Eytan; Yadin's recollections in Bashan, "Yigael Yadin"; Eytan, "Three Nights"; Dayan, *The Story of My Life*; and Shlaim, *Collusion*.

Yadin recalled Abdullah et-Tell's proposal to conquer Syria in Bashan, "Yigael Yadin." The reported Syrian offer to underwrite a military coup in Israel is recorded in Rabinovich, *The Road Not Taken*. On the negotiations with Syria, see also Shalev, *Cooperation*. On the futile efforts of the Palestine Conciliation Commission, see Forsythe, *U.N. Peacemaking*; Spungen, "Deadlock at Lausanne"; and Perla, "Israel and the Palestine Conciliation Commission." Yadin's official mission to Prague is documented in Bialer, *Between East and West*, pp. 160, 178.

The official efforts to reduce the size and expense of the Israel Defense Forces beginning in the spring of 1949 are detailed in Gelber, *Emergence*, pp. 483–507. Ben-Gurion's projections on the future of the IDF are quoted in Greenberg, "The Defense Budget." The archival sources for Yadin's rift with Dori are documented in Gelber, *Emergence*, pp. 497–98.

My account of Yadin's appointment as chief of staff is based on his own recollections in Ben-Porath, "Conversations"; an entry in Ben-Gurion's diary on August 26, 1949; Bar-Zohar, *Ben-Gurion*, pp. 942ff.; and Gelber, *Emergence*, pp. 507–509. Yadin's first order of the day as chief of staff was published in Erez and Kfir, *Tzahal be-Helo*, 1:68.

CHAPTER 9: CHIEF OF STAFF

For the geopolitical situation of Israel in the early 1950s, see Bialer, *Between East and West*; Pappé, "Overt Conflict to Tacit Alliance"; Eytan, *The First Ten Years*; and Safran, *Israel*, pp. 334–47. McDonald's account of his visit with Yadin can be found in his *My Mission in Israel*, pp. 195–96.

On the power struggles within the general staff at the beginning of Yadin's term of office, see Gelber, *Emergence*, pp. 509–512, and Shtaigman, *From Independence to Kadesh*.

The account of the establishment of the army reserve system and the expansion of IDF activities in Israeli society is based on contemporary press accounts; material in the Israel Defense Forces Archives; Yadin's recollections in Ben-Porath, "Conversations"; Lorch, "Yadin's Finest Hours;" and an interview with Netanel Lorch.

For the evolving military and political relationship between Israel and Great Britain, see Pappé, *Britain and the Arab-Israeli Conflict*. Ben-Gurion's reprimand to General Robertson is quoted in Bar-Zohar, *Ben-Gurion*, p. 904.

Yadin's remarks to the teachers were issued as a press release on April 4, 1950, by the Government Press Office. An editorial criticizing those remarks appeared in *The Jerusalem Post* on April 12. On the problems of absorbing new immigrants, see the articles in Naor, *Immigrants and Transfer Camps*. I have based my account of the relief mission on the interview with Netanel Lorch and on material in the Israel Defense Forces Archives.

The background and chronology of the 1950 military confrontations with Syria are documented in Shalev, *Cooperation*, and Berger, *The Covenant*. Additional details are from interviews with Yitzhak Rabin, Netanel Lorch, and Meir Amit, and from material in the Israel Defense Forces Archives. On the subsequent maneuvers in the Negev and Yadin's sometimes uneasy relationship with Dayan, see Slater, *Warrior Statesman*, pp. 138–39, and Yadin's recollections quoted in Ben-Porath, "Conversations."

Yadin's memories of Ben-Gurion's reluctance to see wounded soldiers at Latrun and Ben-Gurion's first sight of dead bodies come from an interview with Yadin conducted by Yoav Gelber on December 14, 1978, transcript preserved at the Ben-Gurion Archives. Sapir's evaluation of the Yadin–Ben-Gurion relationship is quoted in Bar-Zohar, *Ben-Gurion*, p. 871.

Ben-Gurion's growing worry about Yadin's behavior and Yadin's eventual resignation is described in Bar-Zohar, *Ben-Gurion*, pp. 943–47. The following account is based on references in Ben-Gurion's diary and material from the Ben-Gurion Archives as well as on Yadin's recollections in the 1978 Gelber interview; Greenberg, "The Defense Budget"; Bashan, "Yigael Yadin"; and interviews with Netanel Lorch, Yitzhak Navon, and Meir Zorea.

Ben-Gurion's love of books and his gift of the bound volumes of Josephus' histories are recalled by Yadin in the 1978 Gelber interview; in Bashan, "Yigael Yadin"; and in Ben-Porath, "Conversations." The inscribed volumes are today in the library of the Hebrew Union College in Jerusalem.

CHAPTER 10: SONS OF LIGHT, SONS OF DARKNESS

For a description of the Petrie Centennial celebrations, see Drower, *Flinders Petrie*, pp. xix–xxi. My account of the Yadins' time in London is based on correspondence in the Hebrew University archives and on interviews with Benjamin Mazar, Avraham Malamat, and Leon and Lily Shalit.

On the career and personality of Mortimer Wheeler, see Hawkes, *Adventurer in Archaeology*.

For details on the last years of Eleazar Sukenik's life, see Yadin, "Biographical Outline." On Yadin's early work on the War Scroll, see the preface to *The Scroll of the War of the Sons of Light Against the Sons of Darkness*.

My account of Yadin's completion of his dissertation, its contents, and its preparation for publication is based on an interview with Benjamin Mazar and on correspondence in the Hebrew University Archives.

Details on the travels of Archbishop Samuel have been provided by Burrows, *The Dead Sea Scrolls*; Trever, *The Untold Story*; and Samuel, *Treasure of Qumran*. Yadin's own account of his secret purchase of the scrolls is in his *Message of the Scrolls*. Additional details come from Orlinsky, "The Dead Sea Scrolls and Mr. Green," and from interviews with Archbishop Samuel, Avraham Harman, and Harry Orlinsky. I would like to thank Hershel Shanks for calling my attention to an item in the *National Jewish Post and Opinion* on April 22, 1992, that explains how Yadin learned about the *Wall Street Journal* advertisement.

Yadin's lecture at the Cambridge congress was later published as "The Earliest Record of Egypt's Military Penetration into Asia?"

Sharett's references to Yadin's future, perhaps as an ambassador to the United States, come from his published *Personal Diary*, entries for February 24, March 16, and April 11, 1954. For Sharett's plan to dispatch him to meet with Nasser, see entries for January 21, 24, and 26, 1955. The secret mission to Egypt is also described in Bar-Zohar, *Ben-Gurion*, p. 1052.

For the official announcement of Israel's acquisition of the scrolls, see Yadin, *Message*, p. 52, and Sharett, *Personal Diary*, February 13, 1955.

On the philanthropic attachments of the Rothschilds, see Schama, *Two Rothschilds and the Land of Israel*. Details of the Yadins' farewell tour of Europe were provided in an interview with Yaacov Yannai.

CHAPTER 11: HEAD OF ALL THOSE KINGDOMS

The basic, nontechnical published sources for the story of the Hazor expedition are Yadin, *Hazor: The Rediscovery of a Great Citadel of the Bible* and Yadin, *Hazor: The Schweich Lectures*. The expedition published interim reports in the *Israel Exploration Journal* and four large volumes of plates and technical reports between 1959 and 1964. I have also based my account of the expedition on contemporary press reports and interviews with Trude Dothan, Moshe Dothan, Aviva Rosen, Joseph Aviram, Benjamin Mazar, Leon Shalit, David Ussishkin, and Amnon Ben-Tor.

On Ben-Gurion's return to office, see Bar-Zohar, *Ben-Gurion*. On his offer of the Ministry of the South and the Negev to Yadin, see Sharett, *Personal Diary*, May 9, 1955.

On the changing physical landscape of Israel after 1948, see, for example, Golan, "The Transfer," and Khalidi, *All That Remains*. For discussions of the perceptual connection between images of modern Arab culture and representations of antiquity, see, for example, discussions in Shenfeld, *From King Messiah*, and Gratz, "The War of Independence."

Yadin's own recollection of the outbreak of the 1956 war is quoted in Goldstein, "Interview."

My account of Yadin's early career at the university is based on interviews with Avraham Malamat, Trude Dothan, Aviva Rosen, David Ussishkin, Amnon Ben-Tor, and Dan Barag. Details on the dispute over Yadin's 1958 European trip have been provided by documents and correspondence in the Hebrew University Archives.

For an intriguing discussion of the Yadin-Aharoni conflict and its impact on Israeli archaeology, see Geva, "Israeli Biblical Archaeology." See also Moorey, *A Century of Biblical Archaeology*, pp. 116–19. For a definitive history of rival territorial conceptions within Zionism, see Shapira, *Land and Power*. For the published versions of Yadin's and Aharoni's lectures at Ben-Gurion's Bible Circle and transcripts of the discussions that followed each presentation, see Rabin, *Studies in the Book of Joshua*.

My account of Ben-Gurion's attempts to persuade Yadin to join the Mapai list for the 1959 elections is based on excerpts from Ben-Gurion's diary and on correspondence in the Ben-Gurion Archives. See also the account in Bar-Zohar, *Ben-Gurion*, pp. 1441–42.

CHAPTER 12: THE CAVE OF LETTERS

The description of the Judean desert expedition is based on interviews with Joseph Aviram and David Ussishkin; on Yadin's books *Bar-Kokhba* and *The Finds from the Bar-Kokhba Period*; and on contemporary press reports.

On the first discovery of Bar-Kokhba documents in Jordan, see Yadin, *Message*, 68–72. On Aharoni's early expeditions to Nahal Hever, see his *In the Footsteps of Kings and Rebels*.

For the announcement of the discovery of the Bar-Kokhba letters in the president's residence, I have relied on interviews with Joseph Aviram, David Ussishkin, Avraham Malamat, and Yitzhak Navon.

Gillon's admiring profile of Yadin was published in *The Jerusalem Post* on February 17, 1961. On the sources of research support during Yadin's sabbatical year in London, see the detailed list in his preface to *The Finds from the Bar-Kokhba Period*.

Yadin's quote about the juxtaposition of past and present during the Judean wilderness expedition comes from Yadin, *Bar-Kokhba*, p. 253.

CHAPTER 13: MASADA

The basic published source on the Masada expedition is Yadin, *Masada: Herod's Fortress and the Zealots' Last Stand*. The final reports were published beginning in 1989 by the Israel Exploration Society under the editorship of Joseph Aviram, Gideon Foerster, and Ehud Netzer. For a review of the scholarly literature on Masada before the final publications, see Feldman, "Masada: A Critique," and Ladouceur, "Masada: A Consideration." For the political and ideological aspects of Masada in Israeli society, see Alter, "The Masada Complex"; Shargel, "The Evolution of the Masada Myth"; and my own essay on Masada in *Between Past and Present*, pp. 87–101.

My account of the organization and work of the Masada expedition is also based on contemporary press reports and interviews with Joseph Aviram, Gideon Foerster, Ehud Netzer, Amnon Ben-Tor, Dan Bahat, Aharon Kempinski, and Leon Shalit.

For the finds from the earlier expedition to Masada, see Avi-Yonah et al., *Masada*.

Details on the initial contact between Yadin and David Astor of *The Observer* were provided in an interview with Chaim Herzog. Yadin's remarks at the first press conference about Masada are quoted in *The Jerusalem Post* on August 12, 1963. His speech to the recruits is quoted in Elon, *The Israelis*, p. 288.

Gavron's report on the opening day of the Masada expedition appeared in *The Jerusalem Post* on October 15, 1963. O'Donovan's first report was published in *The Jerusalem Post* on October 13.

Yadin's first public announcement of the manuscripts and synagogue appeared in *The Jerusalem Post* on November 24, 1963.

Transcripts of the evening meetings of the Masada staff are preserved with the other expedition records at the Institute of Archaeology of the Hebrew University. I would like to thank Dr. Ehud Netzer for allowing me access to them. The discussion of the age and identity of the three fragmentary skeletons in the northern palace took place on the evening of November 26, 1963.

On the political alliance between Levi Eshkol and Achdut Avodah, see Shaham, *Israel*, pp. 211–21. Ben-Gurion's calls for electoral reform were reported in *The Jerusalem Post* on February 28, 1964. His praise for Dayan's role in the 1948 war appeared in an article in *Haboker* on March 6, 1964. The responses of Yadin and Yigal Allon to Ben-Gurion's remarks are quoted in *The Jerusalem Post* on March 9. A report on the Rothschild Science Award ceremony appeared in *The Jerusalem Post* on June 24, 1964.

Details on Ben-Gurion's secret proposal that Yadin vie for the leadership of Mapai before the 1965 elections were provided in his own words in Ben-Porath, "Conversations," and in Urieli and Barzilay, *Rise and Fall*, p. 19. Information about Yadin's post-Masada travels and fund-raising activities was obtained from material in the Hebrew University Archives.

Yadin's quotations about the identity of the human remains in the cave and in the northern palace come from his book *Masada*, pp. 54, 197. His statement about the symbolic importance of Masada for modern Israel appears on p. 201.

For Shaye Cohen's telling criticism of the Masada story and the common use of the suicide motif in ancient literature, see his "Masada: Literary Tradition." Finley's review of Yadin's book appeared on December 2, 1966. Alsop's *Newsweek* columns, in which he first coined the phrase "Masada complex" and in which he quoted Golda Meir's reaction to it, were published on July 12, 1971, and March 19, 1973.

Yadin's demurral about personal political ambitions is quoted in Kohn, "Yadin: Views of a Soldier-Scholar."

CHAPTER 14: PREPARING FOR BATTLE

The account of Yadin's activities during the weeks leading up to the 1967 war is based on his own recollections in Ben-Porath, "Conversations," and on interviews with Yitzhak Rabin, Ezer Weizman, Meir Zorea, Meir Amit, Yaacov Yannai, Joseph Aviram, Aviva Rosen, and Avraham Malamat. For more general accounts of the prewar tension, see Neff, *Warriors for Jerusalem*; for the strategic situation, see Safran, *Israel, the Embattled Ally*; and for the military operations, see Herzog, *The Arab-Israeli Wars*. On the appointment of Dayan as defense minister, from sharply different perspectives, see Dayan, *The Story of My Life*, and Rabin, *The Rabin Memoirs*. On Yadin's ambiguous role in the negotiations, see Ben-Porath, "Conversations"; Urieli and Barzilay, *Rise and Fall*, pp. 18–19, 26–27; and Slater, *Warrior Statesman*, pp. 253–58.

The first, hasty visit to the Rockefeller Museum is based on interviews with Joseph Aviram, Nahman Avigad, and Avraham Biran. On Yadin's long, unsuccessful negotiations for and eventual acquisition of the Temple Scroll, see his own account in *The Temple Scroll*; Hershel Shanks, "Intrigue and the Scroll"; and a highly embroidered account of the confiscation by one of the intelligence officers involved in the operation in Sutton, *Men of Secrets*, pp. 261–78. Additional details of the acquisition and early preservation efforts have been drawn from interviews with Joseph Aviram and Joseph Shenhav. Yadin's first public lecture on the scroll's contents was reported in *The Jerusalem Post* on October 22, 1967. A shortened version of the lecture text was published in *The Jerusalem Post* on December 29, 1967.

On the public dispute between Yadin and Vilnay, see *The Jerusalem Post*, October 22, 1967. Cahane's derogatory comments were reported in *The Jerusalem Post* on October 23, 1967. Yadin's views on the role of archaeology in modern Israeli consciousness are quoted in Kohn, "The Image of the Israeli." On the plans for the reburial ceremony at Masada, see *The Jerusalem Post*, July 7, 1969. A news account of the ceremony itself was published in *The Jerusalem Post* on the following day.

Details about Yadin's honorary degrees and overseas lecture schedule were drawn from material in the Hebrew University Archives. The account of the 1968 excavations at Hazor is based on interviews with Amnon Ben-Tor, Aviva Rosen, Amihai Mazar, and other participants in that expedition.

Yadin's reflections on Israel's spiritual future are quoted in Goldstein, "Interview." Yadin's comments at the meeting of the electoral reform committee were reported in *The Jerusalem Post* on July 20, 1973.

CHAPTER 15: WAR OF ATONEMENT

For the general background of the events leading to the outbreak of the Yom Kippur War, see Safran, *Israel*, and Herzog, *The Arab-Israeli Wars*. For contrasting perspectives, see Dayan, *The Story of My Life*; Bar-Tov, *Dado*; and Ben-Porat, *Neila*. Yadin's memories of his role in the war room during the early days of the fighting are in Ben-Porath, "Conversations." Additional details were drawn from interviews with Yitzhak Rabin, Meir Zorea, and Yaacov Yannai.

My account of Yadin's postwar approach to the Meir government is based on Ben-Porath, "Conversations"; Urieli and Barzilay, *Rise and Fall*, pp. 14–15; and an interview with Yaacov Yannai. Yadin's changing attitude toward the idea of an investigatory commission was reported in *The Jerusalem Post* on November 2 and 18, 1973. For Yadin's appointment and work on the Agranat Commission, I have relied on interviews with Yaacov Yannai, Meir Zorea, and Yoav Gelber, and on the account in Urieli and Barzilay, *Rise and Fall*, pp. 15–18, 29–31. Yadin's own reflections on the commission's deliberations are quoted in Ben-Porath, "Conversations."

The description of Yadin's initial political involvement is based on Urieli and Barzilay, *Rise and Fall*, pp. 32–41, and on an interview with Meir Zorea. Details on the Yadins' home life in late 1975 and early 1976 were provided by interviews with family friends and by Yadin's statements in Ben-Porath, "Conversations." His references to Carmella's role in his growing involvement in politics are quoted in Segev, "Anatomy."

CHAPTER 16: THE RISE AND FALL OF DASH

Yadin's reflections on his image are quoted in Segev, "Anatomy." Virtually every person I interviewed had vivid memories of Yadin's first appearance on *Moked*. A detailed account of the events preceding it and a brief synopsis can be found in Urieli and Barzilay, *Rise and Fall*, pp. 41–44.

My account of the formation, expansion, and Knesset campaign of Dash is based on interviews with Meir Zorea, Amnon Rubinstein, and Meir Amit, as well as on material from the *Jerusalem Post* Archives; Urieli and Barzilay, *Rise and Fall*; Rubinstein, *A Certain Political Experience*; and Torgovnik, "A Movement for Change." Yadin's rueful analysis of the 1977 election results is quoted in Segev, "Anatomy."

For the impact of the 1977 elections on the political right in Israel and its steady rise during the Begin era, see Sprinzak, *The Ascendance*. In addition to newspaper accounts and published sources, I have relied on interviews with Meir Zorea, Amnon Rubinstein, Meir Amit, and Maya Bailey for my account of Dash's coalition negotiations with the Likud government. Ezer Weizman's taunting statement about Yadin to Tamir is quoted in Urieli and Barzilay, *Rise and Fall*, pp. 284–85, and confirmed in an interview.

On Yadin's relatively minor ceremonial role in Sadat's visit to Jerusalem and the subsequent peace negotiations, see Tirosh, "The Man Who Prepared Sadat's Visit to Jerusalem," and Landau, "On the Defensive." It is interesting to note the scant references to Yadin in Weizman's *Battle for Peace* and Dayan's *Breakthrough*.

For the disintegration of Dash, see Urieli and Barzilay, *Rise and Fall*; Rubinstein, *A Certain Political Experience*; Yadin's own recollections quoted in Ben-Porath, "Conversations"; Segal, "Before the Break-up"; and Landau, "Yadin's Choice." Shapiro's characterization of Yadin as an irrelevant messiah is quoted from his article "Bar Kokhba Tradition."

My account of Project Renewal is drawn from interviews with Yoav Gelber and Maya Bailey, and from contemporary newspaper accounts. Of particular importance are Bellos, "A Poverty of Prospects"; Shapiro, "Judging Project Renewal"; and Elazar, "Doomed by the System." The disappointment of foreign supporters in Project Renewal is quoted in Siegel, "Renewed Interest."

Details on Yadin's official trip to Egypt were drawn from interviews with Joseph Aviram and Maya Bailey, from contemporary press reports, and from Cohen, "Double Mystery."

Yadin's polite yet unconvincing refusal of the post of foreign minister is quoted in *The Jerusalem Post* on October 30, 1979. His reluctance to bring the Begin government down is quoted in Landau, "Yadin's Choice." An account of his farewell appearance on *Moked* appeared in the Jerusalem Post on the following morning, February 19, 1981. Yadin's reflections on the destruction of his own myth are quoted in Segev, "Anatomy."

CHAPTER 17: THE BURDEN OF HISTORY

The transfer of Project Renewal to the Housing Ministry was reported in *The Jerusalem Post* on August 14, 1981.

Yadin's reflections on his natural unsuitability for political life are quoted in Shanks, "BAR Interviews Yigael Yadin."

For the chronology of religious relations with archaeology in Israel, see Rubinstein, "Bones of Contention." The account of the dispute over the excavations in the City of David is based on contemporary press reports and on a highly dramatized and polemical account published by the ultraorthodox community; Meshi-Zahav, *Slope of the Temple Mount*. Chief Rabbi Goren's initial comments on the supposed Jewish cemetery at the dig were published in *The Jerusalem Post* on August 8, 1981. Yadin's responses were published on August 8 and 13, 1981. Aviram's opposition to the intervention of the Rabbinate was reported on August 24, 1981. Yadin's opposition to the "bone bill" was reported on December 16, 1981. A photograph of the desecrated graves of Chassiya and Eleazar Sukenik was published in *The Jerusalem Post* on July 27, 1983.

On the preparations for official reburial of the bones from Nahal Hever, see accounts in *The Jerusalem Post* on November 2 and 3, 1981, and April 5, 1982.

An instructive analysis of the ceremony's political symbolism for the Likud government can be found in Aronoff, "Establishing Authority."

Yossi Yadin's recollection of his brother's reactions to the Lebanon war and its aftermath are quoted in *The Jerusalem Post* on July 7, 1984. Yadin's earlier comments on the findings of the Kahan Commission were reported on February 9, 1983. Additional details about his life and work after his resignation from the government come from an interview with Elizabeth Podkaminer.

The account of Yadin's nostalgic reminiscences about the War of Independence and his role in it was based on an interview with Anita Shapira.

For details of the 1983–84 academic year at the Hebrew University Institute for Advanced Studies, I have relied on interviews with Avraham Malamat, Israel Finkelstein, and Amihai Mazar, as well as on Stager, "A Personal Remembrance." For the dramatic changes that took place in the 1970s and 1980s in the archaeological understanding of the Israelite conquest, see Finkelstein, *The Archaeology of the Israelite Settlement*. Yadin's restatement of his position was published in his article "The Transition from a Semi-Nomadic to a Sedentary Society."

Professor Sy Gitin of the Albright Institute in Jerusalem called my attention to Yadin's efforts to foster the study of biblical archaeology in the United States. On Yadin's plans for returning to Hazor, I have relied on interviews with Joseph Aviram and Amnon Ben-Tor, and on a personal communication from Dr. Paige Patterson. On the 1984 Biblical Archaeology conference, see Yadin's "Biblical Archaeology Today." My account of the journey to Shiloh is based on an interview with Israel Finkelstein.

Details on Yadin's last days at Michmoret were provided in an interview with Yossi Yadin.

SOURCES CONSULTED

ARCHIVES

Ben-Gurion Archives, Sde Boker
Ben-Zvi Institute Archives, Jerusalem
Central Zionist Archives, Jerusalem
The Dropsie College Archives of the Annenberg Research Institute, Philadelphia
Haganah Archives, Tel Aviv
Ha-Kibbutz ha-Meuhad Archive, Ephal
Hebrew University Archives, Jerusalem
Israel Defense Forces Archives, Tel Aviv
Jerusalem Municipality Archives, Jerusalem
Jerusalem Post Archives, Jerusalem
Masada Expedition Archives, Institute of Archaeology, Hebrew University, Jerusalem
Yediot Aharonot Archives, Tel Aviv

INTERVIEWS

Meir Amit, Ramat Gan, June 25, 1991
Rita Arnon, Jerusalem, September 15, 1991
Yosef Avidar, Jerusalem, October 17, 1990
Nahman Avigad, Jerusalem, July 2, 1990
Joseph Aviram, Jerusalem, October 22, 1990; June 24, 1991; February 19, 1992
Dan Bahat, Jerusalem, October 24, 1992
Maya Bailey, Jerusalem, February 11, 1992
Dan and Hannah Barag, Jerusalem, February 14, 1992
Amnon Ben-Tor, Jerusalem, October 17, 1990; June 12, 1991
Avraham Biran, Jerusalem, October 16 and 21, 1990
Eliyahu Carmel, Jerusalem, January 9, 1992
Moshe Dothan, Jerusalem, October 20, 1990
Trude Dothan, Jerusalem, October 20, 1990
Walter Eytan, Jerusalem, June 24, 1991
Israel Finkelstein, New Orleans, November 26, 1990
Gideon Foerster, Jerusalem, October 15, 1990
Yoav Gelber, Haifa, February 15, 1992
Hannah (Rabinovich) Gordon, Ramat Gan, June 25, 1991
Nahum Hacohen, Darien, Connecticut, July 24, 1990
Avraham Harman, Jerusalem, June 12, 1991
Chaim Herzog, Jerusalem, June 24, 1991; February 17, 1992
Naomi Kaplanski, Jerusalem, October 16, 1990
Aharon Kempinski, Jerusalem, October 16, 1990
Teddy Kollek, Jerusalem, June 21, 1991
Netanel Lorch, Jerusalem, February 11, 1992
Hava Magnes, Jerusalem, June 22, 1991
Avraham Malamat, New York City, February 14, 1991
Amihai Mazar, Jerusalem, June 21, 1991
Benjamin Mazar, Jerusalem, October 17, 1990
Yitzhak Navon, Jerusalem, October 21, 1990
Ehud Netzer, Jerusalem, October 20, 1992
Harry Orlinsky, New York City, November 1, 1990
Elizabeth Podkaminer, Jerusalem, June 26, 1991
Yitzhak Rabin, Tel Aviv and Jerusalem, June 13 and 19, 1991
Aviva Rosen, Jerusalem, October 18, 1990
Amnon Rubinstein, Jerusalem, June 11, 1991
Athanasius Yeshue Samuel, Lodi, New Jersey, December 26, 1991
Leon and Lilly Shalit, Jerusalem, June 30, 1990
Shlomo Shamir, Tel Aviv, June 13, 1991
Anita Shapira, Tel Aviv, February 18, 1992
Joseph Shenhav, Jerusalem, October 25, 1992
David Ussishkin, Tel Aviv, June 20, 1991
Ezer Weizman, Jerusalem, June 11, 1991
Havah Ya'ari, Jerusalem, September 15, 1991
Yossi Yadin, Michmoret, October 19, 1990
Yaacov ("Jan") Yannai, Zahala, October 18, 1990
Meir Zorea, Ma'agan Michael, February 13, 1992

PUBLISHED SOURCES

Abboushi, W. F. "The Road to Rebellion: Arab Palestine in the 1930s." *Journal of Palestine Studies* 6 (1977): 23–46.

Agra (pseud.). *Arab Armies in Our Generation*. Tel Aviv: Maarachot, 1948. [Hebrew]

Aharoni, Yohanan. *In the Footsteps of Kings and Rebels*. Tel Aviv: Masada Press, 1966. [Hebrew]

Allon, Hemda. "The Scouting Movement from its Beginnings to 1960." *Eidan* 13 (1989): 19–36. [Hebrew]

Alsop, Stewart. "The Masada Complex." *Newsweek*, July 12, 1971, 92.

———. "Again, The Masada Complex." *Newsweek*, March 19, 1973; 104.

Alter, Robert. "The Masada Complex." *Commentary* 56 (July 1973): 19–24.

Amitzur, Ilan. *Bernadotte in Palestine, 1948: A Study in Contemporary Knight-Errantry*. Houndmills, Basingstoke: Macmillan, 1989.

Arbel, Naftali. *The Land on the Verge of Destruction*. Tel Aviv: Revivim Publishers, 1980. [Hebrew]

Arnon-Ohanna, Yuval. "The Bands in the Palestinian Arab Revolt, 1936–1939: Structure and Organization." *Asian and African Studies* 15 (1981): 229–47.

Aronoff, Myron J. "Establishing Authority: The Memorialization of Jabotinsky and the Burial of the Bar-Kochba Bones in Israel Under the Likud." In *The Frailty of Authority*, edited by Myron J. Aronoff, 105–30. New Brunswick, N.J.: Transaction Books.

Avi-Yonah, Michael. "The Third and Second Walls of Jerusalem." *Israel Exploration Journal* 18 (1968): 98–125.

Avi-Yonah, Michael; Avigad, Nahman; Aharoni, Yohanan; Dunnayevsky, Immanuel; Guttman, Shmaryahu. *Masada: Archaeological Survey in the Years 1955–1956*. Jerusalem: Israel Exploration Society, 1957. [Hebrew]

Avidar, Yosef. *On the Way to Tzahal: Memoirs*. Tel Aviv: Israeli Defense Ministry Press, 1970. [Hebrew]

———. "Plan D." *Sifra ve-Sayafa* 2 (1978): 37–48. [Hebrew]

Barshai, Bezalel. "The Hebrew University of Jerusalem, 1925–1935," *Cathedra* 53 (1989): 107–22. [Hebrew]

Bar-Tov, Hanoch. *Dado*. Tel Aviv: Maariv, 1978. [Hebrew]

Bar-Zohar, Michael. *Ben-Gurion*. Tel Aviv: Am Oved, 1977. [Hebrew]

Bashan, Raphael. "Yigael Yadin on the War of Independence." *Maariv*, May 14, 1967.

Bauer, Yehuda. *From Diplomacy to Resistance: A History of Jewish Palestine 1939–1945*. New York: Atheneum, 1973.

Bellos, Susan. "A Poverty of Prospects." *The Jerusalem Post*, March 24, 1978.

Ben-Arieh, Yehoshua. *Jerusalem in the Nineteenth Century: The Old City*. New York: St. Martin's Press, 1984.

———. *Jerusalem in the Nineteenth Century: Emergence of the New City*. New York: St. Martin's Press, 1986.

Ben-Gurion, David. *The Renewed State of Israel*. Tel Aviv: Am Oved, 1969. [Hebrew]

———. *War Diary, The War of Independence 1948–1949*, edited by Gershon Rivlin and Elhannan Oren. Tel Aviv: Israel Defense Ministry Press, 1982. [Hebrew]

Ben-Horin, U. "The Writings of E. L. Sukenik." *Eretz Israel* 8 (1967): 21–27. [Hebrew and English]

Ben-Moshe, Tuvia. "Liddell Hart and the Israel Defense Forces—A Reappraisal." *Journal of Contemporary History* 16 (1981): 369–91.

Ben-Porat, Yeshayahu. "Conversations with Yigael Yadin." *Yediot Aharonot*. March 13, 20; April 3, 10, 1981. [Hebrew]

Ben-Porat, Yoel. *Neila: Locked-On.* Jerusalem: Edanim Publishers, 1991. [Hebrew]

Bentwich, Norman, ed. *Hebrew University Garland: A Silver Jubilee Symposium.* London: Constellation Books, 1952.

Benvenisti, David. *The Streets of Jerusalem, Its Historic Sites and Institutions— Guide for the Resident and Tourist.* Jerusalem: Kiryat Sefer, 1984. [Hebrew]

Berger, Earl. *The Covenant and the Sword, Arab-Israeli Relations, 1948–56.* London: Routledge and Kegan Paul, 1965.

Berkman, Ted. *Cast a Giant Shadow.* Garden City, N.Y.: Doubleday, 1962.

Bethell, Nicholas. *The Palestine Triangle: The Struggle Between the British, the Jews, and the Arabs 1935–48.* London: Andre Deutsch, 1979.

Bialer, Uri. *Between East and West: Israel's Foreign Policy Orientation 1948–1956.* Cambridge: Cambridge University Press, 1990.

Bitan, Dan. "Masada: The Symbol and the Myth." *Eidan* 14 (1990): 221–35. [Hebrew]

Black, Ian. *Zionism and the Arabs 1936–1939.* New York: Garland Publishing, 1986.

Black, Ian; and Morris, Benny. *Israel's Secret Wars: A History of Israel's Intelligence Services.* New York: Grove Weidenfeld, 1991.

Bond, Brian. *Liddell Hart: A Study of His Military Thought.* New Brunswick, N.J.: Rutgers University Press, 1977.

Bowden, Tom. *The Breakdown of Public Security: The Case of Ireland 1916–1921 and Palestine 1936–1939.* London: Sage Publications, 1977.

———. "The Politics of the Arab Rebellion in Palestine, 1936–39." *Middle Eastern Studies* 11 (1975): 147–74.

Brawer, Avraham. "From the Early Days of the Israel Exploration Society." In *Western Galilee and the Coast of Galilee*, edited by Joseph Aviram, 228–36. Jerusalem: Israel Exploration Society, 1965. [Hebrew]

———. *Memoirs of a Father and His Son.* Jerusalem: Mosad ha-Rav Kook, 1966. [Hebrew]

Brener, Uri. *The Firings.* Ephal, Israel: Yad Tabenkin, 1987. [Hebrew]

———. *Toward an Independent Jewish Army, Kibbutz ha-Meuhad in the Hanagah, 1939–1945.* Ephal, Israel: Yad Tabenkin, 1985.

Broshi, Magen. "The Discovery of the Dead Sea Scrolls and Other Manuscripts in the Judean Wilderness." *Eidan* 14 (1990): 198–206. [Hebrew]

———. "Religion, Ideology, and Politics and Their Impact on Palestinian Archaeology." *Israel Museum Journal* 6 (1987): 17–32.

Brownlee, William H. "Edh-Deeb's Story of His Scroll Discovery." *Revue de Qumran* 3 (1961): 483–94.

Burrows, Millar. *The Dead Sea Scrolls.* New York: Viking Press, 1956.

———. *More Light on the Dead Sea Scrolls.* New York: Viking Press, 1958.

Carmel, Alex. "The German Protestant Community in Palestine, 1840–1914." *Cathedra* 45 (1987): 103–12. [Hebrew]

Cavallo, Dominick. "The Politics of Latency: Kindergarten Pedagogy, 1860–1930." In *Regulated Children/Liberated Children: Education in Psychohistorical Perspective*, edited by Barbara Finkelstein, 158–83. New York: Psychohistory Press, 1979.

Charters, David A. *The British Army and Jewish Insurgency in Palestine, 1945–47.* London: Macmillan Press, 1989.

Cohen, Mitchell. *Zion and State: Nation, Class, and the Shaping of Modern Israel.* Oxford: Basil Blackwell, 1987.

Cohen, Naomi Weiner. *The Year After the Riots: American Responses to the Palestine Crisis of 1929–30.* Detroit: Wayne State University Press, 1988.

Cohen, Shalom. "Double Mystery." *The Jerusalem Post,* June 22, 1979.

Cohen, Shaye J. D. "Masada: Literary Tradition, Archaeological Remains, and the Credibility of Josephus." *Journal of Jewish Studies* 33 (1982): 385–405.

Cohn-Reiss, Ephraim. *From the Memoirs of a Jerusalemite.* Jerusalem: Sifriat Ha-Yishuv, 1967. [Hebrew]

Collins, Larry; and Lapierre, Dominique. *O Jerusalem.* New York: Simon and Schuster, 1972.

Crum, Bartley C. *Behind the Silken Curtain: A Personal Account of Anglo-American Diplomacy in Palestine and the Middle East.* New York: Simon and Schuster, 1947.

Davies, Philip R. *1QM, the War Scroll from Qumran: Its Structure and History.* Rome: Biblical Institute Press, 1977.

Dayan, Moshe. *Breakthrough: A Personal Account of the Egypt-Israel Peace Negotiations.* London: Weidenfeld and Nicholson, 1981.

———. *The Story of My Life.* New York: Morrow, 1976.

De Vaux, Roland. *Archaeology and the Dead Sea Scrolls.* The Schweich Lectures, 1959. London: British Academy, 1973.

Dever, William G. *Recent Archaeological Discoveries and Biblical Research.* Seattle: University of Washington Press, 1990.

———. "Yigael Yadin: Prototypical Biblical Archaeologist." *Eretz Israel* 20 (1989): 44*–51*.

Drower, Margaret S. *Flinders Petrie: A Life in Archaeology.* London: Victor Gollancz, 1985.

Efrat, Elisha, ed. *Deborah Kallen: Her Life and Work.* Jerusalem: Deborah Kallen Fund, 1959. [Hebrew]

Elazar, Daniel. "Doomed by the System." *The Jerusalem Post,* April 22, 1981.

Elboim-Dror, Rachel. "The Foci of Decision-making in the Hebrew Education System in Palestine." *Cathedra* 23 (1982): 125–56. [Hebrew]

———. *Hebrew Education in Eretz Israel.* Jerusalem: Yad Yitzhak Ben-Zvi, 1986. [Hebrew]

Eliav, Binyamin, ed. *The Jewish National Home: From the Balfour Declaration to Independence.* Jerusalem: Keter, 1976. [Hebrew]

Elon, Amos. *Herzl.* New York: Holt, Rinehart, and Winston, 1975.

———. *The Israelis: Founders and Sons.* New York: Holt, Rinehart, and Winston, 1971.

Erez, Yaacov and Kfir, Ilan, eds. *Tzahal be-Helo: Encyclopedia of the Army and Security*. Tel Aviv: Revivim, 1982.

Even-Zohar, Itamar. "The Emergence of a Native Hebrew Culture in Palestine: 1882–1948." *Studies in Zionism* 4 (1981): 167–84.

Evron, Yosef. "The Operation That Led to the Hotel of the Roses." *Yediot Aharonot*, January 21, 1966. [Hebrew]

Eytan, Walter. *The First Ten Years: A Diplomatic History of Israel*. New York: Simon and Schuster, 1958.

Eytan, Walter. "Three Nights at Shuneh." *Midstream* (November 1980): 52–56.

Feinsod-Sukenik, Chassiya. *Pirkey Gan*. Tel Aviv: Otsar Ha-Moreh, 1966. [Hebrew]

Feldman, Louis H. "Masada: A Critique of Recent Scholarship," *Christianity, Judaism, and Other Greco-Roman Cults: Studies for Morton Smith*, edited by Jacob Neusner, 218–48. Leiden: E. J. Brill, 1975.

Finkelstein, Israel. *The Archaeology of the Israelite Settlement*. Jerusalem: Israel Exploration Society, 1988.

———. "The Origins of the Israelite Monarchy: Environmental and Socio-Economic Aspects." *Cathedra* 50 (1988): 3–26. [Hebrew]

Finley, M. I. "Josephus and the Bandits." *New Statesman*, December 2, 1966, 832–33.

Forsythe, David. *U.N. Peacemaking: The Conciliation Commission for Palestine*. Baltimore: Johns Hopkins University Press, 1972.

Frankel, Jonathan. "Borochov and the Generation of the Revolution of 1905." *Me'asef* 18 (1988): 127–35. [Hebrew]

———. *Prophecy and Politics: Socialism, Nationalism, and the Russian Jews 1862–1917*. Cambridge: Cambridge University Press, 1981.

Friedman, Isaiah. "The 'Ezra' Society, the German Foreign Office, and the Dispute with the Zionists (1901–1918)." *Cathedra* 20 (1981): 97–122. [Hebrew]

———. *Germany, Turkey, and Zionism 1897–1918*. Oxford: Clarendon Press, 1977.

Fromkin, David. *A Peace to End All Peace: Creating the Modern Middle East, 1914–1922*. New York: Henry Holt, 1989.

Gelber, Yoav. *The Emergence of a Jewish Army: The Veterans of the British Army in the IDF*. Jerusalem: Yad Yitzhak Ben-Zvi, 1986. [Hebrew]

———. *Jewish Palestinian Volunteering in the British Army during the Second World War*. Jerusalem: Yad Yitzhak Ben-Zvi, 1981. [Hebrew]

———. *Masada: The Defense of Palestine During World War II*. Ramat Gan, Israel: Bar Ilan University, 1990. [Hebrew]

———. *Why Did They Break Up the Palmach?* Jerusalem: Schocken, 1986. [Hebrew]

Geva, Shulamit. "Israeli Biblical Archaeology in its Early Days." *Zemanim* (1991): 93–102. [Hebrew]

Gillon, Philip. "Interviewpoints: The Voice of the Voter." *The Jerusalem Post*, February 17, 1961.

Glass, Joseph B. "Land Purchases and Land Use in the Area of Abu Ghosh (1873–1948)." *Cathedra* 62 (1991): 107–22. [Hebrew]

Gliss, Yaacov. *The Neighborhoods of Jerusalem: The Story of the Construction and Development of the New City Outside the Walls.* Jerusalem: Sifriat Rishonim, 1973. [Hebrew]

Golan, Arnon. "The Transfer of Abandoned Rural Lands to Jews During Israel's War of Independence." *Cathedra* 63 (1992): 122–54. [Hebrew]

Golan, Shimon. *Allegiance in the Struggle.* Ephal, Israel: Yad Tabenkin, 1988. [Hebrew]

Goldstein, Dov. "Interview with Rav Aluf Yigael Yadin." *Maariv Independence Day Supplement,* May 6, 1973. [Hebrew]

Goren, Arthur A., ed. *Dissenter in Zion: From the Writings of Judah L. Magnes.* Cambridge, Mass.: Harvard University Press, 1982.

Gottwald, Norman K. "Early Israel and the Canaanite Socio-economic System." In *Palestine in Transition: The Emergence of Ancient Israel,* edited by David Noel Freedman and David Graf, 25–37. Sheffield: Almond Press, 1983.

———. *The Tribes of Yahweh: A Sociology of the Religion of the Liberated Israel, 1250–1050 B.C.E.* Maryknoll, N.Y.: Orbis Books, 1979.

Graicer, Iris. "The Valley of Jezreel: Social Ideologies and Settlement Landscape, 1920–1929." *Studies in Zionism* 11 (1990): 1–23.

Granott, A. *The Land System in Palestine: History and Structure.* London: Eyre and Spottiswoode, 1952.

Gratz, Nurit. "The War of Independence: Conflict Between Models in Israeli Culture." *Ha-Zionut* 14 (1989): 9–50. [Hebrew]

Greenberg, Yitzhak. "The Defense Budget in Ben-Gurion's Policy on National Security, 1949–1952." *Studies in Zionism* 12 (1991): 43–53.

Grose, Peter. *Israel in the Mind of America.* New York: Alfred A. Knopf, 1983.

Hacohen, Devorah. "The IDF and the Absorption of Immigrants." *Eidan* 8 (1987): 115–26. [Hebrew]

Halpern, Baruch. *The Emergence of Israel in Canaan.* Chico, Calif.: Scholars Press, 1983.

Hawkes, Jacquetta. *Adventurer in Archaeology: The Biography of Sir Mortimer Wheeler.* New York: St. Martin's Press, 1982.

Hebrew Gymnasium in Jerusalem. *Anniversary Volume 1909–1959.* Jerusalem: Hebrew Gymnasium, 1962.

Hebrew University of Jerusalem. *The Hebrew University of Jerusalem: Its History and Development.* Tel Aviv: Haaretz Press, 1939.

Herzog, Chaim. *The Arab-Israeli Wars: War and Peace in the Middle East from the War of Independence to Lebanon.* Tel Aviv: Steimatzky, 1982.

Hoffman, Bruce. *The Failure of British Military Strategy Within Palestine, 1939–1947.* Ramat Gan, Israel: Bar Ilan University Press, 1983.

Hurewitz, J. C. *The Struggle for Palestine.* New York: Schocken Books, 1976.

Israel Bible Society. *Studies in the Book of Joshua.* Jerusalem: Kiryat Sefer, 1971.

Kark, Ruth. "Historical Sites—Perceptions and Land Purchase: The Case of Modi'in, 1882–1931." *Studies in Zionism* 9 (1988): 1–17.

———. *Jerusalem's Neighborhoods.* Jerusalem: Yad Yitzhak Ben-Zvi, 1981. [Hebrew]

Katz, Yossi. "Purchase of JNF Land in Gush Etzion and South of Bethlehem." *Cathedra* 56 (1990): 150–60. [Hebrew]

Kempinski, Aharon. "The Impact of Archaeology on Israeli Society and Culture." *Judaica* 45 (1989): 2–20. [German]

————. *Megiddo: A City-State and Royal Centre in North Israel*. Munich: C. H. Beck, 1989.

Keren, Michael. *Ben-Gurion and the Intellectuals: Power, Knowledge, and Charisma*. DeKalb, Ill.: Northern Illinois University Press, 1983.

Khalaf, Issa. *Politics in Palestine: Arab Factionalism and Social Disintegration, 1939–1948*. Albany, N.Y.: State University of New York Press, 1991.

Khalidi, Walid, ed. *All That Remains: The Palestinian Villages Occupied and Depopulated by Israel in 1948*. Washington, D.C.: Institute for Palestine Studies, 1992.

————. "Plan Dalet: Master Plan for the Conquest of Palestine." *Journal of Palestine Studies* 18 (1988): 4–19.

King, Philip J. *American Archaeology in the Mideast*. Philadelphia: The American Schools of Oriental Research, 1983.

Kohn, Moshe. "The Image of the Israeli." *The Jerusalem Post*, April 30, 1968.

————. "Yigael Yadin: Views of a Soldier-Scholar." *The Jerusalem Post*, April 4, 1966.

Ladouceur, D. J. "Masada: A Generation of the Literary Evidence." *Greek, Roman and Byzantine Studies* 21 (1980): 245–60.

Landau, David. "On the Defensive." *The Jerusalem Post*, May 11, 1979.

————. "Yadin's Choice." *The Jerusalem Post*, June 6, 1980.

Liddell Hart, B. H. *Strategy, The Indirect Approach*. New York: Frederick A. Praeger, 1954.

Liebman, Charles S.; and Don-Yehiya, Eliezer. *Civil Religion in Israel*. Berkeley: University of California Press, 1983.

Loewinger, D. S. "Prof. E. L. Sukenik." In *Jewish Scholarship in Western Europe*, 194–205. Jerusalem: M. Neuman, 1965.

Lorch, Netanel. *Israel's War of Independence, 1947–1949*. Hartford, Conn.: Hartmore House, 1968.

————. "Yadin's Finest Hours." *The Jerusalem Post*, July 29, 1984.

Luz, Ehud. *Parallels Meet: Religion and Nationalism in the Early Zionist Movement (1882–1904)*. Philadelphia: Jewish Publication Society, 1988.

Mattar, Philip. *The Mufti of Jerusalem: Al-Hajj Amin al-Husayni and the Palestinian Nationalist Movement*. New York: Columbia University Press, 1988.

McDonald, James G. *My Mission in Israel, 1948–1951*. New York: Simon and Schuster, 1951.

McTaugue, John J. *British Policy in Palestine, 1917–1922*. Lanham, Md.: University Press of America, 1983.

Meltzer, Julian L. "The First Sign of the Cross?" *The American Weekly*, February 24, 1946, 4–5.

Meshi-Zahav, Zvi; and Meshi-Zahav, Yehuda, eds. *The Slope of the Temple Mount: Battle Diary*. Jerusalem: Meshi-Zahav, 1985. [Hebrew]

Milik, J. T. *Ten Years of Discovery in the Wilderness of Judaea*. Studies in Biblical Theology, no. 26. London: SCM Press, 1959.

Miller, Shane. *Desert Fighter: The Story of General Yigael Yadin and the Dead Sea Scrolls*. New York: Hawthorn Books, 1967.

Mockaitis, T. R. *British Counterinsurgency, 1919–60*. London: Macmillan, 1990.

Moorey, P. R. S. *A Century of Biblical Archaeology*. Louisville, Ky.: Westminster/John Knox Press, 1991.

Morris, Benny. *The Birth of the Palestinian Refugee Problem, 1947-49*. Cambridge: Cambridge University Press, 1987.

Naor, Mordecai. "The Struggle for 'Jewish Labor' in Kfar Saba, 1934." *Cathedra* 39 (1986): 141-61. [Hebrew]

———ed. *The First Year of Independence, 1948-1949 (Eidan 10)*. Jerusalem: Yad Yitzhak Ben-Zvi, 1989. [Hebrew]

——— ed. *Immigrants and Transfer Camps, 1948-1952 (Eidan 8)*. Jerusalem: Yad Yitzhak Ben-Zvi, 1987. [Hebrew]

——— ed. *Tenu'ot ha-No'ar, 1920-1960*. Jerusalem: Yad Yitzhak Ben-Zvi, 1989. [Hebrew]

Neff, Donald. *Warriors for Jerusalem: The Six Days that Changed the Middle East*. New York: Simon and Schuster, 1984.

Netzer, Ehud. "Masada: The Survey, the Excavations, and the Reconstruction." *Eidan* 14 (1990): 185-97. [Hebrew]

Oren, Elhannan. *Operation Danni*. Tel Aviv: Maarachot, 1976. [Hebrew]

Orlinsky, Harry M. "The Dead Sea Scrolls and Mr. Green." In *Essays in Biblical Culture and Bible Translation*, edited by Harry M. Orlinsky, 245-56. New York: Ktav Publishing House, 1974.

Pa'il, Meir, *The Emergence of Zahal*. Tel Aviv: Zmora, Bitan, Modan, 1979. [Hebrew]

Pa'il, Meir; and Ronen, Azriel. *Rift in 1948*. Ramat Ephal, Israel: Mercaz Israel Galili, n.d. [Hebrew]

Pappé, Ilan. *Britain and the Arab-Israeli Conflict, 1948-1951*. New York: St. Martin's Press, 1988.

———. "Overt Conflict to Tacit Alliance: Anglo-Israeli Relations 1948-51." *Middle Eastern Studies* 26 (1990): 561-81.

Peri, Yoram. *Between Battles and Ballots: Israeli Military in Politics*. Cambridge: Cambridge University Press, 1983.

Perla, Shlomo. "Israel and the Palestine Conciliation Commission." *Middle Eastern Studies* 26 (1990): 113-18.

Press, Yeshayahu. *A Hundred Years of Jerusalem: Memoirs of Two Generations*. Jerusalem: Rubin Mass, 1964. [Hebrew]

Raanan, Zvi. *Gush Emunim*. Tel Aviv: Sifriat Poalim, 1980. [Hebrew]

Rabin, Chaim, ed. *Studies in the Book of Joshua*. Jerusalem: Kiryat Sefer, 1971.

Rabin, Yitzhak. *The Rabin Memoirs*. Boston: Little, Brown, 1979.

Rabinovich, Itamar. *The Road Not Taken: Early Arab-Israeli Negotiations*. New York: Oxford University Press, 1991.

Rabinowitz (Shamir), Shlomo. "The Lessons of Service in the Jewish Brigade Group." *Maarachot* 38 (1947): 37-50. [Hebrew]

Rinott, Moshe. *Hilfsverein der Deutschen Juden—Creation and Struggle*. Jerusalem: Hebrew University School of Education, 1971. [Hebrew]

———. "The Organization of Teachers, the Zionist Movement and the Struggle for Hegemony in Education in Palestine (1903-1918)." *Ha-Zionut* 4 (1975): 114-45. [Hebrew]

———. "The Struggle over the Formation of a Hebrew Education System in Palestine." *Ha-Zionut* 5 (1978): 78-114. [Hebrew]

Rivlin, Gershon; and Rivlin, Aliza. *The Stranger Cannot Understand: Code Names in the Jewish Underground in Palestine*. Tel Aviv: Maarachot, 1988. [Hebrew]

Rosenthal, Yemima. *The Jewish Community in Palestine–Eretz Israel: A Chronology, 1917–1935*. Jerusalem: Yad Yitzhak Ben-Zvi, 1979. [Hebrew]

——— ed. *Israel State Archives. Documents on the Foreign Policy of the State of Israel, Armistice Negotiations with the Arab States, December 1948–July 1949*. Jerusalem: Israel Government Press, 1983. [Hebrew, English, and French]

Rothenberg, Gunther E. *The Anatomy of the Israeli Army: The Israel Defense Force, 1948–78*. New York: Hippocrene Books, 1979.

Rubinstein, Amnon. *A Certain Political Experience*. Jerusalem: Edanim Publishers, 1982. [Hebrew]

Rubinstein, Aryeh. "Bones of Contention." *The Jerusalem Post*, March 17, 1978.

Running, Leona Glidden; and Freedman, David Noel. *William Foxwell Albright: A Twentieth Century Genius*. New York: Morgan Press, 1975.

Ruppin, Arthur. *Memoirs, Diaries, Letters*. New York: Herzl Press, 1971.

Sadeh, Yitzhak. *What Did the Palmach Introduce?* Merchavia, Israel: Sifriat Poalim, 1950. [Hebrew]

Safran, Nadav. *Israel, The Embattled Ally*. Cambridge, Mass.: The Belknap Press, 1978.

Said, Edward W. *Orientalism*. New York: Pantheon Books, 1978.

Samuel, Archbishop Athanasius Yeshue. *Treasure of Qumran*. Philadelphia: Westminster Press, 1966.

Schama, Simon. *Two Rothschilds and the Land of Israel*. New York: Alfred A. Knopf, 1978.

Schiff, Yehuda, ed. *Zahal be-Helo: Army and Security, 1948–1968*. Tel Aviv: Revivim Publishers, 1982. [Hebrew]

Schoors, Anton. "The Israelite Conquest: Textual Evidence in the Archaeological Argument." In *The Land of Israel: Crossroads of Civilization*, edited by Edward Lipinski, 77–92. Leuven, Belgium: Uitgeverij Peeters, 1985.

Segal, Mark. "Before the Break-up." *The Jerusalem Post*, August 25, 1978.

Segev, Tom. "Anatomy of Failure." *Haaretz Supplement*, October 24, 1980. [Hebrew]

———. *1949: The First Israelis*. New York: Free Press, 1986.

Shaham, David. *Israel—Forty Years*. Tel Aviv: Am Oved, 1991. [Hebrew]

Shalev, Arieh. *Cooperation in the Shadow of Conflict*. Tel Aviv: Maarachot, 1989. [Hebrew]

Shanks, Hershel. "BAR Interviews Yigael Yadin," *Biblical Archaeology Review* 9 (1983): 16–23.

———. "Intrigue and the Scroll: Behind the Scenes of Israel's Acquisition of the Temple Scroll." *Biblical Archaeology Review* 13 (1987): 23–27.

Shapira, Anita. *The Army Controversy, 1948*. Tel Aviv: Ha-Kibbutz Ha-Meuhad, 1985. [Hebrew]

———. *Land and Power: The Zionist Resort to Force 1881–1948*. New York: Oxford University Press, 1992.

Shapiro, Allen E. "Bar-Kokhba Tradition," "*The Jerusalem Post*, August 30, 1978.

———. "Judging Project Renewal." *The Jerusalem Post*, April 12, 1979.

Sharett, Moshe. *Personal Diary*. Tel Aviv: Sifriat Maariv, 1978. [Hebrew]

Shargel, Baila R. "The Evolution of the Masada Myth." *Judaism* 28 (1979): 357–71.

Shavit, Yaacov. " 'Truth Shall Spring Out of the Earth': The Development of Jewish Popular Interest in Archaeology in Eretz Israel." *Cathedra* 44 (1987): 27–54. [Hebrew]

Shefer, Gabriel. "The Principles of British Pragmatism: The Review of British Policy Toward Palestine in the 1930s." *Cathedra* 29 (1983): 113–44. [Hebrew]

Shenfeld, Ruth. *From King Messiah to King of Flesh and Blood*. Tel Aviv: Papyrus Publishing House, 1986. [Hebrew]

Shlaim, Avi. *Collusion Across the Jordan: King Abdullah, the Zionist Movement, and the Partition of Palestine*. New York: Columbia University Press, 1988.

Shtaigman, Yitzhak. *From Independence to Kadesh: The Air Force in the Years 1949–1956*. Tel Aviv: Israeli Defense Ministry Press, 1990. [Hebrew]

Siegel, Judy. "Renewed Interest," *The Jerusalem Post*, April 9, 1979.

Silberman, Neil Asher. *Between Past and Present*. New York: Henry Holt, 1989.

Silberstein, Laurence J., ed. *New Perspectives on Israeli History: The Early Years of the State*. New York: New York University Press, 1991.

Slater, Robert. *Warrior Statesman: The Life of Moshe Dayan*. New York: St. Martin's Press, 1991.

Slutzky, Yehuda, et al., eds. *The Book of the History of the Haganah*. Tel Aviv: Am Oved, 1954–1973. [Hebrew]

Solmsen, Friedrich. "Classical Scholarship in Berlin Between the Wars." *Greek, Roman, and Byzantine Studies* 30 (1989): 117–40.

Sprinzak, Ehud. *The Ascendance of Israel's Radical Right*. New York: Oxford University Press, 1991.

Spungen, Norma, "Deadlock at Lausanne: Six Months of Lost Opportunities for Peace in the Middle East." *Jewish Social Studies* 49 (1987): 265–74.

Stager, L. E. "A Personal Remembrance of Yigael Yadin as a Biblical Archaeologist." *Eretz Israel* 20 (1989): xiv–xvi.

Stein, Kenneth W. "Rural Change and Peasant Destitution: Contributing Causes to the Arab Revolt in Palestine, 1936–1939." In *Peasants and Politics in the Modern Middle East*, edited by Farhad Kazemi and John Waterbury, 143–170. Miami, Fla.: Florida International University Press, 1991.

Sukenik, Eleazar L. "The Ancient City of Philoteria." *Journal of the Palestine Oriental Society* 2 (1922): 101–109.

———. *The Ancient Synagogue of Beth Alpha*. Jerusalem: Hebrew University Press, 1932.

———. *Ancient Synagogues in Palestine and Greece*. The Schweich Lectures, 1930. London: British Academy, 1934.

———. "The Earliest Records of Christianity." *American Journal of Archaeology* 51 (1947): 351–65.

———. "Twenty-Five Years of Archaeology." In *Hebrew University Garland: A Silver Jubilee Symposium*, edited by Norman Bentwich, 43–57. London: Constellation Books, 1952.

Sukenik, Eleazar; and Mayer, L. A. *The Third Wall of Jerusalem*. Jerusalem: University Press, 1930.

Sutton, Rafi. *Men of Secrets, Men of Mystery.* Jerusalem: Edanim, 1990. [Hebrew]

Sweet, Gershon. "Yigael Yadin: Memories of a Jerusalemite." *Hadoar*, June 4, 1954, 578.

Taggar, Yehuda. *The Mufti of Jerusalem and Palestine: Arab Politics, 1930-1937.* New York: Garland, 1986.

Talmon, Naphtali. "Nineteenth-Century German Institutions and Scientific Societies for the Study of the Land of Israel." *Cathedra* 19 (1981): 171-80. [Hebrew]

Teveth, Shabtai. *Ben-Gurion: The Burning Ground, 1886-1948.* Boston: Houghton Mifflin, 1987.

Tirosh, Avraham. "The Man Who Prepared Sadat's Visit to Jerusalem Was Trapped in the 'Faluja Pocket.'" *Maariv—Days and Nights Magazine*, April 13, 1979. [Hebrew]

Torgovnik, Efraim. "A Movement for Change in a Stable System." In *Israel at the Polls: The Knesset Elections of 1977*, edited by Howard R. Penniman, 147-71. Washington, D.C.: American Enterprise Institute, 1979.

Townshend, Charles. *Britain's Civil Wars: Counterinsurgency in the Twentieth Century.* London: Faber and Faber, 1986.

Trever, John C. *The Untold Story of Qumran.* Westwood, N.J.: Fleming H. Revell Company, 1965.

Tzameret, Zvi. "The Affair of the Mediation of Count Folke Bernadotte." *Eidan* 10 (1988): 143-56. [Hebrew]

Urieli, Nachman; and Barzilay, Amnon. *The Rise and Fall of the Democratic Movement for Change.* Tel Aviv: Reshefim Publishers, 1982. [Hebrew]

Weizman, Ezer. *The Battle for Peace.* New York: Bantam Books, 1981.

Weizmann, Chaim. *Trial and Error: The Autobiography of Chaim Weizmann.* New York: Harper and Brothers, 1949.

Yadin, Yigael. "Arabic Inscriptions from Eretz Israel," *Eretz Israel* 7 (1964): 102-16. [Hebrew]

————. *The Art of Warfare in Biblical Lands.* Tel Aviv: International Publishing Company, 1963. [Hebrew]

————. *Bar-Kokhba: The Rediscovery of the Legendary Hero of the Second Jewish Revolt Against Rome.* New York: Random House, 1971.

————. "Biblical Archaeology Today: The Archaeological Aspect." In *Biblical Archaeology Today*, edited by Janet Amitai, 21-27. Jerusalem: Israel Exploration Society, 1985.

————. "Egypt's Earliest Military Penetration into Egypt?" *Israel Exploration Journal* 5 (1955): 1-16.

————. "E. L. Sukenik—Biographical Outline." *Eretz Israel* 8 (1967): 12-20. [Hebrew]

————. *The Excavation of Masada 1963-64: Preliminary Report.* Jerusalem: Israel Exploration Society, 1965.

————. *The Finds from the Bar Kochba Period in the Cave of Letters.* Jerusalem: Israel Exploration Society, 1963.

————. *Hazor: The Rediscovery of a Great Citadel of the Bible.* London: Weidenfeld and Nicholson, 1975.

————. *Hazor. The Schweich Lectures, 1970.* London: The British Academy, 1972.

————. *Masada: Herod's Fortress and the Zealots' Last Stand*. New York: Random House, 1966.

————. *The Message of the Scrolls*. New York: Simon and Schuster, 1957.

————. *The Scroll of the War of the Sons of Light Against the Sons of Darkness*. Oxford: Oxford University Press, 1962.

————. *The Scroll of the War of the Sons of Light Against the Sons of Darkness from the Scrolls of the Judean Wilderness*. Jerusalem: Mosad Bialik, 1955. [Hebrew]

————. *The Temple Scroll: The Hidden Law of the Dead Sea Sect*. London: Weidenfeld and Nicholson, 1985.

————. "The Transition from a Semi-Nomadic to a Sedentary Society in the Twelfth Century B.C.E." In *Symposia Celebrating the Seventy-Fifth Anniversary of the American Schools of Oriental Research (1900–1975)*, edited by F. M. Cross, Jr., 57–68. Cambridge, Mass.: American Schools of Oriental Research, 1979.

Yanait, Rachel, et. al, eds. *The Haganah in Jerusalem*. Jerusalem: Kiryat Sefer. [Hebrew]

Yitzhaki, Arieh. *Latrun: The Campaign for the Road to Jerusalem*. Jerusalem: Cana, 1982. [Hebrew]

Yuval, Ruth. "An Archaeological Exploration—To Scenes of Childhood." *Kol Ha-'Ir*, April 24, 1981. [Hebrew]

Zweig, Ronald. "Britain, the Haganah, and the Fate of the White Paper." *Cathedra* 29 (1983): 145–72. [Hebrew]

INDEX

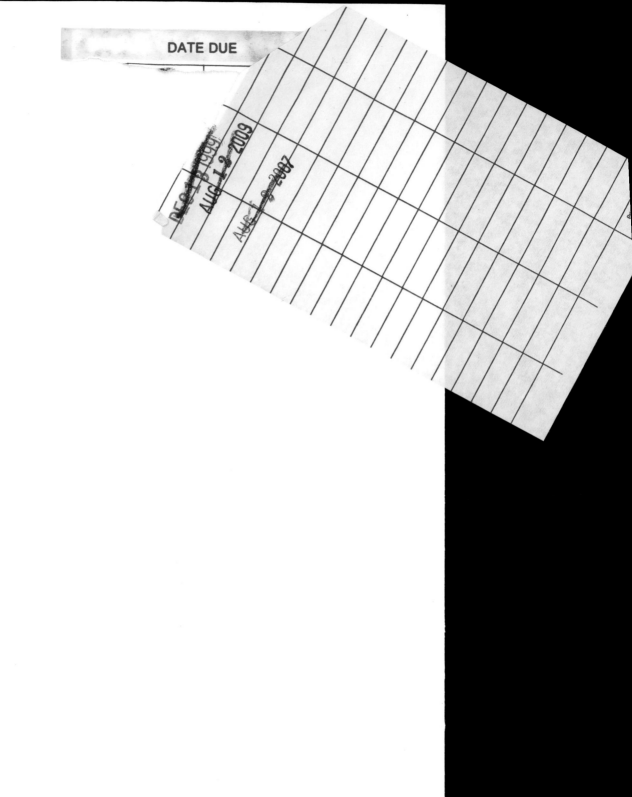